Mathew Summa
25191 Butternut Ridge Rd.
North Olmsted, OH 44070

Assembler Language for Application Programming

Assembler Language for Application Programming

DON H. STABLEY

a petrocelli
book
new york / princeton

Copyright © 1982 Petrocelli Books, Inc.
All rights reserved.

Designed by Diane L. Backes
Typesetting by Backes Graphics

Printed in the United States of America
1 2 3 4 5 6 7 8 9 10

Library of Congress Cataloging in Publication Data

Stabley, Don H.
   Assembler language for application programming.

   Bibliography: p.
   Includes index.
   1. Assembler language (Computer program language) I. Title.
QA76.73.A8S77   001.64'24   81-22749
ISBN 0-89433-176-0   AACR2

Contents

Part I

INTRODUCTION TO MODERN COMPUTING   *1*

1. **The Programmer and the Computer**   *3*
   - A. An Introduction to the Computer Programmer
   - B. System/360 and System/370 Third Generation Computer Systems
   - C. Nomenclature and Terminology

2. **Computer Systems in General**   *13*
   - A. Programming Languages
   - B. Peripheral Hardware
     1. Magnetic Tape
     2. Card Reader/Punch Units
     3. Printer Units
     4. Direct Access Storage Devices
     5. Display Devices
     6. Micrographics

Part II

INTRODUCTION TO ASSEMBLER LANGUAGE   *31*

3. **Numeric Representation and Number Systems**   *33*
   - A. Binary Value Representation
   - B. Fixed-point Value Representation
   - C. Hexadecimal Representation
   - D. The Packed Decimal Number System
   - E. Numeric Character Representation

4. **Assembler Language Instruction Formats**   *59*
   - A. The Instruction Statement Coding Format
     1. The Label or Symbol
     2. The Op Code
     3. The Operands
   - B. Coding Sheet Conventions
   - C. Machine-Language Instruction Formats
   - D. Condition Codes
   - E. Register Concepts and Applications
   - F. Data Format
     1. Character Data
     2. Packed Decimal Data
     3. Fixed-Point Data
     4. Special Data

5. Specifying the Instruction Statement   77
   A. Addressing
   B. Length Attributes
      1. Fixed Length Attributes
      2. "Implied" Length Attributes
      3. "Explicit" Length Attributes
   C. Self-Defining Characters and Values
      1. Literals
      2. Immediate Characters or Values
      3. Absolute Values
   D. Basic Program Initialization

Part III
LOGICAL APPLICATIONS OF ASSEMBLER LANGUAGE   99

6. Creating Work Areas Within the Program   *101*
   A. Establishing Storage Areas
      1. Defining the Areas
      2. Overlaying Field Descriptions
      3. Boundary Alignments
   B. Defining Constants and Literals
      1. What is a Constant
         a. The Duplication Factor
         b. The Type of Constant
         c. The Length Modifier
         d. The Actual Constant Data
         e. The Literal Version of a Constant
         f. Expressing the Constants
      2. The 'C' Constant (Character)
      3. The 'X' Constant (Hexadecimal)
      4. The 'B' Constant (Binary)
      5. The 'F' Constant (Fullword Fixed-Point)
      6. The 'H' Constant (Halfword Fixed-Point)
      7. The 'D' Constant (Doubleword)
      8. The 'P' Constant (Packed Decimal)
      9. The 'Z' Constant (Zoned Decimal)
      10. The Address Constants—A,S,V, and Y
         a. The 'A' Address Constant
         b. The 'Y' Address Constant
         c. The 'S' Address Constant
         d. The 'V' Address Constant

7. Comparing Data and Conditions   143
   A. The Instructions for Comparing Data
   B. The Applications of the "Compare" Instructions
      1. Logical Compares
         a. Compare Logical (CL)
         b. Compare Logical Characters (CLC)
         c. Compare Logical Immediate (CLI)
         d. Compare Logical Registers (CLR)

       e. Compare Logical Long (CLCL)
       f. Compare Logical Characters Under Mask (CLM)
    2. Fixed-Point Compares
       a. Compare (C)
       b. Compare Halfword (CH)
       c. Compare Registers (CR)
    3. The Packed Decimal Compare
       a. Compare Packed (P)

8. Program Branching Logic   *171*

  A. The Instructions for Program Branching Logic
  B. The Use of Branching Logic in the Program
    1. Conditional Branching Instructions
       a. Branch On Condition (BC)
       b. Branch On Condition To Register (BCR)
       c. Branch On Count (BCT)
       d. Branch On Count To Register (BCTR)
       e. Branch On Index High (BXH)
       f. Branch On index Low Or Equal (BXLE)
    2. Branch And Link Instructions
       a. Branch And Link (BAL)
       b. Branch And Link Registers (BALR)
    3. Extended Mnemonics For Branch Instructions

9. Moving, Storing, and Loading Data   *195*

  A. The Data Movement Instructions
  B. The Application of the Move, Store, Load, Insert, and Shift Instructions
    1. Moving Data Within the Problem Program
       a. Move Immediate (MVI)
       b. Move Characters (MVC)
       c. Move Long (MVCL)
       d. Move Numeric (MVN)
       e. Move Zone (MVZ)
    2. The "Store" Instructions
       a. Store Character (STC)
       b. Store Characters Under Mask (STCM)
       c. Store Halfword (STH)
       d. Store (ST)
       e. Store Multiple (STM)
    3. The "Load" And "Insert" Instructions
       a. Insert Character (IC)
       b. Insert Characters Under Mask (ICM)
       c. Load Halfword (LH)
       d. Load (L)
       e. Load Register (LR)
       f. Load Multiple (LM)
       g. Load Address (lA)
       h. Load & Test Register (LTR)
       i. Load Complement Register (LCR)
       j. Load Positive Register (LPR)
       k. Load Negative Register (LNR)

4. "Shifting" Operations
   a. "Logical" Shifting Operations and Instructions
      (1) Shift Left Logical (SLL)
      (2) Shift Left Double Logical (SLDL)
      (3) Shift Right Logical (SRL)
      (4) Shift Right Double Logical (SRDL)
   b. "Algebraic" Shifting Operations
      (1) Shift Left Algebraic (SLA)
      (2) Shift Left Double Algebraic (SLDA)
      (3) Shift Right Algebraic (SRA)
      (4) Shift Right Double Algebraic (SRDA)

10. **Packed Decimal Arithmetic Operations** *271*
    A. The Packed Decimal Arithmetic Instructions
    B. Packed Decimal Arithmetic Operations
       1. Packed Decimal/Fixed-Point Conversion Processes
          a. Pack (PACK)
          b. Unpack (UNPK)
          c. Convert to Binary (CVB)
          d. Convert to Decimal (CVD)
    C. Performing Arithmetic Operations with Packed Decimal Values
       1. Zero & Add Packed Decimals (ZAP)
       2. Add Packed (AP)
       3. Subtract Packed (SP)
       4. Multiply Packed (MP)
       5. Divide Packed (DP)
       6. Move With Offset (MVO)
       7. Shift and Round Packed Decimals (SRP)
    D. Packed Decimal Logic with Assumed Decimal Points

11. **Fixed-Point Arithmetic Operations** *333*
    A. The Fixed-Point Arithmetic Instructions
    B. Performing Arithmetic Operations with Fixed-Point Values
       1. The Fixed-Point "Add" Instructions
          a. Add (A)
          b. Add Halfword (AH)
          c. Add Registers (AR)
          d. Add Logical (AL)
          e. Add Logical Registers (ALR)
          f. Summation of Fixed-Point "Add" Instructions.
       2. The Fixed-Point "Subtract" Instructions
          a. Subtract (S)
          b. Subtract Halfword (SH)
          c. Subtract Registers (SR)
          d. Subtract Logical (SL)
          e. Subtract Logical Registers (SLR)
          f. Summation of Fixed-Point "Subtract" Instructions.
       3. The Fixed-Point "Multiply" Instructions
          a. Multiply (M)
          b. Multiply Registers (MR)
          c. Multiply Halfword (MH)
          d. Summation of Fixed-Point "Multiply" Instructions

   4. The Fixed-Point "Divide" Instructions
    a. Divide (D)
    b. Divide Registers (DR)
  C. Fixed-Point Decimal Logic with Assumed Decimal Points

12. Boolean Logic Applications   *399*

  A. The Boolean Algebra Logic Instructions
  B. Utilizing the Boolean Binary Logic Instructions
   1. The "And" Instructions
    a. And (NI) Immediate
    b. And (N)
    c. And (NC)
    d. And (NR)
   2. The "Or" Instructions
    a. Or Immediate (OI)
    b. Or (O)
    c. Or (OC)
    d. Or (OR)
   3. The "Exclusive Or" Instructions
    a. Exclusive Or Immediate (XI)
    b. Exclusive Or (X)
    c. Exclusive Or (XC)
    d. Exclusive Or (XR)
  C. Boolean Logic Instructions in Data Searches

13. Using Switches and Indicators for Program Logic Control   *435*

  A. The Test Under Mask Instruction
  B. The Concepts of Switches and Indicators
   1. Character-Switches and Indicators
  C. General Applications of Switches
   1. End-Of-File Routine Multiple Conditions.
   2. Has a Routine Been Completed?
   3. What Subroutine or Routine Passed Control?
   4. Special Conditions During Processing
   5. Embedded Switches Within Data Records
   6. Multiple Conditions

14. Loop Controls and Table Look-Ups   *455*

  A. Loop Controls
  B. Sequential Look-ups and Scans
  C. Sectored Look-Up Techniques
  D. Direct Addressing of Table Segments
  E. Tables Containing Mixed Data

15. Editing Data   *497*

  A. The Editing Instructions
  B. The Application of the Editing Instructions
   1. The Necessity of Editing
   2. The Composition of the Edit Instruction Statements
    a. The Source Field
    b. The Edit Pattern
    c. The Significant Trigger

  3. Functional Characteristics of Editing
   a. Edit (ED)
   b. Edit and Mark (EDMK)

16. **Printing Data Listings**   *529*
    - A. Defining the Output Areas
    - B. Line Spacing and Line Control
    - C. Page Control
    - D. Formatting Titles, Headings and Sub-Headings
        1. The Title
        2. Headings and Subheadings

17. **Data Validation**   *543*
    - A. Data Validation
        1. Validation of Numeric Values
        2. Auditing for Special Characters or Conditions
            a. Translate (TR)
            b. Translate & Test (TRT)

18. **Interpreting Hexadecimal-Formatted Storage Dumps**   *581*

Part IV
ACCESS METHODS AND DATA SET FORMATS   *595*

19. **Data Sets and Data Set Record Formats**   *597*
    - A. Record Formats
        1. Fixed-Length Records
        2. Variable-Length Records
        3. Undefined Records
    - B. Printed, Punched, or Displayed Records
    - C. Magnetic Tape Data Sets
    - D. Direct Access Data Sets

20. **The General Access Methods**   *609*
    - A. General Terminology and Descriptions
    - B. Basic Versus Queued Access Methods
        1. I/O Overlap Synchronization
        2. Anticipatory Buffering
        3. Blocking and Unblocking
        4. I/O Operation Completion and Error Exits
    - C. Direct Access Methods
    - D. Sequential Access Methods
    - E. Indexed Sequential Access Methods
    - F. Basic Partitioned Access Method

Part V
TABLES AND GLOSSARY *619*
    A. Table Of Contiguous Bit Position Values and Respective "Powers-Of-Two Values
    B. Hexadecimal/Decimal Conversion Table
    C. Table of Condition Code Settings
    D. Table of Program Interrupt Conditions
    E. EBCDIC Character Table
    F. Table of Assembler Language Instructions by Hexadecimal Code
    G. Answers to Review exercises
    H. Glossary of Terms and Nomenclature

Index *663*

Preface

This book was developed to fill the existing need for a comprehensive treatment of Third Generation concepts, particularly System/360, System/370, and the 303X Processors. I consider Assembler Language the best choice of programming languages for the purpose of education, because:

- Assembler Language relates directly to all the concepts of these computers.
- Nearly every installation utilizing such hardware requires Assembler Language programmers, regardless of other languages that the installation might be using.
- Certain other high-level languages, such as PL/I, are capable of producing an Assembler Language listing of program instructions. That listing represents the code generated by the original program source code statements and may be effectively used for program analysis and interpretation.

In order to establish the characteristics of this book, the intended audience had to be defined. After reviewing the advice of recognized professionals in data processing education, I decided to use a straightforward approach in the basic terminology of the programming profession. Therefore, this text accomodates technical schools, universities, colleges, and industrial and commercial training programs, rather than being a specialized presentation for a particular type of education program. Prepublication testing of the effectiveness of the manuscript proved its potential application within a wide range of educational environments. My only assumption is that the reader has completed a general high school education and has a working knowledge of program logic flowcharting.

The opening chapters present a generalized coverage of Third Generation computer hardware and terminology. This basic knowledge makes it possible to develop an understanding of the subsequent presentations of hardware systems concepts, Assembler Language instructions, and programming techniques. These items are approached in the logical sequence of appropriate number systems (base-2, base-10, base-16), data representation concepts, the individual Assembler Language instructions, and the programming techniques in which each are applied. The final chapters present an overview of the concepts of file organization and data retrieval in their relationship to the data management routines, including sequential, indexed sequential, and random (direct) file organizations and access methods.

A glossary of terms, designed to aid the reader with an expedient reference source, follows the main portion of the text.

In my opinion, it is as important for students to be able to measure their progress as it is for them to receive an evaluation from an instructor. Practice exercises, therefore, must be an integral part of a good textbook. Unlike written examinations for formal quizzes, these should be designed to point out any weakness, even at the lowest level of the student's knowledge and understanding of the subject material. Absolute detail, rather than conceptual responses, is required. The review exercises and examples contained within this book have evolved as a result of my involvement in the sophisticated environment of large-scale computer systems and programming; an environment in which every professional is a perennial student, part-time instructor, writer, and lecturer. These exercises are based almost entirely upon the necessity of understanding the detailed and explicit performance of each of the individual Assembler Language instructions. This effort to emphasize minute details of language performance should result in greater efficiency and accuracy when applied by the student to actual programs.

The logical arrangement of language instructions into a program structure must also be practiced. Just as review exercises are important to a good textbook, the coding of practice programs is essential to the effectiveness of a programming course. Unfortunately, this presents unique problems. What is the "correct" answer to a practice program problem? Speaking in broader terms, what are the "most acceptable" instruction statements that should make up a particular program?

There is a maxim, "If 500 programmers were given an exact set of requirements for a program, the finished products would be 500 unique programs." Admittedly, a large number of those programs would be quite similar in content, but that would depend greatly upon the similarity in education of the programmers. Based on this assumption, the supporting practice coding programs should originate with the individual instructors who utilize this book. This allows each instructor to establish his or her own evaluation of the correctness or inefficiencies of the student's application of the language. For this reason the coding of complete practice programs has not been included.

Because of the inherent flexibility of Third Generation computers and the vast range of possible hardware and system configurations, certain areas of technology and supporting functions have been excluded which would otherwise be desirable; such material as input/output control statements, macroinstructions, job control language, and other types of instructions or parameter definitions. Regardless of the apparent need for such information, it is not unreasonable to exclude it from this text. Just as the content of a single program would vary when written by different programmers, computer centers vary in the configuration of the computer systems they maintain. It must therefore be assumed that the required control statements for input/output operations, data management, job control, and file descriptions will be supplied to the students by the instructional staff of the computer center.

Any attempt to list completely the names of persons and organizations to whom acknowledgements and statements of appreciation are due would most certainly result in numerous, although inadvertent, omissions. Many persons over an extended period of time have contributed directly and indirectly to this book. Within this profession, knowledge is not singularly extrapolated from any one source or individual—it is derived from the day-to-day contact with associates, whether they are students, trainees, or seasoned professionals. My statement of appreciation, accordingly, must be directed to all of those with whom I have shared the exciting challenge of the constantly evolving technology of electronic data processing.

Photographs of IBM computer hardware have been furnished through the courtesy of International Business Machine Corporation.

Don H. Stabley

Webster, New York
1982

Part I

INTRODUCTION TO MODERN COMPUTING

1
The Programmer and the Computer

AN INTRODUCTION TO THE COMPUTER PROGRAMMER

The present-day computer is probably the most misunderstood aid to mankind ever developed. Revered by some, distrusted by others, it has been the target of both humorous and serious attack, based conversely on its tremendous capabilities and its supposed shortcomings.

When "Average Citizen" receives a monthly account statement from the local credit emporium and finds it in error, the computer is spotlighted as the culprit. When a computerized payroll system deducts too much money from the employees' paychecks, the computer becomes infamous for its sins. This goes on and on—the rocket that goes astray, the purchase order automatically written for 1 million gizmos instead of 100, the lines of conglomerate gibberish which suddenly appear in the middle of the news story in the evening newspaper—these are all credited to the antics of a mischievous computer.

Unfortunately, it will probably be many years before the general public recognizes and understands the overall concept of computers and their capabilities. Until that time, however, this fascinating maze of electronic equipment continues to bear the brunt of puns and disdain of those who believe they have suffered from the erratic whims of its flashing lights and massive memory banks. Someday, perhaps, the responsibility for all of the capricious evils of the computer finally will be laid at the feet of that which spawns those misdeeds—the human element.

Programmers have nearly as much to learn about human nature as they do about the electronic nature of the computer that does their bidding. The programmer can slyly attempt to bypass responsibility for a program abortion by blaming it on a "computer malfunction." By its own inability to generate a truly unique thought, therefore, the computer becomes the "fall guy" for many a programmer's errors. After all, it cannot defend itself to the data processing manager. It would be of considerable interest to know the infinitesimally small percentage of processing errors for which the computer is truly responsible, in comparison to the overwhelming number of errors for which it is blamed.

At long last, computer programmers gradually are gaining justified recognition as artists in their own right. Programs can literally be a work of art—an efficient masterpiece of the use of human logic processes—or they might be a collection of garbage (a term frequently used in data processing), a monument of misguided concepts and misapplied techniques. Once computer programming has been accepted as a constructive challenge, it offers a wealth of potential originality to the programmer. What each person makes of this challenge is the difference between the professional programmer and the ordinary "coder."

SYSTEM/360 AND SYSTEM/370–THIRD GENERATION COMPUTER SYSTEMS

Modern data processing concepts possibly originated with the advent of the punched card application, in which the cards were stored, sorted, and arranged into a desired sequence according to the locations of the holes in the cards. This type of equipment really preceded the birth of what was to become the First Generation of computer hardware.

The term *generation,* as used in reference to computers is frequently identified as the period of time during which the internal electronics of the computer uses certain electronic principles and equipment. In this context, First Generation computers were those which contained vacuum tubes for electronic circuitry and processing. These forerunners of the present-day computers were literally ovens, giving off such heat that it was difficult to maintain a reasonable temperature within the computer rooms.

With the initial application of the transistor came the Second Generation of computers, those capable of greater storage and faster logic processes, yet requiring less physical space than their older brothers. As the electronics industry progressed in the design of yet smaller and smaller components, microcircuitry became a reality. Solid-state devices were miniaturized to a point where an entire electronic logic circuit was smaller than the surface of a postage stamp . "Chip" transistors were created so small that 50,000 would fit into an ordinary sewing thimble. These components were the type used in the design and production of the first of today's computers—the Third Generation.

However, electronics technology is advancing so rapidly that even within Third Generation computers newer and more compact circuitry and storage components are being implemented. For example, some of the System/370 computers contain MOSFET transistors for main memory. MOSFET (Metal Oxide Semiconductor Field Effect Transistor) technology uses silicon chips which measure only 0.15 inch by 0.18 inch by 0.013 inch, each containing over 14,000 monolithic components. With this density, one megabyte (1,000,000+ characters) of memory is packaged in approximately 0.4 cubic foot. Yet even by the time you read these paragraphs, newer technological advances undoubtedly will have progressed beyond the state-of-the-art described here.

There are several definitions of computer generations, depending on who is making the analysis of the term. Some say the Third Generation of computers really represents the satisfactory merger of a scientific computer and a commercial application computer into one modular system. Prior to the Third Generation equipment, data processing installations usually procured a particular type of computer according to the scientific versus commercial applications for which it was to be used. In this respect, the newer computer systems appear to satisfy the needs of both the scientific or research programmer and the commercial data processing installations.

As the circuitry within the new computers became more compact, the internal processing speeds increased. Electric pulses and electronic data flow had less distance to travel between components and logic sections of the computer, establishing a performance level that tended to become more and more difficult to comprehend. Terms such as *nanoseconds* and *picoseconds,* representing billionths of a second and trillionths of a second respectively, were now associated with certain internal functions of the computer. Accordingly, it became necessary to design peripheral support equipment such as input/output devices capable of performing data transmission at speeds that would not adversely degrade the performance of the computer's processing functions. To expect peripheral equipment to physically match the speed of the computer's solid-state components would be unrealistic; peripheral equipment uses physical movement of some type as part of its operational functions. Therefore, it cannot be expected to keep pace with a processing unit that depends solely on electronic circuitry. However, disk storage devices were developed for System/360 that provide data transmission speeds of 312,000 characters per second, and drum-type storage devices capable of 1,200,000 characters per second data transmission were implemented. More recently, with the advent of System/370, it is not surprising to find other disk storage and input/output devices being introduced. Among these is a moveable-head disk storage device capable of transmitting data at a rate exceeding 1,198,000 characters per second, and a fixed-head disk storage unit with an effective data transfer rate greater than 3,000,000 characters per second.

Aside from their speed and great capacity, one of the primary advantages of Third Generation computers is the "modular" concept by which they are designed. This allows upgrading of the computer itself, or addition of peripheral equipment, as the users' needs increase for such capability. For example, assume that a particular data processing department had installed a System/370 computer system configured as follows:

>System/370 Model 158, with 512K (524,288) bytes main storage
>Card reader punch
>Appropriate control units
>Two printer units
>Six magnetic tape drives
>Two 2314 Direct Access Storage Facilities (eight disk packs each)
>(466,000,000-byte total storage capacity)

As the work load of the computer center increases, additional direct access storage space is needed, so management procures two 3330-11 Disk Storage Facility units to replace the 2314 DASF units. Later, to accomodate additional users, an additional 1.5 megabytes of main storage as well as another printer unit are required. Subsequent to that, management decides to increase magnetic tape processing, so six additional tape drive units are ordered.

After all of these modifications have been completed, the computer system is now configured as:

>System/370 Model 158, with two megabytes (2,097,152 bytes) main storage
>Card reader punch
>Appropriate control units
>Three printer units
>Twelve magnetic tape drives
>Two 3330-11 Disk Storage Facilities (eight disk packs each)
>(3,000,584,960-byte total storage capacity)

The original system has been modularly incremented to a rather powerful computer system capable of performance satisfactory to many data processing installations. The ability to upgrade a computer system in this manner is highly desirable so that the ever—expanding requirements of computerized business systems and research projects may be accommodated.

For years the would-be oracles of the working class have been warning that the computer spells doom to the security of many jobs, yet as computers are installed the spiral of net manpower required continues on an upward trend, not downward as forecasted. Each year more and more college students select studies in Computer Science and computer-related educational programs. Industry serves to justify the need for those studies by seeking larger quantities of such students as they graduate. The increase in net manpower results in a much greater output of the data necessary for rapid management decisions and customer service. An order may be placed with a sales representative in Los Angeles in the morning and by evening the distribution center in New York City could have the shipping orders prepared, the invoices calculated, and the ordered material waiting for shipment to the customer—all of the related functions having been expedited by means of a computerized telecommunications system for order processing.

As implied, the Central Processing Unit (CPU) of a computer system (Figures 1-1 and 1-2) is the center of its control and operation. Despite that, it is merely a well-planned maze of electronic circuits, incapable of any self-initialized action. In order for these circuits to be activated and perform in a predictable pattern, the computer must be provided with a set of master control programs, often referred to collectively as the *Supervisor* or *Monitor*. The Supervisor, as well as the computer system, may be considered to be modular in that it consists of fixed and optional sets of smaller modules and control programs. The completed package of any given Supervisor control program is generally dependent on the following:

- The intended operating system and the control modules required by that system.
- The hardware configuration of the computer system.
- The selection of optional data management routines.
- The programming languages to be supported.
- The Utility programs to be made available to the users.

The overall Supervisor package is created by a process of merging and extracting control program modules. This is referred to as a *System Generation* or *SYSGEN*. A System Generation by each using installation is necessary in order for the completed system to meet the needs and requirements of its unique hardware configuration. An operating system, therefore, may be generated in many different formats. These variations are created through the inclusion or exclusion of data parameters at the time the system generation is accomplished. Using packaged routines provided by the computer manufacturer, the selected optional routines and modules for the desired operating system configuration are specified, processed through the computer, then compiled and stored as the completed Supervisor. This becomes the master control program package that is "loaded" into the computer CPU. Thereafter it supervises the day-to-day execution of the users' programs.

Within the scope of Third Generation computers, the using installation has a choice of operating systems. The most commonly used are the *Disk Operating System* (DOS), the full *Operating System* (OS), the *Disk Operating System with Virtual Storage* (DOS/VS), and the full *Operating System with Virtual Storage* (OS/VS). Each of these systems may be considered as being designed for computers of somewhat different physical capabilities, although in many instances a particular computer system configuration could utilize several of these operating systems.

DOS and DOS/VS are generally considered applicable to computer systems in a range of sizes, from small to moderate. Despite the possible implication of their names, these two oper-

Figure 1-1.

IBM System/370 Model 168 showing CPU and its console and control panels.
(Photo courtesy of International Business Machines Corporation.)

Figure 1-2.
IBM 3033 Processor for System/370.
(Photo courtesy of International Business Machines Corporation.)

ating systems do not limit peripheral equipment to disk storage devices. Magnetic tape drives, telecommunication gear and many other types of peripherals may be part of the configuration of a computer environment controlled by one of the disk operating systems.

The largest and most flexible of the operating systems are OS and OS/VS. They are compatible on a practical basis with computers ranging from medium-small to the largest available. As such, they offer the data processing installation a wealth of variation in support programs, utilities, access methods, file organization techniques, languages, and overall potential for the most sophisticated assortment of hardware and software.

OS and DOS are operating systems whose main storage capabilities consist of *real* storage only. That is, the amount of memory available to the users is limited to the physical main storage capacity of that particular computer. For example, if a computer's main storage capacity is 512K (524,288 bytes/characters), that space might be allocated as follows:

```
Storage required for supervisor and control programs   112K
Partition No. 1 (for users)                            200K
Partition No. 2 (for users)                            200K
Total main storage                                     512K
```

In this example there would be two user *regions* (partitions) of 200K each. Although two users could run jobs on the computer at the same time, neither one could execute programs exceeding 200K of storage.

DOS/VS and OS/VS, introduced for System/370, uses both real and *virtual* storage. Virtual storage may be thought of as auxiliary storage. For all intents and purposes, virtual storage is an overflow area where the operating system can place, and retrieve, a portion of the contents of active programs when main storage has become full. Under such a system the amount of storage being used at any one time may far exceed the real storage capacity of the computer system.

To illustrate this, assume there is a computer with 1024K (1 megabyte) real storage, and the operating system is OS/VS. After reducing the total real storage by the approximate space required for the Supervisor and control programs (128K), the amount of remaining real storage available to the users is 896K. Further assume that the tasks currently being executed require the following amounts of storage:

User No. 1	...	208K
User No. 2	...	256K
User No. 3	...	512K
User No. 4	...	368K
User No. 5	...	576K
User No. 6	...	720K
Total		2640K

This amount of storage required by the users greatly exceeds the available real storage. To compensate for this, the operating system keeps some portion of each user's task within real storage and places the remainder into virtual storage. Whenever a portion of a user's program residing in virtual storage is needed for execution, the operating system selects a seldom-used section of that same program from real storage, places it into virtual storage, and brings the needed program section from virtual storage into real storage. This process is referred to as *paging*. Admittedly, this example over-simplifies an extremely complex control process, but it is enough to provide an impressive flavor of one of the services provided by the OS/VS and DOS/VS operating systems.

Each of the operating systems utilize control programs that are, to some degree, unique from those of other operating systems. Although a particular access method may be supported by more than one operating system, it would be activated by macroinstructions which differ somewhat among the supporting systems. For this reason the contents of this book cannot possibly attempt to explain input/output macroinstructions, job control language, or functional system and language macroinstructions. Not only would it be impossible to anticipate the unique hardware configurations and corresponding variations of operating systems of the computer installations where this text might be used, but the attempt to explain and evaluate all of these variations would be prohibitive in terms of written volume alone. The educational center, university, college, or industrial complex that finds this text to be of value in the education of their students or programmers must, therefore, bear the respective responsibility for providing the necessary technical information. As indicated, this supplemental information would consist of applicable job control language, device references and addresses, and the macroinstructions necessary for their operating system, language levels, and access methods.

NOMENCLATURE AND TERMINOLOGY

The study of System/360 and System/370 programming brings with it a host of new words and terms that might be totally unfamiliar to the student programmer. Certain words may be entirely within the scope of everyday language, yet when they are used in association with computer programming they take on an entirely different interpretation. For example, drum, channel, word, terminal, register, bit, and switch are all standard nouns and verbs within the grasp of anyone not familiar with computer systems. When these same terms are used to relate to computers, they assume the identity of nouns with peculiar and distinct interpretations. Mention a drum and the initial association by a noncomputer-oriented person would be either a percussion musical instrument or a barrel-like metal container; yet to the programmer it is a direct access storage device! To aid the reader in understanding and interpreting some of these computer-related terms, a glossary has been provided at the end of this text. It contains the majority of terms and descriptive nomenclature required to be of assistance.

Some of the nomenclature for System/360 and System/370, as with other computers, requires additional explanation and discussion. Such is the case with the terms "hardware" and "software." Computer *hardware* is considered to be any physical device or piece of equipment that is a part of the overall configuration of the computer system. The CPU, direct access devices, display units, terminals, cables, tape drives, control units, printer units, console typewriters, and such related equipment are all considered to be hardware. Even data preparation devices, such as key-punch units (Figure 1-3) or key-disk stations (Figure 1-4), can be considered as hardware even though they are not connected to the computer system.

The term *software* is associated with utility programs or with any or all sets of control programs required by the computer in order for it to act on the users' programs in a desired and predictable manner. Although "software" is often used to refer to the specialized control programs furnished by the computer manufacturer, it is a term that is equally applicable to specialized programs written by the using installation, routines which provide a particular service to the operating system or to the everyday user. A program of the latter type might be an accounting routine of computer usage. As such it would accumulate the run time for each job processed during the day, record that job time to a particular charge number on an accounting log, and print a message on the run scroll for each job as to the extent of time required for completion of that task. A software program could also be one that is available to all users to aid them in performing a certain function within their operational programs. This might take the form of a set of routines which performs special arithmetic calculations, based on parameters passed to it by a user's "calling" program, and then returns the resulting values determined by that calculation to the "calling" program.

Throughout this text, certain terms and phrases are used that might not be sufficiently described at that point, or that might not have been previously clarified to the reader's satisfaction. In such instances, it is recommended that the reader refer to the Glossary of Terms and Nomenclature.

Figure 1-3.
IBM 129 Card Data Recorder (Keypunch).
(Photo courtesy of International Business Machines Corporation.)

Figure 1-4.
IBM 3741 Data Entry Station (Diskette Recorder).
(Photo courtesy of International Business Machines Corporation.)

2
Computer Systems in General

PROGRAMMING LANGUAGES

In order to communicate the logic of your program to the computer, you must express the information in such a way that it will be understood by the computer's control programs. The common ground for this understanding between human and machine is the programming language.

In reality, a programming language does not constitute a direct link with the computer. It is only the programmer-related portion of a two-step communication process that defines the action to be accomplished. Using the parameters, keywords, operands, and limitations of the language desired, the programmer encodes language source statements to specify the task to be performed.

Upon completion of this coding, a series of logical steps have been established that must be translated into a form of instruction that can be understood by the internal functions of the computer. This translation is accomplished by a language compiler, or assembler.

The compiler, or language compiler, is one of the control program packages contained within the operating system. Each language, or level of a language, requires a separate compiler program in order to translate the source language coding. The operating system used by any given computer installation, however, needs to contain only a compiler for each of the specific languages or levels thereof used at that installation.

The language source statements, together with the control cards necessary to identify the language compiler, are given to the computer to process. Once all of that source coding has been introduced into the compiler work area, the compiler begins to identify each statement and relate it to a function to be performed by the computer at program execution time. When a statement is identified as relating to a specific function, the compiler translates that action into one or more machine-language instructions. After all the source statements have been translated into machine-language form, the resulting data is considered to be an *object module,* the program that will be linked to the system control programs and executed.

The object module may be punched into cards as an *object deck* or it may be written out onto a storage device as part of a *program library.* After the language compiler completes execution, a print-out lists the source statements from which the object module was generated. This source listing usually "flags" any coding discrepancies and, in some language compilers, might issue warnings about possible error conditions that could occur during the execution of the object program. This is not to imply that the compiler audits the correctness of the flow of logic. It does not! Instead, the flagged errors are usually misspelled keywords and operands, misplaced position-dependent parameters, and violations of statement formats and restrictions.

Programming languages generally fall within two categories—*low-level* languages or *high-level* languages. A low-level language is one that is very closely related to the actual machine-language, almost on a one-for-one basis of programming language instructions to machine-language instructions. Within System/360 and System/370, Assembler Language is considered to be low-level language.

A high-level language is usually referred to as a *statement* language or an *expression* language, wherein each coded instruction statement might generate many machine-language instructions. Typically, a high-level language instruction statement might appear as, "If A equals B then do C until Y equals Z."

There are many valid arguments for both low-level and high-level languages, but too often one is chosen without consideration for the benefits of the other. There is a definite place and a definite need for both types of languages in almost every computer installation. However, the author believes that it is a definite advantage to the programmer to first learn a low-level language because of the direct relationship of such a language to the working concepts of the computer itself. Indications are that this conclusion has also been arrived at by many others, as evidenced by an apparent trend among data processing and programming educational centers. Once the student programmer has grasped the use of the low-level language, simultaneously absorbing the concepts of the computer, any subsequent training required in high-level languages is more easily comprehended.

As mentioned, Assembler Language is a widely used low-level language for both System/360 and System/370. What, then, are the high-level or statement-level languages applicable to these computers? Rather than listing all of them, it will suffice to state that PL/I, COBOL, FORTRAN, and ALGOL are probably the most commonly used. The names of these languages generally imply the environment and application for which they were designed. The name COBOL is derived from COmmon Business Oriented Language; FORTRAN from FORmula TRANslation; ALGOL from ALGOrithm Language; and PL/I, an IBM-developed language, from Programming Language I (One). As its name suggests, COBOL is generally used for business and commercial applications, FORTRAN and ALGOL are quite fitting for scientific and engineering applications, and PL/I contains such a wide range of features that it is suitable to almost any application.

Present high-level languages, such as the four mentioned here, are continually being improved and updated in their techniques. Undoubtedly, new languages of this type will be introduced from time to time, as well as the announcement of new versions of the existing languages. Despite the appropriateness of certain languages to certain applications, there are no rigid standards to determine the type of programming language that should be used by any computer installation. About the only type of meaningful suggestion to be offered is the possible separation of high-level languages between a scientific or engineering environment and the commercial or business programming environment. Certain high-level programming languages are directed more specifically to a particular type of application, but this does not preclude their use for other purposes. On the other hand, Assembler Language as a low-level language enjoys the privilege of being applicable in any type of programming environment, whether it be commercial, scientific, computer research, or software development.

PERIPHERAL HARDWARE

As a part of every computer system, there must be some type of hardware available to provide input data to the operating programs and to receive output data in return. These input and output functions need not be handled both by the same device; one device may accomodate the in-

Computer Systems in General 15

put data and another the output. This equipment may be quite varied in form and configuration, allowing each computer system to be structured to the needs of the user's installation. The peripheral I/O hardware, as it is referred to, may consist of several units of the same type or may comprise many units of numerous types. Each of the devices has a channel (cable) connection with the Central Processing Unit, either directly or through a control unit that interfaces with the CPU.

Within the descriptions of the devices contained on the following pages is sufficient information to become familiar with their general physical characteristics and attributes, and their common application in respect to a functional computer system. Because this text is intended for education in computer programming, rather than computer sciences, these descriptions do not delve deeply into the technical and electronic principles of this equipment.

Magnetic Tape

The use of magnetic tape for storing and retrieving data has been a universally accepted method of accomplishing these functions. Although it is now being challenged by the direct access storage devices of Third Generation computer systems, it probably continues to be the largest single medium of data input/output operations.

Magnetic tape used in computer-driven I/O devices is quite similar in composition to the tape used in voice/music recording devices. It consists of a thin plastic film base that has an oxide coating. This oxide surface accepts electrical impulses, a process which generates structured magnetic groupings of the oxide atoms, sometimes referred to as *bits*. The arrangement of these groupings represents the *bit arrangement* of the data contained on the tape. The data remains in that configuration until altered by a subsequent electrical impulse. The bits are arranged in rows across the face of the oxide surface, from side to side. In some types of magnetic tape equipment, each row of bits represents a single byte of data (a character); in some other equipment it requires two rows of bits to represent a character. These rows of bits are also spaced differently in linear form (along the length of the tape) among the various models of magnetic tape drives. This spacing between rows of bits is referred to as the *density* at which the tape was recorded. Third Generation computers generally utilize magnetic tapes at a density of 800 BPI, 1600 BPI, or 6250 BPI—BPI representing bits per inch, or rows of bits per inch of magnetic tape. A tape created at 1600 BPI density has 1600 rows of magnetized data bits for every inch of tape that contains data. The term BPI may be described elsewhere as bytes per inch, generally when one row of bits comprises a single byte of data.

Magnetic tape does not contain an unending string of contiguous bit rows. After a logical block of data is *written* (recorded) onto the tape surface, the system skips over a portion of the tape prior to writing the next logical block of data. This portion of the tape not containing data is referred to as an *inter-record gap,* or *IRG*. In addition to its use by other control functions, this gap is used by the system as a logical and physical means of distinguishing between blocks of data contained on the tape.

Magnetic tape drives (Figure 2-1) are available in a wide variety of configurations and models within System/360 and System/370. Some units process one particular density of magnetic tape, others process several types. The speed at which the magnetic tape is processed (reading or writing) by the tape drive units is measured as a KBS factor—K bytes per second, wherein K is equal to 1024. A tape drive unit that processes magnetic tape at a rate of 90 KBS is actually capable of 92,160 bytes per second. Some tape drive units process data at the rate of 15 KBS, while others can process as fast as 1250 KBS.

Figure 2-1.
IBM 3420 Magnetic Tape Drive.
(Photo courtesy of International Business Machines Corporation.)

Magnetic tape represents a fairly inexpensive means of storing bulk data. The reels of tape may be readily filed or stored for safekeeping in vaults or tape libraries, thereby providing both privacy and physical protection for the data until it is needed. One of the very practical uses for magnetic tape is to use it as an output medium in lieu of a printer unit connected to the main computer system; the data (reports, invoices, etc.) to be printed as the output of a program is instead written onto magnetic tape. The print-out of that data may then be accomplished at a more convenient time, or on another computer system or off-line printer system.

Card Reader/Punch Units

Data contained on punched cards is probably the oldest form of input/output medium that is still associated with the computer. Punched cards were used as a system of storing data long before the days of magnetic tape, direct access storage devices, and display terminals. Its present-day applications include initial data input, source program coding input, problem program object modules, and task management control statements. Standard punched card concepts, as used in System/360 and System/370, utilize a flexible cardboard card, 3 1/4 by 7 3/8 inches. Each card contains 80 columns with 12 vertical positions per column. To represent data, small rectangular holes are punched into any of these 960 positions. The combination of holes, or single hole, punched into a vertical column is interpreted by the system as data content, either hexadecimal, binary, or EBCDIC formatted.

The *reader* portion of a combination reader/punch unit transmits data to the CPU based on the "sensing" of the holes as the card passes over the sensing mechanism. The actual reading, or sensing, of the holes is usually accomplished by small wire brushes or by photoelectric cells. In the brush-type mechanism, the card is passed under a set of 80 brushes, one for each vertical column on the card. If a hole is present, the brush contacts a sensing plate beneath the card and registers an impulse. All of the impulses received for each vertical column are then interpreted by the system and the next card is read. In reader units that use a light-sensing device, a light source replaces the brushes, and photoelectric cells perform the function of the sensing plate. As the card holes pass over the sensor cells, the light shines through and the existence of the hole is recorded.

The *punch* portion of the reader/punch combination unit may be considered as having the reverse process of the reader logic, but it is somewhat slower because of physically punching the required holes into the cards. Data to be punched is converted into card-code form and transmitted to the punch unit. As the card passes under them, the punch heads are electronically activated according to the positions of the holes that are to be punched into the vertical columns of the card. Cards which are punched as output data from one task are often subsequently used as input to another task or operation. In some hardware configurations the card reader and card punch are separate units (see Figures 2-2 and 2-3).

PRINTER UNITS

Printer units are a means of creating visual data output in *hard-copy* form, in either single or multiple copies. The term *printer* most commonly refers to a unit that is used solely for the output of data. Under some circumstances a typewriter unit, capable of both input and output, may be loosely considered to be a printer, but because of its comparatively slow speed it is a very expensive means of printing output data in any quantity. True printer units are generally high-speed printing devices using either a type-bar or a type-chain/train mechanism to reproduce the data output.

Figure 2-2.
IBM 3505 Card Reader.
(Photo courtesy of International Business Machines Corporation.)

Figure 2-3.
IBM 3525 Card Punch.
(Photo courtesy of International Business Machines Corporation.)

The type-bar printer unit contains repetitive segments of printable characters mounted on a bar that moves back and forth horizontally in a straight-line motion. Each position on the printer unit has a print hammer to drive a selected segment of the print bar forward against the printer ribbon, causing the impression of that character segment onto the paper. As the print bar shuttles back and forth, each print position hammer is activated when a print bar segment, passing in front of it, corresponds to the character to be printed in that position. Many print positions may be simultaneously printed if the segments are properly aligned.

Printer units using either a *type-chain* or a *type-train* perform the printing function in basically the same manner, except that the physical characteristics of the type transport are somewhat different.

A type-chain consists of a series of character-slugs (each slug containing two characters) which are linked together to form a continuous chain. This chain, mounted on two gears and forming an oblong pattern, travels horizontally in one direction at a very high rate of speed. Similar to a type-bar unit, each print position is represented by a print hammer which is activated when the selected character is opposite the hammer. The actual print impression on the paper is created differently, however, in that the print hammer drives the paper against the interceding ribbon to print the character-slug.

A type-train differs from a type-chain in that the print-slugs, each of which contain three characters, are not interconnected. Instead, the print-slugs are consecutively mounted within a track in which they slide freely, driven in a horizontal oblong path by a drive gear at one end and an idler gear at the other. The print-slugs contain the corresponding teeth that are meshed with the drive gear to send them along the track. The printing of each character is conceptually the same as with a type-chain, but the physical characteristics of the hammer mechanism differ somewhat.

The speed at which some printer units perform, such as 2000 lines per minute, is often more impressive to an observer than the internal workings of the computer. The printer offers a mechanical operation that can be more easily comprehended by the novice than the electronic workings of the processing unit; the speed of the printer can be compared and related to an active physical operation.

Printer units normally use assorted widths of continuous-form paper that is perforated to create a fold-point for stacking and separation. The length of each assumed print-page is governed by the distance from one row of perforations to the next. Many paper suppliers produce specialized forms for computer printer applications, such as continuous-form envelopes, federal withholding tax statements, labels, invoices, checks, individualized form letters, etc.

As with any other component of computer systems, printer technology is advancing dynamically. Various equipment manufacturers offer matrix printers, ink-spray printers and laser printers, all utilizing conceptually different techniques for creating printed data and reports. Notable among these advancements is the IBM 3800 Printing Subsystem (Figure 2-4) which combines both laser and electrophotographic technology. This unit can generate "printed" characters in three different sizes, interspersed on the same line or on a line-to-line basis, at speeds up to 13,000-plus lines per minute.

Direct Access Storage Devices

Direct access storage devices derive their name from their ability to allow the operating system, or users' programs, to directly access any single data record, block, or region without first

Computer Systems in General 21

Figure 2-4.
IBM 3800 Printing Subsystem.
(Photo courtesy of International Business Machines Corporation.)

processing all preceding data within the volume or data set. Most direct access devices are used in applications that require the following:

- Storage of large quantities of data.

- Storage of data to be retrieved in some manner other than by sequential processing, but not excluding sequential processing.

- Storage of data that must remain actively accessible to a program or system on an "on demand" basis.

It is not always one of these factors, but sometimes a combination of two or three, that dictates the requirements for a direct access storage device application.

Although this class of device comprises an assortment of hardware using a variety of physical operating concepts, the most common storage units are disk storage devices. Within a disk storage device data is recorded onto oxide-coated *platters* along prealigned paths referred to as *tracks*. Conceptually, a platter can be thought of as similar to a phonograph record, and the tracks as grooves in that record. Unlike a phonograph, however, the tracks do not spiral in toward the center of the disk platter. Instead, each track is concentric—each complete circular path ends at an index marker point just short of where it began. Another difference is that the tracks are not visible—they are only paths of magnetically-encoded oxide atoms.

Each disk platter has tracks on both the upper and lower surface, the number of tracks on either surface dependent upon the type of device with which the platter is associated. For example, the IBM 3330 Disk Storage Facility (Figure 2-5) utilizes disk platters that contain either 404 or 808 addressable tracks per surface, depending upon whether it is a 3330-1 or 3330-11. The platters for the IBM 3350 Direct Access Storage units (Figure 2-6) contain 1,110 tracks per surface.

Figure 2-5.
IBM 3330 Disk Storage Facility.
(Photo courtesy of International Business Machines Corporation.)

Figure 2-6.
IBM 3350 Direct Access Storage Facility.
(Photo Courtesy of International Business Machines Corporation.)

Differing from magnetic tape recording techniques, which build rows of bits across the width of the tape, data placed onto a platter is recorded serially, bit by bit, along each track. The amount of data, in terms of bytes or characters, that can be stored on a single track also varies among direct access storage devices, but every track on one device is capable of holding the same amount of data. For example, each track on an IBM 3330 Disk Storage Facility can hold up to 13,030 bytes; each track on a 3350 Direct Access Storage unit can hold up to 19,069 bytes; a 3340 Disk Storage Facility (Figure 2-7) can hold 8,368 bytes per track.

When considering that every track on a single platter surface is a different length, it appears illogical that each of those tracks would have the same byte capacity. If no two tracks on a single surface are the same length, how can every track hold the same amount of data? Although the answer certainly is not obvious, it is logical in principle—each track on a single surface also has a unique recording density. This variance of recording density between every track on a single surface is caused by the condition that each track, from the outermost track to the innermost track, has a different velocity as it passes beneath the read/write head. Coupled with the constant recording pulse, this causes the actual variance in density; the density of the bits along the outermost tracks is low, on the innermost, high.

For the equipment described within this text, the platters are contained in a stacked assembly called a *disk pack*. The number of platters per disk pack varies according to device, ranging from six to eleven platters per pack. They are mounted on a vertical shaft, spaced far enough apart to allow the read/write heads to access each surface.

Some direct access storage devices contain only one disk pack, others as many as eight. Another variation is that certain devices permit the removal and replacement of the disk packs, allowing them to be taken off and stored in a vault, much like magnetic tape reels. For this type of device, the computer center usually has many more disk packs than drive units. Accordingly, each programming group might have their own private disk packs, calling for those packs to be mounted on the device only when that particular set of data is needed. Other direct access storage devices contain permanently-mounted disk packs. For this equipment, only the service engineer of the device manufacturer can remove or replace the disk packs. The using installation must, therefore, have enough of the devices to meet their storage requirements.

The reading or writing (recording) of data on disk storage devices is accomplished by small read/write heads. On some devices these heads are immobile; others have movable heads. Devices with immobile read/write heads, referred to as *fixed-head* devices, have a stationary head mounted over every track on every platter. *Movable-head* devices contain either one or two read/write heads for each platter surface. These heads are attached to a movable *access arm mechanism*, a comb-like assembly which moves across the surface of all platters simultaneously, positioning the heads over the tracks to be accessed.

The extremely fine limits of tolerance involved in the physical operation of direct access storage devices deserves recognition. For example, a band of 808 tracks on a platter surface is only several inches wide. This is nearly equivalent to placing 100-plus tracks on a conventional 8-track stereo tape cartridge. Despite this density, the access arm mechanism of a movable-head device can accurately reposition the read/write heads from one set of tracks to the adjoining tracks in 10 milliseconds. Of even more delicate tolerance is the clearance between the read/write heads and the platter surface. The heads do not touch the oxide surface of the platters; instead, they float just off the surface, held only by the air pressure generated by the velocity of the spinning platters. On both the IBM 3340 Disk Storage Facility and the 3350 Direct Access Storage unit, the clearance between the heads and the platter surface is equivalent to one-half the

Figure 2-7.
IBM 3340/3344 Disk Storage Facility.
(Photo courtesy of International Business Machines Corporation.)

thickness of a molecule of smoke. This clearance must be maintained at all times—if a read/write head makes contact with the platter surface during normal operations (an occurrence referred to as a *head crash*), both the head and the oxide surface are damaged.

The IBM 3850 Mass Storage System (Figure 2-8), developed to support the increasing need for greater data storage resources, provides System/370 computer systems with a new magnitude of stored data capacity. Although it is not a direct access storage device in the true sense, the Mass Storage System deserves mention here because of its interface with such devices. Within the 3850 Mass Storage System, data is stored on magnetic tape within cylindrical data cartridges. These cartridges measure about two inches in diameter and four inches in length and contain a spool of magnetic tape capable of holding 50.4 million bytes of data. Depending upon the final configuration of the Mass Storage System selected, the data storage capacity of that system can range from 35 billion bytes to 472 billion bytes. The operating principle of this equipment is that the data to be accessed by a user's program is extracted from one or more cartridges and *staged* onto a conventional direct access storage device. The user's program then accesses the data under control of normal data management routines. Once the user's program has completed its need for the data, any units of new or updated data are *destaged* back onto the appropriate data cartridge. The staging and destaging of the user's data is accomplished under the control of the operating system.

A benefit of such a system is that it can significantly reduce the total number of disk packs, or even direct access storage devices, required for data storage for an installation. This can be pointed out more clearly by noting that a 472 billion byte Mass Storage System has the same data capacity as 4,720 disk packs (100,000,000 bytes each) for the IBM 3330 Disk Storage Facility.

Display Devices

Within the range of I/O devices servicing business data processing applications, no others can compare in quantity to the proliferation of the cathode-ray tube display devices—also referred

Figure 2-8.
IBM 3850 Mass Storage System.
(Photo courtesy of International Business Machines Corporation.)

to as *scopes, CRT terminals, display stations,* or *VDU's* (Figures 2-9 and 2-10). These units contain a cathode-ray tube that is quite similar to the "picture tube" in a home television receiver. Unlike a TV set, however, the CRT display device functions through a control unit which serves as an interface between it and the CPU of the computer system. It is the control unit, more than the CRT display device, that determines the quantity of lines per screen, the quantity of characters per line, the screen format, and the capabilities of the display unit. Data is transmitted to the control unit from the computer, or received from the display device keyboard, and held in *buffers*–limited-size storage areas. The data represented within these buffers is continually displayed on the screen of the CRT. To do this, the electron-gun of the cathode-ray tube sweeps across the face of the screen many times per second, restoring the image lines as quickly as they begin to fade. It is not until the buffer contents are either altered, deleted, or replaced by the problem program or a request from the display device keyboard that the screen image is changed.

In addition to the cathode-ray tube, these display devices have a keyboard for data entry or interaction with an operating program. In most instances the basic portion of this keyboard is similar to that of a typewriter keyboard, with the exception of the numeric keys and special characters. Those keys may be placed similarly to a conventional typewriter, arranged in the format of a keypunch or data entry keyboard, or placed in a special arrangement. Along with the regular keyboard, many CRT display devices offer a *control-function keyboard*. This separate group of keys may each be programmed to perform a particular function or special subroutine related to the task currently being run. Also referred to as PFKs (Program Function Keys), these keys can be assigned activities such as formatting a particular data display, deleting lines of data, searching the displayed lines for particular data or conditions, moving or replacing lines of data, and many other activities.

CRT terminals, as these display devices are more commonly known, are available with *character-formatted* screens or *grid-formatted* (dot-matrix) screens. Character-formatted CRT terminals are used for applications limited to sending and/or receiving data in alphanumeric character form, including some special characters or symbols. These devices are well-suited for either *local*

Figure 2-9.
IBM 8775 CRT Terminal.
(Photo courtesy of International Business Machines Corporation.)

Figure 2-10.
IBM 3278 CRT Display Station.
(Photo courtesy of International Business Machines Corporation.)

or *remote* mode applications. Local mode applications are those in which data is transmitted directly between the terminal/control unit and the CPU via a channel connection. In remote mode operations, the terminal/control unit transmits and receives data via transmission lines, such as telephone lines, which interface with the CPU through a transmission control unit. Some CRT terminal applications in remote mode also provide for communication between terminals or even to control communication between several CPUs.

Character-formatted CRT terminals are an excellent tool for applications requiring on-line data inquiry, time-critical updating of data files, submission of data to active programs in lieu of keypunched data, and the interactive development of programs. This latter activity, interactive programming, is gaining wide acceptance as an expedient means of program development.

On CRT terminals having grid/dot-matrix formatted screens, the flexible configurations provide a capability for character data, illustrations, charts, graphs, tables, drawings, or any of an assortment of similar representations. These devices also offer control-function keyboards in which the PFKs may be programmed to accomplish unique screen display tasks. A somewhat classical example of this would be to program the PFKs to simulate the three-dimensional configuration of a model, allowing the figure to be "turned" to different viewing angles in order to see all perspectives of the object.

Another feature of some CRT terminals is the *optic-fibre light-pen*. By touching the pen to the face (screen) of the CRT, elements of the display may be altered, deleted, or moved about. For example, a blueprint of the circuitry of an electronic device may be displayed on the screen after being extracted from a direct access storage device where it had been stored in array format; by using the light-pen, an engineer could replace or eliminate components of the circuitry contained on the blueprint and return the corrected drawing to the storage device.

Although CRT terminals do not perform at the speeds normally thought of in association with computerized devices, they are capable of expedient processing. The inherent fact that they are intended for on-line visual applications deters the need for extremely high-speed performance—they need only be as fast as the ability of the display device operator to read, search, absorb, alter or produce the data that is to be transmitted.

Micrographics

The use of *microfilm* as a compact means of document storage is not new. For many years businesses and government agencies have been using microfilming equipment to photographically reduce and store cancelled checks, customer information, reports, research papers, legal documents, publications, etc. To accomplish this, documents were fed onto a layout frame, photographed, and preserved for future reference at a reduced size as a tiny section of film. Microfilm *viewers* or *readers* contained magnification equipment to enlarge the small photographic images, displaying them in a format large enough to be easily read. Microfilmed data of this type was generally stored on film strips or rolls of film.

But, as one might anticipate, any process relating to the storage and retrieval of data will sooner or later find itself embraced within the technology of computer-based systems. Microfilm has been no exception.

COM, or the *Computer Output Microfilmer,* is rapidly spreading as a major medium for computer-generated output documents. But unlike earlier processes, computer-generated microfilm is not created from hard-copy documents. It is generated, either directly or indirectly, from data stored on magnetic tape or direct access storage devices, or from data being output from an executing program. The two most widely used forms of computer-generated microfilm are roll film and *microfiche* (pronounced "my-crow-feesh"). Roll microfilm is created on 16mm film, not unlike the microfilm output from a unit which photographs hard-copy documents. One of the key differences, however, is that computer-generated roll microfilm can take advantage of many new processing features provided by the computer and the COM device. For example, each frame (individual document image) of the roll can be keyed with a unique code beside it that allows microfilm readers to automatically search for the desired frame. Additionally, a specialized form can be superimposed on the data by photographing it onto the film at the same time the data is photographed. The resulting image gives the appearance of a frame photographed from a hard-copy document.

Microfiche is a significant departure from roll microfilm. It is a section of film measuring 105mm by 148mm (approximately 4 1/2 inches by 5 7/8 inches), containing numerous frames. The frames are aligned in rows and columns, the quantity of each depending upon the reduction ratio used to create the fiche and the assumed size of the original document image. Assuming the use of 11" x 14" documents (the approximate size of computer print-out pages), the quantities would be as follows:

reduction ratio	*columns*	*rows*	*total frames*
42x	16	14	224
48x	18	16	288
72x	27	24	648

Referring to the 48x reduction ratio, one piece of microfiche could contain the equivalent of 288 pages of printed output. As this indicates, the use of microfilm represents significant savings in terms of storage space for "printed" output data. At the same time, it is more durable than paper and, due to recent advances in microfilm viewers, faster to use for retrieval of stored listings or reports. If a "hard copy" page is required, the viewer being used may have the capability of producing an enlargement of that frame, printing it on regular paper.

Micrographics technology, like computer technology, is in a state of dynamic advancement. Consequently there is already a broad assortment of COM hardware available, enough to meet almost any need. COM processors exist which operate off-line or on-line with intelligence supplied by an all-purpose computer system; others can operate off-line or on-line with intelligence supplied by a computer built into the COM unit. The reference to "intelligence" indicates the ability of the COM unit to format the layout of the display to be filmed. If the COM unit is not intelligent, the frame formats, titles, headings, etc., must be developed by the central computer system; if the COM unit is intelligent, the main computer needs only to pass the COM records resembling typical print-out lines—the COM will format the lines. For purposes of providing an overview, a discussion of only two types of this equipment should suffice.

The off-line COM unit uses magnetic tape input and an internal cathode-ray tube for displaying the data to be filmed. To prepare for the microfilming, a program is run on a computer to extract the required data, arranging it into a planned sequence before writing it out onto a reel of magnetic tape. Thereafter the tape can be processed through the stand-alone COM unit as scheduling permits. "Stand-alone" means that the COM hardware is not driven by the computer that created the tape—it is independent. As the COM unit reads the tape, it transforms the contents into pages of data, pages which are displayed on the face of the cathode-ray tube. A microfilm camera photographs each screen display as a single frame. Whether these frames are aligned into roll film or microfiche format depends upon the COM hardware and the user's request. After all the data has been filmed, the microfilm is processed for distribution.

Another significant type of COM unit utilizes a laser image-generator. Not only is the functioning technology of this equipment far more advanced, but it offers a wider range of interfaces and stand-alone capabilities. Data received by the COM unit is inscribed onto the microfilm by a laser beam. The process is so fast that this type of unit can produce 10,000 frames of microfilm per hour. Assuming that a frame (a document page) contains 60 "printed" lines, this is equivalent to 600,000 lines per hour or 10,000 lines per minute, a speed greater than most hardcopy printer units in use today.

More than likely the widespread use of microfilm is transparent (no pun intended) to the general public. They probably see its use frequently without recognizing what it is. So the next time you visit the parts department of your auto dealer to make a purchase—or visit your local lawn and garden store to order a part for your lawnmower—or go to the payroll department of your employer to follow-up on a deduction from your paycheck—or ask your college for a transcript of your grades—watch what happens! It is very likely the person you talk to will search out the necessary information from a tiny section of microfilm.

Part II
INTRODUCTION TO ASSEMBLER LANGUAGE

3
Numeric Representation and Number Systems

Within the scope of this text, there are five types of numeric representation. Four of these number systems probably are not familiar to the student programmer—hexadecimal, binary, fixed-point, and packed decimal. The fifth is the standard numeric character representation in its extended form, or EBCDIC.

The descriptions and explanations within this section are introductory. They should provide enough basic knowledge of the numeric structures of Assembler Language to allow you to understand the logic and execution processes of the system. At certain points within the text these subjects will be reopened for review, and additional information of a more technical nature will be presented.

BINARY VALUE REPRESENTATION

The "bi" of the word binary infers the basis of this scheme of numeric representation. The entire logic is based on two numeric values—0 (zero) and 1 (one). Either of these digits, if written alone, expresses its "face value;" however, when a series of these digits such as '10010101' is interpreted as a value, each successive digit position to the left is construed to represent a value of exactly twice that of the digit position to its right. This value is only counted as being an effective addition to the sum of all digit positions when it is a one-bit. This is known as the "Powers-of-Two" binary representation and is in reality a "base-2" number system.

The contiguous bit positions of any half-byte, byte, or series of bytes may be evaluated as a "Powers-of-Two" binary representation. The potential base-2 value of such a set of bit positions is shown in the following illustration, representing the 16 bit positions contained within a two-byte field.

(respective bit position from the right)   two bytes

16	15	14	13	12	11	10	9	8	7	6	5	4	3	2	1
0	0	0	0	0	0	0	0	0	0	0	0	0	0	0	0
32768	16384	8192	4096	2048	1024	512	256	128	64	32	16	8	4	2	1

(potential bit position value in base-2)

As stated previously, the assumed value representation of any single bit position is not considered to be effective unless a one-bit occupies that position. Therefore, the preceding illustration can be considered to have an absolute value of zero since there are no one-bits within the field. Using this same two-byte field, but containing various bit configurations, the following examples define the accumulation of the assumed one-bit values into the sum value of the entire field as a binary "Powers-of-Two" notation.

Example 1

Example 2

Example 3

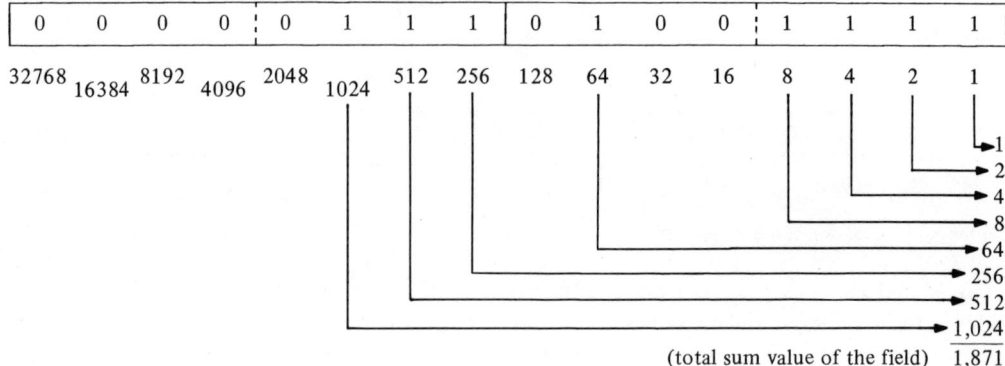

The maximum potential Powers-of-Two value of any field is limited to the number of bit positions within the field. This maximum value for various lengths of fields, in half-byte increments, is as follows:

field byte length	maximum Powers-of-Two value
½	15
1	255
1½	4,095
2	65,535
2½	1,048,575
3	16,277,215
3½	268,435,455
4	4,294,967,295
4½	68,719,476,735
5	1,099,511,627,775

The assumed value of any single bit position within a 32-bit field may be determined by referring to the Powers-of-Two table in Part V of this text. Each successive increment of that table represents the relative bit position of a binary field, from right to left.

A value expressed solely in true binary notation does not have a definitive sign; the sign of the value must, therefore, be considered to be positive. Because of the restriction of having only a positive assumption, true binary representation has limited use in itself as a means of expressing numerics. On the other hand, it is the entire basis for the fixed-point value system.

FIXED-POINT VALUE REPRESENTATION

The fixed-point value system is the principal arithmetic process employed by an operating system in maintaining addressing, displacements, and register assignments. It is available to the programmer as a means of compact and expedient arithmetic operations via Assembler Language fixed-point instructions. The representation of fixed-point value is based on binary value representation with the additional capability of expressing both negative and positive values. The sign of the fixed-point value is determined by the left-most high-order bit of the field. All other bits are combined in binary representation to create the integer value of the field. Using a 16-bit field as an example, the following illustration points out the single sign-bit and the 15 bits comprising the integer.

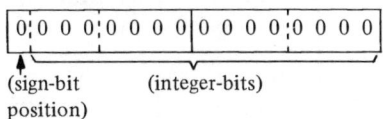

(sign-bit position)   (integer-bits)

Because a fixed-point value may commonly be expressed either as a halfword or as a fullword, depending on the size of the value, the number of integer bits vary in accordance with the size of the field. A halfword fixed-point value contains 1 sign-bit and 15 integer-bits; a fullword fixed-point value contains 1 sign-bit and 31 integer-bits.

A positive fixed-point value is expressed as a 31-bit integer in true binary representation and a sign-bit consisting of a zero-bit. The significant digits of the integer are considered to represent the Powers-of-Two value of their respective positions within the integer field and are summed together to arrive at the whole of the fixed-point value. Using halfword fixed-point values to illustrate this concept, the following examples are presented in the same manner as those for a binary value representation.

A negative fixed-point value is expressed as a 31-bit or 15-bit integer in *"Two's Complement Notation"* and a sign-bit consisting of a one-bit. In Two's Complement Notation, a significant

Numeric Representation and Number Systems

digit-bit is considered to be a zero-bit because it is the opposite of the sign-bit. The interpretation of a negative fixed-point value may be accomplished by:

1. Subtracting a one-bit from the low-order (right-most) bit position of the field.
2. Reversing the configuration of all bit positions.
3. Summing the representative value of all significant integer bits.

This process is indicated in the following illustrations.

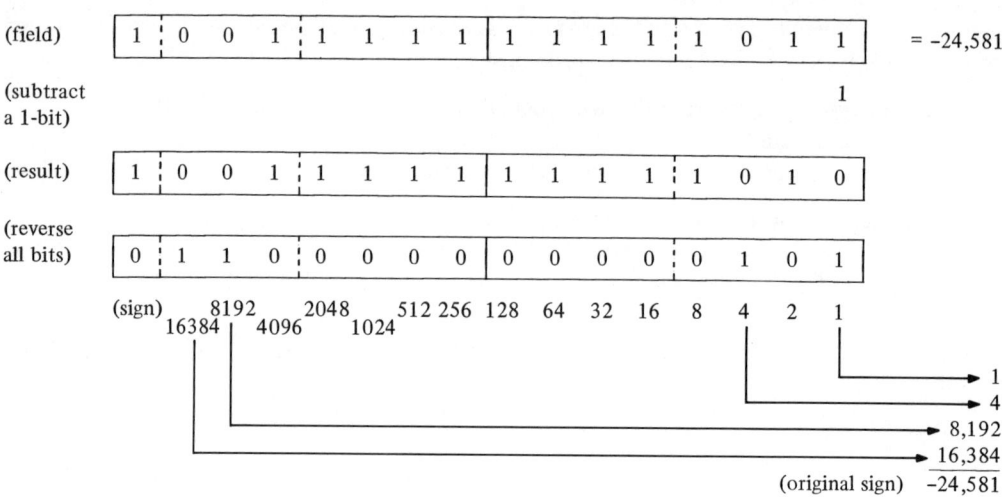

The maximum negative and positive values that can be contained within a halfword or fullword location, and the configuration of those values, are displayed in the examples below:

Maximum halfword positive fixed-point value = + 32,767

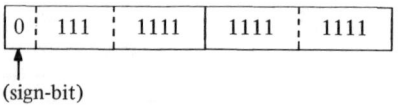

(sign-bit)

Maximum halfword negative fixed-point value = – 32,768

1	000	0000	0000	0000

Maximum fullword positive fixed-point value = + 2,147,483,647

0	111	1111	1111	1111	1111	1111	1111	1111

Maximum fullword negative fixed-point value = 2,147,483,648

1	000	0000	0000	0000	0000	0000	0000	0000

Note that the maximum positive fixed-point value of a fullword (+2,147,483,647) is not so great as the maximum binary value representation of a fullword (+4,294,967,295). This is because the fixed-point value may only use 31 bit positions of the field as integer bits, whereas the true binary value representation can utilize all 32 bit positions as representing the value.

The addition of fixed-point values, as well as true binary representations of values, is based on the schedule of sums and results shown in Table 3-1.

Numeric Representation and Number Systems

TABLE 3-1. Bit Values

Field 'A'		Field 'B'		Sum	
0	plus	0	equals	0	
0	plus	1	equals	1	
1	plus	0	equals	1	
1	plus	1	equals	0	with a carry-over of 1 to the next higher bit position

The following illustration represents a series of additions of a value of +1 to a halfword fixed-point field.

(original field)

0	0	0	0	0	0	0	0	0	0	0	0	0	0	0	0

(plus 1)   1
(equals 1)

0	0	0	0	0	0	0	0	0	0	0	0	0	0	0	1

(plus 1)   1
(equals 2)

0	0	0	0	0	0	0	0	0	0	0	0	0	0	1	0

(plus 1)   1
(equals 3)

0	0	0	0	0	0	0	0	0	0	0	0	0	0	1	1

(plus 1)   1
(equals 4)

0	0	0	0	0	0	0	0	0	0	0	0	0	1	0	0

(plus 1)   1
(equals 5)

0	0	0	0	0	0	0	0	0	0	0	0	0	1	0	1

(plus 1)   1
(equals 6)

0	0	0	0	0	0	0	0	0	0	0	0	0	1	1	0

(plus 1)   1
(equals 7)

0	0	0	0	0	0	0	0	0	0	0	0	0	1	1	1

(plus 1)
(equals 8)

| 0 | 0 | 0 | 0 | 0 | 0 | 0 | 0 | 0 | 0 | 0 | 0 | 1 | 0 | 0 | 0 |

(plus 1)   1
(equals 9)

| 0 | 0 | 0 | 0 | 0 | 0 | 0 | 0 | 0 | 0 | 0 | 0 | 1 | 0 | 0 | 1 |

(plus 1)   1
(equals 10)

| 0 | 0 | 0 | 0 | 0 | 0 | 0 | 0 | 0 | 0 | 0 | 0 | 1 | 0 | 1 | 0 |

(plus 1)   1
(equals 11)

| 0 | 0 | 0 | 0 | 0 | 0 | 0 | 0 | 0 | 0 | 0 | 0 | 1 | 0 | 1 | 1 |

(plus 1)   1
(equals 12)

| 0 | 0 | 0 | 0 | 0 | 0 | 0 | 0 | 0 | 0 | 0 | 0 | 1 | 1 | 0 | 0 |

(plus 1)   1
(equals 13)

| 0 | 0 | 0 | 0 | 0 | 0 | 0 | 0 | 0 | 0 | 0 | 0 | 1 | 1 | 0 | 1 |

(plus 1)   1
(equals 14)

| 0 | 0 | 0 | 0 | 0 | 0 | 0 | 0 | 0 | 0 | 0 | 0 | 1 | 1 | 1 | 0 |

Fixed-point subtraction is accomplished by first reversing the configuration of the subtrahend to its complement value and then adding the two fields together. (See Examples 1, 2 and 3.)

Example 1
+ 245 less + 83 = + 162   or   + 245 plus − 83 = + 162

| 0 | 000 | 0000 | 1111 | 0101 | (+ 245)

| 1 | 111 | 1111 | 1010 | 1101 | (plus − 83)

| 0 | 000 | 0000 | 1010 | 0010 | (equals + 162)

Example 2
+ 175 less − 10 = + 185   or   + 175 plus + 10 = + 185

| 0 | 000 | 0000 | 1010 | 1111 | (+ 175)

| 0 | 000 | 0000 | 0000 | 1010 | (plus + 10)

| 0 | 000 | 0000 | 1011 | 1001 | (equals + 185)

Example 3

+ 2938 less + 5961 = − 3023   or   + 2938 plus − 5,961 = − 3023

| 0 | 000 | 1011 | 0111 | 1010 |

(+ 2938)

| 1 | 110 | 1000 | 1011 | 0111 |

(plus − 5961)

| 1 | 111 | 0100 | 0011 | 0001 |

(equals − 3023)

Notice that in example 2 a negative value is to be subtracted from a positive value. The subtrahend (the negative value) is first reversed to its complement, resulting in the true binary notation form of a positive value. It is then added to the first value (the minuend), and the correct difference obtained.

HEXADECIMAL REPRESENTATION

The hexadecimal number system figures prominently in System/360 and System/370 programming. It is a *"base-16"* numeric structure wherein every four bits of the binary configuration of the data or value is represented by a single hexadecimal digit. Storage dumps, a printed listing of the contents of certain areas of main storage at a planned point in time or as the result of an abnormal termination of processing, are listed in hexadecimal format. Addresses and instructions on an Assembler Language compiler source listing are referenced in hexadecimals, as are many other functional values within the overall scope of these computers. Even fixed-point and true binary values are more easily interpreted when written in hexadecimal notation, as opposed to the format of individual bit configuration expressions. It is, therefore, of prime importance that you obtain a very solid grasp on the fundamentals and concepts of the hexadecimal number system and arithmetic operations.

The range of hexadecimal digit representation is from 0 through 9 and from A through F. The configuration of these hex digits is shown in Table 3-2.

TABLE 3-2

numeral	hexadecimal	bit configuration
0	0	0000
1	1	0001
2	2	0010
3	3	0011
4	4	0100
5	5	0101
6	6	0110
7	7	0111
8	8	1000
9	9	1001
10	A	1010
11	B	1011
12	C	1100
13	D	1101
14	E	1110
15	F	1111

The decimal value of any hexadecimal digit is directly related to the Powers-of-Two value of the significant bits within the four bit positions of the hexadecimal. This can be illustrated by using the true binary format of the hexadecimal digit 'E' and interpreting its value by Powers-of-Two summation.

A single hexadecimal digit may, therefore, represent any decimal value within the range of '0' through '15'. However, it is seldom that a single hexadecimal digit is used as a solitary value. More often multiple hex digits are used to represent a value or set of data. A compound hexadecimal field, one which consists of more than one hexadecimal digit, may represent many kinds of character or numeric data. It is necessary to know the intended construction of the field and the type of value it is supposed to contain, before attempting to analyze the magnitude of that value. In the paragraphs that follow, an appropriate relationship will be established between hexadecimal formats of fields and the type of data represented by those fields.

When the hexadecimal digits are used to interpret the decimal value of a binary or a fixed-point value, each hexadecimal digit is considered to be a base-16 unit of increment. The rightmost hex digit has a maximum value of 15, the next higher-order digit has a maximum value of 240, the next a maximum value of 3840, etc. Each successive hex digit, from right to left, has a potential maximum value sixteen times greater than the potential maximum value of the digit to its right.

The potential range of each hexadecimal digit of a four-byte binary field is indicated in this illustration:

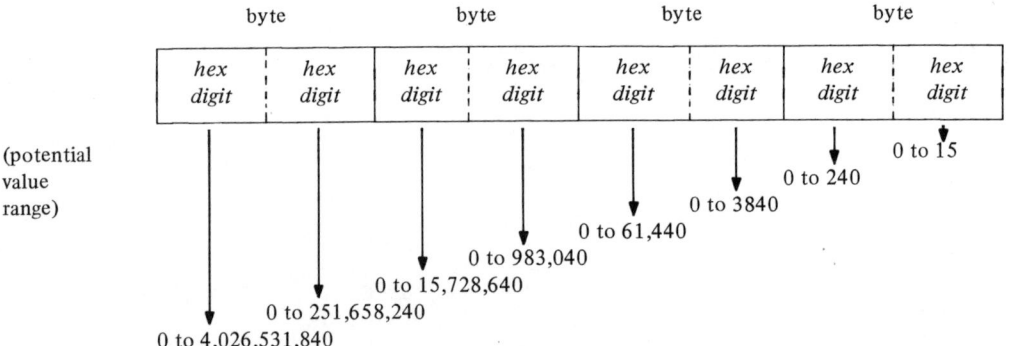

The Hexadecimal/Decimal Conversion Table (see Part V) should be used to aid in interpreting binary values comprising more than one hexadecimal digit. It is an expedient method of converting the positional hex digits into their relative base-16 value.

The following examples consist of binary values, illustrated in both their binary and hexadecimal format, which have been interpreted as the decimal value they represent by using the Hexadecimal/Decimal Conversion Table.

Numeric Representation and Number Systems

In using the table to interpret Example 1, the standard procedure of beginning at the right-most hex digit is used. The right-most hex digit of '5' assumes its own value. The next hex digit, '2', has its value determined by looking at the corresponding column of values within the table—0 = 0, 1 = 16, 2 = 32, etc. The next higher-order hex digit, '9', is evaluated by the corresponding table column—0 = 0, 1 = 256, 2 = 512, 3 = 768, etc.

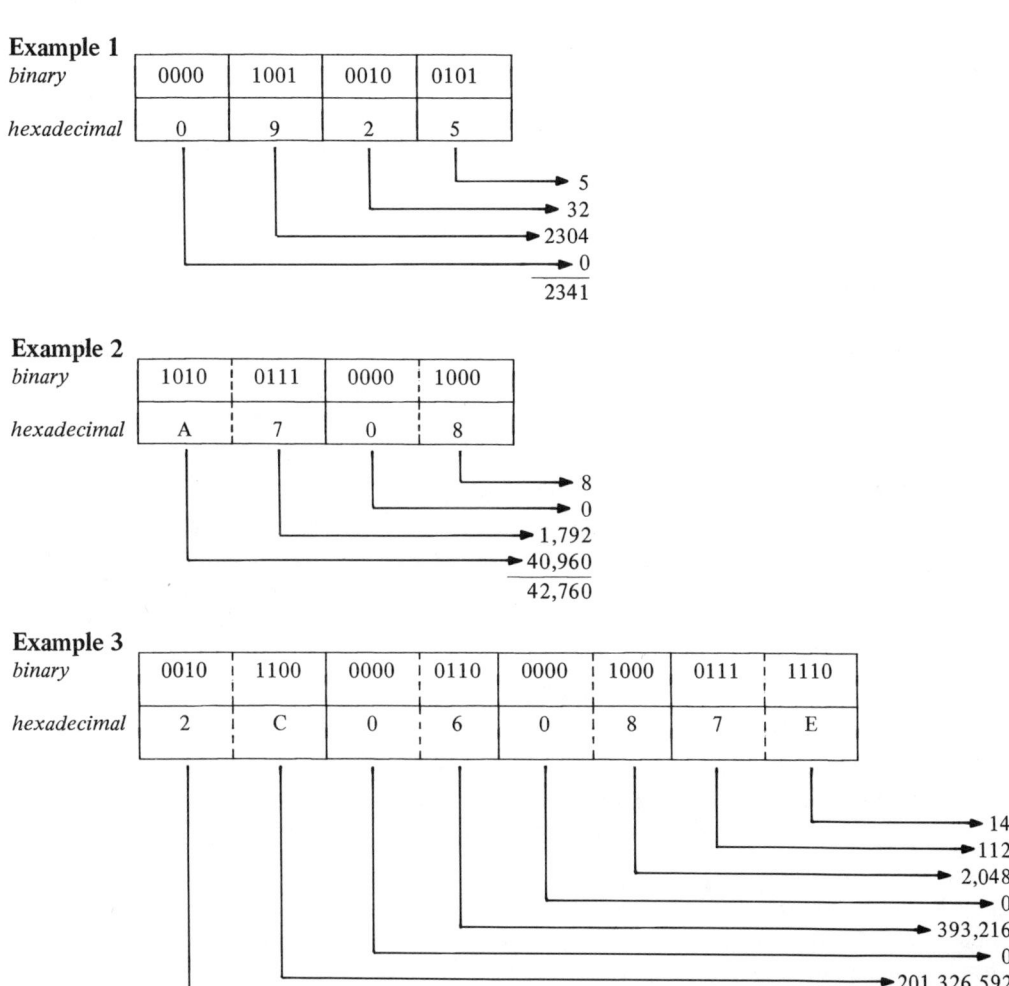

It is quite likely you will want to convert a decimal-to-hexadecimal from time to time. This too becomes a relatively easy task when using the Hexadecimal/Decimal Conversion Table. The decimal value to be converted to hexadecimals is used to find a relative value range on the Conversion Table. The value sought on the table should be equal to the decimal value or else the next value smaller than the decimal value. The corresponding representative hex digit is recorded and the table value is subtracted from the decimal value. The remaining decimal value balance is now searched for and the process is repeated. A detailed example of this action is shown on the following page.

The decimal value to be converted is 15,931.

Step a. 15,931
Step b. 12,288 = 3
Step c. 3,643
Step d. 3,584 = E
Step e. 59
Step f. 48 = 3
Step g. 11
           11 = B
Step h.   hex value = '3E3B'

Step a. Write down the decimal to be converted.

Step b. Scan the table to find a value equal to or nearest to but less than, the value of 15, 931. The closest value in the table is 12,288 (in column 4 from the right) so this number is set down to be subtracted from the decimal value. The hex digit '3' represents the value of 12,288 in that column of the table, so it is also recorded.

Step c. Subtract the table value from the original value, determining the balance of the original value that is yet to be converted.

Step d. Scan the table again, this time in order to find the value closest to, but not greater than, 3643. All subsequent scans of the table should always be to the values that are one column to the right of the column in which the last value was found. In this example a value of 3584 is found in the column to the immediate right of the column in which the value of 12,288 was found. Being the nearest value to 3643, the table value of 3584 is noted along with its hexadecimal representation 'E'.

Step e. Subtract the value of 3584 from the previous remaining balance for a new balance of 59. This amount represents the value that will next be searched for on the table.

Step f. In looking for the value nearest to 59 in the next right column, the value of 48 is found. It is the single value within the table that is closest to, but not greater than, the balance value of 59. The value of 48 and its hexadecimal representation of '3' are recorded.

Step g. Subtract the newest value from the latest balance, resulting in the newest balance. Because the search has now progressed to the right-most column of the table, the new balance cannot exceed a value of 15—otherwise a mistake has occurred during the conversion process. In this instance, the exact value of 11 is found on the table and its hexadecimal representation of 'B' is noted.

Step h. The hexadecimal digits recorded from the table are now taken from top to bottom and are set down from left to right as a compound hexadecimal expression. This results in the hexadecimal '3E3B', which in base-16 is equal to a decimal value of 15,931.

In describing these steps, each time a value was found in a table column, the subsequent search began in the next column to the right. Carefully note that if a satisfactory value is not found in that column during the subsequent search, a hex '0' digit should be recorded and the search should then progress to the next column to the right of that one. If a hexadecimal zero-digit is not recorded for each column in which a satisfactory value was not found, the resulting compound hexadecimal configuration will be grossly incorrect. The following examples illustrate the procedure of recording hex '0' digits during the conversion process.

Numeric Representation and Number Systems

Example 1. The decimal value to be converted is 47,621.

$$
\begin{array}{rll}
47{,}621 & & \\
\underline{45{,}056} & = \text{B} & \text{(found in column 4} \\
2{,}565 & & \text{from the right)} \\
\underline{2{,}560} & = \text{A} & \text{(found in column 3)} \\
5 & & \\
& = 0 & \text{(no comparable value} \\
& & \text{in column 2)} \\
5 & = 5 & \text{(found in column 1)}
\end{array}
$$

The hex value is expressed as 'BA05'.

Example 2. The decimal value to be converted is 36,908.

$$
\begin{array}{rll}
36{,}908 & & \\
\underline{36{,}864} & = 9 & \text{(found in column 4)} \\
44 & & \\
& = 0 & \text{(no comparable value} \\
& & \text{in column 3)} \\
\underline{32} & = 2 & \text{(found in column 2)} \\
12 & & \\
12 & = \text{C} & \text{(found in column 1)}
\end{array}
$$

The hex value is expressed as '902C'.

Example 3. The decimal value to be converted is 11,863,712.

$$
\begin{array}{rll}
11{,}863{,}712 & & \\
\underline{11{,}534{,}336} & = \text{B} & \text{(found in column 6} \\
329{,}376 & & \text{from the right)} \\
\underline{327{,}680} & = 5 & \text{(found in column 5)} \\
1{,}696 & & \\
& = 0 & \text{(no comparable value} \\
& & \text{in column 4)} \\
\underline{1{,}536} & = 6 & \text{(found in column 3)} \\
160 & & \\
\underline{160} & = \text{A} & \text{(found in column 2)} \\
0 & = 0 & \text{(found in column 1)}
\end{array}
$$

The hexadecimal value is expressed as 'B506A0'.

The importance of inserting a hexadecimal zero-digit when a value is not extracted from each successive column is reflected in these examples. If the zero-digit had not been placed into Example 1, the hex configuration would have resulted in 'BA5'—equal to a decimal value of 2981. If the zero digits had not been inserted in Example 3, the resulting hex configuration would have been 'B56A'—equal to a decimal value of 46,442. The general rule to follow is this: "Once the column containing the first value to be subtracted has been found, each successive column to the right must be represented by either a significant hex digit or a hex zero-digit." Even if the total decimal value has been reduced to a zero balance prior to exhausting all columns to the right, each of the remaining columns must be represented by zero-digits.

Decimal value to be converted is 720,896.

$$
\begin{array}{rll}
720{,}896 & & \\
\underline{720{,}896} & = B & \text{(found in column 5} \\
& & \text{from the right)} \\
0 & = 0 & \text{(found in column 4)} \\
0 & = 0 & \text{(found in column 3)} \\
0 & = 0 & \text{(found in column 2)} \\
0 & = 0 & \text{(found in column 1)}
\end{array}
$$

The hexadecimal value is expressed as 'B0000'.

Fixed-point values expressed in hexadecimal format vary somewhat from true binary values similarly expressed, in that the value of the sign-bit is included in the high-order hexadecimal digit. By looking at that high-order hex digit, it can be immediately determined whether or not the fixed-point value is of a positive or a negative configuration. Because a positive value contains a zero-bit in the high-order binary bit position of the high-order hex digit, a positive fixed-point value will always contain a high-order hex digit of '7' or less. Conversely, a negative fixed-point value will always contain a high-order hex digit of '8' or greater.

The positive-signed decimal equivalent of a positive fixed-point value is interpreted from hexadecimal digits as shown in the next examples.

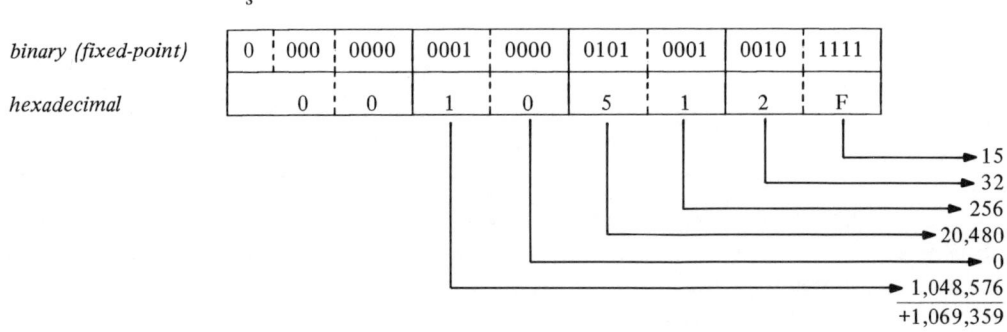

As shown in the previous illustrations, there is no apparent difference between the process of interpreting binary values from hexadecimal fields or interpreting positive fixed-point values from hexadecimal fields. This can be attributed to the fact that a positive fixed-point value always contains a zero-bit sign-bit. A negative fixed-point value always contains a one-bit sign-bit, which is not considered to be a part of the overall value of the integer. Therefore, it is necessary to modify the representation of the high-order hexadecimal digit prior to manually converting the negative fixed-point values from hexadecimal to decimal. Because a negative value of this type is in Two's Complement form, the interpretation of the base-16 values of the hex digits will not present the real negative value of the field. This problem may be circumvented by converting the hexadecimal digits of the negative value to the decimal equivalent of those digits and then subtracting that decimal value from the maximum negative fixed-point value containable in a field of equal length. For example, a negative value that is to be interpreted resides in a halfword storage location. The value is then—14,965.

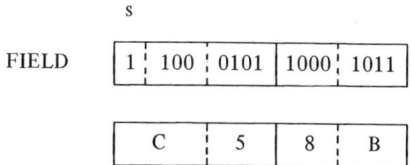

Because the high-order hex digit is greater than seven, the value must be of a negative power. In order to convert the integer value of this number, it is necessary to exclude the one-bit sign-bit from the value of the high-order hex digit; 'C' minus '8' (the hex value of the sign-bit) equals '4'. The hexadecimal digits could now be converted as:

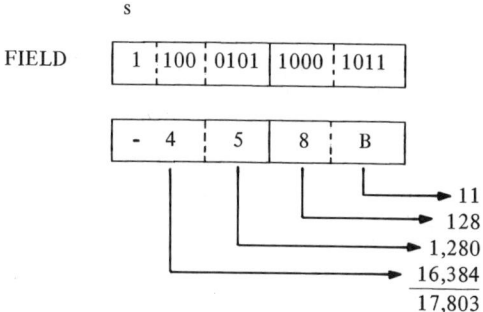

Now that the decimal equivalent of the Two's Complement form of the negative fixed-point value has been determined, subtract that decimal value from the maximum negative fixed-point value possible within a halfword field.

```
Maximum negative fixed-point value                              32,768
Subtract Two's Complement of decimal equivalent of FIELD        17,803
Actual negative fixed-point value of FIELD                      14,965
```

48   *Assembler Language for Application Programming*

The correct decimal equivalent has now been determined by hexadecimal/decimal conversion. This same process is utilized in the following examples.

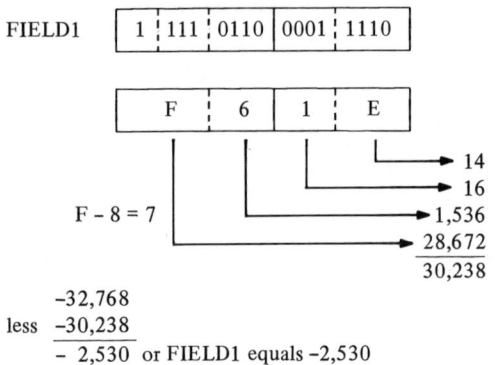

```
   -32,768
less -30,238
   - 2,530  or FIELD1 equals -2,530
```

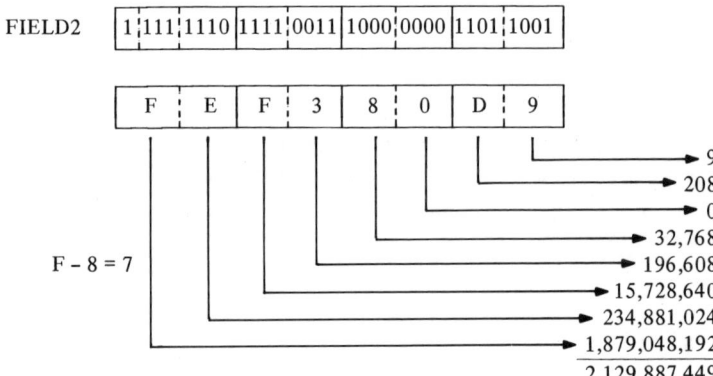

```
   -2,147,483,648
less -2,129,887,449
   -    17,596,199  or FIELD2 equals -17,596,199
```

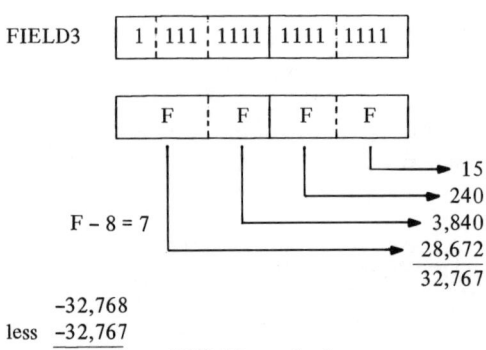

```
   -32,768
less -32,767
   -      1  or FIELD3 equals -1
```

Numeric Representation and Number Systems

As you become more involved with hexadecimals and hexadecimally expressed values, you will find the Hexadecimal/Decimal Conversion Table becoming more important for expedient interpretation. As you become more proficient with this type of arithmetic expression, the use of this table will become second nature, and portions of it will probably be committed to memory. In addition to the table, there are procedures for adding and subtracting hexadecimals that will be of considerable assistance in determining relocatable addresses, displacement factors, and table increments.

The rules for adding together any type of values follow the corresponding parameters for the "base" of those values. Accordingly, the addition of hexadecimal digits must follow the value parameters of a base-16 concept. For example:

```
    F              F  (15)           F  (15)
   +A     or      +A  (10)    or    +A  (10)
    ?              ?  (25)          19  (25)     (25 less 16 equals 9 with a carryover of 1)
```

Carefully examine the following examples of multiple hexadecimal digit addition.

Example 1. Hex '0C3' plus hex '175' equals?

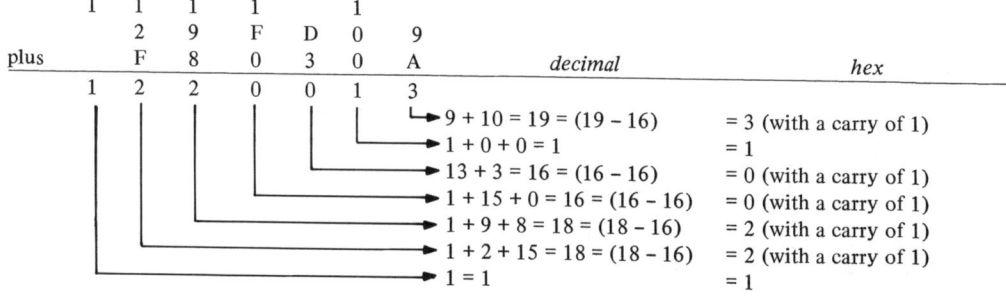

Example 2. Hex '3F268' plus hex '91433' equals?

Example 3. Hex '29FD09' plus hex 'F8030A' equals?

Example 4. Hex '49DE2' plus hex '5F6' equals?

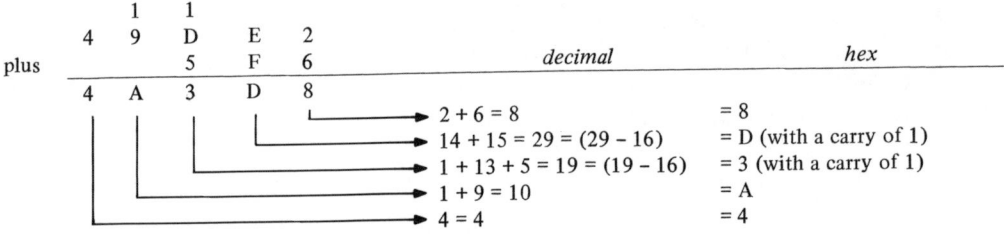

Subtracting hexadecimal digits follows the general rules of subtraction that apply to any base number system. For example, when a unit is "borrowed" from the next higher hex digit it assumes a value of 16 to the column that is borrowing it.

The following examples illustrate the process of "borrowing" as it is applied during the subtraction of hexadecimal digits.

```
                         C  16               C
            D  8         D̸  8                D̸  24
      or           or
  less  1  9    less  1  9         less  1  9
        ?             B  F                B  F
                (12 - 1 = 11 = B)   (24 - 9 = 15 = F)
```

Example 1. Hex '39F48' less hex '17058' equals?

Example 2. Hex 'F20351' less hex '30D21B' equals?

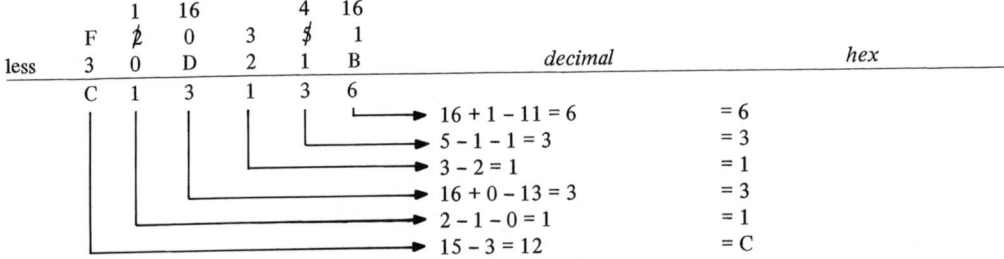

Numeric Representation and Number Systems

Example 3. Hex 'C27835' less hex 'B4339D' equals?

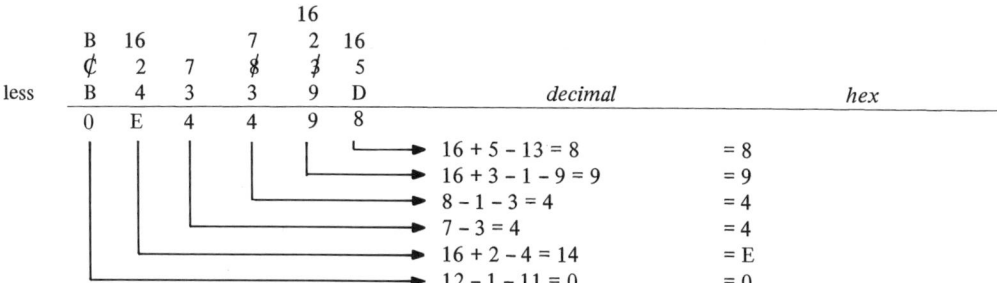

It is understandable that hexadecimals are often looked upon with apprehension by the student programmer. This is primarily because most number systems are composed solely of numeric representation structures, rather than including alpha characters such as those utilized by hexadecimal logic. Once you become accustomed to thinking of the hexadecimal alpha digits in their numeric sense, such as A = 10, B = 11, C = 12, etc., much of the apprehension of hexadecimal configurations should vanish.

In addition to representing a base-16 number system, hexadecimals are used to express packed decimal digits and to define the half-byte configurations of EBCDIC alpha-numeric characters. The packed decimal number system is explained within this section; the hexadecimal configuration of EBCDIC alpha-numeric characters is explained throughout the entire text.

At this point you should perform a task of self-evaluation of acquired knowledge of the concepts of hexadecimals. If the discussions presented within this section have not yet provided a reasonable working knowledge of hexadecimal/decimal conversions and simple hexadecimal arithmetic operations, such as subtraction and addition, it is strongly suggested that the entire section be reviewed.

THE PACKED DECIMAL NUMBER SYSTEM

In the packed decimal number system the value field usually consists of a single sign-digit and one or more numeric digits, all of which are represented by hexadecimal digits. In this application, the hexadecimal digit is not considered to be a base-16 value. Instead it represents a self-expressing base-10 digit. Logically, since the packed decimal digits are represented by hex digits, each packed decimal number occupies only one-half byte. The configuration of a packed decimal value may be in signed or unsigned representation, but it must be a signed value if it is to be used in packed decimal arithmetic operations or converted to a fixed-point value. In an unsigned packed decimal value, every half-byte is represented by a hexadecimal numeric digit; in a signed value, all half-bytes except the low-order (right-most) half-byte are represented by hexadecimal numeric digits. The sign of a packed decimal field must always appear in the low-order half-byte and must be one of the hexadecimal alpha digits of 'A' through 'F'. The standard positive (+) sign for a packed decimal value is a hex 'C' or 'F'; the standard negative (−) sign is a hex 'D'. Both signed and unsigned packed decimal values and their equivalent decimal values are contained in the illustration shown on the following page.

	packed decimal fields	assumed decimal equivalent
1.	`0 3 5 5 6 C`	+ 3,556
2.	`9 9 7 5`	9,975
3.	`0 0 0 0 0 C`	+ 0
4.	`7 5 8 4 4 1 2 6`	75,844,126
5.	`9 C`	+ 9
6.	`0 0 0 0 1 8 8 D`	− 188
7.	`0 6 2 0`	620
8.	`1 9 5 3 3 D`	− 19,533

As indicated by these examples, the hexadecimal configuration of a packed decimal field is self-expressing of its decimal equivalent. Fields 1, 3, and 5 are signed positive values; fields 6 and 8 are signed negative values; fields 2, 4, and 7 are unsigned values, assumed to be positive in lieu of a sign. Fields 2, 4, and 7 could not be used in conjunction with packed decimal arithmetic operations in their present format.

NUMERIC CHARACTER REPRESENTATION

The EBCDIC (Extended Binary Coded Decimal Interchange Code) numeral is the standard numeric character representation. A group of these numerals may be considered to be a numeric value or merely a set of characters that might be intended to create an identification. The composition of any EBCDIC character consists of eight binary bit positions; one full byte. The leftmost four bits are considered to comprise the zone of the character; the right-most four bits comprise the numeric portion. Numeric characters may be signed or unsigned. An unsigned EBCDIC numeral is assumed to be a positive value (+) or a neutral numeric; a signed EBCDIC numeral represents a positive (+) or negative (−) value, as the sign denotes.

The unsigned EBCDIC numeral of zero through nine is represented by the hexadecimal digit sets of 'F0' through 'F9'. The entire range is shown in Table 3-3.

Numeric Representation and Number Systems

TABLE 3-3

one byte	bit configuration	unsigned EBCDIC numeral
F 0	1111 0000	0
F 1	1111 0001	1
F 2	1111 0010	2
F 3	1111 0011	3
F 4	1111 0100	4
F 5	1111 0101	5
F 6	1111 0110	6
F 7	1111 0111	7
F 8	1111 1000	8
F 9	1111 1001	9

These unsigned numeric characters are considered to be positive values in lieu of having a signed configuration.

A signed EBCDIC numeral is referred to as a *"zoned decimal"* configuration. The right-most byte of a signed value expressed in EBCDIC numerics is the only one containing a zoned decimal numeral. The positive and negative signed zoned decimals are represented in Table 3-4.

TABLE 3-4

Signed Positive Zoned Decimals

value	hex	bit configuration	EBCDIC character
+0	C 0	1100 0000	(blank)
+1	C 1	1100 0001	A
+2	C 2	1100 0010	B
+3	C 3	1100 0011	C
+4	C 4	1100 0100	D
+5	C 5	1100 0101	E
+6	C 6	1100 0110	F
+7	C 7	1100 0111	G
+8	C 8	1100 1000	H
+9	C 9	1100 1001	I

Signed Negative Zoned Decimals

value	hex	bit configuration	EBCDIC character
-0	D 0	1101 0000	(blank)
-1	D 1	1101 0001	J
-2	D 2	1101 0010	K
-3	D 3	1101 0011	L
-4	D 4	1101 0100	M
-5	D 5	1101 0101	N
-6	D 6	1101 0110	O
-7	D 7	1101 0111	P
-8	D 8	1101 1000	Q
-9	D 9	1101 1001	R

As indicated by these tables, a signed EBCDIC numeric (zoned decimal) creates a standard EBCDIC alpha character in all instances except for a zero. A signed zero, either negative or positive, creates a configuration for which there is no valid character representation.

Unsigned EBCDIC numeric fields:

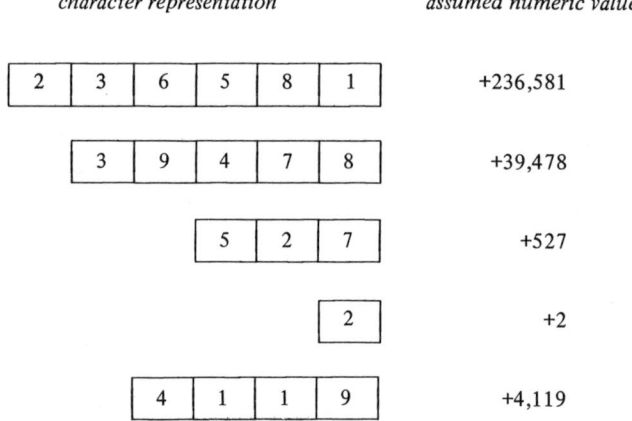

Signed positive-value EBCDIC numeric fields:

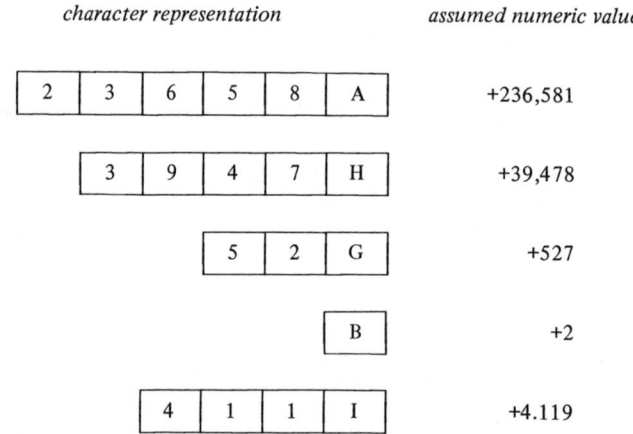

Signed negative-value EBCDIC numeric fields:

character representation	assumed numeric value
2 3 6 5 8 J	−236,581

| 3 | 4 | 9 | 7 | Q | -34,978

        | 5 | 2 | P | -527

                | K | -2

    | 4 | 1 | 1 | R | -4,119

REVIEW EXERCISES

1. The binary number system is comprised of two numeric digits. These are the numbers _____ and _____.
2. The high-order (left-most) bit position of an expressed fixed-point value is considered to contain the _____-_____. All other bit positions are considered to comprise the _____.
3. The integer of a fullword value is construed as consisting of the right-most _____ bit positions.
4. The "base-16" number system utilized in System/360 and System/370 is referred to as _____ representation.
5. EBCDIC alphanumeric characters are represented as consisting of _____ bit positions.
6. The hexadecimal digit 'C' represents a decimal value (base-10) of _____.
7. Packed decimal digits are graphically represented as synonymous with _____ digit representation.
8. An EBCDIC character that represents a signed (positive or negative) numeric value is referred to as a _____ _____.
9. Provide the bit configuration of the following *binary* values:

    a. 48,763

    b. 219,465

    c. 11,557

10. Determine the *fixed-point* value of each of the following fields and express them in decimal form.

a. _____ | S:0 | 111 0000 | 0110 1101 |

b. _____ | S:0 | 000 0000 | 0010 0001 | 1101 0011 | 0101 1101 |

c. _____ | S:0 | 000 1010 | 0111 1110 |

d. _____ | S:0 | 000 0000 | 1001 1111 | 0100 1000 | 0000 0011 |

e. _____ | S:1 | 110 0010 | 0001 0101 |

f. _____ | S:1 | 111 1111 | 1111 1011 | 1100 0011 | 1110 1110 |

11. Complete the bit configuration for the following *fixed-point* values:

a. A halfword value of + 26,715

b. A halfword value of − 8901

c. A fullword value of + 14,211,536

d. A fullword value of − 397,827

12. Determine the *binary* value of each of the binary-expressed fields and indicate that vlaue in decimal form:

a. _____ | 1001 0001 | 1100 0000 | 1001 0111 |

b. _____ | 1111 1111 | 1111 1111 |

c. _____ | 0000 | 0000 | 0000 | 0000 | 0101 | 1000 | 1110 | 1100 |

d. _____ | 0110 | 0111 | 1000 | 0110 | 0101 | 1001 |

13. Add each of the following sets of hexadecimals, expressing the sum of each set in hexadecimal and in decimal (base-10) form.

	a.	2CA1 3029	b.	59F 3082	c.	600C 514D 2953	d.	A0FF 2B33 05C2
hex		_____		_____		_____		_____
decimal		_____		_____		_____		_____
	e.	0C00 31D6 281C	f.	6FF6 2A1D 2177	g.	A37 6C9F	h.	2001 300F
hex		_____		_____		_____		_____
decimal		_____		_____		_____		_____

14. Complete the bit configuration for the following sets of hexadecimals:

a. 3FA6C1

b. D587

c. F347E

d. 189C4B

15. Subtract the following sets of hexadecimals, expressing the resulting difference for each problem in hexadecimal and as a positive decimal value:

	a.	2C356 1D0F7	b.	3A29 B36	c.	A59F 34B5	d.	7B73D 42ACF
hex		_____		_____		_____		_____
decimal		_____		_____		_____		_____

16. Indicate the implied decimal value of these *packed decimal* fields:

a. _____ | 4 | 0 | 0 | C |

b. _____ | 0 | 0 | 3 | 0 | 9 | 7 | 0 | D |

c. _____ | 0 | 0 | 0 | 0 | 6 | 5 | 0 | 0 | 2 | C |

d. _____ | 0 | 8 | 7 | 0 | 0 | D |

e. _____ | 1 | 0 | 7 | 8 | 6 | 0 | 3 | 9 |

17. Define the implied numeric character value of the following *zoned decimal* character representations:

a. _____ | 3 | 0 | 2 | 2 | 5 | 7 | 0 | 6 | 4 | R |

b. _____ | 0 | 0 | 7 | 0 | 3 | M |

c. _____ | 5 | 5 | 8 | A |

d. _____ | 4 | 0 | 0 | 6 | 7 | 9 | 9 | P |

4
Assembler Language Instruction Formats

The Assembler Language of System/360 and System/370 provides a means of program coding that enables the programmer to control the individual logic operations of a program to the smallest degree. It is technically referred to as a low-level language—that is, the structure and relationship of the actual coding instructions are quite close to the machine-language level. Although a single machine-language instruction may cause the computer to perform several internal functions, it is generally considered that a machine-language is the lowest level of instructions that can be coded for the computer.

The individual Assembler Language *instruction*, which may be considered to be a *command* or *statement* to the computer, generates a machine-language instruction, along with certain implied or specified parameters relating to that instruction. If you attempted to code in pure machine-language, it would be necessary to maintain constant surveillance of boundary alignments, register applications and assignments, displacements, lengths, addresses, and many other features that you would soon find overwhelming. However, the Assembler Language compiler interprets the individual instruction statements in such a way as to supervise control of many of these functions. It is still your responsibility to assign and maintain register controls, but not nearly to the degree required in machine-language coding.

Programming with Assembler Language includes the use of *macroinstructions* as provided by the operating system and access methods to be used. A macroinstruction is a unique instruction, or command, that may be stated with a variable number of operand parameters. A single macroinstruction *generates* a series of Assembler Language instructions and macrocoding that provides a service without requiring you to become involved in complex coding. The term generate, as used here, may be somewhat misleading in that the macroinstruction does not really create any unique coding. All of the related instruction statements for each macroinstruction are contained in an operating system library if their inclusion was specified at system generation time. The use of a macroinstruction in the problem program results in a *call* to this library in order to provide the system with the instructions necessary to perform the task for which that macroinstruction was designed. The names, as well as the performance, of the macroinstructions may vary considerably between access methods and operating systems. This text will make no attempt to discuss macroinstructions other than an occasional use of one or two in examples of program coding routines. Even then the use of such macros will be referred to in the most general terms.

The individual Assembler Language instructions described in this text are the Standard Instruction Set and the Decimal Feature Instruction Set. Floating-Point Logic and Floating-Point Feature Instructions of Assembler Language are not to be included in these discussions. In the author's opinion, floating-point arithmetic operations in Assembler Language are not required for the majority of programming students at this stage of their education; the complexity of floating-point applications lends itself to a high-level language of the nature of PL/I or FORTRAN. This could well be a controversial opinion, but with all due apologies, it is the basis on which this portion of the text is presented.

As the study of Assembler Language progresses, supplemented by the discussions and examples within this text, so will your concept of the versatility and scope of System/360 and System/370 progress. In learning the performance of these instructions, one cannot help but derive a better understanding of the detailed processes used by the computer's system control programs in executing those instructions.

The instruction format has two distinct variations. The first format may be interpreted as the way that an instruction statement is written by the programmer. The second format is the way that the system compiler interprets that coding and rearranges it into an executable machine-language sequence. Although these two format groupings are directly related, you will at first need to be more thoroughly familiar with the coded instruction statement format. Once you have begun to write problem programs, you will find that the knowledge of the machine-language format of these intructions will assist in the analysis and interpretation of errors and coding problems.

THE INSTRUCTION STATEMENT CODING FORMAT

An instruction statement, as coded by the programmer, may consist of three sections of data. These are:

- The *LABEL* or *SYMBOL*
- The mnemonic *OP CODE*
- The *OPERANDS*, consisting of from one to three per statement.

These sections comprise an individual instruction statement in its maximum form. Of these, only the op code and the operands are required in order to create a valid statement.

The Label or Symbol

The label is referred to as a symbol, a tag, a name, or an identifier, depending on the nomenclature to which the individual has been exposed. Overall, regardless of the reference, it is used to identify the address of an instruction statement, a defined area, a constant, or the beginning of a routine or subroutine. Whenever a label is used as a part of one of these, the compiler cross-references that label as the address point within the program for that data. Any separate references to that label would then be the same as to use the actual address to which the label relates. A label, therefore, is merely a convenient means of referring to a certain address for a section or a part of the problem program. If no reference is required it is unnecessary to use a label for identification.

The configuration of the label has certain restrictions. The maximum number of characters that may be used in the label varies among different operating systems. For use within OS or OS/VS, the label may consist of from one to eight characters. Although these characters may be mixed alpha-numerics, the first character of the label must be alphabetic. The label may not contain special characters or embedded blanks. The following list consists of valid label references:

Assembler Language Instruction Formats

```
SKIP      PACKRT1
K23456    R
PTS32R    BRANCH
ADD       MOVE
M3M3M3    MVO
```

Note that the last label (MVO) is also the op code for the Move With Offset instruction. This is a valid label as long as it is coded in the proper position of the coding sheet. Any combination of alpha-numerics you can originate are valid if you follow the composition restrictions for a label. Because a unique label is used to reference any single address within the problem program, it is understandable that an identical label may not be used to reference two different addresses within that program.

The Op Code

The op code is the mnemonic representation of the function to be performed by the instruction statement. It represents an activity that the system compiler translates into a machine-language instruction, telling the object program just what action to accomplish. The op code usually represents a single Assembler Language instruction, although it may also represent a macroinstruction identity. In most instances, the alphabetic characters forming the op code have a noticeable relationship to the descriptive name for the instruction that they represent. This relationship is shown in the following op codes for Assembler Language instructions:

```
AR      Add Registers
CL      Compare Logical
EDMK    Edit & Mark
CVD     Convert to Decimal
LPR     Load Positive Register
STM     Store Multiple
DP      Divide Packed
EX      Execute
```

The Operands

A macroinstruction statement need not necessarily have any operands; however, any single Assembler Language instruction statement may contain from one to three operand parameters. Each individual Assembler Language statement may contain from one to three operand parameters. Each individual instruction has a set number of operands that must be specified in order to compose a valid instruction statement. The operand(s) provide the problem program with the address of the field(s) or data to be affected by execution of the op code. For example, the Move Characters (MVC) instruction requires two operands when it is coded into an instruction statement—one operand identifying the area from which the data is to be moved and another operand identifying the field into which the data is to be placed. The unique characteristics of the op code for each instruction determines the use and application of the address generated by the operands. In most instances, the contents of the area or the value specified by the second operand is used to alter the contents, or value, of the first operand. There are exceptions to this performance, so it is necessary to be completely aware of the activity generated by each instruction.

Included with the individual summarized descriptions of the Assembler Language instructions within this text will be an item referred to as a *Format*. For that particular format description, the operands will be shown as consisting of elements, such as $R_1,D_2(X_2,B_2)$. In this instance R_1 represents the first operand of a completed instruction statement and $D_2(X_2,B_2)$ represents the second operand. As implied, a comma not within parentheses separates operands. The use of the parentheses indicates that the elements within them may be used to further modify the operand with which they appear.

The following is a complete listing of all of the elements used in operand formats.

- B The *base register* for the operand in which it is specified.
- D The *displacement*; an actual or symbolic address or value.
- I An *immediate* or self-defining character or value.
- L An explicit *length* attribute for the operand in which specified.
- M A *mask* value, defined as either a literal or a constant.
- R A *general register* used as an operand; or a label or symbol that has been equated to a general register.
- X An *indexing*, or incrementing, general register.

In order that these codes be related directly to the operand for which they apply, a numeric character is also used to identify the component of the instruction statement to which they belong.

1 The number *1*, paired with a format component of the instruction statement, identifies that component as being a part, or the whole, of the first operand.
2 The number *2*, paired with a format component, identifies that component as being a part, or the whole, of the second operand.
3 The number *3*, paired with a format component, identifies that component as being the whole of the third operand. When used with multiple register operands, it identifies the ending register in a sequential range of general registers.

Applying this information to sample coded instruction statements, the identity of the various operands and components would be considered to be as shown in Figure 4-1.

The general forms taken by the instruction statement formats are grouped as follows.

RR FORMAT:
- R_1,R_2
  Both operands refer to general registers.

- M_1,R_2
  The first operand is a *mask* value; the second operand is a general register.

RS FORMAT:
- $R_1,R_3,D_2(B_2)$
  R_1 and R_3 refer to general registers; $D_2(B_2)$ refers to a displacement or storage address, either as an actual value or as a symbolic reference to an address.

- $R_1,D_2(B_2)$
  R_1 refers to a general register; $D_2(B_2)$ refers to a displacement or storage address, either as an actual value or as a symbolic reference to that address.

- $R_1,M_3,D_2(B_2)$
  R_1 refers to a general register; M_3 refers to a mask value; $D_2(B_2)$ refers to a displacement or storage address either as an actual value or as a symbolic reference to that address.

Assembler Language Instruction Formats

SYSTEM / 370 ASSEMBLER CODING FORM

LABELS	OP Codes	OPERANDS
GOTO	BC	8,THERE
		M1 D2
PASS12	MVC	FIELD1(10),FIELD2+6
		D1 L1 D2
	STM	3,9,FULLWDS
		R1 R3 D2
	CLC	0(5,9),TABLE(7)
		D1 L B1 D2 B2
MVI	MVI	SWITCH,X'00'
		D1 I2
	ZAP	FLD1+6(5),FLD2(3)
		D1 L1 D2 L2

FIGURE 4-1

RX FORMAT:
- $R_1,D_2(X_2,B_2)$
  R_1 refers to a general register; $D_2(X_2,B_2)$ refers to a displacement or storage address, either as an actual value or as a symbolic reference to an address.
- $M_1,D_2(X_2,B_2)$
  M_1 refers to a mask value; $D_2(X_2,B_2)$ refers to a displacement or storage address, either as an actual address value or as a symbolic reference to an address.

SI FORMAT:
- $D_1(B_1),I_2$
  $D_1(B_1)$ refers to a displacement or storage address, either as an actual value or as a symbolic reference to an address; I_2 refers to a self-defining or *immediate* character, value or reference.

SS FORMAT:
- $D_1(L_1,B_1),D_2(B_2)$
  Both operands refer to displacement or storage addresses, either as actual values or as symbolic references to addresses.
- $D_1(L_1,B_1)D_2(L_2,B_2)$
  Both operands refer to displacement or storage addresses, either as actual values or as symbolic address references.
- $D_1(L_1,B_1),D_2(B_2),I_3$
  $D_1(L_1,B_1)$ and $D_2(B_2)$ both refer to a displacement or storage address, either as actual values or as symbolic address references; I_3 refers to a self-defining or immediate character or value.

The operand components contained within the parentheses are optional—that is, they may be specified by their inclusion in the coding or they may be implied by their exclusion from the coding. For example, if the defined length of a field labeled AREA was six bytes, and the instruction statements were coded as:

```
MVC     AREA (4) , DATA
MVC     AREA , DATA
```

the first statement would move four bytes of data from DATA into AREA because the length attribute of "4" was specified. The second statement would move six bytes of data because the implied length of AREA is six bytes.

There is also a group of instruction statements which are categorized as "S Format." These are "privileged" instructions and as such should only be used by experienced systems programmers who are fully aware of the potential effect these instructions can have on the operating system.

CODING SHEET CONVENTIONS

As a follow-up to the format of instruction statements, it is appropriate to describe an accepted practice of writing down the coded instructions. Although the Assembler Language compiler allows a certain amount of free-form instruction statement entry, it is far more desirable for the programmer to adhere to a clean, aligned form of coding. This means the labels, op codes, and the first operand should each be aligned at a specified starting point, instruction statement after instruction statement.

Using the standard 80-column coding form an acceptable convention would be formatted as follows:

Column 1. The LABEL must always start in this column. It may be eight positions in length if written for the Operating System (OS) or OS/VS.

Column 10. The OP CODE should begin in this column. Because a blank must always separate a label from the op code, this practice will assure that there is always at least one blank between the op code and a maximum-length label of eight bytes.

Column 16. The first character of the first **operand** should begin here. This allows at least one blank between the op code and the operands. In some instances wherein a macroinstruction op code is used, that op code may be longer than a regular Assembler Language instruction op code; therefore, in order to leave a blank prior to the first character of the first operand, it might be necessary for the first operand to begin in a higher-numbered column.

By following this suggested format, the source listing printed out by the compiler is quite easily read and interpreted. Using these standards, a set of coded instruction statements to be keypunched would appear as in Figure 4-2.

As shown in this illustration, the labels, op codes and operands are all consistently aligned in their respective starting positions. Also, several new items are introduced in this example for the convenience of the programmer. Some of these are the two different ways of entering *comments* information on the coding sheets without affecting the compiler interpretation of the program instructions. In the middle of the example are four lines that contain an asterisk (*) in column 1. This symbol indicates to the compiler that these are "comments lines" that are to be included within the source compilation listing, but are not to be included as a part of the object module. As they are shown here, they are being used to create a visual separation between two subroutines, as well as to document the second routine by providing a "comment heading." You may write any type of information on such a line and insert these lines wherever you wish—even between two lines of sequential instruction logic—without any effect on the performance of the program.

The second type of "comment" entry is shown on the line labeled FINDIT, line 0011. The words "LOAD BASE REGISTER" are shown following the operands for this instruction, with several blanks between the end of the last operand and the comment. A comment to be written on the same line with an instruction statement may occupy up to, and including, column 71 of the coding sheet, but it must be separated from the operands by *at least* one blank position.

By using these two means of entering comments, you can thoroughly document the logic of your coding, skip spaces between subroutines, general headings and explanations of the routines, and provide a brief explanation of the intent of each instruction if that is desired. Good documentation of the source program is a highly desirable feature and, in many instances, it is a required standard set by data processing management.

Columns 73 to 80 of the coding sheet contain spaces for entering sequence numbers for the individual instruction statements or lines of coding. Any or all of these columns may be used for line identification. The sequence numbers are punched into the source code cards at the same time that the coding statements are keypunched, providing identities that allow them to be resequenced or sorted in the event that the card *deck* is dropped. The sequence numbers also allow

SYSTEM / 370 ASSEMBLER CODING FORM

Name	Operation	Operand	Comments	Seq
START	MVC	FIELD1,DATA		0001
	STM	2,13,SAVEAREA		0002
	L	5,FWD1		0003
BRANCHED	BAL	6,FINDIT		0004
	ZAP	PACKFLD1,=PL1'0'		0005
	BCT	5,BRANCHED		0006
*				0007
*		FINDIT LOOKUP ROUTINE		0008
*				0009
FINDIT	LA	9,10		0010
	CLI	0(9),C'S'	LOAD BASE REGISTER	0011
	BCR	8,6		0012
	MVI	0(10),C'X'		0013
	BCR	15,6		0014
*				0015
				0016

TABLE 4-2

the programmer to change any single source statement by merely following the sequence numbers through the source deck until the proper card is located. The sequence numbers contained on the source deck cards are also listed on the compiled source listing so that you may cross-reference any single source statement.

MACHINE–LANGUAGE INSTRUCTION FORMATS

Some knowledge of the format of the machine-language instruction, as created by the Assembler Language compiler, is helpful in analyzing program error conditions and interpreting *dumps* of program storage. A storage dump may be explained as a printed listing, in hexadecimal format, of the contents of the main storage areas occupied by the problem program and the related system Supervisor. A dump is normally produced whenever the problem program encounters various types of programming infractions or data set inconsistencies that result in error interruptions. A storage print-out of this type may be requested by the programmer, requested by the computer operator, or automatically provided by certain error conditions. At that time the programmer may need to understand the machine-language instruction formats in order to follow the phase of programming accomplished immediately prior to the program termination.

These formats, by category of type of instruction, are as follows:

RR FORMAT

RX FORMAT

RS FORMAT

SI FORMAT

SS FORMAT

The small numeric figures under each example represent the relative bit positions occupied by that portion of the machine-language instruction format.

The component codes used for these formats are the same as those used for the instruction statement formats. An example of an RX formatted instruction (in machine-language format) can be followed from the instruction statement format as shown in the following example. The instruction statement is:

    LA   9 , 83

The machine-language format for this statement would be:

    4 1 9 0 0 0 5 3

Assembler Language Instruction Formats

This would be interpreted in a diagram in the following manner:

op code	R_1	X_2	B_2	D_2	
4 1	9	0	0	0 5 3	= *hexadecimal*
0100 0001	1001	0000	0000	0000 0101 0011	= *binary*
LA	9	0	0	+83	= *actual*

CONDITION CODES

The *Condition Code* is represented by two bit positions within the *Program Status Word* (PSW). It is, in effect, an indicator of a condition that was created by, or resulted from, the execution of a previous instruction statement. By testing the configuration of the Condition Code the programmer is able to make program logic decisions based on the configuration. Not all Assembler Language instructions affect the bit configuration of the Condition Code bits, as will be noted during the discussion of the individual instructions. Some of the questions that can be answered by the Condition Code are:

- Was the comparison high, low, or equal?
- Was the resulting answer zero?
- Was the resulting answer a positive value or a negative value?
- Did an arithmetic overflow occur?

Certain instructions test the Condition Code and then react according to the parameters coded for that instruction statement. Although it is not necessary to become technically involved with the form and use of the Condition Code at this time, throughout this text is additional detailed information regarding the composition and utilization of the Condition Code. The chapter on "Program Branching Logic" will go into specific detail about the bit configuration of the Condition Code within the PSW and the means of coding instructions to create a "branch" to another section of the problem program.

REGISTER CONCEPTS AND APPLICATIONS

System/360 and System/370 have a special set of internal storage areas that are referred to as registers. As a part of the system there are sixteen *"general registers,"* referenced by number as "0" through "15". In addition, if the hardware was so ordered, the user may have four additional registers that are referred to as *"floating-point"* registers, each of which have twice the physical number of bit positions of a general register. Because the floating-point registers are not a standard hardware feature on all models and because the floating-point operations are not included within this text, all further references to registers will imply a general register.

A general register is considered to be one fullword in length—four bytes or 32 bit positions. They are located in a contiguous arrangement, "0" through "15", similar to a chain of fullwords. The technical descriptions of the applications of registers will be found throughout this text, but a basic knowledge of their use should be acquired at this point.

The primary use of a register in Assembler Language is to establish a *"base"* range for referencing a set of instruction statements. When a register is used for this purpose it is called a *"base register.*" Simply expressed, the system requires that a base register be assigned for at least every 4096 bytes of object coding generated by the source coding. This includes the areas occupied by constants, literals, and program work fields. The base register creates a type of linkage between the various machine-language instructions contained within the 4096 bytes to which that register has been assigned. If a program is anticipated to generate more than 4096 bytes of object module coding, then enough base registers must be assigned to encompass the number of bytes generated. These assignments would normally be in increments of 4096 bytes.

There are a number of ways to establish base register assignments. If you have the ability to estimate the object coding generated by the program statements, you could assign the base registers throughout the coding of the program as they are required. However, this can result in poor utilization of the registers because it is nearly impossible to determine in advance the exact point within a program where a new base register assignment is necessary. A very convenient means of base register assignment is the "stringing" of base registers together at the beginning of the problem program coding. A rough estimate of the program size is all that is necessary to initialize several base registers at this point in the program. They are established in such a manner that each 4096 bytes covered by a single base register is consecutive in assignment to the next 4096 bytes. The manner of applying this technique is described within the section "Basic Program Initialization." Because all base register assignments are made at one point in the program, this method of creating the base register assignments allows the addition or deletion of extra base registers without difficulty.

A word of caution should be given on the use of certain general registers as base registers. The various operating systems use several of the general registers to perform special linkage tasks. When the system takes control of any of these registers, it destroys the value contained previously within that register. For example, when executing an Assembler Language program operating under OS or OS/VS, it is almost a certainty that the system will use general registers 0, 1, 13, 14 and 15 during the operation of that program. In addition, the Assembler Language Translate & Test instruction will destroy any prior contents of general register 2. Using this information as a guide, it is therefore safe to assume that general registers 3 through 12 are available for your exclusive use, either as base registers, or as control registers to be used in conjunction with instruction statements.

Using registers as a part of the instruction statement is well defined within the description of each appropriate instruction, and governed by certain basic rules. Data being loaded into a register from a storage location must come from a storage area which is aligned on a *fullword boundary* address. A fullword boundary is any main storage location address which is within the range of the problem program and is divisible by four. Likewise, data being stored from a general register to a storage location must have the storage location residing on a fullword boundary address.

Registers are required for the performance of fixed-point arithmetic operations. Although the values to be used by fixed-point operations may reside in storage areas, *at least* one value must be loaded into a register in order to accomplish the arithmetic operation. Depending upon the type of fixed-point instruction to be performed, either one, two or three general registers might be utilized by the instruction statement.

DATA FORMAT

Other than special coding or conversion of information created by the problem program, the *logical* concept of data is represented in three forms: EBCDIC character data, packed decimal numeric data, and fixed-point arithmetic data. As stated, these are the logical concepts of data

Assembler Language Instruction Formats

format, although any of these may also be thought of as binary bit configurations or hexadecimal digit configurations. As a rule, however, there will be a general relationship between the concept of the data format and the identification of its configuration.

Special codes or converted information created by the problem program must also be thought of in terms of one of the data formats or configurations. There is no standard for selecting this information inasmuch as it is your prerogative to determine how it would be more easily decoded or reconverted to standard form.

Character Data

Character formatted data, as it is used within this text, is an alpha numeric or special character representation comprised of eight binary bit positions and constituting a graphically defined number, letter or symbol. This includes alphabetics "A" through "Z", numerics "0" through "9", and such symbol-characters as), (, #, ?, ', $, /, -, etc. A complete listing of the characters that comprise character formatted data can be found in the EBCDIC Character Table in Part V of this text. EBCDIC (which may be pronounced Ē-BICK-DICK), or "Extended Binary-Coded Decimal Interchange Code," represents a standard character-set code in which the graphic characters are identified by unique bit configurations, the bit positions being numbered from 0 through 7, from left to right. Inasmuch as it requires eight bit positions to constitute a single graphic EBCDIC character, it may be stated that a single graphic EBCDIC character requires one byte.

Using the letter "F" and the numeric "4" as examples of one-byte EBCDIC characters, the configurations of these characters can be perceived in three ways.

	1 Byte	*1 Byte*
character format	F	4
hexadecimal digit configuration	C | 6	F | 4
binary bit configuration	1100 | 0110	1111 | 0100

Although it is seldom necessary to know the binary bit configuration of character data, it is often useful to remember the hexadecimal digit composition of alphanumeric characters. This is particularly true when interpreting problem program dumps, which contain untranslated hexadecimal digits as the storage representation.

As indicated, any character that is considered to be a standard EBCDIC graphic character consists of a unique eight-bit configuration. Even though a single byte can contain any one of 256 unique bit configurations, there are only 63 EBCDIC graphic characters. The remaining 193 unique bit configurations do not normally represent characters in the sense that character-formatted data implies.

Packed Decimal Data

Packed decimal data is in a form synonymous with hexadecimal digit configuration; each packed decimal digit is composed of four binary bit positions, equal to one-half byte or one *nibble*. The data itself consists of packed decimal numeric digits (0 through 9) and sign-digits (alphabetic hex digits A through F). Each validly signed packed decimal value must have a single sign-digit residing in the low-order (right-most) half-byte of the field occupied by that value. The remaining packed decimal digits forming the whole of the value must be numeric digits only. It is possible to create a packed decimal value in which all digit positions are represented by numeric digits, but this type of packed decimal cannot be used for packed decimal arithmetic operations. Only validly signed packed decimal values may be used in conjunction with Assembler Language packed decimal arithmetic instructions or operations.

Because of their hexadecimal digit configuration, packed decimal values are easily recognized whenever it is necessary to interpret hexadecimal-configurated storage dumps. This will become evident in the analysis of the examples within this section and others.

The packed decimal format may be considered to be a compressed means of expressing a conventional character-formatted decimal value. Each byte of packed decimal digits contains two numeric digits except for the low-order byte, which usually contains one numeric digit and one sign-digit. A series of decimal values is shown in Table 4.1, along with their corresponding packed decimal format as they would appear within a four-byte field. Although the length of the fields shown for these values is four bytes, the length need only be as many bytes as are required to contain the left-most significant (nonzero) packed decimal digit. Note that the sign-digits for the

TABLE 4-1

decimal value	equivalent packed decimal value format
+254	0 0 | 0 0 | 2 5 | 4 C
+395,116	0 3 | 9 5 | 1 1 | 6 C
+0	0 0 | 0 0 | 0 0 | 0 C
+1	0 0 | 0 0 | 0 0 | 1 C
−45,926	0 0 | 4 5 | 9 2 | 6 D
−0	0 0 | 0 0 | 0 0 | 0 D
+0096	0 0 | 0 0 | 0 9 | 6 C
+7,134,298	7 1 | 3 4 | 2 9 | 8 C
−0	0 0 | 0 0 | 0 0 | 0 B
+3,655	0 0 | 0 3 | 6 5 | 5 A
+116,644	0 1 | 1 6 | 6 4 | 4 E
+00882	0 0 | 0 0 | 8 8 | 2 F

Assembler Language Instruction Formats

illustrated values vary for similar positive or negative configurations. A valid plus sign (+) may be represented by a hexadecimal 'A', 'C', 'E', or 'F'; a valid negative sign may be represented by 'D' or 'B'. However, the usual representation for a packed decimal value is a 'C' for a signed positive value and a 'D' for a negative or minus value.

The purpose of creating packed decimal fields is for performing packed decimal arithmetic operations, compressing numeric data for file storage, and for using editing instructions to put numeric digits to graphic output devices, such as a printer, display terminals or typewriter terminals, in a formatted manner. Whenever eight-bit EBCDIC character data is packed, creating a packed decimal value, the left-most four bits of the EBCDIC characters are discarded. When that packed decimal value is unpacked into eight-bit EBCDIC character format, all character bytes, with the exception of the low-order byte, are supplied with the left-most four bits of a numeric character zone, a hexadecimal 'F'. It is useless, therefore, to attempt to compress EBCDIC alphabetics into packed decimal format; when that same data is later unpacked, it will have permanently lost its alphabetic identity and appear as numeric character data.

The functions of packed decimal values and the means of converting them are thoroughly explained in the section "Packed Decimal Arithmetic Operations" and "Packed Decimal/Fixed-Point Conversion," as well as in numerous other places throughout this text.

Fixed-Point Data

Fixed-point data may be considered to be binary arithmetic values that are contained in increments of halfwords, fullwords, or registers. The data itself is not necessarily used for arithmetic operations, but may be used as an address, an increment, or an absolute value. Fixed-point values are thought of as a binary-configured integer in which the "Powers-of-Two" values of the bits within the contiguous bit positions are summed together to arrive at the overall value of the integer. In a fixed-point value, the sign of the value is represented by the left-most (high-order) bit position of the field or register. A one-bit in the high-order bit position indicates a negative integer value; a zero-bit indicates a positive integer value.

Utilizing the binary bit configuration of fixed-point values, Table 4-2 represents a logical concept of the signed integer expression.

TABLE 4-2

fullword	0 000 0000 0001 0000 0010 0000 0010 1001	+1,056,809
fullword	1 111 1111 1111 0111 0011 1111 1001 0011	−573,549
fullword	0 000 0000 0000 0000 1111 0010 1001 1110	+62,110
halfword	0 000 0011 1111 0000	+1,008
halfword	1 111 1111 1111 0111	−9
halfword	0 000 0101 1001 1101	+1,437

Using the last halfword illustrated in Table 4-2 (+ 1437), the summing of the "Powers-of-Two" values of the one-bits would appear as:

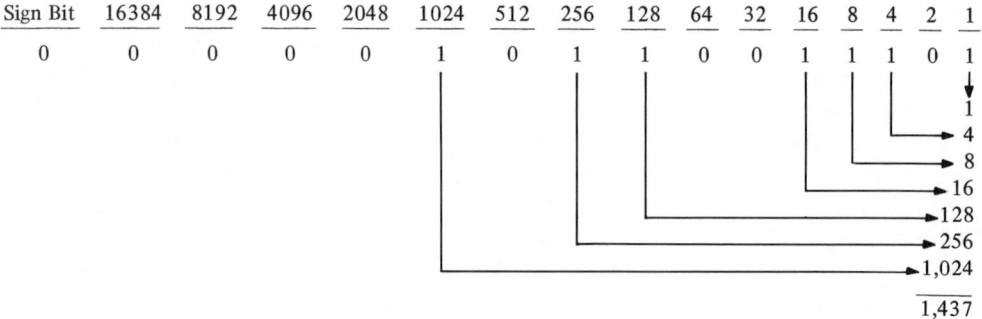

Specific detailed information about interpreting fixed-point values, translating negative fixed-point values, and hexadecimal computation of fixed-point values may be found in the following sections of this text:

Fixed-Point Arithmetic Operations
Packed Decimal/Fixed-Point Conversions
Hexadecimal/Decimal Conversion Table
"Powers-of-Two" Table
Comparing Data and Conditions

A direct and understandable relationship also exists between hexadecimal digit configuration (arithmetic base-16) and the binary bit configuration (arithmetic base-2) of fixed-point values. By using the Hexadecimal/Decimal Conversion Table (see Part V), the hexadecimal digit configuration of a fixed-point value can be calculated directly into the integer value of the number. This type of value conversion is extremely useful; fixed-point values and addresses generated by a problem program are accessible only as a hexadecimal configuration unless the programmer wishes to calculate the binary bit configuration and then sum the "Powers-of-Two" values of those bits. It will be found that the hexadecimal conversion to fixed-point value is considerably more expedient.

Special Data

Special data is not in itself a data format, but rather an interpretation of information that has been configured in any one of the three logical data format arrangements—character, packed decimal, or fixed-point. Quite often the desired information is expressed by the lowest possible configuration, binary bit format, and yet it could coincidentally comprise a valid packed decimal field or an EBCDIC character. This possibility can readily be illustrated: assume that the programmer has established a single byte of storage that is intended to contain eight condition switches, wherein each bit position of the byte is used as a "yes/no" indicator or switch. The bit positions, from left to right, are considered to be Switch 1 through Switch 8. If a switch position contains a one-bit, the implied condition is "yes;" if it contains a zero-bit, the condition is "no." It is quite probable that the circumstances would arrive at any time wherein a "yes" condition could

Assembler Language Instruction Formats   75

be simultaneously reflected for Switches 2, 3, 4, 5 and 6. If this occurred, the bit configuration of the entire byte would appear as:

one byte

0	1	1	1	1	1	0	0
Switch 1	Switch 2	Switch 3	Switch 4	Switch 5	Switch 6	Switch 7	Switch 8

This particular binary bit configuration also represents a hexadecimal configuration of '7C' as shown below.

binary configuration | 0111 | 1100 |

hexadecimal configuration | 7 | C |

This representation may also be construed to be two other valid data formats.

| 7 | C | = a one-byte packed decimal field for a value of +7

| 7 | C | = the EBCDIC character '@'

Insofar as the programmer's intent is concerned, however, the real configuration of this data is the "yes/no" condition reflected by the bit position digits. If the programmer were to use a data code consisting of hexadecimal digits, it is quite likely that this coded data would assume at some time the appearance of a packed decimal field or EBCDIC character data.

Worthy of repeating is the fact that a strong recognition of hexadecimal configurations is a valuable asset to any programmer. Any type of data format can be readily interpreted through its hexadecimal representation.

1. Two hexadecimal digits can represent an EBCDIC character.
2. Two or more hexadecimal digits can represent a packed decimal field.
3. The hexadecimal digits comprising a fixed-point value can be quickly converted into the sign-bit and integer combination.
4. Binary bit values are readily distinguishable from the hexadecimal digits they comprise.

REVIEW EXERCISES

1. A general register has a byte capacity of _____ bytes, equal to one _____.
2. An Assembler Language Op Code, when used in conjunction with applicable operands, comprises an instruction_____.
3. A name that has been used to designate an instruction statement, a defined area, a constant, or the beginning of a routine is referred to as a _____.
4. There are _____ general registers available to the Assembler Language programmer.

5. The first character of a label must be an _____ character.
6. What are the register numbers assigned to the general registers? _____
7. A byte consists of _____ bit positions.
8. The mnemonic representation of an Assembler Language instruction is referred to as an _____ _____.
9. Packed decimal digits are the same configuration as _____ digits.
10. Regular binary values are considered to be a _____ value even though they are not signed.
11. A fullword boundary is any main storage position address that is evenly divisible by_____.
12. An Assembler Language instruction statement may consist of a label, an op code, and from one to three _____.
13. Fixed-point values may be signed as either a _____ or a _____ configuration.
14. A halfword boundary is any main storage position address that is evenly divisible by_____.
15. When creating a label to define any portion of the program, the first character of the label must begin in column # _____ of the coding sheet.
16. A positive fixed-point halfword has a maximum value of _____; a negative fixed-point halfword has a maximum value of _____.
17. An instruction statement that is expressed in RR format has a fixed-length attribute that will affect _____ bytes of data.
18. A "comment" line may be indicated to the Assembler Language compiler by coding an _____ in the first column of that line on the coding sheet.
19. An _____ length attribute may sometimes be used in order to alter or guarantee the number of bytes of data to be affected by an instruction statement.
20. An RR format instruction statement indicates that both operands of that statement should be _____ operands.

5

Specifying the Instruction Statement

The abilities to properly interpret logic problems and apply the appropriate Assembler Language instructions are not the only prerequisites to becoming an efficient programmer. The logic path created by any programmer should be coded so that it may be easily interpreted and followed by another programmer of similar experience and training. Just as the Assembler Language instruction op codes are mnemonic to their performance, so should the labels and symbols used in the instruction statement relate to a program function or task. Compare the following instruction statements:

```
PT111      CLC    CMP1 (3,8) , R45
LOOKUP1    CLC    TABLE (3,8) , KEY
```

For all intents and purposes both statements perform an identical task. The first statement by itself gives no indication of what type of application is being performed. The second statement clearly infers that it is a part of a look-up routine and is comparing the three-byte table segment to a key. Creating labels and fields with names that are synonymous to their applications becomes more valuable with time. If a particular program has been operational for a year, and it is then determined that a change in the logic should be made in order to accept a new condition, even the author of the program would have to review the coding closely to become familiar with it again. Quite possibly, the original programmer is no longer responsible for its maintenance. It would now become evident that logical label and field name assignments are of considerable importance. This application, coupled with sufficient instruction line documentation (comments made on source coding lines), can reduce program maintenance and debugging time to the lowest possible level. Whenever coding a program, it is a good rule to consider that you may be asked to change it two years later; let the comments and logical naming techniques be a map to help you find your way through it at that time.

The unique naming of routines, subroutines, areas, and constants is the one option during the coding of instruction statements over which the programmer has the most control. There are other functions that also give the programmer a range of coding variations for any given instruction. These relate to the technical specification of the operands, which includes addressing elements, length specifications, and self-defining values. Although the results of compounded or complex operands must address or create a required value, the means of accomplishing that end can be properly applied in many ways.

ADDRESSING

Even though there are a number of ways to generate any given address within the problem program, the only concern at this time is with the most obvious, and direct, means of doing so.

One of the methods of creating an address for any given point in a program is to *"tag"* that point with a label or symbol. Labels can be used to identify the address of a constant, a defined storage area, a routine or subroutine, a table, or any particular individual instruction statement. A label, by itself, always generates an address that points to the left-most byte of a field or instruction; this represents the lowest point in storage of the area identified by the label. If the label points to a field of data, then this concept might be somewhat confusing—the address will be that of the left-most byte of that field, which in reality is the lowest point in storage for that field, and yet that byte of the field may be referred to as the high-order byte. It is evident that there are two types of address values to keep clear and separate from each other—the storage address value and the content value of the field itself. For any given field these might appear as:

Any reference to an address generated by a nonmodified label reference will hereafter refer to the lowest storage position address of the overall field, or value, pointed to by that label. As the address of a label is *"modified"* or adjusted, such as FIELDA+5, it will be construed that the address to be generated is a point located that many bytes higher in storage position than the address of the label itself.

Address adjusting is usually performed to locate a specific nonlabeled storage position within a data field or to increment a search through a series of data segments. It can be used to modify the length attribute of an instruction, though this is recommended only after some experience in programming.

One example of address adjusting can be seen in the routine shown in Figure 5-1. In this instance, a five-byte field contains five separate character positions. If certain configurations are found in each of those positions, the program logic intends to branch out to a respective subroutine, process some kind of information, and then return to the main routine again. At this point the logic assumes that the field, FIELD5, now contains data from an input stream.

The first instruction statement compares the first byte of FIELD5 to a character "L"; if the compare is unequal the logic branches to the next "compare" instruction, CHEK2. Each one of the compare statements is checking at an address that is one byte higher than the one addressed by the previous compare statement—FIELD5, FIELD5+1, FIELD5+2, FIELD5+3, FIELD5+4 —after which all five bytes of FIELD5 have been checked. If the byte addressed by the compare is not equal, a branch is taken to the next compare instruction statement. If the compare is equal, the program logic falls through to the Branch & Link instruction statement. The BAL instruction

Specifying the Instruction Statement

SYSTEM / 370 ASSEMBLER CODING FORM

NAME	OPERATION	OPERAND		SEQ
CHEKFLDS	CLI	FIELD5,C'L'		000001
	BC	7,CHEK2		000002
	BAL	9,RTNEL		000003
CHEK2	CLI	FIELD5+1,C'A'		000004
	BC	7,CHEK3		000005
	BAL	9,RTNEA		000006
CHEK3	CLI	FIELD5+2,C'M'		000007
	BC	7,CHEK4		000008
	BAL	9,RTNEM		000009
CHEK4	CLI	FIELD5+3,C'P'		000010
	BC	7,CHEK5		000011
	BAL	9,RTNEP		000012
CHEK5	CLI	FIELD5+4,C'S'		000013
	BC	7,CHEKDUN		000014
	BAL	9,RTNES		000015
CHEKDUN	BC	15,ENDCHEK		000016
*				000017
*				000018
FIELD5	DC	CL5' '		000019
*				000020
				000021

FIGURE 5-1

causes the processing to go out to a unique subroutine, perform a task, and then return to the instruction immediately following the BAL statement. The address adjustments can be shown as:

This type of address adjusting is not always practical to use, especially when incrementing through a series of data segments or a table of values. For that type of application, it is more efficient to load the address of the first segment into a general register and then add a value (equal to the length of a segment) to the register each time the logic wishes to check the next higher segment. The value of the register containing the address is then used as the base register with the operand specifying a zero displacement.

To illustrate this, assume that the problem program contains a very large table that is to be searched for certain values. The table contains many segments, each 10 bytes long. The table might be defined within the program as shown in Figure 5-2.

The value to be searched for on the table is contained in the third and fourth bytes of each table segment. The basic way of coding the primary portion of the routine could be established in several ways. Two different sets of coding are shown in Figure 5-3.

Statement 001, Example 1, loads the address of the *first* byte of TABLE into general register 9.

Statement 001, Example 2, loads the address of the *third* byte of TABLE into general register 9.

Statement 002, Example 1, compares the third and fourth byte of the current table segment to a literal. The third byte is addressed by a displacement of "0+2" plus the current address of TABLE as contained in general register 9. The "2," as contained in (2,9), signifies that the comparison is to be for a length of two bytes.

Statement 002, Example 2, performs the same comparison. Because the address loaded into general register 9 was that of TABLE+2, it is not necessary to specify any displacement factor other than zero.

Statement 003 for both examples causes a branch to PASSBAL if the comparison in Statement 002 resulted in an unequal condition.

Statement 004 for both examples is a Branch & Link statement to an assumed subroutine.

Statement 005 for both examples is another compare of the same TABLE bytes used in Statement 002. The logic used in Statement 005 is applicable for the respective examples.

Statement 006 for both examples is a "Branch on Equal Condition" instruction statement that tests the results of Statement 005 and decides whether or not to branch.

Statement 007 adds the value of the length of one table segment to general register 9. On the second pass through the LOOP routine, register 9 would contain an address equivalent to TABLE +10 for Example 1 and TABLE+12 for Example 2. On the third pass through LOOP, register 9 would contain an address equivalent to TABLE+20 for Example 1 and TABLE+22 for Example 2, etc.

Statement 008 for both examples is a *forced branch* back to the first instruction of the LOOP cycle routine.

Both of these coding examples would accomplish identical tasks. The only difference between them is the value of the address loaded into general register 9 by Statement 001 and the subsequent use of that address in Statements 002 and 005.

Specifying the Instruction Statement 81

FIGURE 5-2

FIGURE 5-3

SYSTEM/370 ASSEMBLER CODING FORM

```
       NAME      OPERATION  OPERAND
*                                                              #1                    001
*      ENTER     LA         9,TABLE                                                  002
       LOOP      CLC        0+2(2,9),=CL2'47'                                        003
                 BC         7,PASSBAL                                                004
                 BAL        3,FOUNDIT                                                005
       PASSBAL   CLC        0+2(2,9),=CL2'99'                                        006
                 BC         8,END                                                    007
                 AH         9,=H'10'                                                 008
                 BC         15,LOOP

*                                                              #2                    001
*      ENTER     LA         9,TABLE+2                                                002
       LOOP      CLC        0(2,9),=CL2'47'                                          003
                 BC         7,PASSBAL                                                004
                 BAL        3,FOUNDIT                                                005
       PASSBAL   CLC        0(2,9),=CL2'99'                                          006
                 BC         8,END                                                    007
                 AH         9,=H'10'                                                 008
                 BC         15,LOOP
*
```

Specifying the Instruction Statement

As shown in these examples, the address pointer register can be incremented by adding a halfword fixed-point value to the contents of that register. The value to be added in this case is the length of the table segments, or +10. Any of the sets of instruction statements shown in Figure 5-4 could have been used to replace Statements 001 and 007, and the end result would have been the same.

Statement Set *A loads the address of TABLE into general register 9. It then effectively states, "Load the actual address value of +10, including the address presently contained in register 9, into register 9." If that general register first contained the address of TABLE as "30563" the instruction increment of general register 9 would create an operation as:

+10 plus register 9 (30563) = register 9 (30573)

Statement Set *B also loads the address of TABLE into general register 9 as its first step. It then loads an absolute address value of +10 into general register 4. The incrementing of register 9 is accomplished by an Add Register instruction statement that adds the increment value contained in register 4 (+10) to the address value in general register 9.

Statement Set *C has defined a fullword constant with a fixed-point value of +10. After general register 9 has been loaded with the address of TABLE, the routine increments that address by a fixed-point ADD instruction statement, adding the fullword constant of +10 to the value contained in register 9.

LENGTH ATTRIBUTES

A length attribute is the controlling factor that determines the number of bytes to be affected by an instruction statement. Certain instruction op codes allow the programmer a choice of using either explicit or implied length attributes. Still other instruction op codes have a fixed length attribute. With the exception of packed decimal operation instructions, all of the Assembler Language Standard Instruction Set have a single length attribute control. Packed decimal instructions have two length attributes—one for each operand. It is quite important to be fully aware of the length attribute characteristics of each of the Assembler Language instructions. These are defined in the following paragraphs.

"Fixed" Length Attributes

Instruction op codes whose statement formats do not include an 'L' component, indicating that a length attribute may be specified, are considered to have a *"fixed"* length attribute. This means that these instruction statements inherently contain a length factor that cannot be altered during the coding of that statement. The actual number of bytes or fullwords controlled by the fixed length attribute varies among the different instruction op codes that fall within this category. This includes all of the RR, RX, RS, and SI formatted instructions. The majority of the "register" instructions, such as CLR, AR, LTR, SR, etc., affect only four bytes (a register or fullword) of data. The fixed-point arithmetic multiply and divide instructions affect a pair of registers. Multiple Load and Multiple Store instructions affect as many fullwords and registers as are covered by the range specified by, and implied between, the registers whose numeric representations form the R_1 and R_3 operands. The remaining instructions affect only one byte of data—such instructions as CLI, STC, IC, and MVI.

SYSTEM/370 ASSEMBLER CODING FORM

```
*A
ENTER   LA   9,TABLE    (REPLACES STATEMENT 001)
        LA   9,10(9)    (REPLACES STATEMENT 007)
*B
ENTER   LA   9,TABLE    (REPLACES STATEMENT 001)
        LA   4,10
        AR   9,4        (REPLACES STATEMENT 007)
*C
ENTER   LA   9,TABLE    (REPLACES STATEMENT 001)
        A    9,INCRMNT  (REPLACES STATEMENT 007)
*
INCRMNT DC   F'10'      (FULLWORD CONSTANT OF +10)
```

FIGURE 5-4

Specifying the Instruction Statement 85

Any attempt to specify a length attribute for an instruction that contains a fixed length attribute will result in either a program compile error or a misinterpretation of the intended use of the value; the compiler could interpret a length attribute to be a base register or a displacement register if the value specified was within the numeric range of 1 to 15.

"Implied" Length Attributes

If a particular Assembler Language instruction format contains the option of specifying a length attribute, it is your decision whether or not the coded statement requires a length attribute specification. Should you choose not to indicate the length attribute, it is considered to be *"implied."* In an instruction statement containing an implied length, the length is construed to be the length of the field addressed by the first operand in the statement.

Examine this set of instruction statements.

```
RECVR     DC    CL6 'ƀƀƀƀƀƀ'
SEND1     DC    CL4 'ABCD'
SEND2     DC    CL4 'EFGH'
*
MOVEIT    MVC   RECVR , SEND1
```

The instruction statement labeled MOVEIT would result in the move of six bytes of data (ABCDEF) into the field labeled RECVR. The implied length for this statement's execution is the length of the first operand, which is six bytes. At the time this statement is executed, the system would commence sending data bytes from the point specified by the second operand and would continue until the implied length of the first operand had been fulfilled. This would result in four bytes of data in SEND1 being moved, immediately followed by the first two bytes of SEND2. The opposite reaction to this is also true in an instance wherein the second operand field is longer than the first operand field.

```
RECVR     DC    CL3 'ƀƀƀ'
SENDR     DC    CL5 '139B2'
*
MOVEDATA  MVC   RECVR , SENDR
```

As a result of the statement shown here, only the first three bytes of SENDR (139) would be moved into RECVR. Since the implied length of the first operand field determines the number of bytes of data to be moved, the move operation is terminated once the length of that operand has been exhausted. Note carefully that if address adjusting is used, such as . . . MVC RECVR + 2, SENDR . . . , the implied length of the receiving field is still effective. Three bytes of data, commencing at SENDR, would be moved into the three bytes of data commencing at RECVR + 2.

Packed decimal instructions are unique in that both operands of the completed statement may be considered to have implied length attributes. Because of this, executing packed decimal instruction statements containing fields of unlike length factors requires adequate knowledge of the peculiarities of those instructions. If the field length of the first packed decimal operand is greater than that of the second packed decimal operand, there is usually no difficulty in completing a satisfactory statement execution. However, if the field length of the second operand is greater than that of the first operand, packed decimal arithmetic routines can possibly result in a decimal overflow exception and a program interrupt. It might be suggested that you acquire the habit of using explicit-length attribute coding for those instructions that allow a defined length characteristic.

"Explicit" Length Attributes

The use of explicit length attributes refers to the coding of an actual length value within an operand. This application may be used to confirm or ensure the stated length attribute of a field, or it may be used to change or alter the implied length. There are many instances in the average program in which this type of specification may be of considerable value. A large section of data may be held in storage under a single label, but through the use of address adjusting and explicit length attributes, small sections of that data field can be moved in or out of the area or manipulated as desired. Regardless of the length of any field of data, a length attribute as great as allowed by the particular instruction op code involved may be used to move data into that field and subsequent fields if so desired. Remember that an explicit length attribute can only be used within those Assembler Language instructions whose instruction statement format indicates the optional use of a length attribute.

The following set of examples illustrate some of the applications for which explicit length attributes may be applied.

Example 1. The data fields to be affected and the instruction statements to be performed are:

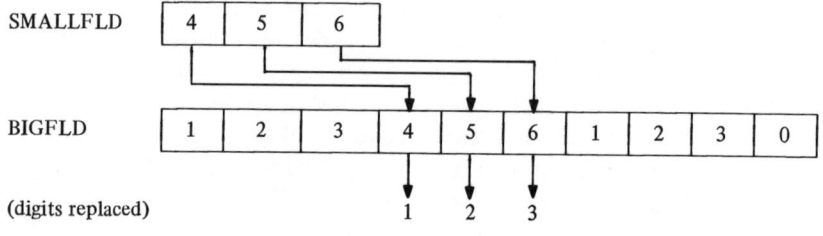

```
BIGFLD      DC    CL10 ' 1231231230 '
SMALLFLD    DC    CL3 ' 456 '
*
            MVC   BIGFLD+3(3) , SMALLFLD      001
            MVC   BIGFLD+9(1) , SMALLFLD      002
```

Statement 001 is interpreted as stating, "Move three bytes of data (as indicated by the explicit length attribute of 3), from the field SMALLFLD into the fourth, fifth, and sixth bytes of BIGFLD (BIGFLD+3)." This performance would appear as:

Specifying the Instruction Statement 87

Statement 002 states, "Move one byte of data, as indicated by the length attribute parameter of '1', from the address generated by SMALLFLD into the tenth byte of BIGFLD (BIGFLD+9)," as shown in the next illustration.

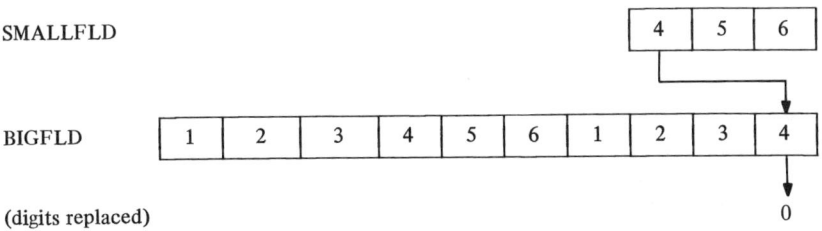

(digits replaced)

This example has shown how a portion, or all, of a "sending" field may be moved into any portion of a receiving field for any explicit length, so long as the length attributes do not exceed the number of bytes allowed to be affected by that instruction.

Example 2. The definition of the data fields and the expression of the instruction statement is:

```
        FIELDA   DC    CL2'AB'
        FIELDB   DC    CL1'C'
        FIELDC   DC    CL6'DEFGHI'
        FIELDD   DC    CL6'JKLMNO'
        *
                 MVC   FIELDD (6), FIELDA
```

This instruction statement specifies, "Commencing at the address generated by FIELDA, move six bytes of data into FIELDD." Because this statement specifies a data length of six bytes to be moved, FIELDA (two bytes), FIELDB (one byte), and the first three bytes of FIELDC are moved into the overall length of FIELDD. The performance of this statement can be illustrated as:

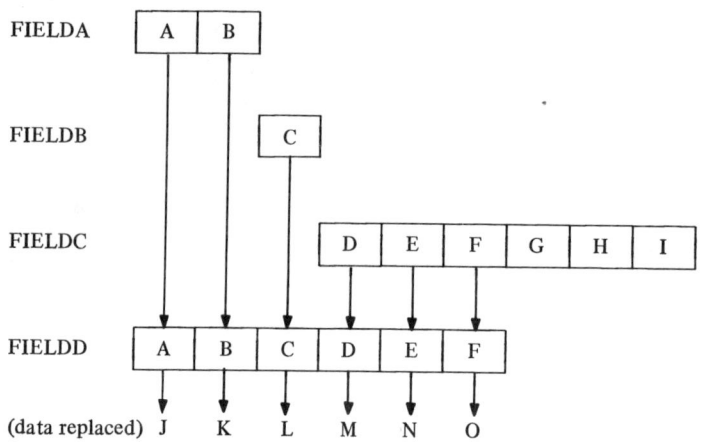

Example 3. This example relates to the comparison of a portion of each of two data fields. The overall definition of these fields and the ensuing instruction statement are:

```
INFLD     DC    CL4 '1AB7'
OUTFLD    DC    CL6 '235CB9'
*
          CLC   OUTFLD+3 (2) , INFLD+1
```

The bytes of data to be compared by the performance of this instruction statement would be:

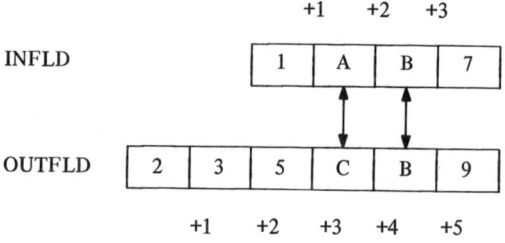

As shown, only the two bytes of alphabetic characters would be compared.

Specifying the Instruction Statement 89

Example 4. This example illustrates how part of a packed decimal field may be added to the whole of a larger packed decimal field. The data contained in the fields appear as:

ADDPACK | 3 | 4 | 0 | 0 | 8 | 2 | 3 | C |

PACKSUM | 0 | 1 | 1 | 0 | 5 | 4 | 9 | C |

The instruction statement that is to be performed is:

AP   PACKSUM (4) , ADDPACK+2 (2)

The operation of this statement may be shown by:

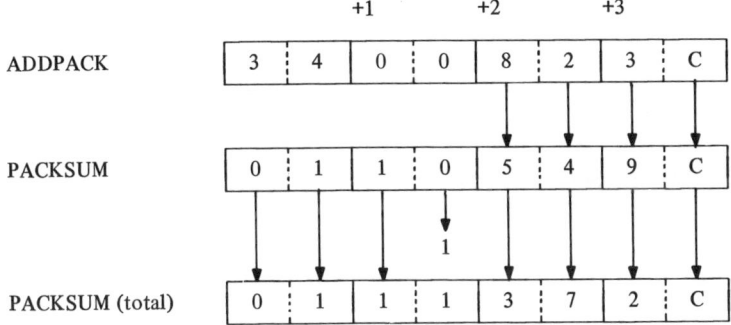

As illustrated, the last two bytes of ADDPACK, containing a packed decimal value of +823, would be added to the whole of PACKSUM. The resulting sum would be considered to be contained in the entire four bytes of PACKSUM.

In addition to these examples of the use of explicit length attributes, many of the various other examples throughout this text also demonstrate this application.

SELF-DEFINING CHARACTERS AND VALUES

A *self-defining* character or value is one that is written in its own representation as an operand. These are generally construed to be literals, immediate character representations, and absolute values. The attributes of each are defined in the following paragraphs.

Literals

Although another section of this text is devoted to the construction and composition of literals, it is necessary to include a general overview of their functions at this point. As a rule, a literal is a relatively small number of data bytes, or a self-defining value, that is to be used as an operand. This would be mostly applicable in instances where the intended value or data content of the literal is to remain unchanged. Because a literal does not have a label by which it may be referenced, it cannot be cross-referenced by the programmer at any other point within the problem program.

If a literal of the same value is to be used at multiple points in the problem program, it must be rewritten in its entirety in each place. A complete explanation of the various types of literals and their respective representations is contained within the section entitled "Defining Constants and Literals."

The instruction statements that follow each contain a literal. The use of the literal is defined following the statement in which it appears.

    AP   PAKCNTR (3) , = PL1 ' 1 '

This instruction statement specifies that a packed decimal value of +1, as represented by the literal, is to be added to a three-byte area referenced by the label PAKCNTR. The programmer could have established a labeled one-byte packed decimal constant and used the label as the second operand in this statement in lieu of the literal. This particular instruction might be part of the logic to keep count of, or control, the number of times that the logic processing passes through a given section of the program.

    CLC   PACKFLD (3) , = X ' 00000C '

This statement compares the three bytes of a field of packed decimals, addressed by the label PACKFLD, to a three-byte hexadecimal literal. The literal represents a three-byte packed decimal field of plus-zero (+0). In this particular instance, the programmer wants to know only if that field, PACKFLD, contains a bit-for-bit configuration of the +0 value. The programmer could have used the Compare Packed instruction except for the fact that the CP instruction considers a plus-zero and a minus-zero to be equal values.

    CLC   RECORD+5 (2) , = CL2 ' ID '

In this instance, the statement compares the sixth and seventh bytes of a field defined as RECORD to a two-byte literal containing the alpha characters 'ID'. It is assumed that the data contents of RECORD will change every time a new data record is used by the program. The literal is used to check the contents of each new section of data for the characters 'ID', so it is just as practical to use that literal as to establish a two-byte constant containing 'ID'. It is often easier to follow the logic of a program containing this type of literal than it is to interpret a statement in which the second operand is a label that references a constant.

Compare the three sets of instruction statements in Figure 5-5, each of which are expressed using a literal and similarly expressed using a label that addresses a constant of the same configuration as the literal.

In each instance, the literal defines itself not only as to data content, but also as to format and length. The statements using the labeled data as the second operand are not self-explanatory as to the value or data content of that operand. Someone tracing these logical instructions in a problem program would have to find the location of the definition of the label of the second operand in order to become familiar with its characteristics and contents.

Immediate Characters or Values

As indicated in the descriptions of some of the Assembler Language instructions, certain instruction statement formats require the use of immediate data. The written configuration of immediate data is very similar to the manner in which a literal is written, with the following exceptions.

- It is not preceded by an equal sign (=).
- It may only consist of one byte of data.
- It cannot be replaced by a constant or symbol.

Specifying the Instruction Statement

SYSTEM / 370 ASSEMBLER CODING FORM

NAME	OPERATION	OPERAND
*		
	ZAP	PKAREA,=PL1'0'
	ZAP	PKAREA,PKZERO
*		
	CLC	DATA+2(2),=CL2'MV'
	CLC	DATA+2(2),DATACHEK
*		
	MVC	CARDOUT(4),=CL4'0001'
	MVC	CARDOUT(4),SEQNO
*		

FIGURE 5-5

91

The functional Assembler Language instructions that use an immediate character or representation are:

AND IMMEDIATE (NI)
EXCLUSIVE OR IMMEDIATE (XI)
OR IMMEDIATE (OI)
COMPARE LOGICAL IMMEDIATE (CLI)
MOVE IMMEDIATE (MVI)
TEST UNDER MASK (TM)

The configuration of the immediate data may be expressed in character, binary bit, or hexadecimal configuration. It may not be expressed as a "P" or packed decimal byte. The decision of which configuration to use would probably depend on the type of instruction statement. The CLI and MVI instruction statements would probably use character configuration. The remaining instructions would be written more often using a hexadecimal configuration or a binary bit configuration, inasmuch as the one byte of immediate data used for these instructions represents a mask comprising binary bit conditions.

Figure 5-6 presents instruction statements using a single byte of immediate data. In each instance the statement is shown twice, utilizing two different configurations for the expression of the immediate data. Because all of these instructions are limited to acting on one byte of data, there are no length attributes reflected in these statements. Note that the data byte used to represent the immediate character must be self-representing. An immediate character of P'4' is not valid inasmuch as the compiler would have to convert it to a hex configuration of X'4C'. However, an immediate character expressed as X'4C' is valid.

Each statement within any of these sets is interpreted by the compiler as identical to the other statement within the set. Therefore, the programmer has the option of configuring the byte of immediate data in whichever mode is preferred.

Absolute Values

An absolute value is a decimal self-defining term or expression. It is written in its basic numeric digit form and should contain no symbols that would indicate the "sign" of the value.

A typical example of the use of an absolute value may be found in its association with a Load Address instruction statement, such as when that statement is used to load a loop control value into a register. This type of use is shown by:

```
          LA    5,1024
          ↑     ↑ ↑
      (op code)/ (absolute value)
           (register)
```

This instruction statement tells the system to load the absolute value of 1024 into general register 5. Upon execution of that instruction statement, general register 5 will contain a value of +1024.

An absolute value may also be used to indicate a displacement parameter in an operand of many Assembler Language instructions. Its most general application in this type of assignment is to reference an unlabeled point within a defined field, creating an explicit address.

Specifying the Instruction Statement

Name	Operation	Operand
	CLI	DATA,C'X'
	CLI	DATA,X'E7'
	XI	SWITCHES,X'04'
	XI	SWITCHES,B'00000100'
	MVI	TABLE+5,X'C1'
	MVI	TABLE+5,C'A'
	TM	ID,B'01011110'
	TM	ID,X'5E'
	CLI	AMNT,C'9'
	CLI	AMNT,X'F9'
	NI	TESTBIT,X'11'
	NI	TESTBIT,B'00010001'
	MVI	KEYBYTE,C'3'
	MVI	KEYBYTE,X'F3'
	OI	0+4(10),X'4B'
	OI	0+4(10),B'01001011'

FIGURE 5-6

```
TABLE      DC    50CL14' b'
*
MODULE   LA    6, TABLE
         MVC   4(2,6),=CL2'ID'
```

The constant TABLE is defined as consisting of 50 segments of 14 bytes each. The Load Address (LA) instruction statement has loaded the address of the first byte of TABLE into general register 6. The Move Characters (MVC) instruction states, "Into the address that represents the fifth byte of TABLE (a displacement of four plus the address of TABLE as contained in general register 6), move the two-byte literal supplied by the second operand." The MVC instruction statement is broken down as:

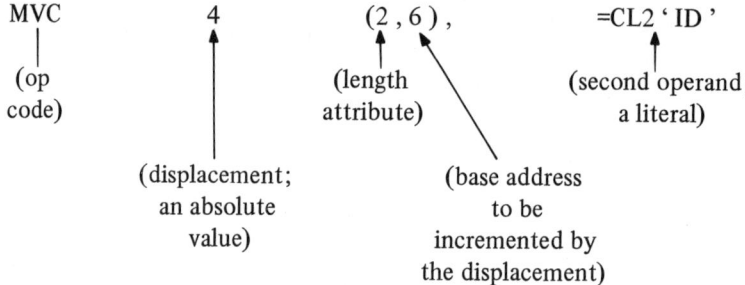

If, at program execution time, the decimal address of TABLE was 23410, then the first operand in the MVC instruction statement just shown would generate an address of 23414.

Logically the value used to represent a register (0 through 15) as a part of an operand, or as an operand in itself, is also an absolute value. This does not mean to imply that every time the compiler encounters a value in the range of 0 through 15 that it will assume that value to represent a general register; this will only be effected when the value stated occupies a statement parameter that requires a register specification.

BASIC PROGRAM INITIALIZATION

In progressing through this text, you will probably want to test out your knowledge of the concepts. Rather than requiring you to study register assignments, *"save"* areas, control sections, etc., at the very beginning of this material, a set of basic coding is provided here that will establish the necessary housekeeping.

Using the instruction statements contained on the coding sheets shown in Figure 5-7, you may insert small coded routines within the control section and compile your program.

The first section, from the label INITL through to the label SAVEREG, sets up the initialization of the program and the base register assignments. This model has been organized with three contiguous base register assignments of 4096 bytes each, so you will have approximately 12,288 bytes of program logic area to work with.

Item 2, the label START, should contain the first instruction statement of the program to be tested.

Item 3 identifies the area where you may place all of the instruction statements of the program. These should be stated between the statement labeled START and the one labeled FINIS.

Specifying the Instruction Statement

SYSTEM / 370 ASSEMBLER CODING FORM

NAME	OPERATION	OPERAND		IDENTIFICATION SEQUENCE NO
INITL	CSECT			00001
BEGIN	SAVE	(14,12),,*		00002
	BALR	BR3,0		00003
	USING	BR3,R3		00004
BR3	L	R4,BR4		00005
	L	R5,BR5		00006
	USING	BR3+4096,R4	(1)	00007
	USING	BR3+8192,R5		00008
	ST	R13,SAVEREG+4		00009
	LA	R13,SAVEREG		00010
	BC	15,START		00011
*				00012
*				00013
BR4	DC	A(BR3+4096)	(2)	00014
BR5	DC	A(BR3+8192)		00015
SAVEREG	DS	18F	(3)	00016
*				00017
*				00018
START		Insert as many program logic source statements here as necessary		00019

FIGURE 5-7a

SYSTEM / 370 ASSEMBLER CODING FORM

Name	Operation	Operand	Comments	Identification
FINIS	L	R13,SAVEREG+4		00500
	RETURN	(14,12)		00501
*				00502
*	LTORG			00503
*				00504
*		PROGRAM CONSTANTS AND WORK AREAS (4)		00505
*				00506
*				00507
R3	EQU	3		00508
R4	EQU	4	Insert program DS and DC statements here (5)	00509
R5	EQU	5		00510
R13	EQU	13		00511
				00512
				00513

FIGURE 5-7b

Specifying the Instruction Statement

FIGURE 5-7c

Item 4 is a *"literal org"* statement that assigns the proper program alignments to any literals you may have included within your instruction statements.

Item 5 contains several "Equate" statements that assign symbolic references or labels to several general registers. Any other reference to these registers may be made by specifying the register only, or by specifying the symbolic label, such as shown in Item 1 of this set of coding. Also included here is the area into which you should place all of the DS (Define Storage) and DC (Define Constant) statements to be used.

Item 6 may contain the data control block statements for the input or output units that are used by the program. The exact form of these statements depends on the operating system and the quantity and type of devices being used for input/output operations to the program. The requirements for the format of this data should, therefore, be supplied by the users' data processing installation.

Item 7, the END statement, is the final statement in the problem program. Any coding to be inserted should have been included within the areas indicated, somewhere prior to this statement.

Both the compilation of the source module and the subsequent testing of the object program will require "Job Control Language" cards. These are necessary in order for the task to be identified by name, to advise the system what type of function is to be performed, which devices are to be used, and several other related types of information that the operating system requires for each task execution.

The statements within this set of coded logic have been formatted for use with **OS** or **OS/VS**. In the event that you use a different operating system, some of the instruction formats may have to be altered.

Part III
LOGICAL APPLICATIONS OF ASSEMBLER LANGUAGE

6
Creating Work Areas Within the Program

ESTABLISHING STORAGE AREAS

The concept of storage areas, as discussed in this section, relates to the fields and work areas used by the problem program to hold data, accumulate data, or manipulate data. This type of storage area might be used to hold input or output records, to build tables and indexes, arithmetic work areas such as the Quotient-Remainder combination, register storage areas, or any other such fields in which the data will change during the execution of the program.

Defining the Areas

The op code used to reserve a contiguous number of bytes of storage area is DS, the Define Storage instruction. Use of this instruction reserves an allocation of main storage within the problem program; however, unlike the Define Constant (DC) op code, DS does not create a configuration of data within the area of storage that it is reserving. Until the logic of the problem program places some type of data into the area established by a DS instruction statement, the contents of that area would be totally unpredictable. Data stored in that particular area of storage by a previous problem program would probably still reside within that area.

A typical DS statement might appear as:

```
RECORD     DS     CL300
```

This particular statement would assign the label RECORD to 300 bytes of contiguous storage as a part of the problem program.

The programmer might want to reference smaller units of storage within a large storage area without using address adjusting. Such an allocation might appear as:

```
DATAFLD    DS     0CL100
NAME       DS     CL20
ADDRESS    DS     CL40
PHONE      DS     CL9
DETAIL     DS     CL31
```

The statement for DATAFLD assigns that label to 100 bytes of storage, but it is not actually reserving or allocating that storage. The zero (0) that precedes the 'CL' in the first statement is a parameter that may be used to indicate that no storage is to be allocated for this statement. It does indicate, however, that if 100 bytes of data are moved into the address referenced by DATAFLD, that data will be placed into the areas reserved by any subsequent DS or DC statement. The obvious logic for establishing this set of statements is that the program intends to place a 100-byte data record into the area that is addressed as DATAFLD. The detail contained within this record will consist of a name, address, telephone number, and some additional detail data. The data to be placed into this overall area can be moved there by referencing the label DATAFLD. Once that data is in storage, it can be referred to in whole by the label DATAFLD, or in part by referencing the labels for the subfields. Take note that the aggregate storage area actually reserved by the subfield DS statements is exactly equal to the length of the DATAFLD label assignment— 100 bytes. In this type of application, it is very important that the subfield space allocations are equal to the length of the area referenced by the primary label. If this rule is not followed, it is quite likely that storage data may be inadvertently destroyed or altered. For instance, the storage definition statements within a problem program might appear as:

```
DATE        DS      0CL6
MONTH       DS      CL2
DAY         DS      CL2
ENDCARD     DC      CL9 'DELIMITER '
```

As shown here, the label DATE is used to reference six bytes of storage. The subfields defined within DATE have only declared four bytes of storage. Because of this, any reference to DATE would imply reference to MONTH, DAY, and the first two bytes of ENDCARD. At the time that the program is initialized, these fields, and the way that the labels would apply, would appear as:

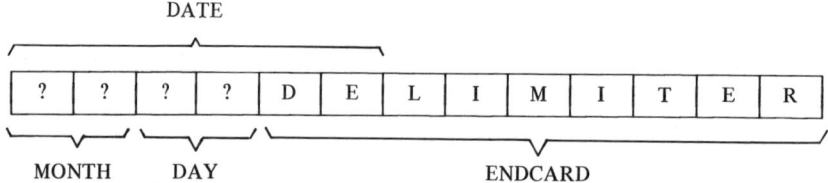

Now assume that the program intends to move some data from another area, which happens to contain "031579" (March 15, 1979), into the area referenced by the label DATE. It then intends to compare a card input area to the constant ENDCARD to see if the card input area contains the word "DELIMITER," indicating the end of the input card data stream. The instruction statements to be executed within the problem program are coded as:

```
MVC     DATE, SOMEAREA      (001)
CLC     CARDIN, ENDCARD     (002)
BC      8, JOBDONE          (003)
```

Statement 001 moves the data contained within SOMEAREA (031579) into the area that is addressed by DATE. The contents of DATE and ENDCARD would now contain this data:

Because DATE is specified to reference six bytes of storage, all six bytes of data are moved from SOMEAREA to DATE. The last two bytes of SOMEAREA (79) have now overlayed and destroyed the first two bytes of the constant ENDCARD (DE).

Statements 002 and 003 are intended to compare a card input field to the contents of END-CARD (which is supposed to be "DELIMITER") and then branch to the end-of-job routine on

Creating Work Areas Within the Program 103

an equal condition. Even though the card input area (CARDIN) eventually would contain the word "DELIMITER," the comparison would not result in an equal condition due to the fact that the constant ENDCARD now would contain "79LIMITER." Accordingly, the appropriate branch to JOBDONE would not be taken and the program would probably terminate abnormally.

The nonreserving attribute of a DS statement may also be used within a previously defined or labeled area.

```
INRECORD    DS      0CL55
NAME        DS      CL15
ADDRESS     DS      0CL40
STREET      DS      CL15
CITY        DS      CL15
STATE       DS      CL5
ZIPCODE     DS      CL5
```

This set of statements specifies a storage area to be used to hold input records of data. The overall length of the area is 55 bytes and it can be referred to in its entirety by the label INRECORD. The first subfield within INRECORD is the NAME field, consisting of the first fifteen bytes of INRECORD. Following the NAME field is a label reference, ADDRESS, which refers to the remaining 40 bytes of INRECORD. STREET, CITY, STATE, and ZIPCODE are the subfields of both INRECORD and ADDRESS, and they are actually reserving the storage positions that are referred to by ADDRESS and INRECORD. The cross-reference of all of these labels would now appear to be:

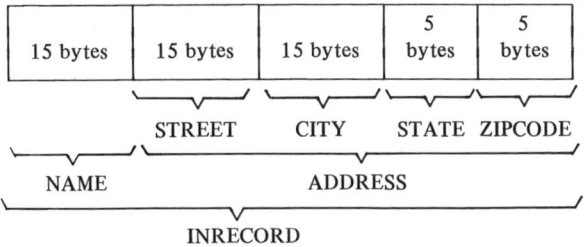

The fields of STREET, CITY, STATE, and ZIPCODE can be moved or altered individually by referring to any one of those labels; or they can be moved or altered collectively by referring to the label ADDRESS. In the same manner, it is possible to move all of INRECORD at one time or any portion of it by the other labels.

DS statements and DC statements can be intermixed in the same manner as just shown for DS statements. The DS statement must be used if a label is to be tagged to an area that is to be subdefined in line without direct storage allocation for that label. An example of this type of application could be coded as:

```
DATAHOLD    DS      0CL9
PACKFLD1    DC      PL2'0'
SWITCH1     DC      X'40'
PACKFLD2    DC      PL2'0'
SWITCH2     DC      X'40'
CODE        DS      0CL3
PREFIX      DC      X'40'
SUFFIX      DC      X'4040'
```

The logical and hexadecimal configuration of the areas defined by these statements would appear as:

As these statements have indicated, the entire nine-byte area may be referred to by the label DATAHOLD. The fields labeled PACKFLD1 and PACKFLD2 contain packed decimal values of +0, which would allow them to be used for packed decimal arithmetic operations by references to either label. SWITCH1 and SWITCH2 are each one-byte areas containing the hexadecimal configuration of a valid "blank." CODE, another subfield of DATAHOLD, is further subdefined by PREFIX and SUFFIX, and contains valid blanks (X '40').

Overlaying Field Descriptions

In some instances, you might find it helpful to be able to define an area in several formats or in different subfields. This can be accomplished by the use of the DS statement and the ORG instruction. The ORG statement effectively causes the next assigned byte of storage to begin at the address specified by the single operand of the ORG instruction statement. A practical example of the combined use of the DS statements and ORG statements might be within a program that reads data cards into its logic. The normal definition of the card input field would usually suffice, but in this instance the program will be reading cards formatted in three different ways. The first character contained on the card identifies which of the three formats apply to that particular card. In order to efficiently work with the unique data fields on each type of card, the overall card input field is first defined in whole and then completely redefined for each of the three different content formats. Using labels that might be applicable to a purchasing system, the card layouts could be defined by the statements in Figure 6-1.

As each card is brought into storage via the I/O (input/output) data management routines, it can be read into the area referenced by the label CARDIN. Once the card data resides in CARDIN, allowing it to be referred to by CARDIN, CODE, or DATA, it may also be referred to by any of the other labels indicated by the list of DS statements. If the card should happen to contain data pertaining to a purchase requisition, it is a CODE1 data card. The information for that card is aligned in the format of the labels shown for a CODE1 card and any field defined by those labels may be accessed by that definition. As indicated, a CODE2 card contains purchase order data and a CODE3 card contains receiving report information. Once the program logic has determined what type of data is contained on the card and has been passed to the program data input area, it would branch to one of three different routines. Each routine would be unique in such a way as to process the appropriate data representation contained on the respective cards.

Note that in each case the card format contains a different number of bytes of data and the unreferenced data bytes have been allowed for by the MT (empty) label for each code. This is the means that is used to account for all of the bytes that have been assigned to the next higher

Creating Work Areas Within the Program

SYSTEM / 370 ASSEMBLER CODING FORM

NAME	OPERATION	OPERAND	SEQ
*			0001
CARDIN	DS	0CL80	0002
CODE	DS	CL1	0003
DATA	DS	CL79	0004
*			0005
	ORG	CARDIN	0006
CODE1	DS	CL1	0007
REQSTNNO	DS	CL8	0008
PARTNO1	DS	CL12	0009
REQDATE	DS	CL6	0010
REQQTY	DS	CL8	0011
MT1	DS	CL45	0012
*			0013
	ORG	CARDIN	0014
CODE2	DS	CL1	0015
PURCHNO1	DS	CL7	0016
VENDOR	DS	CL6	0017
PARTNO2	DS	CL12	0018
PODATE	DS	CL6	0019
POQTY	DS	CL8	0020
BUYER	DS	CL8	0021
MT2	DS	CL32	0022
*			0023

FIGURE 6-1a

SYSTEM / 370 ASSEMBLER CODING FORM

Punching Instructions — GRAPHIC: `I . 7`   PUNCH: `12/7/8  11/7/8`

PAGE 2 OF 2   ASSIGN NO. 6-1B

NAME	OPERATION	OPERAND	IDENTIFICATION SEQUENCE NO.
CODE3	ORG	CARDIN	0024
RECVGNO	DS	CL1	0025
PURCHNO2	DS	CL7	0026
PARTNO3	DS	CL7	0027
RECQTY	DS	CL12	0028
BACKORDR	DS	CL8	0029
MT3	DS	CL4	0030
	DS	CL41	0031
*			0032

FIGURE 6-1b

Creating Work Areas Within the Program

level of label reference. Even though these area definitions have effectively created unique representations for four different card format areas, including the basic input area, the net result has only allocated a total of 80 bytes of storage area.

It is not necessary that the ORG instruction statement refer to the first character byte in the data field that is to be subdefined. If a field is to be similarly defined in multiple subdefinitions, it can be referred to by the first label by which it was defined. This idea is shown in Figure 6-2 using the same basic subdefinitions as in the previous set of DS statements.

In this instance, each subsequent subdefined area is able to use the same labels previously defined for other fields. In a side-by-side listing, these areas would overlap as:

CARDIN	CODE	(CODE)	(CODE)	(CODE)
	DATA	PARTNO	(PARTNO)	(PARTNO)
		QTY	(QTY)	(QTY)
		REQSTNNO	PURCHNO	(PURCHNO)
		REQDATE	VENDOR	RECVGNO
		MT1	PODATE	BACKORDR
			BUYER	MT3
			MT2	

The labels within the parentheses do not appear in the statements because their interpretation and field length is identical to a previous definition. Notice that this type of definition is accomplished in a "step-down" mode, that is, each unique subdefinition must be accomplished at a lateral level or subsequent field level.

Boundary Alignments

Storage areas and data fields used directly in fixed-point arithmetic operations or in the performance of register instructions are required to be aligned on halfword, fullword, or doubleword boundary alignments, depending on the particular instruction statement to be executed. The valid boundary alignments are:

- Halfword   A decimal storage location evenly divisible by 2.
- Fullword   A decimal storage location evenly divisible by 4.
- Doubleword A decimal storage location evenly divisible by 8.

It is not anticipated that the average programmer would know exactly where each storage area or data area would be aligned when a program is compiled. Therefore, the programmer is given the 'H', 'F', and 'D' type of operands for both the DS and DC op codes. These operands automatically provide halfword, fullword, and doubleword boundary alignment respectively. The illustrations that follow provide examples of some of the ways that these operands may be expressed in a Define Storage (DS) statement.

```
FULLWD    DS    F
```

This statement reserves four bytes of storage, aligned on a fullword boundary and referenced or addressed by the label FULLWD.

Name	Operation	Operand	Seq
*			0001
CARDIN	DS	0CL80	0002
CODE	DS	CL1	0003
DATA	DS	CL79	0004
*			0005
	ORG	DATA	0006
PARTNO	DS	CL12	0007
QTY	DS	CL6	0008
REQSTNNO	DS	CL8	0009
REQDATE	DS	CL6	0010
MT1	DS	CL47	0011
*			0012
	ORG	REQSTNNO	0013
PURCHNO	DS	CL7	0014
VENDOR	DS	CL6	0015
PODATE	DS	CL6	0016
BUYER	DS	CL8	0017
MT2	DS	CL34	0018
*			0019
	ORG	VENDOR	0020
RECVGNO	DS	CL7	0021
BACKORDR	DS	CL4	0022
MT3	DS	CL43	0023
*			0024

FIGURE 6-2

Creating Work Areas Within the Program

```
SAVEREG    DS      18F
```

This statement assigns the label SAVEREG to 18 contiguous fullwords of storage—72 consecutive bytes. Every fourth byte of this overall area is aligned on a main storage boundary location divisible by four. This is the type of storage area that is established in every problem program for the purpose of saving register contents at program initialization.

```
HAFWDS3    DS      3H
```

As suggested by the label, this statement defines a storage area that consists of six bytes—three consecutive halfword locations. Because it would not be known which halfword also happens to be aligned on a fullword boundary, it would be impractical to attempt to use any two of these halfwords as a fullword location.

```
ALIGN      DS      0F
DATABITS   DC      B'01001100'
CHEKBITS   DC      X'4C4C'
NULLBITS   DC      B'00000000'
```

The first statement in this group represents a means of establishing fullword boundary alignment for small segments of data that form less than a four-byte fullword. The statement labeled ALIGN creates a reference to the nearest fullword boundary alignment from the point in the program at which the statement was encountered. It does not reserve those storage positions. The one-byte area, DATABITS, which immediately follows ALIGN, commences at the fullword boundary specified by ALIGN. CHEKBITS (two bytes) and NULLBITS (one byte) are allocated so as to complete the remainder of the fullword area. Although this entire set of statements could have been created with the same data by calculating the fixed-point value of the bit configuration and establishing a single fullword constant, this is considerably more expedient. In addition, each of the three defined subfields can be referenced directly by their own labels.

```
           DS      0D
DUBPAK     DC      PL8'0'
```

This set of statements creates an eight-byte field, containing a packed decimal value of +0, aligned on a doubleword boundary. This is one way of establishing the typical packed decimal doubleword area that is required as an operand in the Convert to Binary (CVB) and Convert to Decimal (CVD) instruction statements. This area could also have been defined as:

```
DUBPAK     DS      D
```

This latter form of assignment would have required that the programmer use the ZAP instruction to move the packed decimal field into DUBPAK prior to a CVB instruction statement, or required that the field be formatted as packed decimal prior to an application requiring a packed decimal field.

DEFINING CONSTANTS AND LITERALS

What is a Constant?

Within programming terminology, the term *"constant"* would seem to imply, "an item of expression that maintains its configuration unless expressly altered." In Assembler Language this implication is justified. A constant consists of data such as a value, an expression, or characters, any of which have been defined within the problem program by a Define Constant statement. This data, once defined, may be referenced or used by any subroutine or routine within that program, retaining its defined configuration until directly altered by the program logic. Actual program storage locations are assigned to the constant so that it may be addressed by a symbolic label or by an actual address.

Because the existence of a constant is based on the assumption that some subroutine or statement will use its contents, it is logical that such reference be made via a symbolic label. It is much easier to address a constant by referring to its symbolic label than to state the address at which it would reside. Therefore, even though a Define Constant statement indicates that the symbolic reference of a label is optional, it is an accepted practice to "label" all constants.

The Define Constant is written as:

SYMBOLIC LABEL   DC   DATA

The purpose of the symbolic label has already been described. It may consist of any valid EBCDIC alpha numeric character data, ranging from one to eight bytes in length. The standard rules regarding the composition for labels applies equally to the labels of constants: (a) the first character must be an alphabetic letter; (b) remaining characters may be all alpha, all numeric, or any combination of these; (c) it may not contain any blanks within it; and (d) it may not contain any special characters.

valid symbolic labels	invalid symbolic labels
P124689	86523
RTE	GO THERE
ROUTINE2	3FINIS
GOTDATA	DATAFIELD
KX7RC6	NOW_ GO
M345N346	244MASK

The mnemonic op code for the Define Constant instruction is written as DC. This advises the Assembler Language compiler to create the constant data specified in the data portion of the statement, and to assign the address where it is generated to the symbolic label.

The data portion of the DC statement may comprise four specification factors or subfields. These are:

- The duplication factor
- The type of constant
- The length modifier
- The actual data or value expressed as the constant

The Duplication Factor

The duplication factor defines the number of times that the constant is to be generated. If no duplication factor is specified the default is to one. Therefore, if only a single constant is required, the duplication factor may be omitted. To establish a constant that contained the characters "1234123412341234" the DC statement would be written as:

Creating Work Areas Within the Program   111

In this instance the constant SERIES is to be generated as five groups of four bytes, each group containing the numeric characters '1234'. It is important to note that the implied length of the constant addressed by the label "SERIES" is four bytes. Even though twenty bytes of data have been established, an instruction to move data into "SERIES" without supplying a specific length attribute would terminate after moving only four bytes.

The Type of Constant

The constant must be defined as to the type of data format it is intended to represent. The identity of the type of constant is a single character that provides the Assembler Language compiler with the proper information for creation of that constant in machine-language format. The types of constants, such as 'C' for character format, 'B' for binary, 'X' for hexadecimal, etc., will be fully discussed in this section. If a duplication factor is coded as part of the DC statement, the type of constant indicator immediately follows it; otherwise the type of constant is the first factor coded in the operand field of the statement.

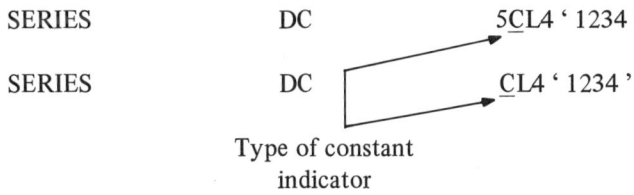

The Length Modifier

The length modifier defines the actual length of the constant. If no length modifier is specified in the DC statement, the created length of the constant will be equal to the length of the expressed constant itself, or equal to the length implied by the type of constant specified. Certain types of constants do imply a given length, i.e., an 'F' constant implies a fullword, an 'H' constant implies a halfword, etc. The following list of DC statements provide some examples of lengths that are implied or specified to constants.

```
CONST1    DC    C ' NOW '        Implied length of three bytes
CONST2    DC    CL5 ' DATE '     Specified length of five bytes
CONST3    DC    F ' 23968 '      Implied length of four bytes
CONST4    DC    H ' 1 '          Implied length of two bytes
```

The manner in which the data is formatted and aligned within the various types of constants will be analyzed as each type of constant is discussed. There are four explicit types of length modifier factors.

- Constant byte-length modifier
- Bit-length specification modifier

- Scale modifier for fixed-point values
- Exponent modifier for fixed-point values

Because of their more general application in Assembler Language programming, the first two types will be discussed and illustrated throughout this section.

The constant byte-length modifier is used to state the number of actual bytes assigned to the constant regardless of its apparent or implied length. It is written as Ln, wherein "n" is a decimal value representing the number of bytes.

The bit-length specification modifier states the actual number of bit positions assigned to the constant. It is written as L.n wherein "n" is a decimal value indicating the number of bit positions to be assigned to the constant. This type of length modifier would normally only be used with B, F, H, or D types of constants. If the value of the constant does not create a length equal to that indicated by the bit-length modifier, a sufficient number of additional high-order zero-bits will be added to the value of the constant in order to complete the bit-length specification.

It is important to know, and remember, that boundary alignments are not provided when a length modifier is used within a fixed-point constant of a halfword, fullword, or a doubleword.

The Actual Constant Data

The actual data which form the intended content of the constant is the last operand factor of the DC statement. If it is an A, S, V, or Y type constant, the actual data is enclosed within parentheses—all other types should have the actual data enclosed within apostrophes. Although many examples of all types of constants appear throughout this section, a few are presented here in order to associate the components of the constant to the way that it is written.

1.	CHARCONS	DC	CL6 ' ABCDEF '	character
2.	BINCON	DC	B ' 10110001 '	binary
3.	FIXDCON	DC	4F ' 398 '	fixed-point
4.	HEXCON	DC	XL3 ' DF236C '	hexadecimal
5.	PACKCON	DC	PL4 ' 253774 '	packed decimal
6.	ADCONST	DC	A (15975)	address constant

* * * * *

1. CHARCONS is a character constant of six bytes containing the characters 'ABCDEF.' The modifiers determine the following:

   C   A character-type constant.
   L6   An explicit length of six bytes.
   ' ABCDEF '   The actual data content of the six bytes.

When compiled, this constant would be generated so that it could be interpreted in any one of these formats:

	A	B	C	D	E	F
character						
hexadecimal	C 1	C 2	C 3	C 4	C 5	C 6
binary	1100 0001	1100 0010	1100 0011	1100 0100	1100 0101	1100 0110

* * * * *

Creating Work Areas Within the Program

2. BINCON is a one-byte binary constant. Because no length attribute is specified, the length of the constant defaults to the implied length of eight bit positions, one byte. The modifiers determine that this constant will be as follows:

   B   A binary constant.

   '10110001'   The binary configuration of the constant. Eight bits are specified with no conflicting specified length attribute; the constant is therefore compiled as one byte.

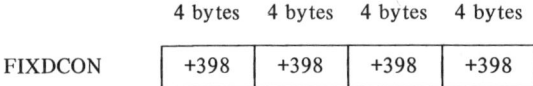

* * * * *

3. FIXDCON is a fullword fixed-point constant. The modifiers are interpreted by the compiler as:

   4   A duplication factor of four; whatever the single constant value is expressed as, it will be generated a total of four times in contiguous storage positions.

   F   It is a fullword fixed-point constant. Because no explicit length modifiers are present each iteration of the constant will consist of four bytes aligned on a fullword boundary.

   '398'   A fixed-point value of +398.

   Inasmuch as a duplication factor of four is applied to a constant consisting of four bytes, the overall storage allocation for FIXDCON will be 16 bytes; 4 times 4 bytes equals 16 bytes.

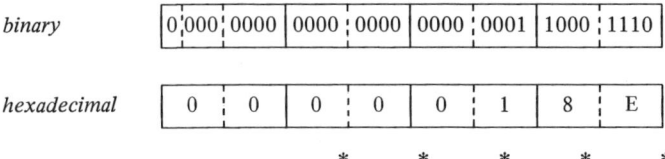

The first four bytes of FIXDCON, and each subsequent four-byte increment, would appear as:

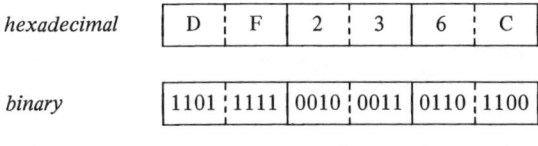

* * * * *

4. HEXCON is a three-byte hexadecimal constant. The compiler would interpret the modifiers as:

   X   A hexadecimal constant.

   L3   A byte-length attribute of three bytes.

   'DF236C'   The hexadecimal digits comprising the constant data.

| hexadecimal | D | F | 2 | 3 | 6 | C |

| binary | 1101 | 1111 | 0010 | 0011 | 0110 | 1100 |

* * * * *

5. PACKCON is a four-byte packed decimal constant containing a value of +253,774. The modifiers are interpreted as:

P A packed decimal constant.
L4 A byte-length attribute of four bytes.
'253774' The packed decimal value of +253,774 that is to occupy the four-byte constant area.

Because the stated value is not sufficiently large enough to occupy the whole of the length specified for the constant, the high-order half-byte is padded with a hex zero-digit.

PACKCON

hexadecimal | 0 | 2 | 5 | 3 | 7 | 7 | 4 | C |

6. ADCONST is an address constant. The lack of a specified length attribute will cause the length of the constant to default to a four-byte fullword. The modifiers are interpreted as:

A An address constant of four bytes.
(15975) An address contained within the fullword ADCONST as a fixed-point value.

ADCONST

hexadecimal | 0 | 0 | 0 | 0 | 3 | E | 6 | 7 |

binary | 0000 0000 | 0000 0000 | 0011 1110 | 0110 0111 |

A more thoroughly detailed examination of the various constants will be supplied during the discussions of each particular type of constant.

The Literal Version of a Constant

The general interpretation of a constant is that a label, or a symbolic reference, is assigned to a particular configuration of data or value in order that it might be referenced via that label from any point within the problem program. A literal, however, is considered to be an "on-the-spot" constant—in other words, a literal interpretation of the data or value that is expressed within an instruction statement. The same literal may be used any number of times within a program, but each time that it is used it must be expressed in its entirety and may not be cross-referenced from any other point within the program.

A literal is written in the same format as the operand portion of a constant except that it must be preceded by an *equal-sign* (=). Other rules regarding the use of a literal are stated below:

- A literal may not specify multiple operands.
- A duplication factor of zero may not be indicated.
- Duplication factors and length modifiers must be expressed as self-defining, unsigned decimal values.
- A literal may not specify an S-type address constant.

The two sets of instruction statements that appear in Figure 6-3 reflect the difference between the use of a constant and the use of a literal.

Creating Work Areas Within the Program

SYSTEM / 370 ASSEMBLER CODING FORM

```
NAME      OPERATION  OPERAND

*
*
PACKS     DC         PL4'31649'         * USING A CONSTANT *
*
ROUTE1
          AP         BIGFIELD,PACKS
          SP         PACKTWO,PACKS
          MP         PACKANSR,PACKS
*
*                                       * USING A LITERAL *
*
ROUTE1
          AP         BIGFIELD,=PL4'31649'
          SP         PACKTWO,=PL4'31649'
          MP         PACKANSR,=PL4'31649'
```

FIGURE 6-3

In the first set of coding statements PACKS has been defined as a four-byte packed decimal constant with a value of +31,649. Any subsequent reference to that amount needs only to state the symbolic label that creates the address of that constant.

The second set of statements reiterates the entire value of the literal each time that it is used. It is somewhat obvious that defined constants can result in faster and more efficient program coding as well as lessening the chance for error in the repeated writing of the value. When a literal is compiled, the language compiler cannot tell if the value stated is correct or not, other than for general format. However, if the name of a constant is misspelled, the compiler can indicate an "undefined symbol error," as long as that misspelling does not create a symbolic reference that is validly designated elsewhere within the program.

If a value or character data is to be used only once or twice throughout the entire program, it is quite practical to use a literal in lieu of a constant.

Expressing the Constants

The means by which a constant is expressed, and the interpretation of that expression by the compiler, depends largely on the type of constant being created. This section discusses the alternatives and requirements to be considered for the twelve most commonly used types of constants. These are shown in Table 6-1.

TABLE 6-1

Code Character	Type of Constant	General Application
C	Character	To define EBCDIC character representation, either as alpha, numeric, or symbols.
X	Hexadecimal	To express a binary format, a hexadecimal configuration, fixed-point values, or packed decimal values.
B	Binary	To indicate a bit-by-bit format of the constant.
F	Fullword	To define a four-byte fixed-point value aligned on a fullword boundary location. (It is aligned providing that no length modifier is specified.)
H	Halfword	To define a two-byte fixed-point value that will be aligned on a halfword boundary location if no length modifier is specified.
D	Doubleword	To define an eight-byte floating-point assignment. That value will be aligned on a doubleword boundary location if no length modifier is specified.
P	Packed decimal	To define a packed decimal value.
Z	Zoned decimal	To express a decimal value in extended zoned format wherein each digit occupies one byte, the right-most byte containing the sign of the field.
A	Address	To define an address constant, consisting of a four-byte fullword unless specified otherwise.
Y	Address	To define an address constant, consisting of a two-byte halfword unless specified otherwise.
S	Address	To define an address constant expressed in base-displacement form, consisting of a maximum of a two-byte halfword.
V	Address	To define a reserved storage area for the address constant of an external symbol. Although this would normally generate a four-byte fullword area, a smaller length may be specified.

Creating Work Areas Within the Program

Each of the various types of constants has an intended application for which it was designed. However, they are by no means restricted to that particular application. It is often the programmer's personal choice that determines the type of constant used for any given application, although it must be stated that this choice should be based on reasonable logic and clarity of definition. For example, if the program logic requires a bit-by-bit binary configuration, the constant could readily be defined as a binary constant, a hexadecimal constant, or even as a halfword or fullword constant. Of these four choices the hexadecimal format is most often preferential—it is not lengthy to write and yet the bit structure can be easily identified.

As the various types of constants are described on the following pages, attempt to visualize all of the practical applications for which they might be used.

The 'C' Constant (Character)

The character constant is the "workhorse" of most business application programs. Data messages, output fields for printed data, data insertion, search arguments, and many other concepts equally utilize this type of constant. A character constant may have a length attribute range of from 1 to 256 bytes. The manner in which the constant is expressed, however, may limit the length to less than 256 bytes, a fact that is not readily pointed out in most texts. If the programmer attempted to create a Define Constant statement wherein the expressed constant itself physically occupied 256 positions on the Assembler Language coding form, the language compiler would flag the last two lines of the constant as an error. This is because the maximum number of continuation lines permissible for a regular instruction statement is two lines plus the original line, or a maximum of 165 bytes after allowing one byte to define the type of constant and one byte each for the opening and closing apostrophes that enclose the constant. (See Figure 6-4.) If it is necessary to actually create a constant with a length greater than 165 bytes in which each and every byte must be relatively unique, it is possible to do so by creating two smaller contiguous constants. In order to use the overall combined data contained in both, it is only necessary to refer to the label of the first constant and state a specific length attribute of the combined length of both constants.

When a character constant is defined, each character indicated in the expressed constant is compiled as a one-byte EBCDIC character. If a length modifier is not expressed, the assigned length of the constant will be determined by the number of characters that form the expressed constant. If a length modifier is specified and it differs from the number of characters contained in the constant expression, one of the following will occur:

> If the specified length attribute is less than the number of characters in the constant, any right-most bytes of the constant in excess of the specified length will be dropped.

> If the specified length attribute is greater than the number of characters in the constant, the bytes to the right of the expressed constant will be supplied with blanks, X'40'.

An exception to the rule of "one character equals one byte" exists when an ampersand (&) or an apostrophe (') is to be included as a part of the constant itself. In order to include either of these characters within the constant, the character must be stated twice in succession—this would appear as && or ''. When considering the length of the constant, however, the two characters only count as one byte.

FIGURE 6-4

Creating Work Areas Within the Program 119

In the character-type constants of the following examples, the DC statement is shown along with the resulting constant field. The individual units within all illustrated fields are considered to be in one-byte increments.

Example 1

```
         DATA1      DC      C'RECORD'
```

DATA1 | R | E | C | O | R | D |

No length modifier is specified; consequently, the length attribute is determined by the number of characters in the constant expression.

Example 2

```
         DATA2      DC      CL7'DEVICES'
```

DATA2 | D | E | V | I | C | E | S |

The length modifier and the number of bytes of constant data agree; therefore, the constant is established exactly as stated.

Example 3

```
         DATA3      DC      CL6'123456789'
```

DATA3 | 1 | 2 | 3 | 4 | 5 | 6 |

Although the constant expression contains nine characters, the length modifier of L6 controls the length of the compiled constant. The three excess bytes '789' are ignored.

Example 4

```
         DATA4      DC      CL10'SERIAL#'
```

DATA4 | S | E | R | I | A | L | # | ƀ | ƀ | ƀ |

A compiled constant of ten bytes is created from the specification of a length modifier of L10. Because the constant expression does not contain enough characters to fill the ten bytes, the rightmost three bytes of the defined area are created as blanks (the symbol 'ƀ' representing a blank).

Example 5

```
        DATA5       DC          C'TO&&FRO'
```

DATA5	T	O	&	F	R	O

The exception regarding ampersands (and apostrophes) is shown in this example. It is necessary to indicate a set of ampersands in order for the compiler to generate a single byte containing an ampersand. Even though seven characters appear within the constant expression, the compiler recognizes the single-byte implication of the double ampersand; therefore, only a six-byte constant is created.

Example 6

```
        DATA6       DC          5CL2 ' A '
```

DATA6	A	ɴ	A	ɴ	A	ɴ	A	ɴ	A	ɴ

In this example a one-byte expression is used to create a two-byte single constant, resulting in a blank being placed in the right-most byte of the pair. In addition, a duplication factor of five is indicated, creating an overall field length of ten bytes.

Example 7

```
    DATA7    DC    CL250 ' ɴ '
```

This constant would be compiled as a 250-byte area, each byte containing a valid blank, X '40'. The first byte of the area is created as a blank because of the 'blank' representation of the expression itself; the remaining 249 bytes are configured as blanks because the length modifier of L250 is greater than the specified characters in the constant expression.

The literal version of a character constant is written exactly the same as the constant operand fields except that it is preceded by an equal-sign. Literals used in instruction statements appear as:

```
    MVC    DATARECD (4) , =CL4 ' 1222 '
    CLC    INPUT (5) , =C ' MERGE '
    MVC    TABLE (20) ,=10CL2 ' DF '
```

The 'X' Constant (Hexadecimal)

The hexadecimal constant has many applications in creating data fields or values throughout the program. It can be suitably used to originate mask configurations, fixed-point values of various lengths, or even to establish packed decimal values and fields.

The hexadecimal constant may have an overall byte length of from 1 to 256 bytes, equal to a range of from 2 to 512 hexadecimal digits. Any of the valid hexadecimal digits may be used to create the constant—0 through 9 and A through F.

The length of the generated 'X' constant is determined much like the 'C' constant, but with a slight variation. If a length modifier is stated, the constant will be generated in accordance with the specified length. If a length modifier is not stated, the hexadecimal expression will determine the constant length by one of the following rules.

> If the number of hexadecimal digits expressed in the DC statement is an even number, the byte length of the constant will be generated at half of that number. This is because there are two hex digits to every byte.

> If the number of hexadecimal digits expressed in the DC statement is an odd number, the byte length of the constant will be generated as half of that number plus one more byte. The left-most (high-order) half-byte will be supplied with a hexadecimal zero-digit. For example, 15 hexadecimal digits will compile into an 8-byte constant—$15 \div 2 = 7 + 1 = 8$.

In the event that the length modifier stated does not logically coincide with the number of hexadecimal digits expressed, one of the following will occur:

> If the length modifier specifies a byte length in excess of the number of bytes required for the hexadecimal digits expressed within the constant, the high-order half-bytes will be supplied with enough hex zero-digits to complete the field.

> If the length modifier specifies a byte length less than that required to contain all of the expressed hexadecimal digits of the constant, any high-order half-bytes in excess of the length modifier will be ignored.

In the examples of hexadecimal constants that follow, the generated constant fields are represented in half-byte increments. They could also be interpreted in character or binary format, depending on the use for which they were intended.

Example 1

HEXCON1   DC   X'39FD1E'

HEXCON1	3	9	F	D	1	E

In this example, the length of the generated constant is determined by the number of hexadecimal digits within the constant expression. No length modifier is stated, so there is no other confirmation or confliction of the length attribute implied.

Example 2

HEXCON2   DC   XL5'069F41'

HEXCON2	0	0	0	0	0	6	9	F	4	1

The length modifier specifies a generated constant length of five bytes (L5). Because there are not enough hex digits to fill this length, the high-order unfilled half-bytes are supplied with hexadecimal zero-digits.

Example 3

	HEXCON3	DC	X ' FFFE1 '

HEXCON3	0	F	F	F	E	1

The rule for creating a generated length for a constant containing an odd number of hex digits is demonstrated here—five digits divided by two equals a whole quotient of two bytes, plus one byte equals three bytes. The high-order additional half-byte required to complete the constant in full-byte format is supplied with a hex zero-digit.

Example 4

	HEXCON4	DC	XL3 ' 06914DE7C '

HEXCON4	1	4	D	E	7	C

The length modifier in this DC statement specifies a total length of three bytes to be generated for the constant. Because nine hex digits are expressed as the constant, the high-order three hexadecimal digits (1½ bytes) are dropped by the compiler.

Example 5

Although the length modifier specifies two bytes for the configuration of the constant expression, only three hex digits are indicated. A high-order hex digit of zero is supplied to the constant in its singular form. The duplication factor of '3' causes the two-byte constant to be generated three times, requiring a total of six storage bytes.

Example 6

	HEXCON6	DC	XL4 ' C '

HEXCON6	0	0	0	0	0	0	0	C

Creating Work Areas Within the Program 123

In this example, a valid four-byte packed decimal field containing a value of +0 is created through the use of X-type constant. The hex digit 'C' (a standard plus-sign for packed decimal values) is placed into the low-order half-byte and the remaining high-order half-bytes supplied with hex zero-digits.

The hexadecimal literal may be written exactly the same as the operand portion of the hexadecimal constant except that it must follow the rule of literals by being preceded by an equal-sign. The following instruction statements include hexadecimal literals.

```
MVC    CHEXFLD (3) ,=X ' 050505 '
MVC    PRTLINE (1) ,=X ' 40 '
OC     SOURCE (4) ,=XL4 'FEFEFEFE '
CLC    DATAFLD (2) , =XL2 ' C1C2 '
```

The 'B' Constant (Binary)

The binary constant is restricted to the use of bit-symbols in the expression of the actual constant data. This would mean that the constant must be expressed in 1's and 0's or all of either of these. The minimum length of a binary constant is one byte—the maximum length is 256 bytes. Experience has indicated that the binary constant may be cumbersome for coding purposes and that a hexadecimal constant would usually suffice as well. The unique ability to define small groups of bits, as provided by this constant, does justify its existence.

The implied length of a binary constant is in eight-bit bytes. If a fractional number of bits are expressed in the constant, the compiled constant will be padded on the high-order with sufficient zero-bits to complete a byte.

If the constant is given a specific byte length that does not agree with the logical number of bits expressing the constant data, one of two actions will occur.

> If the specific byte count of the length modifier is greater than logically required to contain the number of bits expressed by the constant, the high-order undefined bit positions will be filled with zero-bits.

> If the length modifier indicates a byte length less than that required to contain all of the expressed bits, a sufficient number of the bits of the high-order will be dropped to coincide with the specific byte length.

The following examples of binary constants relate these variations to their respective positioning within the byte fields. The generated fields are illustrated only in binary bit configuration format.

Example 1

```
            BINCON1    DC        B ' 0110000010100101 '
```

BINCON1	0110	0000	1010	0101

The implied length of this constant is exactly two bytes, or 16 bits.

Example 2

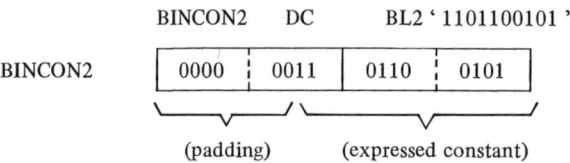

```
BINCON2    DC    BL2 ' 1101100101 '
```

BINCON2 | 0000 | 0011 | 0110 | 0101 |
         (padding)   (expressed constant)

The length modifier of this constant specifies a byte length of 'L2' (16 bits) even though only 10 bits are indicated as the expressed constant. The unspecified six bit positions are supplied in the form of six high-order zero-bits.

Example 3

```
BINCON3    DC    BL1 ' 01101010110 '
```

BINCON3 | 0101 | 0110 |

The explicit length attribute for this constant is stated as one byte (8 bits), although 11 bits are contained in the expressed constant data. Accordingly, the three high-order bits (0 1 1) of the expressed constant are ignored when compiling the constant.

The literal version of the binary constant is expressed in the same manner as the operand portion of the DC statement. As in the case of all literals, it must be preceded by an equal sign. All of the rules conventional to the binary constant apply to the binary literal. Literals of this type would appear as:

```
CLC    HOLDBYTE (1) ,=BL1 ' 1101 '
MVC    INSERT (2) ,=B ' 1111000000001111 '
IC     6 ,=BL1 ' 10110011 '
```

The 'F' Constant (Fullword Fixed-Point)

The fullword constant is used to create a four-byte fixed-point value that is expressed in the constant statement as a decimal value. The fullword alignment is true under the condition that a length modifier is not specified within the constant. In the event that a length modifier is stated, the constant assumes that length and the boundary alignment is no longer guaranteed.

Although there are many variations of the fullword constant (F), the halfword constant (H), and the doubleword constant (D), all of these variations will not be discussed. Constants involving scaling, scale modifiers, exponents, exponent modifiers, and implied or specified variable fractions are not considered by the author to be an integral requirement of the Assembler Language programming portion of this text. Any need for additional data on these factors may be easily referenced within the computer manufacturers' technical manuals.

The fullword constant may be expressed as a signed or unsigned decimal value. If the sign of the value is not specifically expressed, the value is considered to be positive.

Creating Work Areas Within the Program

As mentioned, a fullword constant may be given a length modifier, the maximum range of which is eight bytes. It would appear to be contradictory to create a fullword constant with a length specification of eight bytes, but this allows you to originate a fixed-point value in a field larger than four bytes without first setting up a doubleword area and loading the fixed-point value into it.

The examples for the fullword constant consist of four-byte aligned fullwords including the variations of specifically-signed values. The decimal value in the expressed constant is converted to a fixed-point value expressed in both binary form and hexadecimal configuration.

Example 1

FULLWD1   DC   F '3295'

	s						
FULLWD1 (binary)	0000	0000	0000	0000	0000	1100	1101	1111
(hex)	0	0	0	0	0	C	D	F

Example 2

FULLWD2   DC   F '-661327'

	s					
FULLWD2 (binary)	1111	1111	1111	0101	1110	1000	1011	0001
(hex)	F	F	F	5	E	8	B	1

Example 3

FULLWD3   DC   F '12593446'

	s					
FULLWD3 (binary)	0000	0000	1100	0000	0010	1001	0010	0110
(hex)	0	0	C	0	2	9	2	6

In each of the foregoing examples, the hexadecimal configuration of the resulting constant has been provided to enable a meaningful conversion of the fixed-point value to its decimal equivalent. This can be readily accomplished by the use of the Hexadecimal/Decimal Conversion Table.

126   Assembler Language for Application Programming

The fullword literal follows the conventions of other literals; it is preceded by an equal sign and the content is that of the operand field of the constant.

```
A    10 ,=F ' 675021 '
L     6 ,=F ' 32596 '
LM    6 , 8 , =3F ' 4096 '
```

In the last statement, a Load Multiple instruction statement, the literal generates three consecutive fullwords, each containing a fixed-point value of +4096. The first fullword is loaded into general register 6, the second into general register 7, and the third into general register 8.

The maximum values that may be expressed in a four-byte fullword constant are +2,147,483,647 or −2,147,483,648.

The 'H' Constant (Halfword Fixed-Point)

Ignoring the same variations excluded from the description of the fullword constant, the halfword constant is generally used to establish a two-byte fixed-point value aligned on a halfword boundary location. A length modifier may be specified, in which instance the boundary alignment of the constant is no longer applicable. A halfword constant may contain a length specification of up to eight bytes.

The value of the constant may be expressed specifically as a signed value, or the sign may be implied, in which case the value is assumed to be positive. The maximum values that can be contained within a two-byte halfword are +32,767 or −32,768.

The following examples of halfword constants are considered to be two-byte aligned halfwords representing fixed-point values. The representation of the value is illustrated in both binary and hexadecimal form, the latter allowing a ready interpretation of the decimal conversion process.

Example 1

Example 2

Example 3

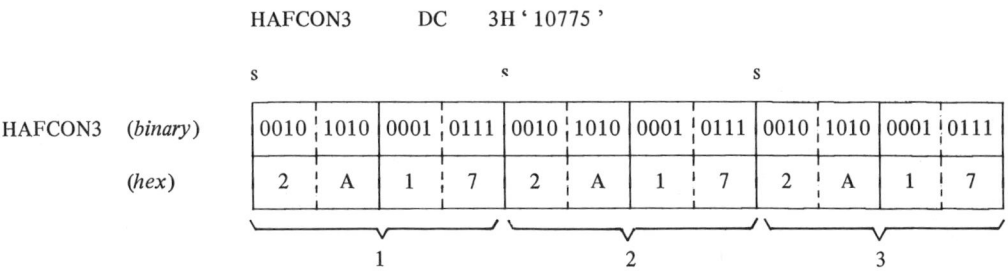

The halfword literal is preceded by an equal sign as shown in its application in the following instruction statements:

```
AH    5 ,=H ' 24 '
LH    10 ,=H ' -13006 '
MH    6 ,=H ' 256 '
```

The 'D' Constant (Doubleword)

Although a doubleword constant is generally assumed to be within the category of floating-point arithmetic operations, it has a very functional use in normal fixed-point applications. Because the need for a value in excess of the capability of a fullword is seldom found in the Assembler Language programming of commercial applications, the primary use of a doubleword constant might be considered to be the initialization of an eight-byte area containing zero-bits.

For example, the program logic might intend to create two individual fullword values within a defined doubleword constant and later place the overall doubleword, assumed to consist of two values, into two consecutive registers via the Load Multiple instruction. The creation of such a field, originally containing a zero value, would be coded as:

```
DUBCON    DC    D ' 0 '
```

Each four bytes of this field would also be on fullword boundary alignment. Data or values could then be loaded out of, or stored into, and manipulated within any section or portion of this field by utilizing address adjusting or length specifications (wherever necessary) as a part of the instruction statement. This might appear as:

```
L       8 , DUBCON+4
STM     5 , 6 , DUBCON
CVB     9 , DUBCON
MVI     DUBCON+7 , X ' 00 '
```

The 'P' Constant (Packed Decimal)

The packed decimal constant is probably the second most widely used type of constant in commercial programming with Assembler Language. Its form of expression is quite similar to that of hexadecimal constants in that each expressed digit occupies a half-byte of the compiled constant. The sign of the packed decimal constant may be expressed within the constant or omitted, which in the latter case is assumed to be a positive value. When the compiler creates the packed decimal constant, the right-most digit of the expressed constant is paired with the sign of the constant to fill the right-most byte. The remaining bytes of the compiled constant are filled with the pairs of digits of the remaining expressed constant.

If the number of digits in the expressed value do not fit equally into the implied length of the constant, a single high-order hexadecimal zero-digit is provided to complete the high-order byte.

When an explicit length modifier is stated as part of the constant and the quantity of expressed decimal digits do not combine to a byte length equal to that of the length modifier, one of two events occur:

> If the explicit length attribute is greater than the number of bytes required for the expressed value, excess high-order half-bytes are padded with hex zero-digits.

> If the explicit length attribute is less than the number of bytes required for the expressed value, the surplus high-order digits of the expressed value are ignored.

The length of a packed decimal constant may be a minimum of one byte and a maximum of 16 bytes. For the purpose of data clarity and implied alignment, a decimal point may be expressed within the decimal value. This decimal point is entirely ignored by the compiler and the constant is compiled as though the decimal point had never existed in the DC statement. It is intended solely for the purpose of aiding the programmer in the interpretation of the value of the constant for alignment purposes. Other than the sign of the packed decimal value and the inclusion of a decimal point when so desired, the expressed constant must be written in decimal form.

The following examples of packed decimal constants contain the DC statement and a hexadecimal representation (half-bytes) of the data field that would be created by the compiler.

Example 1

PAKCON1   DC   P'32'

(padding)

Even though the expressed constant contains only two digits, it is necessary to create the constant as a two-byte field. This is caused by the fact that the implied sign requires the right-most half-byte of the compiled constant. When the length is forced to two bytes, there are not sufficient digits to fill the field; therefore, a hex zero-digit is placed into the vacant high-order half-byte.

Example 2

(padding)

The length modifier of the DC statement forces the compiler to create a six-byte packed decimal constant field. The value of the expressed constant is not great enough to fill these bytes, so zero-digits are supplied to the additional high-order half-bytes.

Example 3

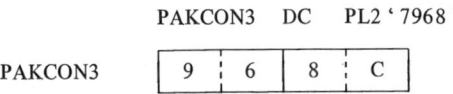

In this example, the programmer apparently did not give any consideration to the necessity of allowing a half-byte for the sign of the constant. An explicit length of two bytes is specified, leaving only three half-bytes for packed decimal digits. Accordingly the high-order digit of the expressed constant is ignored.

Example 4

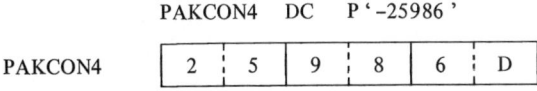

The expressed constant is stated as a negative value. The constant, therefore, contains a standard negative sign applicable to packed decimals.

Example 5

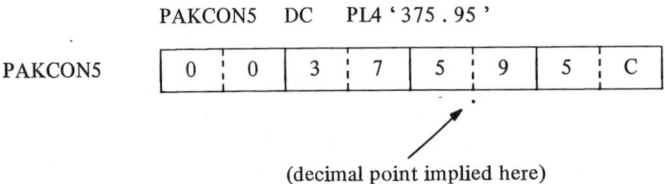

(decimal point implied here)

The expressed constant in this example contains an embedded decimal point. The compiler has ignored the decimal point and has created the actual constant without it. The primary purpose of specifying the decimal point within the DC statement is to remind the programmer that any subsequent use of this constant should consider it to contain an implied decimal point at this position.

Example 6

```
PAKCON6     DC      3PL2 ' 0 '
```

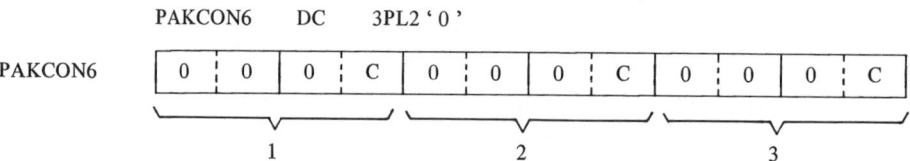

This DC statement effectively creates three two-byte packed decimal fields, each containing a value of +0. Each of the two-byte constants could be addressed separately, such as by PAKCON6, PAKCON6+2, and PAKCON6+4. If an operation is to be executed using any single field of the three, an explicit length attribute should be included in the instruction. This would appear as:

```
    AP      PAKCON6+4 (2) , PAKDATA
```

The literal form of the packed decimal constant is writtten with an equal sign preceding it. All of the rules applicable to the generation of a packed decimal constant apply as well to its literal form. Examples of this type of literal would be:

```
    AP      PACOUNTR , =PL1 ' 1 '
    SP      BIGPACK ,=P ' 32964 '
    CP      PAKCHECK (3) ,=PL3 ' -1597 '
    MP      PAKQUOT ,=PL2 ' 9 . 95 '
    DP      DIVPAK ,=PL3 ' +17 . 82 '
```

The 'Z' Constant (Zoned Decimal)

The zoned decimal constant is used to create an EBCDIC numeric constant in which the rightmost byte contains the sign of the decimal value expressed by the constant. Each digit of the constant expression of the DC statement will construct one byte of the compiled constant if the length attributes coincide.

If a length modifier is not stated, the compiled constant will have a length attribute equal to that implied by the number of digits within the expressed constant.

If a length modifier is specified that does not agree with the number of numeric digits contained within the expressed constant, one of the following will occur:

> If the length modifier is greater than the number of expressed constant digits, the unfilled high-order bytes of the compiled constant will be supplied with EBCDIC zero numerics.

> If the length modifier is less than the expressed constant digits, the excessive expressed digits will be ignored by the compiler.

The maximum length of a zoned decimal constant is 16 bytes. The expressed constant may contain a positive or a negative sign to determine the configuration of the compiled constant. If

Creating Work Areas Within the Program 131

a sign is not specified, the constant is assumed to be a positive value. A decimal point may be written within the expressed constant, but only for the purpose of information and assumed alignment. The decimal point is ignored by the compiler and the constant is created without any reference to it.

The fields representing the compiled zoned decimal constants in the following illustrations are stated both in character and in hexadecimal form. Note that a signed, zoned decimal assumes the identity of an EBCDIC alpha character.

Example 1

ZONECON1   DC   Z '9236'

ZONECON1	9	2	3	F
	F 9	F 2	F 3	C 6

The right-most character, 'F', represents a positive-signed zoned decimal of '6'.

Example 2

ZONECON2   DC   ZL6 '2048'

ZONECON2	0	0	2	0	4	H
	F 0	F 0	F 2	F 0	F 4	C 8

The right-most character, 'H', represents a positive-signed zoned decimal of '8'.

Example 3

ZONECON3   DC   ZL4 '1651'

ZONECON3	1	6	5	A
	F 1	F 6	F 5	C 1

The right-most character, 'A', represents a positive-signed zoned decimal of '1'.

Example 4

ZONECON4   DC   Z '-296883'

ZONECON4	2	9	6	8	8	L
	F 2	F 9	F 6	F 8	F 8	D 3

The right-most character, 'L', represents a negative-signed zoned decimal of '3'.

Example 5

ZONECON5   DC   ZL5 ' 763 . 13 '

ZONECON5	7	6	3	1	C
	F | 7	F | 6	F | 3	F | 1	C | 3

The right-most character, 'C', represents a positive-signed zoned decimal of '3'. The decimal point is not compiled as a part of the constant itself, but appears on the program source listing as a reminder to the programmer of its implied position.

The zoned decimal literal is written in the instruction statement in the same manner as that operand portion of a zoned decimal constant is written within a DC statement. As with all literals, it must be preceded by an equal sign.

```
MVC   DATAHOLD (5) ,=Z ' 23965 '
CLC   ZONEDEC (2) ,=ZL2 ' 99 '
MVC   OUTPUT (4) ,=ZL4 ' +377 . 7 '
```

The Address Constants—A, S, V, and Y

The address constants are used to provide the program with storage address constants. The address used to generate the constant operand may be generally in absolute or relocatable form, such as a symbolic label. One of the principle applications of address constants is to aid in the initialization of the base register assignments for program storage. The symbolic label of the constant itself addresses the area containing the respective address of the symbol or value contained within the statement operand. Address constant expressions are contained within parentheses, rather than within apostrophes. Only the 'A' and 'Y' address constants may be expressed as literals.

The 'A' Address Constant

The 'A' address constant has an implied length of four bytes that results in fullword boundary alignment. If an explicit length modifier is used, word boundary alignment is not applicable.

The 'A' type of address constant is written as:

```
START1    DC    A (BASE1)
START2    DC    A (BASE1+4096)
START3    DC    A (BASE1+8192)
SETADDR   DC    A (TABLE)
```

The 'Y' Address Constant

The implied, and maximum, length of a 'Y' address constant is two bytes. Unless a length modifier is specified, the constant is aligned on a halfword boundary location. Any program to be processed and executed under OS or OS/VS *should not* contain any 'Y' address constants specified in relocatable form. This same restriction is applicable when the processing hardware CPU has a main storage capacity of 32,767 bytes or more.

The 'Y' address constant might appear as:

```
SUBRTE    DC    Y(ENTRY1)
SUBRTEA   DC    Y(ENTRY1+16394)
```

The 'S' Address Constant

The 'S' type of address constant is compiled as a two-byte halfword if no length modifier is specified. It has a maximum length restriction of two bytes, and the presence of a length modifier prevents forced halfword boundary alignment. When the constant has been compiled, the high-order four bit positions will indicate the base register assignment—the low-order 12 bit positions representing the displacement value.

The expressed constant itself may be specified either as:

- A set of absolute expressions representing the displacement portion of the address and the base register assignment. This type of expression would appear as S(512(4)) wherein the '512' indicates the displacement value and the '4' indicates the base register.
- An absolute or relocatable address factor, such as S(BASE1).

The 'V' Address Constant

The 'V' constant differs somewhat from the other address constants in that it compiles with an absolute value content of zero. Its actual purpose within Assembler Language is to allocate storage space for the address of an external symbol. This address is not provided until the program with the external symbol reference is loaded.

Unless a length modifier is specified, the 'V' address constant is compiled as a four-byte fullword, with proper boundary alignment of a fullword. The expressed constant itself is specified as a single relocatable symbol.

```
ADCONVA   DC    V(EXREF)
ADCONVB   DC    V(OUTMOD)
ADCONVC   DC    V(PROG2)
```

In each of these examples the constant expression contained within parentheses has no compiled identification within the program in which it was compiled.

REVIEW EXERCISES

The following problems consist of the constants that have been coded by the programmer via the use of DC instruction statements. Analyze the individual instruction statement and then complete the contents of the field for that constant as it would be generated by the Assembler Language compiler. Express the contents of each field as specified—in character, hexadecimal, or bit-by-bit configuration. Wherever there is insufficient room to place the length of an entire field on one line, subsequent lines represent the contiguous storage allocation for that field. Please note that the character form of a blank (X'40') is shown as ƀ.

1.   HEXCONA   DC   XL6 'C1C2C3E7E8E9'

character format

hex format

2.   HEXCONB   DC   X'F7F8F9'

character

hex

3.   HEXCONC   DC   3XL3 'F7F8C9'

character

hex

4.   HEXCOND   DC   XL5 '5B4B4B6161'

character

hex

5.   HEXCONE   DC   XL2 '4040'

character

hex

6.   HEXCONF   DC   2XL4 '5BF6F1F0'

character

hex

Creating Work Areas Within the Program

7.   CHARA   DC   CL3 ' ABC '

8.   CHARB   DC   5CL1 ' 9 '

9.   CHARC   DC   2CL4 ' A♭B '

10.   CHARD   DC   CL2 ' $- '

11.   CHARE   DC   CL6 ' ADHLPT '

12.   CHARF   DC   4CL2 '135 '

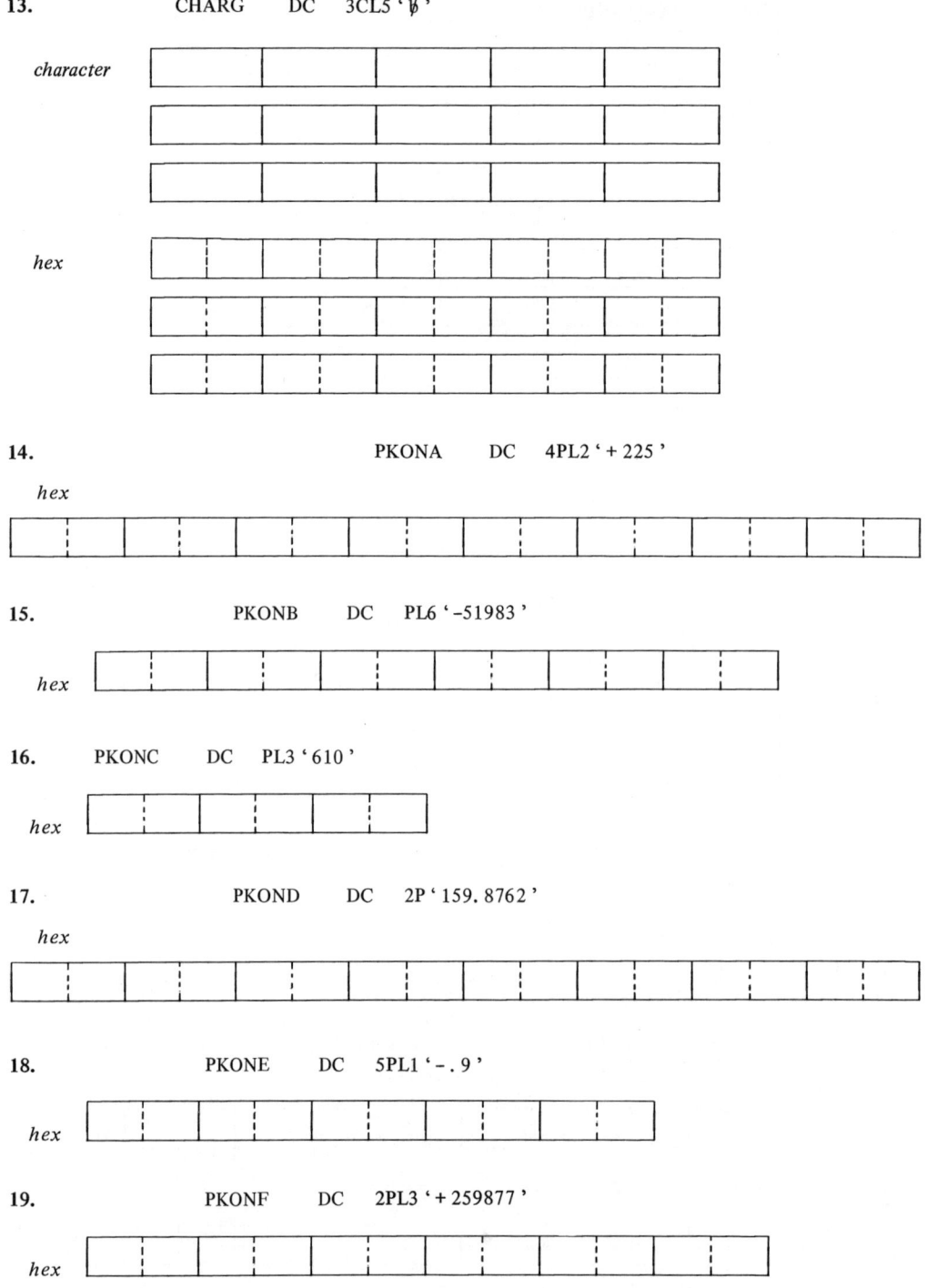

Creating Work Areas Within the Program

28.   BINCONC   DC   2BL.2'11111111'

hex

binary

29.   BINCOND   DC   3BL.1'11101110'

hex

binary

30.   BINCONE   DC   BL3'1111111111111111'.

hex

binary

31.   FXCONA   DC   3H'32767'

hex

binary

fixed-point value _____ _____ _____

32.   FXCONB   DC   2F'32768'

hex

binary

fixed-point value _____ _____

Creating Work Areas Within the Program 139

33.   FXCONC   DC   D'0'

hex

binary

34.   FXCOND   DC   F'295315647'

hex

binary

35.   FXCONE   DC   H'-6153'

hex

binary

36.   FXCONF   DC   2F'-386995'

hex

binary

fixed-point value

The following exercises are intended to further test your understanding of the Define Storage and Define Constant statements.

37. The two op codes that are used to create data fields and work areas are the _____ and the _____.
38. A define Storage statement __(does) (does not)__ clear the storage area that it defines.
39. The label of an area that has been defined by a DS or a DC statement addresses the first (high-order) byte of that area. __(True) (False)__

40. An area established by the following statement will create six 50-byte fields and each field will be singularly addressed by the label WORKFLD. (True) (False)

    WORKFLD   DS   6CL50

41. What would be the total number of bytes of storage reserved by the following statements? _____

    DATAFLDS   DS   0CL54
    DATA1   DS   CL20
    DATA2   DS   0CL34
    SUBDATA1   DS   CL15
    SUBDATA2   DS   CL12
    SUBDATA3   DS   CL7
    DATA3   DS   CL6

42. In the following set of instruction statements, will the field RECNO be aligned on a halfword, fullword, or doubleword boundary? (Use only the largest possible boundary.)

                DS   0D
    FIELDS   DS   CL6
    IDNO   DS   CL5
    CONSTIN   DS   CL1
    RECNO   DS   CL4
    SUBRES   DS   CL15

43. How many bytes of storage would be allocated by each of the following statements?

    a. _____ b. _____ c. _____

    a. SAVEFLD   DS   9H
    b. WORDTABL   DS   15F
    c. PACKAREA   DS   0D

44. Place a check mark in front of each of the following names that could be used as valid labels.

    ____ SETDATA1   ____ DC   ____ ADDFIELDS
    ____ R6SET   ____ INTR '1'   ____ G
    ____ 5TBARD   ____ BACK IN   ____ M3M265911
    ____ FLDA1   ____ INITIATES ____ 360SYS
    ____ Z32MSG   ____ Y   ____ ORG

45. The maximum length of a C-type (character) constant is _____ bytes.

46. How many bytes of storage will be allocated to the constant shown below? _____.

    XFIELD   DC   XL3 '5296874C'

47. A valid "blank" has a hexadecimal configuration of X '_____'.

Creating Work Areas Within the Program

48. ─────── bytes of storage would be allocated to this constant.

    TITLE   DC   C 'WAGES && TAXES'

49. Fill the character contents (EBCDIC) resulting from this DC statement.

    LINEHD   DC   CL8 ' START '

LINEHD								

50. A total quantity of ─────── storage bytes would be allocated to this DC statement.

    STATUSFLD   DC   15CL3 ' INTO '

51. Indicate the hexadecimal contents created by this constant.

    VALUESET   DC   3XL2 ' 5C '

VALUESET												

52. Define the bit configuration resulting from this constant.

    BITSETS   DC   3BL1 ' 100010001 '

BITSETS						

53. Define the hexadecimal configuration resulting from this constant.

    SETHALF   DC   H ' 15999 '

SETHALF			

54. The maximum length of a Z-type (Zoned Decimal) constant is ─────── bytes.

55. What would be the hexadecimal contents generated by this constant?

    PAKFLDS   DC   2PL3 ' 15 '

PAKFLDS												

7
Comparing Data and Conditions

THE INSTRUCTIONS FOR COMPARING DATA

Before studying the general applications of the Assembler Language "compare" instructions, the technical composition and restrictions of each instruction must be presented. This same requirement is equally applicable to subsequent chapters of this text in which logical applications of other Assembler Language instructions are presented. Each of these chapters will, therefore, be preceded by an introductory section consisting of concise technical descriptions for all of the instructions that are to be introduced within that chapter.

It is advised that you thoroughly study the technical description for each of the instructions before proceeding to the application phase of the chapter. The introductory sections for these chapters may thereafter be used as a quick technical reference guide to the Assembler Language instructions.

*   *   *

Instruction: Compare Logical

mnemonic	hex code	operand format
CL	55	$R_1, D_2 (X_2, B_2)$

The Compare Logical instruction activates a binary comparison of the bit configuration of the first operand register to the second operand field. The comparison is from left-most bit to right-most bit. If an unequal condition is encountered prior to the end of the comparative fields, the compare is terminated and the Condition Code bits are set accordingly. The address generated by the second operand (D_2) must be a fullword boundary alignment.

Condition Code (CC)	Branch Condition (BC)	Condition
0	8	The first and second operands are equal.
1	4	The first operand is less than the second operand.
2	2	The first operand is greater than the second operand.

*   *   *

Instruction: Compare Logical Characters

	mnemonic	hex code	operand format
	CLC	D5	$D_1 \,(L, B_1), D_2 \,(B_2)$

The Compare Logic Characters instruction causes the execution of a binary comparison of the storage data specified by the first operand to the storage data specified by the second operand. The comparison is bit-by-bit, from left-most bit (high-order) to right-most bit. If an unequal condition should happen to be encountered prior to the end of the comparative fields, the compare is terminated and the Condition Code is configured accordingly. Up to 256 bytes of data may be compared with one instruction statement.

CC	BC	Condition
0	8	The first and second operands are equal.
1	4	The first operand is less than the second operand.
2	2	The first operand is greater than the second operand.

* * *

Instruction: Compare Logical Immediate

	mnemonic	hex code	operand format
	CLI	95	$D_1 \,(B_1), I_2$

The Compare Logical Immediate instruction creates a binary comparison of one byte of storage data (referred to by the first operand) to one byte of immediate data as defined by the second operand (I_2). The comparison is bit-by-bit, from left-most bit (high-order) to right-most bit. If an unequal condition is encountered prior to the end of the comparative fields, the compare is terminated and the Condition Code bits are set to the representative configuration.

CC	BC	Condition
0	8	The first and second operands are equal.
1	4	The first operand is less than the second operand.
2	2	The first operand is greater than the second operand.

* * *

Instruction: Compare Logical Registers

	mnemonic	hex code	operand format
	CLR	15	R_1, R_2

The Compare Logical Registers instruction causes a binary comparison of contents of the first operand register to the contents of the second operand register. The comparison is from left-most bit to right-most bit. If an unequal condition is encountered prior to the end of the comparative registers, the compare is terminated and the Condition Code is set appropriately.

Comparing Data and Conditions 145

CC	BC	Condition
0	8	The first and second operands are equal.
1	4	The first operand is less than the second operand.
2	2	The first operand is greater than the second operand.

*   *   *

Instruction: Compare Logical Long (System/370 Only)

mnemonic	hex code	operand format
CLCL	0F	R_1, R_2

The Compare Logical Long instruction causes a binary comparison between the storage data addressed by the first operand and the storage data addressed by the second operand. The first operand (R_1) and the second operand (R_2) each represent an even-odd pair of general registers. The even-numbered register of each pair must be the one specified by the operands. Strings (fields) of data of up to 16,777,215 bytes each may be compared by this instruction. Unlike other "logical compare" instructions, the two strings of data being compared may be of different lengths. If unequal-length data fields are to be compared, the programmer is expected to supply a padding character for the shorter field. The comparison is made, bit-by-bit, commencing at the left-most bit (low storage address) of each data string and proceeds toward the right-most bit (high storage address). The comparison terminates upon encountering an unequal condition or the end of the longer field, whichever occurs first.

CC	BC	Condition
0	8	The operands are equal, or else both fields have a length of zero.
1	4	The first operand is less than the second operand.
2	2	The first operand is greater than the second operand.

*   *   *

Instruction: Compare Logical Characters Under Mask (System/370 Only)

mnemonic	hex code	operand format
CLM	BD	$R_1, M_3, D_2 (B_2)$

The Compare Logical Characters Under Mask instruction creates a binary comparison of the second operand ($D_2 (B_2)$) to a portion or all of the first operand (R_1), under control of a mask (M_3). The mask consists of four bit positions, each corresponding to the position of the four bytes within the first operand register. For each one-bit specified in the mask, the corresponding byte within the register is compared to the second operand. A zero-bit in the mask indicates that the corresponding byte position in the register is to be ignored. Selected bytes in the register, though possibly non-contiguous, are considered to be contiguous for the purpose of the comparison. The second operand must be a contiguous field in storage equal in length to the number of bytes selected from the first operand register. The comparison is made from left to right, bit-by-bit. The comparison is terminated upon encountering the first unequal condition or upon completing the comparison of both fields, whichever occurs first.

CC	BC	Condition
0	8	The selected bytes are equal or else the mask was zero.
1	4	The selected bytes of the first operand are less than the second operand.
2	2	The selected bytes of the first operand are greater than the second operand.

*   *   *

Instruction: Compare

mnemonic	hex code	operand format
C	59	$R_1, D_2 (X_2, B_2)$

This Compare instruction compares the contents of the first operand register to the contents of the second operand (algebraically as 32-bit signed integers), and sets the Condition Code bits as a result of that comparison. The operands are not altered by the execution of the instruction. The address generated by the second operand should be that of a fullword boundary alignment.

CC	BC	Condition
0	8	The first and second operands are equal.
1	4	The first operand is less than the second operand.
2	2	The first operand is greater than the second operand.

*   *   *

Instruction: Compare Halfword

mnemonic	hex code	operand format
CH	49	$R_1, D_2 (X_2, B_2)$

Prior to the actual compare operation, this instruction expands the 16-bit value of the second operand contents to a 32-bit value by creating 16 additional high-order bits, each having the same value as the original sign-bit of the second operand. It then algebraically compares the first operand register contents to the expanded second operand, as 32-bit signed integers, and sets a Condition Code as a result of the comparison. The operands are not altered by the execution of this instruction. The address generated by the second operand should be located on a halfword boundary alignment.

CC	BC	Condition
0	8	The first and second operands are equal.
1	4	The first operand is less than the second operand.
2	2	The first operand is greater than the second operand.

*   *   *

Comparing Data and Conditions

Instruction: Compare Registers

mnemonic	hex code	operand format
CR	19	R_1, R_2

The Compare Registers instruction compares the contents of the first operand register to the contents of the second operand register, algebraically as 32-bit signed integers. It then sets the Condition Code as a result of that comparison. The contents of the operands are not altered.

CC	BC	Condition
0	8	The first and second operands are equal.
1	4	The first operand is less than the second operand.
2	2	The first operand is greater than the second operand.

* * *

Instruction: Compare Packed Decimals

mnemonic	hex code	operand format
CP	F9	$D_1 (L_1, B_1), D_2 (L_2, B_2)$

This instruction compares the packed decimal contents of the first operand against the packed decimal contents of the second operand. The comparison is from right to left, through all digits of both operands. If the length attributes of the two operands are not equal, the shorter field is expanded to the length of the longer field by the insertion of high-order zero-digits. The actual bit configuration of the sign-zone nibbles (the right-most four bit positions of each field) is not checked other than to determine if the sign is a plus sign or a minus sign. Any valid plus sign compares equal to any other valid plus sign; any valid minus sign compares equal to any other valid minus sign. However, a plus-zero (+0) value of one field will compare equal to the minus-zero (-0) value of another field. The operand contents are not altered by the execution of the compare. The maximum implied, or explicit, length for either field is 16 bytes.

CC	BC	Condition
0	8	The first and second operand contents are equal.
1	4	The first operand is less than the second operand.
2	2	The first operand is greater than the second operand.

THE APPLICATION OF THE "COMPARE" INSTRUCTIONS

It would be illogical to assume that a program could be written in which the execution of a comparison statement did not take place. Although not all comparison instructions or actions are under the programmer's direct control (the operating system itself performs many decision functions based on comparisons), the average program will probably contain many decisions and decision points, the result of which are based on a comparison.

Since the majority of Assembler Language instructions set the Condition Code bits in the Program Status Word as a result of their performance, it could be loosely interpreted that each of these instructions, in their own way, are a "compare." If we were to disregard the setting of the Condition Code bits as the criteria for distinguishing a compare instruction, there are still a number of instructions that do not clearly define themselves as compare instructions by using that term in their names. Instructions such as Branch on Count, Branch on Index High, and Test Under Mask are quite logically a compare instruction. For the purpose of this section, however, the instructions and techniques to be explained will be only those that contain the term "compare" within their descriptive names. These will be set forth in three categories: logical compares, fixed-point compares, and the packed decimal compare.

Logical Compares

The instructions which fall within the grouping of logical compares are Compare Logical, Compare Logical Characters, Compare Logical Immediate, Compare Logical Long, Compare Logical Characters Under Mask, and Compare Logical Registers instructions. This type of compare instruction is not concerned with the character format of the operand fields on which the comparison is based. Each of these instructions starts at the left-most bit positon (high-order) of the operands fields and compares the binary bit position contents rightward. Each bit position in the first operand is compared to a corresponding bit position within the second operand. As soon as the instruction encounters a single unequal bit position, the compare terminates and the Condition Code in the Program Status Word (PSW) is set according to the status of the inequity. If an unequal condition is not found, the compare continues through the length of the operand fields, bit positon by bit position, until the implied, or explicit, length of the comparison is depleted. Since the logical compare is one in which the individual bit positions create the equal, or unequal, condition, a signed binary decimal integer of -365 would compare high to a signed binary decimal integer of +365. These two operand fields would appear as:

| -365 | 1 111 | 1111 | 1111 | 1111 | 1111 | 1110 | 1001 | 0011 |

| +365 | 0 000 | 0000 | 0000 | 0000 | 0000 | 0001 | 0110 | 1101 |

The first bit position to be compared would be the sign-bit, in which case the negative value of -365 would have a one-bit in the sign-bit position and the positive value of +365 would have a zero-bit in the sign-bit position. The logical compare would terminate at this point and the condition code would be set to indicate that the logical value of -365 (as a fixed-point value) was greater than the logical value of +365 in comparable format. This would be a true condition inasmuch as the comparison was made for the logical value of the operands, not the fixed-point arithmetic value.

Compare Logical (CL)

This instruction is used to logically compare the contents of a register to the contents of a fullword of data in storage. It could be used to logically compare the configuration of a general register to a preestablished bit configuration in a constant in order to determine if a particular condition or point within the program had been reached.

Comparing Data and Conditions 149

In order to understand the various representations that a data field might assume, the logical sequences of translation are shown in the following illustrations. Assume that a particular full-word in storage, referenced by the label CONA, contains the bit configuration required to form the EBCDIC alphabetic characters "ABCD". The transition from EBCDIC format to an interpretation in bit configuration format for the contents of CONA would appear to be:

character	A	B	C	D
hexadecimal	C 1	C 2	C 3	C 4
binary	1100 0001	1100 0010	1100 0011	1100 0100

Using this field as one of the operands, a compare statement is coded as:

    CL   6,CONA

At the time of execution of this instruction statement, general register 6 contains a bit configuration of:

general register 6

```
| 1100 1010 | 1111 0101 | 1111 1100 | 1100 0100 |
```

The sequence of the comparison by bit positions would be:

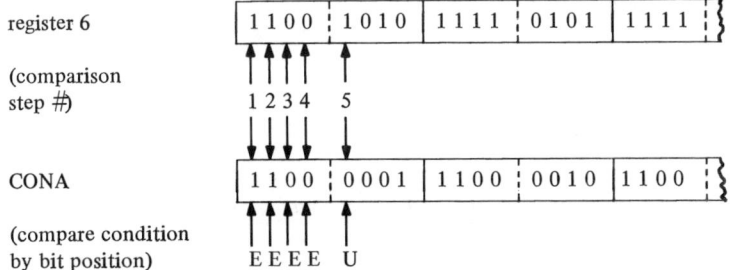

The compare action would terminate on the fifth comparison of the relative bit positions because an unequal condition is encountered. The Condition Code would then be set to reflect that general register 6 contains a bit configuration logically higher in value than the bit configuration of CONA.

Another illustration of the Compare Logical instruction, wherein CONA contains the same value but general register 6 contains a different value, might indicate the following steps of comparison:

150   *Assembler Language for Application Programming*

In this instance, the comparison would terminate on encountering the tenth relative bit positions. The Condition Code would then be set to indicate that general register 6 contains a bit configuration logically lower in value than the bit configuration of CONA.

Compare Logical Characters (CLC)

The CLC instruction would normally be used to logically compare the zoned alpha numeric contents of two fields of storage data. The inference is that both fields of data contain EBCDIC data in character, numeric, or special character form, although it is not restricted to this. The instruction could be used to identify input data through the use of sets of control data, check fields for data stored prior to branching decisions, establishing criteria for the selection or exclusion of data to be processed, or any unique use in which this instruction might lend itself to the programmer's intended logic path.

To illustrate the performance of this instruction in the following example, FIELDA and FIELDB both contain three bytes of EBCDIC character data. FIELDA contains the criteria control data on which the prefix fields in certain records are to be matched. If the prefix field for a record (FIELDB) creates an equal compare to FIELDA, the programmer might wish to use certain data from within the overall data record. The action of the Compare Logical Characters instruction can be interpreted as shown following this instruction statement.

    CLC   FIELDA , FIELDB

The character-formatted contents are considered to be:

FIELDA (control data) | P | O | S |

FIELDB (record prefix data) | P | R | S |

The interpretation of the hexadecimal configuration of these fields would be:

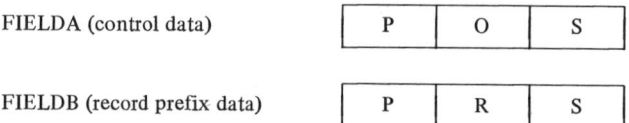

The binary bit configuration of the fields and the resulting action of the CLC instruction statement might appear as:

Comparing Data and Conditions 151

As indicated by this illustration, the compare action would terminate at the 13th bit position (from the left) because an unequal condition occurs at that point. The Condition Code would be set to indicate that FIELDA is of a lesser value than, or unequal to, FIELDB and, based on this result, the programmer's logic coding would determine what the program decision function would be.

Numerals in EBCDIC format can also be readily checked with this instruction. Assume that a programmer wishes to check a three-byte field of data for its EBCDIC numeric contents to ascertain if these numerals are in excess of a value of 099. If the comparative value of 099 is a constant in a data storage area labeled NUMBRA and the data to be checked is in a field in data storage labeled NUMBRB, the instruction statement might appear as:

    CLC   NUMBRB , NUMBRA

If the comparative value of 099 was not already established as a constant, the programmer could use a literal in lieu of the second operand. At program compile time, the compiler would assign a storage address for the literal value. The instruction statement in this instance of the use of a literal would appear as:

    CLC   NUMBRB , =CL3 ' 099 '

In either case the compare would be processed similarly if the contents of all fields in both instructions are comparable.

character format:

NUMBRB	2	3	0

NUMBRA	0	9	9

hexadecimal configuration:

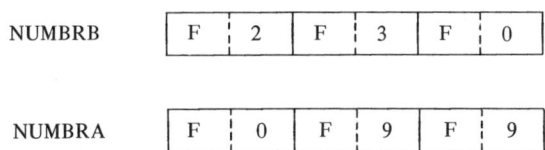

The bit configuration and comparison action would be:

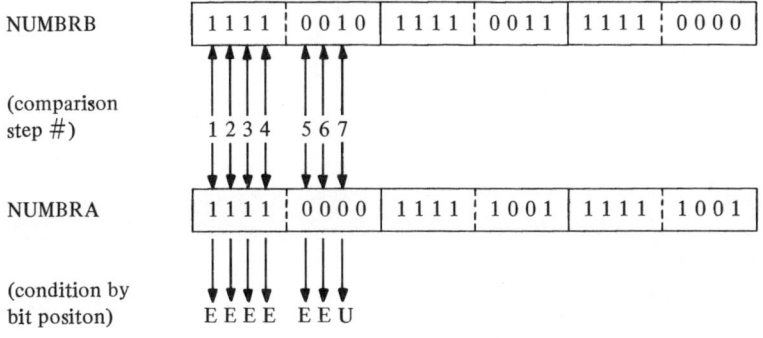

Upon encountering the seventh relative bit position of both fields, the instruction statement operation would find an unequal condition and terminate the compare. The Condition Code would be configured to indicate that field NUMBRB is unequal to, or higher than, field NUMBRA.

Compare Logical Immediate (CLI)

Because this instruction compares only fields of one-byte length, it can readily be used to test the "on-off" condition of a one-byte "switch" or to look for a one-byte control character in data fields. The first operand would contain the label or symbolic address of one byte of storage data; the second operand would be a one-byte self-defining (immediate) character or value.

For example, a programmer plans to check a one-byte control field on each record of input to determine if that byte contains an alphabetic "D" in EBCDIC format. This one-byte field, CHEXA, could be compared in any of the following ways, using the Compare Logical Immediate instruction.

```
CLI    CHEXA,C'D'
CLI    CHEXA,X'C4'
CLI    CHEXA,B'11000100'
```

In each of these three instruction statements, the comparison would be identical. Note that the configuration of the second operand, whether expressed as a character, as hex, or as binary is interpreted as an alphabetic character "D" in all three instances. Assuming that CHEXA contained a character "X," the breakdown of the data could be construed to be:

character format:

CHEXA	X

Immediate character	D

hexadecimal configuration:

CHEXA	E	7

Immediate character	C	4

The action of the CLI instruction on the bit configuration of these two bytes would appear to be:

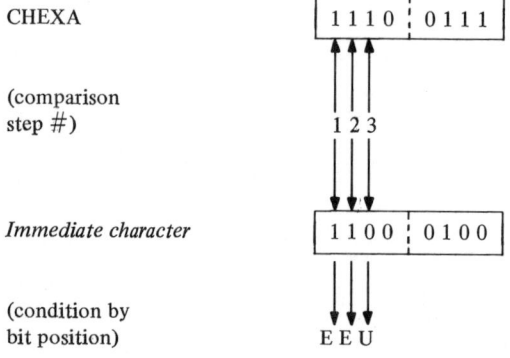

Comparing Data and Conditions 153

During the comparison of the third respective bit positions, the instruction statement would encounter the unequality of the bit values and terminate the compare. The resulting Condition Code setting would enable the programmer to determine that an unequal comparison was made, one in which the first operand contains the greater character value.

Compare Logical Registers (CLR)

The CLR instruction, as its title implies, logically compares the bit configuration of the contents of two general registers. As with the other logical compare instructions, the respective bit positions are compared from left to right, bit by bit.

Assuming that general register 6 is to be compared to general register 8, the instruction statement would be coded as:

    CLR   6,8

The following illustration defines the comparison action that might result from this instruction statement, depending on the contents of the registers.

The bit configuration comparison would be equal until the 17th respective bit positions. At that time, the instruction statement would note the unequal condition, terminate the compare, and change the present Condition Code bits in the Program Status Word to indicate that general register 6 is of a lesser logical value than general register 8.

Compare Logical Long (CLCL) (System/370 Only)

The CLCL instruction would normally be used for purposes similar to those for which the Compare Logical Characters (CLC) instruction is used. Unlike the CLC instruction, however, the CLCL instruction can:

- Compare up to 16,777,215 bytes
- Compare data fields of unequal length
- Readily identify the point at which an unequal condition occurred

The comparison of the data pointed to by the two operands commences at the left-most bit (high-order/lowest storage address) and moves to the right, bit-by-bit, until an unequal condition is found or the end of the longer field is encountered, whichever occurs first.

Two pairs of even-odd general registers must be used to address the strings of data, with the even-numbered register of each pair used to specify the first and second operands, respectively.

The odd-numbered register of each pair is used to specify the length of the data field pointed to by the appropriate even-numbered register.

Assuming that the programmer is going to use general registers 6 and 7 for the first operand and 8 and 9 for the second operand in comparing two fields of equal length, the registers would contain the following information.

The instruction statement necessary to execute the use of these registers is:

    CLCL   6 , 8

If data fields of unequal length are compared, the programmer is expected to provide a "padding" character prior to execution of the instruction statement. This one-byte character, or bit configuration, must be loaded into the high-order byte of the odd-numbered register of the second operand. Even though it is resident in the second operand, it will be used to "pad" out the shorter of the two data fields, regardless of whether the first or second operand points to that shorter field. If general registers 4 and 5 are used as the first operand and registers 10 and 11 are used as the second operand, they would be formatted as follows.

Comparing Data and Conditions 155

The instruction statement would be:

    CLCL   4 , 10

The step-by-step coding to set up both a comparison of fields of equal length and a comparison of fields of unequal length is reflected in the following examples.

Example 1

The two data strings (fields) to be compared are NEWMASTR and OLDMASTR. Both fields are 1,420 bytes in length.

    LA   6 , NEWMASTR   0101
    LA   7 , 1420   0102
    LA   10 , OLDMASTR   0103
    LA   11 , 1420   0104
    CLCL   6 , 10   0105

After completion of the execution of Instruction Statement #0104, the registers would contain:

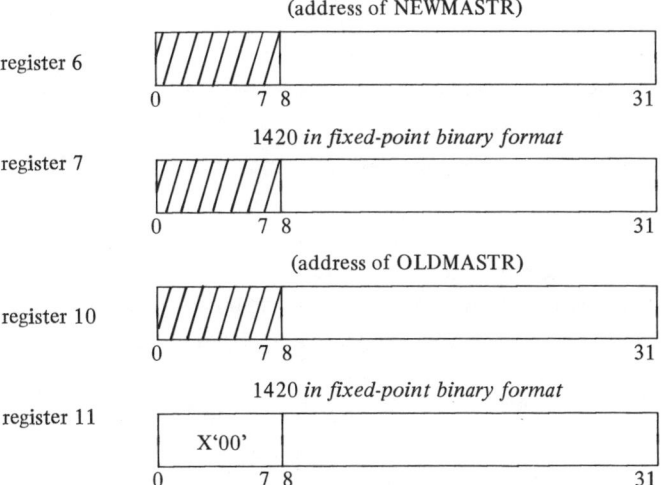

Note that bit positions 0–7 in register 11 contain X'00' rather than a configuration representing a padding character. Inasmuch as the fields being compared were of equal length, it is not necessary to provide a padding character. Therefore the X'00' placed into those bit positions by the Load Address (LA) instruction remains unchanged.

Example 2

The two fields to be compared are MATRIX and TABLE. MATRIX has a length of 2,680 bytes and TABLE has a length of 2,000 bytes. The register pairs to be used are 4-5 and 8-9.

```
    LA    4,MATRIX            0220
    LA    5,2680              0221
    LA    8,TABLE             0222
    LA    9,2000              0223
    ST    9,HOLDFLD           0224
    MVI   HOLDFLD,X'F1'       0225
    L     9,HOLDFLD           0226
    CLCL  4,8                 0227
```

After completion of the execution of Instruction Statement 0226, the registers would contain:

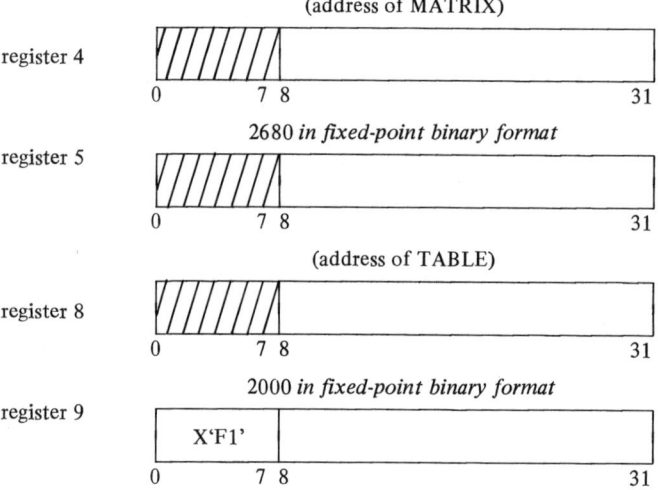

If, during the execution of Instruction Statement 0227, the comparison does not encounter an unequal condition prior to the end of the shorter field (TABLE), the remaining bytes in the longer field (MATRIX) would be compared bit-by-bit against the pad character for each of the bytes remaining in MATRIX.

Note the technique used here to load the pad character into general register 9.

> Statement 0224 Stores (ST) the contents of register 9 into a four-byte fullword-aligned field labeled HOLDFLD.
>
> Statement 0225 uses the Move Immediate (MVI) instruction to move the hexadecimal configuration of an alphanumeric "1" into the high-order byte of HOLDFLD.
>
> Statement 0226 Loads (L) the contents of HOLDFLD back into register 9.

Comparing Data and Conditions

This technique has been used for ease of understanding even though the Insert Character Under Mask (ICM) instruction could have accomplished the same action in one statement.

Another feature to be noted is that the CLCL instruction is interruptible; that is, the operating system can temporarily divert processing to a higher priority task, then return and continue processing the CLCL instruction statement. If and when such an interruption occurs, the odd-numbered register of each operand will have been decremented by the number of bytes already compared; the even-numbered register of each operand will have been incremented to the address of the next byte to be compared. When processing of the CLCL resumes, it picks up at the appropriate location. As implied, even though the action of the comparison is bit-by-bit, the interruption will occur only at a byte address.

The decrementing of the odd-numbered registers and the incrementing of the even-numbered registers provides another service; if the execution of the CLCL instruction results in an unequal condition, the contents of the registers can be interrogated to find the actual location (byte-count or address) of the unequal comparison.

Compare Logical Characters under Mask (CLM) (System/370 Only)

The CLM instruction can be used to compare selected bytes contained within a general register to an equal number of bytes contained within a field in main storage. The selection of the bytes from the general register is controlled by a four-bit mask, each bit position in the mask representing a corresponding byte within the register. A zero-bit in the mask indicates that the corresponding byte in the register is to be excluded; a one-bit in the mask specifies that the corresponding byte in the register is to participate in the comparison. This would appear as:

mask	register bytes selected			
0100		X		
0011			X	X
1101	X	X		X
1111	X	X	X	X
1001	X			X

For purposes of the comparison, bytes selected from the register are considered to be contiguous. Conversely, the data bytes referred to by the second operand *must* be physically contiguous in storage. The field addressed by the second operand must also be equal in length to the quantity of bytes selected from the register.

To represent the action of this instruction, assume general register 9 contains the following hexadecimal representation:

0	3	F	B	C	3	8	C

Given a variation of mask and data fields, the register byte selection and comparisons would occur as follows.

Definition of the data fields:

```
DATA1    DC    X'8C'
DATA2    DC    X'038C'
DATA3    DC    X'03BF8C'
```

Statement examples to be executed:

```
Example 1    CLM    9,B'1001',DATA2
Example 2    CLM    9,B'0010',DATA1
Example 3    CLM    9,B'0001',DATA1
Example 4    CLM    9,B'1010',DATA2
Example 5    CLM    9,B'1101',DATA3
```

The action taken by these statements would be:

example #	register contents selected	data field contents	result of comparison
1	X'038C'	X'038C'	Equal
2	X'3C'	X'8C'	Unequal
3	X'8C'	X'8C'	Equal
4	X'03C3'	X'038C'	Unequal
5	X'03FB8C'	X'03BF8C'	Unequal

In each instance the instruction statement extracts the appropriate bytes from the register as a contiguous representation and compares them (bit-by-bit from left to right) to the contents of the data field specified by the second operand. Although the result of the comparison has been shown only as "equal" or "unequal" in these examples, the Condition Code setting would further define an unequal condition to be either "low" or "high." Neither the contents of the register nor the data field are altered by this instruction.

Fixed-Point Compares

A series of instructions, consisting of the Compare, Compare Halfword, and Compare Registers instructions, are for the comparison of fixed-point values. Each of these instructions compares the first operand to the second operand, setting a Condition Code as a result of the comparison. The contents of both operands are construed to consist of a 32-bit signed integer, comprising a 31-bit integer and a high-order sign-bit. The actual comparison, therefore, is algebraic, based on the fixed-point value of each operand. In essence, the instruction determines the value of the 31-bit integers, evaluates the sign of each, and makes the comparison. The value of a positive-signed (+) integer is determined by summing the Powers-of-Two value for each bit position that contains a

Comparing Data and Conditions 159

one-bit. The value of a negative-signed (-) integer, expressed in Two's Complement form, can be determined by summing the integer as if it were a positive number and subtracting that value from the maximum negative value, -2,147,483,648 for a fullword and -32,768, for a halfword.

Compare (C)

This instruction is used to algebraically compare the fixed-point value of the contents of a general register to the fixed-point value of the contents of a fullword of storage data. In order to understand the execution logic of this instruction, assume that general register 10 and a fullword in storage, FLWDA, are to be compared. The instruction statement itself would be coded as:

    C   10, FLWDA

The data to be compared by this instruction statement resides within the respective areas with this configuration:

bit configuration:

register 10 | 0 000 0000 | 0000 0000 | 0001 1100 | 1001 1101 |

FLWDA | 0 000 0000 | 0000 0000 | 0011 1010 | 1000 1100 |

hexadecimal configuration:

register 10 | + 0 | 0 | 0 | 0 | 1 | C | 9 | D |

FLWDA | + 0 | 0 | 0 | 0 | 3 | A | 8 | C |

You can determine the value of these fields by converting the individual hexadecimal values, in their contiguous arrangement, to the fixed-point value that they represent. The Powers-of-Two Table and the Hexadecimal/Decimal Conversion Table will aid in making this conversion. The method is shown in the following illustration.

	Register 10		FLWDA	
Right to Left Order	*Hex*	*Decimal*	*Hex*	*Decimal*
First hex digit	D	13	C	12
Second hex digit	9	144	8	128
Third hex digit	C	3,072	A	2,560
Fourth hex digit	1	4,096	3	12,288
Integer value		7,325		14,988
Sign-bit		+		+
Signed fixed-point value		+ 7,325		+ 14,988

The algebraic comparison would indicate that the fixed-point value of FLWDA is greater than the value contained in general register 10. The Condition Code bits of the PSW would be set to indicate that the first operand of the instruction statement is of a lower value than that of the second operand.

Another example of this instruction, in which different values are contained in the operands, is:

```
C    6, FLWDB
```

bit configuration:

register 6 | 0 000 | 0000 | 0001 | 0110 | 0000 | 0001 | 1101 | 0110 |

FLWDB | 0 000 | 0000 | 0001 | 0001 | 1001 | 0010 | 1011 | 1010 |

hexadecimal configuration:

register 6 | + 0 | 0 | 1 | 6 | 0 | 1 | D | 6 |

FLWDB | + 0 | 0 | 1 | 1 | 9 | 2 | B | A |

Hexadecimal to fixed-point conversion:

	Register 6		FLWDB	
Right to Left Order	Hex	Decimal	Hex	Decimal
First hex digit	6	6	A	10
Second hex digit	D	208	B	176
Third hex digit	1	256	2	512
Fourth hex digit	0	0	9	36,864
Fifth hex digit	6	393,216	1	65,536
Sixth hex digit	1	1,048,576	1	1,048,576
Integer value		1,442,262		1,151,674
Sign-bit		+		+
Signed fixed-point value		+ 1,442,262		+ 1,151,674

Execution of the Compare instruction statement would determine that the algebraic value of general register 6 is greater than the value contained in FLWDB. The Condition Code bits would indicate that the first operand of the instruction statement is of a greater fixed-point value than that of the second operand.

It is necessary to understand the conversion of binary bit configuration to fixed-point values through the interpretation of the hexadecimal value arrangements in order to fully appreciate the mechanisms of fixed-point instructions. The previous two examples illustrate the conversion of standard positive-signed (+) values. Of equal importance is the knowledge and understanding of the concept of Two's Complement values and their interpretation. Although the subject is adequately covered within other sections of this text, a repetition of some of the basic rules and fundamentals is in order. The negative-signed value of the contents of any fixed-point field may not be of direct and immediate importance insofar as the coding of the Compare instruction statement is concerned; the coding is created in the same manner regardless of what the format of the contents of the operands might be. It is possible, however, that you might wish to verify the

Comparing Data and Conditions

results of a Compare instruction statement in order to confirm the data that is being passed through your program logic. If one of the values you are attempting to verify is a Two's Complement value, representing a negative fixed-point value, it may be interpreted in this manner:

bit configuration:

register 3 | 1 111 1111 | 1110 1100 | 0111 1001 | 1101 0010 |

hexadecimal configuration:

register 3 | - 7 | F | E | C | 7 | 9 | D | 2 |

Fixed-point conversion:

	Register 3		
Right to Left Order	Hex	Decimal	
First hex digit	2	2	
Second hex digit	D	208	
Third hex digit	9	2,304	
Fourth hex digit	7	28,672	
Fifth hex digit	C	786,432	
Sixth hex digit	E	14,680,064	
Seventh hex digit	F	251,658,240	
Eighth hex digit	7	1,879,048,192	(Excludes the sign-bit)
Integer value		2,146,204,114	
Maximum negative value of a fixed-point fullword			2,147,483,648
Integer value of general register 3			2,146,204,114
Difference			1,279,534
Sign-bit			-
Negative fixed-point value of register 3			- 1,279,534

The unsigned integer portion of register 3 can be verified by converting it back to a positive value through reversal of the Two's Complement form, as follows:

general register 3 | 1 111 1111 | 1110 1100 | 0111 1001 | 1101 0010 |

(subtract a one-bit)   -1

(result) | 1 111 1111 | 1110 1100 | 0111 1001 | 1101 0001 |

(reverse the bit notation) | 0 000 0000 | 0001 0011 | 1000 0110 | 0010 1110 |

(convert to hexadecimal) | + | 0 | 0 | 1 | 3 | 8 | 6 | 2 | E |

	Register 3	
Right to Left Order	Hex	Decimal
First hex digit	E	14
Second hex digit	2	32
Third hex digit	6	1,536
Fourth hex digit	8	32,768
Fifth hex digit	3	196,608
Sixth hex digit	1	1,048,576
Integer value		1,279,534

In converting the negative configuration of general register 3 back to a positive value, the calculation verifies the accuracy of the original negative configuration interpretation.

Compare Halfword (CH)

The Compare Halfword instruction algebraically compares the contents of a general register to the contents of a halfword of storage data. The instruction statement first accesses the halfword location and picks up the data stored there. It will then expand that 16-bit halfword to a 32-bit fullword by creating 16 additional high-order bits of the same value as the halfword sign-bit. The instruction then proceeds with the algebraic comparison of the two operands.

The action of this instruction is demonstrated by the following illustrations.

  CH 12 , HAFWDA

Original bit configuration of the fields in this instance:

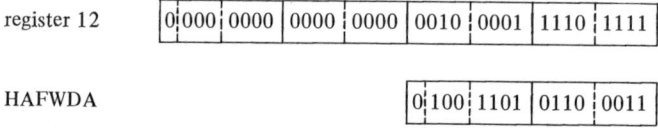

Bit configuration after expansion of the halfword HAFWDA:

Hexadecimal interpretation of these fields:

register 12 | + | 0 | 0 | 0 | 0 | 2 | 1 | E | F |

HAFWDA | + | 0 | 0 | 0 | 0 | 4 | D | 6 | 3 |

Comparing Data and Conditions 163

Hexadecimal to fixed-point conversion:

	Register 12		Expanded HAFWDA	
Right to Left Order	*Hex*	*Decimal*	*Hex*	*Decimal*
First hex digit	F	15	3	3
Second hex digit	E	224	6	96
Third hex digit	1	256	D	3,328
Fourth hex digit	2	8,192	4	16,384
Integer value		8,687		19,811
Sign-bit		+		+
Signed fixed-point value		+ 8,687		+19,811

The algebraic comparison would find that the value of HAFWDA is greater than that of register 12. The Condition Code bits in the PSW would be set to reflect this condition.

A halfword in storage that contains a negative value would be expanded by the addition of 16 additional high-order bits, each bit having the configuration of the negative sign-bit of the original halfword.

HAFWDB | 1 111 | 1010 | 0011 | 1011 |

(expanded) HAFWDB | 1 111 | 1111 | 1111 | 1111 | 1111 | 1010 | 0011 | 1011 |

The value of HAFWDB has not changed, but it is now of a size to facilitate comparison with a register content. The original data, still stored at location HAFWDB, is not altered by the Compare Halfword instruction.

Compare Registers (CR)

The Compare Registers instruction is used to algebraically compare the fixed-point value of the contents of two general registers. The contents of the first operand register are compared to the contents of the second operand register. This instruction, as with the other fixed-point compare instructions, treats both operands as 32-bit signed integers, consisting of a sign-bit and a 31-bit integer.

The evaluation of the contents of two registers that are being used in a CR instruction statement could be accomplished as follows:

    CR   6,9

Bit configuration of the registers:

register 6 | 0 | 000 | 0000 | 0000 | 0001 | 0110 | 1101 | 0010 | 0001 |

register 9 | 0 | 000 | 0000 | 0000 | 0001 | 0110 | 1011 | 0111 | 1000 |

Hexadecimal configuration of the registers:

register 6	+	0	0	0	1	6	D	2	1

register 9	+	0	0	0	1	6	B	7	8

Hexadecimal to fixed-point conversion:

	Register 6		Register 9	
Right to Left Order	Hex	Decimal	Hex	Decimal
First hex digit	1	1	8	8
Second hex digit	2	32	7	112
Third hex digit	D	3,328	B	2,816
Fourth hex digit	6	24,576	6	24,576
Fifth hex digit	1	65,536	1	65,536
Integer value		93,473		93,048
Sign-bit		+		+
Signed fixed-point value		+93,473		+93,048

As a result of this comparison, the Condition Code bits in the PSW would be set to indicate that the first operand, general register 6, contains a value greater than the one in general register 9, the second operand.

Following are several other examples of the Compare Register instruction statement that indicate the interpretation of the values of the operands. In each instance, interim illustrations indicating the means of determining the value of the fields have been omitted.

```
CR    10 , 7
```

register 10	0	000	0000	0000	0001	1011	1000	1001	0100

register 7	0	000	0000	0000	0001	1011	1000	1001	1000

register 10 equals + 112,788
register 7 equals + 112,792

The condition reflected by the Condition Code bits would be that the value of the first operand, general register 10, is of a lesser fixed-point value than that of the second operand, general register 7.

```
CR    5 , 15
```

register 5	1	111	1111	1111	1111	1111	1110	1101	0001

register 15	0	000	0000	0000	0000	0000	0001	0010	1111

register 5 equals −303
register 15 equals +303

Comparing Data and Conditions 165

The Condition Code setting resulting from this instruction statement would indicate that the fixed-point value of the first operand, register 5, is less than the fixed-point value of the second operand, register 15.

The Packed Decimal Compare

The only instruction that falls within this category is the Compare Packed Decimals (CP) instruction. The comparison is between fields of storage data and follows the rules of packed decimal operations. The data is compared from right to left, one-half byte at a time. Inasmuch as a single hexadecimal digit contains four binary bit positions (one-half byte, sometimes referred to as a nibble), the representations and discussions for this instruction will refer to packed decimal digits and hex characters synonomously.

Compare Packed (CP)

The general action of this instruction has been basically covered by the preceding paragraph. It should be noted, however, that unlike other compare instructions, this one has length requirements for both operands. The maximum length for either operand is 16 bytes. If the operand fields are not of equal length, the instruction will expand the shorter field by adding additional bytes of hex zero-digits until the lengths of the two fields agree. The additional bytes are supplied to the high-order side of the shorter field.

As in the case of all packed decimal instructions, a plus sign (+) is represented as a hex character 'A' (1010), 'C' (1100), 'E' (1110), or 'F' (1111); a valid minus sign (-) is either a hex 'B' (1011) or 'D' (1101). The fields to be compared should be validly signed in their low-order nibble (half-byte) with one of these hex digits. Any hex digit with a value of less than ten (A) is construed to be a packed numeric digit and is not acceptable as a sign for a packed decimal field. Any one of the valid positive signs (+), hex 'A', 'C', 'E', or 'F', will compare as equal with one another. Accordingly, a negative sign (-) of hex 'B' will compare equal to a hex 'D'. Somewhat contrary to the general rules is the fact that a packed decimal value of +0 will compare as being equal to a packed decimal value of -0.

In the examples of this instruction, the binary bit configuration of the fields is not used as it was with the fixed-point compare interpretations. The hex digit representation for each nibble is used instead since this gives the clearest illustration of the values of the packed decimal fields. In some instances, the instruction operands contain explicit length attributes. This is done to point out the length differences between operands and the manner in which the instruction adjusts the length of the shorter operand.

```
    CP    PAXA , PAXB
```

PAXA	0	0	0	0	7	3	3	C

PAXB	0	0	9	8	2	4	2	D

As indicated, PAXA contains a packed decimal value of +733; the contents of PAXB is a packed decimal value of -98,242. As a result of the CP instruction statement, the Condition Code bit setting would indicate that the value of the first operand is greater than the value of the second operand.

CP   PACK1 , PACK2

PACK1 | 0 | 9 | 1 | 5 | 3 | C |

PACK2 | 0 | 9 | 1 | 5 | 3 | F |

The Condition Code bit setting resulting from this compare would indicate that both operands contain equal values—both the 'C' sign-digit and the 'F' sign-digit are valid plus signs for packed decimal fields.

CP   PACK3 (2) , PACK4 (3)

PACK3 | 3 | 9 | 7 | C |

PACK4 | 0 | 0 | 2 | 4 | 4 | C |

Prior to the actual comparison of the values, the instruction would extract the shorter field from its data storage location and expand it to match the length of the longer field.

PACK3 | 0 | 0 | 3 | 9 | 7 | C |

PACK4 | 0 | 0 | 2 | 4 | 4 | C |

The comparison shown here would set the Condition Code bits to indicate that the packed decimal value of the first operand, PACK3, is greater than the packed decimal value of the second operand, even though the length attribute of the PACK3 field is the shorter one. The contents of the original storage field, PACK3, are not altered by the execution of the CP instruction statement even though the length of the field is expanded for purposes of comparison.

REVIEW EXERCISES

1. The "logical" compare instructions begin their comparison with the _____-order bit position and compare toward the _____-order bit position. The comparison terminates as soon as a non-match is found between two corresponding _____ positions.
2. The second operand of a CLI (Compare Logical Immediate) instruction statement must consist of an "_____" character or value.
3. If the two fields addressed by the operands of a CLCL instruction statement are of unequal length, a _____ character is required as part of the second register of the second operand.

Comparing Data and Conditions 167

4. The Compare, Compare Halfword, and Compare Registers instructions are considered to be _____-_____ arithmetic comparisons.
5. The CLM instruction can select up to _____ bytes from a general register for comparison to a field of stored data.
6. What are the valid hexadecimal sign-digits for a negative packed decimal value? _____
7. What is the maximum allowable length of a packed decimal field that is indicated as the second operand in a Compare Packed (CP) instruction statement? _____
8. If execution of a CLCL instruction is interrupted, the comparison will resume with the last character previously compared in each field. (True) (False)
9. A packed decimal sign-digit of X'C' will compare as (equal) (unequal) (high) (low) to a packed decimal sign-digit of X'A'.
10. In executing a Compare Logical (CL) instruction statement, a fixed-point value of -39,510 would compare as (high) (low) (equal) to a fixed-point value of +39,510.
11. The register bytes selected by the CLM instruction must be physically contiguous within the register. (True) (False)
12. The maximum lengths for any two fields to be compared by the Compare Logical Characters (CLC) instruction is _____ bytes per field.
13. The following two fields are being compared via a logical type of compare. Circle the single bit position in each field at the point at which the comparison would terminate.

| 0000 | 1010 | 1100 | 0100 | 1101 | 1011 | 1111 | 1000 |

| 0000 | 1010 | 1100 | 0100 | 1101 | 1010 | 1111 | 1000 |

14. If a field labeled BYTE contained an EBCDIC alpha character "S" the following instruction statement would set the Condition Code bits to indicate that BYTE compared as (high) (low) (equal) to the second operand literal.

   CLI   BYTE , B ' 11100010'

15. A mask of '0000' would select _____ bytes from the general register specified by the first operand of a CLM instruction statement.
16. General register 6 contains a fixed-point value of +3,175,815. A fullword of storage, FWDTWO, contains a hexadecimal configuration of X'00307588'. After execution of the following instruction statement, the Condition Code bits would indicate that the value within general register 6 is (greater than) (less than) (equal to) the fixed-point value of the contents of FWDTWO.

   C   6 , FWDTWO

17. In executing a CLCL instruction statement, the field addressed by the first operand must always be equal to or longer than the second operand. (True) (False)
18. A fixed-point value of zero can be represented in either positive or negative form. (True)(False)

Carefully analyze each of the following instruction statements. Place a check mark in front of the instruction statements that contain incorrect types of operands, incorrect length attributes, or that consist of incorrect operand formats. In most instances, register operands have been coded as R3, R4, R5, R6, R7, R8, R9, etc., indicating that the referenced register has been equated to such a symbolic label for the purpose of clarity and to assist the reader in determining which operands are registers.

#	Op	Operands
19.	CP	DATAPAK , =X ' 03952C '
20.	CLR	R12 , R15
21.	CLC	INDATA , 0 (5)
22.	CLI	VALUE , X ' 40 '
23.	CL	DATAFLD , INPUT
24.	CR	R9 , R8
25.	CLM	R3 , B ' 101 ' , DATA
26.	CH	HAFWD , R7
27.	C	DATA , 0 (8)
28.	CP	PACKSUM (6) , DATAPAK (3)
29.	C	R8 , =F ' 32957 '
30.	CLC	0+5 (3 , 9) , R7
31.	CLI	7 (5) , B ' 10110001 '
32.	CLCL	4 , 10
33.	CP	R13 , DUBLPACK
34.	CL	R3 , R2
35.	C	R12 , FULLWD6
36.	CLR	R10 , R11
37.	CLM	R3 , B ' 1101 ' , 86 (R3)
38.	CLI	R6 , F ' 6 '
39.	CLC	DATA (95) , BIGSET
40.	C	R3 , R12
41.	CR	R6 , DATA (9)
42.	CP	0+10 (6 , 8) , 5+7 (10 , 7)
43.	CLI	SWITCH , =C ' X '
44.	CH	R9 , HAFWD7
45.	CLCL	R5 , R8
46.	CL	R6 , FULLWD5RG
47.	CP	SETPACK+20 (3) , INSET+52 (3)
48.	CLI	SETUP , C ' 1 '

Comparing Data and Conditions 169

49.	_____	CP	PACKIT (25) , INPACK (25)
50.	_____	CLR	SETVALUE , R6
51.	_____	CLC	0 (4 , 3) , 5 (4 , 6)
52.	_____	C	R10 (7) , FULLWD8
53.	_____	CL	R6 , 4 (8)
54.	_____	CH	R3 , FULLWD
55.	_____	CLR	0 (4 , 9) , R3
56.	_____	CLI	TWOBYTE (2 , 6) , C ' AB '
57.	_____	CLC	INDATA+9 (6) , CONSTA
58.	_____	CR	R3 (6) , R11
59.	_____	C	R9 , 8 (3)
60.	_____	CP	PACKINITL+15 (3) ,=PL3 ' 519 '
61.	_____	CLI	0+95 (11) , X ' C1 '
62.	_____	CLR	R9 , R13
63.	_____	CLM	6 , B1010 , FIELDA
64.	_____	CH	R12 , HAFWD4

8
Program Branching Logic

THE INSTRUCTIONS FOR PROGRAM BRANCHING LOGIC

Instruction: Branch on Conditon

mnemonic	hex code	operand format
BC	47	$M_1, D_2 (X_2, B_2)$

The Branch on Condition instruction uses the bit configuration of the first operand mask as a comparator to the Condition Code setting within the Program Status Word. If a matching condition is found, the instruction statement will cause a program logic branch to the address referenced by the second operand.

The Condition Code setting is not changed by this instruction.

* * *

Instruction: Branch on Condition to Register

mnemonic	hex code	operand format
BCR	07	M_1, R_2

The Branch on Condition to Register instruction causes a program logic branch to the address contained within the second operand register if the bit configuration of the first operand mask compares equal to the Condition Code setting.

The Condition Code is not changed by this instruction.

* * *

Instruction: Branch on Count

mnemonic	hex code	operand format
BCT	46	$R_1, D_2 (X_2, B_2)$

The Branch on Count instruction causes a program logic branch to the address referenced by the second operand as long as the value of the first operand register is not zero. Each time this instruction is executed it algebraically decrements the value of the first operand register by "1".

Once the value of the first operand register reaches zero, the branch is not taken and the processing logic "falls through" to the next sequential program instruction statement.

The Condition Code setting is not changed by this instruction.

*　　　　　*　　　　　*

Instruction: Branch on Count to Register

mnemonic	hex code	operand format
BCTR	06	R_1, R_2

The Branch on Count to Register instruction creates a branch to the address contained within the second operand register as long as the value of the first operand register is not zero. Each time the processing logic passes through this instruction it algebraically decrements the value of the first operand register by "1". When the value of that register reaches zero, the branch is not taken and the processing logic "falls through" to the next sequential program instruction.

The Condition Code setting is not changed by this instruction.

*　　　　　*　　　　　*

Instruction: Branch on Index High

mnemonic	hex code	operand format
BHX	86	$R_1, R_3, D_2 (B_2)$

This instruction requires a trio of *odd-even-odd* registers. The first operand register represents the first odd-numbered general register, the third operand register (R_3) represents the even-numbered register, and the next odd-numbered register is implied. The action of this instruction adds the value of the third operand register (normally a decrementing value such as -1) to the first operand register and then compares that value to the next odd-numbered register that is higher than the assigned third operand register. If the comparison is equal or low, the program processing falls through to the next sequential program instruction statement; if the comparison is high, the program logic branches to the address specified by the second operand.

The Condition Code setting is not changed by this instruction.

*　　　　　*　　　　　*

Instruction: Branch on Index Low or Equal

mnemonic	hex code	operand format
BXLE	87	$R_1, R_3, D_2 (B_2)$

This instruction, functioning somewhat like the BXH instruction, requires a trio of *odd-even-odd* registers. The instruction adds the value of the third operand register (normally a plus-value increment) to the first operand register and compares that value to the next higher odd-numbered register. If the compare is low or equal, the "branch to" address or symbol contained in the second operand will be the route of the program processing action. Once the comparison results in a "high" condition, the program processing falls through the BXLE instruction to the next sequential program instruction statement.

The Condition Code setting is not changed by this instruction..

*   *   *

Instruction: Branch & Link

mnemonic	hex code	operand format
BAL	45	$R_1, D_2 (X_2, B_2)$

The Branch & Link instruction first stores the low-order 32 bits of the updated Program Status Word, containing the address of the next sequential program instruction, into the first operand register. It then proceeds to branch to the address specified, or implied, by the second operand.

The Condition Code setting is not changed by this instruction.

*   *   *

Instruction: Branch & Link Registers

mnemonic	hex code	operand format
BALR	05	R_1, R_2

The Branch & Link Registers instruction stores the low-order 32 bits of the updated Program Status Word, containing the address of the next sequential program instruction statement, into the first operand register and then branches to the address contained in the register specified by the second operand. If the second operand specifies general register 0, the PSW data is stored but the branch is not taken.

The Condition Code is not changed by this instruction.

*   *   *

THE USE OF BRANCHING LOGIC IN THE PROGRAM

The terms *branch* and *branching* may be defined as "a transfer of the program processing logic from one statement to another within the problem program, but not necessarily in the sequential appearance of those instruction statements. The branch is usually taken as the result of a decision based on a prior instruction." In general, the branch instructions can be grouped into two categories—conditional branches and program linkage branches.

Conditional branches are those that may direct the program logic operations through one or more separate paths, depending on the status of the Condition Code bits or a register value. Program linkage branches are usually established to require the program logic to branch to another routine, subroutine or module, perform the instructions contained within that section, and then return to the next logical instruction statement following the statement that forced the branch to occur.

Conditional Branch Instructions

Before discussing any conditional branch instructions, it would be well to evaluate the factor that determines whether or not a conditional branch instruction statement will reroute the program processing logic. This factor is the Condition Code, composed of two binary bit positions. In System/360, the Condition Code resides in bit positions 34 and 35 of the Program Status Word (PSW). In System/370, the Condition Code is in bit positions 18 and 19 of the PSW. These two bit positions have a maximum range of four unique configurations—00, 01, 10, and 11. Most of the Assembler Language instructions, though not all of them, result in the setting of the Condition Code bits upon execution of that instruction. Two of the Conditional Branch instructions (Branch on Condition and Branch on Condition to Register) use the first operand of the instruction statement to mask the Condition Code bits for any specific conditon or conditions.

The Condition Code bit configurations and their corresponding operand mask values for these instructions are shown below.

CC bits within the PSW		equivalent operand for BC and BCR instructions
00	(0)	8
01	(1)	4
10	(2)	2
11	(3)	1

The value of the mask operand in a conditional branch instruction may be an aggregate of several values. This capability is discussed in detail within this section, under Branch on Condition instruction.

The use of conditional branches allows you to utilize multiple logic paths and to predetermine program decisions based on factors encountered during the processing of data by the program. For example, if a certain numeric field is zero, you may want to go to a routine to bypass further arithmetic operations; if the field has a plus value in excess of zero, you might wish to take another route of operation; if the field has a negative value less than minus-zero, you may want the program logic to convert that number to a positive value before continuing the sequential logic path.

Some of the conditional branch instructions, such as the Branch on Count and Branch on Index instructions, do not require a mask operand as a part of the instruction statement. This type of branch instruction has a built-in function that performs a compare and a branch on condition as a part of the overall instruction. They compare the content value of an operand to a numeric value and then decide whether or not to branch as a result of that internal comparison.

Branch on Condition (BC)

Tne Branch on Condition instruction statement creates a branch to the address implied by the second operand if the Condition Code in the Program Status Word is properly masked by the first operand in the instruction statement. The mask operand comprises solely, or as a compounded value, four basic numeric values—8, 4, 2, and 1. Depending on the nature of the instruction statement that set the Condition Code bits, each of these four basic settings could have variable meanings. As an example of this, instructions that compare data fields for logical contents are normally interpreted as setting the Condition Code bits so that the corresponding mask for each setting indicates:

- 8 Both operands are equal.
- 4 The first operand has a lower value than the second operand.
- 2 The first operand has a higher value than the second operand.
- 1 The '1' value is not used for compare instructions.

Instructions that perform arithmetic operations are generally considered to set the Condition Code so the equivalent mask indicates:

- 8 The answer is zero.
- 4 The answer is negative (minus-one or less).
- 2 The answer is positive (plus-one or greater).
- 1 An arithmetic overflow occurred.

In the event that a branch leads to a particular address if any one of a number of possible conditions exist, the mask operand of the Branch on Condition instruction may be an aggregate of any combination of the 8-4-2-1 mask values. Using the Condition Code interpretations for a logical compare instruction as an example of this, there are a number of valid mask code configurations. Because a mask operand of '8' states "branch on an equal condition," it would be permissible to indicate that if the first operand in a previous compare instruction has proved to be low or equal, the branch should be taken on a mask value of "12" within the BC instruction—a value of "8" for the equal condition and a value of "4" for the "lower than" condition. The combination of mask values, assuming a general use, might be defined as shown in Table 8-1.

Table 8-1

Value of Mask Operand	Which Interprets as:	
14	branch on equal, high or low	(8 + 4 + 2)
13	branch on equal, low, or overflow	(8 + 4 + 1)
12	branch on equal or low	(8 + 4)
11	branch on equal, high, or overflow	(8 + 2 + 1)
10	branch on equal or high	(8 + 2)
9	branch on equal or overflow	(8 + 1)
8	branch on equal	(8)
7	branch on unequal (high, low, or overflow)	(4 + 2 + 1)
6	branch on high or low	(4 + 2)
5	branch on low or overflow	(4 + 1)
4	branch on low	(4)
3	branch on high or overflow	(2 + 1)
2	branch on high	(2)
1	branch on overflow	(1)

As stated previously, the exact interpretation for these mixed values will vary among the different instruction statements that set the Condition Code bits. In addition to the foregoing list, a mask value of zero (0) or fifteen (15) may be used as the first operand of the BC instruction statement. When the value of zero is used for the first operand, the branch will not be taken. This is because a zero mask code will never find that condition within the Condition Code setting since it does not exist. This creates an effective *"No Operation"* (NOP) instruction statement. Later, however, you may have the program move a valid value into the mask at any time during the processing and that branch condition will then become effective. In order to create a *"forced branch,"* or a branch that will occur under any of the Condition Code settings, the mask value of the first operand in a BC statement may be specified as "15". This guarantees a successful branch because the Condition Code must be set equal to one of the values comprising the mask value—$8 + 4 + 2 + 1$.

The following examples contain Compare Logical Character instruction statements followed by a Branch on Condition instruction statement.

Example 1

```
CLC    INPUT , HOLDATA
BC     7 , NOGOOD
```

The BC instruction statement in this example specifies, "If the result of the previous compare was an unequal condition, indicating that the first operand of the compare statement was either high or low to the second operand, branch to the address of the instruction labeled NOGOOD."

Example 2

```
CLC    OUTPUT , HOLD1
BC     8 , PROCESS
```

The BC instruction statement specifies, "If the two operands of the previous compare statement were equal, branch to the address of a routine that is labeled PROCESS."

Example 3

```
CLC    FLD1 , FLD2
BC     8 , MOVEIT
BC     4 , SUBTR
BC     2 , ADDIT
```

This is an example of the multiple branching decisions based on the result of a single comparison.

The first BC statement states, "If the operands were equal to each other, branch to a routine labeled MOVEIT." The second instruction statement for a BC states, "If FLD1 was of a lower logical value than FLD2, branch to a routine labeled SUBTR." The third BC instruction statement indicates, "If FLD1 was of a higher logical value than that of FLD2, branch to a routine labeled ADDIT." Because the CLC instruction will set the Condition Code to a value equal to one of the mask operands shown in the BC instruction statements (8, 4, or 2), one of the branches in this set of instruction statements will be taken.

Program Branching Logic

Example 4

    BC   15 , GOTHERE

This instruction statement can be written as shown without regard for the instruction statement that immediately precedes it. It literally states, "Regardless of what configuration now exists in the Condition Code bits, branch to the instruction statement or routine that is labeled GOTHERE." This is referred to as a *forced* or *unconditional* branch.

Branch on Condition to Register (BCR)

This instruction is nearly identical to the Branch on Condition instruction except that the branch, if taken, is to the address contained in the register specified by the second operand. The instruction checks the first operand (the mask operand) against the Condition Code bit setting and, if the appropriate condition exists, effectively causes a branch to occur. All of the general rules and techniques available to the BC instruction also apply here.

In order to illustrate the use of this instruction, several examples are presented in which various packed decimal instruction statements are followed by BCR instruction statements.

Example 1

    CP   PAKFLD1 , PAKFLD2
    BCR   10 , 2
    BCR   4 , 3

The first instruction statement compares two fields of packed decimal data. The first BCR instruction statement specifies, "If the CP statement indicates that PAKFLD1 is equal to (8), or greater than (2) PAKFLD2 then branch to the address contained in general register 2." The second BCR instruction statement states, "If PAKFLD1 is of a lesser value than PAKFLD2, branch to the address contained within general register 3."

Example 2

    LA   9 , BADADDR
    LA   10 , ZEROSUM
    LA   11 , NEGSUM
    AP   SUMPK , INPAK
    BCR   8 , 10
    BCR   4 , 11
    BCR   1 , 9

The first three instruction statements load the addresses of three separate routines into general registers 9, 10, and 11. The Add Packed (AP) instruction statement adds two fields of packed decimal values together, with the resulting sum residing in the SUMPK field. The first BCR instruction statement indicates, "If the total sum now found in SUMPK is zero, branch to the address contained in general register 10." This is the address of a routine called ZEROSUM, loaded into general register 10 by the second Load Address instruction statement. The second BCR instruction statement indicates, "If the total sum now found in SUMPK is a negative value (less than minus-zero), branch to the address contained within general register 11." This would be the address of the routine called NEGSUM, loaded into general register 11 by the third Load Address instruction statement. The third BCR instruction statement specifies, "If an overflow conditon occurs during the addition of these fields, then branch to the address contained within general register 9." This address would be that of a routine labeled BADADDR, loaded into general register 9 by the first LA instruction statement. It is also implied here, with this particular set of instructions, that if the result of the packed decimal addition is a positive value in excess of plus zero, no branch would be taken and the program logic processing would fall through the three branch instruction statements to the next sequential program statement. This can be logically assumed because the branches shown were established to intercept a zero, a negative, or an overflow condition.

Example 3

    BCR   15 , 8

This instruction statement causes a forced branch of the program logic to the address contained within general register 8. The first operand demands a branch, regardless of any particular setting of the Condition Code bits. Prior to this instruction statement, general register 8 should have been loaded with the address of the routine to which the branch leads. This is one means of returning from a routine which, in turn, was branched to by a Branch & Link instruction that specified general register 8 as the linking register.

Branch on Count (BCT)

The Branch on Count instruction branches to the storage address created by the second operand unless the value contained within the first operand register is zero. It is used frequently for table look-ups, loop control, and count control. Each time the program logic encounters this instruction it results in the following action.

1. The value in the first operand register is decremented by a fixed-point value of 1.
2. The general register is then checked to see if it now equals zero.
3. If the register value is not zero, the instruction statement causes a branch to the address specified by the second operand of the statement.
4. If the register contents have been decremented to a zero value, the branch is ignored and the program logic processing falls through to the next sequential program statement.

You may reload the register operand with any value suitable to its reuse, as long as it conforms to correct program logic.

An impractical but easily understood example of the use of this instruction is shown in this set of coding:

```
        SR    5 , 5                 001
        LA    5 , 100               002
LOOP    AP    PAKSUM , =PL1 ' 3 '   003
        BCT   5 , LOOP              004
        ZAP   BIGSUM , PAKSUM       005
```

This set of statements functionally performs a multiplication routine that could have been accomplished with one instruction statement. It does, however, present a simple illustration of the use and performance of the Branch on Count instruction.

Statement 001 subtracts general register 5 from itself, effectively clearing that register.

Statement 002 loads the absolute value of 100 into general register 5.

Statement 003 adds a one-byte packed decimal literal value of +3 into a packed decimal accumulator area.

Statement 004 decrements register 5 by a value of 1 each time that this instruction statement is executed and then branches back to Statement 003.

This action continues until general register 5 is decremented to zero, at which time the branch to LOOP will not be taken and the processing will fall through to Statement 005. Because the value of +100 was originally loaded into general register 5, the processing program will pass through the LOOP instruction statement 100 times including the initial pass through that statement. Each time the program passes through the LOOP instruction statement, it adds an additional packed decimal value of +3 to the accumulator (PAKSUM). When the BCT instruction is executed for the 100th time, general register 5 is decremented by 1 to a value of zero and the branch is not taken. PAKSUM would now contain a packed decimal value of +300—100 loop cycles times the value of +3 added during each loop.

Branch on Count to Register (BCTR)

The BCTR instruction forces the program logic to branch to the address of the second operand unless the value contained within the first operand register is zero. Whenever the program in operation encounters this instruction the following sequence of events takes place:

1. The value of the content of the general register specified by the first operand is decremented by a value of 1.
2. The content of that general register is then compared to a zero value by the instruction.
3. If the content of the first operand register is not zero, the instruction statement creates an effective branch to the address contained, or implied by, the second operand register.
4. If the content of the first operand register has been decremented to zero, the branch is not taken and the processing falls through to the next sequential instruction statement following the BCTR statement.

In order to illustrate the basic capabilities of this instruction, an example similar to the "looping" technique illustrating the BCT instruction is used; however, in this example the "loop within a loop" technique is illustrated (see Figure 8-1).

In this illustrated set of coding the first four instruction statements, Statement 001 through Statement 004, zero out the contents of the general registers to be used for the BCTR instruction statements. The outside loop (LOOPONE), is controlled by general registers 6 and 8; the inside loop (LOOPTWO) by registers 7 and 9.

Statement 005 loads the absolute value of 50 into general register 6, the loop control register for LOOPONE.

Statement 006 loads the address of the LOOPONE routine into general register 8, the "branch to" address referenced by Statement 012. These two instruction statements have now set up the basis for the control of the outer loop, LOOPONE.

Statement 007 loads the absolute value of 100 into general register 7, the loop control register for LOOPTWO.

Statement 008 loads the address of LOOPTWO into general register 9, the "branch to" address that is referenced by Statement 010.

Statement 009 adds a packed decimal literal value of +2 into an accumulator area for LOOPTWO.

Name	Operation	Operand	Seq
*			001
LOOPRTE	SR	6,6	002
	SR	7,7	003
	SR	8,8	004
	SR	9,9	005
	LA	6,50	006
	LA	8,LOOPONE	007
LOOPONE	LA	7,100	008
LOOPTWO	LA	9,LOOPTWO	009
	AP	SMALPAK,=PL1'2'	010
	BCTR	7,9	011
	AP	BIGPAK,SMALPAK	012
	ZAP	SMALPAK,=PL1'0'	013
	BCTR	6,8	014
	BC	15,FINIS	
*			

FIGURE 8-1

Statement 010 is the BCTR instruction statement for LOOPTWO. Each time the LOOPTWO routine is entered, it is executed 100 times before falling through to Statement 011.

Statement 011 adds the packed decimal contents of the LOOPTWO accumulator, SMALPAK, to the packed decimal accumulator for LOOPONE. Each time this statement is encountered, it adds a value of +200 to the accumulator BIGPAK, since 100 cycles through LOOPTWO results in SMALPAK being equal to +200–100 cycles with a value of +2 being added for each cycle equals +200.

Statement 012 uses the ZAP instruction to zero-out the accumulated amount in SMALPAK prior to entering a new loop-control cycle.

Statement 013 is the BCTR instruction statement for LOOPONE, the outside loop. Inasmuch as Statement 005 loaded general register 6 with an absolute value of 50, this instruction is executed 50 times, the branch being taken 49 times before falling through to Statement 014.

Statement 014 is a "forced" branch to a hypothetical routine that ends the program or subroutine.

When the entire series of instructions is completed, the packed decimal value contained in BIGPAK should be +10,000. This can be determined by applying the loop values as:

LOOPONE times (LOOPTWO times 2) equals BIGPAK

or

50 times (100 times 2) equal 10,000

This example is an excellent opportunity to illustrate how the erroneous omission of a single statement can affect the outcome of a desired solution. If the programmer had overlooked the instruction statement that zeroes-out the contents of the inside loop accumulator after each 100 cycles (Statement 012), the resulting value of BIGPAK at the completion of the entire routine would have been 255,000. Follow the logic process through, excluding Statement 012, to prove this result.

The BCTR instruction may also be used to decrement the value of a general register without branching by specifying general register 0 as the second operand register. If this type of instruction statement appeared as BCTR 6,0, the instruction would decrement general register 6 by a value of 1, but would not branch regardless of the value remaining within general register 6.

Branch on Index High (BXH)

The BXH instruction utilizes three registers, two of which are expressed as statement operands along with a symbolic or actual address for branching. The basic functions of the three registers are:

- An accumulator register
- An increment or decrement register
- A comparison value register

Each time that the BXH instruction statement is executed, it performs the following:

1. It adds the value of the contents of the second general register (either as a plus-value increment or as a minus-value decrement) to the contents of the first general register, placing the result of that addition into the first register.

2. It then compares the new value of the contents of the first general register to the value of the contents of the third general register.
3. If the value of the first register compares high to the third register value, the instruction effectively branches to the storage operand address.
4. If the value of the first register compares low or equal to the third register value, the branch is not taken and the program logic falls through to the next sequential instruction statement.

For practical application and consistency, it is suggested that a contiguous trio of odd-even-odd general registers be used for this instruction.

In the example that follows, assume that the programmer has a table containing 50 elements, each element having a length of four bytes. This would bring the total table length to 200 bytes. If the first character in each element is a character "A", a character "D" should be inserted in the second position of that table element; otherwise no change will be made to the table element. The table defininition, values, and instruction statements are presented in Figure 8-2.

Statement 001 loads the address of TABLE incremented by 49 table units (or 196 bytes) into general register 12. This is done because the search of the table is going to commence at the highest storage address position and decrement downward to the beginning point of the table. Register 12 is to be used as a base register that will point directly at the various elements of TABLE.

Statement 002 loads general register 3 with a fullword value of +196, general register 4 with a fullword value of -4, and general register 5 with a fullword value of -4.

Statement 003 performs a Compare Logical Immediate on the first byte of the table element currently addressed by general register 12, comparing it to a character "A".

Statement 004 tests the Condition Code setting that resulted from the CLI instruction in Statement 003. If an unequal condition is indicated by the Condition Code bits, this instruction creates a branch to Statement 006. If the Condition Code indicates that the comparison resulted in an equal condition, the program logic falls through to Statement 005, the next sequential program instruction statement.

Statement 005 performs a Move Immediate (MVI) instruction in order to move a character "D" into the second byte of the table element currently addressed by general register 12.

Statement 006 performs an Add Registers (AR) instruction, adding the value of the contents of general register 5 (a -4 value that effectively results in a subtraction of 4) to the current address in general register 12. This action decrements general register 12 by 4 bytes so that the next time the program logic passes through the instruction statement labeled RELOOK, register 12 will then be addressing the next lower table element.

Statement 007 performs the BXH instruction statement. Each time it is executed, general register 3 is decremented by the value of general register 4 and the result is compared to general register 5. If register 3 contains a higher value than register 5, the program logic is branched back to RELOOK. Once the value contained in register 3 is decremented to a value of -4, it is found to be an equal compare to register 5 (which contains a value of -4) and the branch is not taken. The program logic would then fall through to the next sequential instruction statement.

Statement 008 is a forced branch to an assumed routine that would probably terminate this part of the program.

If this example were listed using the actual decimal storage position addresses, assume that the first byte of TABLE might reside at storage location 15000. TABLE would then occupy bytes 15000 through 15199 or 200 bytes. If these addresses were used, then:

Statement 001 would load the address 15196 into general register 12. This would be the first byte of the last four-byte table element.

Program Branching Logic

SYSTEM / 370 ASSEMBLER CODING FORM

NAME	OPERATION	OPERAND	COMMENTS	SEQ
*				001
SETABLE	LA	12,TABLE+196		002
	LM	3,5,VALUES		003
RELOOK	CLI	0(12),C'A'		004
	BC	7,BYPASS		005
	MVI	1(12),C'D'		006
BYPASS	AR	12,5		007
	BXH	3,4,RELOOK		008
	BC	15,ALLDONE		009
*				010
*		CONSTANTS AND WORK AREAS		011
*				012
TABLE	DS	50CL4		013
VALUES	DC	F'196'		014
	DC	F'-4'		015
	DC	F'-4'		016
*				017

TABLE 8-2

Statement 003 would check position 15196 to see if it contained a character "A". If the equal condition is found, Statement 005 would move a character "D" into position 15197, the second byte of the four-byte table element presently being scanned.

Statement 006 would add -4 (subtracting a value of 4 from 15196) to general register 12, resulting in a value of 15192 now in register 12.

Statement 007, the BXH instruction statement, would add -4 to general register 3 (actually subtracting 4 from 196), compare the new register 3 value of 192 against the register 5 value of -4, and then branch back to RELOOK, Statement 003.

Statement 003 would now be checking storage location 15192 for a character "A". This cycle would continue down through the table elements until general register 3 is equal or low to register 5 at the time the BXH instruction statement is executed.

Branch on Index Low or Equal (BXLE)

The BXLE instruction statement uses the same type of operands as the BXH instruction (i.e., three registers and a symbolic or actual address that is to be branched to). The functions of the registers also perform similarly—the first general register is an accumulator, the second register contains an increment value, and the third register contains a value for the first register to be compared against. It is also suggested here that the three general registers be a contiguous trio of odd-even-odd general registers.

Each time this instruction is executed, it performs in the following manner:

1. It sums the value of the second register (the increment register) with the value of the first register, placing the result into the first register.
2. It then compares the new value of the first register to the value contained within the third register.
3. If the value of the first general register compares low or equal to the third general register, the instruction effectively branches to the storage operand address.
4. If the value of the first register compares high to the third register the branch is not taken and the program logic falls through to the next sequential program instruction statement.

For the purpose of demonstrating the use of this instruction, assume that the programmer has a 75-byte table, one byte per table element, to be put into another table area, but in reverse order. The definition of the table storage area, the values to be used by the general registers, and the coded instruction statements are shown in Figure 8-3.

Statement 001 loads the trio of registers via a Load Multiple instruction statement. The LM instruction loads general register 5 with a fullword value of zero, general register 6 with a fullword value of +1 for incrementing, and general register 7 with a fullword value of +74 that will be used as a comparator.

Statement 002 loads the address of TABLE1, incremented by 74 bytes, into general register 8. General register 8 now contains the address of the highest storage position occupied by TABLE1.

Statement 003 loads the address of TABLE2 into general register 9. This address would be the lowest storage position occupied by TABLE2. Registers 8 and 9 now contain the opposite storage limits for TABLE1 and TABLE2 in order that the sequence of the data contained within TABLE1 can be reversed into TABLE2.

Statement 004 moves one byte of data from TABLE1 (as addressed by general register 8) into one byte of TABLE2 (as addressed by general register 9).

Program Branching Logic

SYSTEM / 370 ASSEMBLER CODING FORM

NAME	OPERATION	OPERAND	COMMENTS	SEQ
*				001
MIXTABLE	LM	5,7,REGVALS		002
	LA	8,TABLE1+74		003
	LA	9,TABLE2		004
REPEAT	MVC	0(1,9),0(8)		005
	AR	9,6		006
	SR	8,6		007
	BXLE	5,6,REPEAT		008
	BC	15,MOVEDIT		009
*				010
*			CONSTANTS AND WORK AREAS	011
*				012
TABLE1	DS	CL75		013
TABLE2	DS	CL75		014
REGVALS	DC	F'0'		015
	DC	F'1'		016
	DC	F'74'		017
*				018
*				

FIGURE 8-3

Statement 005 adds the value of the contents of general register 6 (+1) to the contents of general register 9. Register 9 contains the address of the current table element of TABLE2.

Statement 006 subtracts the value of general register 6 (equal to +1) from general register 8. General register 8 contains the current table element address of TABLE1.

Statement 007 activates the BXLE instruction statement. Each time this instruction is executed, general register 5 is incremented by the value in general register 6 and the result is compared to the value in general register 7. If general register 5 compares low or equal to the contents of general register 7, the branch is taken to REPEAT. However, when register 5 is incremented sufficiently to compare high to register 7, the branch is not taken and the program execution falls through to Statement 008.

Statement 008 is a forced branch to another part of the main-line program logic. This exit is taken once the subroutine of Statements 001 through 007 have completed their cycles.

In order to more clearly visualize the processing of these instruction statements, assume that the actual decimal storage position addresses have been assigned as:

| TABLE1 | Storage locations | 32000 through 32074 |
| TABLE2 | Storage locations | 32075 through 32149 |

Using these addresses, the instruction statements for the previous routine would effectively be executed as follows:

Statement 001 would function as previously explained.

Statement 002 would load general register 8 with the address 32074. This value represents the address of TABLE1 (32000) incremented by 74, or the last one-byte element within TABLE1.

Statement 003 would load general register 9 with the address 32075, the address of the first table element of TABLE2.

Statement 004 would move one byte of data from address 32074 to address 32075. This would be from the last element of TABLE1 to the first element of TABLE2.

Statement 005 would add general register 6 (a + 1 value) to the present contents of general register 9 (+ 32075), resulting in general register 9 now containing +32076.

Statement 006 would subtract general register 6 (+1) from general register 8 (+32074) resulting in general register 8 now containing +32073. At the end of the execution of Statement 007, general register 5 would now contain a value of +1, general register 6 would be +1, and general register 7 would be +74. The branch would be taken back to Statement 004, REPEAT.

Statement 004 would now move one byte of data from address 32073 to address 32076, from the next-to-last table element of TABLE1 to the second element of TABLE2.

Statement 005 would increment the address within general register 9 to +32077.

Statement 006 would decrement the address within general register 8 to +32072.

This action would continue within the cycle from the REPEAT instruction statement through the BXLE instruction statement until general register 5 contains a value of +75, an amount that would compare high to +74, the value within general register 7. At this point the logic execution of the program would fall through to Statement 008.

Branch & Link Instructions

The instructions that fall within this category may be considered to be "forced" branches that provide the problem program with the capability of returning to the next sequential program statement at the discretion of the programmer. They can be used to establish program linkage between routine-to-routine, subroutine-to-subroutine, module-to-module, or any combination

Program Branching Logic

of this type of linkage. A very frequent use of the Branch & Link instructions is to access a common subroutine from many points of the main-line program logic. This enables you to write the subroutine just once and then access it at will instead of rewriting the same logic statements at many points within the program.

Branch & Link (BAL)

The BAL instruction will store the address of the next sequential program instruction statement (as contained within the updated Program Status Word) into the general register specified by the first operand of the statement, and then branch to the address generated by the second operand. Once the routine "branched to" has been completed, you can force the program logic to return to the instruction series that immediately follows the BAL instruction statement by coding a forced branch to the address contained within the general register used as the first operand in the BAL instruction statement. This is based on the premise that the instruction statements executed by the "branched to" routine did not destroy or alter the contents of the linking register.

Assume that the programmer is required to write a simple packed decimal math routine that will be used at numerous places throughout the main-line program logic. The data fields that have been established and the coded instruction statements appear in Figure 8-4.

The implied sequence of execution of these instruction statements is:

001, 002, 085, 086, 003, -, 010, 011, 085, 086, 012, -, 017, 018, 085, 086, 019, 020.

Statement 001 zeroes the PAKANSR field and adds the value of PACK1 into it.

Statement 002 effects a Branch & Link to Statement 085.

Statement 085 multiplies the contents of PAKANSR (now the same value as PACK1) by PAKMULT (a +5 value in packed decimal form).

Statement 086 then branches back to Statement 003. The branch is to that address because the BAL instruction loaded the address of Statement 003 into general register 10.

Statement 003 adds the new value of PAKANSR to an accumulator that is labeled CUMULAT.

Statements 004 through 009 are not shown, but are implied to be obtaining data records, additional processing, etc.

Statement 010 zeroes the PAKANSR field and adds the value contained within PACK2 into it.

Statement 011 causes a Branch & Link to Statement 085, at the same time loading the address of Statement 012 into general register 10.

Statement 085 multiplies the contents of PAKANSR (now the same value as PACK2) by the value contained in PACKMULT, a +5 value.

Statement 086 is a forced branch to the address contained in general register 10. At this point within the program the address is that of Statement 012.

Statement 012 adds the new value of PAKANSR to the accumulator, CUMULAT.

Statements 013 through 016 are implied to be processing additional data, etc.

Statement 017 zeroes the PAKANSR field and adds the value of PACK3 into it.

Statement 018 performs the BAL instruction, loading the address of Statement 019 into general register 10 and then branching to Statement 085.

Statement 085 multiplies the contents of PAKANSR (now the same value as PACK3) by PAKMULT, a value of +5.

Statement 086 branches back to Statement 019 because that is the address contained within general register 10.

Statement 019 adds the new value of PAKANSR to the accumulator, CUMULAT.

Statement 020 is a forced branch to another section of the main-line portion of the program.

Although the overall function performed by this set of instruction statements may not necessarily be the best means of arriving at the proper answer for these calculations, it sufficiently outlines the use of the Branch & Link instruction and the means of returning to the sequence of instruction statements from which it was issued.

Branch & Link Registers (BALR)

The BALR instruction performs the same basic functions as the BAL instruction except that the branch is to the address contained in the register specified by the second operand of the statement. Explicitly, it stores the address of the next sequential program instruction statement into the first operand register and branches to the address contained in the second operand register. Using the same basic instruction statement logic contained in Figure 8-4 for the BAL instruction, the restated instructions would appear as in Figure 8-5.

The primary difference between this illustration and the similar example for the BAL instruction is the PRELOAD statement in which general register 11 is loaded with the address of DOMULT. Thereafter, the BALR instruction statements use the address in general register 11 as the "branch to" address, effectively branching to DOMULT.

Extended Mnemonics for Branch Instructions

In addition to the single value, or combination of values, which may be used as the mask operand for deciding the action to be taken by a branch instruction, a set of extended mnemonics can be used in lieu of stating an absolute value for the mask. For example, the instruction statements

```
    CLC     FLDA , FLDB
    BC      8 , GOTHERE
```

could validly be replaced by

```
    CLC     FLDA , FLDB
    BE      GOTHERE
```

Both of the branch statements indicate that if FLDA and FLDB compare as equal, a branch to GOTHERE should be executed. Note carefully that the mask value (8) in the second set of statements has been eliminated. Its value is implied by the extended mnemonic BE (Branch Equal).

Table 8-2 lists the extended mnemonics for branching, along with their implied usage. As indicated therein, this table also includes extended mnemonics for branching after execution of arithmetic instructions and after the Test Under Mask (TM) instruction.

Inasmuch as extended mnemonics are not necessarily available for Assembler Language on all operating systems or computer models, the user should determine their availability on the computer system on which the programs will be compiled. This caution is also stated because the restrictions shown in Table 8-2 might be altered or expanded by operating systems released subsequent to the publication of this text.

TABLE 8-2

extended mnemonic	replaces		Applicable for System/360	Applicable for System/370	meaning
general use					
B	BC	15, ...	X	X	unconditional branch
BR	BCR	15, ...	X	X	unconditional branch
after compare instructions					
BH	BC	2, ...	X	X	branch on A high
BHR	BCR	2, ...		X	branch on A high
BL	BC	4, ...	X	X	branch on A low
BLR	BCR	4, ...		X	branch on A low
BNE	BC	7, ...	X	X	branch on A not equal B
BNER	BCR	7, ...		X	branch on A not equal B
BE	BC	8, ...	X	X	branch on A equal B
BER	BCR	8, ...		X	branch on A equal B
BNL	BC	11, ...	X	X	branch on A not low
BNLR	BCR	11, ...		X	branch on A not low
BNH	BC	13, ...	X	X	branch on A not high
BNHR	BCR	13, ...		X	branch on A not high
after arithmetic instructions					
BO	BC	1, ...	X	X	branch on overflow
BOR	BCR	1, ...		X	branch on overflow
BP	BC	2, ...	X	X	branch on plus
BPR	BCR	2, ...		X	branch on plus
BM	BC	4, ...	X	X	branch on minus
BMR	BCR	4, ...		X	branch on minus
BNZ	BC	7, ...	X	X	branch on not zero
BNZR	BCR	7, ...		X	branch on not zero
BZ	BC	8, ...	X	X	branch on zero
BZR	BCR	8, ...		X	branch on zero
BNM	BC	11, ...		X	branch on not minus
BNMR	BCR	11, ...		X	branch on not minus
BNP	BC	13, ...		X	branch on not plus
BNPR	BCR	13, ...		X	branch on not plus
after Test Under Mask instruction					
BO	BC	1, ...	X	X	branch if ones
BOR	BCR	1, ...		X	branch if ones
BM	BC	4, ...	X	X	branch if mixed
BMR	BCR	4, ...		X	branch if mixed
BZ	BC	8, ...	X	X	branch if zeros
BZR	BCR	8, ...		X	branch if zeros
BNO	BC	14, ...		X	branch if not ones
BNOR	BCR	14, ...		X	branch if not ones

SYSTEM / 370 ASSEMBLER CODING FORM

NAME	OPERATION	OPERAND	COMMENTS	SEQ
ROUTE1	ZAP	PAKANSR,PACK1		001
	BAL	10,DOMULT		002
	AP	CUMULAT,PAKANSR		003
	ZAP	PAKANSR,PACK2		010
	BAL	10,DOMULT		011
	AP	CUMULAT,PAKANSR		012
	ZAP	PAKANSR,PACK3		017
	BAL	10,DOMULT		018
	AP	CUMULAT,PAKANSR		019
	BC	15,DUNCALC		020
DOMULT	MP	PAKANSR,PAKMULT		085
	BCR	15,10		086
*			* CONSTANTS *	087
PACK1	DC	PL3'0'		088
PACK2	DC	PL3'0'		089
PACK3	DC	PL3'0'		090
CUMULAT	DC	PL6'0'		091
PAKANSR	DC	PL4'0'		092
PAKMULT	DC	PL1'5'		093
*				094
				095

FIGURE 8-4

Program Branching Logic

SYSTEM / 370 ASSEMBLER CODING FORM

NAME	OPERATION	OPERAND	IDENTIFICATION SEQUENCE NO
PRELOAD	LA	11,DOMULT	000
ROUTE1	ZAP	PAKANSR,PACK1	001
	BALR	10,11	002
	AP	CUMULAT,PAKANSR	003
*			-
	ZAP	PAKANSR,PACK2	010
	BALR	10,11	011
	AP	CUMULAT,PAKANSR	012
*			-
	ZAP	PAKANSR,PACK3	017
	BALR	10,11	018
	AP	CUMULAT,PAKANSR	019
	BC	15,DUNCALC	020
*			021
DOMULT	MP	PAKANSR,PAKMULT	085
	BCR	15,10	086
*			087
*			088

FIGURE 8-5

REVIEW EXERCISES

1. In general, the "branch" instructions may be grouped into two categories—conditional branches and _____ _____ branches.
2. The only branch instructions that require a mask value as the first operand of the statement are the _____ and the _____ instructions.
3. A BC or BCR instruction statement containing a first operand mask value of _____ is considered to be an unconditional, or _____, branch.
4. The four individual mask values that are used singlularly or collectively to test the PSW Condition Code are _____, _____, _____ and _____.
5. Each time that a BCT instruction statement is executed the value contained within the _____ operand is automatically decremented by a value of _____.
6. For each of the following sets of instruction statements indicate the comparison relationship that would have to exist between the two operands within the first statement in order for the branch to be successfully taken in the second statement. (This should be expressed as "the first operand would be greater than or equal to the second operand," etc.)

    a.   COMPA   CL   8, FLWDA
                   BC   12, ROUTE1
    b.   COMPC   CH   3, HALFWDA
                   BC   6, ROUTE2
    c.   COMPE   CP   PACKFLDA, =PL3'8952'
                   BC   10, ROUTE3
    d.   COMPG   CLC   DATAFLD+3 (7), INCARD+20
                   BC   2, ROUTE4
    e.   COMPI   CLI   FIELD6+3, X'40'
                   BC   8, BYPASS
    f.   COMPK   CLR   10, 4
                   BC   14, NEWROUTE
    g.   COMPM   C   3, FULLWDG
                   BC   2, ROUTE5
    h.   COMPN   CR   3, 13
                   BC   4, ROUTE6

7. The maximum value that can be represented by the first operand of a BCT instruction statement is _____.
8. In a BCTR instruction statement the "branch to" address is represented within a _____.
9. The BXH and the BXLE instruction statements each utilize a total of _____ registers.
10. In a BCT instruction statement, the processing logic of the program will fail to branch as soon as the value within the first operand register has been decremented to a value of _____.
11. The BAL instruction statement loads the first operand register with the _____ of the next sequential instruction statement.
12. The BALR instruction statement consists of two operands, both of which are _____.

Program Branching Logic

13. An effective "no operation" instruction statement can be created by coding a mask value of _____ as the first operand of a BC or a BCR instruction statement.

14. Assuming that general register 7 contained a fixed-point value of +75 before the execution of the following instruction statement, what would be the fixed-point value contained in register 7 after execution of the statement? _____.

    LOOPUP   BCTR   7,9

15. Assume the following:
    Register 5 contains a fixed-point value of +3275
    Register 6 contains a fixed-point value of −25
    Register 7 contains a fixed-point value of +50

    After execution of the following instruction statement register 5 would contain a fixed-point value of _____, register 6 would contain a fixed-point value of _____, and register 7 would contain a fixed-point value of _____.

    BXH   5,6,RESEEK

16. If general register 9 contained a fixed-point value of +32500 prior to execution of the statement labeled BRNCH, what would it contain immediately following the execution of that statement? _____.

    BRNCH   BAL   9,EXITRTE
    BACK   CLI   SWITCH,C'A'

17. If general register 10 contains a value of +1 prior to executing the BCT instruction labeled ENDLOOP, the program would proceed to the statement labeled _____ after execution of the BCT instruction.

    ENDLOOP   BCT   10,RELOOP
    CONTIG   CLC   DATA,INPUT

18. In each of the following sets of instruction statements, a branch will be taken. Based on the values shown for the fields that are being compared, place a check mark beside the branch that would be successfully taken.

    a. Register 8 contains a fixed-point value of +3598;
        Register 12 contains a fixed-point value of +15,782.

        COMPARA   CR   8,12
                   BC   4,SUBRT1   _____
                   BC   8,SUBRT2   _____
                   BC   3,SUBRT3   _____

    b. Register 9 contains a fixed-point value of −783;
        FLWD2 contains a fixed-point value of +6.

        COMPARB   CL   9,FLWD2
                   BC   4,SUBRT4   _____
                   BC   2,SUBRT5   _____
                   BC   9,SUBRT6   _____

c. PAKFLDA contains a packed decimal value of −0.

    COMPARF   CP   PAKFLDA,=P'0'
                     BC   8,SUBRT7   _____
                     BC   7,SUBRT8   _____

d. FIELD1 contains the EBCDIC characters S1FA;
FIELD2 contains the EBCDIC characters S12A.

    COMPARG   CLC   FIELD1,FIELD2
                     BC   10,SUBRT9   _____
                     BC   4,SUBRT10   _____
                     BC   15,SUBRT11 _____

e. SETBYTE contains an EBCDIC character X.

    COMPARH   CLI   SETBYTE,X'40'
                     BC   15,SUBRT12A _____
                     BC   8,SUBRT12B   _____

f. Register 8 contains a fixed-point value of +9810516;
Register 10 contains a fixed-point value of +5.

    COMPARJ   CLR   8,10
                     BC   15,SUBRT14 _____
                     BC   10,SUBRT15 _____
                     BC   4,SUBRT16   _____

g. Register 9 contains a fixed-point value of +3516;
HAFWORD6 contains a fixed-point value of −3516.

    COMPARK   CH   9,HAFWORD6
                     BC   2,SUBRT17   _____
                     BC   8,SUBRT18   _____
                     BC   4,SUBRT19   _____

9
Moving, Storing, and Loading Data

THE DATA MOVEMENT INSTRUCTIONS

Instruction: Move Immediate

mnemonic	hex code	operand format
MVI	92	$D_1 (B_1), I_2$

This instruction moves one byte of immediate data, defined by the second operand, into the one-byte area specified by the first operand. Regardless of the implied length of the first operand, this instruction moves only one byte of data.

The Condition Code setting is not changed by this instruction.

* * *

Instruction: Move Characters

mnemonic	hex code	operand format
MVC	D2	$D_1 (L, B_1), D_2 (B_2)$

The MVC instruction moves the storage data specified by the second operand into the storage area specified by the first operand. The data is moved one byte at a time, from left to right, for the explicit or implied length of the first operand. The data being moved is not changed or altered. Up to 256 bytes of data may be moved with one instruction statement.

The Condition Code setting is not changed by this instruction.

* * *

Instruction: Move Long (System/370 Only)

mnemonic	hex code	operand format
MVCL	0E	R_1, R_2

The Move Long instruction moves the storage data addressed by the second operand into the storage area addressed by the first operand. The first operand (R_1) and the second operand (R_2) each represent an even-odd pair of general registers. However, the even-numbered register of each pair must be the one specified by the respective operands. The quantity of data bytes moved by a single MVCL instruction may range from one byte to 16,777,215 bytes. Unlike other "move" instructions, the MVCL instruction permits each operand to specify a different length attribute regarding the quantity of data to be moved. In all cases, however, the movement of data from the second operand address to the first operand address will terminate as soon as the first operand length has been exhausted. If the second operand specifies a length less than the length specified for the first operand, the programmer is expected to supply a padding character. This padding character will fill out the remaining bytes of the first operand once the second operand length has been depleted.

The movement of the data is from left to right, high-order to low-order, byte-by-byte. Among other functions performed, a check is made for destructive overlap of the operands at the time of execution. A destructive overlap is one where data already moved into the first operand location becomes addressed by the second operand. In an instance of destructive overlap, the Condition Code is set and no movement of data occurs.

CC	BC	Condition
0	8	The first-operand and second-operand counts are equal.
1	4	The first-operand count is low.
2	2	The first-operand count is high.
3	1	No movement of data was performed because of destructive overlap.

*   *   *

Instruction: Move Numeric

mnemonic	hex code	operand format
MVN	D1	D_1 (L, B_1), D_2 (B_2)

The Move Numeric instruction moves only the right-most four bits (the right nibble) of each byte, which in zoned decimal format would be the numeric portion of the byte. It moves the right-most half-byte of each byte of storage data specified by the second operand into the corresponding position of each byte of the storage area specified by the first operand. The numeric value of the half-bytes being moved is not checked for numeric validity; therefore, it is possible to move a hex value of 'A', 'B', 'C', 'D', 'E', or 'F' with this instruction. The data is moved from left to right, one nibble at a time, for the explicit length or implied length of the first operand. The left-most four bits of each byte of the first operand receiving field are not altered. The alphanumeric character validity of the bit configuration of the bytes resulting from this instruction are not checked; therefore, the generation of nonprintable characters may occur. The right-most four bits of up to 256 bytes of data may be moved with one instruction statement.

The Condition Code setting is not changed by this instruction.

*   *   *

Instruction: Move Zone

mnemonic	hex code	operand format
MVZ	D3	D_1 (L, B_1), D_2 (B_2)

The MVZ instruction moves only the left-most four bits (the left nibble) of each byte specified, which in zoned character format would be the zone portion of the byte. This does not preclude

Moving, Storing, and Loading Data 197

the movement of numeric values that might be contained within the left nibbles being moved. The instruction will move the left-most four bits of each byte of storage data specified by the second operand into the corresponding left-most four bits of each byte of the storage area specified by the first operand. The data is moved from left to right, one nibble at a time, for the explicit or implied length of the first operand. The right-most four bits (the right nibble) of each byte of the receiving field specified by the first operand are not altered. The left-most four bits of up to 256 bytes of data may be moved with one instruction statement.

The Condition Code setting is not changed by this instruction.

*   *   *

Instruction: Store Character

mnemonic	hex code	operand format
STC	42	$R_1, D_2 (X_2, B_2)$

The Store Character instruction takes the low-order eight bits (one byte) from the general register specified by the first operand and places them in the one-byte storage area specified by the second operand. The eight bits stored are not altered from their original configuration.

The Condition Code setting is not changed by this instruction.

*   *   *

Instruction: Store Characters Under Mask (System/370 Only)

mnemonic	hex code	operand format
STCM	BE	$R_1, M_3, D_2 (B_2)$

The Store Characters Under Mask instruction extracts selected bytes from the general register specified by the first operand and places them into the storage location addressed by the second operand. The quantity of bytes to be stored, as well as the specific location of the bytes selected from the register, are controlled by the mask operand. The mask comprises four bit positions, each bit position representing a corresponding byte location within the first operand register. A zero-bit in the mask ignores the respective byte within the register; for each one-bit specified in the mask, the corresponding byte from the register is stored. The selected bytes are stored in order, contiguously, into the location addressed by the second operand. The quantity of bytes stored equals the quantity of one-bits in the mask. The stored data bytes are only copies of the selected register bytes; the contents of the general register will remain unchanged.

The Condition Code is not changed by this instruction.

*   *   *

Instruction: Store Halfword

mnemonic	hex code	operand format
STH	40	$R_1, D_2 (X_2, B_2)$

The STH instruction takes the low-order 16 bits (two bytes) from the general register specified by the first operand, and places them into the halfword storage location that is specified by the second operand. The configuration of the two bytes being stored is not altered. The address generated by the second operand must be on a halfword boundary alignment.

The Condition Code setting is not changed by this instruction.

*   *   *

Instruction: Store

mnemonic	hex code	operand format
ST	50	$R_1, D_2 (X_2, B_2)$

The Store instruction takes the 32-bit contents of the general register specified by the first operand and places them unaltered in the four-byte fullword specified by the second operand. The address generated by the second operand must be on a fullword boundary alignment.

The Condition Code is not changed by this instruction.

*   *   *

Instruction: Store Multiple

mnemonic	hex code	operand format
STM	90	$R_1, R_3, D_2 (B_2)$

The STM instruction stores a multiple quantity of general registers (two, three, four, five, or more) into a contiguous storage area of fullwords. The first operand specifies the beginning register of a multiple register set and the second operand (R_3) specifies the ending register of that set. The storage area addressed by the D_2 operand must be on a fullword boundary alignment and consist of enough fullwords to contain the registers being stored—one fullword for each register. The general registers are stored in ascending sequence from the register specified by the first operand and revert back to general register 0 after storing general register 15 if the register specified by the R_3 operand has not been encountered. For example, if the R_1 operand specifies register 13 and the R_3 operand specifies register 2, this instruction stores general registers 13, 14, 15, 0, 1, and 2, in that order.

The Condition Code setting is not changed by this instruction.

*   *   *

Instruction: Insert Character

mnemonic	hex code	operand format
IC	43	$R_1, D_2 (X_2, B_2)$

The Insert Character instruction takes an eight-bit configuration or character, as addressed by the second operand, and inserts it into the low-order eight-bits of the register specified by the first operand. The high-order 24 bits of the first operand register remains unaltered.

The Condition Code setting is not changed by this instruction.

*   *   *

Moving, Storing, and Loading Data

Instruction: Insert Characters Under Mask (System/370 Only)

mnemonic	hex code	operand format
ICM	BF	$R_1, M_3, D_2 (B_2)$

The Insert Characters Under Mask instruction takes bytes of data from contiguous storage locations addressed by the second operand, and inserts them into the first operand general register under the control of a mask operand. The mask comprises four bit positions, one for each byte position in the first operand general register. The register byte positions corresponding to one-bits in the mask are filled, from left to right, in order of the ascending addresses of the storage bytes. The register bytes corresponding to zero-bits in the mask remain unchanged. As this implies, the length of the data field addressed by the second operand, $D_2 (B_2)$, must be equal to the quantity of one-bits contained in the mask.

CC	BC	Condition
0	8	All data bits inserted are zero-bits or the mask bits are all zero-bits.
1	4	The first (high-order) of the inserted data bits is a one-bit.
2	2	The first (high-order) of the inserted data bits is a zero-bit and not all inserted data bits are zero-bits.

*   *   *

Instruction: Load Halfword

mnemonic	hex code	operand format
LH	48	$R_1, D_2 (X_2, B_2)$

The Load Halfword instruction first extracts the 16-bit halfword stored at the location addressed by the second operand and expands it to a 32-bit fullword by creating 16 additional high-order bits that are identical to the sign-bit of the original halfword. It then loads the expanded 32 bits into the general register specified by the first operand. The configuration of the original halfword in storage is not altered. The address generated by the second operand must be on a halfword boundary alignment.

The Condition Code setting is not changed by this instruction.

*   *   *

Instruction: Load

mnemonic	hex code	operand format
L	58	$R_1, D_2 (X_2, B_2)$

The Load instruction takes the fullword of data stored at the location addressed by the second operand and loads all 32 bits into the general register specified by the first operand. Upon completion of the Load instruction, the contents of the first operand are identical to those of the

second operand. The address generated by the second operand must be on a fullword boundary alignment.
The Condition Code setting is not changed by this instruction.

* * *

Instruction: Load Register

mnemonic	hex code	operand format
LR	18	R_1, R_2

The LR instruction places the exact contents of the second operand register into the first operand register. Upon completion of this operation, the contents of both registers are identical.
The Condition Code setting is not changed by this instruction.

* * *

Instruction: Load Multiple

mnemonic	hex code	operand format
LM	98	$R_1, R_3, D_2 (B_2)$

The Load Multiple instruction loads fullwords of data, beginning at the location specified by the last operand, into the sequence of registers beginning with the first operand and terminating with the R_3 operand register. The sequence of registers to be loaded may go from the high-numbered registers through to the low-numbered registers in contiguous sequence. For example, if the operands specify the R_1 register as register 13 and the R_3 register as register 4, the load sequence would be general registers 13, 14, 15, 0, 1, 2, 3, and 4.
The Condition Code setting is not changed by this instruction.

* * *

Instruction: Load Address

mnemonic	hex code	operand format
LA	41	$R_1, D_2 (X_2, B_2)$

The Load Address instruction generates a 24-bit address as specified by the second operand and places that address into the low-order 24 bit positions of the register specified by the first operand. It also sets the high-order eight bits of the first operand register to zero. The second operand may be an absolute decimal value or a symbolic reference to an address, including indexing and displacement.
The Condition Code setting is not changed by this instruction.

* * *

Moving, Storing, and Loading Data

Instruction: Load and Test Register

mnemonic	*hex code*	*operand format*
LTR	12	R_1, R_2

The Load and Test Register instruction takes the contents of the second operand register and places them into the register specified by the first operand, after which the contents of both register operands are identical. The Condition Code setting is determined by the combined value and sign of the data loaded into the first operand register.

CC	BC	Condition
0	8	The first operand register now contains a zero value.
1	4	The first operand register now contains a value less than zero.
2	2	The first operand register now contains a value greater than zero.

*   *   *

Instruction: Load Complement Register

mnemonic	*hex code*	*operand format*
LCR	13	R_1, R_2

The Load Complement Register instruction takes the contents of the second operand register, reverses the configuration of those contents to their complement value, and places that complement into the first operand register. The same general register may be specified for both operands in order to reverse the configuration contained within a single register. The complement value that is placed into the first operand register determines the setting of the Condition Code bits.

CC	BC	Condition
0	8	The first operand register now contains a zero value.
1	4	The first operand register now contains a negative value.
2	2	The first operand register now contains a positive value.
3	1	The complement value placed into the first operand register created an overflow condition.

*   *   *

Instruction: Load Positive Register

mnemonic	*hex code*	*operand format*
LPR	10	R_1, R_2

If the second operand register contains a negative value, this instruction loads the positive complement of that value into the first operand register. If the second operand register already contains a positive value, the contents of that register are placed unaltered into the first operand register. In the event that the complementation of the maximum number occurs, an overflow condition will exist, setting the Condition Code accordingly.

CC	BC	Conditon
0	8	The first operand register contains a zero value.
2	2	The first operand register contains a positive value.
3	1	An overflow occurred as a result of this instruction.

* * *

Instruction: Load Negative Register

mnemonic	hex code	operand format
LNR	11	R_1, R_2

If the second operand register contains a positive value, this instruction loads the negative complement of that value into the first operand register. If the second operand register already contains a negative value, the contents of that register are placed unaltered into the first operand register. If the second operand register contains a value of zero, that value is placed into the first operand register with a positive sign.

CC	BC	Condition
0	8	The first operand register contains a zero value.
1	4	The first operand register contains a negative value.

* * *

Instruction: Shift Left Logical

mnemonic	hex code	operand format
SLL	89	$R_1, D_2 (B_2)$

This instruction shifts to the left all 32 bits contained within the general register specified by the first operand, for the number of bit positions specified by the second operand. Only the low-order six bits of the address created by the second operand are used to determine the number of bit positions to be shifted. All bits are shifted, including the sign-bit, and any significant-digit bits shifted out of the high-order positions are lost without an overflow condition being indicated. Zero-bits are added to the low-order bit positions to replace bits shifted to the left.

The Condition Code setting is not changed by this instruction.

* * *

Instruction: Shift Left Double Logical

mnemonic	hex code	operand format
SLDL	8D	$R_1, D_2 (B_2)$

The SLDL instruction shifts to the left all 64 bits contained within an even-odd pair of general registers, for the number of bit positions specified by the second operand. The first operand regis-

Moving, Storing, and Loading Data 203

ter must address the even-numbered register of the pair of general registers. Only the low-order six bits of the address created by the second operand are used to determine the number of bit positions to be shifted. All bits are shifted and significant-digit bits that might be shifted out of the high-order positions are lost; the overflow condition is not activated when such a loss occurs. Zero-bits are added to the low-order bit positions to replace bits shifted to the left.

The Condition Code setting is not changed by this instruction.

* * *

Instruction: Shift Right Logical

mnemonic	hex code	operand format
SRL	88	$R_1, D_2 (B_2)$

This instruction shifts to the right all 32 bits contained within the general register specified by the first operand, for the number of bit positions specified by the second operand. Only the low-order six bits of the address created by the second operand are used to determine the number of bit positions comprising the shift quantity. All bits are shifted and any significant-digit bits that are shifted out of the low-order positions are lost; the Condition Code does not reflect the loss of such bits. Zero-bits are supplied to the high-order bit positions to replace bits that were shifted to the right.

The Condition Code setting is not changed by this instruction.

* * *

Instruction: Shift Right Double Logical

mnemonic	hex code	operand format
SRDL	8C	$R_1, D_2 (B_2)$

The SRDL instruction shifts to the right all 64 bits contained within an even-odd pair of general registers, for the number of bit positions specified by the second operand. The first operand register must address the even-numbered register of the pair of general registers. Only the low-order six bits of the address created by the second operand are used to determine the number of bit positions representing the shift quantity. All bits are shifted and any significant-digit bits that might be shifted out of the low-order positions are lost; the Condition Code does not reflect the loss of such bits. Zero-bits are supplied to the high-order bit positions to replace bits shifted to the right.

The Condition Code setting is not changed by this instruction.

* * *

Instruction: Shift Left Algebraically

mnemonic	hex code	operand format
SLA	8B	$R_1, D_2 (B_2)$

This instruction shifts to the left the 31 integer-bits contained within the general register specified by the first operand, for the number of bit positions specified by the second operand. However, only the low-order six bits of the address created by the second operand are used to determine the shift quantity. The sign-bit of the first operand register is not shifted. Low-order zero-bits are supplied to replace the bits shifted from the low-order bit positions. If a significant-digit bit (one unlike the sign-bit) is shifted out of the high-order integer bit position, the Condition Code indicates an overflow condition.

CC	BC	Condition
0	8	The first operand register contains a zero value.
1	4	The first operand register contains a negative value.
2	2	The first operand register contains a positive value.
3	1	An overflow condition occurred during the execution of the shift.

*   *   *

Instruction: Shift Left Double Algebraically

mnemonic	hex code	operand format
SLDA	–8F	$R_1, D_2 (B_2)$

The SLDA instruction shifts to the left the 63 integer-bits of the value contained within an even-odd pair of general registers, for the number of bit positions specified by the second operand of the statement. The first operand register must address the even-numbered register of the pair of registers. Only the low-order six bits of the second operand address are used to determine the shift quantity. The sign-bit of the odd-numbered general register is shifted along with the other bits, but the sign-bit of the even-numbered register is unaffected. Zero-bits replace the bits shifted from the low-order bit positions. If a significant-digit bit (one unlike the even-numbered register sign-bit) is shifted out of the high-order integer-bit position, the Condition Code is configured to indicate an overflow condition.

CC	BC	Condition
0	8	The first operand registers contain a zero value.
1	4	The first operand registers contain a negative value.
2	2	The first operand registers contain a positive value.
3	1	An overflow condition occurred during the execution of the shift.

*   *   *

Instruction: Shift Right Algebraically

mnemonic	hex code	operand format
SRA	8A	$R_1, D_2 (B_2)$

This instruction shifts to the right the 31 integer-bits contained within the general register specified by the first operand, for the number of bit positions specified by the second operand. Only the low-order six bits of the address created by the second operand are used to determine the shift quantity. Any significant-digit bits shifted out of the low-order bit positions are lost; the Condition Code bit settings do not indicate such a loss. The sign-bit of the first operand register

Moving, Storing, and Loading Data

is not affected by the shift, but bits supplied to the high-order bit positions to replace those shifted to the right will be identical to the sign-bit.

CC	BC	Condition
0	8	The first operand register contains a zero value.
1	4	The first operand register contains a negative value.
2	2	The first operand register contains a positive value.

Instruction: Shift Right Double Algebraically

mnemonic	hex code	operand format
SRDA	8E	$R_1, D_2 (B_2)$

The SRDA instruction shifts to the right the 63 integer-bits of the value contained within an even-odd pair of general registers, for the number of bit positions specified by the second operand of the statement. The first operand register must address the even-numbered register of the pair of registers. Only the low-order six bits of the address created by the second operand are used to determine the shift quantity. Significant-digit bits shifted out of the low-order bit positions of the odd-numbered general register are lost. The sign-bit of the even-numbered register is not affected, but the sign-bit position of the odd-numbered register is shifted along with the other integer-bits. Bits supplied to the high-order positions of the pair of registers are of the same value as the sign-bit of the even-numbered general regsiter and are equal in number of bit positions to those shifted out of the low-order bit positions. An overflow condition does not occur for the loss of a significant-digit bit shifted out of the low-order bit positions.

CC	BC	Condition
0	8	The first operand registers contain a zero value.
1	4	The first operand registers contain a negative value.
2	2	The first operand registers contain a positive value.

THE APPLICATION OF THE MOVE, STORE, LOAD, INSERT, AND SHIFT INSTRUCTIONS

During the design and subsequent coding of program logic, it is usually necessary to manipulate and relocate data from one area to another within the program. Such relocation and reassignment of data is controlled almost entirely by the various types of move, load, store, insert, and shift instructions. The move instructions perform data relocation from one storage address to another; the load and insert instructions relocate data from storage areas to registers or from register to register; the store instructions perform data relocation from registers to storage areas; the shift instructions manipulate data within general registers. Examples and illustrations of the use and performance of the individual instructions represented by these four groups are contained within this section. The presentation of certain instructions is superficial in some instances because they are discussed in detail within other sections of this text.

Because of the number of individual instructions discussed within this chapter, the review exercises have been arranged into four groups; one each for the Move, Load and Insert, Store, and Shift instructions. It is suggested that you do the appropriate review exercise group as you complete the respective portion of this chapter.

Moving Data within the Problem Program

Although any data that is transferred from one location to another within the problem program might correctly be assumed to have been "moved," the term "move" is technically representative of the relocation of data between two storage locations only—from one problem program storage address to another. The specific Assembler Language instructions that fall within this category are:

1. MOVE IMMEDIATE (MVI)
2. MOVE CHARACTERS (MVC)
3. MOVE LONG (MVCL)
4. MOVE NUMERIC (MVN)
5. MOVE ZONE (MVZ)
6. MOVE WITH OFFSET (MVO)

The last instruction, Move with Offset, is sufficiently and more appropriately described in "Packed Decimal Arithmetic Operations;" hence, it will not be elaborated on within this section.

As the discussion of these instructions progresses, it will be obvious that the range of data which may be moved by any single instruction statement will vary from one byte to 16,777,215 bytes. Special attention will be given to the movement of large data fields as well as the concept of "sliding" a single data byte through a multiple-byte field.

Move Immediate (MVI)

The Move Immediate instruction is used as an expedient move of one byte of immediate data into a storage area field. It is considerably faster than moving one byte of data with the Move Characters instruction. The difference in performance speed results from the characteristics of the second operand. In a Move Characters instruction statement, the second operand generates an address at which the character that is to be moved is located. In the Move Immediate instruction statement, the one-byte character to be moved is a part of the generated machine-language instruction itself. The operation of the MVI instruction is demonstrated within this illustration:

```
    FIELDA      DC      CL5'123D5'
                MVI     FIELDA+3,C'4'
```

```
                            +1   +2   +3   +4
FIELDA (before MVI)      | 1 | 2 | 3 | D | 5 |

                            +1   +2   +3   +4
FIELDA (after MVI)       | 1 | 2 | 3 | 4 | 5 |
```

Moving, Storing, and Loading Data

The MVI instruction statement shown here would move an EBCDIC numeric character "4" into the fourth byte of the field addressed by the label FIELDA. Because the "4" is constructed as a part of the machine-language instruction itself, it does not require additional storage for that character.

Move Characters (MVC)

This instruction, which is used to move full bytes of data from one storage area to another, moves up to 256 bytes of data with one instruction statement. The number of data bytes to be moved is determined by the implied or explicit length of the area addressed by the first operand of the instruction statement.

```
        FIELD1      DC      CL2 ' ƀƀ '
        FIELD2      DC      CL3 ' 078 '
        INDATA      DC      CL6 ' 246802 '
```

FIELD1 | ƀ | ƀ |

FIELD2 | 0 | 7 | 8 |

INDATA | 2 | 4 | 6 | 8 | 0 | 2 |

```
        MUVIT   MVC     FIELD1 , INDATA         001
                MVC     FIELD2(1) , INDATA+2    002
```

Statement 001 instructs the problem program logic to "move data, commencing at the address generated by INDATA, into the area labeled FIELD1 for the number of bytes implied by the actual length attribute of FIELD1." This would then move the first two bytes of INDATA, containing '24', into the two byte length of FIELD1.

Statement 002 specifies, "From the address generated by INDATA+2, move data into the address referenced by the label FIELD2 for a length of one byte as specified in the first operand of this instruction statement." This statement would move the third byte of INDATA, containing a '6', into the first byte of FIELD2.

After the execution of these two instruction statements, the contents of these same fields would be:

FIELD1 | 2 | 4 |

FIELD2 | 6 | 7 | 8 |

INDATA | 2 | 4 | 6 | 8 | 0 | 2 |

The Move Characters instruction is relatively easy to understand. It can be applied to a number of different tasks as long as both operands refer to storage areas.

One of the unique methods of using the MVC instruction is creating a "sliding" move of a single data byte through a field. Because the movement of data is from left to right, from low to high storage address, the first byte of any given field can be used to set all bytes of that field to an identical configuration. This is not only an expedient means of setting a field to blanks, but it does away with the necessity of creating a constant that contains the same number of blanks as the field length to be cleared. The actual execution of this technique requires two statements— one statement to move a single blank into the first byte of the field to be cleared and one statement to start the "sliding" action.

The following set of illustrations contains the definition of a storage area, the contents of that area at the time the program logic encounters the instruction statements, and the instruction statement themselves.

```
BIGFIELD        DS    CL15
```

BIGFIELD | 1 | R | 3 | 9 | 5 | P | A | R | T | 6 | 5 | 9 | 2 | 2 | Z |

```
        MVI   BIGFIELD,C' '              001
        MVC   BIGFIELD+1 (14) , BIGFIELD  002
```

Statement 001 uses the Move Immediate instruction to place a valid "blank" configuration (Hex '40') into the first byte of BIGFIELD. At this point BIGFIELD would contain:

BIGFIELD | b | R | 3 | 9 | 5 | P | A | R | T | 6 | 5 | 9 | 2 | 2 | Z |

Statement 002 causes the "slide" action of the first byte of BIGFIELD. It indicates that each byte of BIGFIELD, commencing at the first byte of that field, should be moved to the next rightmost byte location. The byte-by-byte movement of the data appears as shown on page 209.

As indicated within Statement 002, the length of the first operand is specified as 14 bytes from a point addressed by BIGFIELD+1, which effectively places blanks (Hex '40') into the remaining 14 bytes of BIGFIELD. This same type of application may be used to configure a field of up to 256 bytes, either with blanks or any other desired configuration.

In some instances, you may need to move data whose field length exceeds the 256-byte allowable maximum of the MVC instruction within a single statement. The Move Long instruction would be the best choice of instructions to accomplish that task. However, if the Move Long instruction is not available to the programmer, the movement of such data between oversized fields can be accomplished by *"chaining"* a series of MVC instruction statements. After the first Move Characters statement is coded for the maximum allowable length, the first and second operands of the next instruction statement reference an address one byte higher in storage than the last byte of the fields addressed by the first and second operands within the previous statement. This can be more easily illustrated than described.

```
        DATAFLD   DS    CL750
        INPUT     DS    CL890
*
                  MVC   DATAFLD (256) , INPUT              001
                  MVC   DATAFLD+256 (256) , INPUT+256      002
                  MVC   DATAFLD+512 (238) , INPUT+512      003
```

Moving, Storing, and Loading Data 209

In this example the data fields described by the Define Storage (DS) statements are considered to contain valid data. The instruction statements coded thereafter are intended to move 750 bytes of data from the INPUT field into the entire area that is defined by DATAFLD.

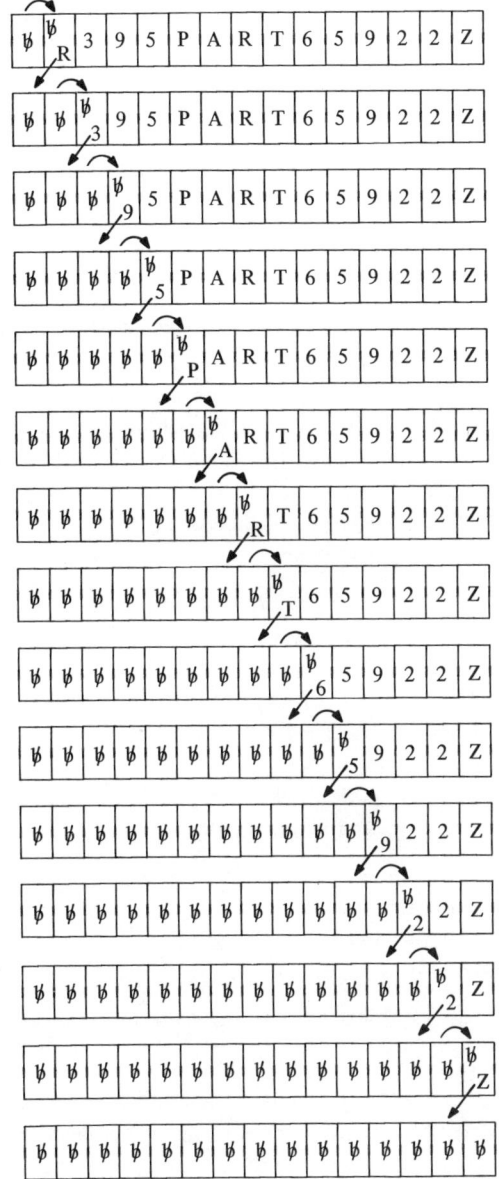

Statement 001 moves the first 256 bytes (from left to right) out of the INPUT field and places that data into the first 256 bytes of DATAFLD.

Statement 002 moves another 256 bytes of data from INPUT to DATAFLD. The data moved by this statement are bytes #257 through #512 of the area labeled INPUT. They are placed into the same relative positions within DATAFLD.

Statement 003 moves bytes #513 through #750 from INPUT into DATAFLD for a total move length of 238 bytes of data. All 750 bytes of data to be placed into DATAFLD from INPUT have now been moved—256 bytes of Statement 001 plus 256 bytes by Statement 002 plus 238 bytes by Statement 003 equal 750 bytes.

This type of chained MVC statements can go on for as long as the programmer desires; thousands of bytes of data may be moved if it is practical to do so.

A combination of the "sliding" MVC technique and the "chained" MVC statements may be used in order to identically configure all bytes of a very large area or data field. This combined application is presented in Figure 9-1.

Based on the combined logic of the "sliding" and "chained" MVC instructions, these statements would effectively place valid blanks (Hex '40') into all 810 bytes of HOLDAREA.

Multiple groups, or segments, of data may be relocated into storage areas throughout the program by use of loop controls and MVC instruction statements. This is a technique sometimes referred to as a *"sliding table,"* or as *"elastic indexing."* It basically consists of adding or deleting segments of data from a large block of data segments formed of equal-length segments arranged in a sequential pattern. Although an example of this type of application would be rather lengthy to present here if it were accompanied by the necessary detailed explanations of the instruction statements themselves, there follows a set of general rules that should enable you to create an example of this technique. Keep in mind that this is a storage-to-storage movement of data. It is intended to delete or sequentially insert any random segment of data into its appropriate ordered position within a block of data consisting of segments of the same length.

The general rules for this application are given below:

- The expansion or contraction of the overall data contained within the block must affect only the high end of the block; any expansion must be from lower storage addresses to higher storage addresses; any contraction must be from the higher storage addresses to lower storage addresses. This indicates that the initial starting address of the overall block of data must not change, although the high-storage address of the last segment of valid data *within the block* may vary as necessary.

- The last valid data segment within the block should be followed by a delimiter segment to indicate this fact, even though the overall length of the block is not occupied by valid segments.

- The last (highest) available position within the area defined by the block itself should contain a block delimiter segment. If the program is coded properly this would prevent any attempt to move a segment outside of the defined limits of the block area.

In order to insert a data segment into its logical sequential position within the block of data segments, the following steps should be taken.

1. Locate the address of the position within the block where the segment belongs. This can be done by comparing the new segment value to the existing segment values in an ascending search. As soon as the new segment compares low to an existing segment, this is the point where the new segment is to be placed. Store this address in a hold area or load it into a register for retention.
2. Scan the remainder of the block to find the segment delimiter.
3. Create a loop routine that will move each data segment, beginning with the segment delimiter, one segment length higher into the addresses within the block. Each cycle through

Moving, Storing, and Loading Data 211

SYSTEM / 370 ASSEMBLER CODING FORM

NAME	OPERATION	OPERAND
*		
MOVELOT	MVI	HOLDAREA,C' '
	MVC	HOLDAREA+1(255),HOLDAREA
	MVC	HOLDAREA+256(256),HOLDAREA+255
	MVC	HOLDAREA+512(256),HOLDAREA+511
	MVC	HOLDAREA+768(42),HOLDAREA+767
	BC	15,BACK
*		
HOLDAREA	DS	CL810
*		

FIGURE 9-1

the loop should decrement the address of both operands in the MVC instruction by the length of one segment. On the first move of a data segment, which will be the segment delimiter, a check should be made to see if this action would overlay the block delimiter. If so, the block is full and the new data segment cannot be added.
4. The loop routine should be written so that the loop cycles are terminated once the segment is moved that occupies the area where the new segment is to be placed.
5. The new segment should then be moved into the proper position within the block. When it is moved into that position, it will destroy the copy of the segment that previously existed there, but that is now also located one segment higher within the block.

In order to delete a data segment from the block of data segments and to contract the remaining segments in order to eliminate the space occupied by the deleted segment, the following steps should be coded.

1. Locate the segment to be eliminated.
2. Load that address into two general registers, X and Y. Add the length of a table segment to the second register.
3. Create a loop routine containing an MVC instruction statement with an explicit length equal to that of a segment. Use the first general register (X) to create an address for the first operand in the MVC statement; use the second general register (Y) to create an address for the second operand in the MVC statement. The MVC instruction statement should then move each segment downward in the block by the length of one segment. The first time that this statement is encountered, it should move the next higher segment into the position occupied by the segment to be deleted.
4. Each time through the loop cycle the logic should increment the values contained in both registers by a value equal to the length of a segment.
5. As each segment is moved downward, the logic should check to see if that segment was in reality a segment delimiter. If so, then the contraction of the segments has been completed.

By using the rules presented here, you should be able to originate the coding required to generate a basic "sliding table" routine. Admittedly, this application might be somewhat complex for a student programmer, but the successful completion of such a routine will add considerably to your understanding and knowledge of data manipulation.

Move Long (MVCL) (System/370 Only)

In a manner similar to the Move Characters (MVC) instruction, the Move Long instruction moves data, one byte at a time, from the storage area addressed by the second operand, placing it into the storage area addressed by the first operand. Although this instruction can move as few as one byte or as many as 16,777,215 bytes of data, it will probably be used most commonly on data fields whose length exceeds the 256-byte maximum capability of the MVC instruction.

One of the unique features of this instruction is that the "sending" field (the second operand) may have a length attribute different than that of the "receiving" field (the first operand). Regardless of the difference or similarity in length of the two operands, the movement of data from the second operand to the first operand will always terminate as soon as the first operand has become full. The specific action regarding this rule is as follows:

- If both operands reference data strings (fields) of the same length, the entire field of data addressed by the second operand is moved into the storage area addressed by the first operand.

Moving, Storing, and Loading Data

- If the data string referenced by the second operand is given a length attribute greater than the length specified for the first operand, only the amount of data necessary to satisfy the first operand data length is moved.
- If the storage area addressed by the first operand is given a length attribute greater than the specified length of the data field addressed by the second operand, all of the data bytes from the second operand address are moved into the first operand data area. Once the contents of the second operand data string have been depleted, the remainder of the first operand data area is padded, byte by byte, with a character supplied by the programmer.

Two pairs of even-odd general registers must be used for addressing. The even-numbered register of each pair must be used to specify the first and second operands, respectively, within the instruction statement. The odd-numbered register of each pair is used to specify the length attribute of the storage areas pointed to by the appropriate even-numbered register.

Assuming that the programmer is going to use general registers 4 and 5 for the first operand and 10 and 11 for the second operand in moving data between two fields of equal length, these registers would contain the following information:

Although bits 0 through 7 of Register 11 would be considered to contain a padding character, none would be needed inasmuch as both fields have identical length attributes. The instruction statement to accomplish the movement of data would be:

```
MVCL    4, 10
```

As stated previously, if the length attribute of the data field addressed by the first operand is greater than the length of the data field addressed by the second operand, the programmer is expected to provide a padding character prior to execution of the MVCL instruction statement. This one-byte character, or bit configuration or pair of hexadecimal characters, must be loaded into the high-order byte of the odd-numbered register associated with the second operand. As soon as all of the data bytes addressed by the second operand have been "moved," the padding character will be supplied to all remaining unfilled bytes addressed by the first operand. To illustrate the step-by-step coding typical for moving data between fields of equal length and fields of unequal length, the following examples of MVCL are presented.

Example 1

Data is to be moved from a storage location identified by the label SUBPOOL, into a main storage area beginning at a location labeled BASEPOOL. Both areas are 3,920 bytes in length.

```
        LA      8 , BASEPOOL    0110
        LA      9 , 3920        0120
        LA      4 , SUBPOOL     0130
        LA      5 , 3920        0140
        MVCL    8 , 4           0150
```

Upon completion of instruction Statement #0140, the registers used would contain the following information:

Note that bit positions 0 through 7 of Register 5 contain a configuration of X ' 00 '. It is not necessary to provide a special padding character because the two storage areas addressed by the operands have identical length attributes. Consequently the X ' 00 ' placed into those bit positions by the execution of statement #0140 (a Load Address) remains unchanged.

Example 2

Data is to be moved from storage commencing at a location labeled REGION2, and placed into storage at a location labeled REGION1. For purposes of the move, REGION1 is considered to have a length of 524,288 bytes and REGION2 a length of 262,144 bytes. The padding configuration desired is X ' FF '.

```
        R1LNGTH   DC      F ' 524288 '             0100
        R2LNGTH   DC      F ' 262144 '             0110
        *                                          0115
        *                                          0120
        DOMOVE    LA      6 , REGION1              0130
                  L       7 , R1LNGTH              0140
                  LA      8 , REGION2              0150
                  MVI     R2LNGTH , X ' FF '       0160
                  L       9 , R2LNGTH              0170
                  MVCL    6 , 8                    0180
```

After completion of the execution of instruction statement #0170, the general registers used in this example would contain:

It is important to point out that the two length values, R1LNGTH and R2LNGTH, are first set up as fixed-point fullword constants and the Loaded (L) into their respective odd-numbered registers. This is necessary inasmuch as an absolute value greater than 4095 cannot be specified as the second operand in a Load Address (LA) instruction. Additionally, prior to loading R2LNGTH into register 9, the padding configuration of X ' FF ' (equal to B ' 11111111 ') is placed into the high-order byte of that field by instruction statement #0160.

During execution of instruction statement #0180, all 262,144 bytes of REGION2 would be placed into REGION1, moving from left to right through both fields. Once all of the data in REGION2 has been moved, the execution would continue by placing X ' FF ' in each of the remaining 262,144 bytes of REGION1.

Whenever the MVCL instruction is executed, it performs a check to determine whether a destructive overlap of the operands will occur. If such a condition is noted, the Condition Code bits in the PSW will be set to "3" and the movement of data will be suppressed. A destructive overlap is the condition under which a section of the first operand, which has already received data, becomes part of the data being moved by the second operand. This occurs whenever the low-order bytes of the second operand extend into the addresses containing the high-order bytes of the first operand. This can be illustrated as:

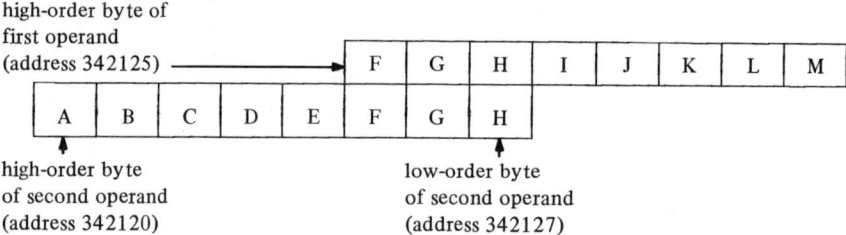

If an MVCL instruction statement had been allowed to move the data from the second operand to the first operand, the byte-by-byte movement would have appeared as:

Moving, Storing, and Loading Data 217

```
              ┌───┬───┬───┬───┬───┬───┬───┐
              │ A │ B │ C │ D │ E │ K │ L │ M │
              └───┴───┴───┴───┴───┴───┴───┘
                              ↑
┌───┬───┬───┬───┬───┬───┬───┐ │
│ A │ B │ C │ D │ E │ A │ B │ C │
└───┴───┴───┴───┴───┴───┴───┘
```

(similar diagrams continue)

As shown by this illustration, the movement of the first byte of data into the first operand storage location also effectively modified the contents of the storage address of the second operand. The destructive overlap prevented the original contents of the second operand from being moved without alteration into the first operand.

Overlapping of a non-destructive nature is permitted with the MVCL instruction. A non-destructive overlap is one wherein the high-order byte of the first operand is to the left of, or coincidental with, the high-order byte of the second operand. Such as:

high-order byte of
first operand
(address 146209)

high-order byte of
second operand
(address 146210)

The MVCL instruction can also be a convenient tool for clearing large sections of storage—setting the contents of storage all to X '00' bytes. This is accomplished by defining the storage area to be cleared as the first operand and then setting both the padding character and the length of the second operand to zero. Inasmuch as the second operand has no length attribute, the padding character of X '00' will be propagated throughout the entire length of the storage area addressed by the first operand.

The MVCL instruction is one of the few interruptible instructions. As such, the operating system can temporarily divert processing to a higher priority task, then return and continue processing the MVCL instruction. If and when such an interrupt occurs, the odd-numbered register of each operand will have been decremented by the number of bytes already moved; the even-numbered register of each operand will have been incremented to the address of the next byte to be moved. When processing of the MVCL instruction statement resumes, it picks up at the appropriate location.

Move Numeric (MVN)

The Move Numeric instruction is one of two Assembler Language instructions that moves data in a fragmented manner. Although the data moves in an orderly method from one storage area to another, this instruction moves only the right-most nibble (four bit positions) of each data byte. EBCDIC alphanumeric characters are so formatted that the right nibble of each byte contains a hexadecimal numeric digit; it is logical then that this instruction should be called the Move Numeric instruction. As indicated, the right nibble of each byte in the sending field is moved to the right nibble of each corresponding byte in the receiving field, for a length implied or specified by the receiving field. The left nibble of each byte in the two fields is not altered in any way. Up to 256 bytes of data may be affected by one MVN instruction statement.

```
        AREA1    DC    CL5 ' 22496 '
        AREA2    DC    CL7 ' 0000000 '
```

```
        MVN    AREA2+2 (5) , AREA1
```

This instruction statement specifies that the right nibble of each byte of AREA1 should be moved into the right nibble of each byte of AREA2+2 (commencing at the third byte of AREA2) for a length of five bytes. This action would appear to be:

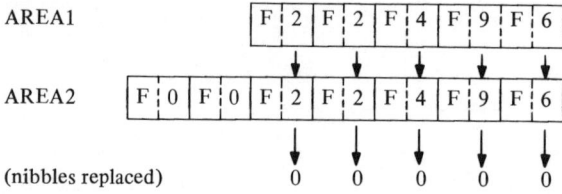

Moving, Storing, and Loading Data 219

This instruction may also be used in an application to convert valid EBCDIC alphabetic characters into their respective right nibble numeric values. This is shown in the following illustration.

```
ALPHAFLD     DC     CL6 ' AKTDNW '
NUMERFLD     DC     CL6 ' 000000 '
```

NUMERFLD *character*

0	0	0	0	0	0

hexadecimal

F￨0	F￨0	F￨0	F￨0	F￨0	F￨0

ALPHAFLD *character*

A	K	T	D	N	W

hexadecimal

C￨1	D￨2	E￨3	C￨4	D￨5	E￨6

```
      MVN    NUMERFLD , ALPHAFLD
```

ALPHAFLD

C￨1	D￨2	E￨3	C￨4	D￨5	E￨6

NUMERFLD

F￨1	F￨2	F￨3	F￨4	F￨5	F￨6

(nibbles replaced)   0 0 0 0 0 0

(resulting EBCDIC data in NUMERFLD)

1	2	3	4	5	6

In this instance, the MVN instruction statement moves only the right nibble (hexadecimal numeric digit) of each byte of ALPHAFLD to the corresponding right nibble of each byte of NUMERFLD, effectively transforming the EBCDIC alphabetic character data into EBCDIC numeric character data.

One of the applications for the MVN instruction is the formatting of a partially numeric character field to a full numeric character field. This type of situation might occur in an instance where a numeric character field is so formed that high-order (leading) zeros of the EBCDIC numeric characters have been stated as blanks. This condition could occur through previous editing of the data in another program. Assume that the problem program expects a set of EBCDIC numeric characters that might range from 0000001 to 9999999. However, because of previous editing the data is read into the problem program in a format range of from ƀƀƀƀƀƀ1 to 9999999. As a peculiarity of the present program, these numeric characters are to be expressed in their full numeric character form. At any given point within the problem program, the fields and respective action might appear as:

```
DATAFLD      DS     CL7
NUMCONV      DC     CL7 ' 0000000 '
*
             MVN    NUMCONV , DATAFLD
```

220   *Assembler Language for Application Programming*

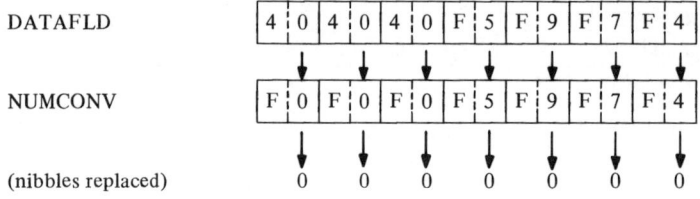

The resulting action would be:

This statement has now changed the data configuration of 'bbb5974' to its full numeric character representation of '0005974'. This same type of transformation can also be accomplished, but by moving the left nibble of each byte instead of the right nibble. This will be described within the analysis of the Move Zone instruction.

Move Zone (MVZ)

Move Zone is the only instruction other than the Move Numeric instruction that moves data by partial bytes, somewhat in a fragmented mode. It is the opposite of the MVN instruction, however, in that it moves only the left nibble of each byte from the sending field to the receiving field. It is generally considered that the left nibble of EBCDIC alphanumeric character data is the "zone" portion of the byte; hence, the Move Zone instruction moves only the left-most four bits of each byte. Up to 256 bytes of data may be affected by one MVZ instruction statement.

The movement of the portions of the data bytes would be in the manner indicated below:

```
    DATA1     DC      CL5 ' PNJLQ '
    CONVRT    DC      X ' C0C0C0C0C0 '
*
              MVZ     DATA1+1 (4) , CONVRT
```

DATA1 *character*	P	N	J	L	Q
hexadecimal	D7	D5	D1	D3	D8

CONVRT *hexadecimal*	C0	C0	C0	C0	C0

Moving, Storing, and Loading Data

Execution of the instruction statement results in the following alteration of the fields:

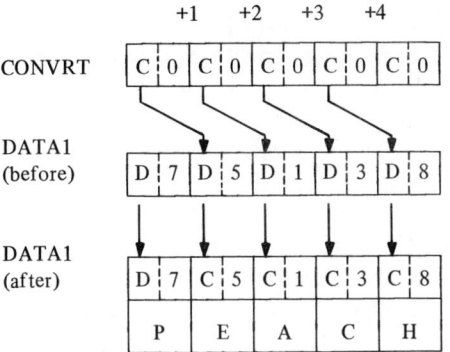

As shown in the illustration, the Move Zone instruction statement has changed the five bytes of data containing 'PNJLQ' so that they now contain 'PEACH'. This is done by altering only the zone portion of each of the last four bytes.

As mentioned within the discussion on the Move Numeric instruction, the Move Zone instruction can be used to expediently configure a field of mixed blanks and numeric characters to a full numeric character field. Because a blank is configured as a hexadecimal '40', it can be converted to a numeric zero (hex 'F0') by moving a hex digit 'F' into the zone portion of each byte. This is shown in the following illustrations:

```
DATAFLD    DC    CL6 ' ƀƀ3922 '
NUMZONE    DC    CL6 ' 000000 '
```

    MVZ   DATAFLD , NUMZONE

The execution of this instruction statement would cause the following action:

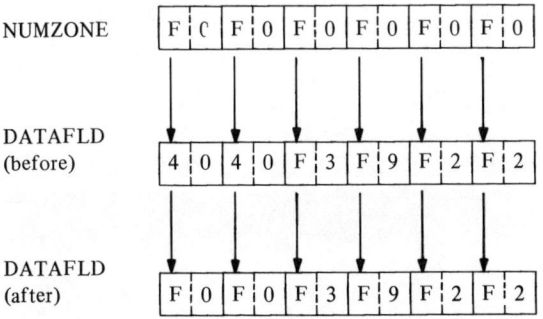

DATAFLD, which was originally a set of numeric characters and leading blanks, has now been configured as a full field of numeric character data. This type of application can be very useful in assuring that an incoming field does not contain a valid blank in the low-order (right-most) byte prior to a Pack instruction. If a Pack instruction operates on a field that contains a blank in the low-order byte, the resulting packed decimal field is invalid for packed decimal arithmetic operations. (Refer to Packed Decimal Arithmetic Operations for further details on this.)

In the preceding examples it was assumed that the numeric data being verified was "unsigned," that is, without a plus or minus zone indicated in the low-order byte other than the standard assumed plus value indicator. For example, when a hex configuration of 'C1' (the character "A") is packed into packed decimal form, it is considered to be a standard value of +1; when a hex configuration of 'D1' (the character "J") is packed, it is considered to be an expressed value of −1; a hexadecimal configuration of 'F1' (the numeric character '1') is considered to be a value of +1. If all of the numeric character data to be affected by the Move Zone instruction are to be considered as valid "plus" numerics, there will be no adverse results from moving a hexadecimal 'F' digit into the left nibble of the low-order byte of the field. If the low-order byte of the field of numeric data contains a negatively signed numeric character, the MVZ instruction "strips" that zone and replaces it with a positive (plus) zone. This can be avoided by not affecting the low-order byte of the numeric field. This would appear as:

```
     NUMERIC    DC    CL5 'b465J'
     ZONEIT     DC    CL4 '0000'
```

NUMERIC *character* | b | 4 | 6 | 5 | J |

hex | 4 0 | F 4 | F 6 | F 5 | D 1 |

ZONEIT *character* | 0 | 0 | 0 | 0 |

hex | F 0 | F 0 | F 0 | F 0 |

```
     MVZ    NUMERIC (4) , ZONEIT
```

The instruction statement indicates the zone portion (left-most four bits) of each byte of ZONEIT is to be moved into the corresponding position of only the first four bytes of NUMERIC. This would appear to be:

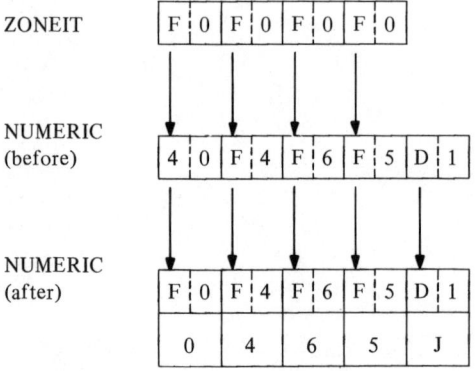

Moving, Storing, and Loading Data 223

The original configuration of NUMERIC represents a set of partially configured numeric character data, of which the low-order numeric is indicated to be a signed zoned decimal character of "J", equal to a value of −1. If the MVZ instruction had moved numeric zones into all bytes of NUMERIC, the hex configuration of the low-order byte would have been 'F1'—equal to a numeric character of "1", which implies a positive value. This would have resulted in a change of the intended sign attached to that numeric character representing a negative zoned decimal.

The "Store" Instructions

The Store instructions are used to move all, or part, of the contents of registers into storage areas. There are five such instructions, and among them they will store one byte, two bytes, four bytes, or up to 64 bytes of data. With the exception of the Store Characters (STC) and the Store Characters Under Mask (STCM) instructions, the data being stored must be directed to an area of storage that is appropriately boundary-aligned. Two-byte storage areas must be halfword-aligned; four-byte storage areas must be fullword-aligned; multiples of four-byte storage areas must be contiguously fullword-aligned.

These instructions are particularly useful in preserving the contents of a register at any point in the processing. This is often necessary, especially when any given general register is to be used for several functions within a single problem program. The data may be stored, held until the required processing logic is completed, and then moved back into the register via a Load instruction.

There are five Store instructions—Store, Store Character, Store Characters Under Mask, Store Halfword, and Store Multiple. The programmer's decision as to which one of these would be used is entirely dependent on the amount of data to be stored.

Store Character (STC)

This Store instruction affects only one byte of data of the four bytes contained within a general register. It derives its name from the fact that the EBCDIC character is represented by one byte—eight bit positions. When the Store Character instruction statement is executed, it takes the low-order byte of data from the general register specified by the first operand and places that data, unaltered, into the one-byte storage area specified by the second operand.

Although there are many conceivable applications for this instruction, one of its primary uses is to modify the length attribute of an existing instruction statement. For example, assume that a problem program contains this instruction statement:

```
MOVEDATA    MVC    FLD1 (6) , FLD2
```

This statement indicates that the problem program is to move six bytes of data from FLD2 to FLD1. The hexadecimal configuration of the first two bytes of the machine-language instruction generated by this statement would appear as:

```
D205
```

The hex 'D2' is the hexadecimal code for the MVC instruction statement; the hex '05' is the machine-language length attribute of '6'. The machine-language length attribute is always one less than the desired decimal length of the operation. If, at a later point within the problem program, the programmer desires to change the length attribute of the MOVEDATA instruction statement so that it would move 11 bytes of data, the necessary statements could be coded as:

```
LA     8 , 10
STC    8 , MOVEDATA+1
```

In the first instruction statement, a fixed-point value of +10 (equal to a machine-language length attribute that would move 11 bytes of data) is loaded into general register 8. The low-order byte of general register 8 now contains a hexadecimal configuration of '0A'. The second instruction statement stores the low-order byte of general register 8 into the address generated by MOVEDATA+1, or the second byte of the machine-language instruction generated by the statement that is labeled MOVEDATA. That portion of the machine-language instruction (which was previously D205) would now appear as 'D20A', indicating a length attribute of 11 bytes for the fields specified within the remainder of the statement. As indicated by this example, the STC instruction can be easily used to modify other instruction statements at will.

Store Characters Under Mask (STCM) (System/370 Only)

The STCM instruction can select one, two, three, or four bytes of data from the contents of a general register and place that data into a storage address. The quantity of bytes selected, and the selection criteria, are controlled by the mask operand of the instruction statement. The mask comprises four bit positions, each representing a corresponding byte within the general register specified by the first operand. A zero-bit in the mask indicates that the corresponding byte in the register is to be excluded; a one-bit in the mask specifies that the corresponding byte in the register is to participate in the "store" operation. Examples of the register-byte selection can be shown as:

mask	register bytes selected by the mask			
1011	X		X	X
0100		X		
1100	X	X		
0101		X		X
1111	X	X	X	X

As the bytes are selected from the general register, from left to right, they are placed into the storage area addressed by the second operand of the instruction statement. Even though the selected bytes might not be contiguous within the general register, they are stored contiguously within the second operand storage address. Therefore, the specified, or implied, length of the second operand storage location must be equal to the number of one-bits in the mask operand.

Moving, Storing, and Loading Data

The following examples demonstrate the action taken by this instruction:

Example 1

register 4 *hex* : 0 0 C 6 0 5 F 8

DATAFLD3 (before STCM): 4 0 4 0 4 0

(instruction executed)   STCM   4 , B ' 1011 ' , DATAFLD3

DATAFLD3 (after STCM): 0 0 0 5 F 8

Example 2

register 9 *hex* : 0 3 0 6 B 7 9 C

DATAFLD2 (before STCM): 0 0 0 0

(instruction executed)   STCM   9 , B ' 0101 ' , DATAFLD2

DATAFLD2 (after STCM): 0 6 9 C

Example 3

register 1 *hex* : 0 0 0 0 0 0 6 E

DATA2FLD (before STCM): C 6 C 4

(instruction executed)   STCM   1 , B ' 0110 ' , DATA2FLD

DATA2FLD (after STCM): 0 0 0 0

In each of these examples the STCM instruction, under control of the mask operand, extracts the selected bytes from the register operand and places them contiguously into the second operand storage address. The original contents of the general register are not altered.

Store Halfword (STH)

The Store Halfword instruction takes the contents of the right-most two bytes of the general register specified by the first operand and places them unaltered into the halfword storage location addressed by the second operand. This instruction may be used to move values into a storage area for retention purposes. Assume:

General register 4 contains a fixed-point value +3926.

```
HAFWD      DC      H'0'
*
           STH     4,HAFWD
```

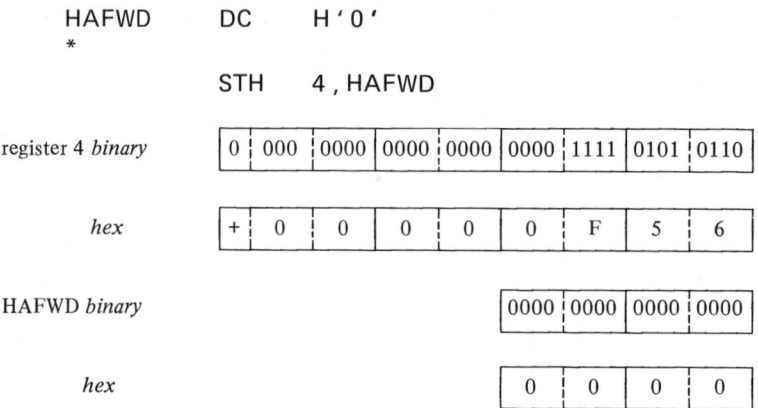

The register and storage area would be affected in the following way:

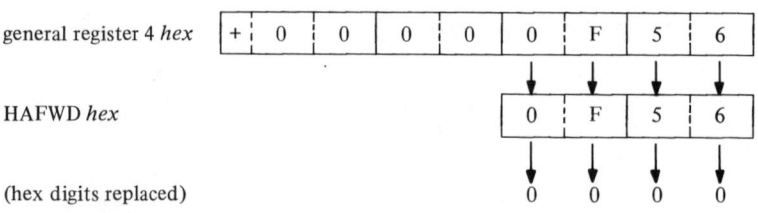

As indicated, the low-order two bytes of general register 4 replace the data originally contained within HAFWD. In general, the Store Halfword instruction might be used to extract halfword values from a register or to selectively pull out and retain address increment values, such as positional pointers to table segments.

Store (ST)

The Store instruction takes the contents of an entire general register and places that data, without change, into a fullword storage location. Because general registers are often used for multiple purposes within a single problem program, it is quite often necessary to temporarily store the contents of a general register, use that register for another application, and then reinstate the register with the original value. This application is useful in arithmetic routines, for holding address increments, and for storing addresses for future reference. The Store instruction is one means of retrieving the results of a fixed-point arithmetic routine for further manipulation. For example:

```
       AR      8,9
       ST      8,FULLWD
```

Moving, Storing, and Loading Data

The first statement adds together the fixed-point contents of registers 8 and 9. The second statement takes the sum that resulted from that operation, residing in general register 8, and places it into a fullword storage location for future reference or use.

Using the Store instruction to allow multiple use of a single general register is indicated in the set of instruction statements shown in Figure 9-2.

Basically these instruction statements perform two rather elementary table lookups. Statements 001 through 005 perform the first table search, using general register 9 as the address pointer to the current table segment within the first table, TABLE1. Whenever an equal condition is found in the first table, the program branches to the second table lookup routine, HITA. HITA, consisting of Statements 006 through 013, also intends to use general register 9 but only as a loop count control register for a BCT instruction. As soon as the HITA subroutine is entered, the problem program stores the address contained in register 9 into HOLDR9 because this address may be used after completion of HITA. Once general register 9 is stored, the logic loads general register 9 with a loop count value of 150 and the logic pattern of the second table lookup commences. If an equal condition is found on TABLE2 the program logic branches to HITB, which now wants to use the address of the table segment pointed to in TABLE1 by the address contained within HOLDR9. HOLDR9 is, therefore, loaded into general register 9 by Statement 014. Statement 015 then uses the address in register 10 (representing a segment in TABLE2) to move data into the table segment of TABLE1 pointed to by the address within general register 9. It is unnecessary to save the loop control value contained in general register 9 upon exit from the HITA routine because this value is reinstated each time that particular routine is entered.

Each unique problem program may have many of its own peculiar needs for using the Store instruction. The performance of this instruction is quite simple, but it may well be used to assist in creating compound, complex routines.

Store Multiple (STM)

The STM instruction is used to move the contents of two or more general registers into a corresponding number of contiguous fullword storage locations. The first and last registers to be stored are specified as the first two operands of the instruction statement; the last operand specifies the first fullword storage area of the set of fullwords into which the registers are to be stored. A Store Multiple instruction statement may be analyzed as:

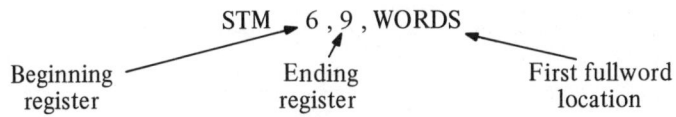

```
                      STM   6 , 9 , WORDS
      Beginning             Ending              First fullword
      register              register             location
```

Although the general registers are numbered from '0' through '15', it is not necessary that the Store Multiple ending register be of a higher value than the beginning register. The following examples indicate some of the different ways that a Store Multiple instruction might be reasonably expressed, in each instance using a similar set of fullword storage locations that are defined as:

SAVEWDS   DS   16F

Name	Operation	Operand	Seq
LOOKUPS	LA	9,TABLE1	001
LOOP1	CLC	0(3,9),KEY1	002
	BC	8,HITA	003
	AH	9,=H'10'	004
	BC	15,LOOP1	005
*			
HITA	ST	9,HOLDR9	006
	LA	9,150	007
	LA	10,TABLE2	008
LOOP2	CLC	0(3,10),KEY2	009
	BC	8,HITB	010
	AH	10,=H'10'	011
	BCT	9,LOOP2	012
	BC	15,NOHIT	013
*			
HITB	L	9,HOLDR9	014
	MVC	4(3,9),0(10)	015
	BC	15,GETOUT	016
*			
HOLDR9	DC	F'0'	017

FIGURE 9-2

Example 1

    STM   8 , 2 , SAVEWDS

This statement would store general registers 8, 9, 10, 11, 12, 13, 14, 15, 0, 1, and 2 into the first eleven fullwords (44 bytes) of SAVEWDS in the exact order shown.

Example 2

    STM   5 , 7 , SAVEWDS

This statement would store general registers 5, 6, and 7 into the first three fullwords of SAVEWDS.

Example 3

    STM   13 , 0 , SAVEWDS+8

This statement would store general register 13 ,14, 15, and 0 into the third, fourth, fifth, and sixth fullwords of SAVEWDS.

Example 4

    STM   9 , 8 , SAVEWDS

This statement would store all sixteen general registers into the whole of SAVEWDS. The first register to be stored would be general register 9, the second would be register 10, etc., until all sixteen general registers had been stored.

The "Load" and "Insert" Instructions

The Load and Insert instructions enable the programmer to insert (or load) data or values into general registers. The amount of data that may be placed into a general register by these instructions ranges from one to four bytes per register. In effect, the Load instructions are the reverse of the Store instructions—data residing within certain types of storage areas, absolute values, addresses, or the contents of other registers may be loaded into one or more general registers.

Insert Character (IC)

Although this particular instruction does not contain the term "load" within its title, it may be considered to be a Load instruction. It is, in effect, a means of extracting one byte of data from a storage location and placing it into the low-order byte of a general register. The insertion of this byte of data into the register does not alter the contents of the three high-order bytes of the register. The IC instruction may be used to alter an address contained within a register, to store or restore a portion of a register to a particular value, and similar other applications. Note the configuration of general register 6 and FIELDA in this illustration:

general register 6	0000	0000	0100	1100	0111	0000	1010	0111

FIELDA	0111	1111	0000	0000	0000	1010	0111	1000

The instruction statement and the resulting action are:

   IC   6, FIELDA

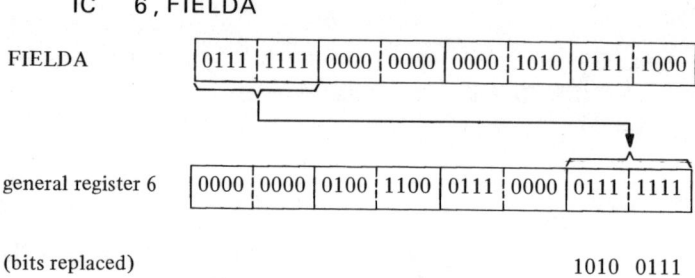

(bits replaced)

As shown, the instruction statement has caused the first byte of FIELDA to be inserted (or loaded) into the low-order byte of general register 6.

Insert Characters Under Mask (ICM) (System/370 Only)

The ICM instruction takes from one to four bytes of data from a storage location and places them into selected bytes within a general register. The placement of the bytes into the register is controlled by the mask operand (M_3) of the instruction statement. The mask operand comprises four bit positions, each representing a corresponding byte location within the general register specified as the first operand (R_1). A zero-bit in the mask indicates that the corresponding byte in the register is not to be altered; a one-bit in the mask specifies the corresponding location in the register to receive a byte of data from the storage location referenced by the second operand ($D_2(B_2)$).

The relationship of the mask bits to the register byte locations is demonstrated in these illustrations:

mask	register bytes selected for insertion of data			
1000	X			
1101	X	X		X
1001	X			X
1010	X		X	
0110		X	X	

Moving, Storing, and Loading Data

The bytes of data are extracted from the storage area (from left to right) and inserted into the selected byte positions of the register. Although the bytes of data are located contiguously within storage prior to their movement, their placement within the register is solely dependent upon the mask configuration, which may or may not represent contiguous bytes. Regardless of the implied length of the second operand storage location, the quantity of bytes inserted into the register is limited to the quantity of one-bits represented in the mask. The following examples illustrate the action taken by the ICM instruction.

Example 1

register 10 (before ICM)	F	F	F	F	3	0	6	D

STORFLD1			0	0	B	6	3	E

(instruction executed)   ICM   10 , B ' 1101 ' , STORFLD1

register 10 (after ICM)	0	0	B	6	3	0	3	E

Example 2

register 3 (before ICM)	0	0	5	C	2	6	A	C

STORFLD2			1	1	3	0	5	C

(instruction executed)   ICM   3 , B ' 0111 ' , STORFLD2

register 3 (after ICM)	0	0	1	1	3	0	5	C

Example 3

register 7 (before ICM)	0	1	1	1	F	1	C	3

STORFLD3							D	4

(instruction executed)   ICM   7 , B ' 0100 ' , STORFLD3

register 7 (after ICM)	0	1	D	4	F	1	C	3

As reflected by these examples, the non-selected byte positions in the register have not been affected. Although not shown here, the original source of the bytes inserted into the register, the storage area, remains unaltered from its configuration before the ICM instruction was executed.

Load Halfword (LH)

The Load Halfword instruction is used to insert the contents of two bytes of storage data, aligned on a halfword storage boundary, into a general register. The halfword value is first extracted from its storage location, expanded to a fullword configuration, and then placed into the general register specified by the first operand of the instruction statement. As in the use of the Insert Character instruction, this instruction is often used to reload a register with the value of a constant. This value may represent an address, a loop control count value, or any other practical application developed by the programmer.

By using the same values as shown in the example for the Insert Character instruction, this example demonstrates the resemblance, and the difference, of the two instructions:

```
       FIELDA      DS     F
*
                   LH     6,FIELDA
```

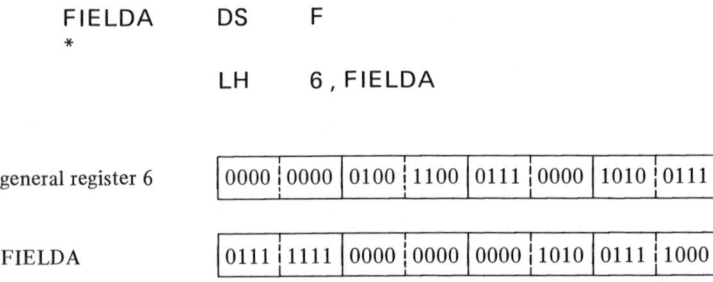

The halfword value contained within the first two bytes of FIELDA is first extracted and then expanded to a fullword by duplicating the sign-bit throughout 16 additional high-order bit positions.

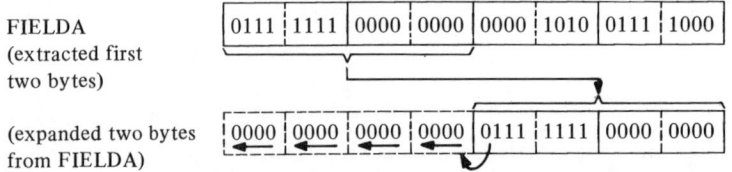

The new fullword configuration is then placed into the general register.

general register 6 | 0000 0000 | 0000 0000 | 0111 1111 | 0000 0000 |

Load (L)

The Load instruction is the reverse of the Store instruction. The four bytes of data (a fullword) addressed by the second operand of the instruction statement is loaded in its entirety into the general register specified by the first operand. The most commonly used application for this in-

Moving, Storing, and Loading Data

struction is to initialize a register or to reinstate a general register with an address or value which, at some previous point within the program, had been stored into a fullword until needed. The same values used in the examples for Insert Character and Load Halfword are also used to illustrate this instruction. Compare the action of the example provided here to the action taken by the Insert Character and Load Halfword instructions.

L   6, FIELDA

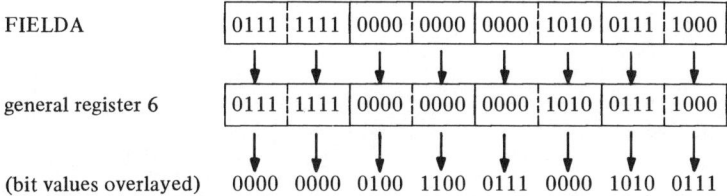

Load Register (LR)

The Load Register instruction merely takes the four-byte contents from one general register (specified by the second operand) and places that configuration into the general register specified by the first operand. The data being moved is not altered in any way. The general register from which the data has been moved still contains the original configuration. In a sense, this instruction and all similar move, load, insert and store instructions may be thought of as a duplication process. Although the data has been placed into another location, the original data configuration remains unchanged.

Suppose that general registers 4 and 8 contain the following bit configuration:

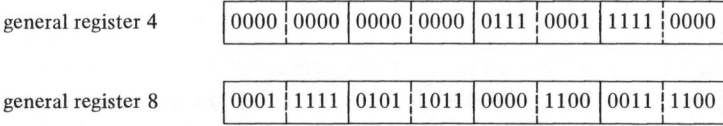

The instruction statement being executed, and the result of the Load Register instruction on those registers, are represented as:

LR   4, 8

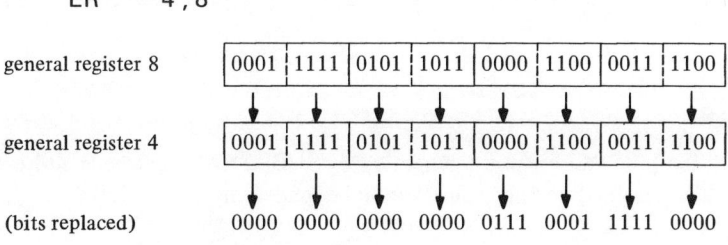

Load Multiple (LM)

The Load Multiple instruction is used to load two or more fullword values, located in a contiguous set of fullword storage locations, into a corresponding quantity of contiguous general registers. The quantity of fullwords loaded is determined by the quantity of registers indicated by the first two operands. The registers are expressed as a range, the first operand indicating the first general register to be loaded and the next operand indicating the last general register to be loaded. For example, a Load Multiple instruction statement might appear as:

```
LM    7,10,DATAFWDS
```

This statement would indicate that general registers 7, 8, 9, and 10 are to be loaded with the values contained in four fullwords beginning at a storage point addressed by the label DATAFWDS. This application is further illustrated in the following example:

```
FULLWD1     DS      F
FULLWD2     DS      F
FULLWD3     DS      F
FULLWD4     DS      F
FULLWD5     DS      F
FULLWD6     DS      F
*
ROUTINEA    LM      8,13,FULLWD1
```

After execution of this instruction statement, general register 8 would contain the value from FULLWD1, general register 9 would contain the value from FULLWD2, general register 10 would contain the value from FULLWD3, general register 11 would contain the value from FULLWD4, general register 12 would contain the value from FULLWD5, and general register 13 would contain the value from FULLWD6.

The use of this instruction permits the loading of multiple contiguous registers at one time by one instruction statement, if the data to be loaded is located in contiguous fullword storage locations.

Load Address (LA)

The Load Address instruction is used to load the address of a specified storage location or an actual value into a general register. The address to be loaded, as indicated by the second operand of the statement, may be represented by a symbolic label or an absolute value expressed in decimal form. It should be noted that the value of the second operand, whether it be a generated address or a stated value, is only loaded into the low-order three bytes of the general register. The high-order byte of the register is set to zero.

The following examples illustrate some of the ways in which this instruction might be expressed.

Example 1

```
LA    11,SUBRTE1
```

If, at program execution time, the address point generated by SUBRTE1 is at storage address 83,596 (or '1468C' in hexadecimals), then that value would be loaded into general register 11.

Register 11 would then be configured as:

address of SUBRTE1

register 11 *binary*	0000	0000	0000	0001	0100	0110	1000	1100
hex	0	0	0	1	4	6	8	C

Example 2

    LA   8 , 300

In this instance, the instruction would load a fixed-point value of +300 into general register 8. This is one way that a loop-control value, or any other type of specific value, may be loaded into a general register.

Example 3

    LA   4 , 2 (0 , 4)

In this example, general register 4 is loaded with a fixed-point value which is equivalent to the current value of general register 4 plus a decimal value of 2. If, in this instance, register 4 contains a value of +3386 prior to the execution of the instruction statement, subsequently it would contain a value of +3388. This may be expressed as:

Displacement + Index + Prior Register 4 equals New Register 4

or

2 + 0 + 3386 equals 3388

The Load Address instruction may, therefore, be readily used for incrementing (systematically "adding to") a general register value.

Load & Test Register (LTR)

The execution of this instruction loads the value of the second operand register into the first operand register, at the same time testing that value for a zero, negative, or positive condition. The action of setting the Condition Code bits of the PSW is the only difference between this instruction and the Load Register instruction. Once the Load & Test Register instruction has been executed, it would be expected that the program logic would encounter another statement to test the setting of the Condition Code, and indicate the action that should occur as a result of that comparison.

The general registers specified by the first and second operands may be different general registers; or a single register may be tested by loading it into itself, specifying the same general register as both operands of the instruction statement. Such a test would be coded as:

    LTR   6 , 6
    BC   8 , ZERORTE
    BC   4 , NEGRTE

In this set of instruction statements, general register 6 would first be loaded into itself and the Condition Code bits would be set according to the value then contained in that register. If the register value is zero, then the program logic would branch out to a routine labeled ZERORTE upon execution of the second instruction statement. If the value is not zero, but rather a negative value, the program logic would branch to a routine labeled NEGRTE when executing the third instruction statement. If neither of those conditions exist, implying that the value in register 6 is a nonzero positive value, the processing logic would fall through to the next sequential program instruction statement.

Load Complement Register (LCR)

The Load Complement Register instruction takes the fixed-point value of the second operand register, converts it to its complement form, and places that complement value into the general register specified by the first operand. If the fixed-point content of the second operand register is a negative value, it is converted to the true Powers-of-Two binary notation; if it is a positive value, it is converted to its complement negative form. This action is illustrated in the following examples.

Example 1

    LCR   4 , 6

General register 4 contains a fixed-point value of +79,327 and general register 6 contains a fixed-point value of +29,231. Initially, the binary configuration of these registers would appear as:

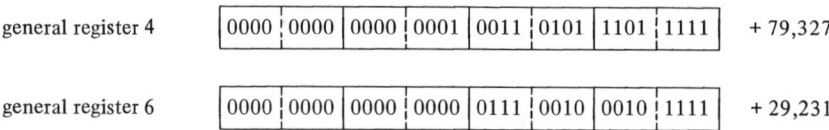

When the instruction statement is executed, the positive fixed-point value contained in general register 6 would be extracted and converted to its negative complement. This conversion can be assumed to be:

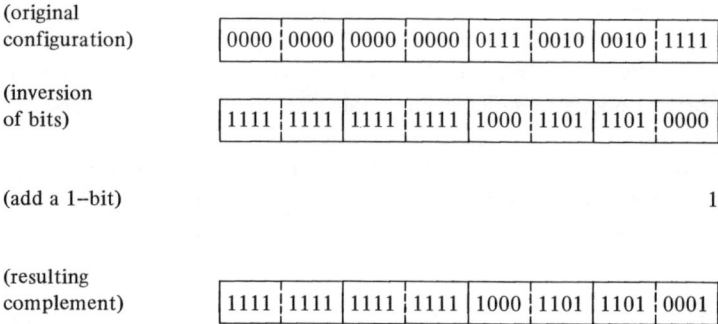

Moving, Storing, and Loading Data

The complement configuration of the value of general register 6 would then be placed into general register 4, after which register 4 would appear as:

general regsiter 4   − 29,231

Example 2

    LCR   9,9

General register 9 contains a fixed-point value of −165,288. The binary configuration of this register would be:

general register 9   − 165,288

The conversion of the contents of register 9 to the complement of the negative value, which is now to be loaded into register 9, may be assumed to be:

general register 9 | 1111 | 1111 | 1111 | 1101 | 0111 | 1010 | 0101 | 1000 |

(subtract a 1-bit)   1

(result) | 1111 | 1111 | 1111 | 1101 | 0111 | 1010 | 0101 | 0111 |

(inversion of bits) | 0000 | 0000 | 0000 | 0010 | 1000 | 0101 | 1010 | 1000 | + 165,288

The inverted bit configuration, representing +165,288, would be placed back into general register 9, overlaying the original configuration of −165,288 that resided there prior to the LCR instruction statement.

Load Positive Register (LPR)

The Load Positive Register instruction will take the fixed-point value contained within the general register specified by the second operand of the statement and place a positive representation of that value into the general register specified by the first operand. If the configuration of that value is negative, it is converted to the positive complement, in true Power-of-Two notation, before it is loaded into the receiving register. If the configuration of the value is already a positive representation prior to encountering the LPR instruction, it is placed unaltered into the receiving register.

A positive configuration of any value contained in a general register can be assured by specifying that register in both operands of a Load Positive Register instruction statement. The performance of this instruction under various conditions can be seen in these examples.

Example 1. In this example the value contained in the second operand register is already a positive configuration. Therefore, when it is loaded into the first operand register it will not be altered by the Load Positive Register instruction. The instruction statement to be executed is:

    LPR   6, 12

If general register 12 contains a value of +693,221, that value would be unaltered during the load into general register 6.

general register 12 (second operand)		0000	0000	0000	1010	1001	0011	1110	0101	+693,221
general register 6 (first operand)	binary	0000	0000	0000	1010	1001	0011	1110	0101	+693,221
	hex	0	0	0	A	9	3	E	5	

Example 2

    LPR   11, 8

This example indicates the conversion of a negative fixed-point value to a positive value during the execution of the LPR instruction. Assuming that general register 8 contains a negative fixed-point value of −219,883 at the time of execution of the instruction statement, the LPR instruction would effectively perform this action.

general register 8 (second operand)	1111	1111	1111	1100	1010	0101	0001	0101	−219,883
(subtract a 1-bit)								1	
(resulting bits)	1111	1111	1111	1100	1010	0101	0001	0100	
(invert all bits)	0000	0000	0000	0011	0101	1010	1110	1011	
(bit configuration now in register 11)	0000	0000	0000	0011	0101	1010	1110	1011	+219,883

Example 3. In this example, a single general register is used for both operands in an LPR instruction statement. This guarantees that the fixed-point value of that general register will have a positive-value configuration, regardless of its configuration prior to the execution of the LPR instruction statement.

    LPR   4, 4

Moving, Storing, and Loading Data

If register 4 originally contains a value of +36,984, it would now still contain that identical configuration. However, had general register 4 contained a value of -2,675,037, it would now contain the configuration for a fixed-point value of +2,675,037.

Load Negative Register (LNR)

This instruction performs the opposite function of the Load Positive Register instruction. The LNR instruction first extracts the fixed-point value configuration from the general register specified by the second operand and examines that value for its positive or negative condition. If the configuration is already a negative value, that same configuration is placed unaltered into the general register specified by the first operand. However, if the configuration of the second operand contents is of a positive value, the LNR instruction converts that value to its complement negative configuration before placing it into the first operand register. This action is demonstrated in the following examples.

Example 1

    LNR   8 , 8

Assuming that general register 8 contains a fixed-point value of +3,965,709 prior to the execution of this instruction statement, the subsequent action of the LNR instruction would be:

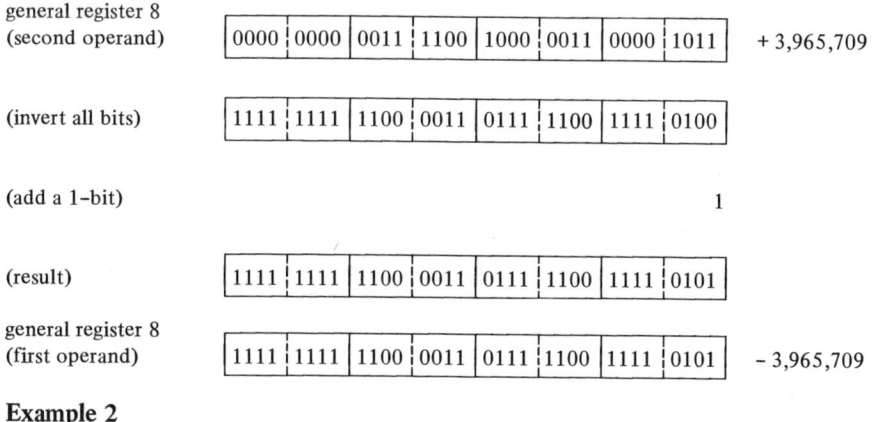

Example 2

    LNR   12 , 2

In this example, it is assumed that general register 2 contains a fixed-point value of -15,299. Since this value already consists of a negative configuration, that configuration is loaded unchanged into general register 12.

general register 2 (second operand)	1111 1111 1111 1111 1100 0100 0011 1101	- 15,299
general register 12 (first operand)	1111 1111 1111 1111 1100 0100 0011 1101	- 15,299

"Shifting" Operations

The terms "shift" and "shifting" describe the sidewise movement of data bits within one or more consecutive general registers. The movement is accomplished on the basis of the number of individual bit positions specified by the second operand of the shift instruction statement. While it is entirely possible to multiply or divide with some fixed-point values by the use of a shift instruction, this practice is generally ignored because the multiplier or divisor may only be a value that is equivalent to an increment of the Powers-of-Two scale—2, 4, 8, 16, 32, 64, 128, etc. The most common use of the shift instructions is to alter, relocate, or isolate certain bit position representations that are contained within one or more general registers. These applications are discussed further within the descriptions of the individual shift instructions. The illustrations of the concepts of shifting contain both the binary and hexadecimal configurations of the general registers.

"Logical" Shifting Operations and Instructions

The Assembler Language instructions for shifting which are defined as "logical" shifts affect all bit positions within all specified register(s) without regard for the sign-bit. Insofar as these instructions are concerned, all bit positions contain a logical configuration of either '0' or '1' and no particular bit position maintains any more significance than another. Therefore, when logical shifting is accomplished, a sign-bit is moved in accordance with the movement of the contents of the other bit positions.

Shift Left Logical (SLL). The Shift Left Logical instruction performs a logical shift within a single general register for a maximum length of 32 bit positions. The contents of the register specified by the first operand move to the left in a logical bit-by-bit manner for the number of bit positions specified by the second operand. The significance of the high-order sign-bit is ignored and it is shifted along with the other bits. As the bit configuration of the specified general register is moved to the left, vacated low-order bit positions are supplied with zero-bits. Bits shifted out of the high-order bit positions are lost as they are replaced by the bits being moved from the lower positions. The loss (shifting out) of a high-order significant-digit bit (a bit unlike the leftmost bit of the original configuration) does not activate a unique setting of the Condition Code within the PSW.

Example 1. This example indicates the ability to alter the configuration of a general register in which program interest is expressed as to the hexadecimal contents of that register. Consequently, assume that general register 7 currently contains a bit configuration representing the equivalent of hexadecimal 'FEDCBA21'. This configuration would appear as:

general register 7

binary	1111	1110	1101	1100	1011	1010	0010	0001
hex	F	E	D	C	B	A	2	1

The instruction statement that is to be executed is:

```
SLL    7,4
```

This statement instructs that the current bit configuration of general register 7 should be logically moved to the left by four bit positions.

Moving, Storing, and Loading Data 241

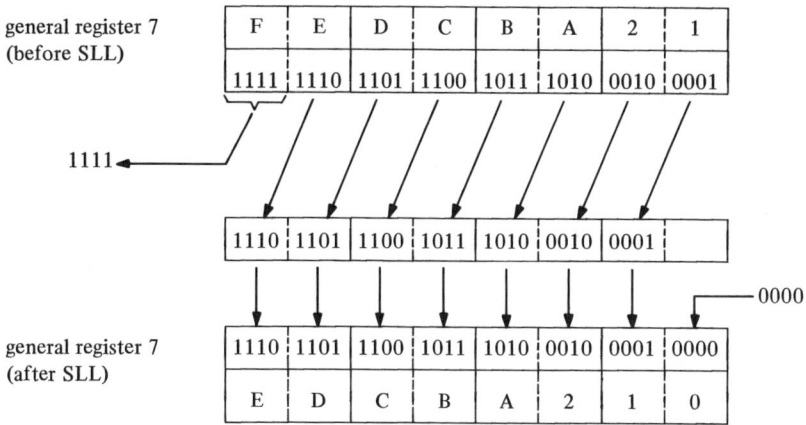

The four high-order bit positions, consisting of bits '1111' (Hex 'F'), have now been lost to general register 7, while the four low-order bit positions have been supplied with zero-bits, comprising a hexadecimal zero (Bits '0000'). The low-order 28 bits have all been moved to the left by four bit positions, so that they now represent the high-order 28 bit positions.

Example 2. In the previous example, the shift was used to move all bit values to the left by four bit positions, the same length as is required to move a single hexadecimal character. Accordingly, each hex digit was merely moved one position higher within the general register, the highest-order hex digit being lost and a new hex digit of zero being supplied to the low-order hex position in the register. This example will show the result of logically shifting the same original value by a number of bit positions that do not preserve the identity of the original hexadecimal digits. The original value of general register 7 will again be X'FEDCBA21'. The instruction statement being executed is:

SLL   7,5

This statement indicates that each bit in general register 7 is to be moved to the left until it occupies the bit position that is five positions higher than the one in which it originally resided. The bits of the five high-order bit positions are shifted out of the general register and lost; the five low-order bit positions vacated during the shift are supplied with zero-bits.

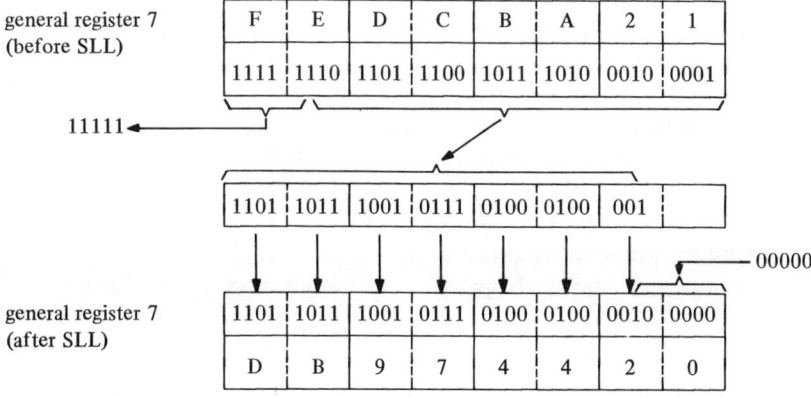

The resulting configuration now bears neither a whole nor a partial resemblance to the original hexadecimal configuration of general register 7. Even so, the programmer could conceivably have many valid reasons for a shift of this type.

Example 3. Although the SLL instruction might likely be used more often to shift character or hexadecimal data within a register, the shifting of fixed-point values may also be accomplished with it. This can be either poorly applied or a useful application because the logical shift does not regard the high-order sign-bit with any particular significance. This example indicates the problem that might be incurred in shifting a fixed-point value with a logical shift. The fixed-point value in general register 5 is +9,180,679, which would appear to be:

general register 5	0000 0000	1000 1100	0001 0110	0000 0111
	0 0	8 C	1 6	0 7

The programmer, wishing to multiply this value by +256, has coded the instruction statement as:

    SLL   5,8

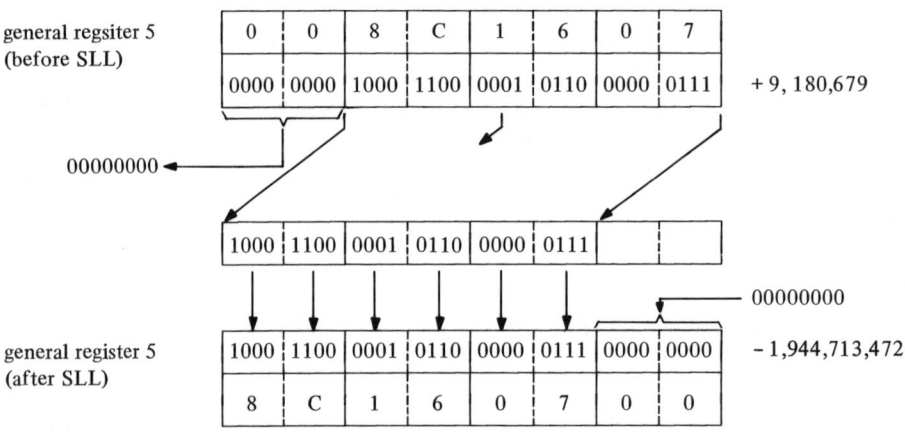

The logical result of the multiplication of +9,180,679 by +256 would be equal to a result of +2,350,253,824. Although no high-order significant-digit bits are shifted out of the register, the inadvertent use of the logical shift has resulted in a one-bit residing in the high-order bit position. This now indicates that the general register contains a negative fixed-point value, the low-order 31 bit positions forming the integer of that value. Instead of arriving at the desired result of +2,350,253,824 the SLL instruction statement has created a negative fixed-point value of −1,944,713,472 or a hexadecimal configuration of X'8C160700'. Because a logical shift, instead of an algebraic shift, was used to accomplish this task the programmer would receive no indication that the application has not performed as anticipated. Therefore, it must be noted that logical shifts should not be used for fixed-point arithmetic operations unless the results of such applications are closely verified.

Moving, Storing, and Loading Data

Shift Left Double Logical (SLDL). The SLDL instruction performs with the same principles as the SLL instruction except that two general registers are utilized. These two registers must consist of an *even-odd* pair of consecutive general registers such as 4 & 5, 8 & 9, 12 & 13, 2 & 3, etc. When using this instruction, or any other shift instruction that utilizes a two-register shift, the first operand of the instruction statement must specify the even-numbered register of the even-odd pair of general registers. A double register shift may be used to move a maximum of 64 bits. Data contained within the high-order byte(s) of a register may be isolated through the use of the SLDL instruction and then extracted into a storage area by use of a Store instruction statement.

Example 1. In this illustration, general register 7 contains data in its high-order byte that is to be isolated for separate use by the program logic. Assuming that general register 6 has been cleared to a +0 value and that general register 7 contains a hexadecimal configuration of 'C30000D3', the process of extracting the high-order byte could be coded with these statements.

```
SLDL    6,8
STC     6,HOLD
```

The first instruction would execute the SLDL instruction, resulting in this shifting of the bits.

general registers 6 & 7 (before SLDL)

0	0	0	0	0	0	0	0	C	3	0	0	0	0	D	3
0000 0000	0000 0000	0000 0000	0000 0000	0000 0000	0000 0000	0000 0000	0000 0000	1100 0011	0000 0000	0000 0000	0000 0000	0000 0000	1101 0011

0000 0000

| 0000 0000 | 0000 0000 | 0000 0000 | 0000 0000 | 0000 0000 | 0000 0000 | 1100 0011 | 0000 0000 | 0000 0000 | 0000 0000 | 1101 0011 | |

0000 0000

0000 0000	0000 0000	0000 0000	1100 0011	0000 0000	0000 0000	1101 0011	0000 0000
0 0	0 0	0 0	C 3	0 0	0 0	D 3	0 0

general registers 6 & 7 (after SLDL)

At this point, the high-order byte of general register 7 shifts into the low-order byte of general register 6. The second instruction statement, Store Character, places that byte into a one-byte area labeled HOLD where it may be manipulated or used as the program requires.

Example 2. For all practical purposes, any single byte or groups of bytes contained within a general register may be isolated for extraction through the use of the shift instructions. This example shows how the middle two bytes of a general register can be isolated by the SLDL instruction and then extracted by the Store Halfword instruction.

```
SLDL    10 , 24
STH     10 , HAFWRD
```

Assume that general register 10 originally contained a hexadecimal configuration of X'003 FC1D2' and general register 11 contained a configuration of X'F0F1F2F3'. The SLDL instruction statement would act on these values in this manner:

general registers 10 & 11 (before SLDL)

0	0	3	F	C	1	D	2	F	0	F	1	F	2	F	3
0000	0000	0011	1111	1100	0001	1101	0010	1111	0000	1111	0001	1111	0010	1111	0011

000000000011111111000001

| 1101 | 0010 | 1111 | 0000 | 1111 | 0001 | 1111 | 0010 | 1111 | 0011 | | | | | | |

000000000000000000000000

| 1101 | 0010 | 1111 | 0000 | 1111 | 0001 | 1111 | 0010 | 1111 | 0011 | 0000 | 0000 | 0000 | 0000 | 0000 | 0000 |
| D | 2 | F | 0 | F | 1 | F | 2 | F | 3 | 0 | 0 | 0 | 0 | 0 | 0 |

general registers 10 & 11 (after SLDL)

The middle two bytes of general register 11, containing hexadecimal digits 'F1F2', have now been shifted into the low-order two bytes of general register 10. The Store Halfword instruction statement now takes those two bytes and places them in a halfword storage location labeled HAFWRD.

Shift Right Logical (SRL). The SRL instruction performs a logical shift of bits within a general register for a maximum length of 32 bit positions. The bit configuration of the general register specified by the first operand is moved to the right in a logical bit-by-bit manner for the number of bit positions specified by the second operand. As in the case of all logical shifts, the significance of the high-order sign-bit is ignored, and it is shifted along with the other data bits. As the bits of the specified register are moved to the right, vacated high-order bit positions are supplied with zero-bits. Bits shifted out of the low-order end of the general register are lost as they are replaced by the bits being moved in from the high-order bit positions. The Condition Code in the PSW will not reflect the loss (shifting-out) of a significant-digit bit. The SRL instruction has limited use as a "divide" instruction, being restricted to the capability of dividing by positive Powers-

Moving, Storing, and Loading Data

of-Two increment values only. When it is used in conjunction with an SLL instruction, it can be used to zero-out a low-order byte or bytes of a general register. Some of its applications are examined in these examples.

Example 1. This example shows how the combined application of the SRL and SLL instructions may be used to clear the right-most three bytes of a general register. This application may also be used to zero-out any number of bits or bytes up to the maximum length of a single register. In this instance, general register 9 contains a hexadecimal configuration of X'C1C2C3C4', representing the EBCDIC characters 'ABCD'. The coded instruction statements will reset the hexadecimal configuration of that register to X'C1000000'.

```
SRL    9 , 24
SLL    9 , 24
```

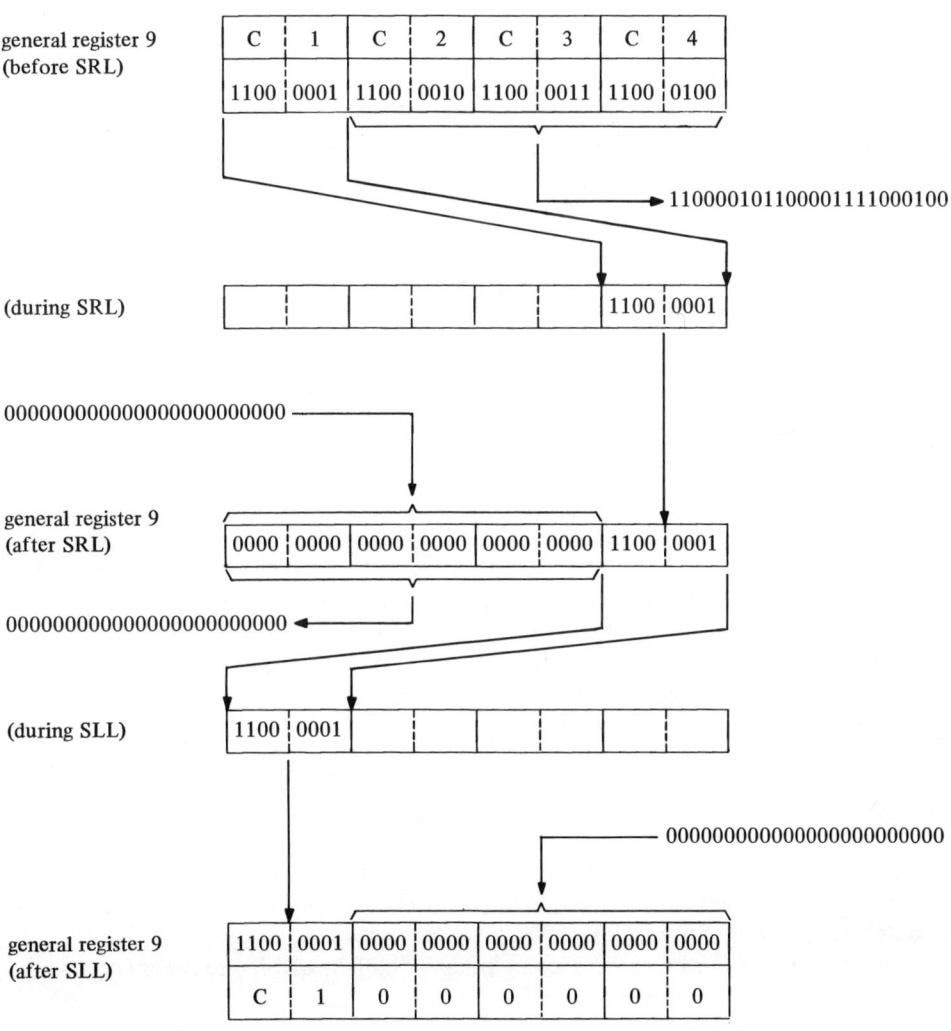

As shown here, the high-order byte of general register 9 (X 'C1') is shifted right until it occupies the low-order byte of that register. It is then reshifted left until it occupies its original position, the latter shift supplying zero-bits to the low-order 24 bit positions in lieu of the former configuration lost during the SRL instruction operation.

Example 2. A simple division by a value of eight is shown in this example, being possible only because that value is one of the increment values of the Powers-of-Two table. This application with a logical shift is also limited to a positive value, resulting from disregard of this instruction for the significance of the sign-bit. Additionally in a single register logical right shift only the quotient of the division is retained; the remainder is shifted out and is lost. Register 3, upon which the shift is being performed, contains a fixed-point value of +39,875. Since this value is to be divided by +8, the shift is for a length of three bit positions. This is determined by the fact that the third increment in the Powers-or-Two table of the value of bit positions has a value of 8—that is, 2, 4, 8, 16, 32, etc.

```
     SRL     3,3
```

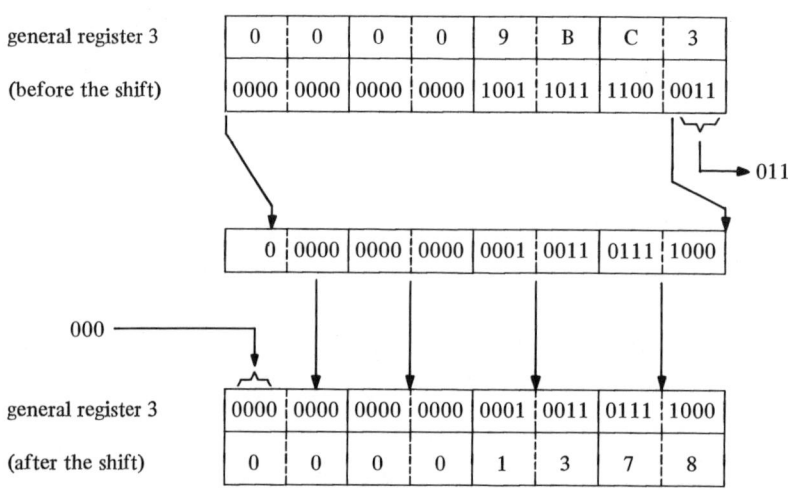

The shift results in general register 3 containing a hexadecimal configuration of significant digits of X'1378', which is equal to 4984—the quotient resulting from the division of +39,875 by +8. You will note that the three bits shifted out of the low-order positions of general register 3 comprise a Powers-of-Two value of +3; the same amount as would be the remainder in a true arithmetic division problem.

Shift Right Double Logical (SRDL). The principle difference between this instruction and the Shift Right Logical instruction is that the SRDL shifts the contents of two consecutive general registers. These two registers must consist of an even-odd pair of general registers. The shift is coded by addressing the even-numbered register as the first operand and by specifying the number of bit positions to be shifted as the second operand. The maximum length of a logical double register shift is 64 bit positions. As with the single register logical right shift, this instruction may be used under limited circumstances to accomplish an arithmetic division routine. The value to be divided must be a positive value and the value of the divisor can only be one of the increment values of the Powers-of-Two table. With this instruction, however, the shift places the remainder into the odd-numbered register and the quotient into the even-numbered register, conditional

Moving, Storing, and Loading Data

that the dividend originated in the even-numbered register. By combining the SRDL instruction in sequence with the other logical shift operations, a great number of variable tasks can be performed within a set of registers. Bytes of data, decimal values, hexadecimal digits and single bit values can be shifted, switched, or altered at will.

Example 1. If the programmer has a particular division to accomplish that meets the qualifications required by the SRDL instruction, this example demonstrates the proper means of aligning the remainder. General register 4 contains a fixed-point positive value of +277,169, which is to be divided by a value of +16. Upon completion of the division by shifting, the remainder must be aligned in general register 5. The instruction statements that have been coded to perform this operation are:

```
SRDL    4 , 4
SRL     5 , 28
```

The action generated by these statements would appear to be:

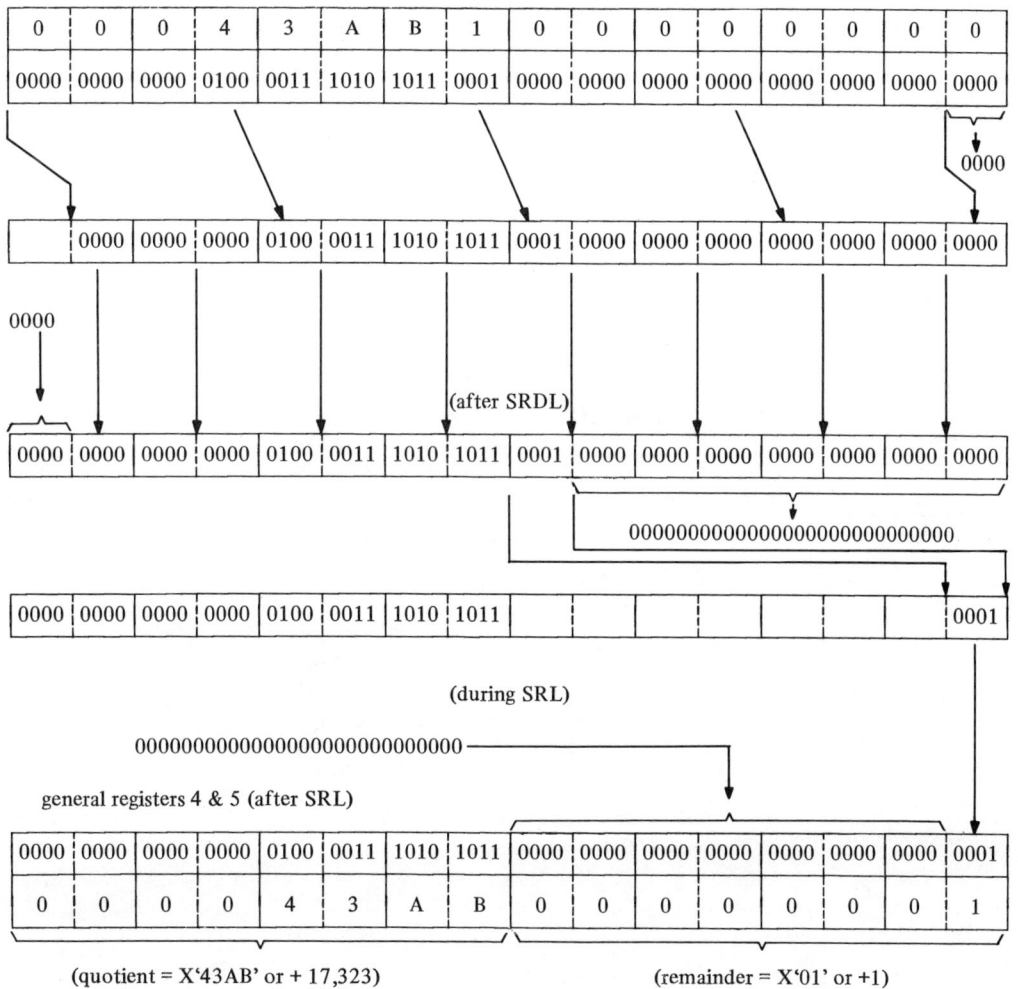

(quotient = X'43AB' or + 17,323)   (remainder = X'01' or +1)

The first instruction statement creates a logical right shift of all bits for a move of four bit positions in length. The four bits shifted out of general register 4 represent the remainder resulting from the divide operation. In order for these four bits to have a fixed-point value of their own, they must be right-aligned within register 5. The four bit positions occupied by the remainder are subtracted from the total number of bit positions contained within a general register (32), the resulting difference of 28 being the number of positions that the remainder must be shifted. The second instruction statement performs the single register logical right shift for a move length of 28 bit positions and the remainder has assumed its own identity as a fixed-point value of +1.

Example 2. This example is presented only for the purpose of indicating the versatility of the combined use of various shift instructions. It is not suggested for any specific application, although it may well have a unique use in some programmers' logic for a problem program. In this instance, the pair of general registers (6 and 7) contains X'D1D2D3D4' and X'C5C6C7C8'. The task to be performed is to move the low-order two bytes (X'D3D4') from general register 6, using them to replace the middle two bytes (X'C6C7') of general register 7. The first and last bytes of register 7 should be cleared to X'00' configuration and the low-order two bytes of general register 6 should be cleared to X'0000'. Although this same task could be performed with the various Store, Load and Move instructions, the means of doing it with Shift instructions only would be:

```
    SRDL    6 , 16
    SLL     6 , 16
    SRL     7 , 16
    SLL     7 , 8
```

See general register 6 and 7 (before SRDL).

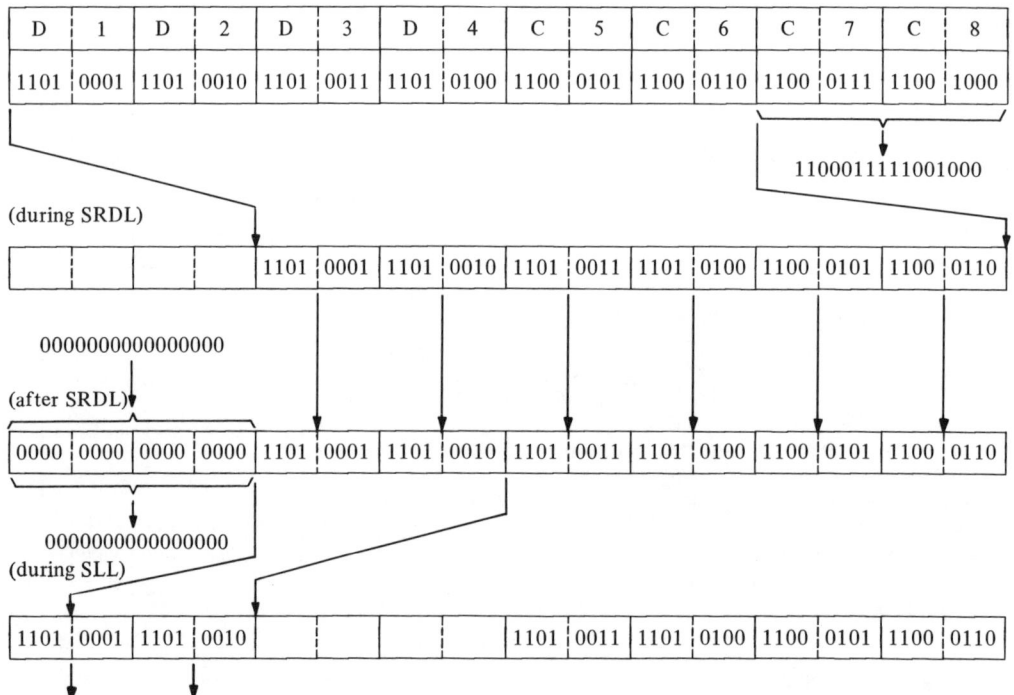

Moving, Storing, and Loading Data

[Figure: Illustration of SLL and SRL shift operations on a 16-byte register, showing bit patterns after SLL, during SRL 7,16, after SRL, during SLL 7,8, and after SLL, resulting in the final pattern: D1 D2 0 0 0 0 0 0 D3 D4 0 0]

The specifications of the task have now been met through the sole use of logical shifting operations.

"Algebraic" Shifting Operations

While the logical shift instructions consider all bit positions as part of the shift operation, the algebraic shift instructions always consider the left-most (high-order) single bit position as being an unmovable sign-bit. The supplying of bit values to vacated high-order or low-order bit positions differ between the logical and the algebraic shift as shown in this illustration.

logical shifts

algebraic shifts

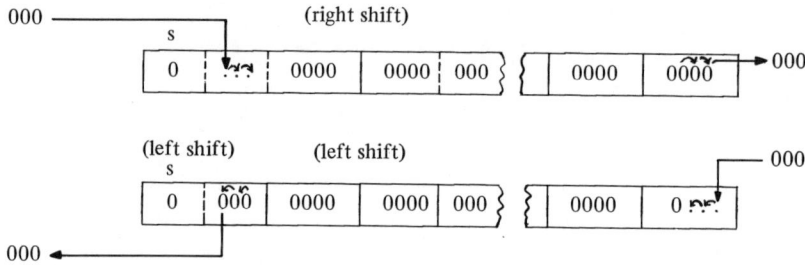

Algebraic shift operations maintain the fixed-point configuration of a general register, regardless of its positive or negative value. This is accomplished by separate functions in the algebraic left shift and the algebraic right shift. In the performance of the algebraic right shift, all bits supplied to the vacated high-order bit positions are of the same value as the sign-bit:

(six bits supplied to a positive value)

(six bits supplied to a negative value)

As shown here, the value of the bits supplied to the vacated high-order bit positions are of the same value as the sign-bit.

In the performance of the algebraic left shift, the continuity of the fixed-point value is preserved by "dropping out" the bit values just prior to the sign-bit. At this point, the left algebraic shifts perform another unique function. If a bit-value unlike the value of the sign-bit is shifted out of the high-order end of the integer bits, a fixed-point overflow exception is signaled and a program interrupt occurs. The bit value that is unlike the sign-bit value is considered to be a significant-digit bit; for a positive value, a one-bit is a significant-digit bit; for a negative value, a zero-bit is a significant-digit bit. The conditions wherein a significant-digit bit being shifted out would cause a program interrupt are:

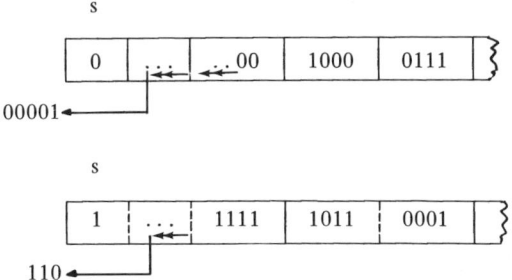

As soon as a significant-digit bit (a bit unlike the sign-bit) is shifted out of the high-order of the integer field, the fixed-point overflow exception occurs. Based on the foregoing information, it is now evident that algebraic shift operations are primarily intended for applications involving fixed-point arithmetic operations and functions.

Shift Left Algebraic (SLA). The SLA instruction shifts all 31 integer-bits contained within the general register specified by the first operand by the number of positions specified by the second operand. For applications with this shift, and all other algebraic shifts, the integer-bits are construed to be all bit positions other than the single high-order bit position. In a regular 32-bit general register, the left-most bit position is understood to be the sign-bit while the remaining 31 bit positions compose the integer value. In a double register algebraic shift operation, consisting of a total of 64 bit positions, the left-most bit position of the combined length of both registers is considered to be the sign-bit and the remaining 63 bit positions contain the bits to be shifted.

As the Shift Left Algebraic instruction is executing, bits are shifted to the left for the specified number of positions. Bits being shifted out of the high-order end of the integer portion of the register are dropped out of the bit position next to the sign-bit. The sign-bit is not shifted or altered. As low-order bit positions are vacated by bits being shifted to the left, the vacated positions are supplied with zero bits. In the event that a significant-digit bit is shifted out of the highest-order integer-bit position, a fixed-point overflow exception occurs. The algebraic shift left may be used for multiplication operations with the limiting factor that the value of the desired multiplier may only be one of the increments of the Powers-of-Two table—2, 4, 8, 16, 32, 128, 256, etc.—and that the multiplicand must be a positive value. If the multiplication operation performed by shifting should happen to result in a product that is too large to be contained within a 31-bit integer, a significant-digit bit is shifted out, resulting in the fixed-point overflow condition. The performance of the SLA instruction is illustrated in the examples shown on the following pages.

Example 1. For this example, general register 3 contains a fixed-point value of +379,518. By using the SLA instruction, the programmer intends to multiply that value by +32. In order to do so, the coding must indicate an algebraic left shift for the length of five bit positions.

    SLA   2,5

The execution of this instruction statement would perform as follows:

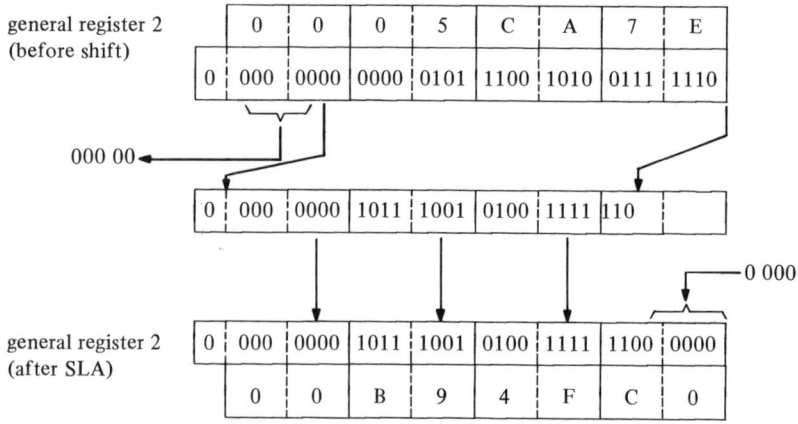

The product resulting from this shift of general register 2 indicates that:

32 times 379,518 equals 12,144,576.

The number of bit positions to be shifted was determined by the fact that the fifth increment of the Powers-of-Two table is a value of 32—2, 4, 8, 16, 32. Hence the shift was indicated to be effective for a move length of five bit positions.

Example 2. In this example, the programmer wishes to find the length of any one of a series of flexible tables contained within the program. There are twelve tables, each composed of four-byte segments. Although each table has a maximum allocated length of 2048 bytes reserved for it (or a maximum of 512 segments), the program logic intends only to use as much of the table as has been loaded with data at program execution time. The amount of data stored into each table has been counted, by segments, and the programmer desires to use shifting to determine the byte length of usable data within each table. Because the length of each segment is four bytes, the proper answer may be obtained by coding this instruction statement:

    SLA   8,2

This instruction statement implies that general register 8 contains the number of valid data segments in any given table and will effectively multiply that number of segments by a value of +4, the length of each segment, in order to arrive at the overall byte length of the valid data seg-

Moving, Storing, and Loading Data

ments portion of the table. If, in this example, the table segment count in general register 8 is +317, the SLA instruction statement would result in this type of performance:

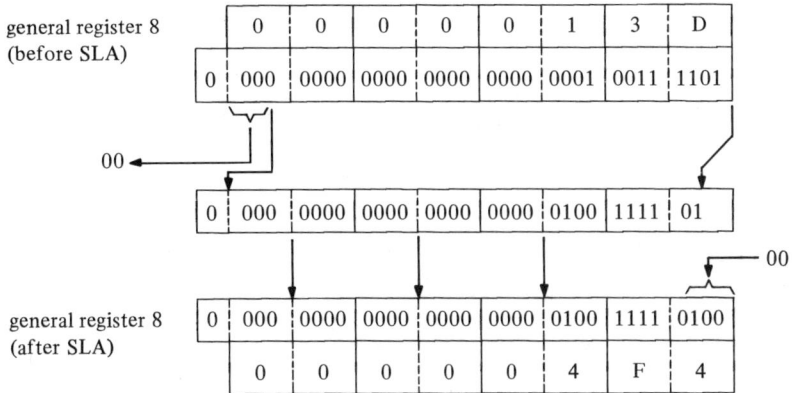

The SLA instruction functioned as a multiplication routine—general register 8 now contains a fixed-point value of +1268, the total length of the valid data segments in that particular table.

Shift Left Double Algebraic (SLDA). The SLDA instruction, another double register shift, considers the combined length of two general registers as consisting of a single high-order sign-bit and 63 integer bits. As in the case of other double register shifts, the set of general registers must be an even-odd consecutive pair and the shift instruction statement must address the even-numbered register as the first operand. The length of the shift of the 63 integer-bits is specified by the second operand of the instruction statement. Bits shifted out of the high-order of the even-numbered register are dropped immediately prior to the sign-bit position, each bit being inspected as it is dropped. If a significant-digit bit is shifted out, the fixed-point overflow exception occurs. Bits shifted out of the odd-numbered register, including its assumed sign-bit, are shifted along into the even-numbered register without inspection. If the fixed-point value in the odd-numbered register is a negative value, the high-order one-bit sign-bit of that register would be shifted into the even-numbered register where it would represent the Powers-of-Two value of its new position. Low-order bit positions vacated as a result of the shift are supplied with zero-bits, regardless of the positive or negative configuration contained within either register.

Using the values of +321,516 and -6810 as the contents of general registers 2 and 3, the bit configuration of these registers would be:

general registers 2 and 3

0	0	0	4	E	7	E	C	F	F	F	F	E	5	6	6
0 000	0000	0000	0100	1110	0111	1110	1100	1 111	1111	1111	1111	1110	0101	0110	0110

If each of these general registers were interpreted individually as containing fixed-point values, the high-order bit position in each would be considered to be the sign-bit. However, if these registers were used in conjunction with an SLDA instruction, only the left-most bit position of the combined registers (the high-order bit of register 2) would be considered to be the sign-bit. An instruction statement such as:

SLDA 2,4

would then shift the entire 63 integer bits in this manner:

general registers 2 and 3 (before SLDA statement)

general registers 2 and 3 (after SLDA statement)

This shift results in the moving of the four high-order one-bits from general register 3 into the four low-order bit positions of general register 2. Register 2 now contains a hexadecimal configuration of X'004E7ECF' that is a fixed-point value of +5,144,271; register 3 contains X'FFFE5660', the fixed-point value of –108,975.

Shift Right Algebraic (SRA). The Shift Right Algebraic instruction shifts the 31 integer-bits of the value contained in a general register. The bits are shifted right toward the low-order positions of that general register, for the length specified by the second operand of the instruction statement. As with other algebraic shift instructions, the high-order sign-bit is not disturbed by the shift of the integer-bits. Bits shifted out of the low-order positions of the register are lost without inspection for significant-digit bits. As high-order integer-bit positions are vacated, bits of the same value as the sign-bit are supplied to the vacated positions:

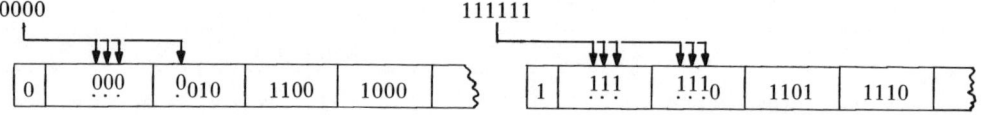

In order to illustrate this action more thoroughly, two examples are presented, one representing the SRA shift of a positive value and the other representing the SRA shift of a negative value.

Moving, Storing, and Loading Data

Example 1. General register 9 contains a fixed-point value of –811,574 that is to be shifted to the right algebraically for a length of six bit positions. The instruction statement that should be coded, and the resulting action, are:

SRA   9,6

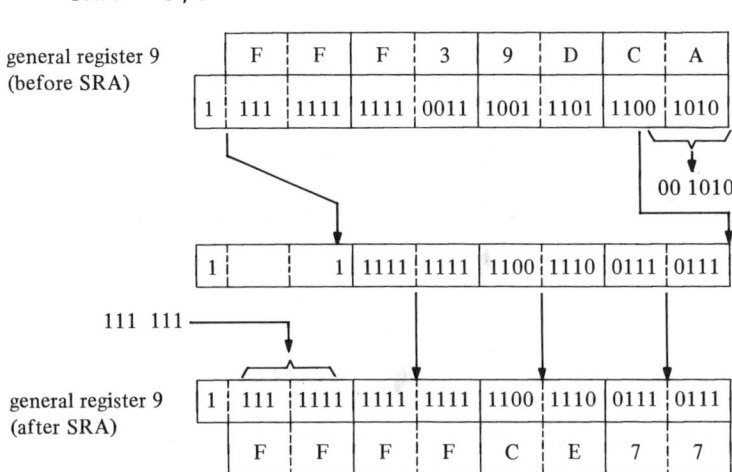

As indicated, the shift causes the shifting-out of significant-digit bits from the low-order positions of the register without signaling this event. The bits supplied to the vacated high-order integer-bit positions are one-bits—the same as the sign-bit of the original negative value occupying that general register.

Example 2. For this example, general register 10 contains a fixed-point value of +14,893,275. This shift is to be for a length of 12 bit positions. The coding and the representative action resulting from the execution of the instruction statement would be:

SRA   10,12

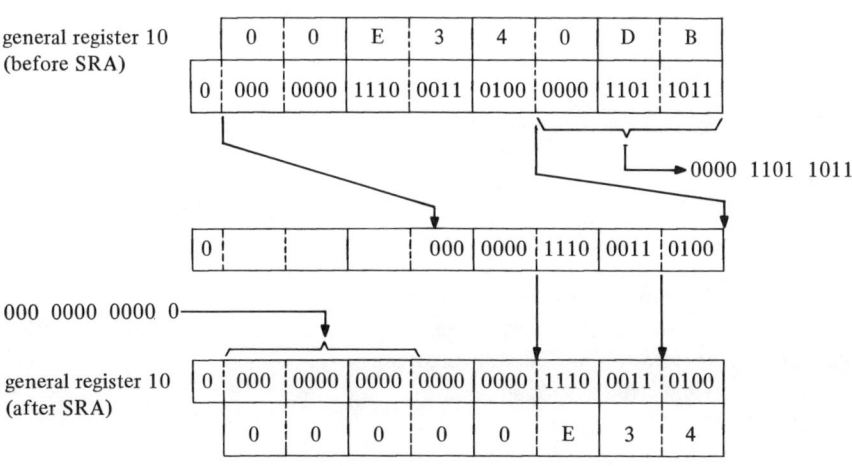

This example in effect divides the original value, as contained in general register 10, by a divisor of 4096. The result contained within register 10 (+3636) represents the unrounded quotient resulting from that divide. The remainder portion of the answer was lost when the low-order integer-bits shifted out. The value of the divisor is determined by the number of bit positions shifted—a shift of 12 positions representing the twelfth increment in the Powers-of-Two table—2, 4, 8, 16, 32, 64, 128, 256, 512, 1024, 2048, 4096.

Shift Right Double Algebraic (SRDA). The SRDA instruction follows the rules of the SRA instruction, except that it performs the shift on an even-odd pair of general registers. Consequently, the maximum shift length of this instruction is the total length of the assumed integer—63 bits. As in all double register shifts, the assumed sign-bit of the odd-numbered register has no significance as a sign-bit. It is considered to be a portion of the overall integer and is shifted along with the other integer-bits. The left-most bit of the combined registers is construed to be the sign-bit for the entire integer and as such it is not moved or altered by this instruction. All bits shifted out of the low-order positions of the odd-numbered register, regardless of their significance, are considered to be lost. Bits supplied to the vacated high-order bit positions of the integer are of the same configuration as the sign-bit—zero-bits for positive values, one-bits for negative values. A positive fixed-point value contained within an even-numbered register can be shifted in its entirety into the consecutive odd-numbered register, at the same time effectively setting the even-numbered register to +0. Using a fixed-point value of +16,295,799 as the contents of general register 4, the proper instruction statement and its execution might appear as:

```
SRDA      4 , 32
```

general registers 4 and 5 (before shift)

general registers 4 and 5 (after SRDA shift)

The configuration that originally existed in general register 4 has now been effectively transferred to general register 5, with register 4 being cleared for future use by the same instruction statement. If this same result were accomplished through the use of the various Load instructions, it would require two complete instruction statements.

Moving, Storing, and Loading Data

A simple "divide" process of positive values, in which the divisor is one of the increments of the Powers-of-Two table, can also be accomplished by using the SRDA instruction. The dividend is shifted to the right and the remainder resides in the right-most (the odd-numbered) register after completion of the shift. A logical right shift is then performed on the odd-numbered register for a length that will move the low-order bit of the remainder into the low-order bit position of that register. In processing such a division routine, wherein the value of +93,268 is to be divided by +8, the statement coding would appear as:

```
SRDA    10 , 3
SRL     11 , 29
```

Although it would make no difference as to the contents of general register 11 at the time these statements are executed, assume that it contained a value of +10. The action of this statement on the contents of the general registers would appear to be:

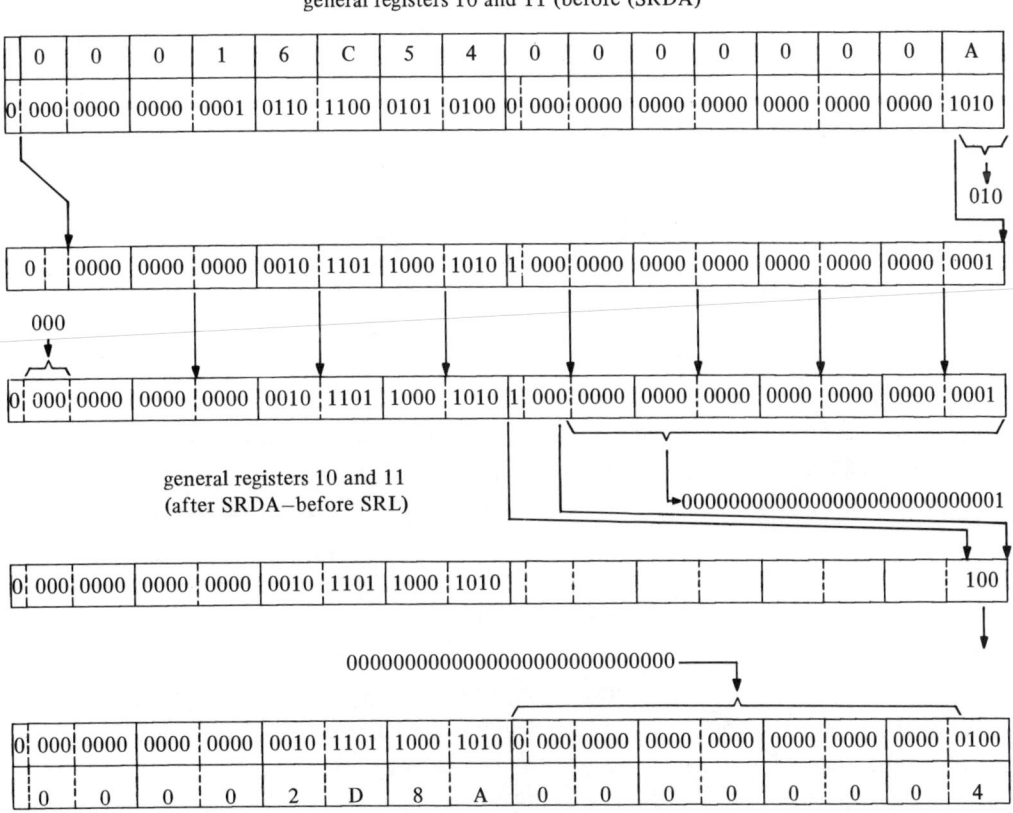

general registers 10 and 11 (after SRL)

The SRDA instruction statement effected the division of "93,268 divided by 8 equals 11,658," with the three bits that are shifted into the high-order of general register 11 comprising the remainder. The SRL instruction statement aligns those three bits into the low-order positions of general register 11, therein creating a valid fixed-point value for representing the division remainder of +4.

Throughout the explanations of the performance of the shift instructions and the applicable examples, comments have basically related to the alteration of character or hexadecimal data representation and fixed-point value manipulation. This relationship has been stressed only for the purpose of clarifying the manner in which these instructions perform, and in no way implies a limitation of their use to this type of function. The various bit positions within one or two general registers can be cleared to zero-bits, set to one-bits or switched around in many different patterns through the combined use of the logical and algebraic left and right shift instruction. "Bit Switches" contained within a register format could easily be cleared to an "off" condition or to an "on" setting by utilizing shifting instructions. Such applications cannot totally be anticipated; more often, the use of a shift will be found to lend itself to a unique or peculiar task that otherwise might require multiple instruction statements. Depending on the conditions leading up to the placement of the value in the registers, and the eventual disposition of the resulting values, it is probable that any of the arithmetic operations performed in the examples within this section could have been accomplished more efficiently with the arithmetic operations instructions that are provided for this purpose.

REVIEW EXERCISES

The "Move" Instructions

1. The three format types of "move" instructions are the SS format, the _____ format, and the _____ format.
2. The Move Numeric instruction moves only the right _____ bits of each byte of the sending field to each byte of the receiving field.
3. The only instruction capable of moving more than 256 bytes in a single statement is the _____.
4. The _____ instruction moves one byte of immediate data, as specified by the second operand of the instruction statement, into the single byte of storage that is addressed by the first operand.
5. The _____ instruction moves the contents of the left nibble of each byte of the storage area addressed by the second operand into the corresponding left nibble of each byte of the first operand storage address, for a maximum of 256 bytes.
6. The following instruction statement would cause a movement of data that is referred to as a "_____" move. After execution of this instruction statement, FIELD7 would consist of data bytes that were all identical to the _____ byte of that field.

```
SETLIKE    MVC    FIELD7+1 (17) , FIELD7
```

Moving, Storing, and Loading Data 259

7. The "padding" character contained in the second operand of a MVCL instruction statement is used to pad out either of the fields addressed by the first or second operands, regardless of which is shorter. (True) (False)

8. If BYTEA contains a valid blank, X'40', and BYTEB contains X'F6', the following instruction statement should have a mnemonic op code of _____ in order for that statement to change the character configuration of BYTEA from a blank to an EBCDIC numeric character of zero.

    ALTERFLD   ———   BYTEA , BYTEB

9. The _____ instruction moves the right nibble of each byte of the storage area addressed by the second operand into the corresponding right nibble of each byte of the first operand storage area, for a length of up to 256 bytes.

10. When an explicit length attribute is not stated within an MVC (Move Characters) instruction statement the length of the move is determined by the implied length of the field addressed by the _____ operand.

11. The _____ instruction moves the storage bytes addressed by the second operand into the storage bytes addressed by the first operand, for the length implied or specified by the first operand but not exceeding 256 bytes.

12. If an MVN instruction statement is executed wherein the sending byte contains X'D7' and the receiving field byte originally contains X'F0', the receiving field byte will subsequently contain an EBCDIC numeric character of _____.

13. Data fields in excess of 256 bytes may be moved from one storage location to another by "_____" a series of MVC instruction statements.

14. In a MVCL instruction, the padding character resides in the high-order byte of the even-numbered register of the second operand. (True) (False)

15. In the following problems, one or more storage areas are defined in the sequence in which they reside in main storage. Examine the contents of the fields and the instruction statement and then fill in the configuration of the receiving field in the blank layout provided. Express the contents of this field in the same format as its original configuration—if it was in hex format before the move, express it as a hex format after the move, etc.

15a. FIELD1 | A | 3 | 9 |

FIELD2 | 5 | 6 |

FIELD3 | G | ɸ | ɸ | 9 | 6 |

MVC   FIELD3+1 (4) , FIELD1

FIELD3 | | | | | |

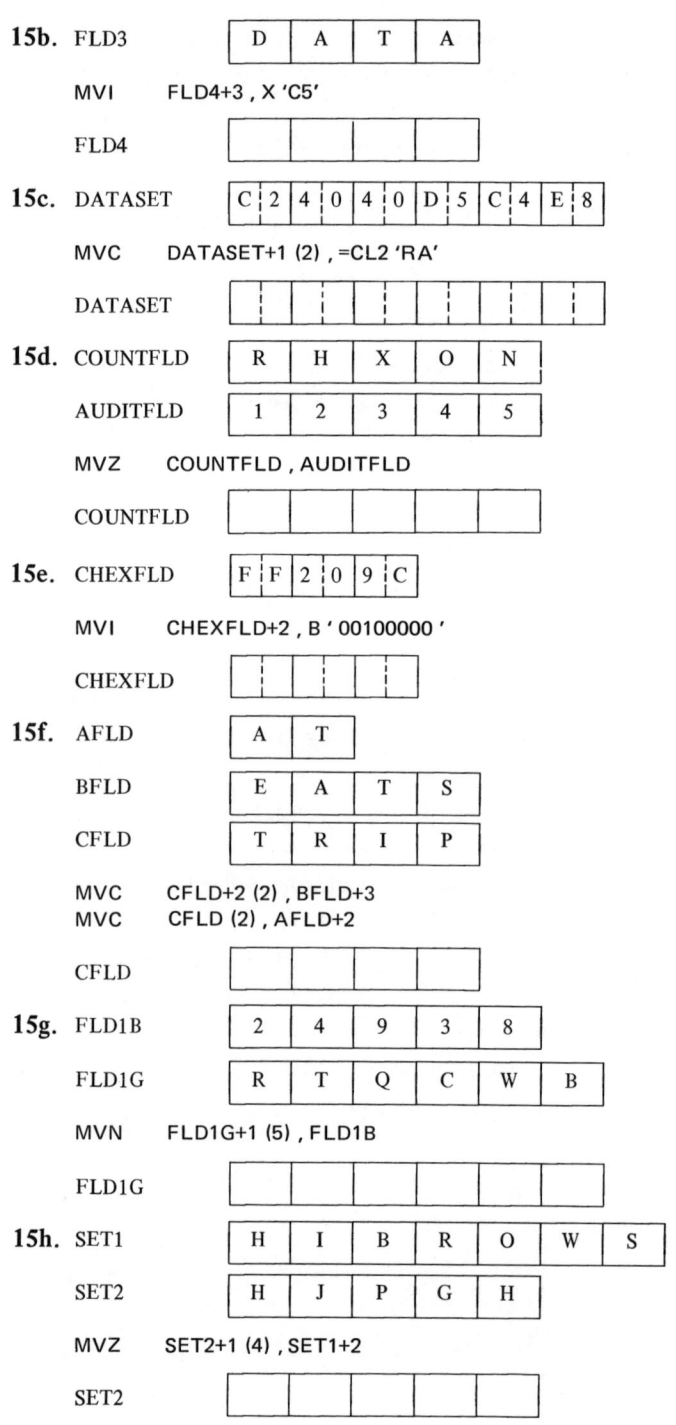

Moving, Storing, and Loading Data 261

15i. SETPAK | 0 | 0 | 0 | 0 |

    MVI   SETPAK , C ' ɓ '
    MVI   SETPAK+1 , B ' 01011100 '

    SETPAK | | | |

15j. INFIELD | D | A | T | A | 9 | 9 |

    MVI   INFIELD , C ' 9 '
    MVC   INFIELD+1 (3) , INFIELD

    INFIELD | | | | | | |

15k. DATAREV | G | L | A | R | E | D |

    MVC   DATAREV (2) , DATAREV+3

    DATAREV | | | | | | |

The "Store" Instructions

16. In the following instruction statement the low-order byte of the first operand register must contain a valid EBCDIC character. (True) (False)

    STC   6 , HOLDBYTE

17. The _____ instruction stores the low-order two bytes of the first operand register into the first two bytes of a halfword-aligned storage location.

18. The mask bits specified in the STCM instruction statement correspond to the high-order bits of the register specified as the first operand. (True) (False)

19. The _____ instruction stores a series of contiguous general registers into an equal quantity of contiguous fullword storage areas.

20. The _____ instruction stores the contents of the first operand register into the four bytes of the fullword-aligned storage area of the second operand.

21. When a Store (ST) instruction statement is executed, only the low-order three bytes of the first operand register are stored into the second operand fullword. (True) (False)

22. The _____ instruction stores the contents of the low-order byte of the first operand register into the single storage byte addressed by the second operand of the instruction statement.

23. If a Store Halfword instruction statement is coded within which the second operand defines a fullword of storage, the low-order _____ bytes of the first operand register will be stored into the _____ two bytes of the fullword.

24. Up to (1) (2) (3) (4)   (bits) (bytes) (nibbles) can be selected from a general register by the STCM instruction.

25. There would be a total of _____ general registers stored into a like number of fullwords by this instruction statement:

    STM   12 , 4 , FULLWDS

26. In the following set of instruction statements, the statement labeled MODFY would alter the statement labeled MVCHAR so that when MVCHAR is executed it would move a total of _____ bytes. (Register 12 contains a hexadecimal configuration of X '00000009'.)

    MODFY   STC   12 , MVCHAR+1
    MVCHAR   MVC   FIELDREC (5) , FIELDSND

27. If general register 10 contains a fixed-point value of –319,771, then the fullword labeled POSTVFWD will contain a fixed-point value of _____ after execution of this instruction statement:

    STOREPOS   ST   10 , POSTVFWD

28. The quantity of bytes stored by the STCM instruction are determined by the quantity of _____ _____ in the M_3 operand.

29. The following instruction statement would store the contents of the specified general registers into a total of _____ contiguous bytes of storage beginning at the point addressed by the label SETWORDS, if that address is on a fullword boundary of storage.

    DATASET   STM   15 , 0 , SETWORDS

30. The following problems define one or more general registers and storage areas. Examine the contents of the specified operands and then fill in the configuration of the receiving field in the blank field layout provided. Express the contents of this field in the same format as originally defined—if it is in hex format before the "store" instruction statement, express it in hex format after it has been stored.

Moving, Storing, and Loading Data 263

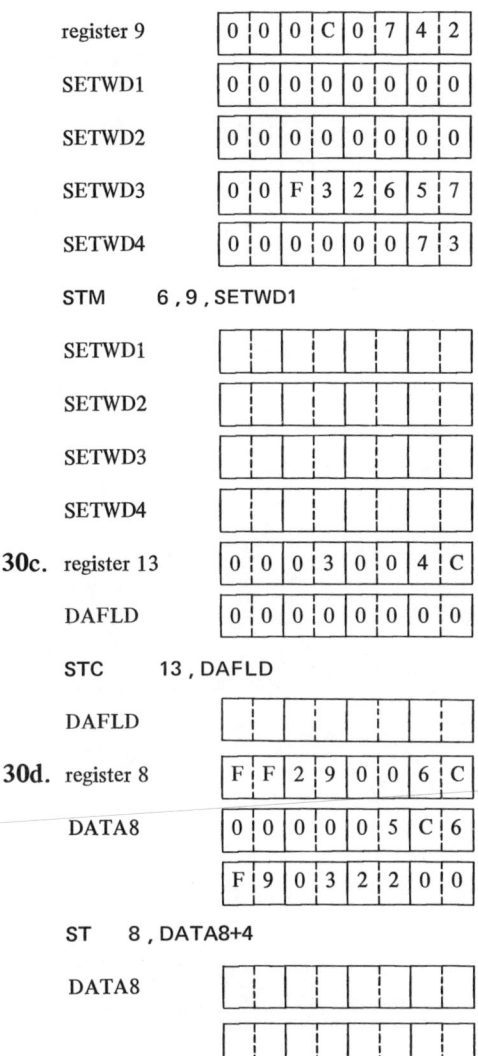

ST   8 , DATA8+4

DATA8

The "Load" and "Insert" Instructions

31. The _____ instruction loads two bytes of storage data, as aligned on a halfword boundary, into a general register in the form of a fullword. The two bytes of data are expanded to a fullword by propagation of the sign-bit throughout sixteen additional high-order bit positions.

32. The data bytes selected from the storage area specified by the second operand of an ICM instruction statement will directly correspond to the unique positions of the one-bits in the mask operand. (True) (False)

33. The _____ instruction takes the address generated by the second operand, either as an actual address or as one created by symbolic reference, and loads it into the low-order three bytes of the first operand register. The high-order byte of the receiving register is set to zero.
34. The _____ instruction loads the first operand register with a positive configuration of the value contained within the second operand register.
35. The instructions that are classified as "load" instructions can cause from _____ to _____ bytes of data to be placed into general registers.
36. One of the primary reasons for utilizing the LTR instruction is to test for the _____ or _____ configuration of a register.
37. The _____ instruction loads the first operand register with the contents of the full-word-aligned four bytes of storage data that are addressed by the second operand.
38. The _____ instruction takes the single storage byte addressed by the second operand and loads it into the low-order byte of the general register specified by the first operand.
39. The _____ instruction loads the first operand register with a negative (Two's Complement) configuration of the value contained within the second operand register.
40. The maximum positive fixed-point value that can be loaded into a register by the Load Half-word instruction is _____.
41. An entire register may be loaded with data from a storage area through the use of the ICM instruction. (True) (False)
42. The following instruction statement would load a total of _____ bytes of storage into the specified general registers.

    RELOAD   LM   9,0,REGAREAS
43. The _____ instruction loads the first operand register with the unaltered contents of the second operand register.
44. The _____ instruction loads the value contained within the second operand register into the first operand register and then sets the condition code to indicate the negative, positive, or zero condition of that value.
45. After execution of the following instruction statement, the high-order byte of register 12 would contain a hexadecimal configuration of X'_____'.

    LOADADDR   LA   12,FIELDB+255
46. Register 8 originally contains a hexadecimal configuration of X'712400FF'. After execution of the following instruction statement register 8 will contain X'_____'.

    LPR   8,8
47. The _____ instruction takes the fixed-point value contained within the second operand register, converts that value to its complement form, and then loads that complement value into the first operand register.

Moving, Storing, and Loading Data 265

48. The _____ instruction loads two or more contiguous fullwords of storage data, as addressed by the last operand, into the range of contiguous general registers specified by the first two operands.

49. Register bytes not selected by the mask bits of an ICM instruction statement will be (set to blanks)(unaltered)(set to X'0') _____ .

50. If a halfword of storage, containing the EBCDIC alpha characters "AB," were loaded into general register 8 via the Load Halfword instruction, the hexadecimal contents of register 8 would then be:

register 8 | | | | | | | |

51. After execution of the following instruction statement, register 3 contains a hexadecimal configuration of X'03040506'. Therefore, register 7 must contain a hexadecimal configuration of X '_____'.

    FLIPREG   LCR   3 , 7

52. If general register 9 contained a hexadecimal configuration of X'003D0E46' after execution of the following instruction statement, general register 10 would have contained a hexadecimal configuration of X '_____' before execution of the instruction statement.

    LTR   9 , 10

53. The following problems define one or more general registers and storage areas. Examine the contents of the specified operands and the instruction statements and then fill in the blank register layouts provided. Express the results in the same format as the register was originally defined—if it is in hex format before the "load" instruction, define and express it in hex format after it has been loaded, etc.

	register 6	F F F 2 0 5 9 F
	LNR 5,6	
	register 5	
53d.	register 3	F F F F 2 1 F 3
	LCR 3,3	
	register 3	
53e.	register 4	0 6 3 9 0 0 F F
	LTR 4,4	
	register 4	
53f.	register 6	0 0 0 6 0 F 9 7
	LNR 6,6	
	register 6	
53g.	register 8	0 0 0 0 C 0 C 0
	register 11	F 0 F F 0 C 0 C
	LR 8,11	
	register 8	
53h.	register 3	0 0 3 9 5 4 2 D
	register 4	F F 3 9 5 4 2 D
	LPR 3,4	
	register 3	
53i.	register 2	0 0 0 0 0 0 0 0
	DATAWD	0 0 0 6 5 1 F F
	L 2,DATAWD	
	register 2	
53j.	register 3	0 0 0 0 0 0 0 0
	register 4	0 0 0 0 0 0 0 0
	register 5	0 0 0 C F D 1 B

Moving, Storing, and Loading Data

FULLWD1

0	0	6	9	3	2	C	D
F	0	F	A	C	D	6	B
F	F	3	9	F	B	D	F
F	F	F	2	9	A	A	6

LM   3,5,FULLWD1+4

register 3

register 4

register 5

53k. register 12

0	0	C	8	0	0	0	0

FULLWD1

3	2	5	1	7	6	5	4

LH   12,FULLWD1+2

register 12

53l. register 12

F	F	3	9	0	6	2	7

register 2

0	0	0	0	7	F	F	D

LCR   12,12

register 12

The "Shift" Instructions

54. The _____ operand of all shift instructions defines the number of bit positions that are construed to be the length of the shift.
55. A bit shift to the left for a length of three positions is the same as multiplying the positive value being shifted by _____.
56. The _____ instruction shifts to the left all bits within a single general register without regard for the significance of the sign-bit.
57. In an algebraic right shift, bits supplied to vacated high-order bit positions are identical to the _____.
58. The _____ instruction shifts all integer-bits within a single register to the right for a maximum shift length of 31 bit positions.
59. In a double register algebraic shift all bits are shifted except the sign-bit of the _____-numbered general register.
60. The _____ instruction shifts all bits contained within two contiguous general registers to the left for a maximum of sixty-four bit positions.

61. In a double register shift the first operand of the instruction must address the _____-numbered register of the contiguous pair of general registers.
62. The _____ instruction shifts all bits to the right within a single register, supplying the vacated high-order bit positions with zero-bits.
63. In an algebraic left shift an overflow exception occurs whenever a bit _____ the sign-bit has been shifted out of the high-order integer-bit position.
64. The _____ instruction shifts the 63 integer-bits of a contiguous pair of general registers to the left for a maximum of 63 bit positions.
65. On a double register shift the sign-bit of the _____-numbered register is considered to be only another integer-bit.
66. The _____ instruction shifts to the right all of the 31 integer-bits contained within a single general register.
67. In all left-shift operations _____-bits are supplied to the vacated bit positions.
68. The _____ instruction shifts the entire 64 bits of a pair of contiguous registers to the right for a maximum of 64 bit positions, supplying the vacated high-order bit positions with _____-bits.
69. A shift to the right for a length of 5 bit positions results in a value that would be the same as a quotient resulting from the division of a positive value by a value of _____.
70. The _____ instruction shifts the 63 integer-bits of a pair of contiguous registers to the right for a maximum of _____ bit positions.
71. A double register logical shift to the right for a length of 32 bit positions results in the even-numbered register containing a value of _____.
72. The following problems define one or more general registers. Examine the contents of the specified operands, study the instruction statements and then express the results in both binary and hexadecimal format.

72a. register 5

1000	0000	1110	1111	1000	0111	0100	0011

    SRA   5 , 7

register 5 *binary*

hex

72b. registers 2 and 3

0000	0000	0011	0110	0011	1111	1110	0000	0000	1111	1111	1110	0101	1001	1000	0100

    SLDL   2 , 18

Moving, Storing, and Loading Data

registers 2 and 3 *in binary and hex*

72c. register 10 | 0000 | 1000 | 1110 | 0010 | 1011 | 1010 | 0111 | 1011 |

    SLL   10 , 32

    register 10 *binary*

                 hex

72d. register 9 | 1111 | 0100 | 1110 | 0101 | 1101 | 1011 | 1110 | 0111 |

    SRL   9 , 12

    register 9 *binary*

                 hex

72e. registers 6 and 7

| 1111 | 1000 | 0111 | 1011 | 1010 | 0000 | 1110 | 0101 | 0000 | 0000 | 0100 | 1101 | 1001 | 1111 | 0101 | 1011 |

    SLDA   6 , 4

    registers 6 and 7 *binary and hex*

72f. registers 10 and 11

| 1000 | 0000 | 0000 | 0000 | 0000 | 0000 | 1000 | 0001 | 0000 | 1111 | 1111 | 0101 | 1011 | 1101 | 0011 | 0000 |

    SRDA   10 , 31

registers 10 and 11 *binary and hex*

72g. register 2 | 0000 | 0000 | 1000 | 1100 | 0001 | 1101 | 0100 | 0010 |

    SLA   2,7

register 2 *binary*

hex

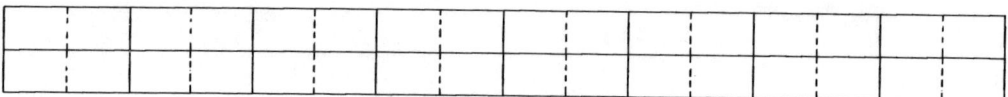

72h. registers 8 and 9

| 0010 | 1000 | 0000 | 1100 | 1111 | 1101 | 0001 | 1000 | 0111 | 1111 | 0000 | 0101 | 1111 | 1101 | 0001 | 1000 |

    SLL   9,16
    SRDL 8,16

registers 8 and 9 *binary and hex*

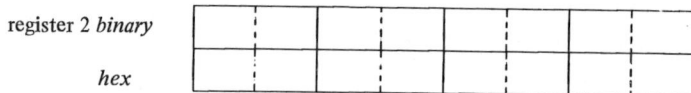

10

Packed Decimal Arithmetic Operations

THE PACKED DECIMAL ARITHMETIC INSTRUCTIONS

Instruction: Pack

mnemonic	hex code	operand format
PACK	F2	$D_1(L_1, B_1), D_2(L_2, B_2)$

The PACK instruction takes the stored data (assumed to be zoned decimals) specified by the second operand and converts it into packed decimal format in the storage address specified by the first operand. The converted data is supplied to the first operand storage area in half-bytes, moving from right to left. The first nibble (half-byte) supplied is the sign of the zone from the right-most (low-order) byte of the sending field (the second operand). This is placed in the low-order four bit positions of the receiving field, the first operand. The next nibble supplied to the receiving field is the numeric value of the same byte from which the sign-zone was taken, the right-most byte of the second operand. These two half-bytes have now reversed their position from the sending field and reside within the receiving field with the zone value in the right nibble and the numeric value in the left nibble of the low-order byte. The instruction at this point now transfers only the right nibble (numeric value) of each byte from the sending field; however, they are placed in the receiving field in contiguous half-byte positions. If the instruction statement should run out of sending field data before the receiving field is filled, it inserts hexadecimal zeros in the remaining high-order nibbles. If the first operand field is filled before the second operand field has run out of sending data, the remaining data to be sent is ignored. Since all data is not transmitted between the operands (only one zone-value nibble is moved), it is obvious that the first operand does not require a byte-length attribute equal to that of the second operand. The formula for computing the byte length of the field that is to contain the packed decimal format is:

> Length of second operand plus 1 divided by 2 equals required length for first operand, rounded high for any fractions.

This formula would apply as:

	example 1	example 2
Length of the second operand field	5	10
Add one byte for the sign-zone	1	1
Sum	6	11
Sum divided by 2	3	5½
Rounded high		6
Required length of first operand	3	6

The maximum explicit, or implied length for either operand is 16 bytes.
The Condition Code setting is not changed by this instruction.

*　　　　　　　　　*　　　　　　　　　*

Instruction: Unpack

mnemonic	hex code	operand format
UNPK	F3	$D_1(L_1, B_1), D_2(L_2, B_2)$

The UNPACK instruction takes the storage data specified by the second operand (in packed decimal format) and converts it into zoned decimal format within the storage address specified by the first operand. The data is moved from right to left of the sending field to the receiving field. The sign of the packed field (the low-order four bits) is placed into the left nibble of the low-order byte of the zoned decimal receiving field. The right-most numeric digit associated with the sign within the packed field is moved into the right-most four bit positions of the receiving field to complete the single low-order signed, zoned decimal. Thereafter, the instruction picks up each contiguous four-bit nibble, expands it to a full byte in zoned decimal format by applying a standard EBCDIC zone (hex digit 'F'), and places that byte into the first operand field, loading the field from right to left. If the area specified by the first operand is longer than the field or area specified by the second operand, the unfilled high-order bytes of the first operand area are supplied with zoned decimal values of zero. If the second operand is longer than the first operand area, the unused high-order digits of the second operand area are ignored. In the event that the packed field contains a sign in the low-order four bits, the formula for computing the byte length of the field to contain the expanded, unpacked data is as follows:

> Length of the second operand times 2 less 1 equals required length for the first operand.

This may be applied as:

	example 1	example 2
Length of the second operand area	3	5
Multiplied by 2	x2	x2
Product	6	10
Less 1 for the packed sign	-1	-1
Required length for the first operand area	5	9

If the field being unpacked is not signed in the low-order four bits, the calculation is "Packed field times 2 equals required length for first operand area."

The maximum implied or explicit length for either operand is 16 bytes.
The Condition Code setting is not changed by the execution of this instruction.

*　　　　　　　　　*　　　　　　　　　*

Packed Decimal Arithmetic Operations

Instruction: Convert to Binary

mnemonic	hex code	operand format
CVB	4F	$R_1, D_2 (X_2, B_2)$

The Convert to Binary instruction takes the packed decimal contents of the second operand and converts that value into a signed, binary integer in the general register specified by the first operand. The address generated by the second operand must be on a doubleword boundary alignment and consist of eight bytes containing packed decimal data. The sign of the packed decimal (the low-order half-byte) creates the sign-bit of the integer. The maximum packed decimal positive value that may be converted to binary format is 2,147,483,647. Any number greater than this creates a fixed-point division interruption during the conversion and results in a program termination.

The Condition Code setting is not changed by this instruction.

*   *   *

Instruction: Convert to Decimal

mnemonic	hex code	operand format
CVD	4E	$R_1, D_2 (X_2, B_2)$

The Convert to Decimal instruction takes the 32-bit signed integer contained within the general register specified by the first operand and converts it to a packed decimal format within the area specified by the second operand. The address generated by the second operand must be that of eight bytes commencing on a doubleword boundary alignment. The packed decimal field is signed in the low-order four bits (right-most half-byte) in accordance with packed decimal conventions.

The Condition Code setting is not changed by this instruction.

*   *   *

Instruction: Zero & Add Packed Decimals

mnemonic	hex code	operand format
ZAP	F8	$D_1 (L_1, B_1), D_2 (L_2, B_2)$

This instruction takes the packed decimal contents of the second operand and places them into the storage area specified by the first operand, setting any additional high-order half-bytes of the receiving field to zero. This instruction is unique from other packed decimal instructions in that it is only necessary for the second operand to be in validly signed packed decimal format. If the length of the first operand field is greater than that of the second operand field, the instruction causes the high-order half-bytes to be filled with zero-digits for the unfilled portion of the first operand field. If the length of the first operand field is shorter than the length of the second operand area and significant hex digits are lost, an overflow condition results. The maximum implied or explicit length for either operand is 16 bytes.

CC	BC	Condition
0	8	The value of the contents of the first operand is zero.
1	4	The first operand contains a value of less than zero (negative).
2	2	The first operand contains a value greater than zero (positive).
3	1	An overflow condition occurred during the execution.

*   *   *

Instruction: Add Packed Decimals

mnemonic	hex code	operand format
AP	FA	$D_1 (L_1, B_1), D_2 (L_2, B_2)$

This instruction algebraically adds the packed decimal contents of the second operand to the packed decimal contents of the first operand. The resulting sum is placed within the field of the first operand, and contains an algebraically determined sign in the low-order half-byte. The packed decimal contents of both operands must have a valid packed decimal sign in the low-order half-byte of their area—a hex value of A through F in the right-most nibble. Two overflow conditions might result from the execution of this instruction:

- If both operand fields are of equal length, a carry-out of a high-order digit might occur, depending upon the values of the operand contents.

- If the second operand length is greater than the length of the first operand, significant high-order digits in excess of the first operand length will be lost.

If the value of the significant digits of a packed decimal field are less than half of the allowable maximum numeric value for that field, the number may be added to itself by coding the same field identity for both operands.

The maximum implied or explicit length for either operand is 16 bytes.

CC	BC	Condition
0	8	The first operand contains a value of zero.
1	4	The first operand contains a value of less than zero (negative).
2	2	The first operand contains a value greater than zero (positive).
3	1	An overflow exception occurred.

*   *   *

Instruction: Subtract Packed Decimals

mnemonic	hex code	operand format
SP	FB	$D_1 (L_1, B_1), D_2 (L_2, B_2)$

The Subtract Packed instruction algebraically subtracts the packed decimal contents of the second operand from the packed decimal contents of the first operand. The net difference between the two operands replaces the contents of the first operand and is algebraically signed as

Packed Decimal Arithmetic Operations

the result of the subtraction. The packed decimal contents of both operands must contain a valid sign in the low-order half-byte (right-most four bits) of their data fields. The maximum implied or explicit length for either operand is 16 bytes.

CC	BC	Condition
0	8	The first operand contains a value of zero.
1	4	The first operand contains a value that is less than zero (negative).
2	2	The first operand contains a value greater than zero (positive).
3	1	An overflow condition occurred during execution of the instruction.

*   *   *

Instruction: Multiply Packed Decimals

mnemonic	hex code	operand format
MP	FC	$D_1 (L_1, B_1), D_2 (L_2, B_2)$

This instruction multiplies the packed decimal contents of the second operand (the multiplier) times the packed decimal contents of the first operand (the multiplicand). The packed contents of both operands must have a valid sign in the low-order half-byte of their data fields. The resulting product occupies the whole of the first operand field. The sign of the product is determined algebraically by the signs of the multiplicand and the multiplier. The length of the multiplier may not exceed eight bytes, nor may the length be equal to, or greater than, the length specified by the first operand. A formula for determining the length of the first operand for a successful MP instruction statement would be:

Length of the multiplier plus length of the multiplicand plus one byte equals the product area.

	example 1	example 2
Multiplicand length	9	6
Multiplier length	4	5
Add one more byte	1	1
Product field length should be	14	12

By using this formula, a product overflow cannot occur. Since the definition of this instruction implies that the "multiplier is multiplied against the multiplicand," it should be mentioned that the following would be the normal sequence of consideration when creating an MP instruction statement.

1. The multiplier should be in a storage location.
2. The multiplicand should be in a storage location.
3. Determine the length required for the product and allocate an area for it.
4. Load the multiplicand into the product area with a Zero & Add Packed instruction statement.
5. Code the Multiply Packed instruction statement.

The maximum allowable length of the product area is 16 bytes.
The Condition Code setting is not changed by this instruction.

*   *   *

Instruction: Divide Packed Decimals

mnemonic	hex code	operand format
DP	FD	$D_1 (L_1, B_1), D_2 (L_2, B_2)$

The Divide Packed instruction divides the packed decimal contents of the second operand (the divisor) into the packed decimal contents of the first operand, which contains the dividend. The contents of both operands must have a valid packed sign in the low-order half-byte of their data fields. The resulting quotient and remainder replaces the dividend in the field of the first operand. The quotient will be in the high-order bytes of the first operand field; its length is the result of the subtraction of the length of the second operand from the length of the first operand field. The remainder from the divide operation resides in the low-order bytes of the first operand field, and is the same number of bytes in length as the second operand field, the divisor. The signs of the divisor and dividend algebraically combine to determine the sign of the quotient; the value of the sign of the dividend creates the sign of the remainder. The length of the divisor may not exceed eight bytes, nor may the length of the divisor be equal to, or greater than, the length specified by the first operand.

The Condition Code setting is not changed by the execution of this instruction.

* * *

Instruction: Move with Offset

mnemonic	hex code	operand format
MVO	F1	$D_1 (L_1, B_1), D_2 (L_2, B_2)$

The MVO instruction moves data by taking each byte of the storage area specified by the second operand and placing it into the storage area specified by the first operand, but offset to the left of the corresponding byte positions by one-half byte. The movement of the data within the fields is right to left in the transfer. Both the first operand and the second operand have their own length attribute for this instruction, but the offset is in the receiving field only. If the second operand is shorter in length than the first operand, the instruction statement places hexadecimal zero-digits into the high-order nibbles of the first operand. If the first operand field is shorter in length than the second operand, the instruction ignores data remaining to be moved once the first operand field is filled.

A maximum length of 16 bytes of data may be moved by this instruction.

The Condition Code setting is not changed by this instruction.

* * *

Instruction: Shift and Round Packed Decimals (System/370 Only)

mnemonic	hex code	operand format
SRP	F0	$D_1 (L_1, B_1), D_2 (B_2), I_3$

The SRP instruction shifts packed decimal data, either to the left or right, within a packed decimal field in storage. Unlike the logical and algebraic shift instructions, which shift individual bits within registers, the SRP instruction shifts hexadecimal characters (four-bit packed decimal digits). Shifting to the left or right is accomplished with the same instruction, the direction of the shift being determined by the second operand of the instruction statement. The first operand, $(D_1 (L_1, B_1))$, is used to specify the address of the packed decimal field to be affected by the SRP instruction. All of the movement of the packed decimal data occurs within the storage area addressed by this operand. The second operand, $(D_2 (B_2))$, is used exclusively to indicate the direction of the shift and the number of positions that each hex digit is to be shifted. Regardless of the combined, implied, or explicit value of the second operand, only the low-order six bit positions of the combined values of the $D_2 (B_2)$ values are used to determine the direction and range of the shift. This must be emphasized again—the second operand does not represent an address as in most other instruction statements; it is a shift value. This second operand may also be stated as an absolute value without a B_2 (base register) segment. In such instances the value of the B_2 segment of the operand is considered to be zero. If the shift value contained within the low-order six bit positions of the second operand is a positive (+) value, it indicates that the shift is to be to the left. If those same six bit positions contain a negative value, in Two's Complement form, it specifies that the shift is to be to the right. The value, either positive or negative, specifies the quantity of hexadecimal positions each hex value within the first operand field is to be moved. If, during a left shift, a significant digit (a value other than zero) is shifted out of the high-order of the packed field, a decimal overflow condition is signalled. The loss of significant digits during a right shift is not considered to be an overflow condition.

Hex characters supplied to the high-order during a right shift, or to the low-order during a left shift, always are packed decimal zero-digits. The sign of the original packed decimal field, contained in the low-order half-byte, is not affected or moved by this shifting.

The third operand (I_3) is used to supply a "rounding" value for right shifts. The absolute value specified as this operand is added to the last packed decimal digit to be shifted out of the low-order end of the data field. If the resulting sum is greater than 9, a "carry" value of 1 is added to the low-order packed decimal numeric digit, the one immediately to the left of the sign-digit. Even though rounding is not applicable for left shifts, the I_3 operand should be stated as zero whenever a left shift is coded. If no rounding is desired for right shifts, the appropriate value to be specified for the I_3 operand is zero. The I_3 operand cannot be omitted.

CC	BC	Condition
0	8	The first operand contains a value of zero.
1	4	The first operand contains a value less than zero (a negative value).
2	2	The first operand contains a value greater than zero (a positive value).
3	1	An overflow exception occurred.

* * *

PACKED DECIMAL ARITHMETIC OPERATIONS

By using Assembler Language, the programmer has access to three basic types of arithmetic instruction sets—fixed-point, packed decimal, and floating-point. For the reasons previously mentioned, floating-point features have been intentionally omitted from this text. Therefore, the subject matter of arithmetic operations will be limited to fixed-point and packed decimal instructions.

When referring to a fixed-point numeric (or a binary format decimal) within this text, it is construed to mean an integer value occupying a halfword, a fullword, or a general register in which the left-most (high-order) bit position identifies the sign of the value and the remaining bit positions form the whole of the integer. There must be at least one register operand in every fixed-point arithmetic instruction.

Packed decimal values are represented by a field of one or more bytes, in which the individual half-bytes (nibbles) represent a decimal value expressed in hexadecimal digit form. For arithmetic operations, the right-most nibble of the packed field must contain a valid packed decimal sign. This would consist of a hexadecimal digit within the range of from X'A' through X'F'.

Packed Decimal/Fixed-Point Conversion Processes

The data used in arithmetic operations of any type often must be converted into the format of the particular type of arithmetic instructions that are coded. Accordingly, prior to investigating the use of the arithmetic instructions, the means of converting the data should be thoroughly explained.

Data received by the problem program in EBCDIC form may be converted first into packed decimal form and then into fixed-point or binary format. Data in binary or fixed-point format may be converted back to EBCDIC form by a reversal of those steps. The transition of the data is as follows:

1. Incoming data is received in EBCDIC.
2. It is converted to packed decimals by the Pack instruction.
3. The packed decimal value is converted to binary or fixed-point by the Convert to Binary instruction.

1. The data is in binary or fixed-point format.
2. It is converted into packed decimals by the Convert to Decimal instruction.
3. The packed decimals are converted into EBCDIC character numerics by the Unpack instruction.

The PACK Instruction

The Pack instruction is used to convert EBCDIC numeric character data into packed decimal form. In converting the data, the instruction takes the sign-zone of the low-order byte of the incoming data and places it into the low-order half-byte of the receiving field.

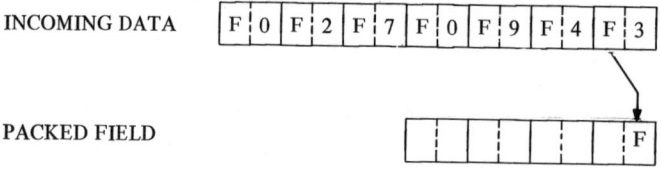

The numeric portion of the low-order byte of the incoming field is then placed into the other half of the low-order byte of the field that is being packed.

Packed Decimal Arithmetic Operations

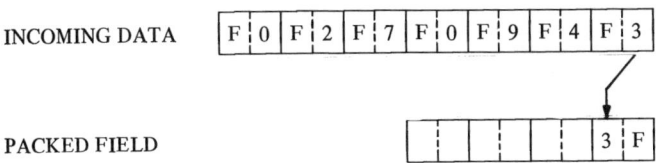

It then proceeds to take the numeric portion of each subsequent higher-order byte and places these hexadecimal digits into the subsequent higher-order half-bytes of the packed decimal receiving field.

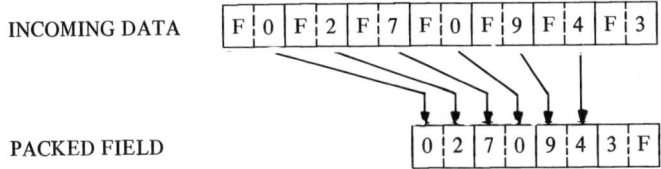

If the EBCDIC field contains more numeric characters than can be accommodated by the packed decimal field, the surplus high-order numeric digits are ignored. This is illustrated as:

    PACK   PACK3 , FIELDIN

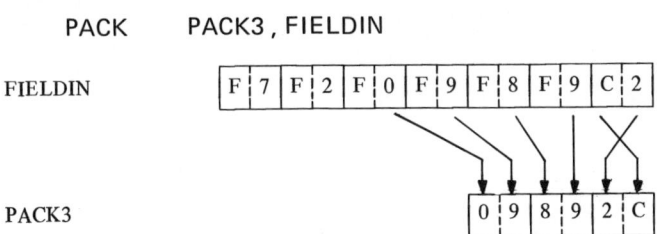

However if the EBCDIC field does not contain sufficient numeric characters to fill the high-order positions of the packed field, the Pack instruction supplies high-order packed decimal zero-digits to those positions.

    PACK   PACK4 , SMALLFLD

EBCDIC alpha characters could be converted into packed decimal format, but they could never be reconverted back into EBCDIC alpha characters again. The reason for this will be shown in the discussion of the Unpack instruction. There could be a reason, however, for desiring a one-way transformation of EBCDIC alpha characters into a packed decimal value. A transformation of this type would be:

    PACK   PACK4 , ALPHA

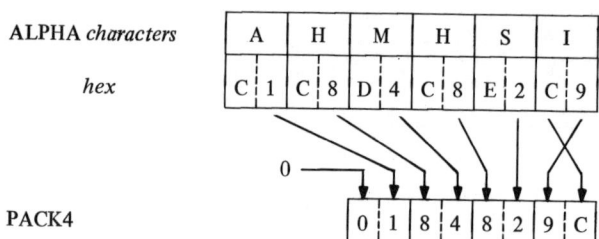

In this illustration, the EBCDIC alpha characters have been converted into a packed decimal value of +184,829.

Further examples of packed decimals are shown in the following illustrations.

Example 1

The EBCDIC numeric zoned decimal field, containing the equivalent of four numeric characters, has been packed into a three-byte field. Because there are not enough numerics to fill all of the half-bytes of the packed field, a high-order zero-digit is supplied.

    PACK   PACK3 , INDATA

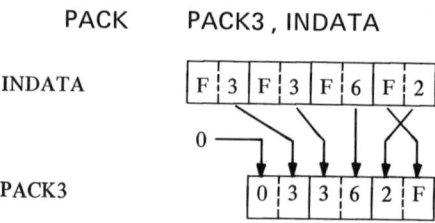

Example 2

    PACK   PACK4+1 (3) , DATA+2 (5)

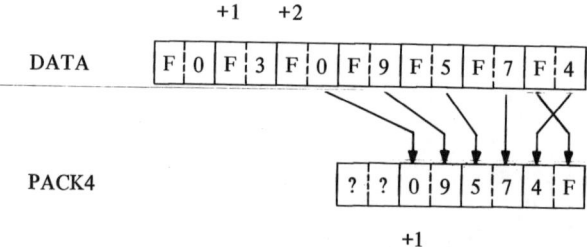

In this example, the low-order five bytes of a seven-byte EBCDIC numeric field have been packed into the low-order three bytes of a four-byte packed field. The contents of the high-order byte of the packed decimal field would remain unchanged from their previous configuration, whatever it was prior to the Pack.

Packed Decimal Arithmetic Operations

The Unpack (UNPK) Instruction

The reverse process of the Pack instruction is created by the Unpack instruction, converting a packed decimal value into an EBCDIC numeric field. The instruction first takes the low-order half-byte of the packed decimal field and places it into the zone portion of the low-order byte of the receiving field.

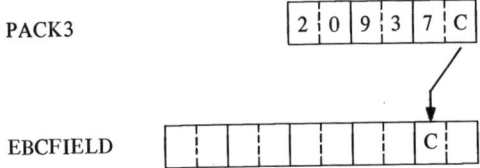

The low-order numeric digit of the packed field is then supplied to the numeric portion of the low-order byte of the receiving field.

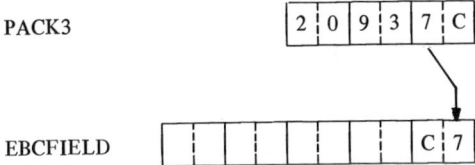

Each successive higher-order packed decimal digit is then inserted into the numeric portion of each successive high-order byte of the EBCDIC receiving field, the zone portion of the bytes being supplied with the standard zone of an EBCDIC numeric character.

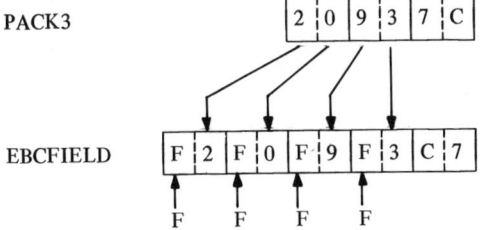

If the packed decimal field contains more numeric digits than the EBCDIC receiving field can accommodate, the surplus high-order packed digits are ignored.

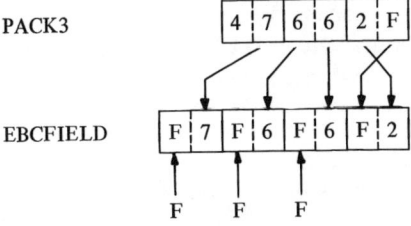

Regardless of the alpha or numeric representation of the data used to create a packed decimal field, if that field were immediately unpacked it would inevitably result in an EBCDIC numeric character field. This is illustrated in the following example of the execution of a PACK instruction statement and an immediately subsequent UNPACK instruction statement.

The reason that the low-order byte does not change is that it represents the zoned decimal portion of the EBCDIC numeric field.

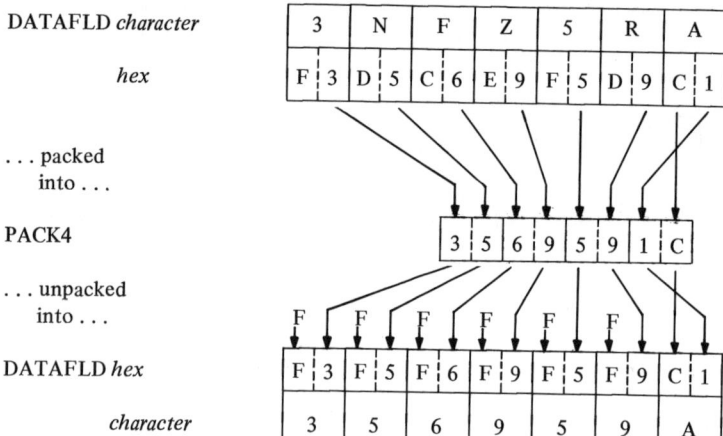

As with many other instructions, an explicit length attribute or address adjusting may be used to modify the portions of the fields that would be affected by the UNPACK instruction. This is illustrated within these examples.

Example 1

    UNPK   DATA+1 (3) , PAK2

In this example, the three numeric digits of the two-byte packed field are unpacked into the low-order three bytes of a field labeled DATA. The high-order byte of DATA would remain unchanged from what it was before execution of the UNPACK instruction.

Example 2

    UNPK   DATAFLD , PAK4+2 (2)

Packed Decimal Arithmetic Operations

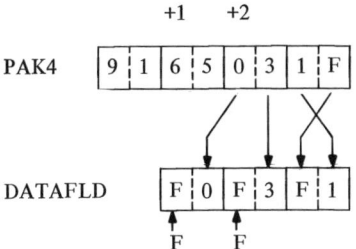

As shown here, the two low-order bytes of a four-byte packed decimal field, containing three numeric digits, are unpacked into a three-byte numeric character field.

Convert to Binary (CVB)

The CVB instruction takes a packed decimal value, as contained within an eight-bit doubleword-aligned field, and converts it to a binary-formatted fixed-point value within a general register. The first operand of the instruction statement indicates the register that is to contain the converted value and the second operand addresses the eight-byte field containing the packed decimal value. This is the second instruction required to convert an EBCDIC numeric character value to a fixed-point value—the first step is to pack the EBCDIC field. In order to establish the eight-byte doubleword field into which a packed value will be placed, the programmer may use either of the following types of statements:

```
BIGDBWDA     DS      D        001
BIGDBWDB     DC      D'0'     002
```

The first statement reserves eight bytes of program storage, aligned on a doubleword boundary, but does not guarantee the contents of that area prior to moving a packed decimal value into it. The second statement creates an eight-byte doubleword, properly aligned, containing a value of +0, or all hexadecimal zero-digits.

In either case, the packed decimal value that is to be converted to binary format should be moved into the doubleword via the Zero & Add Packed (ZAP) instruction. This would guarantee that any previous contents of this doubleword area have been cleared out and the value being moved in will retain a valid packed decimal configuration.

Assume that a packed decimal field of four bytes, LITTLPAK, is to be converted to a binary value. It is first moved into a field labeled DUBLPAK and then converted to binary-formatted fixed-point within general register 7. The configuration of these areas prior to execution of the instruction statements are:

LITTLPAK | 4 | 7 | 1 | 1 | 9 | 7 | 3 | C |

DUBLPAK | 0 | 0 | 0 | 0 | 0 | 0 | 0 | 0 | 0 | 0 | 0 | 0 | 0 | 0 | 0 | 0 |

register 7 | 0 | 000 | 0000 | 0000 | 0000 | 0000 | 0000 | 0000 | 0000 |

The instruction statements to be executed are:

```
ZAP    DUBLPAK , LITTLPAK    001
CVB    7 , DUBLPAK           002
```

Statement 001 effectively places the contents of LITTLPAK into the low-order four bytes of DUBLPAK and resets the four high-order bytes of DUBLPAK to contain hexadecimal zero-digits.

Statement 002 takes the packed decimal value of +4,711,973 as now contained in DUBLPAK and converts it to its fixed-point equivalent in general register 7. After execution of this statement these three areas appear as:

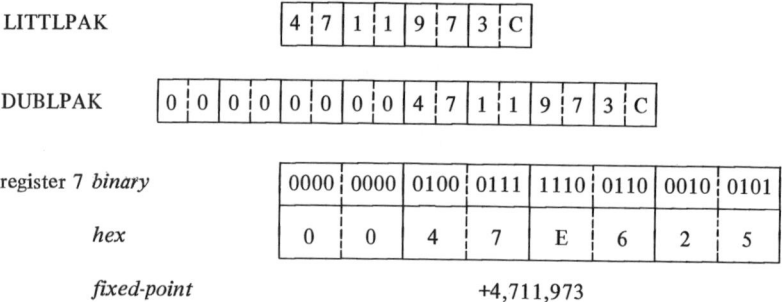

Convert to Decimal (CVD)

The purpose of the CVD instruction is to take a binary-formatted fixed-point value and convert it into its equivalent packed decimal value format. The fixed-point value must reside within a general register and the receiving field must consist of eight bytes aligned on a doubleword boundary. The fixed-point value, contained within the general register specified by the first operand, is converted to packed decimal form and placed into the field addressed by the second operand.

Assuming that the fixed-point value resided in general register 5 and the receiving field is labeled PACK8D, the following examples illustrate various fixed-point values and the resulting packed decimal values after execution of a CVD instruction statement.

```
CVD    5 , PACK8D
```

Example 1

PACK8D

| 0 | 0 | 0 | 0 | 0 | 0 | 0 | 0 | 0 | 0 | 2 | 6 | 6 | 5 | 5 | C |

Example 2

register 5 *fixed-point*	+1,616,642,169							
hex	6	0	5	C	0	0	7	9
binary	0110	0000	0101	1100	0000	0000	0111	1001

PACK8D

0	0	0	0	0	1	6	1	6	6	4	2	1	6	9	C

Example 3

register 5 *fixed-point*	+3							
hex	0	0	0	0	0	0	0	3
binary	0000	0000	0000	0000	0000	0000	0000	0011

PACK8D

0	0	0	0	0	0	0	0	0	0	0	0	0	0	3	C

PERFORMING ARITHMETIC OPERATIONS WITH PACKED DECIMAL VALUES

One of the most frequent decisions made by the programmer results from the question, "Which arithmetic operation mode shall I use—fixed-point or packed decimal?" As might be expected, both types of arithmetic functions have offsetting attributes over the other. One of the key factors in making that decision should be the determination of the use that will be applied to the results of those calculations. A comparison of the performance of individual arithmetic operations between fixed-point and packed decimal instructions (i.e., Add versus Add Packed) clearly indicates that the fixed-point instructions are considerably faster. However, if the data to be processed is entering the program in character format, or packed decimal format, and is to eventually be printed out or stored in a data set in character or packed decimal format, the wisest decision could be to perform all arithmetic functions in packed decimal mode. The instructions required to convert a packed decimal value to binary fixed-point values (CVB) and back to packed decimal format again (CVD) use considerable time. Any time saved by using fixed-point arithmetic routines may well be more than offset by the Convert to Binary and Convert to Decimal instructions. However, if the data to be processed (1) enters the program logic in binary fixed-point format, or (2) will be put out or stored in binary fixed-point format, or (3) will be repetitiously used in fixed-point format, then it may be to your advantage to use fixed-point arithmetic operations. One of the other considerations that must be evaluated is the work area required by each of these types—fixed-point arithmetic operations require the use of *at least* one general register; packed decimal arithmetic operations use storage areas that are set up by the programmer. With fixed point instructions, you might find it necessary to reuse several registers for many different functions. Providing that storage space allocation is not a problem, the packed decimal instructions may be set up to use a separate work area for each set of statements.

General experience has indicated that if data resulting from arithmetic operations is to be printed, displayed, or stored on data sets in character or packed decimal format, it is normally advantageous to perform those arithmetic functions with packed decimal arithmetic instructions. However, there are numerous valid arguments for using either mode.

Before covering the applications of packed decimal arithmetic operations, it is appropriate to review the configuration and rules governing packed decimal arithmetic fields.

The configuration of a packed decimal value is directly related to the hexadecimal character concept. That is, each digit of a packed decimal value is represented by a hexadecimal character —one digit for every four binary bit positions. The hexadecimal characters or digits of '0' through '9' represent valid packed decimal numeric digits; the hexadecimal characters of 'A' through 'F' represent signs/zones for valid packed decimal arithmetic values. In order for a packed decimal value to be used in an arithmetic operation, it must have a valid sign (Hex 'A' though 'F') in the right-most half-byte of the field. All of the remaining hex digits in that field must have a value of hex '9' or less—hex '0' through '9'. If an attempt is made to process an invalidly packed decimal field, a program interrupt will occur, resulting in an abnormal termination (ABEND) of the task. It should be noted that unlike fixed-point arithmetic instructions, packed decimal arithmetic operations do not require word boundary alignment, nor do they use a general register. Therefore, you may use as little as one byte, or as many as 16 bytes, in setting up the work areas for packed decimal arithmetic operations.

Another unique factor regarding any packed decimal instruction statement is the existence of the length attribute on both operands. This should be carefully noted, because the length attribute does exist for both operands whether it is implied or explicit. The reaction of the individual instructions to a variation of length attributes between operands must be considered when using packed decimal instructions.

For the purpose of illustrating packed decimal fields in this section, all graphic presentations will be represented in hexadecimal format only, since this is the only relevant association with packed decimals.

Zero & Add Packed Decimals (ZAP)

This instruction, often humorously referred to as "The ZAP," can effectively perform the initialization of a nonformatted area to a formatted packed decimal work area, clear previous data stored in an area and reinitialize the area to zero, or move packed decimal data from a short packed decimal field to a longer packed decimal field without clearing all of the receiving field in advance. It will act on a maximum of 16 bytes of data for either operand. Upon issuance of a ZAP instruction statement, the system effectively sets all nibbles (half-bytes) in the first operand storage location to contain hexadecimal zero-digits if such nibbles were not directly affected by the data moved into the area as specified by the second operand. If the first operand is greater in length than the second operand, hex zero-digits then occupy the unfilled high-order positions of the first operand. If the first operand is not long enough to contain all of the significant hex digits (nonzeros) of the second operand, a program interruption occurs, indicated by a decimal overflow code contained within the Condition Code bits of the PSW. Some examples of the use of this instruction are presented in the following illustrations.

Packed Decimal Arithmetic Operations

Example 1. The instruction statement to be executed is:

    ZAP   FIELDA,=PL1'0'

Before execution of the statement, FIELDA appears to be:

                  Byte 1 Byte 2 Byte 3 Byte 4

FIELDA | 0 | 9 | F | 3 | 6 | 4 | B | 0 |

After execution of the ZAP instruction statement, the field contains:

FIELDA | 0 | 0 | 0 | 0 | 0 | 0 | 0 | C |

Note that although a one-byte literal is specified as the second operand, the entire length of the first operand is configured with hex zero-digits. This follows the rule that if the second operand is shorter than the first operand, the high-order of the first operand will be supplied with X'0' digits.

Example 2. The instruction statement to be executed is:

    ZAP   FLD1,FLD2+1(2)

Before the ZAP instruction statement is executed, the fields appear as:

FLD1 | 3 | 9 | 4 | 6 | 5 | C |

FLD2 | 0 | 6 | 9 | 8 | 1 | C |

After the execution of the instruction statement these fields would be configured as:

FLD1 | 0 | 0 | 9 | 8 | 1 | C |

FLD2 | 0 | 6 | 9 | 8 | 1 | C |

In this instance, the instruction statement specifies that the data to be moved from FLD2 should commence one byte higher than the address of the first byte of FLD2. Therefore, only two bytes of data are transmitted from FLD2 to FLD1, and the unfilled half-bytes of FLD1 are set to hex zero-digits.

Example 3. The instruction statement to be executed is:

    ZAP   PACKA,PACKB

The packed decimal fields to be affected by this statement are:

PACKA | 0 | 0 | 4 | D |

PACKB | 0 | 0 | 0 | 0 | 0 | 3 | 9 | C |

After the execution of the instruction statement these fields appear as:

PACKA | 0 | 3 | 9 | C |

PACKB | 0 | 0 | 0 | 0 | 0 | 3 | 9 | C |

Although the field length of the first operand is shorter than that of the second operand, a program interrupt (decimal overflow) would not have occurred because no significant digits (non-zero hex values) are lost in the transmission.

Example 4. The instruction statement to be executed is:

    ZAP   SETFLD , SETFLD+2 (1)

The configuration of SETFLD before execution of the ZAP instruction statement is:

SETFLD | 3 | 9 | 4 | 5 | 2 | C |

After execution of the instruction statement, SETFLD would appear as:

SETFLD | 0 | 0 | 0 | 0 | 2 | C |

In this example, the ZAP instruction has effectively cleared the high-order bytes of a packed decimal field by incrementing the starting point of reference in the second operand, but referring to the same field as the first operand. Note that the explicit length attribute of one byte has limited the implied length of the second operand.

Example 5. This example is intended to show the use of explicit length attributes applicable to both operands in a packed decimal instruction. The instruction statement used for this example is:

    ZAP   PACKER1+1 (2) , PACKER2+2 (2)

The configuration of the fields referred to by this instruction are:

PACKER1 | 2 | 4 | 4 | 3 | 6 | 0 | 0 | C |

PACKER2 | 0 | 1 | 0 | 0 | 3 | 2 | 5 | C |

Once the instruction statement has been performed, the configuration of these fields would appear as:

PACKER1 | 2 | 4 | 3 | 2 | 5 | C | 0 | C |

PACKER2 | 0 | 1 | 0 | 0 | 3 | 2 | 5 | C |

Packed Decimal Arithmetic Operations

Note that only bytes #2 and #3 of the PACKER1 field have been altered by the instruction statement. As specified by the first operand, the action to be performed on PACKER1 commences at one byte beyond the high-order point of that field and affects only two bytes of storage. After execution of this instruction statement, any attempt to use the four-byte contents of PACKER1 for arithmetic operations would result in a program interrupt. This is because one hex character position (the sixth half-byte from the left) is a nonnumeric digit residing at a point other than the low-order half-byte. This field could be used for arithmetic operations if the length attribute was specified as three—that is, PACKER1 (3)— and only the left-most three bytes of data are acted upon. Even the single right-most byte of this field could be used if it were specified as PACKER1+3 (1) in the instruction statement.

Add Packed (AP)

This instruction, which adds together two fields of packed decimal data, is visually interpreted rather easily by the programmer. In other words, 4C + 6C equals 10C is easier to comprehend than is fixed-point arithmetics wherein F + F equals 1E. With this instruction, the packed decimal value of the second operand is added to the packed decimal value of the first operand and the resulting sum is placed in the first operand location. If the sum of the addition exceeds the length of the first operand location, a decimal overflow occurs, causing a program interruption. This can occur when the fields of both operands are of equal length, or when the length of the second operand field is greater than that of the first operand field and contains significant digits in the locations that are in excess of the length of the first operand. A validly completed addition resulting in a zero sum always has a positive (+) sign in the low order nibble. A valid positive sign may be a hex digit 'A', 'C', 'E', or 'F'. A valid negative sign may be either a hex digit 'B' or 'D'.

Example 1. Before the AP instruction is executed, the fields specified as the operands appear as:

PKFLD1 | 0 | 0 | 3 | 9 | 7 | C |

PKFLD2 | 0 | 0 | 0 | 9 | 9 | C |

The instruction statement to be executed is coded as:

    AP   PKFLD1 , PKFLD2

After this AP instruction has been executed, the configuration of these fields would be:

PKFLD1 | 0 | 0 | 4 | 9 | 6 | C |

PKFLD2 | 0 | 0 | 0 | 9 | 9 | C |

Note that the data contained in the second operand field is not altered by the execution of the instruction statement. Since this is true in all cases of packed decimal arithmetic operations, any further examples contained in this section will show only the result of the changes to the first operand.

Example 2. The fields used by this example are:

PKA | 0 | 3 | 2 | 2 | 1 | C |

PKB | 3 | 6 | 4 | 4 | 7 | C |

The instruction statement to be executed is:

    AP   PKA , PKB+2 (1)

After this instruction statement has been executed, PKA has the hexadecimal configuration of:

PKA | 0 | 3 | 2 | 2 | 8 | C |

In this instance the second operand specifies an address two bytes beyond the starting point of the PKB field, and also that only one byte should be added to the first operand. Therefore, the addition performed is equivalent to 03221C + 7C = 03228C. The 'C' suffix on each of these values is the packed decimal sign of the values.

Example 3. The configurations of the fields used by this example are:

PACKA | 0 | 0 | 1 | 0 | 8 | 2 | 1 | 0 | 0 | 0 | 5 | C |

PACKB | 3 | 0 | 0 | 6 | 1 | 1 | 1 | C |

The instruction statement to be executed is:

    AP   PACKA , PACKB

After execution of this statement the configuration of PACKA is:

PACKA | 0 | 0 | 1 | 1 | 1 | 2 | 1 | 6 | 1 | 1 | 6 | C |

Example 4. Before the AP instruction statement is executed for this example, the fields are:

PKR1 | 0 | 8 | 5 | C |

PKR2 | 0 | 0 | 0 | 0 | 1 | 5 | 8 | C |

The instruction statement is:

    AP   PKR1 , PKR2

As a result of the performance of this instruction, PKR1 now contains the packed decimal value configured as:

PKR1 | 2 | 4 | 3 | C |

This example would not have resulted in a decimal overflow and subsequent program interruption. Although the length of the second operand is greater than that of the first operand, the excess-length bytes do not contain significant hex digits (nonzeros), nor does the significant sum of the two operands exceed the length of the first operand field.

Example 5. The instruction statement to be executed in this example is:

    AP   FIELDR , FIELDS

The hexadecimal configuration of the fields affected by this statement appears as:

FIELDR | 0 | 0 | 3 | 7 | 5 | 7 | 2 | C |

FIELDS | 0 | 0 | 0 | 4 | 9 | 1 | 6 | D |

After the execution of the instruction statement, FIELDR would appear to contain:

FIELDR | 0 | 0 | 3 | 2 | 6 | 5 | 6 | C |

In this example, FIELDS contained a negative value of –4916 as indicated by the hex digit 'D' in the low-order half-byte of that field. By adding this value to the positive value of +37,572 contained in FIELDR, the resulting sum reflects that a subtraction, in effect, has taken place. If the negative value had been greater than the positive value to which it was added, the resulting sum would have been signed as a negative value.

Subtract Packed (SP)

The Subtract Packed instruction subtracts the packed decimal contents of the second operand field from the packed decimal contents of the first operand field. The difference is placed in the first operand field. Both fields must contain validly signed packed decimal values. A decimal overflow interrupt occurs under similar circumstances as described for the Add Packed instruction.

Example 1. Before the SP instruction statement is acted upon, the fields used by that statement appear as:

PACKERA | 0 | 2 | 2 | 5 | 8 | C |

PACKERB | 0 | 0 | 9 | 9 | 4 | C |

The instruction statement is:

    SP   PACKERA , PACKERB

After the instruction statement has been executed, the first operand field contains:

PACKERA | 0 | 1 | 2 | 6 | 4 | C |

This example has presented a straightforward subtraction. In effect, it states that 2258C less 994C equals 1264C.

Example 2. The instruction statement to be executed is:

    SP   PKFA , PKFB

The configurations of the fields referred to by this statement are:

PKFA | 0 | 0 | 0 | 3 | 4 | 4 | 7 | C |

PKFB | 0 | 0 | 2 | 1 | 1 | 6 | 2 | D |

As a result of the performance of this statement, the configuration of PKFA would be changed to:

PKFA | 0 | 0 | 2 | 4 | 6 | 0 | 9 | C |

This example reflects the application that subtracting a negative value from a positive value results in a net positive value equal to what the sum of the two values would have been, if they had been unsigned.

Example 3. The configurations of the fields for this example are:

ONEPK | 0 | 0 | 0 | 8 | 1 | 7 | 6 | 6 | 2 | C |

TWOPK | 0 | 0 | 0 | 9 | 4 | 4 | 3 | 7 | 5 | C |

The instruction statement that utilizes these fields is coded as:

    SP   ONEPK , TWOPK

The execution of this statement affects the configuration of ONEPK as:

ONEPK | 0 | 0 | 0 | 1 | 2 | 6 | 7 | 1 | 3 | D |

In this instance, the packed decimal value of this second operand is subtracted from the lesser value of the first operand, resulting in a negative difference.

Packed Decimal Arithmetic Operations

Example 4. This example illustrates the type of condition that would cause a decimal overflow program interruption. The configuration of the fields to be used represents their contents prior to execution of the SP instruction statement.

FLDPOS | 6 | 2 | 0 | 0 | 3 | C |

FLDNEG | 3 | 9 | 7 | 7 | 0 | D |

The instruction statement is:

    SP   FLDPOS, FLDNEG

After the SP instruction statement has been executed, the area occupied by FLDPOS would appear as:

FLDPOS | 0 | 1 | 7 | 7 | 3 | C |

This statement's performance creates a value in excess of the length parameter of the first operand field. This condition, called a "carry-out" of the high-order digit position, would have caused a program interruption.

Multiply Packed (MP)

This instruction multiplies the packed decimal contents of the first operand (containing the multiplicand) by the packed decimal contents of the second operand (the multiplier), placing the resulting product in the first operand storage location. In establishing the work areas for this instruction, a number of rules must be followed.

- The length of the multiplier value cannot exceed eight bytes.
- A product area should be established into which the multiplicand value is to be moved prior to the MP instruction statement.
- The length of the product area should be equal to the length of the multiplier plus the length of the multiplicand value.
- The length of the product area cannot exceed 16 bytes.
- The length of the multiplier must be at least one byte less than the length of the product area.
- Once the multiplicand is moved into the product area, the product area must have at least as many high-order zero-digits as to equal the length of the multiplier.
- Both operands must be signed packed decimal values.

If these rules are followed in their entirety, there will be no opportunity for a program interruption to occur as a result of this instruction's performance. This does not preclude the possibility, however, of a program interruption occurring during the execution of this instruction for other reasons, such as using an invalidly signed packed decimal field, etc. If these rules are not followed, a program interruption will most likely occur as a result of a data exception or specification exception.

Inasmuch as the product area will probably be used rather frequently, at least by one set of instruction statements, the best means of getting the multiplicand into the product area is to use the Zero & Add Packed instruction. This will not only right-align the multiplicand into the product area, but it will also clear out any high-order digits that might have contained significant values and set those digit positions to hexadecimal zeros. Upon completion of the Multiply Packed instruction statement, the sign of the product will reside in the right-most nibble of the product field—the low-order half-byte.

The capabilities of using assumed decimal points, and increasing and decreasing decimal point positions for packed decimal arithmetic operations, is discussed within the section entitled "Packed Decimal Logic with Assumed Decimal Points."

The length of the product field may be specified as being shorter than the overall combined length of the multiplier and the multiplicand, but only if the product area contains enough high-order zero-digits to equal the length of the multiplier after the multiplicand has been moved in. By stating this, it is inferred that you would know that the high-order positions of the multiplicand, in its own field, contains at least several zero digits. When the multiplicand is ZAP'd into the product area, there would be more than enough zero-digits on the left (high-order side) of the left-most significant digit of the multiplicand to equal the length of the multiplier. In this instance, the product area could be defined as being reduced by the length of the excess zero-digits. This practice is not recommended for general applications; it requires firm knowledge that the high-order zero-digits contained within the multiplicand field will never be any value other than zero-digits.

The following examples will point out the means of applying the rules and conditions for using the Multiply Packed instruction.

Example 1. The defined constants and the instruction statements for this example are:

```
        MPCAND     DC      PL4 ' 23221 '
        MPLIER     DC      PL3 ' 1176 '
        PRODUCT    DC      PL7 ' 0 '
*
                   ZAP     PRODUCT , MPCAND       001
                   MP      PRODUCT , MPLIER       002
```

Prior to the execution of these statements, the defined packed decimal areas would contain:

MPCAND | 0 | 0 | 2 | 3 | 2 | 2 | 1 | C |

MPLIER | 0 | 1 | 1 | 7 | 6 | C |

PRODUCT | 0 | 0 | 0 | 0 | 0 | 0 | 0 | 0 | 0 | 0 | 0 | 0 | 0 | C |

Statement 001 uses the ZAP instruction to place the multiplicand into the low-order bytes of the PRODUCT field. After execution of this statement the contents of PRODUCT are:

Packed Decimal Arithmetic Operations

PRODUCT | 0 | 0 | 0 | 0 | 0 | 0 | 0 | 0 | 2 | 3 | 2 | 2 | 1 | C |

High-order zero-digits equal to the length of the multiplier

Statement 002 then performs the MP function, after which PRODUCT contains:

PRODUCT | 0 | 0 | 0 | 0 | 0 | 2 | 7 | 3 | 0 | 7 | 8 | 9 | 6 | C |

In effect this routine has shown that 1176 x 23,221 = 27,307,896.

Example 2. The defined areas for this example have been coded as:

```
CASES     DC    PL3 ' 43351 '
PERCASE   DC    PL2 ' 144 '
PRODT     DC    PL5 ' 0 '
```

The configurations of these areas, once they have been defined, appear as:

CASES | 4 | 3 | 3 | 5 | 1 | C |

PERCASE | 1 | 4 | 4 | C |

PRODT | 0 | 0 | 0 | 0 | 0 | 0 | 0 | 0 | 0 | C |

The instruction statements are:

```
ZAP    PRODT , CASES        001
MP     PRODT , PERCASE      002
```

Statement 001 ZAPs the multiplicand into the product area, PRODT, which then contains:

(High-order zero digits equal to the length of the multiplier)

PRODT | 0 | 0 | 0 | 0 | 4 | 3 | 3 | 5 | 1 | C |

Multiplicand

Statement 002 multiplies the multiplier, PERCASE, times the contents of PRODT. PRODT now contains the product, appearing as:

PRODT | 0 | 0 | 6 | 2 | 4 | 2 | 5 | 4 | 4 | C |

or

144 x 43,351 = 6,242,544

Note that although all digit positions in both the multiplier and the multiplicand contain significant digits, the resulting product contains two high-order zero digits. One of these zero-digits results from the fact that although both operands contain a sign-digit in their low-order nibble, the resulting product contains only one sign-digit. The other zero-digit results from the fact that the high-order position of the multiplication does not result in a carry. This can be demonstrated by stating that "two single position units multiplied together may or may not equal a value that would occupy two positions." For instance, 2 x 2 = 4 and 4 x 4 = 16—in either case both the multiplier and the multiplicand are only one-position values, yet the number of positions required by the product has a variance of one position. Therefore, it may be logically concluded that although both the multiplier and the multiplicand fields contain their maximum significant-digit capacity, the resulting product will always contain at least one high-order zero-digit; if the high-order positions of the multiplier and the multiplicand do not combine to create a carry, then the product will contain two high-order zero-digits.

Example 3. The hexadecimal configuration of the packed decimal constants and work areas for this example are given below:

MCAND1 | 0 | 2 | 1 | 5 | 9 | C |

MCAND2 | 8 | 8 | 7 | C |

MCAND3 | 0 | 1 | 6 | 6 | 3 | 4 | 9 | C |

MPLIER | 0 | 5 | 5 | C |

PRODUCT | 0 | 0 | 0 | 0 | 0 | 0 | 0 | 0 | 0 | 0 | 0 | C |

CUMULATE | 0 | 0 | 0 | 0 | 0 | 0 | 0 | 0 | 0 | 0 | 0 | 0 | 0 | C |

The coded definitions of these areas and the instruction statements to be executed are shown in Figure 10-1.

The performance of each of the instruction statements are listed below. In each instance, the current configuration of the field affected is shown.

Statement 001 ZAPs the four-byte multiplicand, MCAND1, into PRODUCT.

PRODUCT | 0 | 0 | 0 | 0 | 0 | 0 | 0 | 2 | 1 | 5 | 9 | C |

Statement 002 multiplies the contents of PRODUCT by the packed decimal contents of MPLIER, resulting in:

PRODUCT | 0 | 0 | 0 | 0 | 0 | 1 | 1 | 8 | 7 | 4 | 5 | C |

Packed Decimal Arithmetic Operations

FIGURE 10-1

```
         OPERATION  OPERAND
*                                                              001
MPSUB    ZAP        PRODUCT,MCAND1                             002
         MP         PRODUCT,MPLIER                             003
         ZAP        CUMULATE,PRODUCT                           004
         ZAP        PRODUCT,MCAND2                             005
         MP         PRODUCT,MPLIER                             006
         AP         CUMULATE,PRODUCT                           007
         ZAP        PRODUCT,MCAND3                             008
         MP         PRODUCT,MPLIER                             009
         AP         CUMULATE,PRODUCT
*
MCAND1   DC         PL3'2159'                                  215
MCAND2   DC         PL2'887'                                   216
MCAND3   DC         PL4'166349'                                217
MPLIER   DC         PL2'55'                                    218
PRODUCT  DC         PL6'0'                                     219
CUMULATE DC         PL7'0'                                     220
*
```

Statement 003 uses the ZAP instruction to initialize the area labeled CUMULATE with the value currently contained within PRODUCT.

CUMULATE | 0 | 0 | 0 | 0 | 0 | 0 | 0 | 1 | 1 | 8 | 7 | 4 | 5 | C |

Statement 004 places the value of the contents of MCAND2 into the low-order bytes of PRODUCT. Note that the previous value contained within PRODUCT has now been entirely overlayed.

PRODUCT | 0 | 0 | 0 | 0 | 0 | 0 | 0 | 0 | 0 | 8 | 8 | 7 | C |

Statement 005 multiplies the current value contained in PRODUCT (that of MCAND2) by the value contained within MPLIER. PRODUCT now contains:

PRODUCT | 0 | 0 | 0 | 0 | 0 | 0 | 4 | 8 | 7 | 8 | 5 | C |

Statement 006 adds the new value of PRODUCT (+48,785) to the current value of CUMULATE (+118,745), resulting in a new total of +167,530 in CUMULATE.

CUMULATE (before AP) | 0 | 0 | 0 | 0 | 0 | 0 | 0 | 1 | 1 | 8 | 7 | 4 | 5 | C |

PRODUCT | 0 | 0 | 0 | 0 | 0 | 0 | 4 | 8 | 7 | 8 | 5 | C |

CUMULATE (after AP) | 0 | 0 | 0 | 0 | 0 | 0 | 0 | 1 | 6 | 7 | 5 | 3 | 0 | C |

Statement 007 now ZAPs the value of MCAND3 into PRODUCT. This represents the movement of the new multiplicand into the low-order bytes of the product area.

PRODUCT | 0 | 0 | 0 | 0 | 0 | 1 | 6 | 6 | 3 | 4 | 9 | C |

Statement 008 uses the MP instruction to multiply the current value of PRODUCT (+166,349, the multiplicand) by the value of MPLIER.

PRODUCT | 0 | 0 | 0 | 0 | 9 | 1 | 4 | 9 | 1 | 9 | 5 | C |

Statement 009 adds the new value of PRODUCT (+9,149,195) to the current value of CUMULATE (+167,530), resulting in a new CUMULATE total of +9,316,725.

CUMULATE (before AP) | 0 | 0 | 0 | 0 | 0 | 0 | 0 | 1 | 6 | 7 | 5 | 3 | 0 | C |

PRODUCT | 0 | 0 | 0 | 0 | 9 | 1 | 4 | 9 | 1 | 9 | 5 | C |

Packed Decimal Arithmetic Operations

CUMULATE | 0 | 0 | 0 | 0 | 0 | 0 | 9 | 3 | 1 | 6 | 7 | 2 | 5 | C |
(after AP)

This example has performed a set of calculations that verifies the fact that:

(55 x 2159) + (55 x 887) + (55 x 166,349) = 9,316,725

Although the length of the multiplier is the same for each MP instruction statement in this last example, the length of the multiplicand is different for each. Since the PRODUCT area length was established for the maximum length of any of the multiplier/multiplicand combinations, the logic was always able to use the same product area.

Also note that the CUMULATE field length is one byte larger than the length of the PRODUCT field. If the results of a packed decimal field arithmetic operation are being accumulated into another packed decimal field, the accumulator field should be *at least* one byte larger than the field from which the data is being accumulated in order to prevent the possibility of an overflow condition.

Divide Packed (DP)

This instruction divides the packed decimal contents of the first operand (containing the dividend) by the packed decimal contents of the second operand, the divisor. The quotient and remainder replace the dividend in the whole of the first operand storage location. The signs of the dividend and the divisor combine algebraically to form the sign of the quotient; the sign of the remainder is of the same value as the sign of the dividend.

The following rules should be followed when establishing the divide work areas and issuing the Divide Packed instruction.

- The length of the divisor cannot exceed eight bytes.
- A QUOREM field (Quotient and Remainder) should be established, into which the dividend is to be moved prior to the DP instruction statement.
- The length of the QUOREM field should be equal to the combined lengths of the dividend and the divisor.
- The length of the QUOREM area cannot exceed 16 bytes.
- The length of the divisor must be at least one byte less than the length of the dividend field.
- The length of the dividend field may not exceed 15 bytes.
- Both operands must contain validly signed packed decimal data.

Adherence to these rules should prevent any possible program interruptions while executing the Divide Packed instruction. The infraction of any single rule, as specified in the preceding list, will most likely result in a specification exception or decimal divide exception, subsequently followed by a program interruption.

As similarly used with the Multiply Packed instruction, the ZAP (Zero & Add Packed) instruction should be used in this instance to move the dividend into the QUOREM field. This will not only assure that the dividend value is right-aligned into the QUOREM field, but it will also reset the high-order digit positions of the QUOREM field to contain zero-digits.

After execution of the Divide Packed instruction, both the quotient and the remainder will occupy the whole of the quorem field. The quotient will be found in the left-most bytes of the field and will have a length attribute equal to "QUOREM length less DIVISOR length." The remainder will be found in the right-most bytes of the quorem field and will have the length attribute of the divisor. Both the quotient and the remainder will be signed in the low-order nibble of their share of the quorem field. This can be illustrated as:

```
DIVIDEND   DC    PL4'0'
DIVISOR    DC    PL3'0'
QUOREM     DC    PL7'0'
```

After the execution of a DP instruction referencing these fields, the interpreted format of the resultant QUOREM field would be:

QUOREM | Q | Q | Q | Q | Q | Q | Q | sz | R | R | R | R | R | sz |

wherein:

Q = Quotient (length of the dividend, including the sign/zone).
R = Remainder (length of the divisor, including the sign/zone).
sz = Sign/zone for each subfield.

The use of arithmetic division operations often requires the concept of utilizing decimal points. An analysis of that method, as applied to the Divide Packed instruction, can be found within the section titled "Packed Decimal Logic with Assumed Decimal Points."

The step-by-step analysis of the following examples should aid in providing a reasonable understanding of the Divide Packed instruction and the format of the fields associated with it.

Example 1. The contents of the fields and work areas used by this example contain the following hexadecimal configurations:

DIVDEND | 0 | 0 | 0 | 8 | 2 | 1 | 6 | 4 | 4 | C |

DIVSOR | 5 | 1 | 0 | C |

QUOREM | 0 | 0 | 0 | 0 | 0 | 0 | 0 | 0 | 0 | 0 | 0 | 0 | 0 | C |

ANSWER | 0 | 0 | 0 | 0 | 0 | 0 | 0 | 0 | 0 | C |

The coding that established these areas and the subsequent instruction statements for this example are presented in Figure 10-2.

Statement 001 uses the ZAP instruction to place the packed decimal value of DIVDEND into the low-order bytes of QUOREM.

QUOREM | 0 | 0 | 0 | 0 | 0 | 0 | 0 | 8 | 2 | 1 | 6 | 4 | 4 | C |

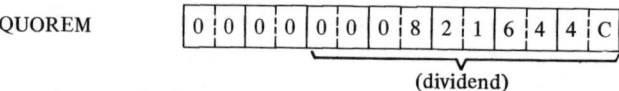
(dividend)

Packed Decimal Arithmetic Operations

```
NAME      OPERATION  OPERAND                  SEQ
*                                             001
DIVSUB    ZAP        QUOREM,DIVDEND           002
          DP         QUOREM,DIVSOR            003
          ZAP        ANSWER,QUOREM(5)
*
DIVDEND   DC         PL5'82164'               072
DIVSOR    DC         PL2'510'                 073
QUOREM    DC         PL7'0'                   074
ANSWER    DC         PL5'0'                   075
*
```

FIGURE 10-2

Statement 002, the Divide Packed instruction statement, would then be executed, after which the contents of QUOREM would appear to be:

QUOREM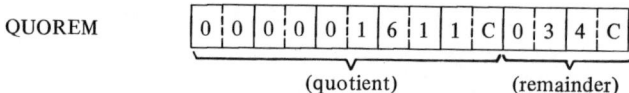
(quotient)   (remainder)

Notice that since the dividend is construed to have a length attribute of five bytes, then the high-order five bytes of the QUOREM field, after the DP instruction statement, are considered to be the quotient. Inasmuch as the length of the divisor is two bytes, the low-order two bytes of the QUOREM field now contain the remainder.

Statement 003 moves the quotient out of the QUOREM field via the ZAP instruction and places it into the field labeled ANSWER. Because the quotient only occupies the first five bytes of the QUOREM field, the second operand of this instruction statement (indicating the "move from" field address) has been given a specific length of five bytes. If this specific length had not been given, this statement would have attempted to move all seven bytes of the QUOREM field into the ANSWER field. This would have resulted in a program interruption, either because of an overflow or because of the fact that the overall data field would have contained a sign/zone in the low-order half-byte of the fifth byte from the left, which is not the low-order byte of the seven-byte field.

Example 2. This example uses both the quotient and remainder resulting from the Divide Packed operation. The contents of the work areas and fields prior to the execution of the statements are:

AMTPAID | 0 | 1 | 2 | 5 | 3 | 9 | 6 | C |

UNITS | 1 | 4 | 4 | C |

QRM | 0 | 0 | 0 | 0 | 0 | 0 | 0 | 0 | 0 | 0 | 0 | C |

AVGCOST | 0 | 0 | 0 | 0 | 0 | C |

FRACTION | 0 | 0 | 0 | C |

The coded instruction statements are represented in Figure 10-3.

Statement 001 uses the ZAP instruction to place the dividend (AMTPAID) into the low-order four bytes of the QRM field. The hexadecimal configuration of QRM then is:

QRM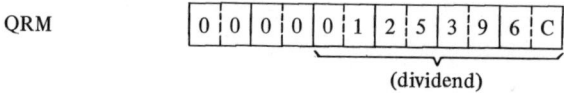
(dividend)

Statement 002 executes the Divide Packed instruction statement, dividing the packed decimal contents of UNITS into the packed decimal contents of QRM, which represents the dividend.

SYSTEM / 370 ASSEMBLER CODING FORM

Name	Operation	Operand	Seq
*			001
DIVRTE	ZAP	QRM,AMTPAID	002
	DP	QRM,UNITS	003
	ZAP	AVGCOST,QRM+1(3)	004
	ZAP	FRACTION,QRM+4(2)	
*			
AMTPAID	DC	PL4'12539.6'	341
UNITS	DC	PL2'144'	342
QRM	DC	PL6'0'	343
AVGCOST	DC	PL3'0'	344
FRACTION	DC	PL2'0'	345
*			

FIGURE 10-3

After completion of this operation, the quotient and remainder are found in QRM in the following form and positions.

QRM | 0 | 0 | 0 | 0 | 8 | 7 | 0 | C | 1 | 1 | 6 | C |
       _____/ _____/
              (quotient)   (remainder)

Statement 003 uses the ZAP instruction to move the *low-order three bytes of the quotient* into an answer field labeled AVGCOST. The second operand in this statement has addressed the first byte beyond the address generated by QRM (QRM+1) and has specified the move length of three bytes of data. The addressing increment points of QRM can be illustrated as:

In this instance the programmer knew that the dividend was being divided by a three-digit divisor; therefore, the quotient was certain to have at least one byte of high-order zero digits. Accordingly, the field that was to contain the stored answer (AVGCOST) was established with a length attribute of one byte less than the dividend. After execution of this instruction, the AVGCOST field would appear as:

AVGCOST | 0 | 0 | 8 | 7 | 0 | C |

Statement 004 uses the ZAP instruction to move the remainder into a storage area. It is assumed that the programmer may have wanted to use this remainder at another point in the program logic. Note the manner in which the remainder is addressed in the second operand of this statement—the starting point of the value of the remainder is four bytes beyond the beginning of the QRM field, hence it is addressed as QRM+4. The two-byte length of the remainder has also been specified, as opposed to allowing it to be inferred as the number of bytes remaining in that field. The contents of the FRACTION field would now be:

FRACTION | 1 | 1 | 6 | C |

Example 3. This example becomes a bit more involved and would have required close attention by the programmer in the use of specific length attributes and address incrementing. The task being performed is to take a single base value and sequentially divide that number and the subsequent quotients by three different values. The hexadecimal configurations of the areas and fields in this example are represented as:

BASE | 0 | 0 | 0 | 0 | 0 | 2 | 6 | 3 | 3 | 5 | 7 | 9 | 5 | 2 | 0 | 0 | 0 | C |

DIVRA | 2 | 0 | 8 | C |

Packed Decimal Arithmetic Operations

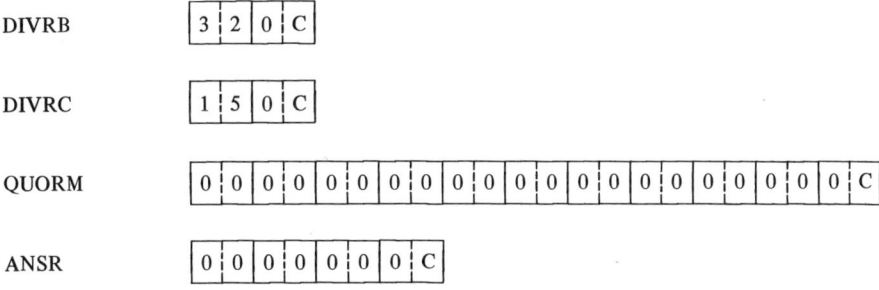

DIVRB | 3 | 2 | 0 | C |

DIVRC | 1 | 5 | 0 | C |

QUORM | 0 | 0 | 0 | 0 | 0 | 0 | 0 | 0 | 0 | 0 | 0 | 0 | 0 | 0 | 0 | 0 | 0 | 0 | 0 | 0 | 0 | 0 | 0 | C |

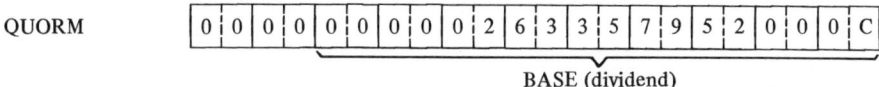

ANSR | 0 | 0 | 0 | 0 | 0 | 0 | 0 | 0 | C |

The coding for this example appears in Figure 10-4.

Statement 001, STARTUP, ZAPs the packed decimal contents of BASE into the division work area labeled QUORM. The hexadecimal configuration of QUORM then appears to be:

QUORM | 0 | 0 | 0 | 0 | 0 | 0 | 0 | 0 | 0 | 2 | 6 | 3 | 3 | 5 | 7 | 9 | 5 | 2 | 0 | 0 | 0 | C |

BASE (dividend)

Statement 002 executes a Divide Packed instruction, dividing the contents of QUORM by the packed decimal contents of DIVRA (+208). The quotient and the remainder then appear in the QUORM field as:

QUORM | 0 | 0 | 0 | 0 | 0 | 0 | 0 | 1 | 2 | 6 | 6 | 1 | 4 | 4 | 0 | 0 | 0 | C | 0 | 0 | 0 | C |

(quotient = 9 bytes)   (remainder = 2 bytes)

Statement 003 uses the ZAP instruction to move the nine-byte quotient into the low-order bytes of the same field, QUORM. Since the next Divide Packed instruction will use this quotient as its dividend, this is an expedient means of getting that value right-aligned into the QUORM field. In order that the ZAP instruction statement would move only the high-order nine bytes (the quotient), the second operand included a specified length of nine bytes. As each DP instruction is encountered during the next several statements, it has been arranged that the assumed length of the QUORM field is decremented by two bytes at a time. Therefore, address adjusting and specific lengths have been assigned to the instruction statements. For the purpose of the problem program at this point, QUORM has now been theoretically reduced to a length of nine bytes and would appear in hexadecimal format as:

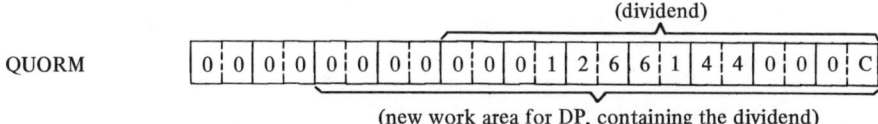

(dividend)

QUORM | 0 | 0 | 0 | 0 | 0 | 0 | 0 | 0 | 0 | 0 | 0 | 1 | 2 | 6 | 6 | 1 | 4 | 4 | 0 | 0 | 0 | C |

(new work area for DP, containing the dividend)

Even though the second operand of the ZAP instruction specifies that only nine bytes of data are to be moved, the first operand still reflects the implied length of QUORM, consequently the high-order two bytes of QUORM are also set to hex zero-digits. In this example, they already contain zeros, but had they contained significant-digits the effect of the implied length for the first operand would have been discernible.

SYSTEM / 370 ASSEMBLER CODING FORM

Name	Operation	Operand	Seq
STARTUP	ZAP	QUORM,BASE	001
	DP	QUORM,DIVRA	002
	ZAP	QUORM,QUORM(9)	003
	DP	QUORM+2(9),DIVRB	004
	ZAP	QUORM,QUORM+2(7)	005
	DP	QUORM+4(7),DIVRC	006
	ZAP	ANSR,QUORM+5(4)	007
*			008
**		* CONSTANTS *	
BASE	DC	PL9'263357952000'	250
DIVRA	DC	PL2'208'	251
DIVRB	DC	PL2'320'	252
DIVRC	DC	PL2'150'	253
QUORM	DC	PL11'0'	254
ANSR	DC	PL4'0'	255
**			256
**			257

FIGURE 10-4

Packed Decimal Arithmetic Operations

Statement 004 now divides the low-order nine bytes of the QUORM field by the two-byte divisor, DIVRB. In order to relate this division to these bytes, the DP instruction addressed the QUORM field as QUORM+2 for a specified length of nine bytes. Inasmuch as the divisor consists of two bytes and the overall specified length of the portion of the QUORM field being used for this instruction is nine bytes, the implication stands that the dividend consists of only seven bytes. Therefore, the quotient will consist of only seven bytes. After execution of this instruction statement, the assumed format of QUORM would be:

QUORM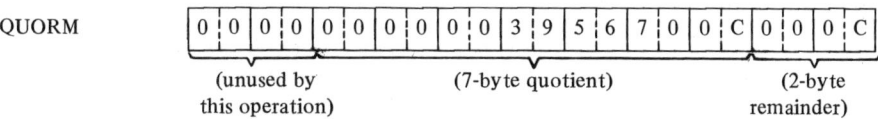

(unused by this operation)   (7-byte quotient)   (2-byte remainder)

Statement 005 uses the ZAP instruction to move the seven-byte quotient, located at QUORM+2, into the low-order bytes of that field, thus right-aligning it in preparation for the next DP instruction. Because the second operand specifies a length attribute of seven bytes, starting at QUORM+2, only the seven bytes of packed decimal representing the quotient are moved. The remainder of QUORM, the high-order four bytes, would be set to zero on the basis that the first operand used the implied length (11 bytes) of QUORM. The hexadecimal format of QUORM would now appear as:

QUORM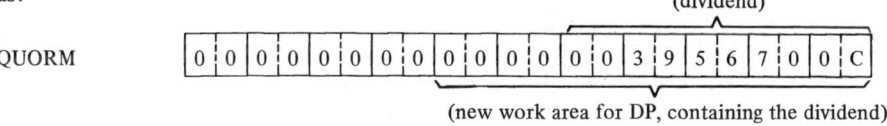

(new work area for DP, containing the dividend)

Statement 006 now divides the low-order seven bytes of the QUORM field by the two-byte divisor, DIVRC. The DP instruction statement has addressed this seven-byte work area as QUORM+4 and has specified a length attribute of seven bytes. This enables the DP instruction statement to perform its operation on that particular part of QUORM, as opposed to utilizing the entire 11 bytes of that field. Because the programmer has, at this point, construed that the overall specified length of the QUORM field to be used is seven bytes and the divisor should consist of two bytes, it is, therefore, to be implied that the dividend, and consequently the quotient, must consist of only five bytes. Upon completion of this instruction statement, the hexadecimal configuration of QUORM would appear to be:

QUORM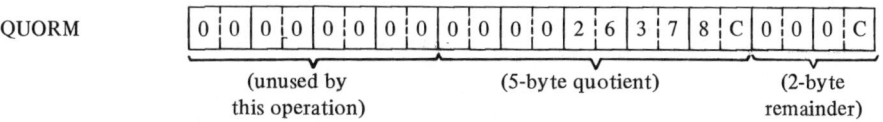

(unused by this operation)   (5-byte quotient)   (2-byte remainder)

Statement 007 uses the ZAP instruction to move the quotient that resulted from the last instruction statement from the QUORM field into a storage area addressed by the label ANSR. Although the quotient is understood to be five bytes of data commencing at QUORM+4, it is known in advance that at least one high-order byte of the quotient will contain zero-digits. The programmer, accordingly, has specified the address of the second operand to commence at QUORM+5 for a length of four bytes. This moves the four low-order bytes of the quotient (bytes 6, 7, 8, and 9 of QUORM) into the ANSR field, whose configuration would then appear as:

ANSR | 0 0 | 2 6 | 3 7 | 8 C |

In coding the instruction statements for this last example, it would not have been necessary to adjust the length attributes of the QUORM field for each successive Divide Packed operation. The programmer could have stipulated that the length of the dividend was always nine bytes and that the divisor always required two bytes, combining to require a work area (QUORM) of 11 bytes for each DP instruction statement. In the format used, however, the logic and means of adjusting field lengths and addresses was well demonstrated.

Move with Offset (MVO)

Although this instruction does not perform a true arithmetic function, it is used so frequently with arithmetic routines that it should logically be discussed at this time.

This instruction takes the data specified by the second operand and moves it to the location specified by the first operand but offset within the field by one half-byte to the left of the low-order position.

If the length of the first operand field (the receiving field) is longer than the length of the second operand field (the sending field), the high-order nibbles of the first operand field are set up as zero-digits. If the length of the first operand field is shorter than the second operand field, the excess nibbles in the second operand field are ignored.

Data is moved from the sending field to the receiving field in four-bit increments, moving from right to left—low-order to high-order. The offset of one half-byte is in the receiving field only.

A frequent application for this instruction is to remove unwanted decimal point positions in a packed decimal value. This application will be illustrated in the section titled "Packed Decimal Logic with Assumed Decimal Points," which follows within this section.

Example 1. The packed decimal field to be manipulated is defined as:

```
PACKFLD5      DC      PL5 ' 32596421 '
```

PACKFLD5 | 0 | 3 | 2 | 5 | 9 | 6 | 4 | 2 | 1 | C |

The instruction statement to be executed is:

```
MVO    PACKFLD5 (5) , PACKFLD5 (3)
```

The resulting action will be accomplished by this statement in the following manner:

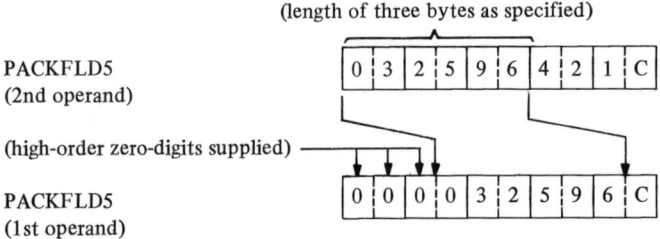

This instruction statement takes the first three bytes of PACKFLD5, as specified by the second operand, and moves them into PACKFLD5, right-aligned and offset by one half-byte. Since the sending field is shorter in length than the receiving field, the high-order digit positions of the receiving field are supplied with zero-digit values.

Example 2. The packed decimal fields to be manipulated in this example are:

```
PKFIELDA    DC    PL5 ' 13376711 '
PKFIELDB    DC    PL3 ' 50 '
```

The MVO instruction statement to be performed is:

MVO   PKFIELDB , PKFIELDA+2 (2)

The movement of the data as specified by this statement would be accomplished in the following manner:

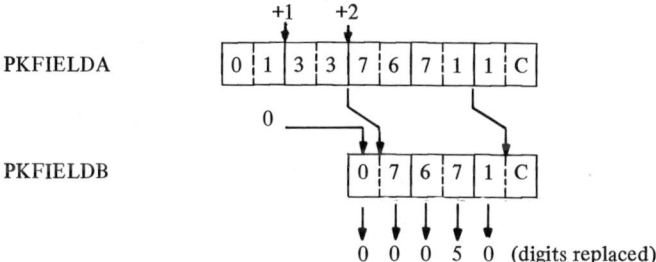

This example states that two bytes of packed decimal data within PKFIELDA, commencing at the third byte of that field (PKFIELDA+2) for a length of two bytes, are to be moved into the whole of PKFIELDB, right-aligned and offset in the low-order position by one half-byte. As requested, the two bytes of data containing the hexadecimal digits '7671' are moved into PKFIELDB, offset to the left by four bits. This effectively creates a validly signed packed decimal value of +7,671 since the standard plus-sign ('C') in the low-order nibble is undisturbed.

Example 3. This example is intended to show the resulting configuration of the movement of an entire field of packed decimal data (containing a sign-digit) into another packed decimal field that already contains a sign-digit. The data fields are:

```
FLDE    DC    PL3 ' 1395 '
FLDF    DC    PL3 ' 00 '
```

FLDE | 0 | 1 | 3 | 9 | 5 | C |

FLDF | 0 | 0 | 0 | 0 | 0 | C |

The instruction statement to be executed, and the resulting action from the performance of that statement, is as follows:

MVO   FLDF , FLDE

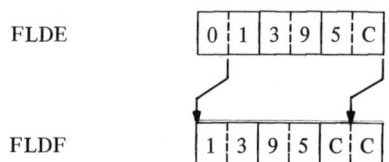

Because the entire sending field is moved and the low-order nibble of the receiving field is not altered, the result is that FLDF has become invalid for packed decimal arithmetic applications; it now has a hexadecimal digit with a value greater than '9' in a position other than the right-most nibble of the field. The proper means of moving FLDE to FLDF, in this instance, would have been to use the ZAP instruction.

Shift and Round Packed Decimals (SRP) (System/370 Only)

The SRP instruction provides the programmer with the capability to cause a lateral shift, either to the left or right, of the hexadecimal numeric digits contained within a packed decimal field of storage. Considering that the maximum length of a packed decimal field is 16 bytes, representing 31 packed decimal numeric digits and a sign-digit, the SRP instruction allows a shift of from one to 31 digits in either direction. The sign-digit is not affected by the shift.

The SRP is a three-operand instruction. Two of those operands, however, are for the purpose of specifying the options available with the instruction. Only the first operand, the $D_1(L_1,B_1)$ portion, is used to address a field of data in main storage. That field must be in valid packed decimal format; it must have a valid sign-digit in the right-most nibble, all other digits must be hexadecimal numerics, and the length may range only from one to 16 bytes.

The second operand, indicated in the instruction format as $D_2(B_2)$, is used to specify the direction of the shift and the number of positions that the field contents are to be shifted. Despite the fact that this operand is identical to operands normally used to create an address from base register and displacement values, its use in the SRP instruction statement does not follow the normal use. It does not represent an address. Instead, it is a coded value that must be carefully established. The concern for emphasizing this point is that regardless of the combined, implied, or explicit value generated by this operand, only the resulting low-order (right-most) six bit positions will be used as the code for indicating the direction and range of the shift. Those six bit positions are interpreted as a fixed-point value, consisting of a high-order sign-bit and five integer bits. A positive value specifies a left shift; a negative value specifies a right shift. Interpretation of the contents of these six bit positions is demonstrated in the following examples:

shift values	direction and range of shift
0 0 0 1 0 1	shift left for five positions
1 1 1 1 1 1	shift right for one position
0 0 0 0 0 1	shift left for one position
1 1 0 1 1 0	shift right for ten positions
0 0 1 1 1 1	shift left for 15 positions
1 1 1 1 1 0	shift right for two positions
1 0 1 1 1 1	shift right for 17 positions
0 1 0 0 0 0	shift left for 16 positions
0 1 1 1 1 1	shift left for 31 positions
1 0 0 0 0 1	shift right for 31 positions

Packed Decimal Arithmetic Operations

There are several ways of expressing the second operand so as to correctly specify the desired six-bit value. It can be accomplished equally well in the form of an absolute value or as variations of base register value and displacement. Examine the second operand in each of the following statements.

1. SRP   PAKFLD1, 23, 0
2. SRP   PAKFLD2, 64-7, 0
3. SRP   PAKFLD3, 0(7), 0
4. SRP   PAKFLD4, 5, 0
5. SRP   PAKFLD5, 64-30, 0
6. SRP   PAKFLD6, 0(10), 0

Statement 1 requests a left shift, moving the contents of PAKFLD1 23 positions to the left. Although the second operand is considered to be comprised of D_2 (B_2) values, the B_2 value is interpreted as zero whenever an absolute value is specified without the base register portion of the operand. The absolute value is interpreted as displacement only.

Statement 2 requests a 7-position shift to the right of all hex numeric digits in PAKFLD2. The notation form of "64-7" is a convenient means of expressing a negative value for a six-bit fixed-point field. This can be shown as:

(halfword value of 64)	0 0 0 0 0 0 0 0 0 1 0 0 0 0 0 0
(less 7)	0 0 0 0 0 0 0 0 0 0 0 0 0 1 1 1
(result)	0 0 0 0 0 0 0 0 0 0 1 1 1 0 0 1
(extract 6 low-order bit positions)	1 1 1 0 0 1
(value)	-7

Statement 3 is not self-defining as to the direction of length of the move. The value contained in the low-order six bit positions of register 7 will determine these factors. It is assumed that a previous statement within the program placed an appropriate value within that register.

Statement 4 specifies a 5-position shift to the left for all packed decimal numeric digits contained in the field PAKFLD4.

Statement 5 calls for a shift to the right of all numeric digits in PAKFLD5, moving each digit 30 positions to the right. The notation of "64-30" creates a validly-signed six-bit negative value of -30.

Statement 6 could only be interpreted by knowing the value contained in register 10. The low-order six bit positions of that value would determine the length and direction of the move.

The third operand of each SRP instruction statement (I_3) is used only for specifying the value to be used for "rounding" after a right shift. However, the I_3 operand *must* be specified at all times, regardless of whether the shift is to the left or right, or whether rounding is desired or not. Expressed as an "immediate" value, the third operand is added to the final packed decimal numeric digit shifted out to the right. If the sum of that addition results in a value greater than 9, a "carry" of 1 is added to the right-most numeric digit remaining within the packed decimal field. This action is demonstrated in subsequent examples.

As the packed decimal field is being shifted, either left or right, packed decimal zero-digits are supplied to the digit positions vacated. The original packed decimal digits shifted out of the length of the field are lost. They cannot be retained or recovered. For a right shift, it makes no difference whether the packed decimal numeric digits shifted out were zero-digits or significant digits (non-zero numeric digits). On a left shift, however, the shifting-out of a significant (non-zero) digit results in a decimal overflow condition.

It is possible, if the programmer has a reason to do so, to create an SRP instruction statement with a shift length of zero. Such a statement might be shown as:

```
    SRP    PACKFLD9,0,0
```

Whenever this statement is encountered, in its illustrated form, no shifting of data would occur. Even though no shift is requested, the statement would be audited for:

- A valid sign in the low-order half-byte.
- Valid packed decimal digits in all other half-bytes of the field.
- A valid value stated as the I_3 operand.

For all intents and purposes, the SRP instruction can be used for multiplying (a left shift) by powers of 10 (10, 100, 1000, 10000, etc.), or for dividing (a right shift) by powers of ten. It might also be construed as a convenient means of eliminating or adding assumed decimal points within a packed decimal field.

The following examples present the specific actions which would occur during various SRP operations.

Example 1

In this example the contents of a field labeled DATAPAK1 are to be shifted eight positions to the right. Rounding is not requested. Before the shift, DATAPAK1 appears as:

DATAPAK1 | 0 | 0 | 0 | 0 | 3 | 0 | 0 | 8 | 9 | 1 | 6 | 2 | 3 | 0 | 5 | C |

The instruction statement is:

```
    SRP    DATAPAK1, 64-8, 0
```

The action taken on the field labeled DATAPAK1 would appear to be:

The original value of +30,089,162,305 as contained in DATAPAK1 has been reduced to +300. This is comparable to having divided the original contents of DATAPAK1 by 100,000,000.

Example 2

The contents of HOLDPAK6 are to be shifted to the left four positions.

HOLDPAK6 | 0 | 0 | 0 | 0 | 0 | 2 | 1 | 7 | 7 | 3 | 5 | C |

The instruction statement being executed is:

SRP   HOLDPAK6 , 4 , 0

The shifting of the data would appear as:

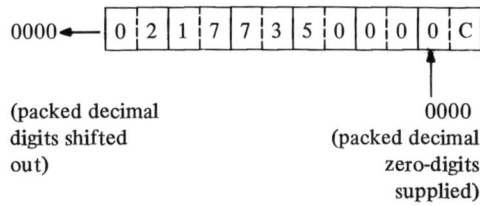

(packed decimal digits shifted out)   0000 (packed decimal zero-digits supplied)

The value of 217,735 originally contained in HOLDPAK6 has been increased to 2,177,350,000. This is comparable to multiplying the original contents by 10,000.

Example 3

The statements to be executed in this example include:

```
PAK6       DC    PL9 ' 32481696907          101
SHIFTR     DC    F ' -4 '                   102
*
SHIFTRTE   LA    3 , SHIFTR                 201
           SRP   PAK6 , 0 (3) , 5           202
```

The intent is to shift the contents of PAK6 four positions to the right and to provide rounding with a value of 5.

Statement #201 uses the Load Address instruction to load a value of '-4' into general register 3.

Statement #202 executes the shift. As controlled by the contents of register 3, specified as the second operand B_2 segment, the shift is to the right for 4 positions. Before rounding, the shifting of PAK6 would appear as:

(packed decimal zero-digits supplied)

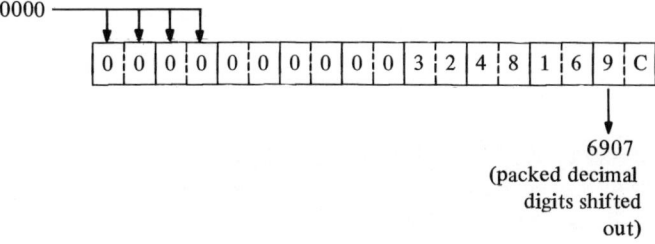

6907
(packed decimal digits shifted out)

The rounding would appear to occur as:

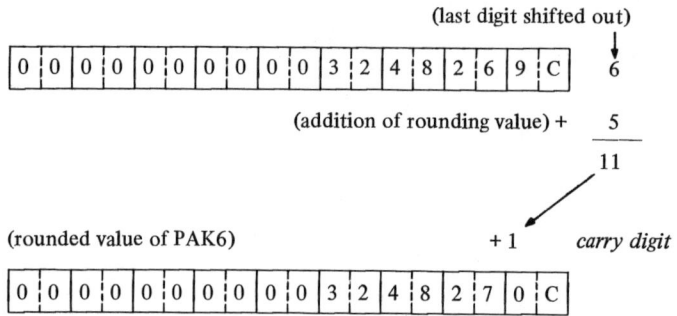

Example 4

The field to be shifted is:

PKHLD

The instruction statement being executed is:

   SRP   PKHLD,5,0

The shifting action would proceed as:

(packed decimal
digits shifted out)

The execution of this example would not have completed successfully due to the high-order shifting out of a significant digit ("3"). As soon as the packed decimal digit "3" had been lost, a decimal overflow condition would have been signalled, interrupting the program.

The following are also offered as examples of SRP instruction statements which would not complete successfully.

Example 1

SETPAKA | 2 | 8 | 9 | 7 | 5 | C | 8 | 3 | 0 | C |

     SRP   SETPAKA,3,0

                Explanation: The sixth digit from the left (Hex "C") is not a valid packed decimal numeric and significant hex digits would have been shifted out.

Example 2

SETPAKB | 0 | 3 | 9 | 8 | 5 | 2 | 6 | 4 |

    SRP   SETPAKB , 64-3 , 5

> Explanation: The field SETPAKB is not validly signed. The operation of this instruction statement would be suppressed.

PACKED DECIMAL LOGIC WITH ASSUMED DECIMAL POINTS

The majority of programmers find that they frequently are required to use decimal point logic in performing packed decimal arithmetic operations. It is reasonably certain, therefore, you will require knowledge of this concept as well as a familiarity with *"rounding"* packed decimal values. As in the case of fixed-point arithmetic operations, extra decimal places can be added or deleted in a packed decimal field by multiplying or dividing by 10, 100, 1000, etc. In working with packed decimal values, it will be noted that the Move with Offset and Shift and Round Packed Decimals instructions may perform many of these tasks in a more efficient manner.

Whether you desire to add decimal point positions or to delete them, there are several ways by which duplicate results may be obtained. It must be your responsibility to determine which method is best suited to your needs, preferably a decision that will be based on the efficiency of the operations, rather than on "likes" and "dislikes." The examples that follow will present a reasonable comparison of these methods on the basis of the coding required. The efficiency of their performance must be rated by the computer system on which they are applied and the requirements of the problem program.

Example 1. The coding sheet illustration shown in Figure 10-5 contains the instruction statements to be executed and the definition of the field and work areas to be used. Wherever applicable, the assumed number of decimal point positions are indicated as a comment on the same line as the field or area.

Statement 001 uses the ZAP instruction to move the value of UNITS into the low-order bytes of WORK. The hexadecimal configuration of WORK would then appear as:

WORK | 0 | 0 | 0 | 0 | 0 | 0 | 0 | 0 | 0 | 7 | 8 | 3 | 5 | C |

Statement 002 multiplies the value of WORK (containing the multiplicand) by the value of COSTPER, the multiplier. The resulting product would be configured in WORK as:

WORK | 0 | 0 | 0 | 0 | 0 | 1 | 6 | 5 | 7 | 1 | 0 | 2 | 5 | C |

                (assumed decimal point)

Since the value of COSTPER contains three assumed decimal point positions, the product is considered to have a similar number of assumed decimal positions. The product, therefore, is

Name	Operation	Operand	Comments	Seq
STARTER	ZAP	WORK,UNITS		001
	MP	WORK,COSTPER		002
	AP	WORK,ROUND1		003
	MVO	WORK(7),WORK(6)		004
	ZAP	GROSS,WORK+3(4)		005
	MP	WORK,DISCOUNT		006
	AP	WORK,ROUND2		007
	MVO	WORK(7),WORK(6)		008
	MVO	WORK(7),WORK(6)		009
	ZAP	NET,WORK+3(4)		010
				011
*				
UNITS	DC	PL3'1835'	(xxxxx. ASSUMED)	460
COSTPER	DC	PL3'2115'	(x.000 ASSUMED)	461
GROSS	DC	PL4'0'	(xxxxx.00 ASSUMED)	462
DISCOUNT	DC	PL2'95'	(x.00 ASSUMED)	463
NET	DC	PL4'0'	(xxxxx.00 ASSUMED)	464
WORK	DC	PL7'0'		465
ROUND1	DC	PL1'5'		466
ROUND2	DC	PL2'50'		467
*				468

FIGURE 10-5

Packed Decimal Arithmetic Operations

construed to have a value of +16,571.025. The desired answer at this point must be rounded off to the nearest cent, which is taken care of by the next instruction statement.

Statement 003 adds a value of +5 to the low-order of WORK, effectively rounding that value to the nearest cent. WORK would now appear as:

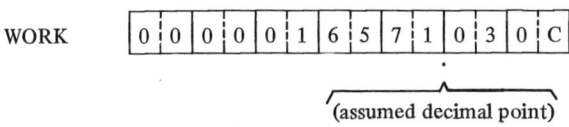

Statement 004 uses the MVO instruction to remove one decimal point position from the value contained in WORK. This is done because that value is to be moved to GROSS by the next instruction statement, and GROSS is set up to accept a value containing only two assumed decimal point positions. The logic of the MVO instruction statement is to move the first seven bytes of WORK into the low-order positions of WORK, offset by one half-byte. The action can be represented by this illustration:

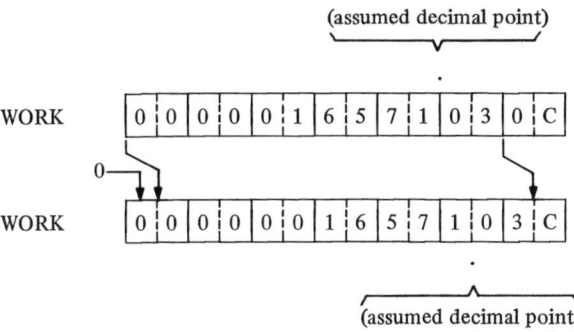

Statement 005 uses the ZAP instruction to move the low-order four bytes of WORK, as specified by the operand WORK+3 (4), into the field labeled GROSS. The contents of GROSS should then appear to contain:

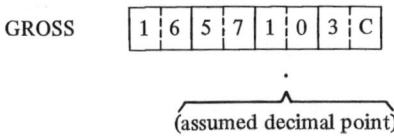

Statement 006 multiplies the contents of WORK (the same value as is in GROSS) by the value of DISCOUNT. Inasmuch as WORK already contained two assumed decimal point positions and DISCOUNT contains two assumed decimal point positions, the resulting product in WORK must be considered to contain four assumed decimal point positions. Upon completion of the execution of this instruction statement, the hex configuration of WORK would be:

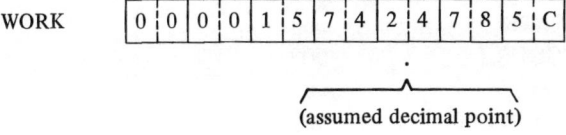

In effect, a 5% discount has been taken against the gross amount (95% of gross) resulting in a net value. This value must now be rounded to the nearest cent and moved to NET.

Statement 007 adds +50 to WORK in order to round that value to the nearest cent. WORK would now appear as:

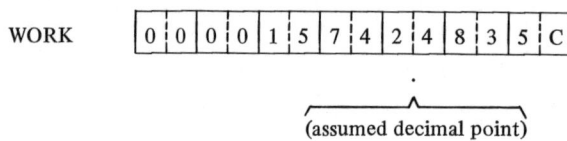

Statements 008 and 009 are a duplicate set of Move with Offset instructions. They would cause the following change on WORK as a result of their execution.

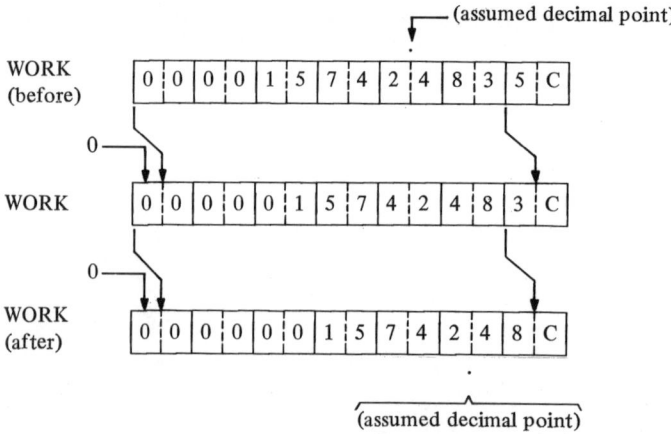

It would have been possible to reduce the value of WORK by two decimal point positions by dividing that value by +100. The use of a duplicate MVO instruction was taken in order to show the action of these instruction sets in an instance where an even number of positions are to be removed.

Statement 010 uses the ZAP instruction to move the low-order four bytes of WORK into an answer field labeled NET. The hex configuration of NET would then appear as:

NET | 1 | 5 | 7 | 4 | 2 | 4 | 8 | C |

(assumed decimal point)

By comparison, if the computer system for which this routine was coded allowed the use of the SRP (Shift and Round Packed Decimals) instruction, this example could have been coded in significantly fewer statements. Compare the following instruction statements to those in Figure 10-5. (The DC statements would remain the same.)

```
        STARTER    ZAP    WORK , UNITS          001
                   MP     WORK , COSTPER        002
                   SRP    WORK , 64-1 , 5       003
                   ZAP    GROSS , WORK+3 (4)    005
```

Packed Decimal Arithmetic Operations

```
MP    WORK , DISCOUNT      006
SRP   WORK , 64-2 , 5      007
ZAP   NET , WORK+3 (4)     010
```

As demonstrated, instruction statements 003 and 007 above have replaced statements 003, 004, 007, 008, and 009 of the original code in FIGURE 10-5. The results are identical, but the revised code would have executed more efficiently.

Example 2. This example is merely a series of MVO instruction statements operating on various fields. It indicates the addressing required to delete low-order decimal point positions in increments of 1, 3, 5, 7, etc., as coded by the instruction statements in Figure 10-6.

Statement 001 uses the MVO instruction to reduce the value of FLDPKA by one decimal point position as it moves it into RECVA. This move would appear to be accomplished as:

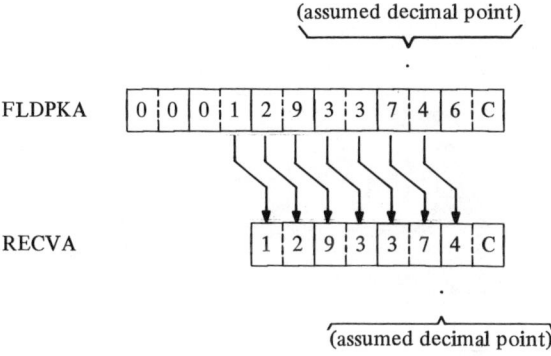

This has now moved the contents of FLDPKA into RECVA and changed the value of its contents from +129,337.46 to +129,337.4.

Statement 002 reduces the value of FLDPKB by three decimal point positions as it moves it into RECVB. This would appear as:

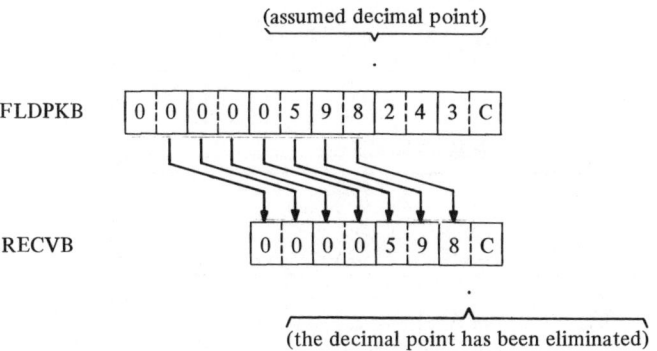

This has moved the packed decimal contents of FLDPKB into RECVB and has changed the value from +598.243 to +598.

Statement 003 moves the value of FLDPKC into RECVC by using the MVO instruction, but is reducing that value by five decimal point positions as the move is accomplished.

SYSTEM / 370 ASSEMBLER CODING FORM

Name	Operation	Operand	Comments	Identification Sequence No
*				
MODRTE	MVO	RECVA,FLDPKA(5)		0001
	MVO	RECVB,FLDPKB(4)		002
	MVO	RECVC,FLDPKC(3)		003
	MVO	RECVD,FLDPKD(2)		004
*				
*				
FLDPKA	DC	PL6'12933746'	(xxxxxxx.00 ASSUMED)	392
FLDPKB	DC	PL6'598243'	(xxxx.xx.000 ASSUMED)	393
FLDPKC	DC	PL6'216597718'	(x.xx.000000 ASSUMED)	394
FLDPKD	DC	PL6'111249003'	(.000000000 ASSUMED)	395
RECVA	DC	PL4'0'		396
RECVB	DC	PL4'0'		397
RECVC	DC	PL3'0'		398
RECVD	DC	PL2'0'		399
*				400
				401
				402

FIGURE 10-6

Packed Decimal Arithmetic Operations

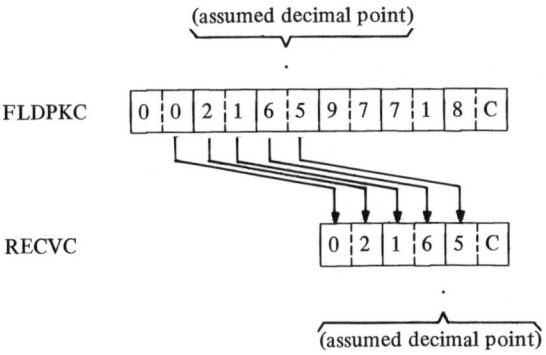

The packed decimal contents of FLDPKC have now been partially moved into RECVC, but in doing so the value of that data has been changed from +216.597718 to +216.5.

Statement 004 uses the MVO instruction to move a portion of the contents of FLDPKD into RECVD, reducing the data by seven decimal point positions during the move. The configuration of the data as it is changed would appear as:

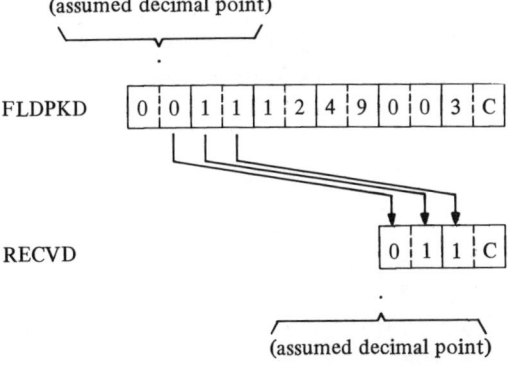

This has effectively reduced the value by seven decimal places during the move from FLDPKD to RECVD, decreasing the expressed value from +.0111249003 to +.011.

To duplicate the action of these instruction statements through the use of the SRP instruction, it would be necessary to code the following:

```
        MODRTE  SRP     FLDPKA , 64-1 , 0              001
                ZAP     RECVA (4) , FLDPKA+2 (4)       002
                SRP     FLDPKB , 64-3 , 0              003
                ZAP     RECVB (4) , FLDPKB+2 (4)       004
                SRP     FLDPKC , 64-5 , 0              005
                ZAP     RECVC (3) , FLDPKC+3 (3)       006
                SRP     FLDPKD , 64-7 , 0              007
                ZAP     RECVD (2) , FLDPKD+5 (2)       008
```

Comparing these instruction statements against those in Figure 10-6 shows that the use of the SRP instruction for this routine requires twice as many statements. This is necessary inasmuch as the SRP instruction addresses only one field of stored data. Therefore, for the sample coding shown, it is necessary to perform the shift in the original field and subsequently move the data into the second field. In the original instruction statements in Figure 10-6 the MVO instruction is able to accomplish both the shifting and the movement of the data to the second field in one statement. At this point it is necessary to admit there has been a bit of subtle deceit in the presentation of this particular comparison. Before reading on, see if you can determine what single condition made the MVO instruction appear more efficient when both a shift and a move between two packed decimal fields is required. The answer to that question is that in all cases of the coding for this example the number of shift positions has been an odd quantity. As illustrated previously within this chapter, a single MVO instruction can reduce a packed decimal field only by an odd quantity (1, 3, 5, 7, etc.) of packed decimal digits. To reduce a packed decimal field by an even quantity (2, 4, 6, etc.) of packed decimal digits would require two consecutive MVO instructions. Therefore, if the program logic requires a reduction of an even-numbered quantity of packed decimal digits and a move of that data to another field, use of the MVO instruction or the SRP instruction would be reasonably comparable.

Example 3. This example demonstrates the method of reducing a value by an even number of decimal point positions or digits, as referred to in the immediately preceding examples. This can be accomplished by a Divide Packed instruction or by two Move with Offset instructions. Both methods will be illustrated (see Figure 10-7).

Statement 001 uses the ZAP instruction to move the packed decimal value of AFLD into the low-order bytes of QUORM in preparation for a divide instruction. The hex configuration of QUORM would now be:

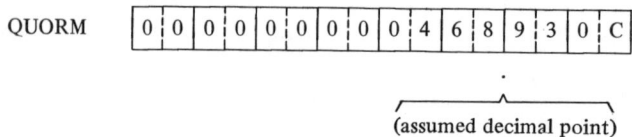

Statement 002 divides the packed decimal value of QUORM by a packed decimal literal value of +100. This action reduces the value contained in QUORM by the two low-order digit positions. As a result of this instruction the configuration of QUORM will appear to be:

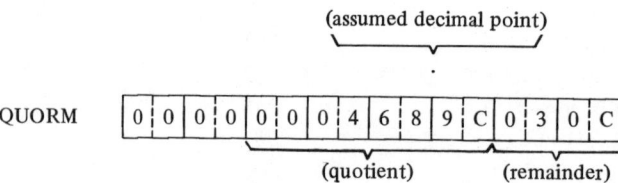

As shown, the original value of the dividend, which is now represented by the quotient, has been reduced from +468.930 to +468.9.

Packed Decimal Arithmetic Operations

Name	Operation	Operand	Comments	Seq
SPECRTE	ZAP	QUORM,AFLD		001
	DP	QUORM+2(6),=PL2'100'		002
	ZAP	HOLDA,QUORM+3(3)		003
	MVO	BFLD(4),BFLD(3)		004
	MVO	HOLDB,BFLD(3)		005
	ZAP	QUORM,CFLD		006
	DP	QUORM,=PL3'10000'		007
	ZAP	HOLDC,QUORM+2(3)		008
	MVO	DFLD,DFLD(2)		009
	MVO	HOLDD,DFLD+3(1)		010
AFLD	DC	PL4'468930'	(xxxx.000 ASSUMED)	685
BFLD	DC	PL4'468930'	(xxxx.000 ASSUMED)	686
CFLD	DC	PL5'126000521'	(xxx.000000 ASSUMED)	687
DFLD	DC	PL5'765994444'	(xxxxxxxxx. ASSUMED)	688
QUORM	DC	PL8'0'		689
HOLDA	DC	PL3'0'		690
HOLDB	DC	PL3'0'		691
HOLDC	DC	PL3'0'		692
HOLDD	DC	PL2'0'		693

FIGURE 10-7

Statement 003 moves the low-order three bytes of the quotient out of the QUORM field and into the HOLDA field. HOLDA would now contain that data as:

Statement 004 performs an MVO instruction to reduce the value of BFLD by one low-order digit. BFLD will then have a value configuration of +468.93 based on the following action:

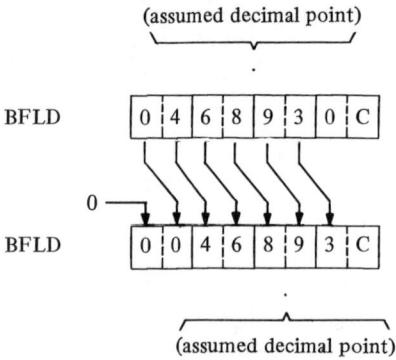

This statement is the first of two steps to delete two low-order digits from the value of BFLD. The deletion of the second digit is accomplished by the next instruction statement.

Statement 005 moves the value of BFLD to HOLDB and at the same time removes one more low-order digit position.

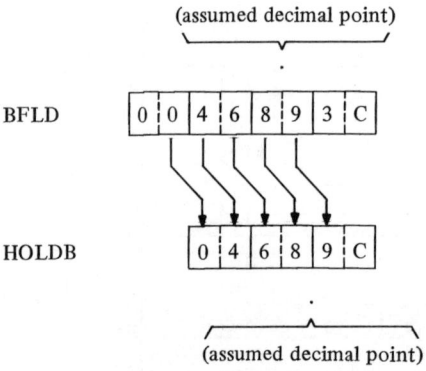

By comparing the results of Statements 004 and 005 to that of Statements 001, 002, and 003 you will note that they create the same final value. Both AFLD and BFLD had the same original value; now HOLDA and HOLDB have identical values.

Statement 006 ZAPs the content value of CFLD into the low-order bytes of QUORM.

QUORM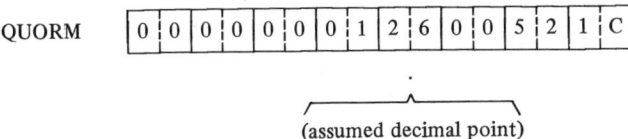

(assumed decimal point)

Statement 007 divides QUORM by a packed decimal literal of +10,000 in order to reduce the value in QUORM by four low-order digits. After execution of this statement, QUORM will appear as:

QUORM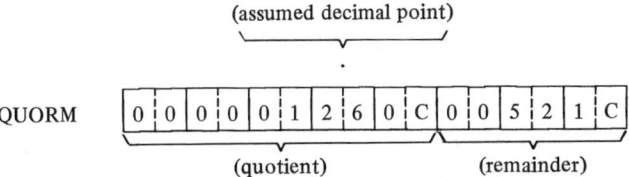

Statement 008 takes the low-order three bytes of the quotient [QUORM+2(3)] and moves it into HOLDC by using the ZAP instruction. CFLD has now been reduced by four low-order digits, changing its assumed value from +12.600521 to +12.60, and that value now resides in HOLDC.

HOLDC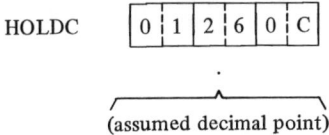

(assumed decimal point)

Statements 009 and 010 use a pair of MVO instructions to reduce the magnitude of the packed decimal value of DFLD by six low-order digits. In doing so the value is also moved to HOLDD by Statement 010. The action accomplished by these two statements is represented by the next illustration.

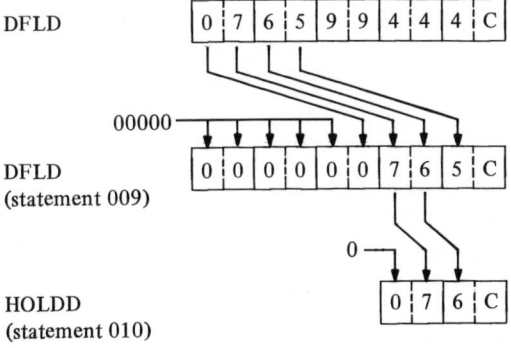

As shown, the low-order six digits of DFLD have been successfully deleted.

By utilizing the SRP instruction, the logic processing produced by the code in Figure 10-7 could have been alternatively coded as:

```
SPECRTE   SRP    AFLD , 64-2 , 0              001
          ZAP    HOLDA (3) , AFLD+1 (3)       002
          SRP    BFLD , 64-2 , 0              003
          ZAP    HOLDB (3) , BFLD+1 (3)       004
          SRP    CFLD , 64-4 , 0              005
          ZAP    HOLDC (3) , CFLD+2 (3)       006
          SRP    DFLD , 64-6 , 0              007
          ZAP    HOLDD (2) , DFLD+3 (2)       008
```

In this instance the reduction of the quantity of instruction statements is not particularly significant, but the technique would be consistent and perhaps easier to understand and interpret.

Example 4. Supplying additional zero-digits to the low-order positions of a packed decimal value can be easily accomplished using the Multiply Packed instruction. This is illustrated using the following coding:

```
VALUE1    DC     PL4 ' 2664 '
VALUE2    DC     PL6 ' 5983 '
VALUE3    DC     PL6 ' 7717 '
VALUE4    DC     PL7 ' 4092 '
*
RTE1      MP     VALUE1 , =PL2 ' 100 '        0001
          MP     VALUE2 , =PL3 ' 1000 '       0002
          MP     VALUE3 , =PL3 ' 10000 '      0003
          MP     VALUE4 , =PL4 ' 100000 '     0004
```

Statement 0001 increases the value of VALUE1 by the increment of two low-order zero-digits. This is accomplished by multiplying its current value by a packed decimal literal of +100. The configuration of the field VALUE1 would appear as:

VALUE1 (before) | 0 | 0 | 0 | 2 | 6 | 6 | 4 | C |

VALUE1 (after) | 0 | 2 | 6 | 6 | 4 | 0 | 0 | C |

Statement 0002 effectively adds three low-order zero-digits to the value of VALUE2 by multiplying that field with a packed decimal literal of +1000.

VALUE2 (before) | 0 | 0 | 0 | 0 | 0 | 0 | 0 | 5 | 9 | 8 | 3 | C |

VALUE2 (after) | 0 | 0 | 0 | 0 | 5 | 9 | 8 | 3 | 0 | 0 | 0 | C |

Statement 0003 increases the content value of VALUE3 by multiplying it by a packed decimal literal of +10,000. This action has added four low-order zero-digits to the original value.

VALUE3 (before): | 0 | 0 | 0 | 0 | 0 | 0 | 0 | 7 | 7 | 1 | 7 | C |

VALUE3 (after): | 0 | 0 | 0 | 7 | 7 | 1 | 7 | 0 | 0 | 0 | 0 | C |

Statement 0004 effectively increases the value of VALUE4 by adding five low-order zero-digits.

VALUE4 (before): | 0 | 0 | 0 | 0 | 0 | 0 | 0 | 0 | 0 | 4 | 0 | 9 | 2 | C |

VALUE4 (after): | 0 | 0 | 0 | 0 | 4 | 0 | 9 | 2 | 0 | 0 | 0 | 0 | 0 | C |

For purposes of comparison, the four MP (Multiply Packed Decimals) instruction statements could also have been coded as:

```
RTE1    SRP     VALUE1,2,0          001
        SRP     VALUE2,3,0          002
        SRP     VALUE3,4,0          003
        SRP     VALUE4,5,0          004
```

The examples shown on these pages should provide you with sufficient material to manipulate any assumed decimal point assignments with packed decimal values. This concept might well be used for general reduction or incrementing of whole values, not necessarily in conjunction with decimal point logic. By utilizing the MP, DP, MVO, SRP, and ZAP instructions, packed decimal values can be rearranged and/or configured in any valid manner that might be required by the problem program.

REVIEW EXERCISES

The following problems are either in the form of questions or instruction statements to be executed. For the questions, select the correct answer, or fill in the missing word or words; for the instruction statements, fill in the field layouts as they would appear after execution of the instruction statement.

1. EBCDIC numeric character data is converted to packed decimal format by the _____ instruction.
2. A left shift of three positions via the SRP instruction is the same as multiplying the value of the packed decimal field by _____.
3. Fixed-point values are converted to packed decimal values by _____ instruction.
4. Packed decimal instruction statements are unique in that both operands have either an implied or explicit _____ attribute.
5. Both the first and second operands of an SRP instruction statement may address a packed decimal field of up to 16 bytes in length (True) (False).

6. INFLD: | 3 | 2 | 5 | 9 | 6 |

   PAKFLD: | 1 | 7 | 0 | 6 | 2 | 3 | 9 | D |

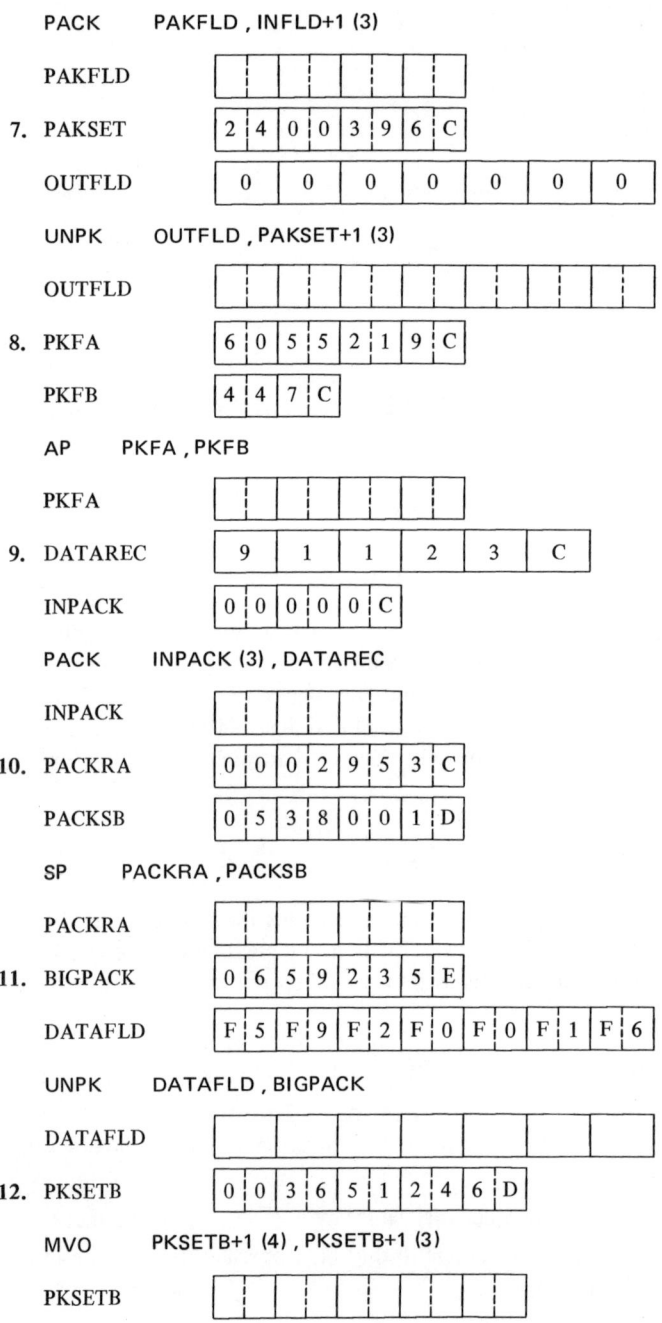

Packed Decimal Arithmetic Operations

13. PKFLD | 0 | 0 | 0 | 0 | 0 | 0 | 0 | 0 | 0 | 0 | 0 | C |

    MPLIER | 0 | 2 | 2 | 1 | 4 | C |

    MPCAND | 0 | 0 | 0 | 3 | 9 | 1 | 1 | C |

    MULRTE   ZAP   PKFLD , MPCAND+1 (3)
                 MP   PKFLD , MPLIER

    PKFLD | | | | | | | | | |

14. In using the SRP instruction, when must a value be specified for the I_3 operand? _____
15. The maximum length of the divisor in a DP instruction statement is _____ bytes.
16. If the multiplicand field is 6 bytes in length and the multiplier field is 4 bytes in length, then the product field of the corresponding MP instruction statement should be _____ bytes long.
17. Packed decimal data to be converted into a fixed-point value must be contained within an _____ byte field that is _____-aligned.
18. With the SRP instruction, a positive (+) value is used to specify a _____ shift.
19. If the EBCDIC alphabetic characters "ABCDEF" are packed and then immediately unpacked they would then be the EBCDIC characters "_____".
20. The work area for a DP instruction, referred to as the "quorem," should be equal in length to the combined lengths of the dividend and the _____.
21. Only the _____ operand in a ZAP instruction statement must represent a validly signed packed decimal field.
22. A right shift of a packed decimal field could be specified as:

    SRP   PAKDATA , 8 (3) , 0

    (True) (False)
23. Fixed-point values may be converted into EBCDIC numeric character form via the combined use of both the _____ and the _____ instructions.
24. If an EBCDIC field that is being packed contains more numeric characters than can be contained within the receiving packed decimal field, then the _____-order numeric digits of the sending field are ignored.
25. The Move with Offset (MVO) instruction moves the contents of the sending field into the receiving field but offset to the _____ by a half-byte within the receiving field.
26. If a signed three-byte packed decimal field is being unpacked into an eight-byte field, the three high-order bytes of the receiving field will each be supplied with a hexadecimal configuration of X '_____'.

27. Would an overflow condition occur if a five-byte packed decimal field containing a value of +395 was shifted by a statement of:

SRP   PAKFIELD , 64-8 , 0

   (Yes) (No)

28. PAKFLDA | 2 | 0 | 4 | 0 | 9 | 3 | 6 | C |

    PAKFLDB | 0 | 0 | 1 | 9 | 0 | 6 | 4 | 5 | 1 | C |

    SP   PAKFLDA , PAKFLDB

    PAKFLDA | | | | | |

29. PAKFLDC | 0 | 0 | 0 | 0 | 0 | 6 | 0 | 0 | 3 | C |

    DATAPAK | 6 | 0 | 0 | 5 | 0 | 0 | 0 | D |

    ZAP   DATAPAK+1 (3) , PAKFLDC+2 (3)

    DATAPAK | | | | | |

30. DIVRPAK | 0 | 4 | 0 | C |

    DIVNDPAK | 0 | 4 | 1 | 6 | 2 | 0 | 6 | C |

    QUOREM | 0 | 0 | 0 | 0 | 0 | 0 | 0 | 0 | 0 | 0 | 0 | C |

    ZAP   QUOREM , DIVNDPAK
    DP   QUOREM , DIVRPAK

    QUOREM | | | | | | | | |

31. SETPAKA | 0 | 0 | 8 | 9 | 2 | 6 | 0 | 0 | 4 | C |

    SETPAKB | 4 | 6 | 2 | 1 | 3 | 9 | 8 | D |

    SP   SETPAKA , SETPAKB

    SETPAKA | | | | | | | |

32. MULTIPAK | 0 | 0 | 0 | 0 | 0 | 0 | 6 | 5 | 9 | C |

    PLIERPAK | 0 | 8 | 4 | C |

    ANSWER | 0 | 0 | 0 | 0 | 0 | 0 | 0 | C |

    MP   MULTPAK , PLIERPAK
    ZAP   ANSWER , MULTPAK+1 (4)

    MULTPAK | | | | | | | |

    ANSWER | | | | | | | |

Packed Decimal Arithmetic Operations

33. XPANDPAK = `0 9 3 4 6 C`

PAKONE = `0 6 8 2 1 C`

PAKTWO = `2 5 9 6 0 7 8 C`

```
MVO    PAKONE (7) , XPANDPAK (2)
```

PAKONE: `0 0 0 0 0 0`

PAKTWO: `0 0 0 3 4 6 C C`

34. DATASFLD = `3 B C D 5 H`

PAKRECV = `0 0 0 0 0 0 0 C`

```
PACK    PAKRECV, DATASFLD
UNPK    DATASFLD , PAKRECV
```

PAKRECV: `0 3 2 3 4 5 8 C`

DATASFLD: `3 2 3 4 5 H`

35. QUOREM = `0 0 0 0 0 6 2 9 4 C`

DIVSOR = `0 1 3 C`

ANSW = `0 0 0 0 0 C`

```
DP     QUOREM , DIVSOR
ZAP    ANSW , QUOREM (3)
```

QUOREM: `0 0 4 8 4 C 0 0 2 C`

ANSW: `0 0 4 8 4 C`

36. REPACK = `0 7 4 3 9 2 6 0 8 C`

```
ZAP    REPACK , REPACK+2 (3)
```

REPACK: `0 0 0 0 9 2 6 0 8 C`

37. MULTAREA = `0 0 0 0 0 1 4 9 2 C`

MPLR = `0 0 3 0 5 C`

ANSWR = `0 0 0 0 0 0 0 C`

```
MP     MULTAREA , MPLR
MVO    ANSWR (4) , MULTAREA (3)
```

MULTAREA: `0 0 0 4 5 5 0 6 0 C`

ANSWR: `0 0 0 0 4 5 5 C`

11

Fixed-Point Arithmetic Operations

THE FIXED-POINT ARITHMETIC INSTRUCTIONS

Instruction: Add

mnemonic	hex code	operand format
A	5A	$R_1, D_2 (X_2, B_2)$

This particular Add instruction adds the 32-bit value of the second operand (consisting of a sign-bit and a 31-bit integer) to the value of the contents of the first operand register. The second operand address must be that of a fullword boundary alignment. The sum of the result resides in the general register specified by the first operand.

CC	BC	Condition
0	8	The first operand register contains a value of zero.
1	4	The first operand register contains a value less than zero.
2	2	The first operand register contains a value greater than zero.
3	1	An overflow condition occurred.

*   *   *

Instruction: Add Halfword

mnemonic	hex code	operand format
AH	4A	$R_1, D_2 (X_2, B_2)$

The Add Halfword instruction first extracts the 16-bit value of the second operand and expands it to a 32-bit fullword by creating 16 additional high-order bits, each additional bit having the same value as the sign-bit for the original value of the second operand. It then adds this expanded value to the 32-bit value (1 sign-bit and 31 integer-bits) of the first operand register and places the sum in the first operand register. The second operand must address a location in storage that is aligned on a halfword boundary.

CC	BC	Condition
0	8	The first operand register contains a value of zero.
1	4	The first operand register contains a value that is less than zero.
2	2	The first operand register contains a value that is greater than zero.
3	1	An overflow condition occurred.

*   *   *

Instruction: Add Registers

mnemonic	hex code	operand format
AR	1A	R_1 , R_2

The Add Register instruction adds the fixed-point value of the second operand register to the fixed-point value of the first operand register, placing the sum of the operation in the first operand. Both general registers contain a value consisting of a sign-bit and a 31-bit integer.

CC	BC	Condition
0	8	The first operand register contains a value of zero.
1	4	The first operand register contains a value less than zero.
2	2	The first operand register contains a value greater than zero.
3	1	An overflow condition occurred.

*   *   *

Instruction: Add Logical

mnemonic	hex code	operand format
AL	5E	R_1 , D_2 (X_2 , B_2)

This instruction adds the 32-bit representation of the value of the second operand to the 32 bits of the first operand register and places the sum of that addition into the first operand register. All bits, including the sign-bits, are logically added together with no change to the resulting sign-bit. An overflow condition does not cause a program interrupt. The address created by the second operand must be that of a properly aligned fullword. When the Condition Code is set by this instruction, it indicates whether or not a carry-out of the sign-bit occurred.

CC	BC	Condition
0	8	The first operand contains a zero value; there was no carry-out of the sign-bit.
1	4	The first operand does not contain a zero value; there was no carry-out of the sign-bit.
2	2	The first operand contains a zero value; a carry-out of the sign-bit occurred.
3	1	The first operand does not contain a zero value; a carry-out of the sign-bit occurred.

*   *   *

Instruction: Add Logical Registers

mnemonic	hex code	operand format
ALR	1E	R_1 , R_2

The Add Logical Registers instruction adds the 32-bit representation of the second operand register to the 32 bits of the first operand register and places the sum into the first operand reg-

Fixed-Point Arithmetic Operations

ister. All bits, including the sign-bits, are logically added together with no change to the resulting sign-bit. An overflow condition does not cause a program interrupt. The Condition Code setting indicates whether or not a carry-out of the sign-bit occurred.

CC	BC	Condition
0	8	The first operand contains a zero value; there was no carry-out of the sign-bit.
1	4	The first operand does not contain a zero value; there was no carry-out of the sign-bit.
2	2	The first operand contains a zero value; a carry-out of the sign-bit occurred.
3	1	The first operand does not contain a zero value; a carry-out of the sign-bit occurred.

* * *

Instruction: Subtract

mnemonic	hex code	operand format
S	5B	$R_1, D_2 (X_2, B_2)$

The Subtract instruction takes the fixed-point signed integer value of the fullword specified by the second operand and subtracts it from the fixed-point contents of the first operand register. This is done by taking the complement of the second operand contents and summing that complement with the fixed-point value of the first operand. The result is placed into the general register specified by the first operand. If an overflow condition occurs as a result of this instruction, the Condition Code is set accordingly and a program interruption normally occurs. The address generated by the second operand must be that of a fullword boundary location.

CC	BC	Condition
0	8	The first operand contains a zero value.
1	4	The first operand contains a value of less than zero.
2	2	The first operand contains a value that is greater than zero.
3	1	An overflow condition occurred.

* * *

Instruction: Subtract Halfword

mnemonic	hex code	operand format
SH	4B	$R_1, D_2 (X_2, B_2)$

This instruction first extracts the 16-bit signed integer halfword from the address specified by the second operand and expands it to a 32-bit signed integer fullword. This is done by creating 16 additional high-order bits of the same value as the sign-bit of the original halfword value. The SH instruction then subtracts the expanded value from the contents of the first operand register. This is done by complementing the bit configuration value of the expanded value and summing that complement with the value contained in the general register specified by the first operand.

The address generated by the second operand must be that of a halfword boundary alignment. If an overflow condition takes place during the execution of this instruction, the Condition Code is set to its respective configuration and a program interruption would normally occur.

CC	BC	Condition
0	8	The first operand contains a zero value.
1	4	The first operand contains a value of less than zero.
2	2	The first operand contains a value greater than zero.
3	1	An overflow condition occurred.

*   *   *

Instruction: Subtract Registers

mnemonic	hex code	operand format
SR	1B	R_1, R_2

This instruction subtracts the second operand register value from the value of the first operand register. This is accomplished by summing the complement of the second operand value with actual value contained within the first operand register. The result of this operation is placed into the first operand register. If an overflow condition occurs as a result of this instruction, the overflow condition is reflected by the configuration of the Condition Code bits.

CC	BC	Condition
0	8	The first operand contains a value of zero.
1	4	The first operand contains a value of less than zero.
2	2	The first operand contains a value greater than zero.
3	1	An overflow condition occurred.

*   *   *

Instruction: Subtract Logical

mnemonic	hex code	operand format
SL	5F	$R_1, D_2(X_2, B_2)$

The Subtract Logical instruction logically subtracts all 32 bits representing the value of the second operand fullword from the 32 bits representing the first operand register value. This is accomplished by summing the complement of the second operand value with the value of the first operand register, and placing the total into the first operand register. The instruction uses all 32 bits, including the sign-bit, of each operand. If an overflow condition should occur, representing a carry-out from the sign-bit position, a program interrupt does not occur. Instead, the resulting Condition Code indicates whether or not a carry-out of the sign-bit did occur during the execution of this instruction.

CC	BC	Condition
1	4	The first operand contains a nonzero value; a carry-out of the sign-bit did not occur.

Fixed-Point Arithmetic Operations

2	2	The first operand contains a zero value; a carry-out of the sign-bit occurred.
3	1	The first operand contains a nonzero value; a carry-out of the sign-bit occurred.

*   *   *

Instruction: Subtract Logical Registers

mnemonic	hex code	operand format
SLR	1F	R_1, R_2

The Subtract Logical Registers instruction logically subtracts all 32 bits representing the value of the contents of the second operand register from the 32 bits representing the contents of the first operand register. This is done by summing the complement of the second operand value with the value of the first operand and placing the total into the first operand register. The instruction uses all 32 bits, including the sign-bit, of each operand as logical digit values. If an overflow condition should occur, representing a carry-out of the sign-bit, a program interrupt does not take place. The Condition Code settings from this instruction indicate whether or not a carry-out of the sign-bit did occur.

CC	BC	Condition
1	4	The first operand contains a nonzero value; a carry-out of the sign-bit did not occur.
2	2	The first operand contains a zero value; a carry-out of the sign-bit occurred.
3	1	The first operand contains a nonzero value; a carry-out of the sign-bit occurred.

*   *   *

Instruction: Multiply

mnemonic	hex code	operand format
M	5C	$R_1, D_2(X_2, B_2)$

In this instruction, the contents of the first operand register (representing the multiplicand residing in an even-odd pair of general registers) are multiplied by the value contained at the address specified by the second operand, the multiplier. Both operands represent 32-bit signed integers, consisting of a sign-bit and a 31-bit integer. The first operand must always reference the even-numbered register of the even-odd pair of general registers. The address of the multiplier created by the second operand must reside on fullword boundary alignment. The resulting product of the multiplication represents a 64-bit signed integer residing in the whole of the even-odd pair of registers referenced by the R_1 operand register. The signs of the multiplier and multiplicand algebraically combine to determine the sign of the product.

The configuration of the Condition Code is not changed by this instruction.

*   *   *

Instruction: Multiply Registers

mnemonic	hex code	operand format
MR	1C	R_1, R_2

In the Multiply Registers instruction, the contents of the first operand register (representing the multiplicand residing in an even-odd pair of general registers) are multiplied by the value of the contents of the second operand register, the multiplier. The first operand register must always reference the even-numbered register of the even-odd pair of registers. The product of the multiplication is contained in the whole of the even-odd pair of general registers. The signs of the multiplicand and the multiplier algebraically combine to determine the sign of the product.

The configuration of the Condition Code is not changed by this instruction.

*   *   *

Instruction: Multiply Halfword

mnemonic	hex code	operand format
MH	4C	$R_1, D_2 (X_2, B_2)$

Although the name of this instruction might seem to imply that both the multiplier and the multiplicand are halfword values, the multiplicand may actually be in excess of the maximum value of a halfword if the multiplier is not of a magnitude that would create a true product in excess of a maximum fullword value. The contents of the halfword at the location addressed by the second operand are first extracted and expanded to a 32-bit fullword by creating 16 additional high-order bits of the same configuration as the sign-bit of the original halfword multiplier. It then takes the 32-bit signed integer field of the first operand register (the multiplicand) and multiplies that value by the 32-bit expanded multiplier. The product resulting from this operation is a 32-bit signed integer residing in the general register specified by the first operand. The signs of the multiplier and the multiplicand combine algebraically to determine the sign of the product. The address created by the second operand must be that of a halfword boundary alignment.

The configuration of the Condition Code is not changed by this instruction.

*   *   *

Instruction: Divide

mnemonic	hex code	operand format
D	5D	$R_1, D_2 (X_2, B_2)$

The Divide instruction divides the 32-bit signed integer specified by the second operand into an even-odd pair of general registers containing the dividend. When the instruction statement is coded, it must always have the first operand register refer to the even-numbered register of the even-odd pair of general registers containing the dividend. The dividend itself resides as a 64-bit signed integer within the even-odd registers. Upon completion of the divide operation, the remainder resides in the even-numbered register and the quotient in the odd-numbered register, both of which appear as 32-bit signed integers. The address created by the second operand must be that of a fullword boundary alignment.

The configuration of the Condition Code is not altered by this instruction.

*   *   *

Instruction: Divide Registers

mnemonic	hex code	operand format
DR	1D	R_1, R_2

The Divide Registers instruction divides the 32-bit signed integer contents of the general register specified by the second operand into an even-odd pair of general registers containing the dividend. When the instruction statement is coded, it must always have the first operand register refer to the even-numbered register of the even-odd pair of general registers containing the dividend. The dividend resides within the pair of registers as a 64-bit signed integer. Upon completion of the divide operation, the remainder is contained within the even-numbered register and the quotient within the odd-numbered register, both of which appear as 32-bit signed integers.

The configuration of the Condition Code is not changed by this instruction.

PERFORMING ARITHMETIC OPERATIONS WITH FIXED-POINT VALUES

To further clarify the value representation of a fixed-point integer, several more pieces of general information should be stated. Along with these, the configuration of the plus-positive or minus-negative value of a fixed-point value is an essential point to review here.

A positive (+) fixed-point value is represented as consisting of a zero-bit sign-bit in the high-order bit position and the value of the integer represented by the true binary Powers-of-Two bit configuration in the remaining bit positions. A negative (−) fixed-point value is represented to consist of a one-bit sign-bit in the high-order bit position with the negative value of the integer represented in Two's Complement notation in the remaining bit positions. Two of the tables that appear in the back of this text, the Powers-of-Two Table and the Hexadecimal/Decimal Conversion Table, can be of considerable value in understanding fixed-point values and bit configurations.

In addition to requiring the use of at least one general register per instruction statement, fixed-point arithmetic operations require that data fields of storage containing arithmetic values must be on fullword or halfword boundary alignments, depending on the particular instruction performed.

The following illustrations present a graphic representation of the bit configurations of positive and negative fixed-point values.

A fullword containing a value of +33,974:

	S							
fixed-point	0000	0000	0000	0000	1000	0100	1011	0110
hex	0	0	0	0	8	4	B	6

A halfword containing a value of +29,878:

	S			
fixed-point	0111	0100	1011	0110
hex	7	4	B	6

A halfword containing a value of −987:

	S			
fixed-point	1111	1100	0010	0101
hex	F	C	2	5

A fullword containing a value of +4,593,211:

	S						
fixed-point	0000	0000	0100	0110	0001	0110	0011	1011
hex	0	0	4	6	1	6	3	B

A fullword containing a value of −3,915,228:

	S						
fixed-point	1111	1111	1100	0100	0100	0010	0010	0100
hex	F	F	C	4	4	2	2	4

A halfword containing a value of −1:

	S			
fixed-point	1111	1111	1111	1111
hex	F	F	F	F

If should be noted that the representation of a negative fixed-point value does not visually agree with the concept of significant digit-bits comprising the value of the whole number. If the last illustration, that of a halfword value of −1, were interpreted to have the Powers-of-Two value of all significant 1-bits, exclusive of the sign-bit, the assumed value would be −32,767. The correct way to determine the true negative value of a negative fixed-point value is to sum the Powers-of-Two value of the significant 1-bits and then subtract that amount from the maximum negative value of the particular field length in which the value appears; a halfword has a maximum negative value of −32,768, a fullword has a maximum negative value of −2,147,483,648. Using the last example shown, the one representing a halfword with a value of −1, the significant 1-bits would sum to a Powers-of-Two value of 32,767. By subtracting this amount from the maximum negative value for a halfword, −32,768, the difference is a −1 value, the true negative value of that halfword.

Fixed-Point Arithmetic Operations

The conversion of a value with a true binary notation (a positive value) to a Two's Complement notation (a negative value) can easily be made. Each bit position content in the positive value is reversed; one-bits become zero-bits and zero-bits become one-bits. Upon completion of the reversal of the value of all bits, add a one-bit to the low-order (right-most) bit position and the transition to the Two's Complement form is completed. For example:

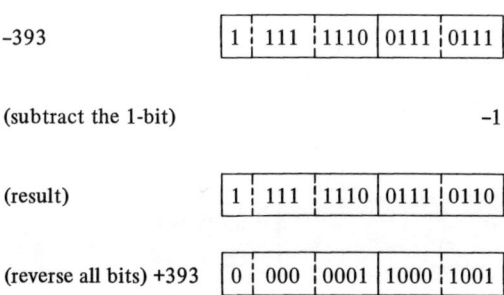

The opposite conversion is accomplished just as easily. The low-order one-bit is first subtracted from the Two's Complement form and then the bit position values are reversed. This reverts a Two's Complement notation back to a positive value in true binary notation. For example:

Halfword containing −393 converted to +393:

−393 | 1 | 111 | 1110 | 0111 | 0111 |

(subtract the 1-bit)   −1

(result) | 1 | 111 | 1110 | 0111 | 0110 |

(reverse all bits) +393 | 0 | 000 | 0001 | 1000 | 1001 |

Halfword containing −1716 to +1716:

−1716

| 1 | 111 | 1001 | 0100 | 1100 |

(subtract the 1-bit)   −1

(result)

| 1 | 111 | 1001 | 0100 | 1011 |

(reverse all bits)
+1716

| 0 | 000 | 0110 | 1011 | 0100 |

These explanations and illustrations should provide enough information on fixed-point numeric formatting to allow the discussions that follow on fixed-point arithmetic instructions to be readily understood.

Throughout the remainder of these discussions of fixed-point arithmetic operations and instructions, the configurations of the storage areas and general registers will be shown as:

0110	0000	1101	0111
6	0	D	7

The '0' and '1' configuration on the upper line represent the binary bit configuration of the fields, while the '0' through '9' and 'A' through 'F' configurations on the lower line are the hexadecimal digit representation for every four bit positions.

The Fixed-Point "Add" Instructions

Add (A)

This instruction adds the fixed-point value of the contents of a four-byte fullword storage area to the fixed-point value contained within a general register. As the addition is completed, the instruction checks for the occurrence of a fixed-point overflow.

The first operand in the instruction statement must be a general register or a symbol or label that has been equated to a general register. The second operand must represent a fullword and generate an address that is resident at a fullword boundary location of storage. The second operand is added to the first operand, the sum of which is placed into the general register specified by the first operand.

Example 1

                    A   6 , FULLWRD1

register 6
(before)

S 0000	0000	0000	1001	0000	1111	0110	1001
0	0	0	9	0	F	6	9

+593,769

Fixed-Point Arithmetic Operations

FULLWRD1	S 0000	0000	0000	0000	0001	0100	1011	0101	+5,301
	0	0	0	0	1	4	B	5	

(sum now in register 6)	S 0000	0000	0000	1001	0010	0100	0001	1110	+599,070
	0	0	0	9	2	4	1	E	

This example had added the fixed-point value of FULLWRD1 (+5301) to the fixed-point value of general register 6 (+593,769), placing the sum of that operation into register 6. The hexadecimal configuration (base-16) for the operands shown may be interpreted as:

```
register 6          + 9 0 F 6 9    or    593,769
FULLWRD1            +     1 4 B 5  or      5,301
register 6 (sum)    + 9 2 4 1 E          599,070
```

By using the Powers-of-Two table and the Hexadecimal/Decimal Conversion table provided in the back of this text, the binary-formatted contents of these examples can be verified as shown above.

Example 2

A   8, =F ' 75963 '

register 8 (before)	S 0000	0000	0000	0000	0000	0000	1111	1111	+255
	0	0	0	0	0	0	F	F	

(literal F'75963')	S 0000	0000	0000	0001	0010	1000	1011	1011	+75,963
	0	0	0	1	2	8	B	B	

(sum now in register 8)	S 0000	0000	0000	0001	0010	1001	1011	1010	+76,218
	0	0	0	1	2	9	B	A	

In this example, a fullword literal with a fixed-point value of +75,963 is added to general register 8, which contains a fixed-point value of +255. The rule that the second operand must consist of a boundary-aligned fullword is adhered to since the literal is established as a fullword value and the compiler will give it the proper boundary alignment.

The addition of the hexadecimal values for this example would appear as:

```
register 8              + F F      or         255
literal                 + 1 2 8 B B  or      75,963
Register 8 (sum)        + 1 2 9 B A  or      76,218
```

Add Halfword (AH)

The Add Halfword instruction adds the fixed-point value of the contents of a two-byte storage area to the fixed-point value contained in a general register. The first operand in the instruction statement must be a general register or a symbol or label that has been equated to a general register. The second operand must represent a halfword and generate an address that is resident at a halfword boundary location of storage. The initial action taken by this instruction is to extract the value of the halfword operand and expand it to a 32-bit fullword. This is done by propagating 16 additional high-order bits of the same bit value as the sign-bit of the halfword. The fixed-point value is not changed by this expansion, nor are the contents of the halfword storage location changed in any way. The expanded operand value is then added to the value of the register operand, the sum of which is placed into the register. A fixed-point overflow is possible and the instruction statement checks for that condition.

Example 1

    AH   3 , HAFWRD2

Before the AH instruction statement is executed the contents of HAFWRD2 appear as:

HAFWRD2

0000	1011	1100	1100
0	B	C	C

+3020

The AH instruction statement extracts the configuration and expands it to a fullword, so that when the addition takes place the operands and the result would appear as:

HAFWRD2 (expanded)

S 0000	0000	0000	0000	0000	1011	1100	1100
0	0	0	0	0	B	C	C

+3,020

register 3 (before)

S 0000	0000	0000	0110	1001	0101	0011	0111
0	0	0	6	9	5	3	7

+431,415

register 3 (sum)

S 0000	0000	0000	0110	1010	0001	0000	0011
0	0	0	6	A	1	0	3

+434,435

Fixed-Point Arithmetic Operations

The addition of the hexadecimal values for this example would be:

HAFWRD2	+ B C C	*or*	3,020
register 3	+ 6 9 5 3 7	*or*	431,415
sum in register 3	+ 6 A 1 0 3	*or*	434,435

Example 2. As in the Add instruction, a literal may be used as the second operand, providing that it meets the halfword alignment specifications that normally apply. This could be coded as:

 AH 5 , =H ' 7721 '

The literal would be established by the compiler on a halfword boundary alignment as the following configuration:

(literal H'7721')

S 0001	1110	0010	1001
1	E	2	9

+7721

The value of the literal would then be extracted, expanded to a 32-bit fullword, and the addition function would result as:

(expanded literal H'7721')

S 0000	0000	0000	0000	0001	1110	0010	1001
0	0	0	0	1	E	2	9

+7,721

register 5 (before)

S 0000	0000	0000	0010	0010	0010	0100	1100
0	0	0	2	2	2	4	C

+139,852

(sum now in register 5)

S 0000	0000	0000	0010	0100	0000	0111	0101
0	0	0	2	4	0	7	5

+147,573

The addition of the hexadecimal values for this example would be:

literal H'7721'	+ 1 E 2 9	*or*	+ 7,721
register 5	+ 2 2 2 4 C	*or*	+ 139,852
sum in register 5	+ 2 4 0 7 5	*or*	+ 147,573

Add Registers (AR)

This instruction, as the name implies, adds together the fixed-point values contained within two general registers. The value of the contents of the first operand register are added to the value of the contents of the second operand register, the sum of which is placed into the first operand register. As the addition is completed, the instruction checks for the occurrence of a fixed-point overflow. Both operands must be general registers, or symbols or labels that have been equated to a general register.

Example 1

General register 7 contains +396
General register 8 contains +4001

The instruction statement to be executed is:

    AR   7 , 8

register 7 (before)

S							
0000	0000	0000	0000	0000	0001	1000	1100
0	0	0	0	0	1	8	C

+396

register 8

S							
0000	0000	0000	0000	0000	1111	1010	0001
0	0	0	0	0	F	A	1

+4001

(sum in register 7)

S							
0000	0000	0000	0000	0001	0001	0010	1101
0	0	0	0	1	1	2	D

+4397

The addition of the hexadecimal values for this example would be:

general register 7	+	1 8 C	or	+ 396
general register 8	+	FA 1	or	+ 4001
sum now in register 7	+ 1 1 2 D	or	+ 4397

The value of a general register may be doubled by adding that register to itself using the Add Register instruction, as shown in the following example.

Example 2. The statement to be executed is:

    AR   8 , 8

This would essentially create the following action:

reigster 8 (1st operand)

S							
0000	0000	0000	0000	0000	1111	1010	0001
0	0	0	0	0	F	A	1

+4001

Fixed-Point Arithmetic Operations

register 8
(2nd operand)

S 0000	0000	0000	0000	0000	1111	1010	0001
0	0	0	0	0	F	A	1

+4001

(sum in register 8)

S 0000	0000	0000	0000	0001	1111	0100	0010
0	0	0	0	1	F	4	2

+8002

The fixed-point value in general register 8 has now been effectively doubled. It is altogether likely that at some time or another you will unintentionally create a fixed-point overflow condition. The following example illustrates, through the use of the AR instruction, how this would occur and what the resulting configuration would be.

Example 3. The instruction statement to be executed is:

   AR   10, 11

The fixed-point value of register 10 is +1,094,788,867.
The fixed-point value of register 11 is +1,057,013,981.

register 10
(before)

S 0100	0001	0100	0001	0010	0111	0000	0011
4	1	4	1	2	7	0	3

+1,094,788,867

register 11

S 0011	1111	0000	0000	1100	0000	1101	1101
3	F	0	0	C	0	D	D

+1,057,013,981

(register 10 as the sum)

S 1000	0000	0100	0001	1110	0111	1110	0000
8	0	4	1	E	7	E	0

Note that the total value in general register 10 should have been +2,151,802,848, but the sign-bit in the high-order bit position has been changed to a negative sign. Because the sum of the addition was of a magnitude exceeding the maximum positive fixed-point value for a general register, the high-order overflow of the integer bits changed the value of the sign-bit. This would signal a fixed-point overflow to the system, the Condition Code would be set to indicate this problem, and a fixed-point interrupt would occur as a program exception.

Add Logical (AL)

The Add Logical instruction is very similar to the Add instruction, except that the data contained within the operands does not necessarily have to be a valid fixed-point value consisting of a signed integer. It logically adds the bit configuration of the data specified by the second operand to the bit configuration of the data contained in the general register specified by the first operand. All 32-bits of each operand are added together without consideration for the existence of a sign-bit and the sum is placed into the first operand register. It is necessary that the address generated by the second operand should represent a four-byte area that resides on a fullword boundary alignment. Unlike the Add instruction, however, the Add Logical instruction does not create an exception condition in the event of a fixed-point overflow. The Condition Code settings for this instruction indicate if a "carry-out" of the sign-bit occurred rather than indicating an overflow condition.

The next example illustrates an Add Logical instruction statement in which the sign-bit is not altered as a result of the addition.

Example 1. The instruction statement to be executed is:

$$AL \quad 7, FULLWD9$$

register 7 (before)

S 0000	0000	0000	1001	0001	1110	0110	0000
0	0	0	9	1	E	6	0

+597,060

FULLWD9

S 0000	0000	0000	0000	0000	0000	1111	1111
0	0	0	0	0	0	F	F

+255

(sum now in register 7)

S 0000	0000	0000	1001	0001	1111	0101	1111
0	0	0	9	1	F	5	F

+597,315

The addition of the hexadecimal values for this example would be:

```
general register 7    + 9 1 E 6 0    or    597,060
FULLWD9               +       F F    or        255
sum in register 7     + 9 1 F 5 F    or    597,315
```

As a result of this example, the Condition Code bits would be set to indicate that "the answer is not zero and no carry-out of the sign-bit occurred."

Example 2. This next example illustrates an Add Logical instruction statement in which a carry-out of the high-order integer-bit occurs, changing the sign-bit of the sum. The instruction statement to be executed:

AL   11, ONEFWRD

Fixed-Point Arithmetic Operations

register 11
(before)

S							
0111	0001	0000	0000	0011	1100	0000	1111
7	1	0	0	3	C	0	F

+1,895,840,783

ONEFWRD

S							
0000	1111	0011	0111	0001	0001	1001	0000
0	F	3	7	1	1	9	0

+255,267,216

register 11
(sum of AL)

S							
1000	0000	0011	0111	0100	1101	1001	1111
8	0	3	7	4	D	9	F

−2,143,859,297

As a result of the addition, the sign-bit has been changed by the overflow of the high-order integer-bit into the sign-bit position. The fixed-point representation created by this overflow is a value of −2,143,859,297. After the execution of this example the Condition Code bits would be configurated to indicate that "the answer is not zero and a carry-out of the sign-bit occurred."

Add Logical Registers (ALR)

The Add Logical Registers instruction bears the same resemblance to the Add Registers instruction that the Add Logical instruction has to the Add instruction. The bit configuration of the value or data contained within the second operand register is added logically to the bit configuration of the value or data contained within the first operand register. This instruction does not cause an exception interruption in the event of an occurrence that would normally be considered to be a fixed-point overflow. In such an instance, a carry-out of the sign-bit is indicated by the particular settings of the Condition Code bits. The sum of the addition resulting from this instruction is placed into the general register specified by the first operand. Both operands must be general registers, or symbols or labels that have been equated to a general register.

Example 1. The instruction statement is:

    ALR   2,7

General register 2 contains −3,596.
General register 7 contains −398,541.

register 2
(before)

S							
1111	1111	1111	1111	1111	0001	1111	0100
F	F	F	F	F	1	F	4

−3,596

register 7

S							
1111	1111	1111	1001	1110	1011	0011	0011
F	F	F	9	E	B	3	3

−398,541

(sum now in register 2)

S							
1111	1111	1111	1001	1101	1101	0010	0111
F	F	F	9	D	D	2	7

−402,137

Note that the bit configuration for the negative fixed-point value is in Two's Complement form. Verification of the bit configuration for these negative values can be established by application of the techniques described earlier in this section under the heading of "Performing Arithmetic Operations with Fixed-Point Values."

Summation of Fixed-Point Add Instructions

Although the five fixed-point Add instructions each have one or two individual peculiarities, they generally perform in a similar manner. A reasonable means of comparison may be found in the following example in which each of these five instructions are used at least once. The coding for this example is shown in Figure 11-1.

Statement 001 subtracts general register 10 from itself by utilizing the Subtract Registers instruction. This effectively configures general register 10 as a zero value.

register 10

S							
0000	0000	0000	0000	0000	0000	0000	0000
0	0	0	0	0	0	0	0

+0

Statement 002 loads the contents of FULLWD4 into general register 7, after which that register contains a fixed-point value of +9000.

register 7

S							
0000	0000	0000	0000	0010	0011	0010	1000
0	0	0	0	2	3	2	8

+9000

Statement 003 adds general register 7 (+9000) to general register 10 (+0), using the Add Registers (AR) instruction. Register 10 now contains a fixed-point value of +9000 that results from the following action:

register 10 (before)

S							
0000	0000	0000	0000	0000	0000	0000	0000
0	0	0	0	0	0	0	0

+0

register 7

S							
0000	0000	0000	0000	0010	0011	0010	1000
0	0	0	0	2	3	2	8

+9000

register 10 (after)

S							
0000	0000	0000	0000	0010	0011	0010	1000
0	0	0	0	2	3	2	8

+9000

Fixed-Point Arithmetic Operations

Name	Operation	Operand	Seq
*			001
ADDRTE	SR	10,10	002
	L	7,FULLWD4	003
	AR	10,7	004
	A	10,FULLWD2	005
	AL	10,FULLWD1	006
	AH	10,HALFWD1	007
	L	9,FULLWD5	008
	L	8,FULLWD3	009
	ALR	10,9	010
	AR	10,8	011
	BC	15,END	012
*			
*		* * * CONSTANTS * * *	620
*			630
FULLWD1	DC	F'256'	640
FULLWD2	DC	F'075'	650
FULLWD3	DC	F'16299'	660
FULLWD4	DC	F'9000'	670
FULLWD5	DC	F'296333'	680
HALFWD1	DC	H'3500'	690
*			700

FIGURE 11-1

Statement 004 uses the Add instruction to add FULLWD2 (+75) to general register 10 (+9000). Register 10 now contains +9075.

register 10 (before)	S 0000	0000	0000	0000	0010	0011	0010	1000	+9000
	0	0	0	0	2	3	2	8	

FULLWD2	S 0000	0000	0000	0000	0000	0000	0100	1011	+75
	0	0	0	0	0	0	4	B	

register 10 (sum of add)	S 0000	0000	0000	0000	0010	0011	0111	0011	+9075
	0	0	0	0	2	3	7	3	

Statement 005 adds FULLWD1 (+256) to general register 10 (+9075) by utilizing the Add Logical (AL) instruction. Because the values are not of a size great enough to affect the sign-bit, this instruction performs as efficiently as a regular Add (A) instruction would have. General register 10 now contains +9331.

register 10 (before)	S 0000	0000	0000	0000	0010	0011	0111	0011	+9075
	0	0	0	0	2	3	7	3	

FULLWD1	S 0000	0000	0000	0000	0000	0001	0000	0000	+256
	0	0	0	0	0	1	0	0	

(sum now in regisger 10)	S 0000	0000	0000	0000	0010	0100	0111	0011	+9331
	0	0	0	0	2	4	7	3	

Statement 006 uses the Add Halfword (AH) instruction to add HALFWD1 (+3500) to general register 10 (+9331). Register 10 now contains +12,831.

register 10 (before)	S 0000	0000	0000	0000	0010	0100	0111	0011	+9331
	0	0	0	0	2	4	7	3	

Fixed-Point Arithmetic Operations

HALFWD1

S							
0000	0000	0000	0000	0000	1101	1010	1100
0	0	0	0	0	D	A	C

+3500

(sum now in register 10)

S							
0000	0000	0000	0000	0011	0010	0001	1111
0	0	0	0	3	2	1	F

+12,831

Statement 007 loads general register 9 with the contents of FULLWD5 (+296,333).

register 9

S							
0000	0000	0000	0100	1000	0101	1000	1101
0	0	0	4	8	5	8	D

+296,333

Statement 008 loads general register 8 with the contents of FULLWD3 (+16,299).

register 8

S							
0000	0000	0000	0000	0011	1111	1010	1011
0	0	0	0	3	F	A	B

+16,299

Statement 009 adds general register 9 (+296,333) to general register 10 (+12,831) by using the Add Logical Registers (ALR) instruction. Register 10 now contains a fixed-point value of +309,164.

register 10 (before)

S							
0000	0000	0000	0000	0011	0010	0001	1111
0	0	0	0	3	2	1	F

+12,831

register 9

S							
0000	0000	0000	0100	1000	0101	1000	1101
0	0	0	4	8	5	8	D

+296,333

register 10 (sum of ALR)

S							
0000	0000	0000	0100	1011	0111	1010	1100
0	0	0	4	B	7	A	C

+309,164

Statement 010 again uses the Add Registers instruction, this time to add general register 8 (+16,299) to general register 10 (+309,164). General register 10 now contains a fixed-point value of +325,463.

	S							
register 10 (before)	0000	0000	0000	0100	1011	0111	1010	1100
	0	0	0	4	B	7	A	C

+309,164

	S							
register 8	0000	0000	0000	0000	0011	1111	1010	1011
	0	0	0	0	3	F	A	B

+16,299

	S							
(sum now in register 10)	0000	0000	0000	0100	1111	0111	0101	0111
	0	0	0	4	F	7	5	7

+325,463

Statement 011 is a forced branch to a routine that is labeled END.

Although this example illustrates the various fixed-point "add" instructions, it is not the most efficient manner in which to arrive at the final result. It could have been coded in many ways, some of which would be considerably more efficient both in coding and in speed. For instance, it could have been more efficiently coded as:

```
ADDRTE   LM    6,10,FULLWD1        001
         AR    6,7                 002
         AR    6,8                 003
         AR    6,9                 004
         AR    10,6                005
         AH    10,HALFWD1          006
         BC    15,END              007
```

In this coding, Statement 001 would load FULLWD1 into general register 6, FULLWD2 into general register 7, FULLWD3 into general register 8, FULLWD4 into general register 9, and FULLWD5 into general register 10. The rest of the statements are self-explanatory. As shown by the coding, the final answer would still be found in general register 10.

The Fixed-Point "Subtract" Instructions

Subtract (S)

This instruction subtracts the fixed-point value of the contents of the second operand from the fixed-point value contained within the first operand register. The second operand must address a four-byte storage area located on fullword boundary alignment. The subtraction is performed by adding together the fixed-point value of the first operand and the complement of the fixed-point value of the second operand. The sum of this operation, representing the difference between the original value representations, is placed into the general register specified by the first operand. The Subtract instruction checks for a fixed-point overflow. If such a condition is found, the Condition Code bits are set to indicate that condition and a program interruption will occur.

Fixed-Point Arithmetic Operations

For the purpose of illustrating this action, assume that general register 8 contains a fixed-point value of +18,793 and that a fullword, FXPONE, contains a fixed-point value of +793. The statement that is to be executed is:

    S   8,FXPONE

Prior to the actual subtraction, the contents of FXPONE would be internally transposed to its Two's Complement notation. This transposition would appear as:

	S							
FXPONE (true binary notation)	0000	0000	0000	0000	0000	0011	0001	1001
+793	0	0	0	0	0	3	1	9

	S							
FXPONE (Two's Complement)	1111	1111	1111	1111	1111	1100	1110	0111
−793	F	F	F	F	F	C	E	7

The subtraction would then be accomplished by adding the value of the contents of general register 8 with the Two's Complement of FXPONE. This addition would appear as:

	S								
register 8 (before)	0000	0000	0000	0000	0100	1001	0110	1001	+18,793
	0	0	0	0	4	9	6	9	

	S								
FXPONE (complement)	1111	1111	1111	1111	1111	1100	1110	0111	−793
	F	F	F	F	F	C	E	7	

	S								
(sum/difference in register 8)	0000	0000	0000	0000	0100	0110	0101	0000	+18,000
	0	0	0	0	4	6	5	0	

If one negative fixed-point value is subtracted from another negative fixed-point value, the second operand would be converted back to the true binary notation (the Two's Complement of the negative configuration) and then added to the value of the first operand.

To illustrate this action, assume that general register 5 contains a fixed-point value of −659,236 and that a fullword of storage, referenced by the label FXPTWO, contains a fixed-point value of −38,523. The instruction statement to be executed is:

    S   5,FXPTWO

The contents of FXPTWO would be first internally transposed as:

FXPTWO
(before)

S							
1111	1111	1111	1111	0110	1001	1000	0101
F	F	F	F	6	9	8	5

−38,523

FXPTWO
(complement)

S							
0000	0000	0000	0000	1001	0110	0111	1011
0	0	0	0	9	6	7	B

+38,523

The subtraction specified by the instruction statement would then be accomplished by adding the contents of FXPTWO to the fixed-point contents of register 5.

register 5
(before)

S							
1111	1111	1111	0101	1111	0000	1101	1010
F	F	F	5	F	0	D	A

−659,236

FXPTWO

S							
0000	0000	0000	0000	1001	0110	0111	1011
0	0	0	0	9	6	7	B

+38,523

(sum/difference
in register 5)

S							
1111	1111	1111	0110	1000	0111	0101	0101
F	F	F	6	8	7	5	5

−620,713

If the instruction statement should specify the subtraction of a field containing a negative value from a register containing a positive value, the negative value configuration (in Two's Complement form) would be reversed to the true binary notation and the two positive values would be added together.

Subtract Halfword (SH)

The Subtract Halfword instruction subtracts the fixed-point value of the contents of a two-byte halfword storage area from the fixed-point value of the contents of a general register. The first operand in the instruction statement must be a general register, or a label or symbol that has been equated to a general register. The second operand must represent a halfword; a two-byte storage area residing at a halfword boundary alignment. The instruction first extracts the value of the contents of the halfword and expands it to a 32-bit fullword by providing 16 additional high-order bits of the same value as the halfword sign-bit. The fixed-point value is not changed by this expansion and the contents of the halfword storage area are not altered. The subtraction is then performed by adding together the fixed-point value of the general register and the Two's Complement of the expanded halfword value. The result of this operation is then placed into the general

Fixed-Point Arithmetic Operations

register specified by the first operand. Since a fixed-point overflow is possible, the instruction checks for that condition. If an overflow has occurred, it is indicated by the Condition Code bit configuration and a program interrupt.

A sample statement using this instruction would be:

    SH   2 , HAFSUB

To illustrate this instruction statement, assume that general register 2 contains a fixed-point value of +3,972,555; and a stored halfword, referenced by the label HAFSUB, contains a fixed-point value of +29,511. The bit configuration of general register 2, the stored halfword HAFSUB, and the expanded 32-bit configuration of HAFSUB, would appear as:

register 2

S 0000	0000	0011	1100	1001	1101	1100	1011
0	0	3	C	9	D	C	B

+3,972,555

HAFSUB (stored)

S 0111	0011	0100	0111
7	3	4	7

+29,511

HAFSUB (expanded)

S 0000	0000	0000	0000	0111	0011	0100	0111
0	0	0	0	7	3	4	7

+29,511

The Two's Complement of the value of the expanded HAFSUB, which would occur prior to the arithmetic operation of the Subtract Halfword instruction statement, would appear as:

HAFSUB (expanded complement)

S 1111	1111	1111	1111	1000	1100	1011	1001
F	F	F	F	8	C	B	9

−29,511

The arithmetic subtraction would then be completed by summing the fixed-point value contained in general register 2 with the complement form of the value of the expanded HAFSUB. This would appear as:

register 2 (before)

S 0000	0000	0011	1100	1001	1101	1100	1011
0	0	3	C	9	D	C	B

+3,972,555

HAFSUB (expanded complement)

S 1111	1111	1111	1111	1000	1100	1011	1001
F	F	F	F	8	C	B	9

−29,511

	S							
(sum/difference in register 2)	0000	0000	0011	1100	0010	1010	1000	0100
	0	0	3	C	2	A	8	4

+3,943,044

Subtract Registers (SR)

The Subtract Registers instruction subtracts the fixed-point value of the contents of the second operand register from the fixed-point value of the contents of the first operand register. As in the performance of the Subtract and Subtract Halfword instructions, the fixed-point value indicated by the second operand is converted to its complement form and added to the fixed-point value of the first operand. This effectively creates the subtraction, after which the net result is placed into the first operand register. The possibility of a fixed-point overflow occurring is tested and the Condition Code bits are configured accordingly. In the event of an overflow condition, a program exception interrupt occurs. The original value of the second register operand is always reversed for the arithmetic operation. If it was originally a positive value, it is changed to the Two's Complement negative form; if it was a negative value, it is changed to the complement of the negative, which would result in the true binary notation of a positive value.

To illustrate this concept, assume that general register 3 contains a value of +7,300,005 and general register 12 contains a value of -839,777. The bit configuration of these registers, prior to the issuance of a Subtract Registers instruction statement, would appear as:

	S							
register 3	0000	0000	0110	1111	0110	0011	1010	0101
	0	0	6	F	6	3	A	5

+7,300,005

	S							
register 12	1111	1111	1111	0011	0010	1111	1001	1111
	F	F	F	3	2	F	9	F

-839,777

The instruction statement to be executed is:

    SR   3,12

This statement would first reverse the negative configuration of the value in general register 12 so that it would appear as:

	S							
register 12 (complemented)	0000	0000	0000	1100	1101	0000	0110	0001
	0	0	0	C	D	0	6	1

+839,777

It would then add together the value of register 12, as complemented, and the value of register 3, placing the sum of that addition into general register 3. This can be illustrated as:

	S							
register 3 (before)	0000	0000	0110	1111	0110	0011	1010	0101
	0	0	6	F	6	3	A	5

+7,300,005

Fixed-Point Arithmetic Operations

register 12

S							
0000	0000	0000	1100	1101	0000	0110	0001
0	0	0	C	D	0	6	1

+839,777

(sum/difference in register 3)

S							
0000	0000	0111	1100	0011	0100	0000	0110
0	0	7	C	3	4	0	6

+8,139,782

The Subtract Register instruction is often used to clear the contents of a general register. By subtracting a register from itself all 32 bit positions of that register are set to zero-bits. An example of this can be shown by using the instruction statement coded as:

    SR   11 , 11

The performance of this instruction statement on general register 11 would be:

register 11
(as 1st operand)

S							
0000	0000	0100	0000	0111	0110	0101	1011
0	0	4	0	7	6	5	B

+4,224,603

register 11
(in complement as 2nd operand)

S							
1111	1111	1011	1111	1000	1001	1010	0101
F	F	B	F	8	9	A	5

−4,224,603

(sum now in register 11)

S							
0000	0000	0000	0000	0000	0000	0000	0000
0	0	0	0	0	0	0	0

+0

Because certain instructions only affect a portion of the bit configuration of a general register, this action would ensure that the high-order bits did not contain a residual value. As in the case of Insert Character, wherein the instruction only changed the low-order byte of the register, you might wish to place a one-byte value into the register and then use that as an actual value. If the high-order bits or bytes are not set to zero, the actual value of the register is not consistent with the value inserted into the low-order byte. This can be prevented by using the Subtract Register instruction and stating the subject general register as both operands.

Subtract Logical (SL)

This instruction executes and performs quite similar to the Subtract instruction. It logically subtracts the bit configuration of the value contained within the second operand from the bit configuration of the value contained within the first operand register. The subtraction is actually performed by converting the bit configuration of the second operand value to its complement form and adding this configuration to the fixed-point value bit configuration of the first operand register. The result of this performance is placed into the general register specified by the first operand. The second operand must represent a four-byte area that is resident on a fullword boundary alignment of storage. The Subtract Logical instruction is different from the Subtract instruction in that it logically subtracts all 32 bits of the second operand from that of the first operand; it does not cause a program interrupt if a fixed-point overflow occurs in the form of a carry-out of the sign-bit. Instead the Condition Code settings have unique interpretations to indicate whether or not a carry-out of the sign-bit did occur. Generally, if the execution of the Subtract Logical instruction did not cause the carry-out of the sign-bit it would perform the same function as the Subtract instruction. The only exception would be in interpreting the Condition Code bits.

Assume that general register 9 contains a fixed-point value of +13,825 and a fullword of storage, labeled SUBT, contains a fixed-point value of +13,663. The configuration of these values within their respective locations would be:

	S								
register 9	0000	0000	0000	0000	0011	0110	0000	0001	+13,825
	0	0	0	0	3	6	0	1	

	S								
SUBT	0000	0000	0000	0000	0011	0101	0101	1111	+13,663
	0	0	0	0	3	5	5	F	

The instruction statement that is to be executed is:

    SL   9, SUBT

The first action to be taken by the instruction statement would be to convert the value of the second operand, SUBT, to its complement form. SUBT would then appear as:

	S								
SUBT (complement)	1111	1111	1111	1111	1100	1010	1010	0001	-13,663
	F	F	F	F	C	A	A	1	

The instruction statement would then add together the bit configuration of the complement of SUBT and the bit configuration of the contents of general register 9, placing the sum of that addition into register 9. This action would appear to affect these fields as:

	S								
register 9 (before)	0000	0000	0000	0000	0011	0110	0000	0001	+13,825
	0	0	0	0	3	6	0	1	

	S								
SUBT (complement)	1111	1111	1111	1111	1100	1010	1010	0001	-13,663
	F	F	F	F	C	A	A	1	

Fixed-Point Arithmetic Operations

(sum/difference in register 9)

S 0000	0000	0000	0000	0000	0000	1010	0010
0	0	0	0	0	0	A	2

+162

In this instance, the Condition Code bits are set to indicate that "the difference in general register 9 is not zero and a carry-out of the sign-bit did not occur."

Subtract Logical Registers (SLR)

This instruction logically subtracts the bit configuration of the value contained within the second operand register from the bit configuration of the value contained within the first operand register. The actual subtraction is performed in the same manner as the other "subtract" instructions contained within this section; the bit configuration of the second operand is complemented and added to the bit configuration of the contents of the first operand.

The resulting sum is placed into the first operand register. As indicated, both operands must specify general registers, or a symbol or label that has been equated to a general register. The Subtract Logical Registers instruction does not cause a program interrupt if a fixed-point overflow in the form of a carry-out of the sign-bit occurs. The Condition Code bit settings, however, do have unique interpretations to indicate whether or not a carry-out of the sign-bit did occur.

To illustrate this instruction, consider that general register 9 contains a fixed-point value of +2,147,483,600 and general register 12 contains a fixed-point value of −486. The bit configuration of these registers would appear as:

register 9

S 0111	1111	1111	1111	1111	1111	1101	0000
7	F	F	F	F	F	D	0

+2,147,483,600

register 12

S 1111	1111	1111	1111	1111	1110	0001	1010
F	F	F	F	F	E	1	A

−486

The instruction statement to be executed is:

SLR   9 , 12

As with the performance of all fixed-point "subtract" instructions, the first action that is taken would be to convert the bit configuration of the contents of the second operand to its complement form. After doing this, general register 12 would have a bit configuration that appeared as:

register 12 (complement)

S 0000	0000	0000	0000	0000	0001	1110	0110
0	0	0	0	0	1	E	6

+486

The remaining action taken by the instruction statement logically adds together the fixed-point bit configuration of register 9 and the complement bit configuration of the value contained in general register 12. This would appear as:

register 9 (before)

S							
0111	1111	1111	1111	1111	1111	1101	0000
7	F	F	F	F	F	D	0

+2,147,483,600

register 12 (complement)

S							
0000	0000	0000	0000	0000	0001	1110	0110
0	0	0	0	0	1	E	6

+486

(sum/difference in register 9)

S							
1000	0000	0000	0000	0000	0001	1011	0110
8	0	0	0	0	1	B	6

-2,147,483,210

Notice that the resulting sum is not the value to be expected from a normal operation. The operation results in a carry-out of the sign-bit, changing the positive/negative value of the answer. In this instance the Condition Code bits would indicate that "the difference is not zero and a carry-out of the sign-bit occurred."

Summation of Fixed-Point Subtract Instructions

Having discussed the action and general use of the five fixed-point subtract instructions, it is in order to present a series of instruction statements that use those instructions. This assists in demonstrating the peculiarities and similarities of each of the instructions as they are applied to fixed-point values. The logic path drawn by the sample statements is not necessarily a practical application, but rather is solely intended to graphically offer an application pattern.

The instruction statements for this general example have been coded as shown in Figure 11-2.

Statement 001 is a Load Multiple instruction statement. It loads the contents of LESS2 (+376) into general register 7 and the contents of LESS3 (-49,377) into general register 8. After the execution of this instruction statement, the fixed-point contents of general registers 7 and 8 appear as:

register 7

S							
0000	0000	0000	0000	0000	0001	0111	1000
0	0	0	0	0	1	7	8

+376

register 8

S							
1111	1111	1111	1111	0011	1111	0001	1111
F	F	F	F	3	F	1	F

-49,377

Fixed-Point Arithmetic Operations

SYSTEM / 370 ASSEMBLER CODING FORM

NAME	OPERATION	OPERAND	COMMENTS	SEQUENCE
*				001
SUBTEX	LM	7,8,LESS2		002
	SLR	7,8		003
	SR	3,3		004
	L	3,WORD		005
	S	3,LESS1		006
	SR	3,7		007
	SH	3,HAFSUB		008
	SL	3,LOGWRD		009
	BC	15,FINSUBT		010
*		* * * CONSTANTS * * *		440
*				441
LESS1	DC	F'2590'		460
LESS2	DC	F'376'		480
LESS3	DC	F'-49377'		500
HAFSUB	DC	H'-747'		520
LOGWRD	DC	F'20000'		540
WORD	DC	F'32596'		560
*				580

FIGURE 11-2

Statement 002 is a Subtract Logical Registers instruction statement that subtracts the value contained within general register 8 (−49,377) from the value within general register 7 (+376). The result of the subtraction (+49,753) is placed into general register 7. The content value configuration of general register 8 is first changed to the complement of its original value and then added to general register 7 to effectively perform the subtraction. The configuration of these registers during the execution of the instruction, at which time general register 8 is in complement form of the original value, is shown by the following:

	S								
register 7 (before)	0000	0000	0000	0000	0000	0001	0111	1000	+376
	0	0	0	0	0	1	7	8	

	S								
register 8 (complement)	0000	0000	0000	0000	1100	0000	1110	0001	+49,377
	0	0	0	0	C	0	E	1	

	S								
(sum/difference in register 7)	0000	0000	0000	0000	1100	0010	0101	1001	+49,753
	0	0	0	0	C	2	5	9	

Statement 003 performs a Subtract Register instruction. It will subtract general register 3 from itself. Upon completion of this statement, register 3 contains a fixed-point value of +0.

Statement 004 loads general register 3 with the contents of WORD, a value of +32,596 which is in the fixed-point value format. After execution of this statement, the bit configuration of general register 3 is:

	S								
register 3	0000	0000	0000	0000	0111	1111	0101	0100	+32,596
	0	0	0	0	7	F	5	4	

Statement 005 subtracts the fixed-point value of the contents of a fullword labeled LESS1 (+2,590) from the fixed-point contents of general register 3 (+32,596). The fullword value, LESS1, is first converted to the Two's Complement of its bit configuration value, after which it will be represented as:

	S								
LESS1 (complement)	1111	1111	1111	1111	1111	0101	1110	0010	−2,590
	F	F	F	F	F	5	E	2	

This value configuration is then added to the fixed-point contents of general register 3, constituting the subtraction as requested. The bit configuration of register 3, before and after the execution of the instruction, and the use of the complement of LESS1, can be illustrated as:

Fixed-Point Arithmetic Operations

register 3
(before)

S							
0000	0000	0000	0000	0111	1111	0101	0100
0	0	0	0	7	F	5	4

+32,596

LESS1
(complement)

S							
1111	1111	1111	1111	1111	0101	1110	0010
F	F	F	F	F	5	E	2

−2,590

(result in
(register 3)

S							
0000	0000	0000	0000	0111	0101	0011	0110
0	0	0	0	7	5	3	6

+30,006

Statement 006, a Subtract Registers instruction statement, subtracts the fixed-point value of the contents of general register 7 (+49,753) from the fixed-point value of the contents of general register 3. The bit configurations shown below are for the value of general register 3 before and after the execution of this statement, and for the complement configuration of general register 7 as it is used by the SR instruction.

register 3
(before)

S							
0000	0000	0000	0000	0111	0101	0011	0110
0	0	0	0	7	5	3	6

+30,006

register 7
(complement)

S							
1111	1111	1111	1111	0011	1101	1010	0111
F	F	F	F	3	D	A	7

−49,753

register 3
(result)

S							
1111	1111	1111	1111	1011	0010	1101	1101
F	F	F	F	B	2	D	D

−19,747

Statement 007 subtracts the fixed-point value of HAFSUB (a stored Halfword) from the fixed-point value contents of general register 3 (−19,747). After its expansion to a 32-bit fullword, the bit configuration of HAFSUB is converted to its complement form and then added to the value of general register 3, as shown in the following illustration.

register 3
(before)

S							
1111	1111	1111	1111	1011	0010	1101	1101
F	F	F	F	B	2	D	D

−19,747

HAFSUB
(expanded
complement)

S							
0000	0000	0000	0000	0000	0010	1110	1011
0	0	0	0	0	2	E	B

+747

(sum/difference
in register 3)

S							
1111	1111	1111	1111	1011	0101	1100	1000
F	F	F	F	B	5	C	8

−19,000

Statement 008, a Subtract Logical instruction statement, subtracts the fixed-point value contained within the fullword LOGWRD (−20,000) from the fixed-point value of the contents of general register 3 (−19,000). The effect of the statement on general register 3 when it is added to the complement of LOGWRD can be shown as:

register 3
(before)

S							
1111	1111	1111	1111	1011	0101	1100	1000
F	F	F	F	B	5	C	8

−19,000

LOGWRD
(complement)

S							
0000	0000	0000	0000	0100	1110	0010	0000
0	0	0	0	4	E	2	0

+20,000

register 3
(result)

S							
0000	0000	0000	0000	0000	0011	1110	1000
0	0	0	0	0	3	E	8

+1,000

Statement 009 is a forced branch to a routine that is referenced by the label FINSUBT.

After performing all of the instruction statements listed within this subroutine, the fixed-point value of the contents of general register 3 would be +1000. Unless the values of the fullword constants were changed prior to each time that the subroutine was entered, these instructions would always return the same answer, making it a useless calculation.

The Fixed-Point "Multiply" Instructions

Multiply (M)

The Multiply instruction requires an even-odd contiguous pair of general registers to be used as a work area and product field. The programmer must load the multiplicand into the odd-numbered register prior to issuing the Multiply instruction. When the Multiply instruction statement is executed, it multiplies the fixed-point value contained in the even-odd register pair by the fixed-point value of the multiplier, a fullword value in storage. The resulting product resides in the combined even-odd pair of registers as a 64-bit signed integer (one sign-bit, 63 integer-bits) with the units position of the answer occupying the low-order position of the odd-numbered register. The first operand register must always address the even-numbered register of the pair, otherwise a specifi-

Fixed-Point Arithmetic Operations

cation error interrupt will occur. If the product is known to be small enough to be contained within a single general register, the product may be extracted from the odd-numbered register only; otherwise it must be extracted from the combined length of the even-odd register pair.

To illustrate the performance of this instruction and its effect on the registers that are used as the operand work areas, the following examples are presented.

Example 1. The fixed-point values for this Multiply example are contained in two fullwords of storage. They are:

```
     FULLWD1    DC     F'32973'
     FULLWD2    DC     F'7851'
```

The instruction statements to be executed are:

```
     L    9,FULLWD1           001
     M    8,FULLWD2           002
```

Statement 001 loads general register 9 with the fixed-point value specified by the label FULLWD1. Although the entire product area comprises general registers 8 and 9, the loading of the multiplicand into the odd-numbered register affects that general register only. Register 8 has not yet been affected at this point and its contents are unpredictable and unspecified. After the Load instruction statement has been executed, the configuration of the general registers used in this example is:

general register 8   general register 9 (+32,973)

?	?	?	?	?	?	?	?	S 0000	0000	0000	0000	1000	0000	1100	1101
								0	0	0	0	8	0	C	D

Statement 002 multiplies the fixed-point value of the multiplicand (assumed to be residing in general register 9) by the fixed-point value of FULLWD2, the multiplier. The resulting product is found in the combined length of general registers 8 and 9, residing as a 64-bit signed integer. The bit configuration of the multiplicand, multiplier and product would be:

Multiplicand (before the Multiply instruction statement)

general register 8   general register 9

?	?	?	?	?	?	?	?	S 0000	0000	0000	0000	1000	0000	1100	1101
								0	0	0	0	8	0	C	D

Multiplier   FULLWD2   (+7,851)

S 0000	0000	0000	0000	0001	1110	1010	1011
0	0	0	0	1	E	A	B

General register 8   (+258,871,023)   general register 9

S 0000	0000	0000	0000	0000	0000	0000	0000	0000	1111	0110	1110	0000	1110	1110	1111
0	0	0	0	0	0	0	0	0	F	6	E	0	E	E	F

In this instance, the product does not exceed the length of the odd-numbered register. Therefore, the answer (the product) could be moved out for retention in another area by storing the contents of general register 9 into a fullword storage location. The sign-bit in register 9 is the same as the sign-bit in general register 8. This is because once the multiplication function is completed, the algebraically determined sign-bit is expanded toward the right until the first significant-digit of the product is encountered. In a positive value, the first significant-digit of the product would be a one-bit; in a negative value it would be a zero-bit. This interpretation could be stated as: "A significant product digit is a bit that is unlike (or the opposite of) the sign-bit of the product."

Example 2. This example shows the result of a multiplication in which the product exceeds the length of the odd-numbered general register. The values to be used are stated as:

```
MPCAN    DC    F ' 75968322 '
MPLIER   DC    F ' 59312 '
ANSWER   DS    D
```

The instruction statements are:

```
L      3 , MPCAN        001
M      2 , MPLIER       002
STM    2 , 3 , ANSWER   003
```

Statement 001 loads general register 3 with the fixed-point value of MPCAN, equal to +75,968,322. The bit configuration of general register 3 should then appear to be:

register 3

S 0000	0100	0111	0111	1110	1101	0000	0010
0	4	7	7	E	D	0	2

+75,968,322

Statement 002 multiplies the fixed-point value contained in general register 3 by the fixed-point value of MPLIER, placing the resulting product into the whole of general registers 2 and 3. The bit configuration of the registers affected by the execution of Statement 002 would be:

Multiplicand (before the Multiply statement)

general register 2   general register 3   (+75,968,322)

?	?	?	?	?	?	?	?	S 0000	0100	0111	0111	1110	1101	0000	0010
								0	4	7	7	E	D	0	2

Fixed-Point Arithmetic Operations

Multiplier (MPLIER)

(+59,312)

S 0000	0000	0000	0000	1110	0111	1011	0000
0	0	0	0	E	7	B	0

Product

general register 2   (+4,505,833,114,464)   general register 3

S 0000	0000	0000	0000	0000	0100	0001	1001	0001	1000	1001	0101	0000	1011	0110	0000
0	0	0	0	0	4	1	9	1	8	9	5	0	B	6	0

Notice that the product that resulted from the execution of Statement 002 exceeds the limit of general register 3 and extends into the two low-order bytes of general register 2.

Statement 003 loads the multiple combination of registers 2 and 3 into a doubleword (AN-SWER) field of storage. Because the product value exceeds the length of one general register, the storage area for the answer must be a doubleword in length.

Multiply Registers (MR)

The Multiply Registers instruction is identical to the Multiply instruction with the single exception that the second operand of the statement must refer to a general register. The MR instruction requires an even-odd contiguous pair of registers for the product area. Normally the multiplicand should be loaded into the odd-numbered general register of the pair of registers and the multiplier should be loaded into another general register. An exception to this rule is discussed later in this analysis. When the Multiply Registers instruction statement is executed, it multiplies the fixed-point value contained within the odd-numbered register of the pair by the fixed-point value of the contents of the second operand register. The product resides in the whole of the even-odd pair of registers as a 64-bit signed integer; a sign-bit and a 63-bit integer value. The units position of the product occupies the low-order bit positions of the odd-numbered general register. The first operand register must always address the even-numbered register of the pair, otherwise a specification interrupt occurs. If it is known that the product value will be small enough to be contained within one register, the answer may be extracted from the odd-numbered register only; otherwise the answer must be moved out of the entire pair of registers.

Example 1. The fixed-point values, as contained within fullword storage locations, are:

```
    POINTA    DC    F'3276'
    POINTB    DC    F'991'
    ANSR      DC    F'0'
```

The instruction statements are:

```
LM    5,6,POINTA           001
MR    4,6                  002
ST    5,ANSR               003
```

Statement 001, a Load Multiple statement, loads the fixed-point value of POINTA into general register 5 first and then loads the fixed-point value of the contents of POINTB into general register 6. Register 5, as the odd-numbered register of the pair of registers 4 and 5, now contains the multiplicand. The value now contained in general register 6 is considered to be the multiplier for this example. As this point, the bit configuration of the three registers would be:

general register 4   general register 5   (+3276)

?	?	?	?	?	?	?	?	S 0000	0000	0000	0000	0000	1100	1100	1100
								0	0	0	0	0	C	C	C

general register 6   (+991)

S 0000	0000	0000	0000	0000	0011	1101	1111
0	0	0	0	0	3	D	F

As indicated above, general register 4 contains unpredictable data prior to the execution of the Multiply Registers instruction.

Statement 002 performs the Multiply Registers instruction statement. The fixed-point value of the contents of general register 6 are used as the multiplier against the fixed-point value contained in general register 5. The product resides in the whole of general registers 4 and 5. The bit configuration of the product appears as:

general register 4   general register 5

S 0000	0000	0000	0000	0000	0000	0000	0000	0000	0000	0011	0001	1000	1001	1011	0100
0	0	0	0	0	0	0	0	0	0	3	1	8	9	B	4

+3,246,516

Statement 003 stores the fixed-point value contained in general register 5 into a fullword storage area labeled ANSR. It is assumed that the programmer was aware that the fixed-point value of the product would not exceed the maximum value content of a single general register. After the Store instruction is executed, the bit configuration of ANSR would be:

ANSR

S 0000	0000	0011	0001	1000	1001	1011	0100
0	0	3	1	8	9	B	4

+3,246,516

Fixed-Point Arithmetic Operations

Example 2. The multiply function of the Multiply Registers instruction can also be used to square a number (i.e., multiply a fixed-point value times itself). This is done by loading the value into the odd-numbered register of an even-odd pair of registers and then issuing the even-numbered register as the second operand. Assume that the fixed-point value of +1006 is to be squared by the following instruction statement coding:

```
SQRIT      DC     F ' 1006 '
*
RTE        L      3 , SQRIT            001
           MR     2 , 3                002
```

Statement 001 loads the fixed-point value of +1006 into general register 3. The bit configuration of general registers 2 and 3 would now appear as:

general register 2   general register 3   (+1006)

?	?	?	?	?	?	?	?	S 0000	0000	0000	0000	0000	0011	1110	1110
								0	0	0	0	0	3	E	E

Statement 002 specifies that the instruction should "multiply the fixed-point contents of general register 3 (by addressing general register 2 as the first operand) by the contents of general register 3." This effectively squares the fixed-point value contained in register 3, placing the product in the whole of general registers 2 and 3. After execution of this instruction statement, general registers 2 and 3 would have a bit configuration of:

general register 2   (+1,012,036)   general register 3

S 0000	0000	0000	0000	0000	0000	0000	0000	0000	0000	0000	1111	0111	0001	0100	0100
0	0	0	0	0	0	0	0	0	0	0	F	7	1	4	4

Example 3. By using an application similar to Example 2, the programmer can load both the multiplier and the multiplicand into the product area and multiply them together. Assume that the following fields have been defined:

```
QUANTITY     DC     F ' 395 '
UNITCOST     DC     F ' 75 '
ANSWER       DC     F ' 0 '
```

The instruction statements would then be:

```
LM     6 , 7 , QUANTITY           001
MR     6 , 6                      002
ST     7 , ANSWER                 003
```

Statement 001 performs a Load Multiple instruction, during which the contents of QUANTITY are loaded into general register 6 and the contents of UNITCOST into general register 7. At the completion of this statement the contents of these registers are shown on the following page.

S							S							
0000	0000	0000	0000	0000	0001	1000	1011	0000	0000	0000	0000	0000	0000	0100	1011
0	0	0	0	0	1	8	B	0	0	0	0	0	0	4	B

general register 6 (+395)   general register 7 (+75)

Statement 002 multiplies the contents of general register 6 against the contents of general register 7, even though the operands both refer to general register 6.

Statement 003 stores the result of the multiplication operation into a fullword storage area labeled ANSWER. It is presumed, in this example, that the result of the multiplication will not exceed the maximum value of one general register.

Multiply Halfword (MH)

This instruction may be used to multiply a halfword fixed-point value contained within a general register. In this instruction, the product area required consists of only one general register. The value to be multiplied is first loaded into the product register and then multiplied by the halfword value that resides in storage. The result resides in the whole of the product register. An overflow condition might occur, but a program interrupt does not take place in such an instance. Care should be taken to assure that the values being used do not create an overflow condition because this could alter the sign-bit of the product from its true value.

Example 1. The fixed-point values, contained within storage locations are:

```
MPLIER      DC      H ' 352 '
MPCAND      DC      F ' 49365 '
PRODANS     DC      F ' 0 '
```

The instruction statements have been coded as:

```
L       6 , MPCAND              001
MH      6 , MPLIER              002
ST      6 , PRODANS             003
```

Statement 001 loads the fixed-point value contained in MPCAND into general register 6. At this point the bit configuration of general register 6 would appear as:

register 6

S							
0000	0000	0000	0000	1100	0000	1101	0101
0	0	0	0	C	0	D	5

+49,365

Statement 002 multiplies the fixed-point value contained in general register 6 (+49,365) by the fixed-point value contained in MPLIER (+352). The halfword value of MPLIER is first extracted and expanded to a 32-bit fullword format. The general register is then multiplied by this expanded halfword, with the resulting product residing in the whole of the general register. The bit configuration of MPLIER, before and after expansion, and the product value in general register 6 resulting from the multiplication, are as follows:

Fixed-Point Arithmetic Operations

register 6
(before)

S 0000	0000	0000	0000	1100	0000	1101	0101
0	0	0	0	C	0	D	5

+49,365

MPLIER
(before)

S 0000	0001	0110	0000
0	1	6	0

+352

MPLIER
(expanded)

S 0000	0000	0000	0000	0000	0001	0110	0000
0	0	0	0	0	1	6	0

+352

register 6
(product)

S 0000	0001	0000	1001	0010	0100	1110	0000
0	1	0	9	2	4	E	0

+17,376,480

Statement 003 stores the fixed-point value contents of general register 6 into a fullword storage area labeled PRODANS.

Example 2. This example illustrates the multiplication of two halfword fixed-point values by using the Multiply Halfword instruction. For this example the values to be used are defined as:

```
HAF1    DC    H'4392'
HAF2    DC    H'68'
ANSW    DC    F'0'
```

The instruction statements have been coded as:

```
LH    7, HAF1        001
MH    7, HAF2        002
ST    7, ANSW        003
```

Statement 001 loads the fixed-point halfword value from HAF1 into general register 7. In doing so, the instruction statement expands the halfword configuration to a 32-bit fullword configuration by adding 16 additional high-order bits of the same bit value as the original sign-bit of the halfword. Therefore, it is not necessary to clear general register 7 to a zero value before loading HAF1 into general register 7. The bit configuration of general register 7 now appears as:

register 7

S 0000	0000	0000	0000	0001	0001	0010	1000
0	0	0	0	1	1	2	8

+4392

Statement 002 multiplies the value contained in general register 7 by the fixed-point value contained in HAF2. HAF2 is expanded to a 32-bit fullword configuration after which the multiplication occurs. The bit configuration of the expanded value of HAF2 and the product in general register 7 after the multiplication, would be:

HAF2 (expanded)	S 0000	0000	0000	0000	0000	0000	0100	0100	+68
	0	0	0	0	0	0	4	4	

register 7 (product)	S 0000	0000	0000	0100	1000	1110	1010	0000	+298,656
	0	0	0	4	8	E	A	0	

Statement 003 stores the fixed-point value contained in general register 7 into a fullword storage area referenced by the label ANSW. If it were definitely known that the product contained within general register 7 would never exceed the maximum value of a halfword, then Statement 003 could have been a Store Halfword instruction—from general 7 into a halfword storage location.

Summation of Fixed-Point "Multiply" Instructions

In learning about the three fixed-point multiply instructions it is probably apparent that the concept of the operations performed by these instructions varies quite little. The use of any of these would depend largely on the requirements of the data to be processed, its magnitude and, if all of these considerations were equal, the programmer's personal preference for instruction use.

In order to illustrate these instructions, the following example is presented. Assume that the programmer wishes to determine the total quantity of rivets used to assemble bulk quantities of various pieces of equipment. Although it would not be practical to use a series of multiply instructions such as this, it is shown here in that manner in order to relate the similarity of the fixed-point multiply instructions. Normally, the quantity of rivets used and the quantities of the assemblies would be variable factors dependent on the particular assembly to be completed. Assume that, when processing passes through this particular logic part of the problem program, the data fields contain the values indicated. The coding created for this example is shown in Figure 11-3.

Statement 001 sets the contents of general register 11 to zero by subtracting it from itself. Register 11 is to be used as an accumulator to hold the total sum of the rivets required as calculated by the multiply statements that are coded.

Statement 002 loads general register 3 with the fixed-point value from the stored fullword ITEM1QTY (+593). Because general register 3 is part of a pair of even-odd general registers that are construed to be the product area, the bit configuration of the product area would now appear as:

general register 2								general register 3							(+593)
?	?	?	?	?	?	?	?	S 0000	0000	0000	0000	0000	0010	0101	0001
								0	0	0	0	0	2	5	1

Statement 003 multiplies the multiplicand content (+593) of general registers 2 and 3 by the fixed-point value contained within RIVET1 (+15), resulting in a product of +8895, a figure small

Fixed-Point Arithmetic Operations

SYSTEM / 370 ASSEMBLER CODING FORM

Name	Operation	Operand	Seq
*			001
GOCALC	SR	11,11	002
	L	3,ITEM1QTY	003
	M	2,RIVET1	004
	AR	11,3	005
	LM	5,6,ITEM2QTY	006
	MR	4,6	007
	AR	11,5	008
	L	8,ITEM3QTY	009
	MH	8,RIVET3	010
	AR	11,8	011
	ST	11,TOTALRVT	012
*		CONSTANTS AND WORK AREAS	1110
*			1120
ITEM1QTY	DC	F'593'	1130
RIVET1	DC	F'15'	1140
ITEM2QTY	DC	F'278'	1150
RIVET2	DC	F'38'	1160
ITEM3QTY	DC	F'899'	1170
RIVET3	DC	H'9'	1180
TOTALRVT	DC	F'0'	1190
*			1200

FIGURE 11-3

enough to be contained within general register 3 although the product is construed to be in the whole of general registers 2 and 3. The bit configuration of registers 2 and 3 would now be:

general register 2 (+8895) general register 3

S															
0000	0000	0000	0000	0000	0000	0000	0000	0000	0000	0000	0000	0010	0010	1011	1111
0	0	0	0	0	0	0	0	0	0	0	0	2	2	B	F

Statement 004 adds the fixed-point value that is contained within general register 3 (+8895) to the fixed-point value currently residing within general register 11 (+0), resulting in a new value of +8895 for general register 11.

Statement 005 executes a Load Multiple instruction statement that takes the value from ITEM2QTY and loads it into general register 5, and also loads the value of RIVET2 into general register 6. In effect, this is loading the multiplicand into general registers 4 and 5, and the multiplier into general register 6. After this instruction is executed, the fixed-point value within those registers is:

general register 4 general register 5 (+278)

								S							
?	?	?	?	?	?	?	?	0000	0000	0000	0000	0000	0001	0001	0110
								0	0	0	0	0	1	1	6

register 6

S							
0000	0000	0000	0000	0000	0000	0010	0110
0	0	0	0	0	0	2	6

+38

Statement 006 multiplies the fixed-point contents of general register 5 (+278) by the fixed-point contents of general register 6 (+38), resulting in the product residing in the whole of general registers 4 and 5 (+10,564). This product would have a bit configuration of:

general register 4 general register 5 (+10,564)

S															
0000	0000	0000	0000	0000	0000	0000	0000	0000	0000	0000	0000	0010	1001	0100	0100
0	0	0	0	0	0	0	0	0	0	0	0	2	9	4	4

Statement 007 adds the fixed-point value of the contents of register 5 (+10,564) to the value of the contents of general register 11 (+8895). Register 11 would then contain a new fixed-point value of +19,459, which would appear as:

register 11

S							
0000	0000	0000	0000	0100	1100	0000	0011
0	0	0	0	4	C	0	3

+19,459

Fixed-Point Arithmetic Operations

Statement 008 loads the fixed-point value of the contents of ITEM3QTY (+899) into general register 8. Because the next instruction statement is to be a Multiply Halfword statement, it is only necessary to load that value into a single register, which may be either even-numbered or odd-numbered. Register 8 would then contain a bit configuration of:

register 8

S 0000	0000	0000	0000	0000	0011	1000	0011
0	0	0	0	0	3	8	3

+899

Statement 009 executes the Multiply Halfword instruction. This multiplies the value of the contents of general register 8 (+899) by the value of the contents of RIVET3 (+9). After this operation register 8 contains a value of +8091.

register 8

S 0000	0000	0000	0000	0001	1111	1001	1011
0	0	0	0	1	F	9	B

+8091

Statement 010 performs another Add Registers instruction, adding together the values contained in general register 8 (+8091) and register 11 (+19,459); the resulting sum appearing in general register 11 as:

register 11

S 0000	0000	0000	0000	0110	1011	1001	1110
0	0	0	0	6	B	9	E

+27,550

Statement 011 stores the fixed-point value of the contents of general register 11 into a fullword of storage that is referred to by the label TOTALRVT.

The program routine has now determined, via a series of multiply routines, that the bulk quantities of rivets required for the various part assemblies will total 27,550.

The Fixed-Point "Divide" Instructions

Divide (D)

The Divide instruction like the Multiply instruction, also requires an even-odd contiguous pair of general registers, a set to be used as the area for the dividend, quotient, and the remainder. The dividend must first be loaded into this pair of registers. The instruction statement that loads the dividend may address the odd-numbered register of the pair unless the programmer intends to manipulate the sign of the dividend by shifting. If the dividend is loaded directly into the odd-numbered register, the content of the even-numbered register is unpredictable, but the odd-numbered register will contain the fixed-point value of the dividend. The dividend may be loaded from a fullword in storage or from another general register. When the Divide instruction is executed it divides the fixed-point value contained within the odd-numbered general register by the fixed-point value of the divisor operand. After completion of the divide operation, the quotient is found in the odd-numbered register in fixed-point format. The remainder is contained in the even-numbered register and has the sign of the dividend. The sign of the quotient is algebraically determined. Inasmuch as the dividend is considered to consist of an even-odd pair of registers once it has been moved into the divide work area as a 64-bit signed integer, it is suggested that the even-numbered register be guaranteed the sign of the odd-numbered register. This may be accomplished in several different ways as will be shown. Several examples of the use and function of the Divide instruction follow.

Example 1. The fixed-point values to be used in this example are represented by:

```
DIVDEND     DC      F'48933'
DIVSOR      DC      F'37'
QUOTNT      DC      F'0'
REMNDR      DC      F'0'
```

The instruction statements to be executed are:

```
ROUTE1      SR      8,8                 001
            L       9,DIVDEND           002
            D       8,DIVSOR            003
            ST      8,REMNDR            004
            ST      9,QUOTNT            005
```

Statement 001 subtracts general register 8 from itself, guaranteeing a +0 value for that register. In this instance, it is known that all dividends will be a positive value, so this action assures the 64-bit dividend of a sign of the same configuration as are loaded into the low-order 32 bit positions.

Statement 002 loads the fixed-point value of DIVDEND into general register 9, the odd-numbered register of the even-odd pair of registers. After completion of this instruction statement, those registers appear as:

general register 8   general register 9   (+48,933)

S																
0000	0000	0000	0000	0000	0000	0000	0000	0000	0000	0000	0000	1011	1111	0010	0101
0	0	0	0	0	0	0	0	0	0	0	0	B	F	2	5

Statement 003 divides the contents of general registers 8 and 9 (+48,933) by the fixed-point value contained in DIVSOR (+37). After execution of this instruction statement, the quotient may be found in general register 9 and the remainder, if any, may be found in register 8. The contents of these two registers would be configured as:

general register 8 (remainder, +19)   general register 9 (quotient, +1322)

S							S								
0000	0000	0000	0000	0000	0000	0001	0011	0000	0000	0000	0000	0000	0101	0010	1010
0	0	0	0	0	0	1	3	0	0	0	0	0	5	2	A

Fixed-Point Arithmetic Operations

Statement 004 stores the remainder of +19, as found in general register 8, into a fullword storage area labeled REMNDR.

Statement 005 stores the quotient of +1322, as found in general register 9, into a fullword storage area labeled QUOTNT.

Example 2. This example takes the gross amount of dollars paid for a quantity of items and divides that amount by the number of pieces purchased in order to determine the average dollar cost per piece.

The statements have been coded as:

```
AMTPD      DC    F ' 3927869 '
UNITS      DC    F ' 8346 '
REMAINDR   DC    F ' 0 '
AVGCOST    DC    F ' 0 '
*
DIVRTE     L     4 , AMTPD            001
           SRDA  4 , 32               002
           D     4 , UNITS            003
           STM   4 , 5 , REMAINDR     004
```

Statement 001 loads general register 4 with the fixed-point value contained in AMTPD. This represents the gross dollars paid for the entire quantity of units. After this instruction statement is completed, the configuration of general registers 4 and 5 appears as:

general register 4   general register 5

S 0000	0000	0011	1011	1110	1111	0011	1101	?	?	?	?	?	?	?	?
0	0	3	B	E	F	3	D								

Statement 002 is a Shift Right Double Algebraic instruction with a shift length of 32 bit positions. This shifts the entire contents of general register 4 into general register 5 and replaces the bits shifted out of register 4 with the same value of bits as the sign-bit of general register 4. This has now assured that the sign-bit of the 64-bit signed integer, considered to comprise registers 4 and 5, has the same sign-bit as that of the original dividend, AMTPD. After the shift the configuration of general registers 4 and 5 appears as:

general register 4   general register 5

S 0000	0000	0000	0000	0000	0000	0000	0000	0000	0000	0011	1011	1110	1111	0011	1101
0	0	0	0	0	0	0	0	0	0	3	B	E	F	3	D

Statement 003 divides the contents of registers 4 and 5 (+3,927,869) by the total number of units purchased, which is represented by the fixed-point value contained in UNITS (+8346). After this statement has been executed, general register 4 contains the remainder and general register

5 contains the quotient; the quotient representing the average gross dollar price per unit. The configuration of these appears to be:

general register 4   (remainder, +5249)   general register 5   (quotient, +470)

S								S							
0000	0000	0000	0000	0001	0100	1000	0001	0000	0000	0000	0000	0000	0001	1101	0110
0	0	0	0	1	4	8	1	0	0	0	0	0	1	D	6

Statement 004 performs a Store Multiple operation. It stores the contents of general register 4 (remainder, +5249) into a fullword of storage labeled remainder by the identity REMAINDR and also stores the contents of general register 5 (quotient, +470) into a fullword of storage labeled AVGCOST.

Divide Registers (DR)

The Divide Registers instruction performs identically to the Divide instruction with the single exception that the divisor operand must address a general register rather than a fullword storage location. It too uses a pair of even-odd contiguous general registers as the division work area for the dividend.

Example 1. The values in this example and the instruction statements to be performed have been coded as:

```
        SETSIGN    DC      F'0'
        DIVDEN     DC      F'72833117'
        DIVSR      DC      F'442'
        REMDR      DC      F'0'
        ANSR       DC      F'0'
*
        BEGINDV    LM      6,8,SETSIGN              001
                   DR      6,8                      002
                   STM     6,7,REMDR                003
```

Statement 001 performs a Load Multiple instruction statement. It loads the fixed-point value of SETSIGN into general register 6, the value of DIVDEN into general register 7, and the value of DIVSR into general register 8. This program has assumed that all dividends are to be positive values. Therefore, the loading of a +0 value (SETSIGN) into register 6 assures that the 64-bit signed integer (representing the whole of general registers 6 and 7) has the same sign-bit configuration as the dividend (DIVDEN) which was loaded into register 7. When the forced sign-bits and the dividend are loaded into registers 6 and 7, this statement also loads the divisor (DIVSR) into general register 8. This single instruction statement has effectively replaced three possible individual Load instruction statements. Upon completion of the execution of this statement the configuration of general registers 6, 7, and 8 would appear to be:

general register 6   (+72,833,117)   general register 7

S															
0000	0000	0000	0000	0000	0000	0000	0000	0000	0100	0101	0111	0101	1000	0101	1101
0	0	0	0	0	0	0	0	0	4	5	7	5	8	5	D

Fixed-Point Arithmetic Operations

register 8
(divisor)

S							
0000	0000	0000	0000	0000	0001	1011	1010
0	0	0	0	0	1	B	A

+442

Statement 002 executes the Divide Registers instruction. In this instance, it divides the fixed-point value of general register 8 into the fixed-point 64-bit signed integer represented by general registers 6 and 7. After the execution of this statement, the bit configuration of registers 6 and 7 is:

register 6   (remainder, +357)   register 7   (quotient, +164,780)

S								S							
0000	0000	0000	0000	0000	0001	0110	0101	0000	0000	0000	0010	1000	0011	1010	1100
0	0	0	0	0	1	6	5	0	0	0	2	8	3	A	C

Statement 003 is a Store Multiple instruction statement. It stores the fixed-point value of the contents of register 6 (the remainder) into a fullword storage area labeled REMDR and then stores the fixed-point value of register 7 (the quotient or answer) into a fullword of storage that is addressed by the label ANSR.

Because there are only two fixed-point "divide" instructions, it is not considered necessary to have a summary of their performance included at this point. It is intended that the section that follows, dealing with the application of decimal point concepts in fixed-point math routines, will suffice for a generalization of the use of the Divide and Divide Registers instructions.

FIXED-POINT LOGIC APPLICATIONS WITH ASSUMED DECIMAL POINTS

The task of applying decimal point logic to fixed-point math routines is quite easily accomplished. Basically, it is merely the interim step of multiplying or dividing the various fixed-point values by increments of 10, 100, 1000, 10,000, etc. To increase the value of a whole number so that it retains its whole number value plus two assumed decimal places, it is only necessary to multiply that number by 100. To remove unwanted assumed decimal places from a mixed number containing two decimal places, only the division of the number by 100 is required in order to reduce it to a whole number configuration. "Rounding off" of decimal point values and subsequent reduction to a whole number is similarly accomplished.

For example, assume the programmer desires to multiply a given quantity of units by an even-dollar per unit cost and to arrive at a total cost that includes two decimal places. Using the base data constants stated within the following coding, this could be accomplished by at least two different methods.

```
       UNITCOST   DC    F ' 95 '      (xxxx. assumed format)
       UNITQTY    DC    F ' 863 '     (xxxx. assumed format)
       TOTLCOST   DC    F ' 0 '       (xxxxxxxx. 00 assumed format)
       XPANDIT    DC    F ' 100 '     (x. 00 assumed format)
*
       DORTE      SR    4 , 4                                        001
                  L     5 , UNITCOST                                 002
```

M	4 , XPANDIT	003
M	4 , UNITQTY	004
ST	5 , TOTLCOST	005

Statement 001 clears general register 4 to a +0 value by subtracting it from itself.

Statement 002 loads general register 5 with the fixed-point value contained in UNITCOST. In this instance it is considered to be +$95. The configuration of general registers 4 and 5 would now be:

general register 4 (+0)   general register 5 (+95)

S								S							
0000	0000	0000	0000	0000	0000	0000	0000	0000	0000	0000	0000	0000	0000	0101	1111
0	0	0	0	0	0	0	0	0	0	0	0	0	0	5	F

Statement 003 multiplies the contents of general registers 4 and 5 by a value of +100, the value contained in the fullword storage location, XPANDIT. This action would change the configuration of registers 4 and 5 to:

general register 4 (+9500)   general register 5

S															
0000	0000	0000	0000	0000	0000	0000	0000	0000	0000	0000	0000	0010	0101	0001	1100
0	0	0	0	0	0	0	0	0	0	0	0	2	5	1	C

Statement 004 multiplies general registers 4 and 5 by the total number of units (+863), the value contained in UNITQTY. These registers would now have a configuration of:

general register 4   general register 5
(+8,198,500 – assumed to $81,985.00)

S															
0000	0000	0000	0000	0000	0000	0000	0000	0000	0000	0111	1101	0001	1001	0110	0100
0	0	0	0	0	0	0	0	0	0	7	D	1	9	6	4

Statement 005 stores the value of general register 5 into a fullword storage area labeled TOTLCOST. For the intents and purposes of the programmer, the data being stored there has a format of 81,985.00, even though the physical decimal point does not exist. It is the programmer's responsibility to remember this assumed decimal point if any further operations with this value are to be performed.

The same results could have been accomplished by this series of coded instruction statements:

DORTE	SR	4 , 4	001
	L	5 , UNITCOST	002
	M	4 , UNITQTY	003

Fixed-Point Arithmetic Operations 383

	M	4 , XPANDIT	004
	ST	5 , TOTLCOST	005

In this instance the unit cost and the unit quantity are first multiplied together and the resulting product of that action is then multiplied by +100. The configuration of the registers for the first four instruction statements would then be:

After Statements 001 and 002:

general register 4 (+0) general register 5 (+95)

S															
0000	0000	0000	0000	0000	0000	0000	0000	0000	0000	0000	0000	0000	0000	0101	1111
0	0	0	0	0	0	0	0	0	0	0	0	0	0	5	F

After Statement 003:

general register 4 (+81,985) general register 5

S															
0000	0000	0000	0000	0000	0000	0000	0000	0000	0000	0000	0001	0100	0000	0100	0001
0	0	0	0	0	0	0	0	0	0	0	1	4	0	4	1

After Statement 004:

general register 4   general register 5
(+8,198,500–assumed to be $81,985.00)

S															
0000	0000	0000	0000	0000	0000	0000	0000	0000	0000	0111	1101	0001	1001	0110	0100
0	0	0	0	0	0	0	0	0	0	7	D	1	9	6	4

Statement 005 performs exactly the same function in this instruction statement set as it did in the previous set of statements.

Another frequent use of this method of adding decimal points to a whole number is to increase the magnitude of a value that is to be divided by a similar value, or by a larger value, in order to determine a percentage ratio. This is demonstrated in the following set of coding.

```
       SQUARES   DC    F ' 893 '      (xxxx. assumed format)
       CIRCLES   DC    F ' 995 '      (xxxx. assumed format)
       MULT      DC    F ' 1000 '     (x.000 assumed format)
       RATIO     DC    F ' 0 '        (xxxx.0% assumed format)
       *
       PCTRTE    SR    6 , 6                  001
                 L     7 , SQUARES            002
                 M     6 , MULT               003
```

```
         D      6 , CIRCLES           004
         ST     7 , RATIO             005
```

Statement 001 sets general register 6 to a +0 value by subtracting it from itself.

Statement 002 loads general register 7 with the fixed-point value of the contents of SQUARES. The bit configuration of general registers 6 and 7 would then appear to be:

general register 6   (+893)   general register 7

S 0000	0000	0000	0000	0000	0000	0000	0000	0000	0000	0000	0000	0000	0011	0111	1101
0	0	0	0	0	0	0	0	0	0	0	0	0	3	7	D

Statement 003 multiplies the contents of general registers 6 and 7 (+893) by +1000, the fixed-point value contained in MULT. This has now effectively added three assumed decimal places to the value in general register 7. The configuration of these registers would now be:

general register 6   general register 7
(+893,000—assumed to be 893.000)

S 0000	0000	0000	0000	0000	0000	0000	0000	0000	0000	0000	1101	1010	0000	0100	1000
0	0	0	0	0	0	0	0	0	0	0	D	A	0	4	8

Statement 004 divides the contents of general registers 6 and 7 (+893,000) by the fixed-point value contained within the stored fullword CIRCLES (+995). After execution of this instruction the configuration of these registers would be:

general register 6   general register 7 (quotient, +897)
(remainder, +485)   (assumed to be .897 or 89.7%)

S 0000	0000	0000	0000	0000	0001	1110	0101	S 0000	0000	0000	0000	0000	0011	1000	0001
0	0	0	0	0	1	E	5	0	0	0	0	0	3	8	1

Statement 005 stores the fixed-point contents of general register 7 into a stored fullword labeled RATIO. The programmer has assumed that the configuration of the data at this point is .897 or 89.7%, whichever way the ratio or percentage is to be expressed.

"Rounding off" of decimal places to the nearest whole number value, or to a lesser number of decimal places, is performed in a similar manner. The following two examples, a multiply routine and a divide routine, illustrate the common concept of "rounding off."

Example 1. This example multiplies together several "mixed" values (whole numbers and decimal places) and then "rounds off" the product to the nearest whole number unit. That is, if the first decimal point position is equal to, or greater than, a value of five, the unit position of the whole number is increased by a value of +1.

Fixed-Point Arithmetic Operations

The values to be used in this example and the instruction statements that have been coded are shown in Figure 11-4.

Statement 001 sets general register 2 to a zero balance by subtracting it from itself.

Statement 002 loads the fixed-point value of CASES into general register 3. Registers 2 and 3 would now appear to be:

general register 2   (+4331)   general register 3

S 0000	0000	0000	0000	0000	0000	0000	0000	0000	0000	0000	0000	0001	0000	1110	1011
0	0	0	0	0	0	0	0	0	0	0	0	1	0	E	C

Statement 003 multiplies the contents of general register 2 (+4331) by the fixed-point value of UNITS. Although the visual value of UNITS is +293, for the programmer's application it has an assumed value of .293. After execution of the Multiply instruction, the general registers contain:

general register 2   general register 3

S 0000	0000	0000	0000	0000	0000	0000	0000	0000	0000	0001	0011	0101	1100	1111	0111
0	0	0	0	0	0	0	0	0	0	1	3	5	C	F	7

+1,268,983   (assumed to be +1,268.983)

Statement 004 adds the fixed-point value of +500, contained within ROUNDER, to the value contained within general register 3. The logic of the program has intended that if the first digit to the right of the assumed decimal point is equal to, or greater than, a value of five, then the units position of the whole number should be increased by +1. In adding .500 to the digits to the right of the assumed decimal point, this automatically increases the units position of the whole number by one if the first decimal value to the right of the decimal point is five or greater. After execution of this statement the configuration of the registers is:

general register 2   general register 3

S 0000	0000	0000	0000	0000	0000	0000	0000	0000	0000	0001	0011	0101	1110	1110	1011
0	0	0	0	0	0	0	0	0	0	1	3	5	E	E	B

+1,269,483   (assumed to be 1,269.483)

Statement 005 divides the value of REDUCE (+1000) into the value contained within general registers 2 and 3. In doing this, it effectively reduces the dividend to an assumed whole number value. Because the three assumed decimal point positions had a power of 1000ths, the division of

SYSTEM / 370 ASSEMBLER CODING FORM

Name	Operation	Operand	Comments	Identification Sequence No.
SAMPRTE	SR	2,2		001
	L	3,CASES		002
	M	2,UNITS		003
	A	3,ROUNDER		004
	D	2,REDUCE		005
	ST	3,ANSWER		006
*				
*				
CASES	DC	F'4331'	(xxxx. ASSUMED FORMAT)	770
UNITS	DC	F'293'	(.000 ASSUMED FORMAT)	780
ROUNDER	DC	F'500'	(.000 ASSUMED FORMAT)	800
REDUCE	DC	F'1000'	(X.000 ASSUMED FORMAT)	820
ANSWER	DC	F'0'	(xxxxxx. ASSUMED FORMAT)	840
*				860
*				880
				890
				895

FIGURE 11-4

Fixed-Point Arithmetic Operations

this value by 1000 eliminates all digits to the right of the assumed decimal point. The configuration of the registers would now be:

general register 2

S 0000	0000	0000	0000	0000	0001	1110	0011
0	0	0	0	0	1	E	3

general register 3

S 0000	0000	0000	0000	0000	0100	1111	0101
0	0	0	0	0	4	F	5

(remainder, +483)   (quotient, +1269)

Statement 006 stores the value of general register 3 (+1269) into a fullword of storage labeled ANSWER.

Example 2. This example intends to find a percentage ratio between two values, carried out to an assumed value expression of 0.0000 or 000.00%. This value is then rounded to an assumed value expression of 0.000 of 000.0% and stored into a receiving area. The values to be used and the instruction statements that have been coded are shown in Figure 11-5.

Statement 001 sets the contents of general register 8 to a zero value by subtracting that register from itself.

Statement 002 loads the fixed-point value of RECEIPTS (+2395) into general register 9. The configuration of registers 8 and 9 would now appear as:

general register 8   (+2395)   general register 9

S 0000	0000	0000	0000	0000	0000	0000	0000
0	0	0	0	0	0	0	0

0000	0000	0000	0000	0000	1001	0101	1011
0	0	0	0	0	9	5	C

Statement 003 multiplies the value of these registers by 10,000, the value contained within XPAND. The configuration of the new values now found in these registers is:

general register 8   general register 9

S 0000	0000	0000	0000	0000	0000	0000	0000
0	0	0	0	0	0	0	0

0000	0001	0110	1101	0111	0010	1011	0000
0	1	6	D	7	2	B	0

+23,950,000   (assumed to be 2,395.0000)

SYSTEM / 370 ASSEMBLER CODING FORM

```
NOWRITE  SR   8,8
         L    9,RECEIPTS
         M    8,XPAND
         D    8,SALES
         A    9,ROUND
         SR   8,8
         D    8,CUTOFF
         ST   9,HOLDIT
*
RECEIPTS DC   F'2395'         (XXXX.  ASSUMED FORMAT)
SALES    DC   F'4116'         (XXXX.  ASSUMED FORMAT)
XPAND    DC   F'10000'        (X.0000 ASSUMED FORMAT)
ROUND    DC   F'5'            (.0000  ASSUMED FORMAT)
CUTOFF   DC   F'10'           (X.0    ASSUMED FORMAT)
HOLDIT   DC   F'0'            (XXX.0% ASSUMED FORMAT)
**
```

Identification sequence: 001–008, 845–885

FIGURE 11-5

Fixed-Point Arithmetic Operations

Statement 004 divides the contents of general registers 8 and 9 by the value of SALES. The resulting quotient in register 9 is construed to have the format of an unexpressed percentage (0.0000). The registers would now appear in a configuration of:

general register 8

S 0000	0000	0000	0000	0000	1100	0010	1000
0	0	0	0	0	C	2	8

general register 9

S 0000	0000	0000	0000	0001	0110	1011	1010
0	0	0	0	1	6	B	A

(remainder, +3112)   (quotient, +5818)
                                  (assumed to be .5818 or 58.18%)

Statement 005 adds a value of +5 (assumed to be .0005 or .05%) to general register 9 in order to round off the percentage to the nearest .0% value. After execution of this instruction statement the configuration of general registers 8 and 9 is:

general register 8

S 0000	0000	0000	0000	0000	1100	0010	1000
0	0	0	0	0	C	2	8

general register 9

S 0000	0000	0000	0000	0001	0110	1011	1111
0	0	0	0	1	6	B	F

(+3112)   (+5823 – assumed to be .5823 or 58.23%)

Statement 006 sets register 8 to zero in preparation for the Divide instruction statement that immediately follows. The registers would now appear to contain:

general register 8

S 0000	0000	0000	0000	0000	0000	0000	0000
0	0	0	0	0	0	0	0

general register 9

0000	0000	0000	0000	0001	0110	1011	1111
0	0	0	0	1	6	B	F

(+0)   (+5823 – assumed to be .5823 or 58.23%)

Statement 007 divides general registers 8 and 9 by the value contained within CUTOFF (+10). This effectively reduces the value in general register 9 by one decimal point position. The configuration of the registers now is:

general register 8

S							
0000	0000	0000	0000	0000	0000	0000	0011
0	0	0	0	0	0	0	3

(remainder, +3)

general register 9

S							
0000	0000	0000	0000	0000	0010	0100	0110
0	0	0	0	0	2	4	6

(quotient, +582)
(assumed to be .582 or 58.2%)

Statement 008 stores the fixed-point contents of general register 9 into a fullword storage location that is referenced by the label HOLDIT. The value of +582, which is being stored, has been assigned an assumed identity of 58.2% by the programmer and is recognized as this format at any other point within the program.

The foregoing illustrations and examples should have presented a reasonable basis for understanding the application and manipulation of assumed decimal point locations. In general, to remove unwanted decimal point positions, it is only necessary to divide by 10, 100, 1000, 10,000, 100,000, etc. In order to add a required number of decimal point positions, it is only necessary to multiply by 10, 100, 1000, 10,000, 100,000 etc. At your discretion you may use a combination of both of these concepts to manipulate decimal points in fixed-point arithmetic routines.

REVIEW EXERCISES

1. When an Add Halfword instruction statement is executed, the stored two-byte halfword specified by the second operand is added to the low-order two bytes of general register specified by the first operand register. (True) (False)
2. SLR is the mnemonic op code for the Assembler Language instruction _____ _____ _____.
3. In fixed-point arithmetic instructions, the PSW Condition Code is not altered by the execution of any one of the _____ or _____ instructions.
4. A negative fixed-point value always has a single sign-bit that is formed by a _____ -bit.
5. During the execution of a fixed-point Subtract instruction statement, the value of the content of the second operand is _____ and that new configuration is then algebraically _____ to the value of the content of the first operand.
6. When coding a Multiply or Multiply Registers instruction statement, the first operand of the statement must always specify the _____-numbered register of a contiguous pair of even-odd registers.

Fixed-Point Arithmetic Operations

7. If a Subtract Registers instruction statement is executed in which the first operand register contains a fixed-point value of +2048 and the second operand register contains a fixed-point value of −2048, the first operand register would subsequently contain a fixed-point value of _____.

8. An odd-numbered general register may be validly addressed by the first operand in a Multiply Halfword instruction statement. (True) (False)

9. In an Add Registers (AR) instruction statement the sum of the addition will be placed into the (first) (second) operand register.

10. If a storage halfword, containing a fixed-point value of −32,768, is to be added to a general register via the Add Halfword instruction, the expanded fullword version of that halfword during execution of the statement could be represented in hexadecimal form as:

11. A fixed-point Multiply (M) instruction statement can validly generate a fixed-point value that is greater than the capacity of a single register. (True) (False)

12. In a fixed-point Add _____ instruction statement all bits of the fullword storage area are added to all bits of the general register specified by the first operand without regard for sign-bit significance.

13. Although only a single register is specified as the first operand in a Multiply Halfword instruction statement, it is not possible for a fixed-point overflow to occur as a result of execution of an MH instruction statement. (True) (False)

Using the values defined as residing within the specified general register and storage areas for the following problems, complete both the binary and hexadecimal configuration of the fields as they would appear upon completion of the execution of the instruction statement.

14. register 3 ... contains +23,975
    register 9 ... contains −14,210

                    ADDFLDS   AR   3,9

    register 3 *hex*
            binary

15. register 11 ... contains +392,417
    HAFWD ... contains +32,519

                    SETADDRT   AH   11,HAFWD

    register 11 *hex*
            binary

16. register 7 ... contains 32,416,817
FWD9 ... contains −27,941

                      LOGADD   AL   7 , FWD9

register 7 *hex*

binary

17. register 3 ... contains +31,965,423
register 9 ... contains +7,592,087

                      CALCADD   ALR   9 , 3

register 9 *hex*

binary

18. register 10 ... contains +159,375
register 9 ... contains +2,899

                      SUBRTE   SLR   10 , 9

register 10 *hex*

binary

19. register 4 ... contains −39,541,782

                      SUBRT2   SR   4 , 4

register 4 *hex*

binary

20. register 12 ... contains −389,510
FULLWD6 ... contains +426,877

                      SUMRTE   A   12 , FULLWD6

register 12 *hex*

binary

21. register 7 ... contains +319,586
HALFWDB ... contains −7,853

                      JOBRTE7   SH   7 , HALFWDB

register 7 *hex*

binary

Fixed-Point Arithmetic Operations

22. register 10 ... contains +21,583,910
FULLWRDX ... contains +30,009

                CLRTE5   SL   10 , FULLWRDX

register 10 *hex*

binary

23. register 3 ... contains +325,198
FWORD ... contains -2,768,447

                SETCALC   S   3 . FWORD

register 3 *hex*

binary

24. register 2 ... contains +83,915
register 3 ... contains -5,176,933
register 4 ... contains +213,847
FVALUE1 ... contains +15,006
FVALUE2 ... contains +8,092

                SETVALS   SR   2 , 2
                                LM   3 , 4 , FVALUE1
                                MR   2 , 4

register 2 *hex*

binary

register 3 *hex*

binary

25. register 4 ... contains +3,975
register 5 ... contains +17,842,931
FULLWORD ... contains +800,216
FWMP ... contains +83

                MULTRTE   L   4 , FULLWORD
                                SRDL   4 , 32
                                M   4 , FWMP

register 4 *hex*

binary

register 5 *hex*

binary

26. register 6 ... contains +0
register 7 ... contains +385,910
HAFWD9 ... contains +16,694

              MULRTE8   MH   6 , HAFWD9

register 6 *hex*

      binary

register 7 *hex*

      binary

27. register 8 ... contains +315,876
register 9 ... contains +2,977,310
register 10 ... contains −15,900
FWD1 ... contains +0
FWD2 ... contains +26,985
FWD3 ... contains +204

              DIVRTE3   LM   8 , 10 , FWD1
                             DR   8 , 10

28. register 4 ... contains +3,906,608
register 5 ... contains −21,504
FULLWA ... contains +612,983
FULLWB ... contains +716

              DIVROUT4   L   4 , FULLWA
                              SRDA   4 , 32
                              D   4 , FULLWB

ADDITIONAL REVIEW EXERCISES FOR CHAPTERS 3 THROUGH 11

This review consists of instruction statements that may or may not be valid. The errors include incorrect formatting of statements, incorrect operands, and invalid length and register specifications. Place a checkmark before the incorrect statements.

#	Label	Op	Operands
1. _____	DATARTE	CLI	DATA3+9 , Z ' 6 '
2. _____		AP	DATPAK (5) , 7 (4 , 5)
3. _____	BIN4SET	DC	63BL1 ' 11000001 '
4. _____	LOADEM	L	2 , ADCON1
5. _____		MVC	BIGFLD+1500 (6) , PADDATA
6. _____	LOADSET	LM	13 , 2 , 4 (8)
7. _____		SL	5 , 15 (0 , 8)
8. _____	BRANCHA	BALR	3 , 6
9. _____	SETLARGE	DC	6000XL2 ' 4040 '
10. _____		M	10 , 0 (0 , 3)
11. _____		D	3 , FULLWORD
12. _____	PUTTEM	STM	10 , 9 , 8 (7)
13. _____		AP	DATAPAK , =XL3 ' 004593 '
14. _____		C	DATA1 (6) , DATA2
15. _____	MULTEM	MH	3 , =H ' 328 '
16. _____		SH	11 , =H ' 1 '
17. _____		LH	10 , FULLWRD9
18. _____	ADDUP	A	6 , =H ' 12396 '
19. _____	COMPRTE	CLC	0+260 (260 , 3) , 0 (4)
20. _____		AR	6 (4) , 8
21. _____		SLDA	5 , 12
22. _____		CLC	DATA1+900 (15) , INDATA (15 , 5)
23. _____		LCR	10 , 10
24. _____	CONVRTER	CVB	DUBLPAK , 6
25. _____	ODDSET	DS	0CL393
26. _____		MVI	DATAFLD+56 (4 , 4) , C ' DATE '
27. _____		SR	10 , 1
28. _____		SP	0+19 (15 , 12) , 0 + 45 (12 , 8)
29. _____		SL	3 , 4 , FULLWORDS

30. _____	CALCIT	AP	0+5 (3 , 9) , 8 (2 , 10)
31. _____		MH	5 , HAFWRD1
32. _____		L	6 , 8 , FULWD3
33. _____	REROUTE	A	10 , FLWD (0 , 9)
34. _____	SETCHAR	STC	5 , ONEBYTE
35. _____		S	3 , F ' 820015916 '
36. _____	DIVREG	DR	10 , 4
37. _____		ALR	4 , =F ' 9831 '
38. _____	NULLAREA	DC	0CL6 ' 123123 '
39. _____	LTROUTE	LTR	9 , 0 (10)
40. _____	SETTLERTE	SR	10 , 9
41. _____		M	7 , =F ' 99210 '
42. _____		MVZ	B8 (17) , CONST1
43. _____	S3468F	MVC	G , A (2)
44. _____		SP	DATAPAK (3) , LONGPACK (4)
45. _____		CP	PACKBYTE (1) , PL1 ' 4 '
46. _____		AR	5 , 5 (5)
47. _____	CHEXIT	CH	4 , =H ' 15002 '
48. _____		MVC	DATA+1 (255) , DATA
49. _____		SH	6 (2) , =H ' 32765 '
50. _____		SRA	8 , 8
51. _____		SP	7 (7 , 8) , DATA3+2 (1)
52. _____		A	11 , 4 (3 , 5)
53. _____	PAKITUP	PACK	PAKIT (9) , 0+400 (12 , 5)
54. _____		MVC	0+256 (256) , 0 (8)
55. _____		DP	QUOREM (7) , =P ' 51 '
56. _____		MR	6 , 5
57. _____		SRL	4 , 1
58. _____	CLEARIT	SR	11 , 11
59. _____		BAL	8 , GOBACK
60. _____		SH	H ' 523 ' , HAFWRD
61. _____		LA	6 , 6
62. _____	LEFTITE	SLDL	8 , 60
63. _____		ST	6 , FULLWORDS

Fixed-Point Arithmetic Operations

#	Label	Op	Operands
64. _____		SR	5 , 5
65. _____	DIVIT	D	7 , 11
66. _____		BC	5 , NEWLOOP
67. _____		M	3 , FULLWRD7
68. _____		L	FULLWD , 9
69. _____		SRDR	8 , 32
70. _____		LM	5 , WORD1 , WORD2
71. _____	SUMUP	AH	9 , 2 (8 , 9)
72. _____		DR	6 , 5
73. _____		ST	11 , FULLWORDS
74. _____	TOTALS	AL	6 , =F ' 392566 '
75. _____		S	9 , 10 (0 , 4)
76. _____		LH	3 , HAFWRDA
77. _____		MVZ	DATAHOLD (3 , 5) , CHANGE (3 , 6)
78. _____		AR	3 , =F ' 5932 '
79. _____	LEFTMUV	SLL	2 , 2
80. _____		LTR	8 , 8
81. _____		MH	5 , 0 (0 , 5)
82. _____	DIVQRM	DR	3 , 8
83. _____		C	6 , 4 (0 , 9)
84. _____	VALCONST	DC	PL10 ' + 15356983.333 '
85. _____		MR	8 , 10
86. _____		BXLE	9 , 10 , 12
87. _____	OUTRTE	BCT	7 , RELOOP
88. _____		L	8 , DUBLWD
89. _____		D	6 , FULLWRD9
90. _____		AL	8 , FULLWD1
91. _____	SETTAB	CLI	FIELDA (6,1) , =CL1 ' X '
92. _____		M	11 , 0 (0 , 8)
93. _____		SH	HAFWORD , 2
94. _____		UNPK	DATAFLD (20) , PACKFLD+20 (8)
95. _____		AL	2 , 36 (1 , 11)
96. _____		D	12 , 14 (0 , 8)
97. _____		LM	6 , 15 , WORDS

98. _____	SAVE	STH	3, FULLSWT
99. _____		A	8, 5, (6, 8)
100. _____		SRDA	11, 48
101. _____		MR	10, =F ' 939 '
102. _____		CL	DATAFIELD, =F ' 155220 '
103. _____	SETPAK	PACK	PACKER (18), DATA (18)
104. _____	BCTEXIT	BCT	10, 0 (0, 8)
105. _____		C	10, FULLWD5
106. _____		IC	6, 6 (6, 12)
107. _____		LNR	13, 13
108. _____		MP	MULTPAK (12), MPLIER (10)
109. _____		BC	0, NEXTRTE
110. _____		CH	HAFWRD1, HAFWRD2
111. _____		ST	FULLWD, 7
112. _____		MVC	DATASET+8 (1), =C ' A '
113. _____		CVD	10, PACK8
114. _____		BCTR	8, 8
115. _____	MATCH	CR	9, 10
116. _____		LM	FULLWORD, 6, 9
117. _____		STC	DATABYTE, =CL1 ' X '
118. _____		BAL	6, 3, NEWROUTE
119. _____		AP	DPACK (12), EPACK (11)
120. _____		CLR	10, 0 (3, 4)
121. _____		LA	7, 1932659
122. _____		BXH	5, 9, 10 (11)
123. _____	VALCONS	DS	8CL2 ' 00 '
124. _____	SETREDY	DC	CL9 ' IN && OUT '
125. _____	H	DH	8, HALFWRD

12

Boolean Logic Applications

THE BOOLEAN ALGEBRA LOGIC INSTRUCTIONS

Instruction: And Immediate

mnemonic	hex code	operand format
NI	94	$D_1(B_1), I_2$

The And Immediate instruction (a binary logic "times" instruction) uses the one byte of immediate data, as defined by the second operand, to mask one byte of data specified by the first operand. The operation of this instruction affects the bits in the following manner:

Bit values			Result in
Second operand	First operand		first operand
1	1	equals	1
1	0	equals	0
0	0	equals	0
0	1	equals	0

As indicated, the result of the operation is placed into the first operand location. This instruction acts upon only one byte of data.

CC	BC	Condition
0	8	The first operand is zero (all zero-bits).
1	4	The first operand is not zero (one or more one-bits).

* * *

Instruction: And

mnemonic	hex code	operand format
N	54	$R_1, D_2(X_2, B_2)$

This And instruction (a binary logic "times" instruction) uses the contents of the second operand to mask the contents of the first operand register. The effects of this instruction on the contents of the first operand register are shown on the following page.

Bit values			Result in
Second operand	First operand		first operand
1	1	equals	1
1	0	equals	0
0	0	equals	0
0	1	equals	0

The result of the operation is placed into the first operand register. The address created by the second operand must reside on a fullword boundary alignment.

Both operands must be of the same length, four bytes.

CC	BC	Condition
0	8	The first operand register contains zero (all zero-bits).
1	4	The first operand register does not contain zero (one or more one-bits).

* * *

Instruction: And

mnemonic	hex code	operand format
NC	D4	$D_1 (L, B_1), D_2 (B_2)$

This particular And instruction (a binary logic "times" instruction) uses the storage data specified by the second operand to mask the storage data specified by the first operand. The resulting operation affects the bits of the first operand in the following manner:

Bit values			Result in
Second operand	First operand		first operand
1	1	equals	1
1	0	equals	0
0	0	equals	0
0	1	equals	0

The result of the masking operation is placed into the first operand storage area. This particular And instruction may be used to mask up to 256 bytes of data in one operation.

CC	BC	Condition
0	8	The contents of the first operand are zero (all zero-bits).
1	4	The contents of the first operand are not zero (one or more one-bits).

* * *

Instruction: And

mnemonic	hex code	operand format
NR	14	R_1, R_2

This instruction (a binary logic "times" instruction) uses the contents of the second operand register to mask the contents of the first operand register. The result of this action are:

Bit values			Result in
Second operand	First operand		first operand
1	1	equals	1
1	0	equals	0
0	0	equals	0
0	1	equals	0

The result of the performance of this instruction is placed into the first operand register. As indicated, both operands must be general registers.

CC	BC	Condition
0	8	The first operand register contains zero (all zero-bits).
1	4	The first operand register does not contain zero (one or more one-bits).

* * *

Instruction: Or Immediate

mnemonic	hex code	operand format
OI	96	$D_1(B_1), I_2$

The Or Immediate instruction (a binary logic "add" instruction) uses the one byte of immediate data, as defined by the second operand, to mask the single byte of data that is specified by the first operand. The resulting operations affect the bits of the first operand as follows:

Bit values			Result in
Second operand	First operand		first operand
1	1	equals	1
1	0	equals	1
0	1	equals	1
0	0	equals	0

The result of the execution of the instruction is available in the first operand location. This instruction acts upon only one byte of data.

CC	BC	Condition
0	8	The first operand contains zero (all zero-bits)
1	4	The first operand does not contain zero (one or more one-bits).

*   *   *

Instruction: Or

mnemonic	hex code	operand format
O	56	$R_1, D_2(X_2, B_2)$

This Or instruction (a binary logic "add" instruction) uses the fullword contents of the second operand to mask the contents of the first operand register, wherein the results of the operation are:

Bit values			Result in
Second operand	First operand		first operand
1	1	equals	1
1	0	equals	1
0	1	equals	1
0	0	equals	0

The result of the operation is placed into the general register specified by the first operand. The address generated by the second operand must be located on a fullword boundary alignment.

CC	BC	Condition
0	8	The first operand contains zero (all zero-bits).
1	4	The first operand does not contain zero (one or more one-bits).

*   *   *

Instruction: Or

mnemonic	hex code	operand format
OC	D6	$D_1(L, B_1), D_2(B_2)$

This Or instruction (a binary logic "add" instruction) uses the storage data specified by the second operand to mask the storage data specified by the first operand. The action of this instruction modifies the bits of the first operand field as follows:

Bit values			
Second operand	First operand		Result in first operand
1	1	equals	1
1	0	equals	1
0	1	equals	1
0	0	equals	0

The result of this operation is placed in the first operand location. Up to 256 bytes of data may be masked with a single instruction statement of this type.

CC	BC	Condition
0	8	The first operand contains zero (all zero-bits).
1	4	The first operand does not contain zero (one or more one-bits).

* * *

Instruction: Or

mnemonic	hex code	operand format
OR	16	R_1, R_2

This particular Or instruction (a binary logic "add" instruction) uses the contents of the second operand register to mask the contents of the first operand register. The action of this instruction upon the bits would be:

Bit values			
Second operand	First operand		Result in first operand
1	1	equals	1
1	0	equals	1
0	1	equals	1
0	0	equals	0

The result of the operation is placed into the general register specified by the first operand. Both operands must refer to general registers.

CC	BC	Condition
0	8	The first operand register contains zero (all zero-bits).
1	4	The first operand register does not contain zero (one or more one-bits).

* * *

Instruction: Exclusive Or Immediate

mnemonic	hex code	operand format
XI	97	$D_1 (B_1), I_2$

The Exclusive Or Immediate instruction (a binary logic "modified add" instruction) uses one byte of immediate data, defined by the second operand, to mask a single byte of storage data as specified by the first operand. The resulting operation affects the first operand bits as follows:

Bit values			Result in
Second operand	First operand		first operand
1	1	equals	0
1	0	equals	1
0	0	equals	0
0	1	equals	1

The result of the operation of this instruction is placed into the first operand location. This instruction acts on only one byte of storage data.

CC	BC	Condition
0	8	The first operand contains zero (all zero bits).
1	4	The second operand does not contain zero (one or more one-bits).

*   *   *

Instruction: Exclusive Or

mnemonic	hex code	operand format
X	57	$R_1, D_2 (X_2, B_2)$

This Exclusive Or instruction (a binary logic "modified add" instruction) uses the contents of the fullword specified by the second operand to mask the contents of the first operand register. The results of the operation of this instruction would be as follows:

Bit values			Result in
Second operand	First operand		first operand
1	1	equals	0
1	0	equals	1
0	0	equals	0
0	1	equals	1

The result of the operation is placed into the general register specified by the first operand. The address generated by the second operand must be that of an aligned fullword boundary.

CC	BC	Condition
0	8	The first operand contains zero (all zero-bits).
1	4	The first operand does not contain zero (one or more one-bits).

* * *

Instruction: Exclusive Or

mnemonic	hex code	operand format
XC	D7	$D_1 (L, B_1) , D_2 (B_2)$

This instruction (a binary logic "modified add" instruction) uses the storage data specified by the second operand to mask the storage data specified by the first operand. The resulting action modifies the first operand bit configuration as follows:

Bit values			Result in
Second operand	First operand		first operand
1	1	equals	0
1	0	equals	1
0	0	equals	0
0	1	equals	1

The result of the operation is placed into the storage area addressed by the first operand. Up to 256 bytes of data may be masked with one instruction statement.

CC	BC	Condition
0	8	The first operand contains zero (all zero-bits).
1	4	The first operand does not contain zero (one or more one-bits).

* * *

Instruction: Exclusive Or

mnemonic	hex code	operand format
XR	17	R_1 , R_2

This particular Exclusive Or instruction (a binary logic "modified add" instruction) uses the contents of the second operand register to mask the contents of the first operand register. The execution of this instruction results in the following action on the bits:

Bit values			Result in
Second operand	First operand		first operand
1	1	equals	0
1	0	equals	1
0	0	equals	0
0	1	equals	1

The results of this operation are placed into the general register specified by the first operand. Both operands in the statement coded with this instruction must be general registers.

CC	BC	Condition
0	8	The first operand contains zero (all zero-bits).
1	4	The first operand does not contain zero (one or more one-bits).

Utilizing the Boolean Binary Logic Instructions

Boolean logic, or Boolean binary logic, consists of a set of instructions that manipulates individual bits or groups of bits. The data that is processed by these instructions would not normally be thought of as consisting of character configurations. There are three unique classes of Boolean logic instructions in Assembler Language—the AND, the OR, and the EXCLUSIVE OR. Within each of these groups are several instructions, all of which perform the same type of function but depend on different types and lengths of data fields.

All of these instructions have one common factor in that each uses a "mask" to determine which bit positions in the source field are to be manipulated or altered. This mask may be logically thought of as a bit position pattern, wherein each unique pattern would cause a correspondingly unique reaction on a similar source field. There is no standard configuration for the mask pattern inasmuch as this would depend entirely on the interpretation of the meaning of the individual bit positions and whether or not any action was to be taken against them individually or collectively.

The instruction statements are coded by specifying the source field as the first operand and the mask as the second operand. The actual bit configuration of the source field is altered if the mask creates any resulting action at all—which does not necessarily occur.

The "And" Instructions

The And instructions function as a logical "times" (multiplication) instruction. The logic applied here is that "any value times zero equals zero" or "zero times any value equals zero." Because the Boolean instructions are associated only with bits, the understanding is generated that the multiplication of each bit of the source field by each corresponding bit in the mask must, therefore, be limited to "0 x 1," "0 x 0," "1 x 0," or "1 x 1;" zero and one being the maximum range of any single bit. The resulting configuration of the source field, based on its original content and the content of the mask, would be as follows.

mask bit		corresponding source field bit		resulting source field bit
1	times (x)	1	equals	1
1	times (x)	0	equals	0
0	times (x)	0	equals	0
0	times (x)	1	equals	0

As a result of the execution of any of the And instructions, the PSW Condition Code is set to one of two conditions—the indication that the source field is now zero (consisting of all zero-bits) or it is not zero (containing one or more one-bits).

Boolean Logic Applications

condition code value	corresponding test value	condition indicated
0	8	The result is zero.
1	4	The result is not zero.

The And instructions have a very definite application in being used to turn "bit switches" to an "off" condition.

Three of the four And instructions have an identical name; they do have different mnemonic codes, however, which relate to the type of data fields that they are to be used with.

And Immediate (NI)

The And Immediate instruction uses a one-byte "immediate character" mask to act on a one-byte area of storage. For clarity, it is a good practice to express the "immediate character" in hexadecimal form, thereby making the bit configuration of that character easily identifiable. As with all of the And instructions, the NI instruction is quite useful for setting bit switches to an "off" condition. This particular instruction would mask a single byte, representing eight bit switches if so desired, and for every zero-bit in the mask it would set every corresponding bit in the source field byte to a zero-bit value. For any bit positions in the source field byte that are not to be altered, a one-bit should be constructed in the mask prior to executing the NI instruction statement.

If a single byte of storage data, addressed by the label CHEXBITS, is used as a set of bit switches the logical concept of the switches would be:

```
                                    one byte
CHEXBITS              | 0   0   0   0 ¦ 0   0   0   0 |

(switch number)         1   2   3   4   5   6   7   8
```

Using the concept that a one-bit equals an "on" condition and a zero-bit equals an "off" condition, a value of X'B6' in CHEXBITS would indicate the following switch conditions:

```
                                    one byte
CHEXBITS              | 1   0   1   1 ¦ 0   1   1   0 |

(switch number)         1   2   3   4   5   6   7   8
(switch status)        on  off  on  on off  on  on  off
```

In the following examples, this configuration (X'B6') will be used as the source byte field, which will be altered by various "immediate character" masks.

Example 1. The logic of this program routine intends to reset bit-switches 1, 4, 5, and 8 to an "off" condition prior to reentry to a certain routine. In order to set these bits "off" and leave all other bits unaltered, it is necessary to construct a mask in which bit positions 1, 4, 5, and 8 contain a zero-bit and all other positions contain a one-bit. This mask would be configured as:

	one byte								
	0	1	1	0	0	1	1	0	X'66'
(bit-switch position)	1	2	3	4	5	6	7	8	

Using the source field byte CHEXBITS, the instruction statement and the resulting action would be:

    NI   CHEXBITS, X'66'

	one byte								
CHEXBITS (before)	1	0	1	1	0	1	1	0	X'B6'
X'66' (mask)	0	1	1	0	0	1	1	0	X'66'
CHEXBITS (results)	0	0	1	0	0	1	1	0	X'26'
(switch number)	1	2	3	4	5	6	7	8	
(switch status)	off	off	on	off	off	on	on	off	

As requested by the program task, switches 1, 4, 5, and 8 have been reset, or remain, in an "off" condition. Switches 2, 3, 6, and 7 remain as they were, regardless of their previous condition.

Example 2. The program now requires that all bit switches contained in CHEXBITS be set to an "off" condition. According to the performance of the NI instruction, a zero-bit in the mask guarantees a zero bit in the corresponding position of the source byte. Therefore, the mask should be all zero-bits, or X'00', to assure the program of all zero-bits in CHEXBITS.

    NI   CHEXBITS, X'00'

CHEXBITS (before)	1	0	1	1	0	1	1	0
X'00' (mask)	0	0	0	0	0	0	0	0
CHEXBITS (after)	0	0	0	0	0	0	0	0
(switch numbers)	1	2	3	4	5	6	7	8
(switch status)	off	off	off	off	off	off	off	off

Boolean Logic Applications

All switches contained within CHEXBITS have now been set to, or remain in, an "off" condition.

Example 3. In this example, a destructive test of certain bit positions is being made. The program logic intends to determine whether or not bit switches 5, 6, 7, and 8 are in an "off" status. If they are all "off," the program logic should branch to a subroutine labeled AUDIT; if one or more are "on," the branch is to a subroutine labeled ERROR. Because switches 1, 2, 3, and 4 are not to be tested and the program logic prefers that they be reset to a zero-bit configuration at this time, the mask used is:

0	0	0	0	1	1	1	1	X'0F'
1	2	3	4	5	6	7	8	

(bit-switch position)

This mask turns off bit-switches 1, 2, 3, and 4 if they are "on" and at the same time leaves bit-switches 5, 6, 7, and 8 "on" if they are not "off." The Condition Code indicates whether the result of the operation is zero or not zero. A zero condition would indicate that none of the last four switches were on; a nonzero condition would indicate that one or more of switches 5, 6, 7, or 8 were on. The coding of the instruction statements for this example would be:

```
    NI    CHEXBITS , X ' 0F '        001
    BC    8 , AUDIT                   002
    BC    4 , ERROR                   003
```

CHEXBITS (before)	1	0	1	1	0	1	1	0	X'B6'

X'0F'	0	0	0	0	1	1	1	1	X'0F'

CHEXBITS (after)	0	0	0	0	0	1	1	0	X'06'

(switch number)	1	2	3	4	5	6	7	8
(switch status)	off	off	off	off	off	on	on	off

Statement 001 would execute the And Immediate instruction statement, giving the results shown in the field "CHEXBITS (after)."

Statement 002 specifies, "If the result is a totally zero configuration, branch to the subroutine AUDIT." This branch is not taken in this example.

Statement 003 indicates, "If the result is not zero, branch to the subroutine labeled ERROR." In this example the branch would be made at this point.

These examples illustrate the type of action that is generated by all And instructions. Just as the And Immediate is used to mask only one storage byte with an immediate character, the other And instructions each have individual requirements regarding the source field and mask.

And (N)

This particular And instruction, the mnemonic code of which is 'N', uses a fullword of storage as a mask to audit the bit contents of a general register. The length of the operation is fixed at

32 bit positions. The mask must reside on a fullword boundary location of program storage and the source field must be specified in the first operand of the instruction statement as a general register, either directly or symbolically.

This instruction may be used in a bit-switch application similar to those shown in the examples for the And Immediate instruction. It may also be used to set bits or bytes of a general register to zero.

To illustrate this particular type of And instruction, assume that the following conditions are to be programmed:

- General register 8 contains a value in the low-order three bytes and a code character in the high-order byte.
- The high-order byte is to be cleared by using the 'N' version of the And instruction.
- The value contained within the low-order three bytes of the register must be an "even" number; if it is an odd number it is to be reduced by one to the next lower even number.

At the time of execution of the following instruction statements, general register 8 contains a value of +15,391 and a code character of "D" in the high-order byte.

The fullword mask and the instruction statement to be executed are:

```
            DS    0F
MASK1       DC    X'00FFFFFE'
*
            N     8,MASK1
```

The bit manipulation generated by this statement would appear to be:

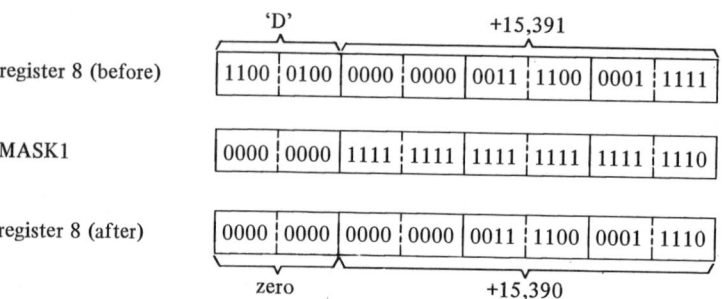

The high-order byte of the mask (X'00') has cleared the high-order byte of general register 8 to all zero-bits. The single low-order zero-bit in the mask has guaranteed that a low-order one bit in the register would be changed to a zero-bit, therefore assuring the program logic that general register 8 now contains an even number.

Note that wherever a one-bit appears in the mask, the corresponding bit position in general register 8 is not altered; wherever a zero-bit appears in the mask, a zero-bit is forced into the corresponding bit position in general register 8.

And (NC)

The NC version of the And instruction utilizes a program storage mask to inspect and alter a similar-length program storage source field. The mask, and the corresponding general storage

Boolean Logic Applications

source field, may each be up to 256 bytes in length. Both operands of the instruction statement may be represented by either symbolic or actual storage addresses.

A unique application for this instruction would be to convert all EBCDIC alpha characters to a range of 'A' through 'I'. Because of the configuration of the high-order four bits of EBCDIC character alphabetics this conversion is possible.

The similarity between these matched character sets may be found by examining the EBCDIC Character Table.

source alphabetics		*converted alphabetics*
A or J	equals	A or X'C1'
B or K or S	equals	B or X'C2'
C or L or T	equals	C or X'C3'
D or M or U	equals	D or X'C4'
E or N or V	equals	E or X'C5'
F or O or W	equals	F or X'C6'
G or P or X	equals	G or X'C7'
H or Q or Y	equals	H or X'C8'
I or R or Z	equals	I or X'C9'

The data field to be converted (where necessary) is a five-byte storage area (DATAFLD) that presently contains the EBCDIC characters 'RAQWS'. The mask that would be used to accomplish the specified conversion of such a five-byte source field is defined as a five-byte constant labeled BIGMASK. Its bit configuration is:

```
BIGMASK    DC    XL5 'CFCFCFCFCF'
```

or

BIGMASK | 1100 1111 | 1100 1111 | 1100 1111 | 1100 1111 | 1100 1111 |

The instruction statement to be executed is:

```
NC    DATAFLD , BIGMASK
```

The execution of this statement would result in the following conversion of the data in DATAFLD:

DATAFLD *character*	R	A	Q	W	S
hex	D 9	C 1	D 8	E 6	E 2
binary	1101 1001	1100 0001	1101 1000	1110 0110	1110 0010

BIGMASK	1100 1111	1100 1111	1100 1111	1100 1111	1100 1111

DATAFLD *binary* (result)	1100 1001	1100 0001	1100 1000	1100 0110	1100 0010
hex	C 9	C 1	C 8	C 6	C 2
character	I	A	H	F	B

Assembler Language for Application Programming

And (NR)

This instruction is the register version of the And instruction—both the mask and the source field must be contained within general registers. Accordingly, the execution of this instruction affects exactly 32 bits, four bytes—the length of a general register. Any of the applications illustrated within the examples shown for the other And instructions may be applied to this one, providing that the length restrictions of registers are observed.

An interesting concept that might be applied to illustrate this instruction would be to use the NR to create a mask for subsequent use by the result register with a third register. This would be to And (NR) general register 'X' (the mask) with general register 'Y', then subsequently And (NR) general register 'Y' (the mask) with general register 'Z'. The logic behind such a technique might be:

- The data content of general register 'Y' has been created through a set of program subroutines that have configured the bits of that register as switches. Any critical bit switches are assumed to be "on."

- Register 'Z' has also been partially configured by program subroutines. The program intends to compare the portion of register 'Z' containing critical bit switches to comparable bit positions in general register 'Y'. The resulting logic would depend on whether or not the comparable critical bit positions were all of opposing conditions prior to the And'ing.

In the example that follows the bit-switches of general register 'Z' are only the even-numbered bit positions, assuming that the positions are numbered from left to right, from 1 to 32. Consequently, the mask in general register 'X' must delete any one-bits that might appear in the odd-numbered bit positions of general register 'Y' inasmuch as register 'Y' will be used as the mask when it is And'ed with general register 'Z'. Instead of a hypothetical assignment of registers as 'X', 'Y', and 'Z', general registers 6, 7 and 8 will be used. Prior to the execution of any of the And (NR) instructions, the configuration of these general registers are:

register 6	0101 0101 0101 0101 0101 0101 0101 0101	X ' 55555555 '
register 7	1101 1111 0010 1101 1111 0111 0101 0011	X ' DF2DF753 '
register 8	0000 0000 0000 0100 0000 0000 0100 0000	X ' 00040040 '

The instruction statements have been coded as:

```
NROUTE    NR    7,6             001
          NR    8,7             002
          BC    4,BADMATCH      003
          BC    8,VALID         004
```

Statement 001 And's the contents of register 6 with register 7, placing the result of that operation into register 7. All one-bits occupying odd-numbered bit positions in general register 7 are

Boolean Logic Applications

replaced with zero-bits. Any remaining one-bits occupy even-numbered bit positions and these are used as the significant mask digits in Statement 002.

Statement 002 uses the new configuration of general register 7 as the mask for the And with general register 8. Only those bit positions within register 7 that contain one-bits test the corresponding positions within register 8. All other bit positions in general register 8 are considered as not participating and are supplied with zero-bits.

Statement 003 tests the Condition Code that resulted from the execution of Statement 002. If one or more one-bits remain in general register 8 after the And is completed, the Condition Code would indicate that the result is not zero and the program would branch out of Statement 003 to a subroutine labeled BADMATCH.

Statement 004 assumes that if the branch in Statement 003 is not taken, then the result of the And must be zero—the only other alternative. Accordingly, this statement tests the Condition Code and branches to a subroutine labeled VALID. Because there would be only two possible conditions resulting from Statement 002, either zero or nonzero, Statement 004 could have been coded as a forced branch (i.e., BC 15,VALID).

The configuration of the general registers as they exist through the two And statements would be:

Statement 001

| register 7 (before) | 1101 | 1111 | 0010 | 1101 | 1111 | 0111 | 0101 | 0011 |

| register 6 (mask) | 0101 | 0101 | 0101 | 0101 | 0101 | 0101 | 0101 | 0101 |

| register 7 (after) | 0101 | 0101 | 0000 | 0101 | 0101 | 0101 | 0101 | 0001 |

Statement 002

| register 8 (before) | 0000 | 0000 | 0000 | 0100 | 0000 | 0000 | 0100 | 0000 |

| register 7 (mask) | 0101 | 0101 | 0000 | 0101 | 0101 | 0101 | 0101 | 0001 |

| register 8 (after) | 0000 | 0000 | 0000 | 0100 | 0000 | 0000 | 0100 | 0000 |

It is not necessary that you be able to find, or completely understand, an application for the technique just illustrated. What is important is that you fully understand the use of the significant and nonsignificant digits in the And mask.

The "Or" Instructions

Forming a "matched set" similar to the And instructions, are four comparable Or instructions. The Or instructions perform as an "add" function, adding together the bits of the mask and the corresponding bits of the source field. Each bit position is treated as a separate add function in binary form and a carry-over from one bit position to the next is ignored. This can be more clearly explained by stating that within this unique function "one plus zero equals one," "zero plus one equals one," "one plus one equals one," and "zero plus zero equals zero." Based on the original configuration of the source field and the bit content of the mask, the Or would affect the source field as follows:

mask bit		corresponding source field bit		resulting source field bit
1	plus (+)	1	equals	1
1	plus (+)	0	equals	1
0	plus (+)	1	equals	1
0	plus (+)	0	equals	0

Note carefully that "1+1 equals 1," with no carry-over to the next higher bit position.

Upon completion of an Or instruction statement, the PSW Condition Code bits indicate one of two possible conditions: (1) the source field is zero (containing all zero-bits) or (2) the source field is not zero (containing one or more one-bits).

condition code value	corresponding test value	condition indicated
0	8	The result is zero.
1	4	The result is not zero.

While the And instructions are used to set bit-switches to an "off" condition, the Or instructions set bit-switches to an "on" condition. If a source field bit position is considered to be "on" (containing a one-bit) either a one-bit or a zero-bit in the corresponding mask position will leave that source bit on. If the source field bit position is "off" (containing a zero-bit), a one-bit in the mask will turn it "on," a zero-bit in the mask will leave it "off." Only one of the Or instructions has a unique name (OR IMMEDIATE), although each of the four instructions do have unique mnemonic codes. The use of any one particular Or instruction is directly related to the type of data fields (either storage or register) that are used for the source field and the mask.

Or Immediate (OI)

The Or Immediate instruction acts upon a one-byte source field of storage by using the immediate character specified as the second operand of the instruction statement as the mask. Each bit of the eight-bit mask is Or'ed with each corresponding bit of the single-byte storage area specified by the first operand of the instruction statement. The sum of the bits represents the result of the Or statement. The PSW Condition Code reflects the status of the sum—zero or not zero.

The configuration of the mask is determined by evaluating the action that is to be taken on the source field byte. A zero-bit in the mask does not alter the configuration of the corresponding source field bit; a one-bit in the mask guarantees that the corresponding bit position in the source field will contain a one-bit.

To illustrate this instruction, assume that a one-byte storage area (BITSET) contains all zero-bits at the beginning of the program subroutine. During the first cycle through the program logic two Or Immediate instructions are encountered. Each of these instruction statements sets a separate bit-switch to an "on" condition. Although these two statements appear relatively close together here, in the program source statements they are separated by a considerable number of instruction statements.

Boolean Logic Applications

```
--   -------
OI   BITSET  X'20'              0011
--   -------


--   -------
OI   BITSET , X'08'             0132
--   -------
```

Statement 0011 Or's the bit configuration of the immediate character X'20' with the bit content of BITSET. At this point within the program BITSET contains a configuration of X'00'.

	one byte							
BITSET (before)	0	0	0	0	0	0	0	0
X'20' (mask)	0	0	1	0	0	0	0	0
BITSET (after)	0	0	1	0	0	0	0	0

Statement 0132 Or's an immediate character mask of X'08' with the current configuration of BITSET.

	one byte							
BITSET (before)	0	0	1	0	0	0	0	0
X'08' (mask)	0	0	0	0	1	0	0	0
BITSET (after)	0	0	1	0	1	0	0	0

Thinking of BITSET as an eight-switch byte, it could be stated that switches 3 and 5 are now "on."

BITSET	0	0	1	0	1	0	0	0
(switch number)	1	2	3	4	5	6	7	8
(switch status)	off	off	on	off	on	off	off	off

The Or Immediate instruction may be used for any application that requires one or more bit positions filled with one-bits.

Or (O)

The 'O' version of the Or instruction Or's a fullword storage mask with a general register source field. All 32 bits of the four-byte mask are used to determine the resulting status of the register bits. The instruction statement is written with the first operand specifying, or referring to, a general register, and the second operand consisting of the actual or symbolic address of the fullword storage location.

As an example of this instruction, the programmer has designed a modular program that consists of eight subroutine modules and a control module. In each of the various subroutines, the program logic loads an address value, in fixed-point form, into the low-order three bytes of general register 10. Once the processing returns to the control module, it is necessary to know which subroutine is responsible for loading general register 10 with the value that now resides there. This problem could be easily solved by considering the eight high-order bits of general register 10 as bit-switches. After any one of the subroutine modules performs the task of loading register 10 that module can immediately set a bit-switch "on" to correspond to the module identity—such as, module 6 could turn "on" bit-switch 6. Then when the address value in general register 10 is passed back to the control module that register would also contain the identity of the sub-module from which it was passed. The instruction statements that follow are assumed to be a part of the coding within subroutine 6:

```
L     10 , NEWVALUE        010
O     10 , MASK6           011
BC    15 , CONTROL         012
```

In this instance MASK6 is a fullword constant containing a hexadecimal configuration of X'04000000'.

Statement 010 loads general register 10 with the address value contained in NEWVALUE. Assume that this value is +385,911.

Statement 011 Or's the fullword at MASK6 with general register 10. Inasmuch as the low-order three bytes of MASK6 do not contain any significant digits, the address value in general register 10 is not affected. The execution of Statement 011 would appear to affect general register 10 as:

```
                              +385,911
                              ╭───────────────────────────╮
register 10 (before)  | 0000 0000 | 0000 0101 | 1110 0011 | 0111 0111 |

MASK6                 | 0000 0100 | 0000 0000 | 0000 0000 | 0000 0000 |

register 10 (after)   | 0000 0100 | 0000 0101 | 1110 0011 | 0111 0111 |
```

Register 10 now contains the address value in the low-order three bytes and an indicator (bit-switch) in the single high-order byte that tells the control module which subroutine module is responsible for loading that address.

Statement 012 is a forced (unconditional) branch back to the control module.

Or (OC)

The storage-to-storage version of the Or instruction uses the mnemonic **OC** as its op code. Both the mask and the source field are located in program-defined storage fields and each may be up to 256 bytes in length. The areas addressed by the first and second operands of the instruction statement must have equal length characteristics, whether specified or implied, if the mask is to affect all of the area specified by the first operand.

Boolean Logic Applications

The example for the 'NC' instruction illustrated the means of converting certain EBCDIC alphabetic character representation into an alphabetic range of from A to I. In order to demonstrate the performance of the 'OC' instruction, the example to be presented will show how to convert any EBCDIC alphabetic character into its comparable EBCDIC numeric character representation. Because every valid EBCDIC alpha character contains a hexadecimal numeric digit in its low-order four bit positions, it is an excellent application for the OC instruction to change the four high-order bits of each character to one-bits, thus converting the alpha character to an EBCDIC numeric character.

This example uses a six-byte storage area labeled CONVRSN as the source field and a six-byte mask that is referred to by the label NUMASK. The data contained within CONVRSN at the time of execution of this example is:

CONVRSN												
character	N		U		M		B		E		R	
hex	D	5	E	4	D	4	C	2	C	5	D	9
binary	1101	0101	1110	0100	1101	0100	1100	0010	1100	0101	1101	1001

The instruction statement to be executed is:

    OC   CONVRSN (6) , NUMASK

Assuming that NUMASK consists of a hexadecimal format configuration of X'F0F0F0F0F0F0', the action generated by the instruction statement would appear to be:

CONVRSN (before)	1101 0101	1110 0100	1101 0100	1100 0010	1100 0101	1101 1001

NUMASK	1111 0000	1111 0000	1111 0000	1111 0000	1111 0000	1111 0000

CONVSN (after)												
binary	1111	0101	1111	0100	1111	0100	1111	0010	1111	0101	1111	1001
hex	F	5	F	4	F	4	F	2	F	5	F	9
character	5		4		4		2		5		9	

By Or'ing a mask of X'F0' with any valid EBCDIC alphabetic character, that character representation becomes a valid EBCDIC numeral of the same numeric value as the right-most hex digit of the original alphabetic character.

Or (OR)

This instruction is coincidentally mnemonically coded the same as its functional name. The instruction name Or states the group of Boolean instructions to which it belongs; the mnemonic OR specifies that it is an "Or Register" instruction op code.

Inasmuch as both operands of the instruction statement (the source field and the mask) must refer symbolically or directly to general registers, it is understood that a length of four bytes, 32 bits, is Or'ed.

The logic to be applied in the example for this instruction is that the programmer needs to assure the next subroutine within the problem program that general register 9 contains a minimum fixed-point value of +65,535. Any sum larger than +65,535 is modified by the insertion of one-bits into any of the 16 low-order bit positions of the source field that contain zero-bits. Because this required minimum value (+65,535) has a configuration of X'FFFF', the programmer may Or that configuration with the low-order two bytes of general register 9. It should also be noted that because general register 9 might contain a negative value the programmer must first guarantee a positive value. At the time of execution of the coded statements general register 9 contains a value of +48,373 and the mask is located within general register 2. The instruction statements to be executed are:

```
LPR    9,9                061
OR     9,2                062
```

Statement 061 is a Load Positive Register instruction statement. This would force the value contained within general register 9 into a positive configuration if it did not already have one.

Statement 062 sets the low-order 16 bits of general register 9 to all one-bits. Register 9 now contains the *minimum* positive value of +65,535 as required by the program logic.

| register 9 (before) | 0000 0000 0000 0000 1011 1100 1111 0101 | +48,373 |

| register 2 (mask) | 0000 0000 0000 0000 1111 1111 1111 1111 | +65,535 |

| register 9 (after) | 0000 0000 0000 0000 1111 1111 1111 1111 | +65,535 |

Because the logic of this application is not necessarily obvious, it should be explained further in order that it might be referenced for possible use. The program in question contains a routine that takes the value contained within general register 9 and assigns blocks of main storage in increments of +65,536 until register 9 has been decremented to less than one block size. At that point, one more block of storage minus one byte (65,536 less 1 equals 65,535) is assigned. The storage location byte immediately following the short (65,535) block is filled with a delimiter character to indicate that this is the final storage block assigned. If the value in register 9 at this point is less than +65,535 it is increased by the Or statement to that minimum value. The resulting block of storage is the only block, and also the short block, with a delimiter character immediately following it. The Or statement has guaranteed that the last, or only, block contains exactly 65,535 bytes.

The "Exclusive Or" Instructions

The Exclusive Or instruction set comprises four comparable instructions, each of which performs identical functions but using different types of data storage area. The action created by any one of the Exclusive Or variations takes the form of a "modified add" function. The basic logic of the "modified add" is that "two similar bits result in a zero-bit." The specific results of every possible combined configuration of the source field and the mask would be:

Boolean Logic Applications 419

mask bit		corresponding source field bit		resulting source field bit
1	plus (m+)	1	equals	0
1	plus (m+)	0	equals	1
0	plus (m+)	0	equals	0
0	plus (m+)	1	equals	1

Because each bit position is treated as a separate and complete entity, there is no carry-over from the modified addition of "1 + 1 equals 0."

The PSW Condition Code bit settings that result from the execution of an Exclusive Or are identical to those of the other Boolean logic instructions—"the result is zero" or "the result is not zero."

condition code value	corresponding test value	condition indicated
0	8	The result is zero.
1	4	The result is not zero.

The Exclusive Or instruction has several practical applications, one of which is the reversing of the status of bit-switches. If a bit-switch is "on" the Exclusive Or can turn it "off"; If it is "off" the Exclusive Or can turn it "on." The explanation of these instructions may be more aptly defined by stating that a one-bit in the mask reverses the corresponding bit of the source field—a zero-bit in the mask does not affect the source field bit.

Exclusive Or Immediate (XI)

The "XI" version of the Exclusive Or uses a one-byte "immediate character" mask to alter the contents of a one-byte storage area. Each significant bit (one-bit) of the mask reverses the configuration of the corresponding bit in the source field byte. A zero-bit in the mask does not alter the corresponding bit in the source field.

Relating once again to the application of bit-switches, assume that a storage byte, labeled BITTS, contains the hexadecimal configuration of X'7D'.

				one byte					
BITTS	0	1	1	1	1	1	0	1	X'7D'
(switch number)	1	2	3	4	5	6	7	8	
(switch status)	off	on	on	on	on	on	off	on	

An Exclusive Or instruction, with an immediate character of X'FF', is to be applied against BITTS and the resulting Condition Code is to be tested to see whether or not the bit-switches are now all in an "off" status.

```
XI    BITTS,X'FF'        001
BC    8,ALLOFF           002
BC    15,NOTOFF          003
```

Statement 001 is the Exclusive Or Immediate instruction statement, applying the X'FF' mask against BITTS. The performance of this statement would appear to be:

one byte

BITTS (before) | 0 | 1 | 1 | 1 | 1 | 1 | 0 | 1 |

X'FF' (mask) | 1 | 1 | 1 | 1 | 1 | 1 | 1 | 1 |

BITTS (after) | 1 | 0 | 0 | 0 | 0 | 0 | 1 | 0 |

The Condition Code would now contain a bit configuration indicating that the result of the operation is not zero.

Statement 002 indicates that if the Condition Code happens to indicate that BITTS is now all zero-bits, the branch should be taken to a subroutine labeled ALLOFF. However, in this particular example the branch would not be taken at this point.

Statement 003 is a forced branch to a subroutine labeled NOTOFF. Because the branch in Statement 002 is not taken the Condition Code result of the XI statement must have been that the result was not zero. An instruction statement of BC 4,NOTOFF would have caused the same branch to take place.

The following examples, presented without detail logic, are for the purpose of illustrating the "modified add" effect of the Exclusive Or Immediate instruction.

Example 1

    XI   BYTE4 , X ' 25 '

BYTE4 (before) | 1000 | 1101 |

X'25' (mask) | 0010 | 0101 |

BYTE4 (after) | 1010 | 1000 |

Example 2

    XI   FIELDA+2 , X ' E6 '

                         +1   +2

FIELDA (before) | 0111 | 1100 | 0100 | 1111 | 0110 | 0011 |

X'E6' (mask) | | | | | 1110 | 0110 |

FIELDA (after) | 0111 | 1100 | 0100 | 1111 | 1000 | 0101 |

                         +1   +2

Boolean Logic Applications

Example 3

    XI   SETBIT , X ' EE '

SETBIT (before)	1110 1110
X'EE'	1110 1110
SETBIT (after)	0000 0000

Exclusive Or (X)

The single mnemonic character 'X' represents the op code for this Exclusive Or instruction. The instruction statement for the 'X' should specify a general register as the first operand and the address of a fullword storage area (either symbolic or actual address) as the second operand. The second operand fullword is expected to contain the mask to be Exclusive Or'ed to the contents of the first operand general register. The operation length of this Exclusive Or instruction is fixed at 32 bit positions—equal to the length of the register source field and the fullword mask.

A fullword mask, residing at an address labeled FULLMASK, contains a hexadecimal configuration of X'FF000000'. The Exclusive Or instruction is to apply this mask against general register 3. At the time of execution of this example, general register 3 is configured as X'EE783D01'. The execution of the instruction statement, and the coded statement itself, would be:

    X   3 , FULLMASK

register 3 (before)	1110 1110 0111 1000 0011 1101 0000 0001
FULLMASK	1111 1111 0000 0000 0000 0000 0000 0000
register 3 (after)	0001 0001 0111 1000 0011 1101 0000 0001

As indicated, the significant one-bits in the high-order byte of the mask reverse the configuration of all of the corresponding bits in general register 3. The zero-bits in the mask have no effect on the relative bits of general register 3.

Exclusive Or (XC)

The 'XC' version of the Exclusive Or is a storage-to-storage type of operation. Both the mask and the data field are program storage areas with a maximum length of 256 bytes; both operands must have the same implied or explicit length attribute.

The example used to demonstrate the performance of this instruction is an EBCDIC alphanumeric conversion routine. Any alphabetic character from 'A' to 'I' is changed to a numeric character from '1' to '9'—or any EBCDIC numeric character of from '1' to '9' is converted to an alpha character of from 'A' to 'I'.

The conversion table would be:

from A to 1   or   from 1 to A
from B to 2   or   from 2 to B
from C to 3   or   from 3 to C
from D to 4   or   from 4 to D
from E to 5   or   from 5 to E
from F to 6   or   from 6 to F
from G to 7   or   from 7 to G
from H to 8   or   from 8 to H
from I to 9   or   from 9 to I

If an invalid alpha character (one other than 'A' through 'I') is encountered, it will be converted as follows:

from J to 'blank' (X'E1', unprintable)
from K to S   or   from S to K
from L to T   or   from T to L
from M to U   or   from U to M
from N to V   or   from V to N
from O to W   or   from W to O
from P to X   or   from X to P
from Q to Y   or   from Y to Q
from R to Z   or   from Z to R

The mask that is to be used for the conversion is stored in a six-byte storage area labeled KEYBITS, and contains a configuration of X'303030303030':

KEYBITS	0011	0000	0011	0000	0011	0000	0011	0000	0011	0000	0011	0000

The data to be converted by this example consists of two six-byte fields labeled TRANSA and TRANSB . . . .

TRANSA	A	H	I	J	2	5

TRANSB	1	3	8	J	K	L

The instruction statements have been coded as:

    XC   TRANSA , KEYBITS
    XC   TRANSB , KEYBITS

The 'XC' instruction statements translate/convert the source field data in the following manner:

TRANSA character (before)	A		H		I		J		2		5	
hex	C	1	C	8	C	9	D	1	F	2	F	5
binary	1100	0001	1100	1000	1100	1001	1101	0001	1111	0010	1111	0101
KEYBITS mask	0011	0000	0011	0000	0011	0000	0011	0000	0011	0000	0011	0000

Boolean Logic Applications

TRANSA binary (after)	1111 0001	1111 1000	1111 1001	1110 0001	1100 0010	1100 0101
hex	F 1	F 8	F 9	E 1	C 2	C 5
character	1	8	9	'blank'	B	E

TRANSB character (before)	1	3	8	J	K	L
hex	F 1	F 3	F 8	D 1	D 2	D 3
binary	1111 0001	1111 0011	1111 1000	1101 0001	1101 0010	1101 0011

KEYBITS mask	0011 0000	0011 0000	0011 0000	0011 0000	0011 0000	0011 0000

TRANSB binary (after)	1100 0001	1100 0011	1100 1000	1110 0001	1110 0010	1110 0011
hex	C 1	C 3	C 8	E 1	E 2	E 3
character	A	C	H	'blank'	S	T

If the two data fields, TRANSA and TRANSB, are now concatenated, their combined data content would appear to be:

1	8	9	∅	B	E	A	C	H	∅	S	T

Many corporations and organizations have data files that are classified as confidential. Various schemes are devised, ranging from very complex to extremely simple, to "scramble" and code the data contained within these files. If unauthorized personnel inadvertently gain access to these files, the information would be useless masses of data bytes unless the proper "key" is supplied with which to unscramble them. The example just presented could be for this type of application—not only is the third and fourth bit of each byte reversed, but also the logical data fields are segmented and placed into separate storage locations.

Exclusive Or (XR)

The register-to-register version of the Exclusive Or instruction uses **XR** as the instruction statement op code. All 32 bits of a general register mask are Or'ed with all 32 bits of a general register source field. The source field data bits are altered whenever the corresponding bit position within the mask contains a one-bit. Both operands of the instruction statement must refer specifically or symbolically to a general register.

In the following illustration of this particular instruction, general register 8 contains a hexadecimal configuration of X'007A91BF', representing the source field; general register 12 contains X'96969696', representing the mask.

The instruction statement to be executed is:

```
XR    8,12
```

register 8 *hex* (before)	0	0	7	A	9	1	B	F
binary	0000	0000	0111	1010	1001	0001	1011	1111

register 12 mask	1001	0110	1001	0110	1001	0110	1001	0110

register 8 *binary* (after)	1001	0110	1110	1100	0000	0111	0010	1001
hex	9	6	E	C	0	7	2	9

BOOLEAN LOGIC INSTRUCTIONS IN DATA SEARCHES

As industry, government, and various other organizations attempt to computerize mass information and store it for selective search criteria, the problem of which media to use to store this data becomes increasingly critical. Even within industry the storage space required to record the background and employment information on one employee may consume thousands of bytes. It has long been an accepted practice to store data in EBCDIC character form, each section of information being assigned to a particular field that is identified as to the type of information it contains. Some fields could contain a single character that would represent the explicit information. For example, a one-byte field used to determine "Marital Status" could contain an 'M' for married or an 'S' for single. Even this abbreviated form of coded data requires considerable data storage space.

The ability to manipulate data bits via Boolean instructions presents a challenge to both the system analyst and the programmer. Information that previously required a single byte, or even more, of storage area on a magnetic tape or disk drive can now be reflected within a single bit position. As many as 16 separate conditions, or answers, may be contained within a single eight-bit data byte.

To illustrate this capability, an information query-byte is utilized in the following examples. Within the data record for each individual employed by Company 'K', there is a single byte of data that contains the following information:

bit position	information	one-bit implies	zero-bit implies
1	Sex	Male	Female
2	Marital status	Married	Single
3	Age group	25 or over	Under 25
4	High school	Graduated	Did not graduate
5	College (4 Year)	Degree	Nondegreed
6	Driver's license	Yes	No
7	Home owner	Yes	No
8	Citizenship	Native-born	Naturalized

If a search were to be made of this file for certain personnel who match multiple selective criteria, it could be accomplished in an absolute minimum of time as compared to a character search of multiple fields on each personnel record. Not only is the minimum length field (one byte) being used, but the real advantage is that multiple conditions may be audited within that single byte via one instruction statement. The type of information provided by the simple query byte

Boolean Logic Applications

illustrated here is very general; this could be refined and expanded to meet the need and scope of almost any type of data inquiry system.

Each example presented in this section is looking for a matching set of data conditions. Each match would either be noted and extracted along with other pertinent data or it would be used to accumulate a tally-count for an analytical survey. Because the Boolean instructions destructively analyze the query byte, that byte is first moved to a work-area byte before the Boolean instruction statement is applied against it.

Example 1. The management of company 'K' requires a list of all male personnel who are 25 years of age or over and have graduated from high school but who do not have college degrees. The company plans to use this listing to advise such personnel of a new college tuitional aid program being made available. The bit conditions to be searched for are as follows:

Bit 1	1-bit equals . . . Male
Bit 3	1-bit equals . . . 25 years of age or over
Bit 4	1-bit equals . . . High school graduate
Bit 5	0-bit equals . . . No college degree

The instruction statements for this example have been coded as:

MVC	HOLDBYTE(1) , DATA+3	001
NI	HOLDBYTE , X ' B8 '	002
XI	HOLDBYTE , X ' B0'	003
BC	8 , HIT	004
BC	15 , MISS	005

To illustrate the effect of these statements, assume that the byte currently being checked contains the following bit configuration:

one byte

HOLDBYTE | 1 | 1 | 1 | 1 | 1 | 1 | 0 | 1 |

Bit position 1 2 3 4 5 6 7 8

These bit conditions indicate the following about the individual:

Bit 1	1-bit equals . . . Male
Bit 2	1-bit equals . . . Married
Bit 3	1-bit equals . . . 25 years old or over
Bit 4	1-bit equals . . . High school graduate
Bit 5	1-bit equals . . . College Degree
Bit 6	1-bit equals . . . Has a driver's license
Bit 7	0-bit equals . . . Does not own his home
Bit 8	1-bit equals . . . Is a native-born citizen

Statement 001 moves the query-byte from the data record into the one-byte work area labeled HOLDBYTE.

Statement 002 executes an And Immediate instruction. The mask contains a one-bit in the bit positions corresponding to the bit positions of the query-byte to be audited.

	one byte							
HOLDBYTE (before)	1	1	1	1	1	1	0	1
X'B8' (mask)	1	0	1	1	1	0	0	0
HOLDBYTE (after)	1	0	1	1	1	0	0	0
(bit position number)	1	2	3	4	5	6	7	8

This instruction statement forces zero-bits into all of the bit positions in which the inquiry is not interested. The X'B8' mask has stated, "Maintain the status of the bits of the source field for which there is a corresponding one-bit in the mask."

Statement 003 executes an Exclusive Or Immediate instruction, using a mask of X'B0'.

	one byte							
HOLDBYTE (before)	1	0	1	1	1	0	0	0
X'B0' (mask)	1	0	1	1	0	0	0	0
HOLDBYTE (after)	0	0	0	0	1	0	0	0
(bit position number)	1	2	3	4	5	6	7	8

The mask of X'B0' causes the result to be zero if the proper bit-settings are present in HOLDBYTE prior to the 'XI' instruction statement. The analysis of this would be based on the following assumptions:

bit position	should be	indicating	mask	desired result after 'XI'
1	1-bit	Male	1-bit	0-bit
3	1-bit	25 or over	1-bit	0-bit
4	1-bit	High school graduate	1-bit	0-bit
5	0-bit	No college degree	0-bit	0-bit

In this example, however, the result is not zero—the individual whose record is being checked had received a college degree. Therefore, when bit position 5 of HOLDBYTE is Exclusive Or'ed with the corresponding zero-bit of the mask, the result is a one-bit.

Statement 004 tests the PSW Condition Code that results from the Exclusive Or Immediate. If the result contained within HOLDBYTE is zero, the branch would be taken at this statement.

Statement 005 is a forced branch to a subroutine labeled MISS, implying that the personnel record for this particular employee did not meet the search criteria.

Boolean Logic Applications

Example 2. In this file search, the management of company 'K' has asked to be provided with a count of all unmarried native-born employees under 25 years of age who are not high school graduates. These combined characteristics would require a search for the following bit conditions:

Bit 2	0-bit equals	... Unmarried
Bit 3	0-bit equals	... Under 25 years old
Bit 4	0-bit equals	... Not a high school graduate
Bit 8	1-bit equals	... A native-born citizen

The instruction statements have been coded as:

```
        MVC     HOLDBYTE (1) , DATA+3           001
        NI      HOLDBYTE , X ' 71 '             002
        XI      HOLDBYTE , X ' 01 '             003
        BC      4 , EXIT                        004
        AP      COUNT , =PL1 ' 1 '              005
EXIT    BC      15 , NEXTCHEK                   006
```

For this example, the byte moved into HOLDBYTE is:

one byte

HOLDBYTE	1	0	0	0	0	1	0	1
(bit position)	1	2	3	4	5	6	7	8

Statement 001 moves the query byte out of the fourth byte position of DATA and into the HOLDBYTE work area.

Statement 002 is the And Immediate instruction statement. The configuration of the mask places zero-bits into bit positions 1, 5, 6, and 7 of the source field but does not alter the bits that reside in positions 2, 3, 4, and 8.

HOLDBYTE (before)	1	0	0	0	0	1	0	1
X'71' (mask)	0	1	1	1	0	0	0	1
HOLDBYTE (after)	0	0	0	0	0	0	0	1
(bit position)	1	2	3	4	5	6	7	8

Statement 003 is the Exclusive Or Immediate instruction statement. The mask of X'01' creates the following action:

one byte

HOLDBYTE (before)	0	0	0	0	0	0	0	1

X'01' (mask)	0	0	0	0	0	0	0	1
HOLDBYTE (after)	0	0	0	0	0	0	0	0
(bit position)	1	2	3	4	5	6	7	8

The program logic searches for a zero-bit in bit positions 2, 3, and 4. In order to confirm this condition, a zero-bit is placed in the mask in these positions. If any one of those positions contains a one-bit in the source field, the one-bit would have carried through to the result. Because the logic checks for a one-bit in the eighth position bit of HOLDBYTE, a one-bit is also used in the mask at this position. If the one-bit exists in the source byte the execution of the Exclusive Or would place a zero-bit there in the result. Upon completion of the 'XI' instruction statement, HOLDBYTE contains all zero-bits, indicating that the necessary conditions were found for including this record in the count analysis.

Statement 004 is a conditional branch instruction statement. It specifies, "If the result field does not contain a zero value, branch to the instruction labeled EXIT." The result field is zero in this example and the branch from this statement is not taken.

Statement 005 assumes that because the program logic is passing through to it and does not branch out of Statement 004, then the value in HOLDBYTE must be zero. This is a valid assumption. The Add Packed instruction statement is, therefore, adding a packed decimal literal of +1 to the counter to indicate that a selected record has been found.

Statement 006 is a forced branch to a point within the program labeled NEXTCHEX. That routine would probably bring in another data record and pass through Statements 001 to 006 again. The program logic has arrived at Statement 006 by one of two ways—either the branch was taken from Statement 004 directly to Statement 006 in which case the value of +1 would not have been added to COUNT; or the processing logic fell through Statements 004 and 005 in sequence.

The examples for this application could go on and on, almost endlessly. Two bytes, three bytes, four bytes, or many bytes could be utilized to contain information in the bit-indicator form. Consider the effective savings of stored data space when four bytes (32 bit positions) can supply as much information as 32 bytes—a savings of 28 bytes per individual record. Compound this savings by 15,000 employees (28 times 15,000) and the overall result is a savings of 420,000 bytes of data storage—on only one file. Even though some hardware and methods of storing data are relatively inexpensive, computer time is not. Actual processing time saved by the examples shown is approximately a "1 to n" ratio, wherein "n" represents the number of compare statements necessary to accomplish the same task via EBCDIC character data comparisons.

REVIEW EXERCISES

1. The Boolean Logic instructions are generally considered to be useful in manipulating individual _____ or groups of _____.
2. The _____ instructions are useful in setting or forcing bit-switches to an "off" condition.

Boolean Logic Applications 429

3. The Or series of Boolean instructions perform an "_____" function wherein "one plus zero or one plus one equals one."
4. The performance of the Exclusive Or instructions generates results in which similar bits in corresponding bit positions in the mask and the source field combine to create a _____-bit; unlike bits in corresponding bit positions in the mask and the source field combine to create a _____-bit.
5. Up to 2048 bit positions can be altered by the _____ mnemonic op code version of the Exclusive Or instructions.
6. In all Boolean Logic instruction statements, the content of the second operand is considered to be a "_____," whether it is represented by an immediate character, register, or a storage field.
7. When executing any one of the Or instructions, a one-bit in the resulting source field may be guaranteed by coding a _____-bit in the corresponding bit position of the mask as represented by the second operand.
8. A mnemonic op code of X, as contained in a valid instruction statement, causes action against all of the _____ bit positions represented by the first operand.
9. When executing an And instruction statement, a one-bit in the mask and a corresponding one-bit in the source field results in a _____-bit in the source field; a zero-bit in the mask and a corresponding one-bit in the source field results in a _____-bit.
10. The O version of the Boolean Logic Or instructions requires that the first operand of the statement in which it is used be specified as a _____ and that the second operand represent a valid-aligned _____ storage location.
11. A coded instruction statement containing the mnemonic op code of XI indicates that the first operand addresses a single byte of storage and that the second operand is represented by an _____ character.
12. The And instructions function on the data bits as a logical "_____" or _____ instruction.
13. The NC version of the Boolean Logic series of _____ instructions utilizes defined storage areas as both operands of the statement, and may affect from one to _____ bytes of source field data.
14. The NR instruction statement is considered to be a _____-to-register operation.
15. The mnemonic op code of OR indicates that the first operand of the instruction statement should be a _____, and the second operand of the instruction statement should be a _____.
16. The Boolean Logic Or instructions are useful in bit-switch applications inasmuch as they may be used to guarantee that any single bit position, or bit-switch, is set to an/a "_____" condition.
17. When utilizing an Or instruction to perform an operation, a _____-bit in the mask (the second operand) is used to guarantee that the corresponding bit position of the source field is not altered.

18. Upon execution of an Exclusive Or instruction statement, any _____ -bit in the second operand mask results in the reversal of the content of the corresponding bit position of the source field; a one-bit is changed to a zero-bit, a zero-bit is changed to a one-bit.

In each of the following problems is one or more source fields and a masking value defined. Apply the mask against the source field(s) using the Boolean instruction indicated, and supply both the hexadecimal configuration and bit configuration of the source field(s) as they would be after execution of the statement(s).

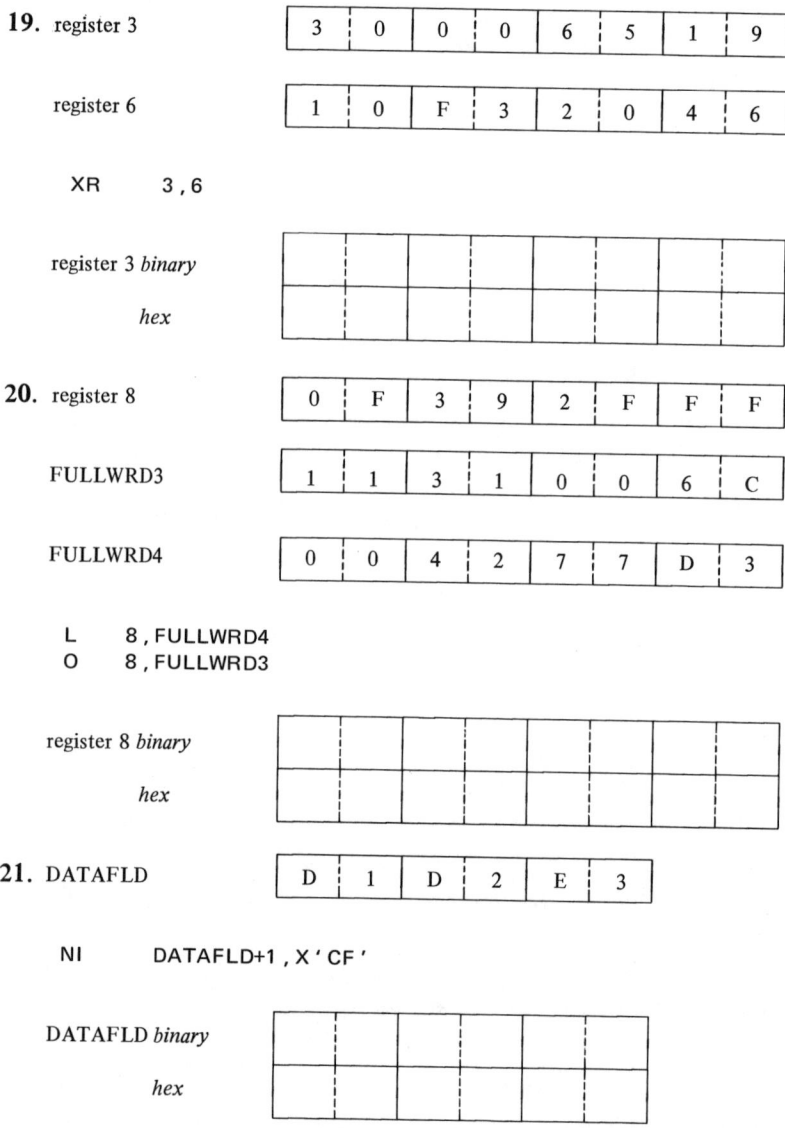

Boolean Logic Applications

22. DATATEST: | D | C | E | 7 | E | 0 | 3 | C | E | 9 |

MASK22: | 4 | 0 | 2 | 4 | 1 | 8 | 1 | 4 | 2 | 4 |

```
XC    DATATEST(3), MASK22+2
```

DATATEST result:

binary	1100	0100	1111	0011	1100	0100	0011	1100	1110	1001
hex	C	4	F	3	C	4	3	C	E	9

23. register 12: | 0 | 0 | C | 3 | 5 | 6 | 9 | 8 |

WORDTWO: | 0 | 0 | 0 | 4 | 0 | 4 | 0 | 4 |

```
O    12, WORDTWO
```

register 12 result:

binary	0000	0000	1100	0111	0101	0110	1001	1100
hex	0	0	C	7	5	6	9	C

24. DATASET: | C | 7 | C | 8 | D | 7 | D | 9 | C | 1 |

MASK1: | 0 | 2 | 0 | 2 | 0 | 2 |

```
NC    DATASET+2(3), MASK1
```

DATASET result:

binary	1100	0111	1100	1000	0000	0010	0000	0000	0000	0000
hex	C	7	C	8	0	2	0	0	0	0

25. CHKFLD: | 2 | D | 8 | C | C | 1 | E | 6 | F | 3 |

```
         LA    6, 3
         LA    7, CHKFLD+1
DATALOOP XI    0(7), X'33'
         AH    7, =H'1'
         BCT   6, DATALOOP
```

CHKFLD result:

binary	0010	1101	1011	1111	1111	0010	1101	0101	1111	0011
hex	2	D	B	F	F	2	D	5	F	3

Assembler Language for Application Programming

26. FLDSET | C | 3 | 6 | B | 4 | B | 9 | C |

    OI   FLDSET , X ' 21 '
    OI   FLDSET+2 , X ' 12 '

FLDSET *binary*
        hex

27. register 4 | F | F | 3 | 9 | 2 | 6 | 7 | 8 |

    FWORD | 0 | 0 | F | F | F | F | F | F |

    N   4 , FWORD

register 4 *binary*
        hex

28. SWITCHES | 0 | 0 | 0 | 0 | 1 | 1 | 0 | 1 |

    OI   SWITCHES+1 , X ' 2A '
    OI   SWITCHES+2 , X ' 5E '

SWITCHES *binary*
        hex

29. register 8 | 0 | 0 | 0 | C | 3 | B | 6 | 4 |

    register 7 | F | 2 | F | 2 | F | 2 | F | 2 |

    NR   8 , 7

register 8 *binary*
        hex

Boolean Logic Applications

30. DATASW

0	4	4	0	8	2	A	3	C	6

OC   DATASW (2) , DATASW+2

DATASW *binary*

hex

31. WORDBASE

F	3	F	5	D	4	D	1	D	7

SETCHNGE

F	F	C	D	C	3

NC   WORDBASE+2 (2) , SETCHNGE+1

WORDBASE *binary*

hex

32. register 6

8	2	8	7	8	5	8	8

register 10

4	0	4	0	4	0	4	0

OR   6 , 10

register 6 *binary*

hex

33. register 5

F	F	F	F	F	F	F	3

FULLWD3

F	F	F	F	F	F	F	F

X   5 , FULLWD3

register 5 *binary*

hex

13

Using Switches and Indicators for Program Logic Control

THE TEST UNDER MASK INSTRUCTION

Instruction: Test Under Mask

mnemonic	*hex code*	*operand format*
TM	91	$D_1(B_1), I_2$

This instruction takes the single byte of immediate data, defined by the second operand, and uses it to test the bit configuration of the single byte of data addressed by the first operand. The execution of this instruction does not change the bit configuration of the data being tested. The second operand, which is considered to be the mask, is constructed by the programmer as follows:

- For each bit to be tested in the data, the corresponding bit within the mask should be a one-bit.

- For each bit to be ignored within the data-byte, the corresponding bit within the mask should be a zero-bit.

The instruction then tests only the bits in the data field that have corresponding one-bits in the mask. When the actual test is performed the instruction creates a work-byte in the image of the data-byte that has been addressed. Each mask-bit that is a one-bit tests for a one-bit in the corresponding position of the data/work-byte; if a corresponding one-bit is found, a similar one-bit is placed, or remains, in the work-byte. If a corresponding one-bit is not found, a zero-bit is placed into the work-byte. At the end of the test operation, the instruction reviews the contents of the result and sets a Condition Code based on the contents. This instruction allows you to test the "on/off" condition of any single bit-switch, or the bit configuration of an entire byte of data, without altering that bit configuration.

CC	BC	Condition
0	8	The result-bits are all zero bits.
1	4	The result-bits are both zero-bits and one-bits.
3	1	The result-bits are all one-bits.

THE CONCEPTS OF SWITCHES AND INDICATORS

In the computer equipment existing prior to the Third Generation systems, any reference to a switch or indicator might well have been understood to pertain to a physical device or signal unit.

Certain problem program functions could relate to the requirement of altering a physical switch on the computer console panel in order for the program to perform its functions. Physical and electronic switches do exist in Third Generation systems, but these are more often related to the performance of peripheral equipment, such as a two-channel switch on a direct access device or tape drive control unit. This type of a switch is normally not under problem program control or even directly related to the performance of the problem program insofar as knowledge of its status is concerned.

The switches and indicators to be discussed herein may be thought of as existing in the form of stored data or characters. The condition of these switches may be considered to signal many variations of status, such as "yes" or "no," "on" or "off, " "branch" or "fall through," and as many other decisions as there are questions requiring such an answer.

Unfortunately, there is often a lot of controversy about the practice of using switches within the program logic. Improper manipulation of logic switches can create havoc with any problem program, and is too often of such magnitude that it is extremely difficult to pinpoint the errant or omitted instruction. The omission of a single instruction statement to turn a switch to "on" or "off" at the proper logic point can result in a complete reversal of the intended logic pattern. On the other hand, by following a set of proper programming conventions and by adequate flowcharting, a single switch is often all that is needed to replace an entire subroutine of logic or data interpretation.

Setting a switch to an "on" condition, or turning it "off," does not in itself create any resulting action by the problem program. The condition of the switch is merely established for subsequent testing of that condition and a logic decision based on the result of that test. The application of setting and testing a switch or indicator will be thoroughly discussed and illustrated within this section.

As a rule, there are two types of switches and indicators—the character-switch and the bit-switch. Each have their own peculiar characteristics and functions, although the applications for which they are used can often be interchangeable. For the purpose of this text, each type is reviewed in relationship to the environment in which they are most frequently used. The similarity of use will point out their interchangeability without discussing that factor in detail.

Character-Switches and Indicators

A character-switch or indicator is construed to consist of one byte of data; therefore, it may also be referred to as a byte-switch. Inasmuch as one byte of data may be any one of 256 unique bit configurations, it is conceivable that a byte-switch, or character-switch, could be considered to represent 256 unique conditions. For all practical purposes, however, the usual application is that a byte-switch has only two conditions. This is not meant to imply that it is not good logic to have a switch represent multiple conditions, but the main reason usually justifying the existence of a switch will normally be found to be an "on" or "off" condition.

Because character-switches inherently consist of one byte of data, it is logical to use an instruction that processes only one byte in order to set or test the switch. These are referred to as the "immediate" type of instructions. For the purpose of setting a byte-switch to a desired condition, the Move Immediate (MVI) instruction is ideally suited; for the purpose of testing a byte-switch, the Compare Logical Immediate (CLI) instruction holds precedent. Both of these instructions, the MVI and the CLI, are far more expedient than a regular "move" or "compare" instruction. In each instance, the second operand is a self-defining character value. The overall performance of these instructions is considerably faster than if the second operand generated an address which, in turn, contained a character.

A common means of using a switch is to first establish a constant labeled by a unique name. Because the original value of the switch, before it is ever used, should be a null value, it is good practice to create the switch as a one-byte constant containing a valid blank. This might be expressed as:

```
SWITCH1    DC     CL1'b'
```

or

```
SWITCH1    DC     XL1'40'
```

The symbol 'b' as used here, and in other places within this text, is considered to represent a legitimate blank, configured as hexadecimal '40'.

Assuming that this particular switch is to represent an "on" or "off" condition, it has been arbitrarily decided that an "X" indicates that the switch is on, and a blank that it is off. In order to alter the setting of the switch at will, two instruction statements are applied:

```
MVI    SWITCH1,C'X'
```

or

```
MVI    SWITCH1,C'b'
```

The first instruction statement moves a character "X" into the one-byte field labeled SWITCH1. This is considered to turn the switch on. The second instruction statement moves a valid blank (hex '40') into SWITCH1, turning the switch off.

The routine shown in Figure 13-1 demonstrates the application of a byte-switch. This routine, although not a practical application in itself, illustrates setting the switch on, testing the condition of the switch, and turning the switch off. The assumed logic here appears to be that the switch is first set to an "on" condition, followed by an unspecified number of instruction statements and then the switch is tested to see if it is still on. If it is on, a branch is taken to a subroutine to check the accumulated value of a particular packed decimal field. If that packed decimal value is equal to +2999, the logic falls through to OFFIT. At this point, the switch is turned off, the logic branches back to REPEAT, processes, checks the switch at ONOFF and finds that it is off (not equal to "X"), so the logic falls through to the branch to END. In this particular example, the switch concept could have been eliminated and the Compare Packed instruction statement labeled CHECKIT could have replaced the ONOFF instruction statement, eliminating the need for the entire CHECKIT subroutine. This example would then appear as:

```
REPEAT     AP     FIELD,=PL1'1'
           --     ------
           --     ------
           --     ------
           CP     FIELD,=PL3'3000'
           BC     7,REPEAT
           BC     15,END
```

As previously mentioned, a byte-switch may represent more than two conditions. Consider an instance in which the problem program has three types of record input—a type-1 record, a type-2 record, and a type-3 record. As the problem program brings each new record into storage, a switch is set by inserting either a 1, 2, or 3 into it. Further on in the program logic it is necessary to

SYSTEM / 370 ASSEMBLER CODING FORM

Name	Operation	Operand	Identification-Sequence No.
TURNON	MVI	SWITCH1,C'X'	0040
REPEAT	AP	FIELD,=PL1'1'	0041
ONOFF	CLI	SWITCH1,C'X'	0063
EQUALB	BC	8,CHECKIT	0064
	BC	15,END	0065
*			
CHECKIT	CP	FIELD,=PL3'2999'	0066
	BC	7,REPEAT	0067
OFFIT	MVI	SWITCH1,C' '	0068
	BC	15,REPEAT	0069
*			

FIGURE 13-1

Using Switches and Indicators for Program Logic Control   439

check again for the type of record being processed, and to branch to one of three subroutines based on the value contained within the switch. One compare instruction statement would test the switch, as shown following:

```
            CLI     SWITCH , C ' 2 '
            BC      4 , RECORD1      (Switch low)
            BC      2 , RECORD3      (Switch high)
  RECORD2   MVC     FLDB , FLDA      (Switch equal to ' 2 ')
```

The first instruction statement compares the one-byte character content of SWITCH to a character '2'. The next instruction causes a branch to RECORD1 subroutine if SWITCH compares low to the '2'. The next instruction causes a branch to the RECORD3 subroutine if SWITCH compares high to '2'. If a branch is not taken via the second or third statements, then the comparison must have been equal (SWITCH contains '2'), so the processing falls through to the RECORD2 routine.

Another application for switches is in a multipurpose program that gives the user a choice of output options. For this example, assume that the problem program creates output to any or all of three output devices—a magnetic tape drive, a card punch unit, and/or an output printer unit. At the time that the problem program is read into the computer, the user must supply a control card indicating which output types he desires. The control card should have an "X" in card column 5 for the magnetic tape output option, an "X" in card column 6 for the punched card output option, and/or an "X" in card column 7 for the printed output option. One of the very first routines in the program is to read the control card and set the output switches that are indicated by the user. This routine could appear as shown in Figure 13-2.

Statement 001 is a standard QSAM macroinstruction that reads the control card into a data area labeled CARD.

Statement 002 checks card position 5 of the input (CARD+4) for an "X". If it does not contain an "X", then Statement 003 causes a branch around the next statement, Statement 004.

Statement 004 sets a switch to indicate that magnetic tape output is desired.

Statement 005 checks card position 6 of the input (CARD+5) for an "X". If it does not contain an "X", Statement 006 causes a branch around Statement 007.

Statement 007 sets a switch to indicate that punched card output is desired.

Statement 008 checks card position 7 of the input (CARD+6) for an "X". If it does not contain an "X", then Statement 009 causes a branch around Statement 010.

Statement 010 sets a switch to indicate that printed output is desired.

Now that the switches are set, the program logic continues on until it is time to create the output. The instruction statements for testing the switches and branching to the output routines as required could appear as illustrated in Figure 13-3.

Statements 001, 004, and 007 test the three switches so as to determine what form of output is to be created. If the switch is not set to the "on" condition, the subsequent instruction statement causes a branch to the next switch-test statement. The branch decision is expressed as:

```
       BC       7 , . . .
```

which states, "If the preceding compare instruction statement resulted in an unequal comparison, branch to . . . . " If the CLI instruction statement resulted in an equal comparison, indicating that the switch was on for that output method, the program logic would fall through the BC instruction statement to the BAL (Branch & Link) instruction statement. The BAL instruction

SYSTEM / 370 ASSEMBLER CODING FORM

Name	Operation	Operand	Identification Sequence No.
READCON	GET	CARDER, CARD	001
	CLI	CARD+4, C'X'	002
	BC	7, PASS1	003
	MVI	SWTAPE, C'T'	004
PASS1	CLI	CARD+5, C'X'	005
	BC	7, PASS2	006
	MVI	SWPUNCH, C'P'	007
PASS2	CLI	CARD+6, C'X'	008
	BC	7, PASS3	009
	MVI	SWPRINT, C'W'	010
PASS3			011
*			
CARD	DC	CL80' '	520
SWTAPE	DC	CL1' '	525
SWPUNCH	DC	CL1' '	530
SWPRINT	DC	CL1' '	535
*			540
			545

FIGURE 13-2

Using Switches and Indicators for Program Logic Control

SYSTEM / 370 ASSEMBLER CODING FORM

Name	Operation	Operand	Identification Sequence No.
*			001
WHATOUT	CLI	SWTAPE,C'T'	002
	BC	7,SKIP1	003
	BAL	10,MAGTAPE	004
SKIP1	CLI	SWPUNCH,C'P'	005
	BC	7,SKIP2	006
	BAL	10,PUNCHER	007
SKIP2	CLI	SWPRINT,C'W'	008
	BC	7,SKIP3	009
	BAL	10,PRINTER	010
SKIP3			011

FIGURE 13-3

would, in turn, force a branch back to the next sequential instruction statement after completing the subroutine it is branching to.

Another means of loading, or setting, switches of this type is to move the contents of the control card directly into the switches. Assume that as in the previous example, columns 5, 6, and 7 of the control card contain any mixture of X's or blanks in order to specify the output mode. Accordingly, the three switches are established in storage in a contiguous manner such as:

```
SWTAPE      DC      CL1'b'
SWPUNCH     DC      CL1'b'
SWPRINT     DC      CL1'b'
```

The instruction statements required to set the switches to "on," or to leave them "off," according to the contents of the control card, would be:

```
READCON     GET     CARDER, CARD
            MVC     SWTAPE (3), CARD+4
```

The second statement would move the contents of card columns 5, 6, and 7 (either an "X" or a blank in each) into SWTAPE, SWPUNCH and SWPRINT. Notice that this has been accomplished in two instruction statements as compared to the ten statements required to set the switches in the previous example. The only other difference would be that when the routine to test the switches is entered, each test would be for an "X" rather than for a unique character for each switch.

As you become more proficient in these techniques you will discover many additional ways to use byte-switches. Perhaps the greatest failing by programmers attempting to use "switch" techniques is the lack of care in clearing, or turning off, switches at the proper time and logic point.

Bit-Switches and Indicators

While character-switches utilize a full byte of data and may contain many condition signals, a bit-switch consists of only one binary bit position and can represent a maximum of two conditions. On the other hand, a single byte of data can contain eight individual bit-switches—one for each bit position.

These switches are of particular value when the program logic depends on a set of information as can be provided by a group of switches or indicators. For example, one byte of detail can contain a string of switches that would answer eight conditional tests, individually or collectively, such as:

(yes or no) and/or (yes or no) and/or (yes or no) and/or
(yes or no) and/or (yes or no) and/or (yes or no) and/or
(yes or no) and/or (yes or no)

A sample test of the yes/no or the on/off condition of the eight bit-switches might possibly follow the logic of:

"If bit-1 is yes and bit-2 is yes/or bit-3 is no, then . . . ."

Establishing the single byte of data that is to contain from one to eight switches is accomplished in a similar manner as for a byte-switch. The exception, however, is that the defined value of the field being established for bit-switches should contain a fixed-point value of zero instead of a

Using Switches and Indicators for Program Logic Control 443

blank. A one-byte fixed-point value of zero will create eight zero-bits (00000000); a blank (Hex '40') will create a bit configuration of '01000000'. The constant used to create the bit-switch field would appear as:

```
SWITCHES    DC      X'00'
```

For manipulating the configuration of the bit-switches, it is expedient to use the Boolean logic instruction statements. For turning bit-switches "on" in a single byte of data, the Or Immediate Logical (OI) instruction may be used. For turning bit-switches "off" in a single byte of data, the And Immediate Logical (NI) instruction is used. By using these two instructions, you have the capability of setting any one bit position, or combination of positions, to an "on" or an "off" condition. The condition of one or more bit-switches may be tested by using the Test Under Mask (TM) instruction. This instruction tests selected bit positions without altering the configuration of those positions. The means of using these three instructions will be pointed out and illustrated in the paragraphs that follow.

As stated, the Or Immediate Logical instruction is used to set bit-switches to an "on" condition; that is, to insert a one-bit in the particular bit position representing that switch. Using a one-byte storage area labeled CHEX, it could be interpreted that the eight bit positions of that area would each constitute a bit-switch. Graphically this would appear as:

	SW-1	SW-2	SW-3	SW-4	SW-5	SW-6	SW-7	SW-8
CHEX	0	0	0	0	0	0	0	0

one byte

Each bit position would represent an individual switch, capable of indicating a yes/no condition – '0' for no, '1' for yes. By using the Or Immediate Logical instruction, any one or multiple bit positions can be set to a "yes" condition. A few examples of this application follow.

Example 1. Set switch 5 (SW-5) to a yes (or on) condition.

The first task to be accomplished is to establish the mask for the OI instruction. This can be done by visualizing the switch positions.

switch number	*Is it to be turned on?* *0 = No, or do not change* *1 = yes*
SW-1	0 ... No
SW-2	0 ... No
SW-3	0 ... No
SW-4	0 ... No
SW-5	1 ... Yes
SW-6	0 ... No
SW-7	0 ... No
SW-8	0 ... No

The mask for this example can, therefore, be construed to be configured as bits of 0-0-0-0-1-0-0-0. This configuration represents a hexadecimal value of X'08', so the mask to be used with the OI instruction should be coded as X'08'. The instruction statement would be:

```
OI      CHEX,X'08'
```

The execution of this instruction statement would act on CHEX in the following manner:

	SW-1	SW-2	SW-3	SW-4	SW-5	SW-6	SW-7	SW-8
CHEX (before)	0	0	0	0	0	0	0	0
X'08' (mask)	0	0	0	0	1	0	0	0
CHEX (after)	0	0	0	0	1	0	0	0

Switch 5 has now been successfully set to a "yes" or an on condition.

Example 2. The task is to "turn on" SW-2, SW-4, and SW-8. The mask for this example would be determined as follows:

switch number	Is it to be turned on? 0 = No, or do not change 1 = Yes	
SW-1	0	... No
SW-2	1	... Yes
SW-3	0	... No
SW-4	1	... Yes
SW-5	0	... No
SW-6	0	... No
SW-7	0	... No
SW-8	1	... Yes

This indicates that the mask should be coded as a set of bits consisting of 0-1-0-1-0-0-0-1, or hexadecimal '51'. The instruction statement itself would be written:

```
OI    CHEX , X ' 51 '
```

	SW-1	SW-2	SW-3	SW-4	SW-5	SW-6	SW-7	SW-8
CHEX (before)	0	0	0	0	0	0	0	0
X'51' (mask)	0	1	0	1	0	0	0	1
CHEX (after)	0	1	0	1	0	0	0	1

Example 3. The problem in this instance is to assure the program that SW-1, SW-2, SW-6, SW-7, and SW-8 are set to a "yes" condition. If they are off, turn them on; if they are already on, leave them in that condition. In presenting this example, it shall be assumed that SW-1 and SW-8 are already in an "on" condition. When setting up the mask, however, this fact is not known so the

Using Switches and Indicators for Program Logic Control 445

provision for activating all of these switches must be taken. The mask comprises a bit configuration of 1-1-0-0-0-1-1-1 or X'C7' and the instruction statement is:

    OI   CHEX , X ' C7 '

	SW-1	SW-2	SW-3	SW-4	SW-5	SW-6	SW-7	SW-8
CHEX (before)	1	0	1	0	0	0	0	1
X'C7' (mask)	1	1	0	0	0	1	1	1
CHEX (after)	1	1	1	0	0	1	1	1

Two reactions occur in this example which had not been illustrated in the previous examples. First, whenever a one-bit in the mask encounters a one-bit in the switch position the resulting condition is a one-bit. This follows the request to assure that it would be set to an "on" condition even if the switch already indicates that condition. Second, when a zero-bit in the mask encounters a one-bit in the switch position, the one-bit is not altered. This follows the request that "if the switch is already on, leave it that way." This action is shown by the condition of SW-3—it was on before the instruction statement was executed and it is left on after a zero-bit in the mask is matched to it.

Conversely, the And Immediate Logical (NI) is used to "turn off" switches, or to set them to a "no" condition. The basis for establishing the mask to be used with the NI instruction is also the opposite of the OI instruction usage. If a bit-switch is to be turned off, then a zero-bit must be placed in the corresponding position in the mask; if a switch is to be left unaltered, whether it is on or off, then a one-bit is placed in the corresponding position in the mask. The examples that follow demonstrate this activity.

Example 1. The task for the instruction is to turn off SW-3. The mask for this example would be created from the following logic:

switch number	Is it to be turned off? 0 = Yes 1 = No, or do not change		
SW-1	1	...	No
SW-2	1	...	No
SW-3	0	...	Yes
SW-4	1	...	No
SW-5	1	...	No
SW-6	1	...	No
SW-7	1	...	No
SW-8	1	...	No

This would determine that the mask should be configured as 1-1-0-1-1-1-1-1 or hex 'DF'. The instruction statement would be coded as:

    NI   CHEX , X ' DF '

If SW-3 were the only switch currently on, the resulting action from this instruction statement would be:

	SW-1	SW-2	SW-3	SW-4	SW-5	SW-6	SW-7	SW-8
CHEX (before)	0	0	1	0	0	0	0	0
X'DF' (mask)	1	1	0	1	1	1	1	1
CHEX (after)	0	0	0	0	0	0	0	0

Example 2. Regardless of whether they are currently on or off, SW-2, SW-5 and SW-7 are to be set to an "off" condition. The mask for this example would, therefore, be a set of bits appearing as 1-0-1-1-0-1-0-1 or a hexadecimal value of 'B5'. The instruction statement is coded as:

    NI   CHEX , X ' B5 '

If, in this instance, SW-2 and SW-5 were on, the operation would be:

	SW-1	SW-2	SW-3	SW-4	SW-5	SW-6	SW-7	SW-8
CHEX (before)	0	1	0	0	1	0	0	0
X'B5'	1	0	1	1	0	1	0	1
CHEX (after)	0	0	0	0	0	0	0	0

SW-2 and SW-5 have been now set to an "off" condition as requested. Since SW-7 is already off, the corresponding zero-bit in the mask does not alter that condition.

Example 3. The task is to assure the program that SW-1, SW-3, SW-4 and SW-6 are off, or in a "no" condition. If they are off, they should remain that way; if they are on, turn them off. Do not alter the configuration of any of the other switches. For this request, the mask would be a set of bits consisting of 0-1-0-0-1-0-1-1 or X'4B'. The instruction statement would be:

    NI   CHEX , X ' 4B '

	SW-1	SW-2	SW-3	SW-4	SW-5	SW-6	SW-7	SW-8
CHEX (before)	1	1	0	1	0	1	0	1
X'4B' (mask)	0	1	0	0	1	0	1	1
CHEX (after)	0	1	0	0	0	0	0	1

As requested by the program requirements, this instruction statement successfully warrants that SW-1, SW-3, SW-4 and SW-6 are now in an "off" condition. SW-2 and SW-8, which were "on" before execution of this statement, remain as they were because the corresponding one-bit in the mask specifies that they were to stand unaltered.

Now that the means of setting bit-switches to an "on" or "off" condition has been presented, there remains the method of checking the condition of each switch—testing the value of any or all bit positions via the use of the Test Under Mask instruction. As in the instructions used to set the bit-switches on and off, a mask is used as a part of the TM instruction. Because that instruction performs on only one byte of data, the mask is established as a one-byte self-defining immediate character. Bit positions in the data-byte representing the bit-switches to be tested are correspondingly indicated by a one-bit in the mask. That is, for each bit-switch to be tested, the mask contains a one-bit for that indicated position; for bit-switches not to be tested, or to be ignored, the mask contains a zero-bit in the corresponding bit position. During the execution of the TM instruction statement a zero-bit in the mask does not cause a result indication. A one-bit in the mask causes the Condition Code bits to be set in accordance with the result of the match of the mask bit to its corresponding bit-switch. If a one-bit in the mask detects a one-bit in the bit-switch, a one-bit result is stored; if it detects a zero-bit in the bit-switch, a zero-bit result is stored. After all one-bits in the mask have tested all corresponding bit-switches, the Condition Code indicates any one of three possible conditions. These conditions may be construed to be as follows:

CC	BC	Condition
0	8	All result-bits were zero-bits.
1	4	Result-bits were both one-bits and zero-bits.
3	1	All result-bits were one-bits.

The first condition states that all bit-switches tested were off; the second condition states that some were off and some were on; the third states that all bit-switches were on.

The criteria for determining the hexadecimal value of the mask is similar to creating a mask for the OI instruction. If, for example, a TM instruction statement is to be executed for the purpose of testing SW-3, SW-5 and SW-8 the mask would be arrived at by:

switch number	mask 0 = do not test 1 = test this switch	
SW-1	0	... No
SW-2	0	... No
SW-3	1	... Yes
SW-4	0	... No
SW-5	1	... Yes
SW-6	0	... No
SW-7	0	... No
SW-8	1	... Yes

This represents a mask of 0-0-1-0-1-0-0-1 or hex '29'. If the instruction statement were to be subsequently issued as:

    TM   CHEX , X ' 29 '

then only SW-3, SW-5 and SW-8 would be tested. The result of the test of these three bit-switches, and only these three, would determine the status of the Condition Code bits.

Example 1. The data-byte to be tested contains eight bit-switches. The current value of these switches, in their respective "on/off" conditions, represents a hexadecimal value of '9D'. In this example, only switches SW-3 and SW-7 are to be tested, requiring a mask value of X'22'. The instruction statement could be coded as:

```
TM      BITSWIT , X ' 22 '
```

The resulting performance of this instruction statement would appear as:

	SW-1	SW-2	SW-3	SW-4	SW-5	SW-6	SW-7	SW-8
BITSWIT (before)	1	0	0	1	1	1	0	1
X'22' (mask)	0	0	1	0	0	0	1	0
(result bits)			0				0	

Note that although several switches are equal to an "on" condition, there are only result-bits for the particular switches tested by the one-bits within the mask. For this example, the Condition Code would have indicated that "all result bits were zero-bits."

Example 2. The byte of bit-switches to be tested has a value of hexadecimal 'FF'. The individual switches to be tested are SW-1, SW-2 and SW-4.

```
TM      BITSWITB , X ' D0 '
```

	SW-1	SW-2	SW-3	SW-4	SW-5	SW-6	SW-7	SW-8
BITSWITB (before)	1	1	1	1	1	1	1	1
X'D0' (mask)	1	1	0	1	0	0	0	0
(result bits)	1	1		1				

The resulting Condition Code for this example would indicate that "all result bits were one-bits." This would signal that all three switches tested were of a configuration that represented an "on" condition.

Example 3. The byte of data to be tested within this example has a hexadecimal value of '27'. The instruction statement is to test for an "on" condition of SW-2, SW-3, SW-5 and SW-8.

```
TM      BITSWITC , X ' 69 '
```

	SW-1	SW-2	SW-3	SW-4	SW-5	SW-6	SW-7	SW-8
BITSWITC (before)	0	0	1	0	0	1	1	1

Using Switches and Indicators for Program Logic Control 449

X '69' (mask) | 0 | 1 | 1 | 0 | 1 | 0 | 0 | 1 |

(result bits)   0   1   0   1

After execution of the instruction statement, the PSW Condition Code bits would be interpreted as stating, "the result bits are both one-bits and zero-bits."

GENERAL APPLICATIONS OF SWITCHES

The particular circumstances under which character-switches or bit-switches may be effectively applied are innumerable. They do, however, fall within major groupings, each of which might have many variations based on the logic of the individual problem program. A detailed listing of some of these major groupings of switch applications appears in the following paragraphs.

End-of-File-Routine Multiple Conditions

A program that utilizes parallel multireel magnetic tape input and output quite often presents a logic problem in the closing routines when those multiple reels represent different sets of data. This would be exemplified by a sizable merge or update routine wherein several separate tape data sets are being simultaneously merged into a master tape file. In this type of situation, it is usually not known which tape will reach an EOF (End-of-File) condition first; therefore, some type of indicator or switch is quite often used in order to allow the program to check if certain tapes have already been closed out.

For example, if TAPE1, TAPE2 and TAPE3 are to be sequentially merged with MASTER1, the program logic would require knowledge of whether MASTER1 reaches the end of its data first, or if any one or all of the updating tapes are the first to be exhausted. If TAPE2 reaches an EOF condition prior to any of the other three tapes, the program should continue merging TAPE1 and TAPE3 with MASTER1, ignoring or bypassing the existence of TAPE2. Any further attempts to read TAPE2 would now result in a program interrupt by the system, so the possible application of a switch would be evident. Upon the completion of TAPE2, an EOF routine could be entered, within which the program logic could set a switch to indicate that TAPE2 had been depleted. Any further attempts to read TAPE2 could be deterred by a test of that switch immediately prior to the "read" routine.

This same logic is applicable to "closing" routines. Peculiar program logic could present the condition that one or more of these tape data sets might possibly be closed during the execution of the main-line logic. When the entire program has been completed, it would be necessary to know if this condition had occurred, and which particular tape data sets had been affected. If a tape data set was closed during the execution of the main-line logic, it would have been a simple application for the programmer to set a switch indicating this fact. Then, at the completion of the program and within the final closing routines, the logic could test an individual switch for each tape data set used by the program—if the switch was "on," the logic would know that this data set had already been closed and it would bypass further action; if the switch was "off," the logic would know that the tape data set was still "open" and could issue the necessary macroinstructions required to close it. Although this application has been used in reference to tape data sets, it applies equally well to any type of data set, whether it resides on a disk, drum, or any other type of storage device.

Has a Routine Been Completed?

Any given routine, or subroutine, may consist of stages of execution using a common logic module. The performance of this module might well vary in accordance with the completion, or partial completion, of the controlling routine. By setting a variable switch at unique points within the control routine and then testing that switch for various conditions within the common module, many alternatives can be applied to the execution of the common module.

What Subroutine or Routine Passed Control?

This type of application is similar to the one just described. A common module may be used from many different logic points in the problem program, each one accessing it by a Branch & Link instruction statement. Each exit point in the main logic may require one or more unique functions within the common module, but not to such a point as to require a separate module. Prior to exiting from the main logic by the BAL instruction, a single switch can be given a unique setting so as to identify the exit point from which the common module was entered. That module, in turn, can test this switch and establish the criteria demanded by that unique condition.

Special Conditions during Processing

There are so many possibilities within this group that it precludes mentioning even a general application; however, one example that may give some indication of this type of use is the previously mentioned application of updating master files. When the update is in process, it might be assumed that input data will match to a currently existing master record. If this is so, then certain functions might be bypassed since the control data already exists on the master record. If a record of input data is encountered for which there is no master record, certain additional functions that are located noncontiguously throughout the program logic could be required to create a master record. Once again here is a logical task for a switch. When comparison of the input record to the master file determines that no master records exist for this data, a switch can be set, indicating this exception. As sequential logic is performed, this switch is tested at critical points—if the switch is off, certain additional routines are bypassed by branches; if the switch is on, the branches are not taken and the logic falls through in order to build the additional data required to create the master record.

Embedded Switches within Data Records

The use of embedded switches is often a major factor in the maintenance of data files that are time-dependent. In this type of maintenance, the records themselves are "flagged" by the setting of a switch embedded in the data as a part of the record. One concept of this is that the record is flagged and a subsequent listing of flagged records is produced. If no action is taken to reinstate the "keep" status of these records prior to the next update, all such records are deleted from the data file.

Multiple Conditions

This application, primarily using bit-switches, depends on the status of two or more switch conditions in order to make a decision. If bit-switches are set whenever a record of data was input to the problem program (in this instance a Purchase Order System), some of the switches might represent:

Using Switches and Indicators for Program Logic Control 451

		switch settings	
		Yes	No
SW-1	Has the material been received?	1	0
SW-2	Has the material been back-ordered?	1	0
SW-3	Back-ordered for more than 60 days?	1	0
SW-4	Has an invoice been received?	1	0
SW-5	Was there more than a 5% price variance from the P.O.?	1	0
SW-6	Was it a partial shipment?	1	0
SW-7	Any defects found during Purchase Material Inspection?	1	0
SW-8	Should invoice payment be withheld?	1	0

Based on the contents of these switches for each data record, certain records might be extracted for special use. For example, an Accounts Payable Department might wish to obtain a listing of all records for which switches, SW-1, SW-4, SW-5 and SW-8 were set to an "on" condition. These would be the records indicating that the material has been received, an invoice for the material had been received from the vendor, the vendor price varied more than 5% from the quoted price on the purchase order, and payment of this invoice was to be withheld at this time. It is true that each of these conditions could have been tested individually from embedded switches or indicators within the record. In a system of this type, however, many phases of logical extracts test for similar conditions. By setting a series of bit-switches in the input routines, each phase can test for the particular conditions it is interested in, merely by using one TM (Test Under Mask) instruction statement. In the example described for the Accounts Payable Department extract, a mask of X'99' would give a satisfactory test for the questioned conditions.

REVIEW EXERCISES

1. Using the concept of bit-switches, a single byte of storage can represent a total of _____ unique switches or indicators.
2. When it is necessary to compare the contents of a character-switch to a particular configuration, the _____ _____ _____ instruction proves to be the most expedient method of doing so.
3. Nondestructive testing of the condition of bit-switches can be accomplished by the use of the _____ _____ _____ instruction.
4. A byte-switch may also be referred to as a _____ switch.
5. A single bit position of a source byte can be tested by coding a _____-bit in the corresponding bit position of the mask operand within a Test Under Mask instruction statement.
6. The Assembler Language instruction that would be the most efficient for setting the configuration of a byte-switch or character-switch is the _____ _____.
7. A character-switch could be configured so as to represent _____ different switch conditions.

In each of the following problems, a one-byte set of switches is defined. Logical action to be taken against each byte is defined in terms of the bit positions, numbered from left to right as bit-switch 1 through bit-switch 8. Fill in the appropriate Boolean Logic instruction mnemonic op code and the hexadecimal configuration of the mask that would be required to perform the task as requested, assuming that the contents of the source byte is not known prior to the execution of the instruction statement. Then complete the blank field representing the source byte as it would appear after execution of the instruction statement.

8. ABITS | 0 1 1 0 | 0 0 1 0 |

Task: Turn on switches 1, 3, and 5:

                 ──OI── ABITS , X '──A8──'

ABITS | 1 1 1 0 | 1 0 1 0 |

9. KBITS | 0 1 1 0 | 1 0 0 1 |

Task: Define KBITS after execution of the following statements:

             NI   KBITS , X ' C3 '
             XI   KBITS , X ' 17 '
             OI   KBITS , X ' 4D '
             NI   KBITS , X ' A0 '

KBITS | 0 0 0 0 | 0 0 0 0 |

10. HBITS | 0 0 1 1 | 0 1 1 1 |

Task: Turn off all switches except switch 4:

                 ──NI── HBITS , X '──10──'

HBITS | 0 0 0 1 | 0 0 0 0 |

11. BBITS | 1 0 0 1 | 0 0 1 1 |

Task: Turn on switches 1, 4, 6, 7 and 8:

                 ──OI── BBITS , X '──97──'

BBITS | 1 0 0 1 | 0 1 1 1 |

12. EBITS | 0 0 1 0 | 1 0 1 1 |

Task: Turn off switches 1, 3 and 8; turn on switches 2 and 5:

                 ──NI── EBITS , X '──5E──'
                 ──OI── EBITS , X '──48──'

Using Switches and Indicators for Program Logic Control   453

EBITS [|]

13. CBITS [0 1 0 0 | 1 1 0 1]

Task: Turn off switches 2, 4 and 6:

————— CBITS , X '—————'

CBITS [0 0 0 0 | 1 0 0 1]

14. FBITS [1 0 0 1 | 1 1 1 1]

Task: Reverse the individual conditions of switches 3, 4, 5 and 7. If they are on, turn them off; if they are off, turn them on.

————— FBITS , X '—————'

FBITS [1 0 1 0 | 0 1 0 1]

15. GBITS [0 1 1 0 | 0 0 0 1]

Task: Non-destructively test the conditions of switches 2, 5, 7 and 8.

TM   GBITS , X '—————'

GBITS [0 1 1 0 | 0 0 0 1]

16. DBITS [1 1 1 0 | 1 0 1 1]

Task: Turn off switches 1, 2, 6, 7 and 8:

————— DBITS , X '—————'

DBITS [0 0 1 0 | 1 0 0 0]

14
Loop Controls and Table Look-Ups

This chapter provides a basis for applying index and/or table look-up logic utilizing loop control techniques and direct addressing manipulation. In essence, look-up techniques generally involve incremental addressing through a contiguous field or block of data under the control of a loop count value or conditional compare. In some instances it is possible to manipulate the key value of the segments being sought and create the actual address of that segment as it resides within the parent table or index. Prior to a detailed discussion of the actual look-up techniques, it is essential that the means of using loop controls be thoroughly understood.

LOOP CONTROLS

The quantity of cycles through any given loop pattern may be controlled by using any of the "Branch on Count" or "Branch on Condition" instructions. Most often, the instructions used are the Branch on Count, Branch on Count to Register, Branch on Condition, and Branch on Condition to Register instructions. Less frequently used, but equally effective, are the Branch on Index High, and Branch on Index Low or Equal instructions. Because of the similarity and general applications of all of these instructions, this discussion uses only the Branch on Count and Branch on Condition instructions to demonstrate and review loop control functions. Any of the other instructions mentioned may be suitably applied to these functions, as a review of their capabilities would indicate.

If the total length of a field, table, or index is fixed and unvariable, the loop control may be assumed to be a constant value that should not be exceeded. In this instance, a Branch on Count instruction may be used to terminate a complete set of cycles through that field, table, or index. If the length of the area to be scanned is a variable, changing from time to time, a Branch on Condition instruction may be more practical to apply. The common logic for this application would be to insert a number of unique characters, or an entire table segment of unique characters, at the end of the data and then check for the occurrence of those characters each time the area address is incremented. When those characters are encountered, the program logic should signal that the entire area has been scanned without finding the original argument for which the search was being made.

SEQUENTIAL LOOK-UPS AND SCANS

Sequential look-ups or scanning is construed to mean the sequential checking of contiguous data elements, whether or not those elements are in a logically sequential value arrangement. Such groups of elements may be organized in either a sequential or random pattern of the value of the identifier (key) field. "Sequential look-up" means that the elements of the table or index are looked at in an element-by-element physical pattern regardless of whether or not their values correspond to that arrangement. A physically sequential table array, arranged in a logically sequential mode, would be:

001/002/003/005/006/007/009/010/012/013/017/018
/019/020/021/023/025/026

A physically sequential table array, arranged in a random value pattern, would be:

006/005/047/001/012/017/075/065/066/063/014/019
/003/008/010/009/088/027

Sequential look-up processing may be applied to either format. In some instances, however, it might be considerably more expedient to use another type of look-up for a table or index that is both physically and logically sequential; perhaps a binary or a sectoring look-up.

The performance of a sequential look-up is based on a series of loop cycles, each cycle containing a comparison of the present table segment being addressed, a decision based on that comparison, and an instruction statement to increment the current table address setting to the next segment. In this type of scan, or look-up, the search is normally initialized at the beginning point of the table and increments its way through the table by one segment at a time. Many variations of this scheme are possible—the search may start at the end of the table and decrement downward one segment at a time; or the search may proceed in both directions at the same time. Several of these variations will be shown in the examples that follow.

Example 1. This routine consists of a table look-up that converts a three-byte EBCDIC numeric to a one-byte EBCDIC alphabetic character. The organization of the table is physically sequential and logically random. Each table segment consists of four bytes—a three-byte numeric and a one-byte character. The table consists of 50 segments plus an end-of-table delimiter. If a "hit" is encountered, the logic branches to a subroutine to pick up the character from the table segment; if a "hit" is not encountered the entire table is scanned and the logic then falls through to the next statement.

The coded instructions shown in Figure 14-1a and b may be defined as performing in the manner described in these following statements.

Statement 0101 is a Branch & Link to an assumed routine that reads a card into the CARDIN area.

Statement 0102 moves the third, fourth, and fifth characters from CARDIN (assumed to be containing a three-byte numeric key) to HOLDKEY. HOLDKEY now contains the three-byte code (argument) used to search the table.

Statement 0103 loads the address of the first byte of TABLE into general register 6. This value (address) can now be incremented for "stepping" through the table in a sequential manner.

Statement 0104 uses the Load Address instruction to place a value of +50 into general register 7. Register 7 is the Branch on Count register for loop control. Because there are only 50 valid segments in the table, the value of +50 in general register 7 allows a maximum of 50 increments to the table starting-point address.

Statement 0105 is the initial statement within LOOP. It compares the three bytes of HOLDKEY to the data located at the current address in general register 6. Each time that general register 6 is incremented, this instruction compares HOLDKEY to a new table segment—the one pointed to by register 6.

Loop Controls and Table Look-Ups

SYSTEM / 370 ASSEMBLER CODING FORM

TABLE LOOK-UP ROUTINE

NAME	OPERATION	OPERAND	COMMENTS
*		PROGRAM WORK AREAS	
*			
CARDIN	DC	CL80' '	- CARD INPUT AREA
HOLDKEY	DC	CL3' '	- HOLD AREA FOR RECORD KEY
CONVKEY	DC	CL1' '	- HOLD AREA FOR 1-BYTE CHARACTER
*			
*		TABLE	
*			
TABLE	DC	CL28'010A015D020E031B045A048C242C'	
	DC	CL28'026B053G056A096B100C177D316G'	
	DC	CL28'049A098E072C039D176E134A410F'	
	DC	CL28'092C121B165H073A016F265C259H'	
	DC	CL28'071D041A083F030A088B085G047F'	
	DC	CL28'110E318D059A237B103A025A196H'	
	DC	CL28'051F283B075E066A217C291D019J'	
	DC	CL8'035C999X'	
*			

FIGURE 14-1a

SYSTEM / 370 ASSEMBLER CODING FORM

TABLE LOOK-UP ROUTINE

Name	Operation	Operand	Comments	Identification
*		ROUTINE LOGIC		
*				
GO	BAL	8,GETCARD		0101
	MVC	HOLDKEY(3),CARDIN+3		0102
	LA	6,TABLE		0103
	LA	7,50		0104
LOOP	CLC	HOLDKEY(3),0(6)		0105
	BC	8,FOUND		0106
	AH	6,=H'4'		0107
	BCT	7,LOOP		0108
	BC	15,GO		0109
*				
FOUND	MVC	CONVKEY(1),0+3(6)		0110
	BAL	8,PUTDATA		0111
	BC	15,GO		0112
*				

FIGURE 14-1b

Loop Controls and Table Look-Ups 459

Statement 0106 is a Branch on Condition instruction statement, specifying that if HOLDKEY is equal to the table segment being addressed by register 6, then the problem program logic should branch to the FOUND routine.

Statement 0107 adds a value of +4 to general register 6. Because the branch in Statement 0106 was not taken, the logic knows that an equal condition was not found in the compare between HOLDKEY and the current table segment pointed to by the address contained in register 6. Therefore, the address in register 6 is increased by one table segment (four bytes) so that if Statement 0105 is encountered again it will be comparing HOLDKEY to the next higher table segment.

Statement 0108 is the Branch on Count loop control statement. Each time that this statement is encountered, the value in general register 7 is reduced by a value of +1. As long as general register 7 is greater than zero the branch to LOOP will be taken. As soon as register 7 is decremented to zero, indicating that the entire table has been scanned, the branch will not be taken and the program execution will fall through to Statement 0109.

Statement 0109 is a forced branch back to GO. Because the key held in HOLDKEY was not found, the program is designed to branch back to GO, get a new card, move in the new key value, reset the loop controls, reset the pointer to the beginning of TABLE, and then enter LOOP to see if that new key is within the TABLE.

Statement 0110 is the beginning of the subroutine that is followed if a "hit" is made against the table. It moves the fourth byte of the current TABLE segment into a one-byte area labeled CONVKEY. This segment is pointed to by the address contained in general register 6, and the one-byte of data is accessed by incrementing that address by +3—pointing to the fourth byte in that segment.

Statement 0111 is a Branch & Link to an assumed routine to perform an output operation using the character that was moved into CONVKEY.

Statement 0112 is a forced branch to GO that will start through the series of instruction statements again, getting a new input card, moving in the look-up argument, reinitializing the loop control, etc.

In this example, the BCT instruction is used to determine when the entire table had been checked. Because there are 50 valid table segments, the value of +50 is loaded into the BCT register. In reality, the table consists of 51 segments, the last segment being a table delimiter segment. In the set of instruction statements just explained, it would have been assumed that the table would always consist of 50 valid segments. By utilizing the table delimiter segment, it would make no difference what the length of the overall table would be. Compare the instruction statements in Figure 14-2 to the first set of statements of the preceding example.

This set of coding gives no consideration to the number of segments in the table. It continues incrementing through the table and terminates the look-up only when a "hit" has occurred or when Statement 0107 encounters the table delimiter segment. As soon as Statement 0107 creates an equal comparison, Statement 0108 knows that the entire table has been scanned without a "hit" and the processing logic falls through to Statement 0110. Although Statements 0107 and 0108 have been added to this set of instructions, Statement 0104 and 0108 have been eliminated from the previous set of instructions, resulting in exactly the same number of statements to perform the task. Either method is logically correct to use, but the latter method has definite merit if the overall length of the table might possibly vary from time to time.

In many instances the table used by a problem program exists only as a defined area within that program and actually contains no data. The data that belongs within the table is not supplied until execution time of the program. It exists as a supplement to the program object module, or

Name	Operation	Operand	Seq
*			0101
*			0102
GO	BAL	8,GETCARD	0103
	MVC	HOLDKEY(3),CARDIN+3	0104
	LA	6,TABLE	0105
LOOP	CLC	HOLDKEY(3),0(6)	0106
	BC	8,FOUND	0107
	AH	6,=H'4'	0108
	CLC	0(3,6),=CL3'999'	0109
	BC	7,LOOP	0110
	BC	15,GO	0111
*			0112
*			
FOUND	MVC	CONVKEY(1),3(6)	
	BAL	8,PUTDATA	
	BC	15,GO	
*			
*			

FIGURE 14-2

Loop Controls and Table Look-Ups 461

as an input data set, and is loaded into the table area by the problem program itself. This is generally referred to as a "loadable" table. For example, if the problem program is being input to the computer via the card reader, the data to be supplied to the table could be a set of additional card data that follows the object module delimiter card. The problem program begins execution and as one of its first tasks it commences reading-in the table data cards and placing their data into the defined table area.

Once again, a table delimiter segment may be used, but this time for two purposes. As the cards are being read in, this card signifies the end of the table input; when the table is actually being searched, the delimiter card signals that the end of the table has been reached. This is also an excellent use of the application of a variable-length table concept. When loading the card data into the table, both the check for the table delimiter segment card and the Branch on Count loop control makes sure that the number of table segment data cards do not exceed the maximum overall length of the table area. If the defined area for the table within the problem program allowed for a maximum of 500 table segments and the program encounters a table delimiter segment card on the 400th read, only 400 table segments would be loaded—and only that many would be utilized in subsequent searches if the search compare was looking for a table delimiter segment. If the problem program tried to read 510 table segments into the storage area, the Branch on Count loop control instruction would not allow the branch to be taken once the 500th segment had been read. The program logic could fall through to the next sequential instruction, one which might well be a message to the computer operator advising him that the table capacity had been exceeded. The following example presents a set of data as described for this type of an application.

Example 2. The instruction statements and defined areas have been coded as shown in Figure 14-3.

Statement 0041 defines a label of CARDIN that is to reference the 80 bytes of storage defined following this statement. The zero preceding the 'CL' indicates that no storage area is to be reserved by this define-statement. The card data to be placed in the next 80 bytes of storage may be referenced by this label or by the labels subdefined by the DC statements 0042 and 0043.

Statement 0042 actually reserves four bytes of storage, tagged with the label IDNO. This represents the first four bytes of each of the table cards to be read in, these bytes containing the unique identification number of an employee record that is to be part of the data loaded into the table.

Statement 0043 reserves 76 more bytes of storage, completing the area of 80 bytes referenced by CARDIN. Only the first 16 bytes of this field are important because they contain the name to be loaded into the table along with the associated identification number field of four bytes that immediately precedes this field.

Statement 0044 reserves a total of 16,000 bytes of storage, labeled TABLE, for the "Employee I.D. and Name" table. It is estimated that the table consists of a maximum of 800 segments of 20 bytes each—four bytes for the I.D. number and 16 bytes for the name associated with that number. Any quantity of table segments within the range of one to 800, including the table delimiter segment, may be loaded into this table. As the number of employees varies from week to week, the table accepts these variances.

The remaining statements of this particular illustration are those that control the loading of the table segments from card form into the problem program table area.

Statement 0015 loads the address of the first byte of the TABLE area (16,000 bytes long) into general register 6.

```
         NAME    OPERATION  OPERAND                                    COMMENTS
*
CARDIN   DS      0CL80                                                                          0041
IDNO     DC      CL4' '                                                                         0042
MISC     DC      CL76' '                                                                        0043
TABLE    DC      800CL20' '                                                                     0044
*
*
STARTIN  LA      6,TABLE                 LOAD TABLE ADDRESS IN REGISTER 6                       0051
         LA      7,800                   LOAD TABLE CAPACITY IN REGISTER 7                      0052
GETDATA  BAL     5,CARDGET               BRANCH TO CARD READING ROUTINE                         0053
         MVC     0(20,6),CARDIN          MOVE SELECTED CARD DATA INTO TABLE                     0054
         CLC     IDNO,=CL4'9999'         CHECK FOR LAST CARD                                    0055
         BC      8,ALLIN                 BRANCH IF LAST CARD                                    0056
         AH      6,=H'20'                INCREMENT TABLE ELEMENT ADDRESS                        0057
         BCT     7,GETDATA               BRANCH IF TABLE NOT FULL                               0058
         WTO     'ID TABLE EXCEEDED - ABEND'                                                    0059
         ABEND   400                                                                            0060
*
*
ALLIN                                                                                           0070
```

FIGURE 14-3

Loop Controls and Table Look-Ups 463

Statement 0052 loads a value of +800 into general register 7, to be used for loop control in the BCT instruction in Statement 0058. This assures that a maximum of 800 table segments are all that can be loaded into TABLE.

Statement 0053 is a Branch & Link instruction statement to an assumed data access routine that reads a card into the area addressed by CARDIN. Once this data has been read in, it may be referenced in whole by CARDIN or in part by IDNO or MISC.

Statement 0054 moves the first 20 bytes of the CARDIN field into the current table segment that is pointed to by general register 6. These 20 bytes contain a four-byte I.D. number and a 16-byte employee name, forming one table segment. When the first card is read, register 6 points to the address generated by TABLE+0, on the second card it points to TABLE+20, on the third to TABLE+40, on the fourth to TABLE+60, etc.

Statement 0055 compares the first four bytes of CARDIN (as subdefined by the label IDNO), the same four bytes that have just been moved into the table, to a four-byte literal constant of '9999'. This particular program is using a card containing '9999' as its combined input delimiter and table delimiter segment value. Because the logic wants this end-of-table delimiter indicator to be a part of the table, the comparison looking for the input delimiter card is not made until the data has been moved into the table.

Statement 0056, a Branch on Condition statement, causes a branch to be taken if the comparison in Statement 0055 creates an "equal" condition setting of the Condition Code bits. If the condition is "equal," the branch leads to a routine that begins additional problem program processing on the assumption that all current table segments have been loaded.

Statement 0057 adds a halfword value of +20 to general register 6 if the preceding statement, Statement 0056, did not cause a branch to be taken. This is incrementing general register 6 so that it points to the next logical table segment to be loaded with data.

Statement 0058 is the Branch on Count loop control. Because general register 7, the first operand in this statement, is loaded with a value of +800, this instruction statement allows up to 800 table segments to be loaded before dropping through to Statement 0059. If fewer than 800 segments are loaded, the input card delimiter is encountered and the branch in Statement 0056 is taken before general register 7 can be decremented to zero.

Statement 0059 is an OS macroinstruction, referred to as the "Write to Operator" (WTO) macro. It causes the system data management routines to type out the message, as contained within quotes, onto the computer console typewriter. In this case, the message advises the computer operator that the number of table segments has exceeded 800 and that the program is unable to process further.

Statement 0060 is an ABEND macroinstruction that advises the system to terminate the current problem program with an *ab*normal *end* condition, using a termination condition code of '400'. The program is terminated and the related data remaining in the job input stream is "flushed," or passed through the card reader without further action.

Now that the table has been loaded with an "X" amount of segments, the problem program can search it by using the second version of logic as shown under Example 1 in this section. That is, instead of using a Branch on Count instruction to signal the problem program when the entire table has been searched, a compare statement should be issued that looks for the '9999' code, indicating the end of the active table segments.

Whenever programming a sequential look-up on a table or index that is arranged with the data in a logically sequential identity pattern, another shortcut in processing time is available. This option is a Branch on Condition instruction statement that causes a branch whenever the argument (the data being compared to the table) compares "low" to the current table segment. In effect, such a condition indicates that the table segments have been sequentially scanned to a point where the logical value of the table key is now greater than that of the argument key, indicating that the table does not contain a segment comparable to the argument. It would then be appropriate to branch out of the table look-up loop inasmuch as any further scanning of the table would be useless—all remaining table keys being even greater than the one for which the search is being made. This technique is illustrated in the next example.

Example 3. The logic to be applied within this routine is that KEYCHEX is compared to the index to seek an address contained within the last four bytes of each INDEX table segment. If a "hit" occurs, the routine moves the corresponding address from INDEX into the ADDRESS field. If a "hit" is not encountered, the table look-up loop terminates as soon as KEYCHEX compares "low" to INDEX or when the table delimiter segment of '999' is encountered. The routine assumes that the table has already been loaded with an unspecified number of index table segments arranged in ascending sequential order of the value of the first three bytes of each segment. (See Figure 14-4)

Statement 0061 is a Branch & Link instruction, branching to an assumed subroutine for the purpose of accessing a tape data set and placing the incoming data records into the field labeled TAPEIN.

Statement 0062 loads the address of the first byte of INDEX into general register 10. That register is used as the pointer register for incrementing through the seven-byte segments of INDEX.

Statement 0063 moves three bytes of data from TAPEIN into the KEYCHEX field. This data is assumed to be the three-byte key that will be compared to the contents of the INDEX segment keys.

Statement 0064 is the first statement within the table look-up loop. It compares the three bytes of data in KEYCHEX to the first three bytes in the single INDEX segment that is currently pointed to by general register 10. As a result of this comparison, the Condition Code bits in the PSW are set so as to indicate the existing condition—high, low, or equal.

Statement 0065 indicates that if Statement 0064 results in an "equal" compare, then the program logic should branch to an assumed subroutine that moves the last four bytes of the current table segment into ADDRESS. Otherwise, the logic "falls through" Statement 0065 and the branch is not taken.

Statement 0066 specifies that if the comparison in Statement 0064 indicates that KEYCHEX is of a lower logical value than the current INDEX segment referenced by general register 10, then the program should branch back to GONOW. This condition would indicate that since the current table segment key is of a higher logical value than KEYCHEX, the portion of the INDEX where a corresponding key to KEYCHEX would have been found has already been passed. Therefore, it is concluded that no match to KEYCHEX exists within INDEX and there is no reason to search that table any further. If the branch is not taken, the logic "falls through" to the next instruction statement.

Statement 0067 adds a halfword value of +7 to general register 10. This increments general register 10 so that the address contained therein points to the next INDEX segment that is higher than the one just checked.

Statement 0068 compares the first three bytes of the table segment now addressed by general register 10 to a three-byte character literal to see if the end of INDEX has been reached. The last segment of INDEX would be the table delimiter segment containing '999' in its first three bytes.

Statement 0069 indicates that as long as Statement 0068 does not create an "equal" setting of the Condition Code bits, then the logic should branch back to the first instruction in the loop

Loop Controls and Table Look-Ups

SYSTEM / 370 ASSEMBLER CODING FORM

NAME	OPERATION	OPERAND	COMMENTS	IDENT.
*				
GONOW	BAL	5,GETAPE	BRANCH TO TAPE READ ROUTINE	0061
	LA	10,INDEX	PUT INDEX ADDRESS INTO REGISTER 10	0062
	MVC	KEYCHEX(3),TAPEIN+14	MOVE KEY TO HOLDING AREA	0063
LOOPCHEX	CLC	KEYCHEX(3),0(10)	COMPARE KEY TO INDEX SEGMENT	0064
	BC	8,GOTADDR	BRANCH IF EQUAL	0065
	BC	4,GONOW	BRANCH IF KEY COMPARES LOW	0066
	AH	10,=H'7'	INCREMENT INDEX SEGMENT ADDRESS	0067
	CLC	0(3,10),=CL3'999'	COMPARE FOR END OF INDEX	0068
	BC	7,LOOPCHEX	BRANCH IF NOT END OF INDEX	0069
	BC	15,GONOW	KEY NOT IN INDEX – READ TAPE AGAIN	0070
NOHIT				0071
*				
GOTADDR	MVC	ADDRESS(4),3(10)	MOVE ADDRESS FROM INDEX	0072
*				
*				
TAPEIN	DC	CL25' '		0840
KEYCHEX	DC	CL3' '		0850
INDEX	DC	300CL7' '		0860
ADDRESS	DC	CL4' '		0870
*				
*				

FIGURE 14-4

cycle, LOOPCHEX. If Statement 0068 results in an equal compare, the program logic would fall through to Statement 0070 on the assumption that the entire table had been searched.

Statement 0070 is a forced branch to GONOW. Because a match to the current value in KEYCHEX is not found in the table, the logic of this particular routine wishes to now bypass that record and get a new key field value from the next tape record.

As mentioned previously, this particular type of look-up routine, utilizing an exiting branch when the argument is of a lower value than the corresponding table value, is applicable *only* when the table is organized in the ascending or descending sequential order of the value of the table segment keys.

SECTORED LOOK-UP TECHNIQUES

The concept of a sectored look-up routine, or sectoring the table by search arguments, is based on the technique of arranging a table into logical sections, each section containing approximately an equal number of segments. The overall contents of the table, however, should be arranged in a logical sequence of values. When activating a look-up of this type of file table, the inquiry may start at any sector point within that table, based on the subsequent program logic. In explaining this technique further, Table 14-1 is used to reference the types of sectoring logic.

This table consists of 250 segments of four bytes each, a total of 1000 bytes. It is broken down into five primary sectors, each sector having a unique name and each containing 50 individual table segments. For example, the segments within sector PTA may be addressed as PTA+0, PTA+4, PTA+8, PTA+12, etc., through to PTA+196. The table segment that follows PTA+196 is the first segment within sector PTB; it could, however, also be addressed as PTA+200. Note that the first segment in sector PTA (0000) and the last segment in sector PTE (9999) represent the maximum low and high limits of the segment keys. By initializing the table with '0000' and ending it with '9999', the table may now be scanned in ascending or descending sequence without overrunning the table boundaries. This statement is made with the assumption that the programmer will issue the proper comparative statements to these values to prevent such an overrun. If the table is being checked in ascending sequence a comparison should be made to branch out if the KEY compares less than '9999', or equal to '9999', once it reaches that segment. If the table is being checked in descending sequence, a comparison should be made to branch out if the KEY compares equal to or higher than '0000' once it reaches that segment. The degree of detail used in any sectoring technique is dependent on the programmer's skill as well as the size of the file table being scanned.

In order to understand the basic idea of sectored look-ups, apply the following cases of simple sectoring to Table 14-1. In each case the argument is referred to as KEY and the table segment sectors are referred to as PTA, PTB, PTC, PTD and PTE, respectively. The reference to these diagrams (Type 1, Type 2, etc.) is merely to relate to these techniques during subsequent discussions.

Type 1

In this type of sectoring technique (Figure 14-5), the sector segments are sequentially checked in their logical ascending order. PTA+0 is not checked since it is already known that the value of its KEY contents is '0000'. Under the worst possible conditions this particular sectoring technique, as applied to this table, would require a maximum of 54 comparisons—one compare each for PTB, PTC, PTD, and PTE, and one compare for each segment within the PTE sector.

TABLE 14-1. Logical Arrangment of a Sectored Table

	+4	+8	+12	+16	+20	+24	+28	+32	+36
PTA →	0000	0008	0010	0012	0014	0018	0023	0024	0025	0027
+40	0029	0030	0033	0041	0042	0043	0045	0046	0047	0049
+80	0051	0060	0061	0062	0065	0066	0067	0068	0069	0070
+120	0072	0074	0076	0078	0079	0080	0082	0083	0085	0086
+160	0087	0088	0092	0094	0095	0096	0097	0100	0101	0103
PTB →	0105	0106	0107	0109	0110	0112	0114	0116	0117	0118
+40	0119	0120	0122	0123	0124	0127	0128	0129	0130	0132
+80	0133	0134	0135	0136	0137	0138	0139	0140	0144	0146
+120	0147	0149	0150	0151	0152	0153	0154	0155	0156	0157
+160	0158	0159	0160	0161	0162	0163	0164	0165	0166	0168
PTC →	0169	0170	0171	0172	0173	0174	0175	0176	0177	0178
+40	0180	0181	0182	0183	0184	0185	0186	0187	0189	0191
+80	0192	0193	0194	0195	0196	0197	0198	0200	0202	0203
+120	0204	0205	0206	0207	0208	0210	0211	0212	0213	0214
+160	0215	0216	0217	0218	0219	0220	0221	0222	0224	0225
PTD →	0226	0228	0230	0235	0237	0238	0239	0240	0241	0242
+40	0245	0246	0247	0248	0250	0252	0254	0256	0257	0259
+80	0260	0261	0263	0264	0265	0266	0267	0268	0269	0270
+120	0271	0272	0273	0274	0275	0276	0279	0280	0282	0284
+160	0295	0310	0311	0312	0315	0317	0321	0322	0330	0331
PTE →	0332	0335	0336	0337	0338	0339	0340	0341	0342	0343
+40	0344	0350	0351	0352	0353	0354	0355	0356	0357	0358
+80	0360	0362	0364	0365	0366	0380	0384	0385	0387	0390
+120	0391	0392	0393	0394	0395	0402	0403	0405	0407	0410
+160	0411	0412	0413	0414	0424	0425	0426	0429	0431	9999
	+164	+168	+172	+176	+180	+184	+188	+192	+196

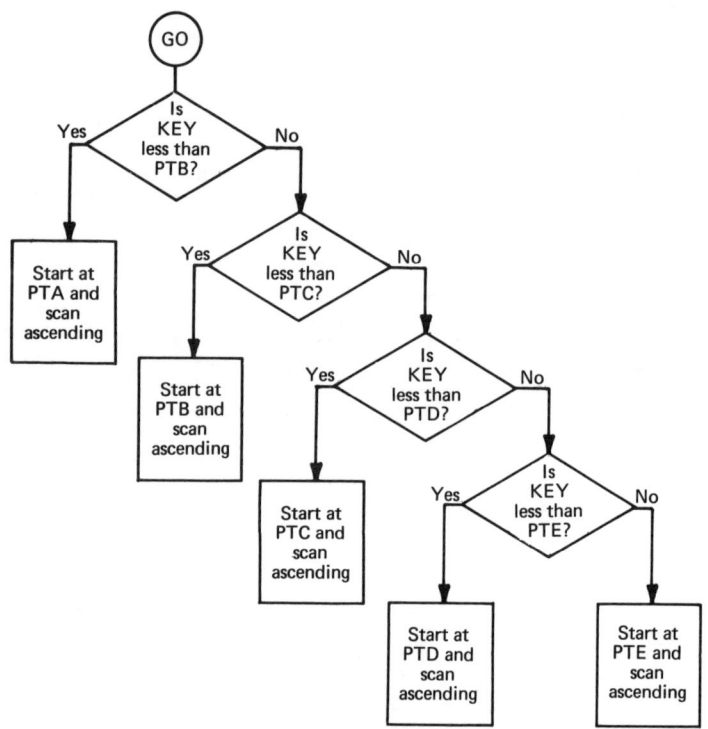

FIGURE 14-5

Type 2

This type of sectored look-up (Figure 14-6), starting at the approximate middle of the table, would require a maximum of 53 comparisons during the search for the data within Table 14-1. Depending on the number of defined sectors within a table, as well as the size of the table itself, this type of look-up could reduce search time by a considerable amount.

Type 3

This particular logic pattern (Figure 14-7) is an expansion on the Type 2 sectoring lookup.

Pick any number at random and follow this logic through to find that number on the table. Using the logic pattern shown for this particular sectored look-up, a maximum of 29 comparisons would be made to find any given table key, although this number would occur only under the most adverse conditions. Note that the logic flow of these graphs of sectoring techniques does not provide for an equal condition during one of the indicated comparisons. Even though an equal condition does not appear thereon, the programmer would have to check after each comparison for such a condition and arrange the program logic to accept that condition as a "hit."

The three preceding types of sectoring techniques are noncomplex in nature and are intended only to start you thinking about the many variations on this theme. Literally dozens of sectoring schemes might be developed to expedite search time, the design of which would be *relatively*

Loop Controls and Table Look-Ups

dependent on the size and format of the table to be searched and *quite dependent* on your ingenuity and ability.

Once the logic pattern for any given sectoring technique has been developed, the coding of the instruction statements merely follows the logic path for that technique. Referring to Table 14-1, the following program coding contains the statements necessary to define those table segments and sectors. The subroutines contained in this example represent the typical statements for a Type 1 sectoring technique. Assume that the program in which these routines are coded has already accessed a data record and placed a four-byte set of numeric characters into the field labeled KEY. (See Figure 14-8a and b.)

Statement 0201 compares the characters in KEY to the table segment addressed by the label PTB. In this case, using the contents of the sectored table (Table 14-1), PTB would be referring to the four bytes of storage containing '0105'.

Statement 0202 specifies, "If KEY compares high to PTB, branch to Statement 0205." This result would indicate that the corresponding value to KEY is not contained in the table segements from PTA to PTB. However, if KEY had compared low to PTB, this would indicate that a corresponding value to KEY would fall within the table segments between PTA and PTB. In the latter condition, the branch would not be taken and the program processing would fall through to Statement 0203.

Statement 0203 loads the address of the first byte of PTA into general register 10. This address is to be used by a common subroutine labeled SCANITA.

FIGURE 14-6

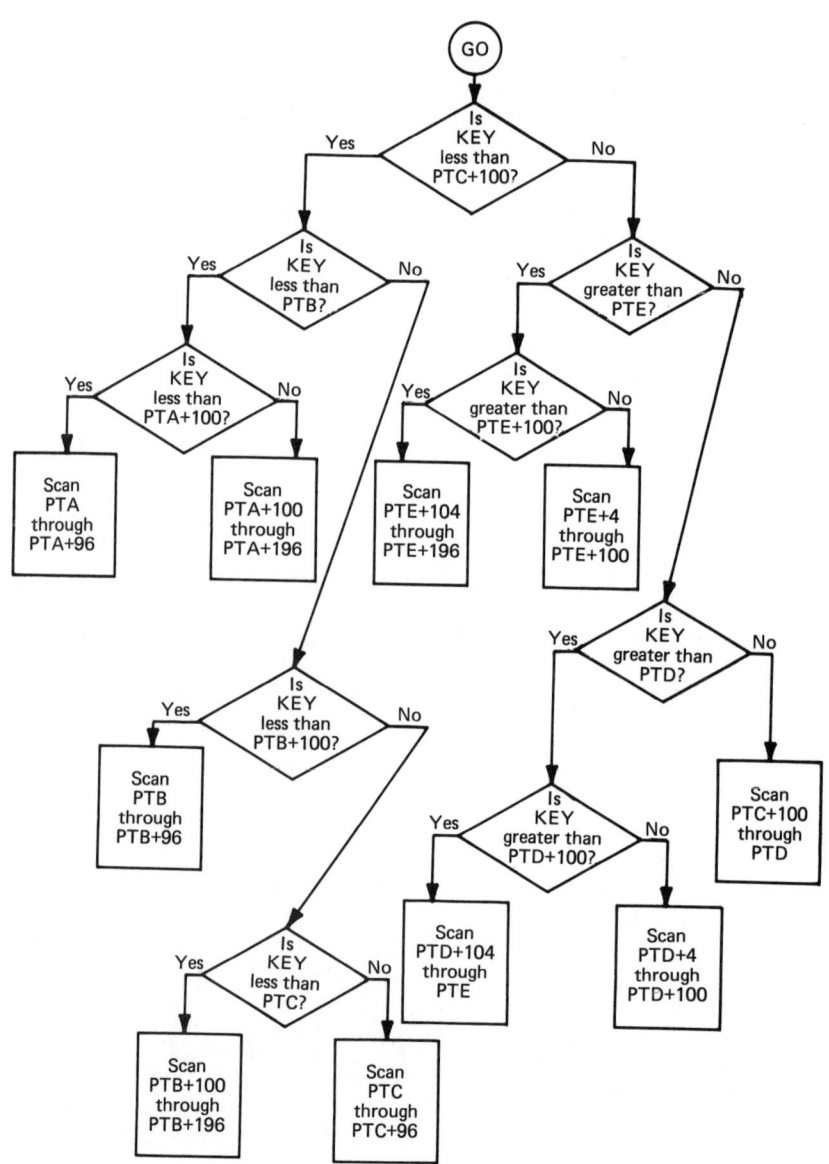

FIGURE 14-7

Loop Controls and Table Look-Ups

SYSTEM / 370 ASSEMBLER CODING FORM

Type #1 Sectoring Technique

PAGE 1 OF 2
ASSIGN NO. 14-8A

NAME	OPERATION	OPERAND	SEQ
TABLE	DS	0CL2000	0094
PTA	DC	50CL4' '	0095
PTB	DC	50CL4' '	0096
PTC	DC	50CL4' '	0097
PTD	DC	50CL4' '	0098
PTE	DC	50CL4' '	0099
*			0100
KEY	DC	CL4' '	0101
*			
GOTDATA	CLC	KEY(4),PTB	0201
	BC	2,SKIP1	0202
	LA	10,PTA	0203
	BC	15,SCAN1TA	0204
*			
SKIP1	CLC	KEY(4),PTC	0205
	BC	2,SKIP2	0206
	LA	10,PTB	0207
	BC	15,SCAN1TA	0208
*			

FIGURE 14-8a

SYSTEM / 370 ASSEMBLER CODING FORM

Type #1 Sectoring Technique
PAGE 2 OF 2
ASSIGN NO. 14-8b

Name	Operation	Operand	Identification Sequence No.
SKIP2	CLC	KEY(4),PTD	0209
	BC	2,SKIP3	0210
	LA	10,PTC	0211
	BC	15,SCANITA	0212
*			
*			
SKIP3	CLC	KEY(4),PTE	0213
	BC	2,SKIP4	0214
	LA	10,PTD	0215
	BC	15,SCANITA	0216
*			
*			
SKIP4	LA	10,PTE	0217
	BC	15,SCANITA	0218
*			
*			
SCANITA	LA	11,50	0219
SCANIT	CLC	KEY(4),0(10)	0220
	BC	8,HITKEY	0221
	BC	4,NOGO	0222
	AH	10,=H'4'	0223
	BC	15,SCANIT	0224
*			

FIGURE 14-8b

Loop Controls and Table Look-Ups

Statement 0204 is a forced branch to SCANITA, the subroutine that checks the table segments of the sector pointed to by the address in general register 10.

Statement 0205, SKIP1, is entered if the branch in Statement 0202 was taken. This statement compares KEY to the first four-byte table segment address by PTC—the segment containing '0169'.

Statement 0206 states, "If KEY compares high to PTC, branch to Statement 0209." If the branch is taken it would indicate that the range of value that would correspond to KEY is not within the table segments from PTB to PTC, but is at a higher table segment location. If the branch is not taken, the program logic falls through to Statement 0207, indicating that the comparable value range of KEY is to be found somewhere between PTB and PTC. This can be proved by noting that in order to get to Statement 0205, KEY had to compare high or equal to PTB, and in order to get to Statement 0207, KEY had to compare low to PTC.

Statement 0207 loads the address of the first byte of PTB into general register 10. This address is used by SCANITA to check the table segments from PTB to PTC for a match to KEY.

Statement 0208 is a forced branch to SCANITA, the subroutine that checks the table segments of the sector pointed to by the address within general register 10.

Statement 0209, SKIP2, is entered if the branch in Statement 0206 is taken. This statement compares KEY to '0226', the first four bytes addressed by PTD.

Statement 0210 causes a branch to be taken to Statement 0213 if the value of KEY compares high to PTD in Statement 0209. By taking the branch, the program would indicate that KEY is of a value equal to, or greater than, PTD. If the branch is not taken, this would indicate that the table value range comparable to KEY is somewhere between PTC and PTD. Statement 0205 and the branch from Statement 0206 to Statement 0209 have already indicated that KEY is higher than PTC; because the compare in Statement 0209 does not result in a branch in Statement 0210, KEY must have a value that fits the table range between PTC and PTD.

Statement 0211 loads the address of the first byte of the table segment pointed to by PTC. General register 10 is used as the address pointer register in the SCANITA subroutine.

Statement 0212 is a forced branch to SCANITA. If entered from this point, SCANIT checks the table segements from PTC to PTD in an attempt to find a match for KEY.

Statement 0213, SKIP3, would be entered only if the branch in Statement 0210 is taken. This would indicate that KEY is of a higher value than the table segment addressed by PTD. This statement now compares KEY to the table segment addressed by PTE.

Statement 0214 causes a branch to Statement 0217 if KEY compares high to PTE in Statement 0213. If KEY compares low to PTE, indicating that the table values comparable to KEY are between PTD and PTE, the processing logic falls through this statement to Statement 0215.

Statement 0215 loads the address of PTD into general register 10, pointing to the first byte of the table segment referenced by PTD. Register 10 is used as the pointer register in SCANIT.

Statement 0216 is a forced branch to SCANITA. If SCANIT is entered from this point, it checks the table segments from PTD to PTE for a matching value to KEY.

Statement 0217 loads the address of PTE into general register 10. This statement is entered only if the branch in Statement 0214 is taken, indicating that KEY contains a logical value equal to, or greater than, PTE. Because PTE is the last sector of the segments in the table, the logic assumes that the corresponding value range for KEY is somewhere between PTE and the end of the table. General register 10, now containing the address of the first byte of the table segment referenced by PTE, is used by the SCANIT subroutine.

Statement 0218 is a forced branch to Statement 0219, SCANITA. When SCANIT is entered from this point, it checks the table segments from PTE to the end of the table.

Statement 0220 is the second statement in the SCANITA subroutine. The preceding statement loaded the Branch on Count register for this subroutine with the maximum number of items within a single table sector. This statement now compares KEY to the table segment pointed to by the address in general register 10, for a length of four bytes. When this instruction statement is first entered at the beginning of a loop cycle, general register 10 will point to sector:

> PTA, if SCANITA was branched to from Statement 0204.
> PTB, if SCANITA was branched to from Statement 0208.
> PTC, if SCANITA was branched to from Statement 0212.
> PTD, if SCANITA was branched to from Statement 0216.
> PTE, if SCANITA was branched to from Statement 0218.

Each time this statement is entered from Statement 0223, the address in general register 10 is incremented in order to step through the table segments of the table sector being scanned. This subroutine, SCANITA, is therefore an effective "common" set of instruction statements shared by five different logic points of the main-line logic, the five forced branches represented by Statements 0204, 0208, 0212, 0216 and 0218.

Statement 0221 is a test for an equal condition as a result of the comparison (in Statement 0219) of KEY to the table segment pointed to by general register 10. If the equal status is indicated by the Condition Code bits, this statement causes a branch to an assumed routine, HITKEY. HITKEY proceeds with whatever logic the programmer intended to accomplish once a "hit" was made against the table. If the Condition Code indicates that the comparison is not equal, the processing action falls through to Statement 0222.

Statement 0222 tests the current setting of the Condition Code bits for an indication that KEY is of a lower logical value than the table segment that it was compared to in Statement 0220. If this condition exists, indicating that an exact match for KEY does not exist within the table, this instruction statement branches to NOGO. NOGO is assumed to be a routine that tells the program logic that the value of KEY was not found and that it is to proceed with whatever corresponding action the programmer intended to take under such circumstances. If KEY does not compare low to the current table segment, the branch is not taken here and the processing logic falls through to Statement 0223.

Statement 0223 increments the address contained in general register 10 by a halfword value of +4. This has now pointed general register 10 to the next table segment beyond the one just tested by Statement 0220.

Statement 0224 is a forced branch back to Statement 0220, SCANIT, for the purpose of comparing KEY to the new table segment pointed to by register 10.

In order to visually follow the logic pattern of these instruction statements as the table is scanned for a particular value, trace the action represented by the search for these values. The keys to be sought are assumed to be on Table 14-1.

(a) The key to be found is . . . 0185.
(b) The sequence of the instruction statements performed would be . . .
0201, 0202, 0205, 0206, 0209, 0210, 0211, 0212, 0219, 0220, 0221, 0222, 0223, 0224, 0220, 0221, 0222, 0223, 0224, 0220, 0221, 0222, 0223, 0224, 0220, 0221, 0222, 0223, 0224, 0220, 0221, 0222, 0223, 0224, 0220, 0221, 0222, 0223, 0224, 0220, 0221, 0222, 0223, 0224, 0220, 0221, 0222, 0223, 0224, 0220, 0221, 0222, 0223, 0224, 0220, 0221, 0222, 0223, 0224, 0220, 0221, 0222, 0223, 0224, 0220, 0221, 0222, 0223, 0224, 0220, 0221, 0222, 0223, 0224, 0220, 0221, 0222, 0223, 0224, 0220, 0221, HITKEY.

Loop Controls and Table Look-Ups

(a) The key to be found is ... 0107.
(b) The sequence of the statments executed would be ...
0201, 0202, 0205, 0206, 0207, 0208, 0219, 0220, 0221, 0222, 0223, 0224, 0220, 0221, 0222, 0223, 0224, 0220, 0221, HITKEY.

(a) The key to be found is ... 0236.
(b) The sequence of the statements executed are ...
0201, 0202, 0205, 0206, 0209, 0210, 0213, 0214, 0215, 0216, 0219, 0220, 0221, 0222, 0223, 0224, 0220, 0221, 0222, 0223, 0224, 0220, 0221, 0222, 0223, 0224, 0220, 0221, 0222, 0223, 0224, 0220, 0221, 0222, NOGO.

(a) The key to be found is ... 0332.
(b) The sequence of the statments would be ...
0201, 0202, 0205, 0206, 0209, 0210, 0213, 0214, 0217, 0218, 0219, 0220, 0221, HITKEY.

Utilizing these same field descriptions and the values shown in Table 14-1, the instruction statements that could be used to code the Type 2 sectoring technique might appear as shown in Figure 14-9a and b.

The performance of these statements should be similar enough to the previous set of instruction statements so as to be easily understood. To prove the logic of these instruction statements, follow these value keys as the routine searches the table for their corresponding match.

(a) The value of the key to be found is ... 0014.
(b) The sequence of the statements executed in this search would be ...
0301, 0302, 0303, 0304, 0305, 0306, 0319, 0320, 0321, 0322, 0323, 0319, 0320, 0321, 0322, 0323, 0319, 0320, 0321, 0322, 0323, 0319, 0320, 0321, 0322, 0323, 0319, 0320, HITKEY.

(a) The key to be found is ... 0333.
(b) The sequence of the statements executed would be ...
0301, 0302, 0309, 0310, 0313, 0314, 0317, 0318, 0319, 0320, 0321, 0322, 0323, 0319, 0320, 0321, NOGO.

(a) The key to be found is ... 0226.
(b) The search sequence would be ...
0301, 0302, 0309, 0310, 0313, 0314, 0315, 0316, 0319, 0320, HITKEY.

(a) The value of KEY is ... 0112.
(b) The sequence of the instructions executed during the lookup are ...
0301, 0302, 0303, 0304, 0307, 0308, 0319, 0320, 0321, 0322, 0323, 0319, 0320, 0321, 0322, 0323, 0319, 0320, 0321, 0322, 0323, 0319, 0320, 0321, 0322, 0323, 0319, 0320, 0321, 0322, 0323, 0319, 0320, HITKEY.

The instruction statement coding for the sectoring technique referred to within this section as a Type 3 application becomes somewhat more involved. The more complex the task becomes, the more variation that can be applied to the coding of that task. Therefore, the following instruction statements are only one way of performing the logic pattern for the Type 3 sectoring technique. Note that the field definitions and values are the same as used in the examples for the Type 1 and Type 2 sectoring applications, but that address adjusting has been implemented in some of the instruction statements. (See Figure 14-10a, b, and c.)

SYSTEM / 370 ASSEMBLER CODING FORM

TYPE #2 SECTORING TECHNIQUE

Name	Operation	Operand	Identification
*			
GOTDATA	CLC	KEY(4),PTC	0301
	BC	10,PASS1	0302
	CLC	KEY(4),PTB	0303
	BC	10,SKIP1	0304
	LA	R10,PTA	0305
	BC	15,SCANIT	0306
*			
*			
SKIP1	LA	R10,PTB	0307
	BC	15,SCANIT	0308
*			
*			
PASS1	CLC	KEY(4),PTD	0309
	BC	10,PASS2	0310
	LA	R10,PTC	0311
	BC	15,SCANIT	0312
*			
*			
PASS2	CLC	KEY(4),PTE	0313
	BC	10,PASS3	0314
	LA	R10,PTD	0315
	BC	15,SCANIT	0316
*			

FIGURE 14-9a

Loop Controls and Table Look-Ups

SYSTEM/370 ASSEMBLER CODING FORM

Type #2 Sectoring Technique

Name	Operation	Operand	Comments	Identification
*				
PASS3	LA	R10,PTE		0317
	BC	15,SCANIT		0318
*				
SCANIT	CLC	KEY(4),0(R10)		0319
	BC	8,HITKEY		0320
	BC	4,NOGO		0321
	AH	R10,=H'4'		0322
	BC	15,SCANIT		0323
*				
R10	EQU	10	TO EQUATE R10 AS A VALUE OF 10 TO BE USED FOR REGISTER 10 NOTATION	0324
*				0325

FIGURE 14-9b

SYSTEM / 370 ASSEMBLER CODING FORM

TYPE #3 SECTORING TECHNIQUE

Name	Operation	Operand	Identification Sequence No.
GOTDATA	CLC	KEY(4),PTC+100	0401
	BC	10,SECTB	0402
	CLC	KEY(4),PTB	0403
	BC	10,SECTA	0404
	CLC	KEY(4),PTA+100	0405
	BC	10,SECTC	0406
	LA	R10,PTA	0407
	BC	15,SCANIT	0408
*			
*			
SECTC	LA	R10,PTA+100	0409
	BC	15,SCANIT	0410
*			
SECTA	CLC	KEY(4),PTB+100	0411
	BC	10,SECTD	0412
	LA	R10,PTB	0413
	BC	15,SCANIT	0414
*			
SECTD	CLC	KEY(4),PTC	0415
	BC	10,SECTE	0416
	LA	R10,PTB+100	0417
	BC	15,SCANIT	0418
*			

FIGURE 14-10a

Loop Controls and Table Look-Ups

SYSTEM / 370 ASSEMBLER CODING FORM

Type #3 Sectoring Technique

Name	Operation	Operand		Seq
*				0419
SECTE	LA	R10,PTC		0420
	BC	15,SCANIT		
*				0421
SECTB	CLC	KEY(4),PTE		0422
	BC	4,SECTF		0423
	CLC	KEY(4),PTE+100		0424
	BC	4,SECTG		0425
	LA	R10,PTE+100		0426
	BC	15,SCANIT		
**				0427
SECTG	LA	R10,PTE		0428
	BC	15,SCANIT		
*				0429
SECTF	CLC	KEY(4),PTD		0430
	BC	4,SECTH		0431
	CLC	KEY(4),PTD+100		0432
	BC	4,SECTI		0433
	LA	R10,PTD+100		0434
	BC	15,SCANIT		

FIGURE 14-10b

SYSTEM / 370 ASSEMBLER CODING FORM

TYPE #3 SECTORING TECHNIQUE

PAGE 3 OF 3

Name	Operation	Operand	Comments	Identification Sequence No.
*				
SECTI	LA	R10,PTD		0435
	BC	15,SCANIT		0436
*				
SECTH	LA	R10,PTC+100		0437
	BC	15,SCANIT		0438
*				
SCANIT	CLC	KEY(4),0(R10)		0439
	BC	8,HITKEY		0440
	BC	4,NOGO		0441
	AH	R10,=H'4'		0442
	BC	15,SCANIT		0443
*				
HITKEY				0450
*				
R10	EQU	10	TO EQUATE R10 TO REGISTER 10 OPERANDS	0828
*				0829

FIGURE 14-10c

Loop Controls and Table Look-Ups

At this point in the text, the performance and action of these instruction statements should require little or no explanation. Each step and subroutine generated by these statements is directly related to the logic pattern of the logic flow-chart for the Type 3 sectoring technique. A series of values and the logic flow required to find those values during a table look-up is listed below. Trace the sequence of operation through the instruction statements to verify the search for this data.

(a) The value of KEY is ... 0205.
(b) The search sequence of instructions would be ...
0401, 0402, 0421, 0422, 0429, 0430, 0437, 0438, 0439, 0440, 0441, 0442, 0443, 0439, 0440, 0441, 0442, 0443, 0439, 0440, 0441, 0442, 0443, 0439, 0440, 0441, 0442, 0443, 0439, 0440, 0441, 0442, 0443, 0439, 0440, 0441, 0442, 0443, 0439, 0440, HITKEY.

(a) The value of the key to be found is ... 0066.
(b) The sequence of the instructions executed would be ...
0401, 0402, 0403, 0404, 0405, 0406, 0409, 0410, 0439, 0440, HITKEY.

(a) The value of KEY is ... 0108.
(b) The search sequence would be ...
0401, 0402, 0403, 0404, 0411, 0412, 0413, 0414, 0439, 0440, 0441, 0442, 0443, 0439, 0440, 0441, 0442, 0443, 0439, 0440, 0441, 0442, 0443, 0439, 0440, 0441, NOGO.

(a) The value of KEY is ... 0385.
(b) The sequence of instructions for the search would be ...
0401, 0402, 0421, 0422, 0423, 0424, 0425, 0426, 0439, 0440, 0441, 0442, 0443, 0439, 0440, 0441, 0442, 0443, 0439, 0440, HITKEY.

Even though this example follows the logic flow-chart for the Type 3 sectoring technique almost to the instruction symbol, the same basic task could have been coded in considerably fewer statements. The set of instruction statements shown in Figure 14-11a and b are not conforming entirely to the flow chart of logic for the Type 3 sectoring technique but they are, however, providing a search pattern on a very similar level.

In order to compare this reduced set of coding statements to the previous example, wherein a total of 43 instruction statements were used, look-up sequences are provided here with the same values as those for the previous look-ups.

(a) The value of KEY is ... 0205.
(b) The search sequence of instruction statements would be ...
0501, 0502, 0503, 0513, 0514, 0515, 0507, 0508, 0509, 0510, 0507, 0508, 0509, 0510, 0507, 0508, 0509, 0510, 0507, 0508, 0509, 0510, 0507, 0508, 0509, 0510, 0507, 0508, 0509, 0510, 0507, 0508, 0509, 0510, 0507, 0508, 0509, 0518, 0519, 0520, 0521, 0522, 0518, 0519, HITKEY.

(a) The value of KEY is ... 0066.
(b) The sequence of statements would be ...
0501, 0502, 0503, 0504, 0505, 0506, 0507, 0508, 0509, 0510, 0507, 0508, 0509, 0510, 0507, 0508, 0509, 0510, 0507, 0508, 0509, 0510, 0507, 0508, 0509, 0510, 0507, 0508, 0509, 0510, 0507, 0508, 0509, 0510, 0507, 0508, 0509, 0510, 0507, 0508, 0509, 0518, 1519, HITKEY.

SYSTEM / 370 ASSEMBLER CODING FORM

Name	Operation	Operand	Identification
GOTDATA	LA	R10,PTC+100	0501
	CLC	KEY(4),0(R10)	0502
	BC	10,SECTA	0503
	SH	R10,=H'200'	0504
	CLC	KEY(4),0(R10)	0505
	BC	10,SECTB	0506
DOWN20	SH	R10,=H'20'	0507
	CLC	KEY(4),0(R10)	0508
	BC	10,SCAN1T	0509
	BC	4,DOWN20	0510
*			
SECTB	AH	R10,=H'200'	0511
	BC	15,DOWN20	0512
*			
SECTA	AH	R10,=H'200'	0513
	CLC	KEY(4),0(R10)	0514
	BC	12,DOWN20	0515
	LA	R10,PTE+196	0516
	BC	15,DOWN20	0517
*			

FIGURE 14-11a

Loop Controls and Table Look-Ups

SYSTEM / 370 ASSEMBLER CODING FORM

NAME	OPERATION	OPERAND		IDENTIFICATION SEQUENCE NO.
*				
SCANIT	CLC	KEY(4),0(R10)		0518
	BC	8,HITKEY		0519
	BC	4,NOGO		0520
	AH	R10,=H'4'		0521
	BC	15,SCANIT		0522
*				
*				
HITKEY				0535
*				
*				
NOGO				0550
*				
*				
R10	EQU	10		0578
				0579
				0580

FIGURE 14-11b

(a) The value of the key is . . . 0108.
(b) The search sequence of the executed statements would be . . .
0501, 0502, 0503, 0504, 0505, 0506, 0507, 0508, 0509, 0510, 0507, 0508, 0509, 0510, 0507, 0508, 0509, 0510, 0507, 0508, 0509, 0510, 0507, 0508, 0509, 0518, 0519, 0520, 0521, 0522, 0518, 0519, 0520, 0521, 0522, 0518, 0519, 0520, 0521, 0522, 0518, 0519, 0520, NOGO.

(a) The value of KEY is . . . 0385.
(b) The sequence of instruction statements for the search would be . . .
0501, 0502, 0503, 0513, 0514, 0515, 0516, 0517, 0507, 0508, 0509, 0510, 0507, 0508, 0509, 0510, 0507, 0508, 0509, 0510, 0507, 0508, 0509, 0510, 0507, 0508, 0518, 0519, 0520, 0521, 0522, 0518, 0519, 0520, 0521, 0522, 0518, 0519, HITKEY.

Although this latter set of instructions is composed of fewer statements, the actual search for the table value takes more statement executions to accomplish; consequently, the routine would use more computer time. In this instance, the first set of instructions for a Type 3 sectoring technique would be considerably more efficient in machine utilization, although it requires more coding on the part of the programmer. This is quite often the case—you might spend considerable time devising compact little subroutines only to find in the end that a straight-line approach to the problem would have been more efficient.

It must be explained that the references to the Types 1, 2 and 3 sectoring techniques are intended only to group these techniques by a degree of complexity for the purpose of this section of the text. These references in no way imply a professionally accepted grouping of techniques or an accepted measurement standard of their complexity. Almost needless to say, there are probably more variations of sectoring look-ups than one person could conceive of and, consequently, any attempt to validly group such techniques would be presumptuous.

DIRECT ADDRESSING OF TABLE SEGMENTS

The concept of direct addressing techniques for table look-ups has a number of variations ranging from simple "add" functions to extremely complex numerical conversion schemes. For the purpose of this text, only the basic method of directly addressing a table segment is reviewed. This method is generally applicable in a table that contains a consecutive, contiguous arrangement of key values in ascending sequence. In the discussion that follows, it is assumed that the table to be used is arranged in such a format. The creation of the table itself must be considered so that a table segment must be created for each consecutive value in the numbering sequence to be used, whether or not that value does exist for use within the table. For example, if the values 001, 002, 003, 005, 006, 008 and 009 were valid table arguments, then the table would have to contain segments available for 001, 002, 003, 004, 005, 006, 007, 008 and 009. The values of 004 and 007 would have to be provided in the table in order to "balance" it for the direct addressing technique to be applied. Table 14-2 represents a table of data to be accessed via direct addressing. Notice that all table segments do not contain valid data. The table addresses shown are in decimal format, rather than the normal hexadecimal representation in order that the logic might be more easily followed.

When developing the routine for directly addressing the table segments, the length of the segments themselves must be considered. Multiplication of the key value of the table segment by the number of bytes in each segment is a common way of obtaining a direct address increment.

Loop Controls and Table Look-Ups

TABLE 14-2. A Sequentially Organized Table for Direct Addressing Access

Table segment number	Relative address	Label	Table segment 16 bytes	Assumed address
		PRETAB	dummy record	32,404
1	PRETAB+16	TABLE	D049586746384556	32,420
2	+32		D837465847465837	32,436
3	+48		D002838883746554	32,452
4	+64		D922264537394058	32,468
5	+80		ҏҏҏҏҏҏҏҏҏҏҏҏҏҏҏҏ	32,484
6	+96		D847263949555836	32,500
7	+112		D933650003645572	32,516
8	+128		D003232505926266	32,532
9	+144		D225242829254836	32,548
10	+160		D110584711365934	32,564
11	+176		D004619375137473	32,580
12	+192		D199257364563930	32,596
13	+208		D887423641593211	32,612
14	+224		D613800342746513	32,628
15	+240		D222746143804950	32,644
16	+256		D741109384125135	32,660
17	+272		ҏҏҏҏҏҏҏҏҏҏҏҏҏҏҏҏ	32,676
18	+288		D001145848547522	32,692
19	+304		D011466648347436	32,708
20	+320		ҏҏҏҏҏҏҏҏҏҏҏҏҏҏҏҏ	32,724
21	+336		D391004216756481	32,740
22	+352		D190011458374629	32,756
23	+368		D700121232998414	32,772
24	+384		D774038374157193	32,788
25	+400		D283938474911584	32,804
26	+416		D459941374620293	32,820
27	+432		D120290485650481	32,836
28	+448		ҏҏҏҏҏҏҏҏҏҏҏҏҏҏҏҏ	32,852
29	+464		D696870285630575	32,868
30	+480		D113931146577764	32,884
31	+496		D773000395877392	32,900
32	+512		D033472274635443	32,916
33	+528		D373747485930491	32,932
34	+544		D400113843932114	32,948
35	+560		ҏҏҏҏҏҏҏҏҏҏҏҏҏҏҏҏ	32,964
36	+576		ҏҏҏҏҏҏҏҏҏҏҏҏҏҏҏҏ	32,980
37	+592		D110021137894911	32,996
38	+608		D885693847513394	33,012
39	+624		D775648886978411	33,028
40	+640		D103478576849932	33,044
41	+656		D488576829427836	33,060
42	+672		D774638375856342	33,076
43	+688		D933140405768113	33,092
44	+704		ҏҏҏҏҏҏҏҏҏҏҏҏҏҏҏҏ	33,108
45	+720		D559045551438813	33,124
46	+736		D399993374157738	33,140
47	+752		ҏҏҏҏҏҏҏҏҏҏҏҏҏҏҏҏ	33,156
48	+768		D669484857611332	33,172
49	+784		D390046574847339	33,188
50	+800		D110200678511225	33,204

The illustrated table look-up routine (Figure 14-12a and b) uses a "shift" instruction to calculate the table segment address from the segment key. The format of PRETAB and TABLE have been established in accordance with the table just illustrated. For the purpose of this example, it is assumed that at problem program execution time PRETAB is a storage position address 32,404 and TABLE is at 32,420. Normally, the key of the table segment to be located would be brought in through some type of I/O device in a random pattern. For this example, they have been established as constants in order to illustrate their conversion to a direct address.

The explanation of the instruction statements is given in the order in which they are executed.

Statement 0601, GOSEEK, packs the value of KEYA (+12) into DUBPAK. DUBPAK then appears to be:

DUBPAK | 0 0 0 0 0 0 0 0 0 0 0 0 0 1 2 C |

Statement 0602 converts the packed decimal value of the contents of DUBPAK into fixed-point format in general register 6. KEYA was packed into a doubleword area in Statement 0601 because the second operand in a CVB instruction statement must be a packed decimal value in a doubleword storage location. General register 6 would now have a configuration of:

register 6 | 0 000 0000 | 0000 0000 | 0000 0000 | 0000 1100 | +12

Statement 0603 performs a Shift Left Algebraic instruction statement. The relative address of KEYA (which is +12) is the 12th 16-byte table segment. By shifting left algebraic for four bit positions, the value in general register 6 is being multiplied by 16, resulting in the relative table address for KEYA; 12 times 16 equals 192. The SLA instruction statement would affect general register 6 in the following manner:

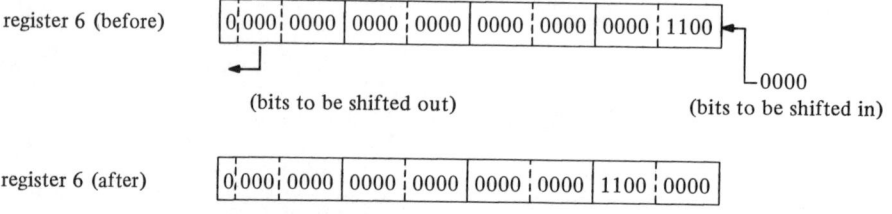

Statement 0604 is a Branch & Link to LOOKUP. At the time the branch is accomplished, general register 3 contains the address of Statement 0605.

Statement 0614, LOOKUP, loads the address of PRETAB into general register 8. Because this example assumes that the address of PRETAB at program execution time is 32,404, general register 8 now appears as:

register 8 *binary* | 0 000 0000 | 0000 0000 | 0111 1110 | 1001 0100 |

hex | 0 | 0 | 0 | 0 | 7 | E | 9 | 4 |

Loop Controls and Table Look-Ups

SYSTEM / 370 ASSEMBLER CODING FORM

Name	Operation	Operand	Identification Sequence No.
*			0601
GOSEEK	PACK	DUBPAK,KEYA	0602
	CVB	R6,DUBPAK	0603
	SLA	R6,4	0604
	BAL	R3,LOOKUP	0605
	PACK	DUBPAK,KEYB	0606
	CVB	R6,DUBPAK	0607
	SLA	R6,4	0608
	BAL	R3,LOOKUP	0609
	PACK	DUBPAK,KEYC	0610
	CVB	R6,DUBPAK	0611
	SLA	R6,4	0612
	BAL	R3,LOOKUP	0613
	BC	15,END	
*			
*			
LOOKUP	LA	R8,PRETAB	0614
	AR	R8,R6	0615
	CLI	0(R8),C'D'	0616
	BC	7,NODATA	0617
	MVC	OUTDATA(16),0(R8)	0618
	BAL	R5,PUTDATA	0619
	BCR	15,R3	0620
NODATA			
*			

FIGURE 14-12a

SYSTEM / 370 ASSEMBLER CODING FORM

NAME	OPERATION	OPERAND	COMMENTS	ID
PUTDATA	, , ,	, , ,		0630
*				
*				
*			CONSTANTS AND WORK AREAS	
R3	EQU	3		0660
R5	EQU	5		0661
R6	EQU	6		0662
R8	EQU	8		0663
*				0664
PRETAB	DC	CL16' '		0665
TABLE	DC	50CL16' '		0666
KEYA	DC	CL2'12'		0667
KEYB	DC	CL2'24'		0668
KEYC	DC	CL2'44'		0669
DUBPAK	DC	D'0'		0670
OUTDATA	DC	CL16' '		0671
*				0672
*				0673
				0674
				0675
				0676
				0677

FIGURE 14-12b

Loop Controls and Table Look-Ups

Statement 0615 adds general register 6 to general register 8, with the sum of this addition then residing in general register 8. Register 6 contains the relative address of table segment 12 and register 8 contains the execution-time address of PRETAB, the resulting sum being the direct actual address of table segment 12. The configuration of general register 8 after the addition would be:

register 8 | 0000 0000 | 0000 0000 | 0111 1111 | 0101 0100 | +32,596

Statement 0616 compares the first byte of table segment 12 to see if it contains valid data. A valid table segment must contain a character 'D' in the first position for the purposes of this example.

Statement 0617 tests the Condition Code that results from the "compare" in Statement 0616. If the compare results in an equal condition, the program logic falls through to Statement 0618. If the compare is unequal, the branch is taken to NODATA in order to avoid attempting to process the table segment. In this particular instance, the compare would have been equal and the branch would not have been taken.

Statement 0618 moves the table segment that is addressed by general register 8 into a field labeled OUTDATA.

Statement 0619 is a Branch & Link to an assumed subroutine that processes the data contained in OUTDATA. When that subroutine is completed the program logic processing should return to Statement 0620.

Statement 0620 is a forced branch to the address contained in register 3. At this point of the program, general register 3 contains the address of Statement 0605.

Statement 0605, the next statement to be executed, packs the contents of KEYB (+24) into DUBPAK. DUBPAK then appears as:

DUBPAK | 0 | 0 | 0 | 0 | 0 | 0 | 0 | 0 | 0 | 0 | 0 | 0 | 0 | 2 | 4 | C |

Statement 0606 takes the value of DUBPAK and converts it to a fixed-point value in general register 6. Register 6 would then appear to contain:

register 6 *binary* | 0000 0000 | 0000 0000 | 0000 0000 | 0001 1000 | +24

hex | 0 | 0 | 0 | 0 | 0 | 0 | 1 | 8 |

Statement 0607 shifts the integer-bits of general register 6 toward the left for a total algebraic shift of four bit positions. This effectively multiplies the value in register 6 by 16, or 24 times 16 equals 384.

register 6 *binary* | 0000 0000 | 0000 0000 | 0000 0001 | 1000 0000 | +384

hex | 0 | 0 | 0 | 0 | 0 | 1 | 8 | 0 |

Statement 0608 is a Branch & Link to Statement 0614, LOOKUP, with the return address of Statement 0609 being placed into general register 3.

Statement 0614 loads the address of PRETAB into general register 8.

Statement 0615 adds the relative address of the current table segment (+384), which is contained in register 6, to the actual current address of PRETAB (+32,404) as contained in register 8—the resulting sum residing in register 8. General register 8 now contains the actual direct address of table segment 24.

Statements 0616 through 0619 perform the processing logic as explained previously.

Statement 0620 is a forced branch to the address contained in general register 3, which at this point in the program is the address of Statement 0609.

Statement 0609 packs the contents of KEYC into DUBPAK. KEYC contains "44," representing the pointer key to table segment 44. DUBPAK would now appear to contain.

DUBPAK | 0 0 | 0 0 | 0 0 | 0 0 | 0 0 | 0 0 | 0 4 | 4 C |

Statement 0610 converts the packed decimal value of DUBPAK to a fixed-point value in register 6.

register 6 | 0000 0000 | 0000 0000 | 0000 0000 | 0010 1100 | +44

Statement 0611 shifts the binary contents of general register 6 toward the left algebraically for a length of four bit positions. This action represents 44 times 16 equals 704, creating the relative address of table segment 44.

Statement 0612 is a Branch & Link to Statement 0614, at the same time placing the address of Statement 0613 into general register 3.

Statement 0614 loads the actual address of PRETAB (+32,404) into general register 8.

Statement 0615 adds general register 6 to general register 8, with the sum residing in register 8. This has added together the actual address of PRETAB (+32,404) and the relative address of table segment 44 (+704) to create the actual direct address for that table segment (+33,108).

Statement 0616 through 0619 are the logic statements that process the data. The branch out of Statement 0617 into Statement 0620 is taken in this instance because table segment 44 does not contain valid data.

Statement 0620 branches to Statement 0613, the address contained in general register 3.

Statement 0613 is a forced branch to an assumed routine, representing the end of this module.

Not all table segment direct addressing computations are achievable with shifting techniques. Assuming that general register 6 contains the binary value of a table segment, in this instance segment 5, Table 14-3 shows the values obtainable by shifting. The factor by which the table segment number is being multiplied implies the byte-length of each individual table segment.

If the table segment length is not one of those specified in this list, a common multiply routine, either fixed-point or packed decimal, may be used to determine the relative address of the table segment. Assuming that the table segment length is 17 bytes and the programmer wishes to compute the relative address of table segment 19, the packed decimal multiply routine could be coded as:

```
        PACK    DUBPAK , KEY            0001
        MP      DUBPAK, =PL2 ' 17 '     0002
        CVB     6 , DUBPAK              0003
```

Loop Controls and Table Look-Ups 491

TABLE 14-3

Table Segment Length (Bytes)	Instruction Statement	Resulting Relative Address in Register 6	Shift Routine is Equal to:
2 bytes	SLA 6,1	10	5 x 2 equals 10
4	SLA 6,2	20	5 x 4 equals 20
8	SLA 6,3	40	5 x 8 equals 40
16	SLA 6,4	80	5 x 16 equals 80
32	SLA 6,5	160	5 x 32 equals 160
64	SLA 6,6	320	5 x 64 equals 320
128	SLA 6,7	640	5 x 128 equals 640
256	SLA 6,8	1280	5 x 256 equals 1280
512	SLA 6,9	2560	5 x 512 equals 2560
Etc....			

Statement 0001 converts the data contents of KEY (the table segment number, now equal to 19) by packing it into DUBPAK. DUBPAK now appears as:

DUBPAK | 0 | 0 | 0 | 0 | 0 | 0 | 0 | 0 | 0 | 0 | 0 | 0 | 0 | 0 | 1 | 9 | C |

Statement 0002 multiplies the contents of DUBPAK by a packed decimal literal of +17, representing the byte-length of each table segment. DUBPAK now contains +323, the relative address of table segment 19.

DUBPAK | 0 | 0 | 0 | 0 | 0 | 0 | 0 | 0 | 0 | 0 | 0 | 0 | 3 | 2 | 3 | C |

Statement 0003 performs a Convert to Binary (CVB) instruction statement, taking the packed decimal value of DUBPAK and placing it into general register 6 in fixed-point format.

register 6 | 0000 0000 | 0000 0000 | 0000 0001 | 0100 0011 | +323

| 0 | 0 | 0 | 0 | 0 | 1 | 4 | 3 |

The fixed-point multiplication routine to accomplish this same process could be coded as:

```
PACK    DUBPAK , KEY        0001
CVB     6 , DUBPAK          0002
MH      6 , =H ' 17 '       0003
```

Statement 0001 packs KEY into DUBPAK; DUBPAK now would contain a value of +19.
Statement 0002 converts the value of DUBPAK (+19) into a fixed-point format value in general register 6.

register 6 | 0 000 0000 | 0000 0000 | 0000 0000 | 0001 0011 | +19

| 0 | 0 | 0 | 0 | 0 | 0 | 1 | 3 |

Statement 0003 multiplies general register 6 by a halfword literal value of +17, the latter value representing the length of the table segements. General register 6 now would contain a fixed-point value of +323, the relative address of table segment 19.

register 6

0	000	0000	0000	0000	0000	0001	0100	0011
	0	0	0	0	0	1	4	3

+323

Both the fixed-point multiply routine and the packed decimal multiply routine have efficiently determined the relative address of table segment 19. It should be carefully noted, however, that this is only the *relative* address of the table segment. This value must be added to an *actual* address available during program execution, to combine to create the *actual direct* address of the table segment.

The actual address of the beginning point of the table can be obtained in several ways. In Table 14-2, the programmer has established a "dummy" field of the same length as a table segment, placing that field immediately prior to the table itself. By doing this, the table key could be multiplied by the number of bytes in each segment and arrive at a relative address to be added to the address of PRETAB. If the relative address of the key had been added to the actual address of TABLE, the resulting direct address would have been 16 bytes higher in the table than the address desired; for example:

$$\frac{\text{Table Segment Key}}{(4)} \text{ times } \frac{\text{Segment Length}}{(16)} \text{ plus } \frac{\text{Address of Table}}{(32,420)} \text{ equals } 32,484$$

The total address of 32,484 points to the beginning of table segment 5, not table segment 4. If you do not want to set up a "dummy" area for preaddressing of the table, you may arrive at the proper direct address by the following type of calculation:

$$\frac{\text{Table Segment Key}}{(4)} \text{ less 1 times } \frac{\text{Segment Length}}{(16)} \text{ plus } \frac{\text{Address of Table}}{(32,420)} \text{ equals } 32,468$$

or by

$$\frac{\text{Table Segment Key}}{(4)} \text{ times } \frac{\text{Segment Length}}{(16)} \text{ less } \frac{\text{Segment Length}}{(16)} \text{ plus } \frac{\text{Address of Table}}{(32,420)}$$

equals 32,468

The values shown in these calculations should be replaced by the actual values of the table segment length and address in each unique table to be created. These examples contain the values relevant to the illustrated table of directly addressed data for the purpose of this presentation only.

If the table segment length was 21 bytes, the two calculations just referred to could have been coded as:

Loop Controls and Table Look-Ups

```
        PACK    DUBPAK , KEY
        SP      DUBPAK , =PL1 ' 1 '
        MP      DUBPAK , =PL2 ' 21 '
        CVB     6 , DUBPAK
        LA      7 , TABLE
        AR      7 , 6
```

or as:

```
        PACK    DUBPAK , KEY
        MP      DUBPAK , =PL2 ' 21 '
        SP      DUBPAK , =PL2 ' 21 '
        CVB     6 , DUBPAK
        LA      7 , TABLE
        AR      7 , 6
```

TABLES CONTAINING MIXED DATA

It is most likely that the average table to be established will contain EBCDIC character-formatted data. However, a table may comprise data that is recognized in hexadecimal format, binary format, fixed-point arithmetic format, packed decimal format, or any combinations of these. The mixed formatting of the table can be organized by the DC statements or by program execution.

For the purpose of defining the logic of this concept, the desired content of the table should first be described. A typical table might be constructed of the following data.

Table = 250 segments
One segment = four fields
    Field 1   three bytes of character data.
    Field 2   four bytes of fixed-point values on fullword boundary alignment.
    Field 3   six bytes of packed decimal data.
    Field 4   three bytes of character data.

This table is initialized in the following way:

1. The table key values, occupying the first three bytes of each table segment, are loaded by the problem program. These three bytes should be initialized as blanks prior to the loading of the key values.
2. Field 2, representing a fullword containing a fixed-point value, should be initialized as a fixed-point value of +0. Fixed-point values may be added to the value of this field and stored there for subsequent use. In some instances it will not be known if a valid fixed-point value has already been entered into the field prior to attempting a fixed-point "add" of this field to another value. This is the reason for initializing the field to a +0 fixed-point value.
3. Field 3, to be used as a six-byte packed decimal field, should be initialized with a packed decimal value of +0 for the same reason that Field 2 was initialized. Packed decimal data may, or may not, be accumulated in the field and the program logic may attempt to use this field for arithmetic operations prior to the insertion into it of any tangible value.
4. Field 4 contains character data in most table segments, but not in all. This data is placed in the table during program execution. This field should be initialized as blanks.

A relatively easy way to meet the requirements of the formatting necessary for this table would be to use hexadecimal formatting when stating the DC (Define Constant). Keep in mind that in this example the first byte of the second field in each segment must always be aligned on a fullword boundary alignment.

```
ALIGN   DC    F'0'
FILL1   DC    CL1'ƀ'
TABLE   DC    250X'404040000000000000000000C404040'
                   \____/_____/_____/\____/
                   Field 1  Field 2    Field 3    Field 4
```

The DC for ALIGN sets that address on a fullword boundary alignment; therefore, every fourth byte after this label is on a fullword boundary. Because it is required that Field 2 be on a fullword alignment and Field 1 is only three bytes long, the one-byte constant FILL1 has been used to move the beginning point of TABLE one byte further in storage. TABLE now starts three bytes short of being on the next fullword boundary. Because the first three bytes of TABLE use up this shortage, Field 2 starts on a fullword aligned location. Inasmuch as each table segment is a total of 16 bytes long (equivalent to four fullwords), all subsequent table segments also have Field 2 on a fullword boundary alignment.

In looking at the DC statement for TABLE, you will note that all fields have now been initialized in accordance with the table requirements.

- Field 1 (three bytes equals six hex digits) is initialized with blanks, represented by '404040.'
- Field 2 (four bytes equals eight hex digits) contains a fixed-point +0 value, X'00000000.'
- Field 3 (six bytes equals twelve hex digits) contains a valid packed decimal value of +0, X'00000000000C'—the low-order 'C' representing the plus sign for the field.
- Field 4 (three bytes equals six hex digits) is also set as blanks, X'404040'.

As shown, all fields are initialized and the DC statement has specified a total table length of 250 of these segments, all formatted identically. The table is now ready to be loaded and utilized.

During the use of this table by the problem program, certain fields may serve as limited accumulators. For example, assume that the six-byte packed decimal field in each table segment is to be used as an accumulator until a certain condition occurs. When that event takes place, the packed decimal value in Field 3 of each table segment is extracted and that field should be reinitialized to a +0 value. Assuming that the values have already been extracted, the subroutine to reinitialize Field 3 in each segment could be coded as:

```
RESETF3   LA    10, TABLE+7         00001
          LA    9, 250              00002
LOOPSET   ZAP   0(6,10),PL1'0'      00003
          AH    10,H'16'            00004
          BCT   9, LOOPSET          00005
          BC    15, ALLSET          00006
```

Statement 00001 loads the address of TABLE+7 into general register 10. The address generated by TABLE+7 operand points to the first byte of the packed decimal field in the first table segment.

Statement 00002 uses the Load Address instruction to place the value of +250 into general register 9. Register 9 is the Branch on Count (BCT) loop control register, and once loaded with this value it allows 250 cycles through the LOOPSET routine.

Statement 00003 uses the ZAP instruction to reset to zero the packed decimal field of the table segment currently pointed to by general register 10. Although a one-byte literal is used as the second operand, the first operand specifies a byte length of six bytes for the statement. The ZAP resets all six bytes of hex digits to zero with the exception of the low-order nibble, which contains a valid packed decimal sign of 'C'.

Statement 00004 increments general register 10 by a count of 16 bytes in order to point to the packed field of the next table segment.

Statement 00005 is the Branch on Count instruction for loop control. Until general register 9 is decremented to zero the branch to LOOPSET will continue to be taken.

Statement 00006 is a forced branch to an assumed subroutine, indicating that the packed decimal fields of the table have all been reset to +0.

As mentioned throughout this entire section on tables and look-up routines, there are many variations and techniques for accomplishing these concepts in actual application. Table formatting and the subsequent searches of the table must be tailored to the needs of the problem program. Even at this, you are given the challenge of discovering, or designing, the most efficient technique for your application.

15

Editing Data

THE EDITING INSTRUCTIONS

Instruction: Edit

mnemonic	hex code	operand format
ED	DE	$D_1 (L, B_1), D_2 (B_2)$

This instruction modifies the contents of the second operand by converting it from packed decimal format to zoned decimal format. The converted data, in zoned decimal, is then further modified by the functional control of the edit pattern. The functional address of the edit pattern is specified by the first operand of the statement.

The processing of data occurs from left to right; one byte at a time is processed for the length specified, or implied, by the first operand.

More definitive information on editing capabilities of this instruction is covered within this chapter.

CC	BC	Condition
0	8	The edit resulted in a zero field.
1	4	The edit resulted in a field value of less than zero (-).
2	2	The edit resulted in a field value greater than zero (+).

*   *   *

Instruction: Edit and Mark

mnemonic	hex code	operand format
EDMK	DF	$D_1 (L, B_1), D_2 (B_2)$

This instruction basically performs the same function as the EDIT instruction. In addition, however, a special audit is made during the time that the second operand source data is being modified under the control of the edit pattern specified by the first operand. This audit consists of a scan in which the instruction, during its left to right modification of the data, looks for the encounter of the first significant character (nonzero resulting character) placed into the edit pattern prior to finding a "significant start" character in the edit pattern itself. If such an encounter occurs, the instruction places the address of that byte (the first significant character) into general register 1. If an edit pattern "significant start" character is encountered prior to the insertion of a significant character into the pattern, the storage of the address into general register 1 is not accomplished. Considerably more information and detail regarding the use of this instruction is presented in the subsequent portions of this chapter.

CC	BC	Condition
0	8	The edit resulted in a zero field.
1	4	The edit resulted in a field value of less than zero (-).
2	2	The edit resulted in a field value of more than zero (+).

THE APPLICATION OF THE EDITING INSTRUCTIONS

The Necessity of Editing

The internal configuration of data and fixed-point or decimal values can alternately, or selectively, be thought of as consisting of binary, hexadecimal, or character representations.

These representations, however, cannot always be visually reproduced on a graphic output device in that same form without some manipulation of the configuration. For the purpose of this discussion, a graphic output device shall be interpreted as any output unit on which data representation appears in a visual character form. This includes printer units, console typewriters, cathode-ray display units, and similar equipment. Regular EBCDIC character representations may be reproduced directly on such devices without alteration of their configuration. Fixed-point and packed decimal values, however, require a certain amount of transformation before being transmitted to the output unit. Some of this transformation is accomplished by the use of the editing instructions and some by the applications of various instructions, depending on the type of data to be presented. Because the edit instructions require that the data to be edited be in packed decimal form, numeric character representation is the only type of data that can be edited with these instructions. During the editing itself, however, alphabetic and special characters may be inserted into various sections of the edited fields as a part of that function.

Several common types of editing are:

- Suppression of leading zeros in a numeric field.
- Insertion of punctuation in a numeric field.
- Identifying positive and negative values by inserting such descriptives as—CR - + etc.
- Addition of dollar-signs ($) to monetary values, either in a fixed-position or with a "floating" capability.

In order to relate these applications to actual practice, Table 15-1 shows the general content of data that is to be edited and the various output forms that the data may assume through editing.

The means of accomplishing these editing routines are discussed in detail in subsequent paragraphs. At this point, however, it is important to understand the necessity of presenting numeric data in a format that is not only easy to read and evaluate, but in a form that also relates to the association of that numeric to its representation. This would mean, for example, that if a numeric field is used to express the quantity of square inches in different sizes of floor space, it would be illogical to present that field as $268.93; the presentation of such a value in the form of "26,893

Editing Data

TABLE 15-1

Data Field Content	Edited Output Data
0 0 3 9 5 6 1 C	395.61
0 0 3 9 5 6 1 F	395.61+
0 0 3 9 5 6 1 F	$ 395.61
0 0 3 9 5 6 1 C	$395.61
2 5 7 8 8 1 4 D	25,788.14–
2 5 7 8 8 1 4 D	25788.14CR
2 5 7 8 8 1 4 D	(25,788.14)
0 0 0 0 0 0 6 F	6
0 0 0 0 0 0 6 F	.06
0 0 0 0 0 0 6 F	6¢

SQ. IN." would be considerably more proper in addition to being self-descriptive. In many instances, data of this type would be in columnar form; therefore, column headings may be used to describe the representation of the numeric values. This might appear as:

```
SQUARE INCHES
   26,893
      426
    5,830
```

Here, the values are correctly expressed and the columnar heading describes their representation. When formatting data to an output device that creates visual information, it is of prime importance for that data to be self-communicating. It must be visually easy to read, logically presented, and bear a descriptive relationship to the overall meaning of what it represents. Proper editing and presentation formatting can accomplish all of these goals. Compare the two sample listings and note the self-descriptive style of the second as compared to the general presentation used in the first listing.

#	LENGTH	WIDTH	WEIGHT	$
0039658	368	36	36-5	95.00
0078621	52	22	3-11	7.00
0113965	89	48	12	25.00
PRODUCT NUMBER	LENGTH (FEET)	WIDTH (INCHES)	WEIGHT PER LINEAR FOOT	COST PER MEASURED UNIT
39658	368 '	36 "	36# 5 oz	$95.00 lin. ft
78621	52 '	22 "	3# 11 oz	$ 7.00 lb
113965	89 '	48 "	12#	$25.00 ea.

In the second listing, the descriptive representation is often presented in both the columnar heading and with the data under that heading; the "length" heading indicates the representation of the values in "quantity of feet" and the numeric value itself is followed by the standard symbol (an apostrophe) for "feet." The printed, or displayed, data that is generated by any single program is normally expected to be used by numerous personnel who are concerned with the overall system. To meet the comprehension level of all personnel, which would normally vary quite considerably, the output data should be in the most logical, explicit form.

The Composition of the Edit Instruction Statements

The actual editing function is performed by either one of two instructions: the Edit instruction or the Edit & Mark instruction. Because both of these perform relatively similar functions, the makeup of the edit functions will be described in detail before approaching the instructions themselves. The components that are active during the execution of an editing routine might well be considered to be separate little instructions in themselves; there are many editing variations made possible by merely using a different combination of these optional components. In general, then, the Edit instruction and the Edit instruction statement consist of the following items:

1. The Source Field
2. The Edit Pattern
    a. Insertion Characters
    b. Digit Select Characters
    c. Significant Start Characters
    d. Field Separation Characters
3. Significant Trigger (S-Trigger)

Each of these items have a number of different rules and variations that determine the manner in which the edit instruction performs.

The Source Field

The source field is the originating data storage area that contains the numeric value to be edited. It may consist of enough data to fill 255 bytes of edited output, under the stipulation that the overall editing process does not involve more than a maximum length of 256 bytes including the length of the edit pattern. The data contained within the source field must be in packed decimal form. The packed value contained within the source field does not have to be a "signed" value, but if it is, then the sign must exist in the right-most half-byte of the field. All other half-bytes within the field must contain valid decimal digits—hexadecimal numeric digits of '0' through '9'. If the edit is to be performed on a source field that contains multiple packed decimal values, each value may contain a "sign" in the right-most nibble (half-byte).

Single value source field

Multiple value source field

The source field is edited into the Edit Pattern which would usually exist in a storage area used as the output location.

The Edit Pattern

The Edit Pattern contains the specifications of what type of editing functions are to be performed. Unlike the source field, each byte of the Pattern must be in unpacked, zoned format. The Pattern is considered to consist of:

- Fill Characters (Insertion Characters)
- Digit Select Character(s)
- Significant Start Character(s)
- Field Separator Character(s)—only in a multiple field edit
- Any character(s) to be placed unaltered into the edited output field

These configurations, some of which do not represent existing printable characters, each participate in their own way to control the editing process. A general description of each of these is offered here. The overall function that they perform is covered in the discussion of Functional Characteristics of Editing.

Fill characters. This is also referred to as an insertion character. It may be any valid character including a blank, $, *,), (, #, etc. The Fill Character is used to replace leading nonsignificant digits that exist in the source field.

Digit Select character. This character consists of a hex configuration of X'20', an unprintable character. It is used to indicate a position within the Edit Pattern that is to be filled with a numeric digit from the source field if one is available. The Digit Select Character is always replaced by either the Fill Character of the Edit Pattern or a numeric digit from the source field.

Significant Start character. An unprintable hexadecimal configuration of X'21' is used to signal to the editing function that all remaining (low-order) numeric digits in the source field are to be considered significant and that suppression of leading zeros is to terminate at this point.

Field Separator character. A hexadecimal configuration (unprintable) of X'22', this character is only used when the edit process is to act on a source field containing multiple numeric values. It effectively separates the multiple values by appearing as a blank between each of the individual values.

Others. In addition, any valid character that is required within the final edited output may be inserted within the Edit Pattern.

The Significant Trigger (S-Trigger)

The Significant Trigger is actually a "switch," or condition setting, that is inspected during the editing process in order to determine various processing decisions. The S-Trigger has two conditions—OFF, which is equal to '0', and ON, which is equal to '1'. During the process of editing, the S-Trigger may be alternately switched ON/OFF several times, depending entirely on the configuration of the Edit Pattern and the contents of the source field being edited. The conditions that turn the S-Trigger ON are:

- Encountering a Significant Start Character in the Pattern.
- Insertion into the Edit Pattern of a significant numeric digit from the source field prior to encountering a Significant Start Character in the Pattern.

The conditions that would turn the S-Trigger OFF (assuming it was in an ON status) are:

- Encountering a Field Separator Character in the Edit Pattern.
- Detection of a plus sign (+) digit in the low-order nibble (half-byte) of a value in the source field.
- Initialization of each edit operation.

In addition, the edit operation uses the status of the S-Trigger to determine the setting of the PSW Condition Code at the end of each edit function. If a multiple field edit has been performed in which values of both positive and negative amounts were present, the resulting Condition Code would indicate only the status of the last value that was edited.

Up to this point, the description of the functions and components of editing operations has been limited considerably to the individual structure of each. This in itself does not tend to present a lucid interpretation of editing characteristics. It is necessary, however, to describe these items merely for the purpose of becoming familiar with the terms and nomenclature used to explain the overall performance of Edit instructions. It is recommended that as the remaining portion of this chapter is presented, an occasional reference and review be made of the preceding paragraphs. This will aid you in comprehending the many facets and variations possible in editing.

Functional Characteristics of Editing

Now that the basic components and their individual actions in an edit instruction statement have been described, it is time to put them all together in order to examine the interaction between them under various circumstances. A preface to the examination should be a brief description of the normal functions of these components. This may be considered to be the general rules of operation for an edit statement and is presented, as follows, in numbered form.

1. The source field (the "sending" field) is changed from packed decimal format to zoned decimal format (EBCDIC) as each numeric digit is edited under control of the Edit Pattern.
2. The editing scan, and the inspection of the Edit Pattern, moves from left to right (high-order to low-order) for the length specified or implied by the length of the Pattern.
3. The edited source field, including any additional characters inserted by the Pattern, replaces the Edit Pattern in its entirety.

Editing Data

4. In order to edit another source field into the same location at a subsequent time, the Edit Pattern must be completely reinitialized.

Because certain characters within the Edit Pattern do not have a printable representation, pseudo-characters will be used at certain points within this text to represent them. These are:

- ƀ   A valid blank; X'40'
- ȡ   Digit Select Character; 'X20'
- $ Significant Start Character; X'21'
- ƒ   Field Separator Character; X'22'

A practical way to prepare for an edit function is to establish the Edit Pattern as a constant. It may then be moved into the output field area before each edit instruction statement, reinitializing that area with the Pattern as required. It is suggested that the Edit Pattern constant be defined in hexadecimal configuration, thus eliminating the need of finding a substitute pseudo-character to represent the nonprintable editing components. A constant of this type might appear as:

In pseudo-character representation this same pattern would be coded as:

    EDPATRN   DC   C ' ƀȡȡȡȡ$ȡ '

When the source program has been compiled, however, and the source listing of the program has been printed, this constant (if coded in pseudo-character form) would appear as:

    EDPATRN   DC   C '   '

Because the constant was expressed as being in character form, the Pattern itself appears as blanks. This is because there is no printable character representation for those components of the Pattern. It is much more practical, therefore, to define the Edit Pattern constant as hexadecimal form in order for the source program listing to contain a printable representation of that Pattern.

Once the Edit Pattern has been moved into the output field, the Edit instruction is coded and the process begins.

The left-most (high-order) byte of the Edit Pattern is evaluated as the "Fill" Character. Source field digits (half-bytes) are then passed to the Edit Pattern one at a time, from left to right. The Fill Character is used to replace nonsignificant numeric digits (hex zero digits) from the source field until the first significant (nonzero) digit from the source field is passed to the Pattern, or until a Significant Start Character is encountered within the Pattern, whichever might occur first. If a significant digit from the source field is passed to the edit prior to encountering a Significant Start Character in the Edit Pattern, that digit and all remaining source field digits for that particular value replace the remaining Digit Select Characters in that portion of the Pattern. Inasmuch as the passing of the significant digit to the Edit Pattern has now turned the S-Trigger ON, any subsequent Significant Start Characters within this portion of the Pattern are ignored. If a Significant Start Character is encountered in the Pattern prior to the time when the source field passes a significant digit, the S-Trigger is set to an ON condition and all remaining digits in the current value replace existing Digit Select Characters remaining within this portion of the Edit Pattern.

These last few statements have been rather lengthy, and quite probably confusing, so a closer, descriptive examination of how this would perform is in order.

Assume that an Edit Pattern exists as a constant, coded in hex format as:

    EDITPAT   DC   X'402020212020'

or

    EDITPAT   DC   C'bdd$dd'

Using this Edit Pattern as the base, the following illustrations will show the editing of two numeric values into this Pattern—one in which the Significant Start Character is encountered prior to a significant digit being passed from the source field; the other in which a significant digit is passed from the source field prior to encountering the Significant Start Character.

Example 1

Step 1

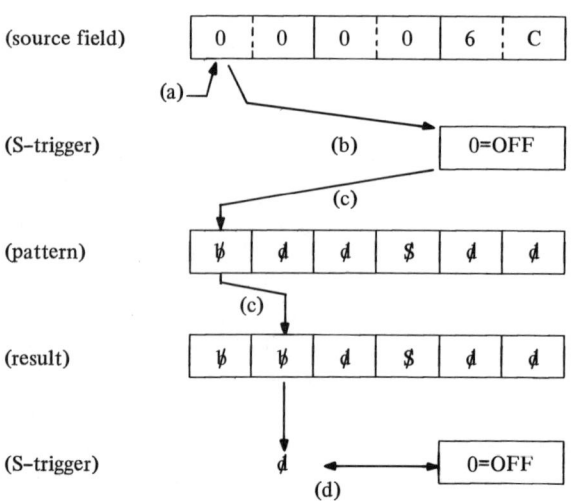

(a) The first digit of the source field is examined to see if it is a significant digit.

(b) Because it is not, the S-Trigger is inspected for an ON condition.

(c) The S-Trigger is OFF, consequently the Fill Character replaces the first Digit Select Character in the Pattern.

(d) The character replaced in the Pattern is inspected to see if it was a Significant Start Character. It was not, so the S-Trigger remains OFF.

Editing Data

Step 2

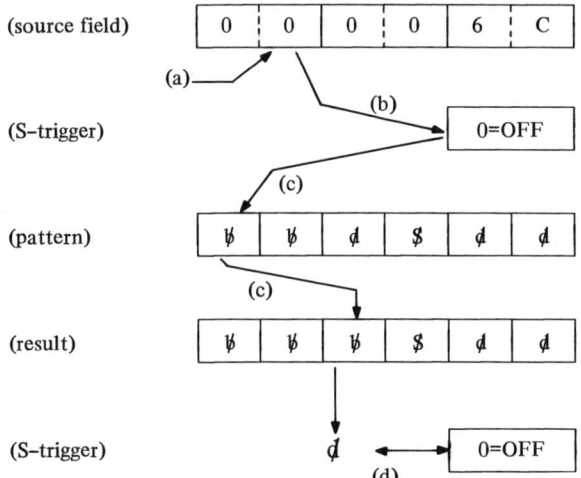

(a) The second digit of the source field is inspected.
(b) It is not a significant digit, so the S-Trigger is checked.
(c) It is OFF, resulting in the Fill Character being used to replace the second Digit Select Character in the Pattern.
(d) The character replaced by the Fill Character is not a Significant Start Character; therefore, the S-Trigger remains OFF.

Step 3

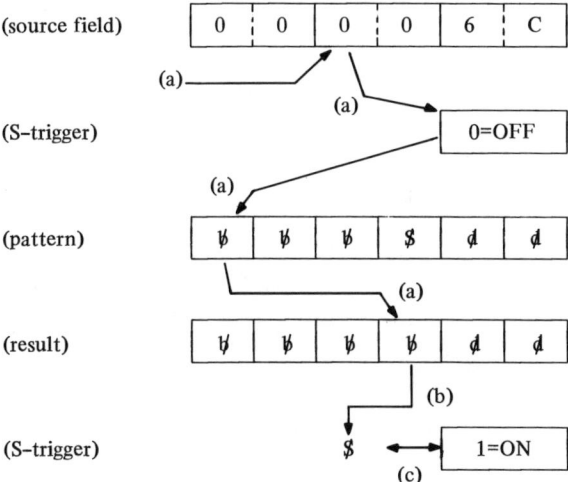

(a) The third digit of the source field is not a significant digit and the S-Trigger is not ON, so the Fill Character is used to replace the next available editing character in the Pattern.

(b) The character replaced by the Fill Character is inspected to see if it was a Significant Start Character.

(c) It was, so the S-Trigger is set to an ON condition. This indicates that remaining digits of the source field, whether significant or nonsignificant, will be placed into the Edit Pattern.

Step 4

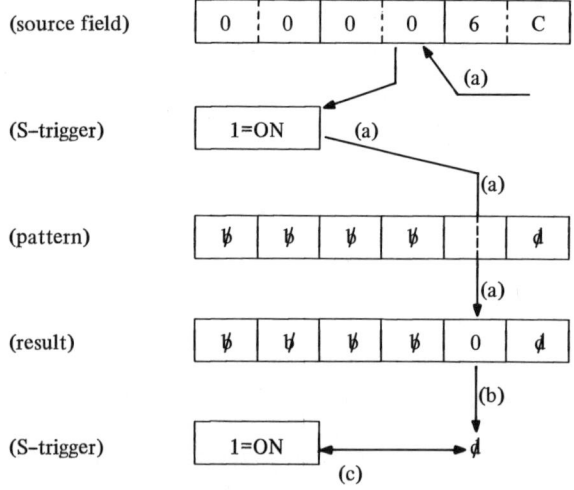

(a) The fourth digit of the source field is found to be nonsignificant, but because the S-Trigger is ON, that digit is sent to the Edit Pattern to replace the next available Digit Select Character.

(b) The character in the Pattern that was replaced by the source field digit is inspected to see if it was a Field Separator Character.

(c) Because it was not, the S-Trigger remains ON.

Step 5

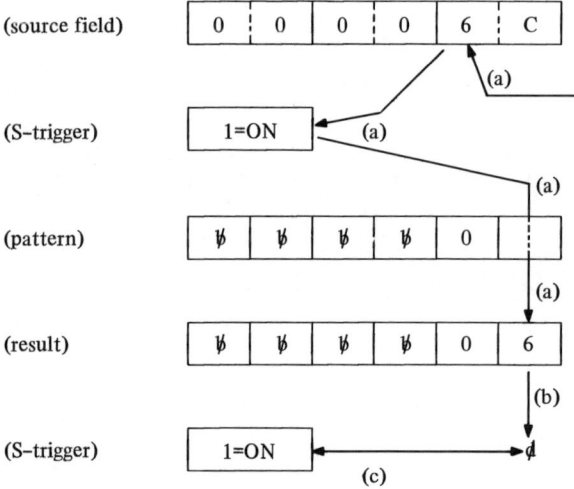

Editing Data

(a) The fifth digit of the source field is sent to replace the next available Digit Select Character in the Edit Pattern. This is done because either: (1) the source field digit was a significant digit, and/or (2) the S-Trigger was ON.

(b) The operation then inspects the character from the Pattern that was replaced by the source field digit to determine if it was a Field Separator Character.

(c) It was not, so the S-Trigger is not altered.

At this point the edit terminates, having completed the length assumed to be specified for this statement. If this Pattern were now printed or displayed on an output device it would appear as ... 06. Had the edit been specified to include one more byte of the source field, the encounter of a valid plus sign would have caused the editing operation to set the S-Trigger to an OFF condition.

Example 2

Step 1

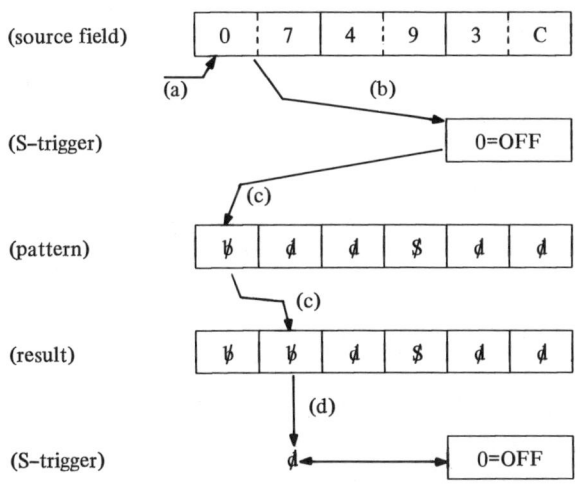

(a) As in the previous example, the first digit of the source field is inspected to see if it is a significant digit.

(b) It is not, so the S-Trigger is checked to see if it is ON.

(c) Because the S-Trigger is OFF, the nonsignificant digit in the source field is suppressed and the Fill Character replaces the first Digit Select Character in the Edit Pattern.

(d) The character from the Pattern that was replaced by the Fill Character is inspected and found not to be a Significant Start Character, so the S-Trigger is not affected.

Step 2

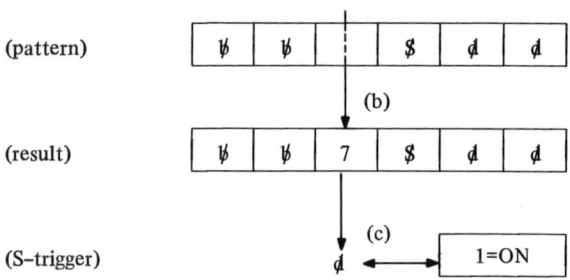

(a) The second character of the source field is inspected and found to be a significant digit.

(b) The S-Trigger is set to an ON condition and the significant source field digit is passed to the Edit Pattern, replacing the next Digit Select Character.

(c) That character, as it is replaced, is examined to determine if it was a Field Separator Character. Because it was not, the S-Trigger is not altered.

Step 3

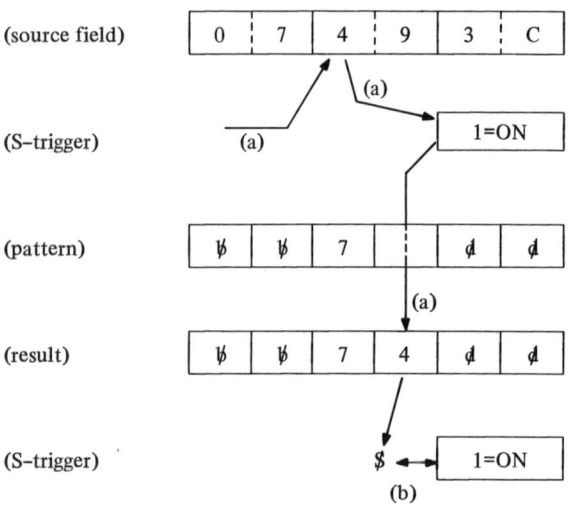

(a) The third character of the source field is passed to the Edit Pattern on the basis that the S-Trigger is ON and the character being passed is a significant digit.

(b) The Significant Start Character that was bumped out of the Edit Pattern does not affect the S-Trigger because it was already ON. Because the replaced character was not a Field Separator Character, the S-Trigger is not set to an OFF condition.

Editing Data

Step 4

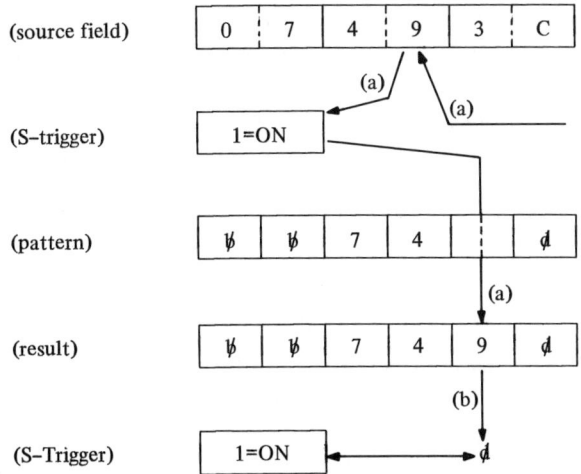

(a) In this step the fourth source field digit is sent to replace the corresponding Digit Select Character in the Edit Pattern; it is a significant digit and the S-Trigger is ON.

(b) The character replaced by the source field digit within the Edit Pattern is tested and found not to be a Field Separator Character. Accordingly, the S-Trigger setting is not changed.

Step 5

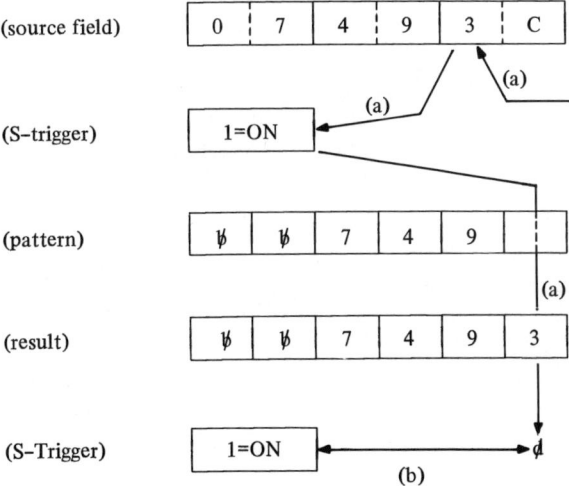

(a) At this point the fifth source field digit is sent to replace the last Digit Select Character in the Edit Pattern. That source field digit is a significant digit and the S-Trigger is ON.

(b) The character that was within the Pattern but was replaced by the source field digit is tested and noted as not being a Field Separator Character. On this basis the S-Trigger setting is not changed.

The length of the edit, as implied by the Pattern length, has been entirely scanned and the editing process terminates. The data residing in the Pattern, if displayed on an output device, would appear as:

    7493

To avoid confusion, it should be explained that the foregoing examples and illustrations are presented in a logical manner that is intended to communicate the process of the editing function. They do not include all of the technical functions performed by the edit, but they are sufficiently accurate and complete to present the concepts required to understand those functions. A more technical discourse on these examples would require considerably more space without really providing the reader with a better understanding.

It has now been explained how the S-Trigger, Significant Start Character, and the Digit Select Character create interacting processes within the editing functions. In effect, the examples so far have demonstrated the simple application of "zero suppression," or suppressing leading nonsignificant digits in a numeric value. Another option that is available, and frequently used, is the insertion of punctuation or characters within the value. This would be a process such as converting a number from '03952867' to '39,528.67'. The Edit Pattern would be initialized containing hexadecimal representation of the punctuation in the proper positions. An Edit Pattern of this type could be defined as a constant, in hexadecimal form, such as:

    EDPATRN   DC   X ' 40206B2020214B2020 '

or

    EDPATRN   DC   C ' ƀd , ddS . dd '

In this Edit Pattern, the source field value is implied to consist of a maximum value of +999999, which would be edited as 9,999.99. If the value edited into this Pattern is less than the maximum, all leading nonsignificant digits would be suppressed until either a significant digit passes from the source field or until after the Significant Start Character in the sixth byte of the Pattern has been encountered. If the first digit of the source field is a nonsignificant digit, the third byte of the Pattern, the comma, would be replaced by the Fill Character. Shown below are a quantity of source field values and the manner in which they would be edited into this Edit Pattern. It may be of help to review the rules regarding the S-Trigger conditions, the Significant Start Character, and the passing of a significant digit, prior to studying these examples.

Example 1

Editing Data

(edited result) | ƀ | ƀ | ƀ | ƀ | 3 | 6 | . | 7 | 5 |

(display output)   36.75

Example 2

(pattern) | ƀ | ȼ | , | ȼ | ȼ | $ | . | ȼ | ȼ |

(source field) | 0 | 0 | 0 | 0 | 0 | 1 |

(edited result) | ƀ | ƀ | ƀ | ƀ | ƀ | ƀ | . | 0 | 1 |

(display output)   .01

Example 3

(pattern) | ƀ | ȼ | , | ȼ | ȼ | $ | . | ȼ | ȼ |

(source field) | 4 | 7 | 1 | 1 | 6 | 9 |

(edited result) | ƀ | 4 | , | 7 | 1 | 1 | . | 6 | 9 |

(display output)   4,711.69

Example 4

(pattern) | ƀ | ȼ | , | ȼ | ȼ | $ | . | ȼ | ȼ |

(source field) | 0 | 8 | 3 | 3 | 5 | 7 |

(edited result) | ƀ | ƀ | ƀ | 8 | 3 | 3 | . | 5 | 7 |

(display output)   833.57

In many instances, especially when listing monetary values, the program may require a visible distinction between positive and negative values such as debits and credits or plus and minus amounts. As stated before, the S-Trigger will be turned OFF whenever the edit process encounters a positive/plus sign indication in the low-order half-byte of a packed decimal value. By utilizing this capability, it is now possible to identify all negative values edited. To apply such an edit, an Edit Pattern could be defined as:

    EDITPT   DC   X'402020214B202040C3D94B'

or

    EDITPT   DC   C'ɃddS.ddɃCR.'

If, when using this Pattern, the edit encounters a valid plus sign in the source field, the S-Trigger will be turned OFF after processing the last numeric digit transmitted from the source field. If the sign is other than a plus sign, the S-Trigger will remain ON and the suffix of 'ɃCR.' will appear immediately following the actual value.

The following packed decimal source fields are shown as they would be transformed into printed or displayed output when using this Edit Pattern.

Example 1

(pattern) | Ƀ | d | d | $ | . | d | d | Ƀ | C | R | . |

(source field) | 0 | 3 | 4 | 5 | 0 | C |

(edited result) | Ƀ | Ƀ | 3 | 4 | . | 5 | 0 | Ƀ | Ƀ | Ƀ | Ƀ |

(output)   34.50

Example 2

(pattern) | Ƀ | d | d | $ | . | d | d | Ƀ | C | R | . |

(source field) | 1 | 3 | 8 | 5 | 3 | D |

(edited result) | Ƀ | 1 | 3 | 8 | . | 5 | 3 | Ƀ | C | R | . |

(output)   138.53 CR.

Example 3

(pattern) | Ƀ | d | d | $ | . | d | d | Ƀ | C | R | . |

(source field) | 0 | 0 | 6 | 0 | 0 | B |

(edited result) | Ƀ | Ƀ | Ƀ | 6 | . | 0 | 0 | Ƀ | C | R | . |

(output)   6.00 CR.

Editing Data

Example 4

| (pattern) | ƀ | ɖ | ɖ | $ | . | ɖ | ɖ | ƀ | C | R | . |

| (source field) | | | | | | 0 | 0 | 0 | 2 | 9 | C |

| (edited result) | ƀ | ƀ | ƀ | ƀ | . | 2 | 9 | ƀ | ƀ | ƀ | ƀ |

(output)   .29

Example 5

| (pattern) | ƀ | ɖ | ɖ | $ | . | ɖ | ɖ | ƀ | C | R | . |

| (source field) | | | | | | 0 | 0 | 0 | 0 | 4 | D |

| (edited result) | ƀ | ƀ | ƀ | ƀ | . | 0 | 4 | ƀ | C | R | . |

(output)   .04 CR.

When using a computer system to create negotiable documents, such as payroll checks, it is desirable to print monetary values in such a way that the suppressed nonsignificant digits are replaced with a character other than a blank. One application of this type is to use an asterisk (*) as a Fill Character. An Edit Pattern using this character could appear as:

    EDITPAY   DC   X ' 5C20206B2020214B2020 '

or

    EDITPAY   DC   C ' *ɖɖ , ɖɖ$. ɖɖ '

In actual use, this Pattern would perform as:

Example 1

| (pattern) | * | ɖ | ɖ | , | ɖ | ɖ | $ | . | ɖ | ɖ |

| (source field) | | | 0 | 0 | 3 | 5 | 6 | 7 | 8 | A |

| (edited result) | * | * | * | * | 3 | 5 | 6 | . | 7 | 8 |

(output)   ****356.78

Example 2

(pattern)	*	¢	¢	,	¢	¢	$	.	¢	¢
(source field)			0	0	0	0	0	2	8	C
(edited result)	*	*	*	*	*	*	*	.	2	8

(output) *******.28

Example 3

(pattern)	*	¢	¢	,	¢	¢	$	.	¢	¢
(source field)			0	1	0	0	4	5	0	C
(edited result)	*	*	1	,	0	0	4	.	5	0

(output) **1,004.50

Example 4

(pattern)	*	¢	¢	,	¢	¢	$	.	¢	¢
(source field)			2	3	0	0	0	0	0	F
(edited result)	*	2	3	,	0	0	0	.	0	0

(output) *23,000.00

In each instance, the asterisks have been inserted up to the first significant digit or to the point where the S-Trigger was set ON by a Significant Start Character. The general purpose of this type of application is to discourage the alteration of monetary amounts on negotiable documents by not allowing any blanks to appear in the high-order positions of the printed value.

Multiple-field editing is accomplished through the use of the Field Separator Character. It is this character that guarantees that the S-Trigger is set to an OFF condition between each successive value encountered during a multiple-field edit. If, for example, an Edit Pattern is established for the purpose of editing three contiguous unsigned numeric fields, the Field Separator Character could be used to assure that zero-suppression is applied to each of the three fields.

When creating the Edit Pattern for a multifield edit, it should be remembered that it is necessary to specify the Fill Character only once—as the first (high-order) character of the Pattern.

Editing Data 515

The multiple fields to be edited, assuming that they are in adjacent program storage areas, and the Edit Pattern used to create the edited output, are:

    EDITMF   DC   X ' 402020212022202020214B2020222120 '

or as

    EDITMF   DC   C ' ƀddЅdϜddЅ . ddϜЅd '

The passing of the digits into the Edit Pattern, and the resulting edited Pattern and the source fields, can be shown as follows:

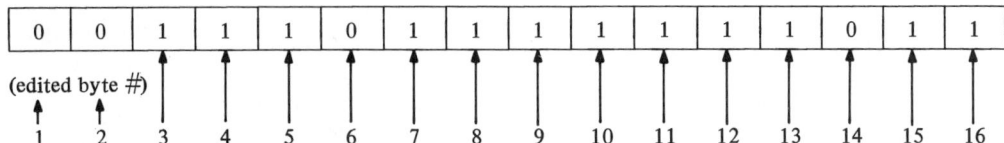

If printed, the edited data would appear as:

    265 3954.27   0

The following list shows the manner in which this edit is accomplished.

1. At initialization of the edit, the S-Trigger is OFF.
2. During the process of editing the value contained in FIELD1, the S-Trigger is turned ON when it encounters the significant digit '2'. As a result, at the completion of the third byte in the Edit Pattern, the S-Trigger is now ON.

3. In processing the sixth byte of the Edit Pattern, a Field Separator Character is detected and the S-Trigger is turned OFF. Zero-suppression is once again effected in the event that the next value to be edited contains leading nonsignificant digits. The Field Separator Character retains its position in the Edit Pattern in the form of a blank.
4. The first digit of FIELD2 happens to be a significant digit; therefore, it is passed directly to the seventh byte of the Pattern, at the same time setting the S-Trigger to an ON condition.
5. Because the S-Trigger is on, the remaining digits are passed to the Edit Pattern, replacing the Digit Select Characters in bytes 7, 8, 9, 10, 12 and 13.
6. Another Field Separator Character is encountered, this time in byte 14 of the Pattern, and once again the S-Trigger is placed in an OFF condition. The Field Separator Character is an effective blank in this position.
7. Byte 15 is a Significant Start Character that sets the S-Trigger ON for subsequent editing of FIELD3.
8. Although the last digit of the source field is a nonsignificant digit, the ON condition of the S-Trigger causes the edit to pass the '0' source digit to byte 16 of the Pattern.
9. After completion of the 16th byte of processing, the operation is terminated, assuming that the implied length of the Edit Pattern was not given as any other specific length.

Having described the components and functions of the editing instructions, it is time to review the instructions themselves and how they are used in an instruction statement.

Edit

The Edit instruction, coded as the mnemonic ED, is used to cause the initialization of any or all of the editing functions described in the preceding paragraphs. It performs in accordance with all of the editing rules heretofore specified. Although the variable functions have been suitably described, the entire means of editing a field of data to an output area in storage have not been detailed.

In many, or at least most, instances wherein data is transmitted to an output device, an output area of program storage has been defined by the programmer. This is usually coded in the form of a Define Storage (DS) statement or a Define Constant (DC) statement. For the purpose of general practice and good housekeeping, one area may be defined to accommodate each output device.

Each defined area is usually stated with a length attribute sufficiently large to accommodate the largest single string of data that is to be sent to that device. For example, a standard output printer unit is considered to have a line length of 132 printable characters; cathode-ray display devices have varying screen size capabilities, some of which utilize 240, 480, or 960 characters; most card punch units are construed to consist of an 80-byte character line. Although each of these devices could have a "storage output" area specifically designated for its maximum data length, the entire length of those areas need not be transmitted to the output unit. Inasmuch as the actual length of the data sent to the device is more likely dependent on the coding of the access method macroinstructions and DCB statements, which in turn may vary between the different types of operating systems, the means of specifying the length of the data to be transmitted will not be discussed here.

It is sufficient to know, at this time, that data sent from a given storage output area to an output device may vary in length. Assume, then, that the programmer has defined an output area labeled PRTLINE, and has then established an Edit Pattern as a constant labeled EDITPRT. Because the

Editing Data 517

intent is to edit a field of data into PRTLINE, print it, edit another value into PRTLINE where the previous data was edited, print that new value, etc., it is necessary to move the Edit Pattern into PRTLINE each time before issuing the EDIT instruction. The Edit Pattern is stated as:

    EDITPRT   DC   X ' 4020206B2020214B2020 '

or as

    EDITPRT   DC   CL10 ' ƀdd , dd$. dd '

The storage area from which the source data is to be extracted for editing is a packed decimal field that has been defined as:

    VALUEFLD   DC   PL4 ' 0 '

The logic of this program example is that the processing reads a data record from tape, packs a particular field from that record into VALUEFLD, edits VALUEFLD into an output area, and then prints the output area onto a printer unit. The GET and PUT macros used in this example are standard OS move-mode QSAM (Queued Sequential Access Method) macros, which generate the necessary action to access the tape file and display the necessary print line. The coding itself could be stated as:

```
BACK    GET    TAPEIN , INAREA                0001
        PACK   VALUEFLD , INAREA+25 (7)       0002
        MVC    PRTLINE+10 (10) , EDITPRT      0003
        ED     PRTLINE+10 (10) , VALUEFLD     0004
        PUT    PRTR , PRTLINE                 0005
        BC     15 , BACK                      0006
```

Statement 0001 is the coding of the OS QSAM GET macro. It reads the file named TAPEIN and places a logical record unit into an area defined as INAREA. A warning should be made that all of the names (labels) used by the operand in these coding statements have been originated by the programmer and in no way represent established naming convention. The file TAPEIN must be defined elsewhere in the program by a DCB macroinstruction and the field INAREA must have been defined by a DS or DC statement.

Statement 0002 packs a hypothetical seven-byte EBCDIC numeric field into the four-byte area VALUEFLD. The data field to be packed is located at a starting point of the 26th byte within the record residing in INAREA. It is, therefore, referred to as INAREA+25, in lieu of subdefining INAREA into labeled fields.

Statement 0003, a Move Character instruction statement, moves the Edit Pattern constant into the output area that is to be used by the printer DCB. This output area, labeled PRTLINE, consists of 132 bytes of storage containing additional data other than the value to be edited. Because the edited value is to start at the 11th byte of PRTLINE, the Edit Pattern has been moved into the address of PRTLINE +10. Because the MVC instruction performs a move for the length implied by the first operand, or the length specified within that operand, a length attribute of ten bytes has been specified in order that only the ten bytes representing EDITPRT are moved.

Statement 0004 is the Edit instruction statement. Once again, the explicit length attribute is used in the first operand to define the length of the operation. The packed decimal source field, VALUEFLD, is edited into the Edit Pattern, which now exists in PRTLINE+10.

Statement 0005 is a conventional OS QSAM PUT macro. It takes the output area PRTLINE and generates the necessary input/output task to place that data onto the output unit defined by a DCB macro labeled PRTR.

Statement 0006 is a forced (unconditional) branch back to the instruction statement defined by the label BACK.

The entire set of statements would then be executed again—read a tape record, pack the value, move the Edit Pattern to the output area, edit the packed value into the output area, put out the print line, branch to BACK, etc. This cycle would continue until an end-of-file (EOF) condition is encountered on the input tape, signaling that the source of input data had been exhausted. This example has made no provisions for line counting, page numbering, etc., all of which are described within the section "Printing Data Listings."

After the completion of an EDIT instruction statement, the PSW Condition Code bits contain an indication as to the value of the source field just edited. The bits are set as follows:

PSW bit setting	comparable BC condition	condition represented
00	8	A zero-value source field was edited.
01	4	A negative-value source field was edited.
10	2	A positive-value source field was edited.

It is possible that the programmer might intend to make a logic decision based on the Condition Code setting. It should be noted that the Condition Code is set to its resulting configuration based on the last value edited—in a multiple-field edit, this would be the right-most value in the multiple field; in a single-value edit this would be that value alone.

As noted previously, the first operand in an Edit instruction statement determines the length of the editing process. A length attribute is not implied, or allowed to be explicitly stated, for the source field value represented by the second operand of the statement. It is suggested, therefore, that a specific length attribute, equal to the legnth of the Edit Pattern, be included as a part of the first operand in the Edit statement.

Edit & Mark

The EDMK performs all of the functions of the regular Edit instruction. In addition, however, it notes the address of the point in the Edit Pattern to which the first significant digit was loaded from the source field, if that digit was passed prior to encountering a Significant Start Character within the Edit Pattern. The address noted is returned to the program in general register 1.

This instruction can be used to load "floating" symbols, such as a dollar sign, into an output print area or display device array that is to be edited. By using this instruction in a subroutine, you can always arrange to print a dollar sign, or any other symbol, within a given range of bytes in the edited data. A listing such as this could appear to be:

```
    $2.56
$3,918.10
    $.06
 $715.75
    $.28
```

Because the address of the first significant digit to be passed from the source field is not always loaded into general register 1, as in the instance when a Significant Start Character is encountered

Editing Data

first, the address of the decimal point may be loaded into register 1 before the Edit & Mark instruction statement is executed. This guarantees that the address in register 1 will never be at a point in the Edit Pattern to the right of the decimal point. The overall logic of this process is:

1. Use the Move Character (MVC) instruction to move the Edit Pattern into the output print area.
2. Load general register 1 with the address of the right-most position plus one byte within the output area Edit Pattern beyond which the dollar sign should not be placed.
3. Code the Edit & Mark instruction statement, addressing the pattern that resides in the output print area as the first operand and the source field as the second operand.
4. Code a statement that subtracts a value of +1 from the address contained in general register 1.
5. Use a Move Immediate (MVI) instruction statement to move a dollar sign into the address pointed to by general register 1.

Assume that an Edit Pattern has been moved into an output area at a point identified as PRTOUT+25. If the first byte of PRTOUT resides at program storage address of 23,516, the first byte of the Edit Pattern would be at address 23,541.

PRTOUT+25	ᛒ	¢	,	¢	¢	$	.	¢	¢
(storage address)	23,541	23,542	23,543	23,544	23,545	23,546	23,547	23,548	23,549

The data that was being passed to the Edit Pattern shown here would determine whether or not general register 1 is reset.

In describing the coding pertaining to this particular Edit Pattern, it must first be determined that you would want the dollar sign to appear somewhere to the left of the decimal point immediately following the Significant Start Character. Because the coding later subtracts a value of +1 from the address contained in general register 1, the address of the decimal point is loaded into general register 1.

    LA   1 , PRTOUT+31

Register 1 now contains a fixed-point value of +23,547, representing the storage address of the decimal point at PRTOUT+31.

The source field to be edited into the Pattern which commences at PRTOUT+25 is a three-byte unsigned packed field labeled PACKAMT. The instruction statement to Edit & Mark this field is:

    EDMK   PRTOUT+25 (9) , PACKAMT

This instruction statement would perform the editing function and at the same time might alter the address contained in general register 1. The determining factor as to whether or not register 1 (+23,547) would be changed is the significance of the numeric digits passed from the source field. If a significant digit is edited from the source field into the Edit Pattern between bytes 23,541 and 23,547 (not including these addresses), the Edit & Mark instruction would load into register 1 the address of the Pattern byte into which that significant digit was placed. If no significant digit is passed to the Edit Pattern prior to storage byte 23,547, the address contained in general register 1 would not be changed.

When the Edit & Mark instruction statement has completed its execution, register 1 contains an address that points to a significant digit or a significant character—the decimal point. Regardless of which address is in register 1, a value of +1 should be subtracted from that address in order that it would point to the first available "blank" immediately preceding the significant digit or character. This could be properly coded using the Subtract Halfword (SH) instruction or a Branch on Count to Register (BCTR) instruction. These two means of reducing the address in general register 1 by a value of +1 could be coded as:

    SH   1,=H'1'

or as

    BCTR   1,0

The Subtract Halfword instruction statement subtracts a halfword literal of +1 from general register 1. The BCTR instruction statement also decrements the value in general register 1 by +1, but the branch is not taken—the second operand of "zero" in a BCTR instruction statement does not allow a branch to take place.

Now that general register 1 points to the storage position where the dollar sign is to be inserted into the edited field, a Move Immediate instruction statement is written as:

    MVI   0(1),C'$'

This statement specifies, "Move a one-byte immediate character, consisting of a dollar sign, into storage address zero incremented by the address in general register 1."

The accumulated set of coding statements used to complete this task can be summarized as:

```
MVC     PRTOUT+25(9), EDITPTRN
LA      1, PRTOUT+31
EDMK    PRTOUT+25(9), PACKAMT
SH      1,=H'1'
MVI     0(1), C'$'
```

The placement of the dollar sign into the edited data under various circumstances as caused by different values is illustrated in these examples.

Example 1

Example 2

Example 3

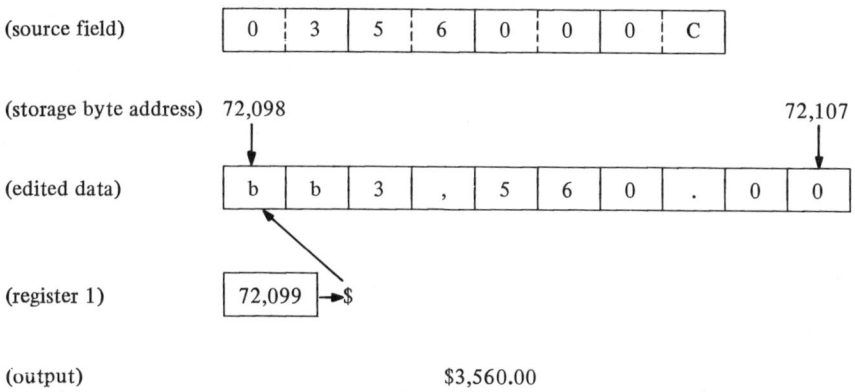

It is possible to substitute any valid symbol, character, or characters, in place of the dollar sign. A minus sign could be used to indicate credit or negative values in front of the amount instead of after it. This would be done by testing the Condition Code resulting from the execution of the EDMK instruction statement. If the value edited is negative, the program could move a hyphen (−) into the address contained in general register 1; if the value is positive, the MVI instruction could move a plus sign (+) into that address, or move nothing at all. Printed output of this type might appear as:

```
 -395.06      2,519.78              -.99
   +.04        -71.63         +15,921.88
```

Using this same basic idea, sets of characters such as 'DR.' and CR.' could be inserted into the high-order portion of the edited data field. Because the data field might contain its full complement of data, an application of this type should be structured so that the several storage bytes immediately preceding the data field area are blank—and must be reset to blanks after each edit. The only difference between a set of instructions for this EDMK routine and the one shown previously would be the amount of the value subtracted from general register 1, the movement of "blanks" to the bytes preceding the edited data field, and the logic for the insertion of the characters by an MVC instruction rather than an MVI instruction. The coding could be stated as shown in Figure 15-1.

Statement 0701 moves the Edit Pattern constant into the data field output area.

Statement 0702 moves blanks into the three bytes immediately preceding the data field edit pattern.

Statement 0703 loads the address of the decimal point of the Edit Pattern into general register 1.

Statement 0704 executes the Edit and Mark instruction statement. The PSW Condition Code is set after completion of this statement.

Statement 0705 is a "branch if the value edited was zero." The program goes to Statement 0712 if this condition exists, consequently neither 'DR.' nor 'CR.' are moved into the edited data field.

Statement 0706 is a "branch if the value edited was negative," taking the logic to Statement 0710 if that condition is noted.

Statement 0707 assumes that the value edited is neither negative nor zero, so it subtracts +4 from the address contained in general register 1.

Statement 0708 moves the characters 'DR.' into the three high-order bytes of the four bytes immediately preceding the first significant digit or character in the edited data field.

Statement 0709 is a forced branch to Statement 0712.

Statement 0710 assumes that the value edited is negative if the logic passes through this statement, so it subtracts a value of +4 from general register 1. If the value edited was either greater than +0 (a positive value) or less than -0 (a negative value), either Statement 0707 or Statement 0710 would be executed, but not both.

Statement 0711 moves the characters 'CR.' into the three high-order bytes of the four bytes immediately preceding the first significant digit or character in the edited data field.

Statement 0712, which is arrived at via a branch from Statement 0705, Statement 0708, or by falling through from Statement 0711, is a forced branch back to an assumed point in the program logic.

Data edited with this routine would probably appear as:

```
DR. 277.07            .00       CR. 3,984.41
   CR. .06     DR. 75.14        DR. 23,109.88
```

Given the capabilities provided by the Edit instruction and the Edit & Mark instruction, you have considerable versatility in the formatting and presentation of numeric data.

Editing Data

SYSTEM / 370 ASSEMBLER CODING FORM

Name	Operation	Operand	Identification Sequence No.
DOEDIT	MVC	PRTOUT+25(9),EDITPTRN	0701
	MVC	PRTOUT+22(3),=CL3' '	0702
	LA	1,PRTOUT+31	0703
	EDMK	PRTOUT+25(9),PACKAMT	0704
	BC	8,BYALL	0705
	BC	4,NEGTV	0706
	SH	1,=H'4'	0707
	MVC	0(3,1),=CL3'DR.'	0708
	BC	15,BYALL	0709
NEGTV	SH	1,=H'4'	0710
	MVC	0(3,1),=CL3'CR.'	0711
BYALL	BC	15,ANYWHERE	0712

FIGURE 15-1

REVIEW EXERCISES

1. Define the proper segment names for the edit pattern characters indicated in the following pattern.

   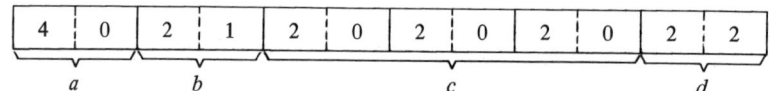

   a. _____
   b. _____
   c. _____
   d. _____

2. Which general register is sometimes used by the Edit & Mark instruction as a part of its regular operation? _____.

3. The _____ _____ is considered to be a switch or condition setting that is inspected during the editing in order for the Edit instruction to make certain processing decisions.

4. The hexadecimal configuration for the edit pattern Significant Start character is X '____'.

5. If the editing function detects a _____-sign in the low-order half-byte of the source field, the S-Trigger will be set to an "off" condition.

6. Even though the source field may contain significant digits, the Edit & Mark instruction does not return the address of the first significant digit if that operation first encounters a _____ _____ character within the edit pattern.

7. Data to be edited must be in _____ _____ form at the time that the Edit instruction is issued.

8. If a source field of four bytes, containing a packed decimal value of +0, were to be edited into the following edit pattern, the total number of zero-digits remaining in the result field after the edit would be _____.

| 4 | 0 | 2 | 0 | 2 | 1 | 2 | 0 | 2 | 0 | 2 | 0 | 2 | 0 | 2 | 0 |

9. The hexadecimal configuration for the edit pattern Digit Select character is X'____'.

10. The _____ _____ character is used to signal the editing functions that zero-suppression is to terminate at this point, provided that the edit has not passed any significant digits from the source field.

11. The direction of the editing scan, during the execution of an Edit or an Edit & Mark instruction, is from _____ to _____.

12. The hexadecimal configuration for the edit pattern Field Separator character is X'____'.

Editing Data

13. If the Edit & Mark instruction encounters the proper conditions to cause it to load register 1 with an address, that address will point to a byte within the particular _____ _____ being utilized by that statement.
14. Upon encountering a _____ _____ character in an edit pattern, the Edit instruction will set the Significant Trigger (S-Trigger) to an "off" condition.
15. The first (high-order) character in an edit pattern is considered to be the _____ _____.
16. A _____ _____ character is used to indicate a position within the edit pattern that is to be filled with a numeric digit from the source field or by the fill character of the pattern.
17. Upon completion of an edit, the Edit operation sets the PSW Condition Code based on the status of the _____ _____.
18. The _____ _____ character is generally used in editing a source field containing multiple values.
19. The _____ _____ is used to replace leading nonsignificant digits of the source field whenever zero-suppression is indicated.

Each of the following problems contains an edit pattern, a source field, an output field in which the editing is to take place, and one or more instruction statements. Analyze the fields and statement(s) and complete the character and hexadecimal format of the output field as it would appear after execution of the statement(s).

20. EDPATA | 40 | 20 | 20 | 21 | 20 | 20 |

    SOURCEA | 00 | 00 | 9C |

    RESULTA | C1 | C2 | 40 | 40 | 40 | 40 | 40 | 40 |

    MVC   RESULTA+1 (6) , EDPATA
    ED   RESULTA+1 (6) , SOURCEA

    RESULTA hex
           character

21. EDPATB | 40 | 20 | 21 | 20 |

    SOURCEB | 38 | 7C |

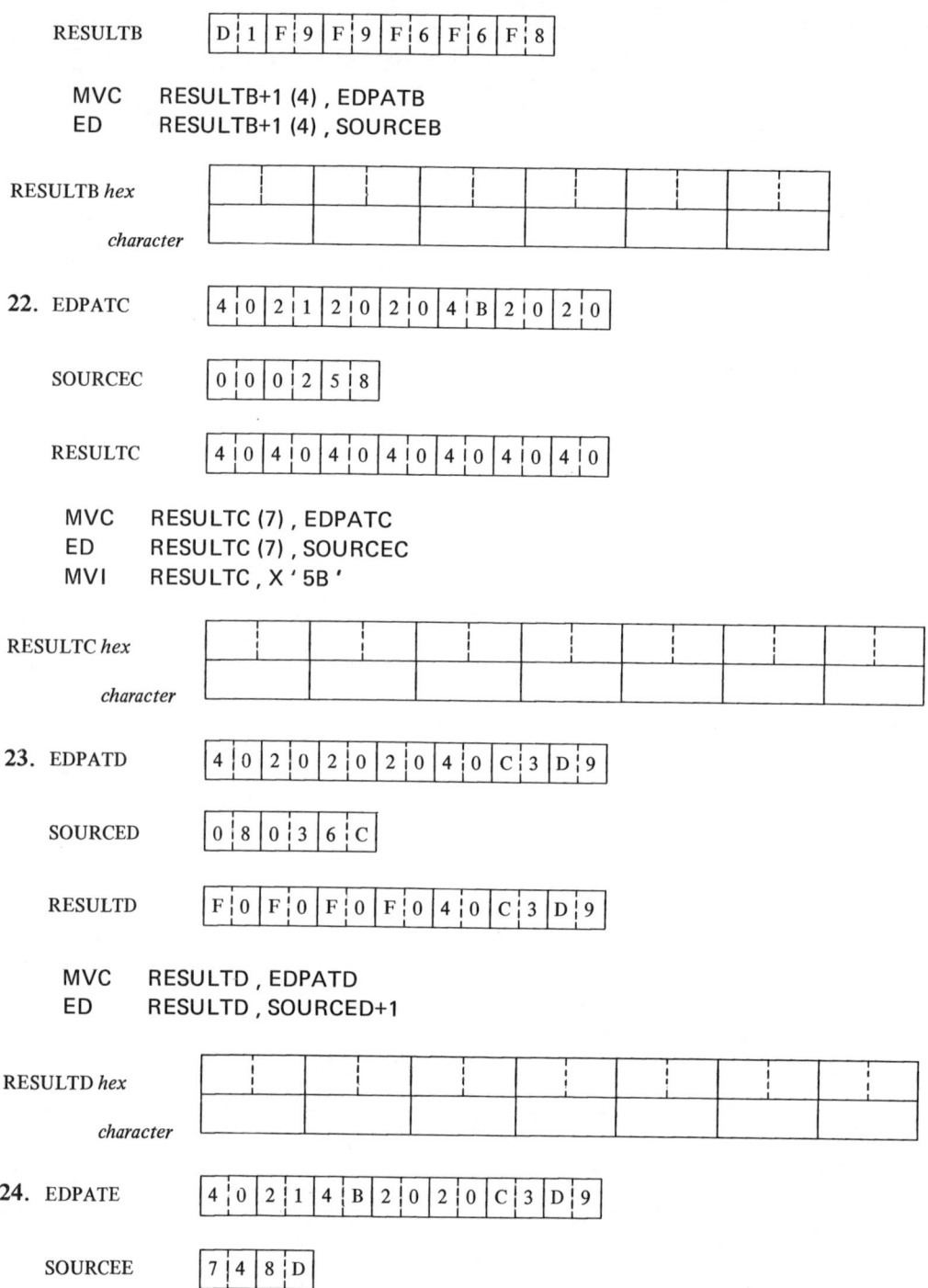

Editing Data

RESULTE | 40 | 40 | 40 | 40 | 40 | 40 | C4 | D9 |

```
MVC   RESULTE , EDPATE
ED    RESULTE , SOURCEE
```

RESULTE *hex*

character

25. EDPATF | 5C | 20 | 21 | 20 | 20 | 20 | 60 |

SOURCEF | 00 | 62 | 9D |

RESULTF | 40 | 40 | 40 | 40 | 40 | 40 | 40 |

```
MVC   RESULTF , EDPATF
ED    RESULTF , SOURCEF
```

RESULTF *hex*

character

26. EDPATG | 40 | 20 | 20 | 21 | 4B | 20 | 20 |

SOURCEG | 06 | 11 | 7D |

RESULTG | C1 | C2 | C1 | C2 | C1 | C2 | C1 |

```
LA      1 , RESULTG+4
MVC     RESULTG (7) , EDPATG
EDMK    RESULTG (7) , SOURCEG
SH      1 , =H ' 1 '
MVI     0 (1) , C ' $ '
```

RESULTG *hex*

character

27. EDPATH `40 20 20 20 21 4B 20 20`

SOURCEH `00 03 3C`

RESULT `40 40 40 40 40 40 40 40`

```
        LA      1 , RESULT+4
        MVC     RESULT (7) , EDPATH
        EDMK    RESULT (7) , SOURCEH
        SH      1 , =H ' 1 '
        MVI     0 (1) , X ' 5B '
```

RESULT hex	40	40	40	5B	F3	4B	F3	40
character				$	3	.	3	

16
Printing Data Listings

In order that the applications explained within this text might be tested under actual computer operating conditions, the general specifications for creating printed output should be discussed at this point. These enable you to code instruction statements and print out listings of the data generated by your program.

Some of the routines used in this section employ the use of OS or OS/VS macroinstructions for input/output functions. It must be noted that these macros are applicable only with OS or OS/VS in their expressed form. If you are using any system other than OS or OS/VS, you will have to be provided with the proper input/output control statements.

DEFINING THE OUTPUT AREAS

Data to be printed or displayed on an output device is usually arranged and formatted in a program-controlled section of storage that may be referred to as an *output area*. Although various devices are capable of accepting data records of different maximum lengths, this discussion shall relate to a standard printer unit capable of printing up to 132 characters per line. In defining the output area from which the I/O instructions extract and transmit the data that is to be printed, it is assumed that this area consists of 132 bytes of contiguous program storage area.

There are several ways in which you might define the output area. It can be defined as a single 132-byte field or it can be subdefined as a group of smaller fields.

```
        PRTRA    DC      CL132'b'
```

or as

```
        PRTRB    DS      0CL132
        FIELD1   DC      CL15'b'
        FIELD2   DC      CL25'b'
        FIELD3   DC      CL10'b'
        FIELD4   DC      CL63'b'
        FIELD5   DC      CL19'b'
```

Data to be moved into the PRTRA output area could be located at different places within PRTRA by address-adjusting the first operand of the move statement. This might be coded as:

```
        MVC     PRTRA+10 (16) , DATA1      0001
        MVC     PRTRA+35 (8) , DATA2       0002
        MVC     PRTRA+88 (12) , DATA3      0003
```

529

Statement 0001 moves 16 bytes of data from the field DATA1 into PRTRA+10, or into the 11th through the 26th bytes of PRTRA.

Statement 0002 moves DATA2 into PRTRA for a length of eight bytes commencing at the 36th byte of PRTRA.

Statement 0003 moves DATA3 into the 88th through the 99th bytes of PRTRA.

Data to be moved into the PRTRB output area could either be moved into the subdefined field labels or into the address-adjusted positions of PRTRB. Each of the instruction statements within the following pairs refers to the same address.

```
MVC    FIELD1 , AREA1
MVC    PRTRB (15) , AREA1

MVC    FIELD3 , AREA2
MVC    PRTRB+40 (10) , AREA2

MVC    FIELD5 , AREA 3
MVC    PRTRB+113 (19) , AREA3
```

Quite often, you will find it to your advantage to define the output area as a single constant. This way, you can readily move the data to different locations for each subsequent print line without becoming confused by the subfield descriptions of the labels. On the other hand, a printed listing that follows one or several distinct formats throughout may be more easily understood and manipulated if the output area is defined by specific subfields. A multiple-defined output area can be established as shown in Figure 16-1.

With the output area PRTROUT defined in this fashion, data can be moved into either type of printed line format as necessary. When the output area is actually printed, it appears in the format into which the data was moved.

Although the output storage area itself has now been explained, it must be noted that a Data Control Block (DCB) macro (or its equivalent) must be coded somewhere within the problem program in order to define the printer output as a data set. The means by which the data set is described varies between the different operating systems. For OS or OS/VS the dataset is described by coding the Data Control Block (DCB) macro.

The DCB contains numerous parameter specifications which, when completed, combine to define most of the information relevant to the type of output data set being utilized. It specifies the length of the records, the record form, the macroinstructions for input/output control, the input/output options, and many other codes that would be totally unfamiliar to you unless completely analyzed and described. Unfortunately, it is impossible, within the scope of this text, to describe the various macroinstructions used by each of the operating systems. The school, university or industrial location at which you might be located may conceivably have any one, or more, of the available operating systems. It is, therefore, necessary that any knowledge of the operating systems I/O macros and functional macros be obtained directly from the installation to which you are assigned.

For the purpose of identifying an I/O (input/output) macro statement to an output printer device, the PUT macro is used. This macro generates a Queued Sequential Access Method I/O task. An I/O statement of this type would be:

```
PUT    PRTR , PRTAREA
```

The PUT macro defines the I/O task as being initiated to write out a data set (PRTR) using the data contained within the storage area PRTAREA. This is a very brief description of this

SYSTEM / 370 ASSEMBLER CODING FORM

NAME	OPERATION	OPERAND
PRTOUT	DS	0CL132
AFLD1	DS	CL25
AFLD2	DS	CL10
AFLD3	DS	CL40
AFLD4	DS	CL5
AFLD5	DS	CL42
	ORG	PRTOUT
BFLD1	DC	CL12' '
BFLD2	DC	CL38' '
BFLD3	DC	CL9' '
BFLD4	DC	CL38' '
BFLD5	DC	CL15' '
BFLD6	DC	CL20' '

FIGURE 16-1

process, but it is intended that full information regarding the operating system macros available to you will be supplied by the computer center with which you are associated.

LINE SPACING AND LINE CONTROL

Another of the features available to you is the ability to control the number of spaces, or blank lines, appearing between the printed lines of your output listing. Printed lines may be single-spaced, double-spaced, triple-spaced, suppressed spacing, or started on a new page. The printed output line spacing can be controlled by a single character representation known as a Carriage Control Symbol. In order for the system to recognize this symbol (when coding under OS or OS/VS), it is necessary to include the code letter 'A' in the RECFM (Record Form) parameter of the DCB macro. A commonly expressed RECFM parameter used for printer files is:

    RECFM=FSA

The code letter 'F' states that the records are fixed length; the 'S' indicates that there should be no "short" blocks or records; the 'A' indicates that Carriage Control Symbols are to be used as part of the output area print line. Once again, it must be stated that the means of advising the system that this type of line space control is to be used differs among the various operating systems.

If the Carriage Control Symbol is used to control line spacing, it must appear in the single byte position immediately preceding the first byte of the data of the record that is to be printed. The character representation of each of the effective Carriage Control Symbols and the resulting action of each are listed as:

Carriage Control Symbol			instructs the printer carriage:
ƀ	(blank)	X'40'	Space one line before printing data (single-spaced)
0	(zero)	X'F0'	Space two lines before printing data (double-spaced)
-	(hyphen)	X'60'	Space three lines before printing data (triple-spaced)
+	(plus)	X'4E'	Do not space before printing (suppressed spacing)
1	(one)	X'F1'	Go to the beginning of new page before printing the data (page-skip)

Although there are a quantity of other Carriage Control Symbols available, the five listed above are more than sufficient for the use of the text and the novice programmer.

Previously within this section, it was mentioned that the standard-length print line would be considered to consist of a maximum of 132 bytes of data. Accordingly, the output data area was shown as being defined as a 132-byte constant. When using a Carriage Control Symbol, however, the first byte of the defined output area is considered to be that symbol. To allow for 132 bytes of printed data, the output storage area should now be defined as 133 bytes in length—a one-byte Carriage Control Symbol followed by 132 printable data bytes. Here again, the thought of sub-defining output data fields becomes applicable. For example:

```
        OUTAREA   DS    0CL133
        CCSYMB    DC    CL1 ' ƀ '
        DATA      DC    CL132 ' ƀ '
```

The input/output macro to print out this field of data could be coded as:

    PUT   PRTR , OUTAREA

Even though OUTAREA is specified as the location containing the output data, consisting of 133 bytes, the system has been told, via the RECFM parameter of the DCB, that a Carriage Control

Printing Data Listings

Symbol is to be used for printed output. Accordingly, the first byte of OUTAREA (the same as CCSYMB) is interpreted to be the Carriage Control Symbol and the remaining 132 bytes (DATA) are assumed to contain the data to be printed.

If the program requires an alteration of the line spacing during the printing of a listing, you would only need to code an MVI instruction statement that would move the appropriate symbol into the Carriage Control Symbol byte at the beginning of the print line. To illustrate this, the next example reflects the effect of altering the Carriage Control Symbol to create different spacings between lines.

The output area is defined as:

```
PRTOUT    DS    0CL133
SYMBOL    DC    CL1'b'
MESSG     DC    CL132'b'
```

In order to represent some printed output data, the message "THIS IS THE WAY DATA LINES ARE SPACED" is considered as occupying the first 37 bytes of the subfield MESSG. The I/O is via the PUT macro referring to an output DCB labeled DEVICE. The instruction statements are:

```
PUT    DEVICE, PRTOUT        00001
PUT    DEVICE, PRTOUT        00002
MVI    SYMBOL, C'0'          00003
PUT    DEVICE, PRTOUT        00004
MVI    SYMBOL, C'-'          00005
PUT    DEVICE, PRTOUT        00006
```

The resulting printed output would appear as:

```
statement 00001        THIS IS THE WAY DATA LINES ARE SPACED
statement 00002        THIS IS THE WAY DATA LINES ARE SPACED

statement 00004        THIS IS THE WAY DATA LINES ARE SPACED


statement 00006        THIS IS THE WAY DATA LINES ARE SPACED
```

In Statements 00001 and 00002, the Carriage Control Symbol byte contains a valid "blank" so the lines of printed data are single-spaced with no blank lines between them.

Statement 00003 moves a zero into the Carriage Control Symbol byte.

Statement 00004 causes the printer to space two spaces before printing the data line. This double-space creates a blank line between the current printed line of data and the one previously printed.

Statement 00005 uses the MVI instruction to move a hyphen into the Carriage Control Symbol byte.

Statement 00006, when executed, causes the printer to space three lines before printing the data line.

The "suppress space" Carriage Control Symbol can be used to enable the program to print twice on the same print line. Although this capability may not have many obvious applications, there are occasions when this function can be useful. Double-character configurations, underscoring, and creating of special characters can be accomplished with the "suppress space" feature. Some of these might appear as:

Ø   θ   ÷   AB   ⊣   ⊦

The "page-skip" Carriage Control Symbol is used to start the line of printed data on a new page. There are several ways and equivalent conditions for which this symbol can be applied. It is good program housekeeping to print a title or descriptor data at the top of each page of printed output. If a listing were printed in unbroken sequence, the printed lines would continue across the perforations of the page separations, page after page. It is desirable, therefore, for the program to keep count of the number of lines printed per page. By doing this, it can determine when it is time to space forward to the beginning of a new page, print any necessary headings or title lines, and then continue on with the data print lines.

PAGE CONTROL

As just indicated in the preceding paragraph, page control is important in producing logical, legible data listings. This is a comparatively easy routine to code, requiring only a knowledge of the size of the printer paper used for the data listing and the spacing for the print lines. The general rules in controlling the number of lines per page are given below:

1. Establish a "counter" into which you can accumulate the number of lines used on each page.
2. After each data line is printed, add the appropriate number to the line counter.
3. Compare the value in the line counter to a constant value equal to the maximum number of lines to be printed on each page.
4. If the counter is equal to or greater than the constant, branch to a routine to space to a new page.
5. Otherwise continue processing on that page.

The following set of instruction statements establish a subroutine of this type.

```
LISTING      PUT    PRTR1 , OUTAREA          00001
             AP     LINECTR , =PL1 ' 2 '     00002
             CP     LINECTR , =PL2 ' 56 '    00003
             BC     10 , NEWPAGE             00004
LISTDONE     BC     15 , GO                  00005
```

Statement 00001 is the PUT macroinstruction statement that causes the data line to be printed.

Statement 00002 adds a packed decimal value of +2, expressed as a literal, to the packed decimal line counter. The increment value of +2 is used because this particular report is being printed in double-spaced format, so for every data line printed, a blank line has also been passed.

Statement 00003 compares the accumulated count of lines for the current page, as contained in LINECTR, to a packed decimal literal value of +56. This implies that the desired number of lines per page for this program is 56. As a result of this comparison, the PSW Condition Code bits are set to reflect an "equal," "less than," or "greater than" condition.

Statement 00004 is a conditional branch statement. If the value in LINECRT is equal to or greater than a value of +56, a branch would be generated to a subroutine labeled NEWPAGE. Although it is not shown here, the function of the NEWPAGE subroutine would be to:

(a) space to the beginning of a new page,
(b) reset the LINECTR to zero,
(c) print any necessary heading or title lines, and then
(d) branch back to LISTDONE.

Statement 00005 is an unconditional branch to another section of the program.

Page control does not necessarily need to be based solely on the number of lines used (either printed or spaced) on a single page. Logical page breaks are just as often the prime reason for skipping ahead to the beginning of a new page. For example, assume that the listing being created by the program represents the purchase orders placed by a quantity of customers. The vendor wishes to start the analysis for each unique customer on a new page so that the listing may be separated by customer number identity in order to forward a copy of that customer's orders for confirmation. The average number of orders placed by each customer is ten; therefore, it would be the rule that the listing for each customer would normally require less than one-half page of printed data. The logic required to properly handle the vendor's request would be that each time a new "customer #" is encountered, the program would branch to a subroutine that skips ahead to the beginning of a new page and performs whatever headings and title lines are required. The customer's data would be listed until another "customer #" is encountered, at which time the program would branch to the new-page routine, etc.

FORMATTING TITLES, HEADINGS, AND SUBHEADINGS

When the program prints data lists, it is almost always desirable to have each page begin with a title line that identifies the contents of the listing, the data to which the listing refers, and the page number. Second in priority is the insertion of headings, which may or may not identify the data on that page as being different in classification than data on other pages. Subheadings are used whenever data lines create columns of items that can be identified by placing a printed explanation at the top of each column.

The formatting and data content of the titles and headings can be widely varied. The decision of how to arrange these items is usually the responsibility of the analysts who have designed the system for which the program is to be written. If prior requirements have not been specified, the programmer is sometimes given the responsibility of the design of the printed output. In this instance, the programmer must strive to create a logical, well-defined listing that will not require cross-referencing to other information sources in order to be understood. The following paragraphs, which describe title lines and headings, are general in nature yet specific enough to create reasonable guidelines for the programmer to follow. There is no "magic formula" to follow—common sense and logic can arrive at a practical data list format.

The Title

The title line for any printed listing should be self-explanatory in content. The actual title itself should contain the name of the listing and possibly the name of the system or program to which the report belongs. This might also include the identification number of the program that generates the report if such a number is applicable. For all practical purposes, the name or actual title portion of the title line should be centered in such a way that it is easily distinguished at first glance. If a 132-byte print line is used, the midpoint of a corresponding report title line would be the 66th byte. Count the number of characters in the title name, divide that number by two, then use the quotient as the number of spaces to back-off from the center (the 66th byte) to a point where the title name should begin.

For example:

>Title name equals . . . 38 bytes.
>Half of name length equals . . . 19 bytes.
>66th byte less 19 bytes equals . . . 47th byte.
>The title name should begin at the 47th byte of the output
>field of the title line.

The title line should also contain two other small fields—one for the page number and one for the effective date of the listing. These may be used to "balance" the title name itself (one on either side of it) or they may both be placed on the right-hand side of the page. General systems practices have advocated that both the date and the page number should appear in the top right corner of the report. This has apparently been determined through system studies as being the most obvious point where the average reader looks for that information. These can be arranged as:

DATE: PAGE #

In order to supply the page number for each page of a listing, you can maintain another counter or accumulator. Each time that the program logic branches to the "new page" routine, it can add a value of +1 to the page counter, edit that value into the title line immediately following the PAGE # field, and then proceed to print the title line.

The date information can be provided from many sources, depending considerably on the programming logic. Some means of obtaining the date are:

- By control card input at the time that the object program is executed. The program logic should include a routine to read in the control card, extract the date from it, and then move the date into the title line output area.
- By console typewriter entry to/from the computer operator. The program logic would include a "Write to Operator" message that would request him to supply a date via the console typewriter. The date portion of his reply would be inserted into the title line output area.
- By extracting the current system date from the computer operating system itself. In most operating systems it is possible for the program logic to interrogate the "supervisor" of the system control program and receive the current system date in reply. This action is all accomplished internally, with no external reference to the task. The only objection to this method is that many data lists contain an effective date other than the date on which the listing was produced.

Although the loading of a date into the title line output area would appear to be a very minor item, it is often necessary to use a date conversion routine to meet the requirements of the personnel using the listing. Sometimes a "Gregorian/Julian" date conversion is necessary; other such conversions are "month/day/year" to "production day," etc. Such dates may appear as:

Printing Data Listings

Month/day/year	November 18, 1980
Month/day/year	11-18-80 or 11/18/80
Year and day-of-year	80-322
Year and production day	80-209
Day/month/year (military)	18 November 1980

Now that the components of the title line have been explained, it would be of assistance to know of a convenient means of establishing that data as a program constant. It is suggested that the title line output area be created as a 133-byte constant, including the Carriage Control Symbol, with each byte of the constant set up in its intended form. The coding statement for this type of constant is shown in Figure 16-2.

Note that the first byte of the output field is a Carriage Control Symbol of '1', indicating that the printer is to skip to the beginning of a new page before printing the title. This enables the program to skip to a new page by just issuing an I/O instruction to print the title. One of the other advantages of establishing a title line output area as a separate constant from the data output area is that the PUT macro, or its equivalent, can directly reference the TITLE1 area, such as:

```
PUT    PRTR1 , TITLE1
```

It is not necessary, therefore, to move the title line information into the data output area in order to print it.

Using the information supplied thus far, the following set of statements are typical of a subroutine to initialize the beginning of a new page.

```
NEWPAGE    AP     PAGECTR , =PL1 ' 1 '              0001
           MVC    TITLE1+126 (4) , PAGEDIT          0002
           ED     TITLE1+126 (4) , PAGECTR          0003
           PUT    PRTR1 , TITLE1                    0004
           BCR    15 , 6                            0005
```

This subroutine assumes that the data has already been moved into the TITLE1 field at the initialization of the program and that the program has logically branched to the address of NEWPAGE at this point in order to print the title line for a new page of data.

Statement 0001 adds a packed decimal literal of +1 to the page count accumulator, the sum of which is the new page number in packed decimal form.

Statement 0002 moves an Edit Pattern into the four bytes of TITLE1 that immediately follow "PAGE #." Information on this editing is provided in the section "Editing Data."

Statement 0003 edits the packed decimal value from PAGECTR, representing the page number, into the Edit Pattern that was moved into TITLE1 by Statement 0002.

Statement 0004 is the PUT macro statement that transfers the data contents of the title output area labeled TITLE1 to the output printer defined as PRTR1. When this macroinstruction is executed, the printer skips to the beginning of a new physical page before actually printing the title line.

Statement 0005 is a "Branch on Condition to Register" instruction statement that causes a forced branch to the address contained in general register 6. That address should be the address of the next instruction following the one that branched to NEWPAGE.

FIGURE 16-2

Printing Data Listings

Headings and Subheadings

The distinction between headings and subheadings is a very slight matter of interpretation. What would be considered to be a heading in one listing could also be properly defined as a subheading in another listing. It would not be incorrect to state that "a subheading is a secondary level of heading that further defines the subject matter associated with the primary headings." Because this appears to be a rather ambiguous statement, the following examples of headings and subheadings are used to clarify its intended meaning.

Example 1

Line 1	J.D.S.S.G. MANUFACTURING CO.–PAYROLL ANALYSIS REPORT PAGE 16				
Line 2	EMPLOYEE 1049	EMPLOYEE NAME:	NANCY HUNT		
Line 3	PAY PERIOD	HOURS	GROSS	DEDUCTIONS	NET AMOUNT
Line 4	1	40.0	$160.00	$33.15	$126.85
Line 5	2	36.0	$144.00	$21.62	$122.38
Line 6	3	40.0	$160.00	$27.87	$132.13

Line 1 is the title line. It indicates the name of the company for whom the report is being created and the type of analysis that the report is listing.

Line 2 may be defined as the heading line. It implies that the report is created with a section or page for each employee. The employee identification number and name are printed as a heading in order to indicate which employee the subsequent data is related to.

Line 3 is a subheading line, consisting of columnar headings to define that data which appears for the employee named in the heading.

Lines 4, 5, and 6 are the data lines, representing the actual data for the employee.

Example 2

Line 1	J.D.S.S.G. MANUFACTURING CO.–PAYROLL ANALYSIS REPORT							
Line 2	EMP. #	NAME	PERIOD	HOURS	GROSS	DEDUCTIONS	NET PAY	
Line 3	1049	Nancy Hunt	1	40.0	$160.00	$33.15	$126.85	
Line 4			2	36.0	$144.00	$21.62	$122.38	
Line 5			3	40.0	$160.00	$27.87	$132.13	
Line 6	1052	James Warren	1	40.0	$140.00	$26.15	$113.85	
Line 7			2	40.0	$140.00	$20.02	$119.98	
Line 8			3	20.0	$ 70.00	$14.80	$ 55.20	
Line 9	1076	Greg Williams	1	40.0	$200.00	$24.95	$175.05	
Line 10			2	40.0	$200.00	$29.95	$170.05	
Line 11			3	40.0	$200.00	$20.95	$179.05	

Line 12	1085	John Scott	1	40.0	$165.00	$31.20	$133.80
Line 13			2	40.0	$165.00	$22.50	$142.50
Line 14			3	32.0	$132.00	$18.20	$113.80

In this second example, there appears only one set of headings in addition to the title line. Rather than necessarily starting a new page and a new set of headings each time another employee number is encountered, this listing format has combined the headings and subheadings of Example 1 into a single set of headings. The identity number and name of the employee is listed only once, at the point where the first line of information for that employee is printed. Line 2 can, therefore, be considered to be a heading or a subheading, depending on the programmer's interpretation of these terms. Generally, a heading can be assumed to be the first definitive print line that follows the title line, and subheadings may be defined as any subsequent lines that further define preceding headings or subheadings. A number of subheading lines may be used if necessary to establish the analysis and identification of the report data lines. This is shown in the next example.

Example 3

					DEDUCTIONS			NET PAY
Line 3	PAY PERIOD	HOURS	GROSS					
Line 4					F.I.C.A.	WITHHOLDING TAX	OTHER	
Line 5	1		40.0	$160.00	5.55	22.15	5.45	$126.85
Line 6	2		36.0	$144.00	5.00	16.62	.00	$122.38

This example uses the third line of Example 1 and relates the association of a subheading line to subsequent subheadings. The columnar heading "Deductions" has been further broken down into additional subheadings.

Regardless of your interpretation or definition of headings and subheadings, they may be established as fixed or variable constants in the same manner as the title lines are originated. A 133-byte constant is coded for each heading line that is to be printed, leaving blanks wherever variable heading data is to be inserted. Using the title line, heading, and subheading illustrated for the "J.D.S.S.G. Manufacturing Co." in Example 1, the coding of the Define Constant (DC) statements could be illustrated as shown in Figure 16-3.

The spacing of the headings represented by these DC statements is not identical to those shown in Example 1. However, all three types of definitive lines have been effectively created by these statements and each may be directly specified as an output area associated with an output device Data Control Block. If only one output area had been designated for the listing it would be necessary to move each set of data into that output area prior to issuing the PUT macro to print that line. By establishing the three output areas for the title and headings, the data may be listed by issuing three consecutive PUT statements.

```
        PUT     PRTDEV , TITLE      00001
        PUT     PRTDEV , HEADING    00002
        PUT     PRTDEV , SUBHEAD    00003
```

Statement 00001 prints the title line. Because the first byte of the constant TITLE is a '1', the printer unit skips to the beginning of a new page prior to printing.

Printing Data Listings

SYSTEM / 370 ASSEMBLER CODING FORM

NAME	OPERATION	OPERAND	COMMENTS
TITLE	DC	CL133'1 * DEFINE PRINT-LINE CONSTANTS *	
		NUFACTURING CO. - PAYROLL ANALYSIS REPORT J.D.S.S.G. MA*	
		PAGE #'	
HEADING	DC	CL133'0 EMPLOYEE # EMPLOYEE NA*	
		ME'	
SUBHEAD	DC	CL133'0 PAY PERIOD HOURS GROSS *	
		DEDUCTIONS , NET PAY ,'	

FIGURE 16-3

Statement 00002 spaces two lines and then prints the data contained within the constant HEADING.

Statement 00003 spaces two lines and then prints the constant SUBHEAD.

Although it was not shown as a part of these statements, the programmer would also have coded the necessary instruction statements to move a page number into the TITLE constant and to move the employee number and employee name into the HEADING constant prior to printing those lines.

The practice of creating more than one output area constant for any given output device applies equally well whenever it is needed. It is not limited in its application to the data list titles and headings as shown herein. Separations between logical groups of printed data can be emphasized by inserting a print line consisting of asterisks or hyphens. Larger gaps of blank lines within a single page can be created by the repeated issuance of a PUT instruction that references a print line of blanks, the Carriage Control Symbol consisting of a hyphen, indicating the request to skip three lines before printing.

In much the same manner, multiple display screen formats for a cathode-ray display device may be established as individual output areas. Each output area is called on as the screen format of data contained within it is required.

Your design capabilities and common sense are often thoroughly tested when the formatting of printed or displayed data lists are entirely your responsibility.

17

Data Validation

Instruction: Translate

mnemonic	hex code	operand format
TR	DC	$D_1 (L, B_1), D_2 (B_2)$

This instruction can be used to convert from one bit configuration code to another bit configuration code. This is applicable as long as both codes refer to a configuration of eight bits or less. It can be used to translate ASCII codes, EBCDIC, paper tape transmission codes, or any code application required by the user, just as long as the configuration requirements are met. The first operand of the statement specifies the location of the data to be translated, and the second operand specifies the beginning location of a translate table.

A translate table would normally consist of 256 contiguous bytes of storage containing the "translated to" data. Provision should be made for all of the 256 possible eight-bit hexadecimal configurations—X'00' through X'FF'. The table should conform to the particular code that the data is being converted to. The sequence of the table would be arranged in the hex value of the character being translating *from*, but that table position would contain the bit configuration of the coded character being translating *to*.

This instruction then takes the beginning address of the translate table, increments the low-order bits of that address by the hexadecimal value of the character to be translated, goes to the total incremented address, picks up the one-byte configuration of the translated code, and replaces the original character bit configuration with the one that it has just picked up from the translate table.

The movement of the translate is from left to right, one byte at a time, through the data field specified by the first operand for the implied, or specified, length of that field.

The Condition Code setting is not altered by this instruction.

*   *   *

Instruction: Translate and Test

mnemonic	hex code	operand format
TRT	DD	$D_1 (L, B_1), D_2 (B_2)$

This instruction performs similarly to the TRANSLATE instruction except that it terminates operation once a byte in the translate table is scanned that does not contain a hexadecimal '00' configuration. The instruction is used primarily to scan a set of data for special characters and to return information to the user when such a character is encountered. The field containing the data to be scanned is specified by the first operand and the translate table beginning address is specified by the second operand.

Referring to the characters in the first operand as the "check" characters, the translate table should be arranged in the hexadecimal sequence of those characters. Provision should be made to allow for all of the 256 possible eight-bit hexadecimal configurations—X'00' through X'FF'. For the characters that are not to be flagged, a hexadecimal value of '00' should be built into the table segment addressed by that character. Each character to be flagged should have a unique eight-bit configuration built into the table segment addressed by that character.

The TRT instruction then begins checking (from left to right) each character of the data field specified by the first operand, against the translate table. If the table segment for that character contains a X'00' value, the instruction continues on to check the next character, etc. However, once the instruction statement checks a character and finds that the appropriate table segment is not a X'00' value, the instruction discontinues the scan. It then inserts the low-order 24 bits of the address of the "check character" into general register 1 and inserts the contents of the unique table segment for that character into the low-order eight bits (one-byte) of general register 2. The Condition Code is then set and the instruction terminates.

CC	BC	Condition
0	8	All of the table segments encountered were X'00'.
1	4	A nonzero table segment was encountered prior to the last "check character" in the first operand of the statement.
2	2	The last check character in the first operand of the statement had a nonzero table segment.

DATA VALIDATION

Almost every commercial program, in one way or another, requires that a certain amount of auditing and certification of data be accomplished. This can range from a single "compare" statement to a very complex auditing subroutine certifying data as a numeric value or as to its character contents. Auditing and validation of this type is required for many reasons, some of which are given below.

- To inspect input data as to its category, such as when there are several classes of input and each class has its own unique processing routines.
- To audit numeric values for valid configurations. This might include checking for the positive or negative configuration of a value or determining its magnitude to confirm that it exceeds or fails to meet a minimum value.
- To audit for special characters. One such application would be to ascertain that an EBCDIC numeric field does not contain any blanks prior to a pack operation.
- To search for certain characters which, if found, are to be converted into another character or set of characters or, in some instances, eliminated altogether.

There are probably hundreds of reasons for unique auditing and validation of data, and an equal or greater number of ways to accomplish those tasks within Assembler Language programming. This section of the text will strive to point out a few of the applicable techniques that might be

Data Validation

used to accomplish this, and to establish the general groundwork that will provide you with some ideas for developing auditing and validation techniques of your own. It must be mentioned once again that there is more than one "correct" programming answer to every problem—and the configuration of the computer system and available storage is often the limiting factor as to the efficiency of that answer.

Validation of Numeric Values

The validation of numeric or decimal value representation might take various forms. Rather than attempting to define these possibilities through many sentences of explanation and description, examples of several types of decimal value validation tasks are presented. In each instance the reason for the auditing is explained, sets of instruction statements are illustrated, and an explanation of the action generated by the coding is offered.

Task 1. A fullword value, supplied by another portion of the problem program, is to be tested for a negative value configuration. If the fullword is a positive value, it is acceptable; if the fullword is a negative value, it must be deleted and replaced with a plus-zero value. The first item in the coding, CHECKAMT, is a fullword defined constant that will be supplied with a fixed-point value by the program prior to entering the audit routine.

```
          CHECKAMT   DC    F'0'
*
          AUDIT      CLI   CHECKAMT , X ' 80 '     0001
                     BC    4 , POSVALUE            0002
                     MVC   CHECKAMT , =F ' 0 '     0003
          POSVALUE   — —   — — — — — — —           0004
                     — —   — — — — — — —
```

Statement 0001 is the first instruction statement in the audit subroutine and is addressed by reference to the symbolic label AUDIT. The Compare Logical Immediate (CLI) instruction statement determines whether or not the left-most bit of the high-order byte (the sign-bit) is a one-bit or a zero-bit. The immediate character of the second operand of this statement represents a bit configuration of '1000 0000'. Because a negative fixed-point value contains a one-bit sign-bit, this comparison results in the PSW Condition Code defining that status of the fullword value. If CHECKAMT is a negative value the Condition Code is set to indicate an "equal" or "greater than" condition.

Statement 0002 is a test of the Condition Code and a branch to POSVALUE if the Condition Code indicates that the first byte of CHECKAMT is less than X'80'. If the first byte of CHECKAMT is not less than X'80', indicating that CHECKAMT contains a negative value, the branch would not be taken and the processing logic would fall through to Statement 0003.

Statement 0003 assumes that because the processing logic has entered this instruction statement, CHECKAMT must contain a negative value. According to the requirements of the task, a negative value must be deleted and replaced with a plus-zero value. The Move Character instruction moves a four-byte fullword, containing a plus-zero value into CHECKAMT.

Statement 0004, addressed by the symbolic label POSVALUE, would contain whatever instruction was the next step in the program logic. If CHECKAMT contains a positive value, this statement would be entered via the branch from Statement 0002.

Task 2. In this program logic, a value has previously been loaded into general register 6. The audit subroutine is to reverse the positive/negative configuration of that value if the integer portion is greater than 32,768; otherwise, the configuration of the value is to remain unaltered.

CHEXRTE	LPR	5,6	0001
	C	5,=F'32768'	0002
	BC	12,NOTGREAT	0003
	LCR	6,6	0004
NOTGREAT	--	------	0005
	--	------	

Statement 0001 is the opening instruction of this subroutine. It takes the value contained in general register 6, regardless of its configuration, and loads it in its positive form into general register 5. This allows the integer portion of that value to be tested with a single compare statement.

Statement 0002 compares the value contained in general register 5 to a fullword fixed-point value literal of +32,768. The PSW Condition Code reflects the high, low or equal result of this comparison.

Statement 0003 tests the result of the comparison made within Statement 0002 by requesting that a branch to NOTGREAT be made if general register 5 contains a value equal to or less than 32,768. If register 5 contains a value greater than 32,768, the processing would fall through to Statement 0004.

Statement 0004 assumes that the integer value in general register 6, regardless of its positive or negative configuration, is greater than 32,768. In accordance with the task logic, the Load Complement Register (LCR) instruction statement loads the current value contained within general register 6 back into register 6 in its complemented form. If the value was originally positive, it is reloaded as a negative configuration; if it was originally a negative configuration, it is loaded in its positive complement.

Statement 0005 represents the next logic step to be executed by the program. This statement would be entered by the branch from Statement 0003 or by natural sequence through Statement 0004.

Task 3. This subroutine receives a series of packed decimal values, each of which may vary in length from two to four bytes, and may or may not contain a valid packed decimal sign in the right-most half-byte. Two objectives are to be accomplished:

- All values are to be expanded to a five-byte packed decimal without altering the decimal value itself.

- Any unsigned values are to be supplied with a hexadecimal 'C' in the right-most half-byte, representing a packed decimal positive sign.

When this subroutine receives the incoming packed decimals, they have already been left-aligned into a four-byte field that is referred to by the symbolic label INFIELD, and the byte-length of the value has been placed into general register 8 in fixed-point form. (See Figure 17-1a and b.)

The general logic of this set of statements accomplishes the task as requested, but requires an application that modifies the length and displacement parameters within an instruction statement.

Statement 0901, SIGNCHEX, uses the Load Address instruction to place a fixed-point value of +4 into general register 9. Because the length of the packed decimal value to be passed is con-

Data Validation

SYSTEM / 370 ASSEMBLER CODING FORM

NAME	OPERATION	OPERAND	COMMENTS	SEQ
*				0880
*			DEFINED CONSTANTS AND WORK AREAS	0881
*				0882
*				0883
*				0884
LENGTH	DC	XL1'00'		0885
PACK5	DC	PL5'0'		0886
PACK1	DC	PL1'0'		0887
SIGNTEST	DC	XL1'00'		0888
OUTPACK	DC	PL5'0'		0889
*				0890
*			AUDIT SUBROUTINE	0891
*				0892
*				0893
*				0894
SIGNCHEX	LA	R9,4		0895
	SR	R9,R8		0896
	SH	R8,=H'1'		0897
	STC	R8,LENGTH		0898
	ZAP	PACK5(5),PL1'0'		0899
	LA	R10,PACK5+1		0900
	MVC	LOADVAL+1(1),LENGTH		0901
	AR	R10,R9		0902
LOADVAL	MVC	0(1,R10),INFIELD		0903

FIGURE 17-1a

SYSTEM / 370 ASSEMBLER CODING FORM

Name	Operation	Operand	Identification Sequence No.
	MVN	SIGNTEST(1),PACK5+4	0911
	CLI	SIGNTEST,X'09'	0912
	BC	12,NOTVALID	0913
	ZAP	OUTPACK(5),PACK5	0914
	BC	15,VALID	0915
NOTVALID	MVI	PACK1,X'0C'	0916
	MVO	PACK5(6),PACK5(5)	0917
	ZAP	OUTPACK(5),PACK5+1	0918
	BC	15,COMPLETE	0919
VALID			0920
*			0921
*			0922
COMPLETE			0923
*			
R8	EQU	8	1430
R9	EQU	9	1431
R10	EQU	10	1432
*			1433
			1434
			1435

FIGURE 17-1b

Data Validation

tained in general register 8, that value is subtracted from register 9 in order to determine the displacement factor for moving the packed decimal into its receiving field.

Statement 0902 subtracts the length of the packed decimal value (that length being contained in general register 8) from the maximum possible length of four as contained in general register 9. The result of this subtraction provides a displacement increment if the length of the packed decimal value is less than four.

Statement 0903 subtracts the halfword fixed-point literal of +1 from the value in general register 8. This prepares that value for insertion as a machine-language length into the instruction statement that moves the incoming packed decimal field into its receiving field.

Statement 0904 stores the low-order byte of general register 8, containing the machine-language length of the packed decimal field, into a one-byte storage area labeled LENGTH.

Statement 0906 clears the five-byte packed decimal field to a value of +0 each time this subroutine is entered. This assures that all high-order bytes of this receiving field are zero-digits.

Statement 0907 loads the address of the second byte of the packed decimal receiving field into general register 10. This address, plus the displacement increment contained in register 9, should properly align the packed decimal value that is to be moved into the PACK5 field.

Statement 0908 moves the machine-language length of the incoming packed decimal value from its storage byte into the second byte of the instruction statement that actually moves the value into PACK5.

Statement 0909 adds register 9, containing the displacement increment, to the contents of general register 10. Register 10 now addresses the byte of the PACK5 field that is to receive the value from INFIELD.

Statement 0910, having been modified by Statements 0908 and 0909, moves the proper number of left-aligned packed decimal bytes from INFIELD into the proper right-aligned bytes of PACK5. The correct number of bytes was inserted from the LENGTH field in Statement 0908; and Statement 0909 adjusted the alignment by adding the displacement increment from register 9.

Statement 0911 uses a Move Numeric instruction statement to move the right-most half-byte of PACK5 into a storage work area.

Statement 0912 compares a one-byte area, containing a high-order hex digit of '0' and a low-order hex digit consisting of the half-byte passed to this field in Statement 0911, to a hexadecimal literal of X'09'. This comparison is made to determine whether or not the packed decimal value in PACK5 contains a sign-digit in the low-order half-byte.

Statement 0913 requests that a branch be taken to NOTVALID if the comparison in Statement 0912 indicates that the low-order half-byte of PACK5 contains a hex digit of X'9' or less. That condition would indicate that it is not a packed decimal sign-digit. If that digit was a valid sign-digit the processing logic would fall through to Statement 0914.

Statement 0914 ZAPs (Zero & Add Packed) all five bytes of PACK5 into the outgoing packed decimal field. Regardless of the byte length of the value when it was moved into PACK5 by Statement 0910, it is put out as a five-byte field containing high-order packed decimal zero-digits.

Statement 0915 is a forced branch to the exit statement for this subroutine.

Statement 0916, NOTVALID, is entered if the branch in Statement 0913 is taken. This would indicate that the packed decimal value in PACK5 does not contain a valid sign in the low-order half-byte. The statement itself moves a hex value of X'0C' into the single byte that immediately follows PACK5 in order to reinitialize that byte each time this routine is entered. The hex 'C' digit supplies the standard packed decimal positive sign to the value in PACK5.

Statement 0917 uses the Move with Offset (MVO) instruction to literally shift the packed decimal value that is in PACK5 to the right by one-half byte and into the high-order half-byte of PACK1. This places that value immediately in conjunction with the hex 'C' digit residing in the low-order half-byte of PACK1, effectively creating a validly signed packed decimal value that now ranges from PACK5+1 through PACK1.

Statement 0918 uses the Zero & Add Packed (ZAP) instruction to move the right-most five bytes of the combined six-byte length of PACK5 and PACK1 into the outgoing five-byte packed decimal field.

Statement 0919, VALID, is the exit from this entire subroutine. It consists of an unconditional branch to an assumed routine that is labeled COMPLETE.

It is suggested that the reader originate several packed decimal values of varying lengths of from one to four bytes, both signed and unsigned, and follow the process of that data through this subroutine.

Task 4. In this task, the subroutine receives a validly signed six-byte packed decimal number. If the passed value contains any low-order zero-digits, they are to be deleted by shifting all other high-order digits to the right one-half byte at a time until a significant digit shares the low-order byte with the sign-digit. For example, if the incoming field contains a packed decimal configuration of:

0	0	6	0	4	5	0	9	0	0	0	C

it should pass through the subroutine and be modified so that its configuration is:

0	0	0	0	0	6	0	4	5	0	9	C

The field is collapsed in half-byte increments until the first significant hex digit is placed adjacent to the sign-digit. If the resulting field is a zero-value, the program logic is to go to a special routine labeled ZEROVALU.

The instruction statements for this routine are:

```
TESTPACK    DC      PL6'0'                          04000
*
TESTRTE     ZAP     TESTPACK , INFIELD              04001
            LA      4 , 11                          04002
LOOPIN      TM      TESTPACK+5 , X'F0'              04003
            BC      5 , TESTDONE                    04004
            MVO     TESTPACK (6) , TESTPACK (5)     04005
            BCT     4 , LOOPIN                      04006
            BC      15 , ZEROVALU                   04007
```

Statement 04001, the entry statement into this subroutine, uses the Zero & Add Packed instruction to move the incoming packed decimal value into the work area labeled TESTPACK.

Statement 04002 uses the Load Address instruction to place a fixed-point value of +11 into general register 4. Register 4 will be the loop control counter register for the BCT instruction in Statement 04006.

Statement 04003 tests the left-most four bits of the low-order byte of TESTPACK. The X'F0' operand of the Test Under Mask instruction statement will only cause a one-bit result-bit if any

Data Validation

of the left-most four bit positions of the right-most byte of TESTPACK have a corresponding one-bit.

Statement 04004 is a conditional branch instruction. It states that if the result of the TM instruction in Statement 04003 indicates that one or more one-bits are found in the left-most four bit positions of TESTPACK+5, the program logic would branch out of this statement to TESTDONE. This would indicate that the packed decimal digit currently residing immediately to the left of the sign-digit is a value other than a zero-digit.

Statement 04005 performs a Move with Offset instruction. All half-bytes within TESTPACK are effectively moved to the right by one-half byte except for the low-order byte. The digit immediately to the left of the sign-digit is replaced by the digit to its left and so on, up through the length of TESTPACK. The vacated high-order digit position of the field is supplied with a zero-digit.

Statement 04006 is the Branch on Count (BCT) instruction that creates the loop control back to the LOOPIN statement. General register 4 is loaded with a value of +11, equal to the number of numeric digits in the six-byte packed decimal field of TESTPACK. Each time the processing logic passes through this statement, the BCT instruction would reduce general register 4 by a value of +1. If general register 4 becomes decremented to zero, the processing logic would not branch, but would fall through to Statement 04007. This would indicate that all eleven numeric digit positions of TESTPACK were inspected without encountering a significant digit.

Statement 04007 is a forced branch to a routine labeled ZEROVAL. In order to get to this instruction statement, the processing logic has to fall through the BCT instruction statement. This would indicate that the original value in TESTPACK was, and still is, a total of zero.

Carefully inspect the following set of instruction statements and evaluate what difference they could have in performing the same task as the foregoing statements.

TESTRTE	ZAP	TESTPACK , INFIELD	05001
	CP	TESTPACK , =PL6 ' 0 '	05002
	BC	8 , ZEROVALU	05003
LOOPIN	TM	TESTPACK+5 , X ' F0 '	05004
	BC	5 , TESTDONE	05005
	MVO	TESTPACK (6) , TESTPACK (5)	05006
	BC	15 , LOOPIN	

This set of instruction statements is equal in quantity to the previous set of statements, but would probably result in less processing time if any input values of zero were encountered. The logic contained in Statements 05002 and 05003 would detect any overall zero values before entering the test loop, rather than processing through the test loop eleven times before concluding that TESTPACK contained a zero value. The Load Address (LA) and Branch on Count (BCT) instruction statements are no longer necessary inasmuch as it is known that if a value enters the testing loop, at least one digit position of that value contains a significant digit.

Auditing for Special Characters or Conditions

Because of the wide range of potential applications for this type of task, it would be impractical to give any typical examples. The tasks illustrated within this subject are merely a means of familiarizing you with the overall scope of such routines.

In most instances, a routine calling for special auditing techniques is aimed at transforming or converting one form of existing data into another representation or form. An example of this could be that a unique data file contains a number of different unprintable characters that are necessary for the interpretation of the data on that file when it is listed in printed form. Unless these unprintable configurations were interpreted into some type of printable character, or combination of printable characters, each one would appear as a blank position on a printed listing.

If the problem program logic for auditing data also requires a conversion of invalid characters to valid characters, the Translate instruction provides an exceptional service.

Translate

The Translate instruction utilizes a table consisting of 256 bytes, each byte representing one of the existing 256 hexadecimal configurations. Each table byte is considered to be an individual table segment whose displacement from the beginning of the table is addressed by the binary value of its hexadecimal representation. For example, if the translate table started at main storage location 32,000, then X'00' would represent the first table segment (32000), X'01' would represent the second table segment (32001), X'02' would represent the third table segment (32002), X'03' would represent the fourth (32003), X'04' would represent the fifth (32004), etc. Each byte (segment) of this table, however, does not necessarily contain the same hexadecimal configuration as the one implied by its relative location to the beginning of the table.

In effect the Translate instruction does the following:

1. Takes a byte of data specified by the first operand of the instruction statement.
2. Adds the binary value of that byte to the address of the translate table, which is referred to by the second operand.
3. Goes to the table segment referenced by this incremented address.
4. Extracts the resident character from that segment and places it into the first operand field in the byte that was used to find the relative table segment position.

The first operand field may consist of multiple bytes, in which case each byte is used to address a table segment in order to extract the byte representation from that segment.

In order to illustrate the use of this instruction, assume that a program is to be written that will delete all punctuation and symbols from data fields by replacing such characters with a slash or diagonal bar. This would mean that any bytes of the table whose relative position to the beginning of the table generates a hex value synonomous to a valid EBCDIC punctuation symbol or character symbol should contain the hexadecimal configuration for a diagonal. The standard EBCDIC configuration for this character is X'61'. (See Table 17-1.) Accordingly, the following relative bytes of the translate table would contain a hexadecimal configuration of X'61'.

All other segments of the table would contain the standard EBCDIC character representations. There are three tables illustrated for the purpose of explaining this concept.

Translate Table 1 (Table 17-2) represents the 256 individual segments used within the table. The hex value shown within each segment represents the binary value of the relative position of that segment to the beginning of the table. The implied decimal representation of that binary value is also included in each segment.

Translate Table 2 (Table 17-3), representing the same 256 segments, illustrates the contents of the table if each segment contained the hexadecimal configuration that is implied by the relative position of the segment to the beginning of the table. In this instance the EBCDIC character representations have been included where applicable.

Data Validation 553

Translate Table 3 (Table 17-4) represents the modified table that the programmer would establish for this particular application. Note that the contents of the EBCDIC punctuation symbols and symbol character segments have now been established to contain a value of X'61'—a diagonal.

In the coding statements shown in Figure 17-2a and b, four fields of data are processed through the Translate instruction using the illustration of Translate Table 3 (Table 17-4). These four fields are FIELDA, FIELDB, FIELDC, and FIELDD. For the purpose of this example, these fields have been defined as constants. In a real application, however, the data to be audited would be continually replenished into a work area.

Statement 04001, TRANSOUT, loads general register 6 with a value of +4. This amount in register 6 will be used as a loop control count for the BCT instruction in Statement 04009.

Statement 04002 loads the address of the translate table, TRANSTAB, into general register 7. For the purpose of this example, assume that at program execution time TRANSTAB resides at storage location 53,200. General register 7 would now contain a fixed-point value of +53,200 in the low-order three bytes.

TABLE 17-1

Hex Configuration for EBCDIC Punctuation Symbol or Character Symbol	Character Represented by that Configuration		Relative Byte Position of the Table that will Contain X'61'
4A	Cent sign	¢	4A
4B	Period	.	4B
4C	Less than	<	4C
4D	Left parenthesis	(	4D
4E	Plus sign	+	4E
4F	Concatenate symbol	|	4F
50	Ampersand	&	50
5A	Exclamation	!	5A
5B	Dollar sign	$	5B
5C	Asterisk	*	5C
5D	Right parenthesis	)	5D
5E	Semicolon	;	5E
5F	Not sign	¬	5F
60	Dash	-	60
61	Diagonal	/	61
6B	Comma	,	6B
6C	Percent	%	6C
6D	Bar	—	6D
6E	Greater than	>	6E
6F	Question mark	?	6F
7A	Colon	:	7A
7B	Pound sign	#	7B
7C	At sign	@	7C
7D	Apostrophe	'	7D
7E	Equal sign	=	7E
7F	Quote sign	"	7F

SYSTEM / 370 ASSEMBLER CODING FORM

Name	Operation	Operand	Comments	Identification Sequence No.
*				03900
*		* DEFINING THE TRANSLATE TABLE		03901
TRANSTAB	DS	0CL256		03902
	DC	XL16'000102030405060708090A0B0C0D0E0F'		03903
	DC	XL16'101112131415161718191A1B1C1D1E1F'		03904
	DC	XL16'202122232425262728292A2B2C2D2E2F'		03905
	DC	XL16'303132333435363738393A3B3C3D3E3F'		03906
	DC	XL16'404142434445464748494A4B4C4D4E4F'		03907
	DC	XL16'505152535455565758595A5B5C5D5E5F'		03908
	DC	XL16'606162636465666768696A6B6C6D6E6F'		03909
	DC	XL16'707172737475767778797A7B7C7D7E7F'		03910
	DC	XL16'808182838485868788898A8B8C8D8E8F'		03911
	DC	XL16'909192939495969798999A9B9C9D9E9F'		03912
	DC	XL16'A0A1A2A3A4A5A6A7A8A9AAABACADAEAF'		03913
	DC	XL16'B0B1B2B3B4B5B6B7B8B9BABBBCBDBEBF'		03914
	DC	XL16'C0C1C2C3C4C5C6C7C8C9CACBCCCDCECF'		03915
	DC	XL16'D0D1D2D3D4D5D6D7D8D9DADBDCDDDEDF'		03916
	DC	XL16'E0E1E2E3E4E5E6E7E8E9EAEBECEDEEEF'		03917
	DC	XL16'F0F1F2F3F4F5F6F7F8F9FAFBFCFDFEFF'		03918
*				03919
*				03920

FIGURE 17-2a

Data Validation

SYSTEM / 370 ASSEMBLER CODING FORM

NAME	OPERATION	OPERAND	IDENTIFICATION SEQUENCE NO.
*			03921
*			03922
FIELDA	DC	CL15'AMT. #15 PER'	03923
FIELDB	DC	CL15'ID IS 23-A65-76'	03924
FIELDC	DC	CL15'RATIO 15%PCT EA'	03925
FIELDD	DC	CL15'DATE: 7-15-79'	03926
*			03927
OUTFLDA	DC	CL15' '	03928
OUTFLDB	DC	CL15' '	03929
OUTFLDC	DC	CL15' '	03930
OUTFLDD	DC	CL15' '	03931
*			03932
TRANSOUT	LA	6,4	04001
	LA	7,TRANSTAB	04002
	LA	8,FIELDA	04003
	LA	9,OUTFLDA	04004
	TR	0(15,8),0(7)	04005
NEXTRAN	MVC	0(15,9),0(8)	04006
	AH	8,=H'15'	04007
	AH	9,=H'15'	04008
	BCT	6,NEXTRAN	04009
	BC	15,DONE	04010
*			04011

FIGURE 17-2b

TABLE 17-2. Translate Table 1

a	X'00'	X'01'	X'02'	X'03'	X'04'	X'05'	X'06'	X'07'	X'08'	X'09'	X'0A'	X'0B'	X'0C'	X'0D'	X'0E'	X'0F'
b	0	1	2	3	4	5	6	7	8	9	10	11	12	13	14	15
	X'10'	X'11'	X'12'	X'13'	X'14'	X'15'	X'16'	X'17'	X'18'	X'19'	X'1A'	X'1B'	X'1C'	X'1D'	X'1E'	X'1F'
	16	17	18	19	20	21	22	23	24	25	26	27	28	29	30	31
	X'20'	X'21'	X'22'	X'23'	X'24'	X'25'	X'26'	X'27'	X'28'	X'29'	X'2A'	X'2B'	X'2C'	X'2D'	X'2E'	X'2F'
	32	33	34	35	36	37	38	39	40	41	42	43	44	45	46	47
	X'30'	X'31'	X'32'	X'33'	X'34'	X'35'	X'36'	X'37'	X'38'	X'39'	X'3A'	X'3B'	X'3C'	X'3D'	X'3E'	X'3F'
	48	49	50	51	52	53	54	55	56	57	58	59	60	61	62	63
	X'40'	X'41'	X'42'	X'43'	X'44'	X'45'	X'46'	X'47'	X'48'	X'49'	X'4A'	X'4B'	X'4C'	X'4D'	X'4E'	X'4F'
	64	65	66	67	68	69	70	71	72	73	74	75	76	77	78	79
	X'50'	X'51'	X'52'	X'53'	X'54'	X'55'	X'56'	X'57'	X'58'	X'59'	X'5A'	X'5B'	X'5C'	X'5D'	X'5E'	X'5F'
	80	81	82	83	84	85	86	87	88	89	90	91	92	93	94	95
	X'60'	X'61'	X'62'	X'63'	X'64'	X'65'	X'66'	X'67'	X'68'	X'69'	X'6A'	X'6B'	X'6C'	X'6D'	X'6E'	X'6F'
	96	97	98	99	100	101	102	103	104	105	106	107	108	109	110	111
	X'70'	X'71'	X'72'	X'73'	X'74'	X'75'	X'76'	X'77'	X'78'	X'79'	X'7A'	X'7B'	X'7C'	X'7D'	X'7E'	X'7F'
	112	113	114	115	116	117	118	119	120	121	122	123	124	125	126	127
	X'80'	X'81'	X'82'	X'83'	X'84'	X'85'	X'86'	X'87'	X'88'	X'89'	X'8A'	X'8B'	X'8C'	X'8D'	X'8E'	X'8F'
	128	129	130	131	132	133	134	135	136	137	138	139	140	141	142	143
	X'90'	X'91'	X'92'	X'93'	X'94'	X'95'	X'96'	X'97'	X'98'	X'99'	X'9A'	X'9B'	X'9C'	X'9D'	X'9E'	X'9F'
	144	145	146	147	148	149	150	151	152	153	154	155	156	157	158	159
	X'A0'	X'A1'	X'A2'	X'A3'	X'A4'	X'A5'	X'A6'	X'A7'	X'A8'	X'A9'	X'AA'	X'AB'	X'AC'	X'AD'	X'AE'	X'AF'
	160	161	162	163	164	165	166	167	168	169	170	171	172	173	174	175
	X'B0'	X'B1'	X'B2'	X'B3'	X'B4'	X'B5'	X'B6'	X'B7'	X'B8'	X'B9'	X'BA'	X'BB'	X'BC'	X'BD'	X'BE'	X'BF'
	176	177	178	179	180	181	182	183	184	185	186	187	188	189	190	191
	X'C0'	X'C1'	X'C2'	X'C3'	X'C4'	X'C5'	X'C6'	X'C7'	X'C8'	X'C9'	X'CA'	X'CB'	X'CC'	X'CD'	X'CE'	X'CF'
	192	193	194	195	196	197	198	199	200	201	202	203	204	205	206	207
	X'D0'	X'D1'	X'D2'	X'D3'	X'D4'	X'D5'	X'D6'	X'D7'	X'D8'	X'D9'	X'DA'	X'DB'	X'DC'	X'DD'	X'DE'	X'DF'
	208	209	210	211	212	213	214	215	216	217	218	219	220	221	222	223
	X'E0'	X'E1'	X'E2'	X'E3'	X'E4'	X'E5'	X'E6'	X'E7'	X'E8'	X'E9'	X'EA'	X'EB'	X'EC'	X'ED'	X'EE'	X'EF'
	224	225	226	227	228	229	230	231	232	233	234	235	236	237	238	239
	X'F0'	X'F1'	X'F2'	X'F3'	X'F4'	X'F5'	X'F6'	X'F7'	X'F8'	X'F9'	X'FA'	X'FB'	X'FC'	X'FD'	X'FE'	X'FF'
	240	241	242	243	244	245	246	247	248	249	250	251	252	253	254	255

a Relative position of segment in hex
b Binary equivalent in decimal.

Statement 04003 loads the address of the first of the four data fields into general register 8.

Statement 04004 loads the address of OUTFLDA into general register 9. As each of the input data fields are audited, the translate data is moved into a corresponding output field. OUTFLDA receives the audited data from FIELDA, OUTFLDB receives the audited data from FIELDB, OUTFLDC receives FIELDC, and OUTFLDD receives FIELDD.

Statement 04005 is the Translate instruction. It audits the data field addressed by the contents of general register 8 for a length of 15 bytes. The first time through this instruction general register 8 contains the address of FIELDA as loaded by Statement 04003. The contents of register 8 are

Data Validation

then incremented by a fixed-point value of +15 in Statement 04007 so that the second time through this statement register 8 addresses FIELDB. Each subsequent pass through the instruction set increments register 8 so that it points to FIELDC and FIELDD respectively.

Statement 04006 takes the audited data, as addressed by general register 8, and moves it into the field pointed to by the address in general register 9. On the first pass through this statement register 9 addresses OUTFLDA. On each subsequent pass through the instruction set register 9 is incremented to point to OUTFLDB, OUTFLDC, and OUTFLDD, in that order.

TABLE 17-3. Translate Table 2—Standard Hexadecimal Configurations and Corresponding EBCDIC Representation

X'00'	X'01'	X'02'	X'03'	X'04'	X'05'	X'06'	X'07'	X'08'	X'09'	X'0A'	X'0B'	X'0C'	X'0D'	X'0E'	X'0F'
X'10'	X'11'	X'12'	X'13'	X'14'	X'15'	X'16'	X'17'	X'18'	X'19'	X'1A'	X'1B'	X'1C'	X'1D'	X'1E'	X'1F'
X'20'	X'21'	X'22'	X'23'	X'24'	X'25'	X'26'	X'27'	X'28'	X'29'	X'2A'	X'2B'	X'2C'	X'2D'	X'2E'	X'2F'
X'30'	X'31'	X'32'	X'33'	X'34'	X'35'	X'36'	X'37'	X'38'	X'39'	X'3A'	X'3B'	X'3C'	X'3D'	X'3E'	X'3F'
X'40' ♭	X'41'	X'42'	X'43'	X'44'	X'45'	X'46'	X'47'	X'48'	X'49'	X'4A' ¢	X'4B' .	X'4C' <	X'4D' (	X'4E' +	X'4F' |
X'50' &	X'51'	X'52'	X'53'	X'54'	X'55'	X'56'	X'57'	X'58'	X'59'	X'5A' !	X'5B' $	X'5C' *	X'5D')	X'5E' ;	X'5F' ⌐
X'60' -	X'61' /	X'62'	X'63'	X'64'	X'65'	X'66'	X'67'	X'68'	X'69'	X'6A'	X'6B' ,	X'6C' %	X'6D' _	X'6E' >	X'6F' ?
X'70'	X'71'	X'72'	X'73'	X'74'	X'75'	X'76'	X'77'	X'78'	X'79'	X'7A' :	X'7B' #	X'7C' @	X'7D' '	X'7E' =	X'7F' "
X'80'	X'81' a	X'82' b	X'83' c	X'84' d	X'85' e	X'86' f	X'87' g	X'88' h	X'89' i	X'8A'	X'8B'	X'8C'	X'8D'	X'8E'	X'8F'
X'90'	X'91' j	X'92' k	X'93' l	X'94' m	X'95' n	X'96' o	X'97' p	X'98' q	X'99' r	X'9A'	X'9B'	X'9C'	X'9D'	X'9E'	X'9F'
X'A0'	X'A1'	X'A2' s	X'A3' t	X'A4' u	X'A5' v	X'A6' w	X'A7' x	X'A8' y	X'A9' z	X'AA'	X'AB'	X'AC'	X'AD'	X'AE'	X'AF'
X'B0'	X'B1'	X'B2'	X'B3'	X'B4'	X'B5'	X'B6'	X'B7'	X'B8'	X'B9'	X'BA'	X'BB'	X'BC'	X'BD'	X'BE'	X'BF'
X'C0'	X'C1' A	X'C2' B	X'C3' C	X'C4' D	X'C5' E	X'C6' F	X'C7' G	X'C8' H	X'C9' I	X'CA'	X'CB'	X'CC'	X'CD'	X'CE'	X'CF'
X'D0'	X'D1' J	X'D2' K	X'D3' L	X'D4' M	X'D5' N	X'D6' O	X'D7' P	X'D8' Q	X'D9' R	X'DA'	X'DB'	X'DC'	X'DD'	X'DE'	X'DF'
X'E0'	X'E1'	X'E2' S	X'E3' T	X'E4' U	X'E5' V	X'E6' W	X'E7' X	X'E8' Y	X'E9' Z	X'EA'	X'EB'	X'EC'	X'ED'	X'EE'	X'EF'
X'F0' 0	X'F1' 1	X'F2' 2	X'F3' 3	X'F4' 4	X'F5' 5	X'F6' 6	X'F7' 7	X'F8' 8	X'F9' 9	X'FA'	X'FB'	X'FC'	X'FD'	X'FE'	X'FF'

a Hex contents of each segment.
b EBCDIC representation.

TABLE 17-4. Translate Table 3 (with segments representing EDCDIC punctuation and symbols all changed to contain diagonals)

a / b																
X'00'	X'01'	X'02'	X'03'	X'04'	X'05'	X'06'	X'07'	X'08'	X'09'	X'0A'	X'0B'	X'0C'	X'0D'	X'0E'	X'0F'
X'10'	X'11'	X'12'	X'13'	X'14'	X'15'	X'16'	X'17'	X'18'	X'19'	X'1A'	X'1B'	X'1C'	X'1D'	X'1E'	X'1F'
X'20'	X'21'	X'22'	X'23'	X'24'	X'25'	X'26'	X'27'	X'28'	X'29'	X'2A'	X'2B'	X'2C'	X'2D'	X'2E'	X'2F'
X'30'	X'31'	X'32'	X'33'	X'34'	X'35'	X'36'	X'37'	X'38'	X'39'	X'3A'	X'3B'	X'3C'	X'3D'	X'3E'	X'3F'
X'40' ⌀	X'41'	X'42'	X'43'	X'44'	X'45'	X'46'	X'47'	X'48'	X'49'	X'61'/	X'61'/	X'61'/	X'61'/	X'61'/	X'61'/
X'61'/	X'51'	X'52'	X'53'	X'54'	X'55'	X'56'	X'57'	X'58'	X'59'	X'61'/	X'61'/	X'61'/	X'61'/	X'61'/	X'61'/
X'61'/	X'61'/	X'62'	X'63'	X'64'	X'65'	X'66'	X'67'	X'68'	X'69'	X'6A'	X'61'/	X'61'/	X'61'/	X'61'/	X'61'/
X'70'	X'71'	X'72'	X'73'	X'74'	X'75'	X'76'	X'77'	X'78'	X'79'	X'61'/	X'61'/	X'61'/	X'61'/	X'61'/	X'61'/
X'80'	X'81' a	X'82' b	X'83' c	X'84' d	X'85' e	X'86' f	X'87' g	X'88' h	X'89' i	X'8A'	X'8B'	X'8C'	X'8D'	X'8E'	X'8F'
X'90'	X'91' j	X'92' k	X'93' l	X'94' m	X'95' n	X'96' o	X'97' p	X'98' q	X'99' r	X'9A'	X'9B'	X'9C'	X'9D'	X'9E'	X'9F'
X'A0'	X'A1'	X'A2' s	X'A3' t	X'A4' u	X'A5' v	X'A6' w	X'A7' x	X'A8' y	X'A9' z	X'AA'	X'AB'	X'AC'	X'AD'	X'AE'	X'AF'
X'B0'	X'B1'	X'B2'	X'B3'	X'B4'	X'B5'	X'B6'	X'B7'	X'B8'	X'B9'	X'BA'	X'BB'	X'BC'	X'BD'	X'BE'	X'BF'
X'C0'	X'C1' A	X'C2' B	X'C3' C	X'C4' D	X'C5' E	X'C6' F	X'C7' G	X'C8' H	X'C9' I	X'CA'	X'CB'	X'CC'	X'CD'	X'CE'	X'CF'
X'D0'	X'D1' J	X'D2' K	X'D3' L	X'D4' M	X'D5' N	X'D6' O	X'D7' P	X'D8' Q	X'D9' R	X'DA'	X'DB'	X'DC'	X'DD'	X'DE'	X'DF'
X'E0'	X'E1'	X'E2' S	X'E3' T	X'E4' U	X'E5' V	X'E6' W	X'E7' X	X'E8' Y	X'E9' Z	X'EA'	X'EB'	X'EC'	X'ED'	X'EE'	X'EF'
X'F0' 0	X'F1' 1	X'F2' 2	X'F3' 3	X'F4' 4	X'F5' 5	X'F6' 6	X'F7' 7	X'F8' 8	X'F9' 9	X'FA'	X'FB'	X'FC'	X'FD'	X'FE'	X'FF'

a Hex contents of each segment.
b EBCDIC representation.

Statement 04007 adds a halfword fixed-point literal value of +15 to general register 8, incrementing the address within that register to point to the next input data field.

Statement 04008 adds a halfword fixed-point literal value of +15 to general register 9, incrementing the address within that register to point to the next output data field.

Statement 04009 is the Branch on Count loop control statement. Because Statement 04001 loaded general register 6 with a value of +4, the processing branches back to NEXTRAN three times. On the fourth time through this instruction, general register 6 is decremented to zero and the processing logic falls through to Statement 04010.

Data Validation

Statement 04010 is a forced branch to an assumed end-of-job routine. That routine might possibly extract the data from the four output fields, place new data into the pre-audit input fields and then branch back to TRANSOUT.

Whenever the TRANSLATE instruction is executed on each of the four input data fields, it replaces all punctuation symbols and character symbols with the replacement character of a diagonal. In accordance with the assumption that the first byte of TRANSTAB resides at storage location 53,200 at program execution time, each subsequent segment of TRANSTAB would have an address of "53,200 plus the binary value of the bits that represent the relative position of that segment within the table." For example, the segment with a relative position of X'09' would be at an address of "53,200 plus 9" or 53,209.

The action taken by the Translate instruction on FIELDA is shown in Table 17-5.

The action then taken by the Translate instruction on FIELDB is shown in Table 17-6.

TABLE 17-5

FIELDA Character			Sum of the Value of the Character Added to the Address of TRANSTAB (53,200)	Character contained at this Segment of TRANSTAB		Character Placed into FIELDA by the Translate Instruction
character	hex	binary value		hex	character	
A	C1	193	53,393	C1	A	A
M	D4	212	53,412	D4	M	M
T	E3	227	53,427	E3	T	T
.	4B	75	53,275	61	/	/
ƀ	40	64	53,264	40	ƀ	ƀ
ƀ	40	64	53,264	40	ƀ	ƀ
ƀ	40	64	53,264	40	ƀ	ƀ
$	5B	91	53,291	61	/	/
1	F1	241	53,441	F1	1	1
5	F5	245	53,445	F5	5	5
ƀ	40	64	53,264	40	ƀ	ƀ
ƀ	40	64	53,264	40	ƀ	ƀ
P	D7	215	53,415	D7	P	P
E	C5	197	53,397	C5	E	E
R	D9	217	53,417	D9	R	R

After FIELDA is moved to OUTFLDA, OUTFLDA would contain:

A	M	T	/	ƀ	ƀ	ƀ	/	1	5	ƀ	ƀ	P	E	R

TABLE 17-6

FIELDB Character			Sum of the Value of the Character Added to the Address of TRANSTAB (53,200)	Character Contained at this Segment of TRANSTAB		Character Placed into FIELDB by the Translate Instruction
character	hex	binary value		hex	character	
I	C9	201	53,401	C9	I	I
D	C4	196	53,396	C4	D	D
⁶	40	64	53,264	40	⁶	⁶
I	C9	201	53,401	C9	I	I
S	E2	226	53,426	E2	S	S
⁶	40	64	53,264	40	⁶	⁶
2	F2	242	53,442	F2	2	2
3	F3	243	53,443	F3	3	3
-	60	96	53,296	61	/	/
A	C1	193	53,393	C1	A	A
6	F6	246	53,446	F6	6	6
5	F5	245	53,445	F5	5	5
-	60	96	53,296	61	/	/
7	F7	247	53,447	F7	7	7
6	F6	246	53,446	F6	6	6

After FIELDB has been moved to OUTFLDB, OUTFLDB will contain:

I	D	⁶	I	S	⁶	2	3	/	A	6	5	/	7	6

The action taken on FIELDC by the Translate instruction is shown in Table 17-7.

The action taken on FIELDD by the Translate instruction is shown in Table 17-8.

You may load the translate table segments with any one-byte hex configurations you desire. The contents of each segment will then replace any data being translated that generates the address of that segment.

Translate & Test

The Translate and Test instruction uses the same addressing scheme for the scan-table as used by the Translate instruction. That is, the binary value of the hex configuration of the data byte to be checked is used as an incremental value to the address of the first byte of the Translate table. Unlike the Translate instruction, however, the Translate & Test instruction *does not alter* the configuration of the data field being tested.

The TRT instruction statement takes each byte of the data field of the first operand, generates the unique translate table segment address and inspects that segment. If the contents of that segment are X'00', the TRT instruction continues processing, checking each byte of the data field against the table. If a segment is inspected and found to contain a configuration other than X'00', the scan is terminated. At this point, the TRT instruction loads, into general register 1, the address of the data byte of the first operand that it was checking at the time the exception occurred. It also takes the hex contents of the exception segment from the translate table and places that configuration into general register 2.

Data Validation

TABLE 17-7

FIELDC Character			Sum of the Value of the Character Added to the Address of TRANSTAB (53,200)	Character Contained at this Segment of TRANSTAB		Character Placed into FIELDC by the Translate Instruction
character	hex	binary value		hex	character	
R	D9	217	53,417	D9	R	R
A	C1	193	53,393	C1	A	A
T	E3	227	53,427	E3	T	T
I	C9	201	53,401	C9	I	I
O	D6	214	53,414	D6	O	O
ƀ	40	64	53,264	40	ƀ	ƀ
1	F1	241	53,441	F1	1	1
5	F5	245	53,445	F5	5	5
%	6C	108	53,308	61	/	/
P	D7	215	53,415	D7	P	P
C	C3	195	53,395	C3	C	C
T	E3	227	53,427	E3	T	T
ƀ	40	64	53,264	40	ƀ	ƀ
E	C5	197	53,397	C5	E	E
A	C1	193	53,393	C1	A	A

After OUTFLDC has received the translated data from FIELDC, OUTFLDC will contain:

R	A	T	I	O	ƀ	1	5	/	P	C	T	ƀ	E	A

TABLE 17-8

FIELDD Character			Sum of the Value of the Character Added to the Address of TRANSTAB(53,200)	Character Contained at this Segment of TRANSTAB		Character Placed into FIELDD by the Translate Instruction
character	hex	binary value		hex	character	
D	C4	196	53,396	C4	D	D
A	C1	193	53,393	C1	A	A
T	E3	227	53,427	E3	T	T
E	C5	197	53,397	C5	E	E
:	7A	122	53,322	61	/	/
ƀ	40	64	53,264	40	ƀ	ƀ
ƀ	40	64	53,264	40	ƀ	ƀ
7	F7	247	53,447	F7	7	7
-	60	96	53,296	61	/	/
1	F1	241	53,441	F1	1	1
5	F5	245	53,445	F5	5	5
-	60	96	53,296	61	/	/
7	F7	247	53,447	F7	7	7
9	F9	249	53,449	F9	9	9
ƀ	40	64	53,264	40	ƀ	ƀ

After the data has been moved from FIELDD, OUTFLDD would contain:

D	A	T	E	/	ƀ	ƀ	7	/	1	5	/	7	9	ƀ

A practical application for this instruction would be to locate delimiter or separator characters within variable length fields, records, or messages. For example, assume that a series of records have been completed and created, each record containing several variable-length messages. As each record is created, a one-byte configuration of X'01' is placed between each individual message and also immediately following the last message. These records are now transmitted to another location and it is the task of the receiving location to extract the messages, one at a time, from each of the records. In this instance the location that was programming to receive the message transmission would find it convenient and expedient to use the Translate & Test instruction to find the logical "break" between messages within a record. Because the "break code" used to separate messages is a hexadecimal '01' configuration, the programmer would create a translate table in which all segments contain X'00' except the segment that would be addressed by a relative value of X'01'. As indicated in the previous illustrations, this would be the second physical segment of the table. In the illustration of a translate table for this particular application (Table 17-9), the programmer has chosen to load the exception segment with the same hexadecimal configuration as the one used to address that segment—X'01'.

The coding for this particular application has been created as shown in Figure 17-3.

TABLE 17-9. Translate Table for "TRANSLATE & TEST" Instruction

X'00'	X'01'[a]	X'00'	X'00'	X'00'	X'00'	X'00'	X'00'	X'00'	X'00'	X'00'	X'00'	X'00'	X'00'	X'00'	X'00'
X'00'	X'00'	X'00'	X'00'	X'00'	X'00'	X'00'	X'00'	X'00'	X'00'	X'00'	X'00'	X'00'	X'00'	X'00'	X'00'
X'00'	X'00'	X'00'	X'00'	X'00'	X'00'	X'00'	X'00'	X'00'	X'00'	X'00'	X'00'	X'00'	X'00'	X'00'	X'00'
X'00'	X'00'	X'00'	X'00'	X'00'	X'00'	X'00'	X'00'	X'00'	X'00'	X'00'	X'00'	X'00'	X'00'	X'00'	X'00'
X'00'	X'00'	X'00'	X'00'	X'00'	X'00'	X'00'	X'00'	X'00'	X'00'	X'00'	X'00'	X'00'	X'00'	X'00'	X'00'
X'00'	X'00'	X'00'	X'00'	X'00'	X'00'	X'00'	X'00'	X'00'	X'00'	X'00'	X'00'	X'00'	X'00'	X'00'	X'00'
X'00'	X'00'	X'00'	X'00'	X'00'	X'00'	X'00'	X'00'	X'00'	X'00'	X'00'	X'00'	X'00'	X'00'	X'00'	X'00'
X'00'	X'00'	X'00'	X'00'	X'00'	X'00'	X'00'	X'00'	X'00'	X'00'	X'00'	X'00'	X'00'	X'00'	X'00'	X'00'
X'00'	X'00'	X'00'	X'00'	X'00'	X'00'	X'00'	X'00'	X'00'	X'00'	X'00'	X'00'	X'00'	X'00'	X'00'	X'00'
X'00'	X'00'	X'00'	X'00'	X'00'	X'00'	X'00'	X'00'	X'00'	X'00'	X'00'	X'00'	X'00'	X'00'	X'00'	X'00'
X'00'	X'00'	X'00'	X'00'	X'00'	X'00'	X'00'	X'00'	X'00'	X'00'	X'00'	X'00'	X'00'	X'00'	X'00'	X'00'
X'00'	X'00'	X'00'	X'00'	X'00'	X'00'	X'00'	X'00'	X'00'	X'00'	X'00'	X'00'	X'00'	X'00'	X'00'	X'00'
X'00'	X'00'	X'00'	X'00'	X'00'	X'00'	X'00'	X'00'	X'00'	X'00'	X'00'	X'00'	X'00'	X'00'	X'00'	X'00'
X'00'	X'00'	X'00'	X'00'	X'00'	X'00'	X'00'	X'00'	X'00'	X'00'	X'00'	X'00'	X'00'	X'00'	X'00'	X'00'
X'00'	X'00'	X'00'	X'00'	X'00'	X'00'	X'00'	X'00'	X'00'	X'00'	X'00'	X'00'	X'00'	X'00'	X'00'	X'00'
X'00'	X'00'	X'00'	X'00'	X'00'	X'00'	X'00'	X'00'	X'00'	X'00'	X'00'	X'00'	X'00'	X'00'	X'00'	X'00'

[a] Showing a single exception segment.

Data Validation

SYSTEM / 370 ASSEMBLER CODING FORM

NAME	OPERATION	OPERAND		IDENT
TRANSTAB	DC	256XL1'00'		06001
RECAREA	DC	CL80' '		06002
DUMMY	DC	CL80' '		06003
LENGTH	DC	CL1' '		06004
MSGLENG	DC	CL1' '		06005
MSG	DC	CL80' '		06006
*				06007
INITL	MVI	TRANSTAB+1,X'01'		06008
NEWONE	BAL	6,GETRECD		06009
	LA	7,TRANSTAB		06010
	LA	8,RECAREA		06011
NEXTMSG	TRT	0(80,8),0(7)		06012
	BC	8,NEWONE		06013
	LR	10,1		06014
	SR	10,8		06015
	SH	10,=H'1'		06016
	STC	10,LENGTH		06017
	MVC	MOVER+1(1),LENGTH		06018
MOVER	MVC	MSG(1),0(8)		06019
	BAL	6,ROUTINEB		06020
	LA	8,1(1)		06021
	BC	15,NEXTMSG		06022
*				06023

FIGURE 17-3

Statement 06001 is the Define Constant (DC) that creates a 256-byte translate table consisting of X'00' bytes. In this instance, the programmer has found it convenient to create the entire table in this manner and then move the X'01' code into the exception segment via an instruction statement.

Statement 06008, INITL, uses the Move Immediate (MVI) instruction to place a hexadecimal configuration of '01' into the second segment, the exception segment, of the translate table.

Statement 06009 is a Branch & Link instruction to a subroutine that is to supply the main-line program logic with records containing the messages. The "branched to" subroutine uses blanks to clear out an area labeled RECAREA, places the incoming record into that area, and then returns to the main-line logic via Statement 06010.

Statement 06010 loads general register 7 with the address of the first byte of TRANSTAB, the translate table.

Statement 06011 loads general register 8 with the address of the first byte of the input record work area. This address should also be that of the first byte of the first message within that record. As the routine is processed, general register 8 is incremented to point to the subsequent messages within the record. However, each time a new record is supplied to the routine this statement is executed and general register 8 is reinitialized to the beginning of the record work area.

Statement 06012 is the Translate & Test instruction. As specified by the first operand, it commences processing at the address stated in general register 8 and terminates after testing 80 bytes or when encountering a byte that translates into a table segment that is nonzero. The second operand addresses the translate table that contains the translation segments for the test of the data bytes. As a result of the execution of this statement, the Condition Code will be set to indicate whether or not an exception segment was encountered. Rather than keeping track of the number of bytes already processed within the record area, the programmer has set up an additional dummy area that is located immediately following the record work area. Doing this has made it unnecessary to check if the previous message processed was the last one in the current record. Once the last message in the record has been processed, the TRT instruction statement is executed again. At this time no exception segments are encountered because general register 8 addresses an 80-byte field of blanks. Consequently, the programmer has provided a branch back to the routine that gets a complete new record of messages whenever the Condition Code indicates that no exception segments were encountered during the TRT.

Statement 06013 is the branch just referred to. Whenever the TRT has tested 80 bytes without encountering an exception segment in the translate table, this branch is taken in order to obtain a new set of messages. If a data byte is tested that results in the encounter of an exception segment in the table, the branch would not be taken and the processing logic would fall through to Statement 06014.

Statement 06014 loads the contents of general register 1 into general register 10. At this time, because the TRT must have terminated on an exception segment, general register 1 contains the address of the data byte that caused the encounter of an exception segment. This address is now contained within both register 1 and register 10.

Statement 06015 subtracts general register 8 from general register 10, the resulting difference remaining in register 10. The purpose of this instruction statement is to determine the number of bytes residing between the address where the TRT commences, as represented by the address in register 8, and the address at which it terminates, as represented by the address in register 10. The resulting difference is the total number of valid data bytes that compose the current message to be extracted, excluding the message delimiter of X'01'.

Data Validation

Statement 06016 subtracts a halfword fixed-point literal value of +1 from the contents of general register 10. The purpose of this statement is to reduce the specified byte-length of the current message to be extracted, that length being contained in register 10. General register 10 now contains the length of that message expressed in machine-language, or one byte less than the true physical length.

Statement 06017 stores the low-order byte of general register 10 into a single storage byte. The byte labeled LENGTH now contains the machine-language length of the current message unit to be extracted from the record.

Statement 06018 moves the machine-language length of the current message unit, as contained in LENGTH, into Statment 06019, modifying the length of the move specified by the MVC instruction contained therein.

Statement 06019 extracts the current message segment as pointed to by register 8 in the second operand and moves it into the storage area labeled MSG. The number of data bytes to be moved depends on the length attribute inserted into this statement by Statement 06018.

Statement 06020 is a Branch & Link to another subroutine. It is assumed that this particular subroutine does some type of processing with the message unit extracted in Statement 06019 and then returns to the main-line logic via Statement 06021.

Statement 06021 loads a value of +1 plus the content value of general register 1 into general register 8. Assuming that the contents of register 1 were not altered or destroyed by the subroutine ROUTINEB, that register should point to the message delimiter byte flagged during the preceding TRT instruction. In order to address the next message data byte following that delimiter, it is necessary to increment the value in general register 1 by +1. This statement performs that function, resulting in register 8 now containing the address of the storage byte immediately following the last message delimiter encountered.

Statement 06022 is a forced branch back to the statement labeled NEXTMSG. The processing logic performs the TRT instruction and then as a result of that action:

- Encounters another message unit delimiter and continues processing through Statement 06022 again, or

- Does not encounter a message delimiter within the 80 bytes addressed by register 8, so the logic branches out to Statement 06009 in order to get a new record.

The Translate & Test instruction creates a unique Condition Code configuration if the last byte specified by the length attribute results in an exception segment being noted in the translate table. In this preceding example, however, the length of the data contained within the records was variable, so the programmer created logic to circumvent this problem as explained in Statement 06012.

Aside from the use of the Translate instructions, another real-life example of an auditing technique involves a routine that inspects a rather lengthy field consisting of nearly every conceivable alphanumeric and special character. The requirement for the routine is that upon completion of the audit this field would consist solely of alphanumerics and hyphens, but the hyphens are allowed to exist only if they separate two numeric characters.

On the initial phase of the routine, each byte has to be individually scanned—if it contains anything other than an alphanumeric character, a hyphen, or an "at sign" (@), that byte is to be changed to a hyphen. The next phase is to scan the entire field again, one byte at a time and delete any hyphens that do not separate two numeric characters. As hyphens are deleted, the data field is to be collapsed to the left, keeping the data left-aligned within the field by overlaying the deleted hyphen and subsequent bytes with the data that appeared one byte to the right. When the retention or deletion of the existing hyphens has been determined, and the data record has been collapsed to a left-alignment wherever necessary, the next phase is to scan the field for the '@' symbols. It is necessary, in this phase, to maintain a count of the maximum number of data bytes that may occupy this field, as well as the number of data bytes, left-aligned, which do occupy it.

Whenever an '@' is found within the field, the number of existing data bytes is compared to the allowable maximum number of data bytes in order to determine if the field is full. If the field is not full, all bytes to the right of the '@' are moved one byte to the right. The '@' and the next byte to its right are then replaced with the alpha characters 'AT'. The actual number of bytes occupying the field is incremented by +1 and the scan continues through the field looking for any additional '@' characters. In the event that an '@' is found and the field contains the maximum number of data bytes, no change takes place.

Although the routine just described may sound somewhat imaginary, it is one that has actually been programmed and utilized for a particular application. In reality, the overall audit contained several more phases that were not included within this description because of their complexity. The task examples in the remainder of this section are not as complex, but they should indicate some of the audit techniques that may be used for data validation and transformation other than through the use of the Translate instructions.

Task 1. In this task, the subroutine is passed a field of 200 bytes of mixed data. The subroutine is supposed to check every eighth byte of this data, starting with the first byte, and ascertain whether that byte is a valid EBCDIC alpha character within the range of "A" thorugh "I". If an invalid character is found, that character is to be replaced with an EBCDIC alpha "Z" character (See Figure 17-4.)

Statement 02406 moves 200 bytes of data from INFIELD to a 200-byte work area labeled AUDITFLD.

Statement 02407 uses the Load Address instruction to place a fixed-point value of +25 into general register 5. Register 5 is the loop control register for the process of incrementing through AUDITFLD; the field is 200 bytes long and, therefore, contains 25 eight-byte segments.

Statement 02408 loads the address of the first byte of AUDITFLD into general register 6, which is used as the base register for incrementing through AUDITFLD.

Statement 02409 is the first instruction statement within BIGLOOP. It loads a fixed-point value of +9 into general register 7, the loop control register for passing through the nine bytes of ALPHAS. The loop BIGLOOP is considered to be all of the instruction statements from Statement 02409 through 02417.

Statement 02410 loads general register 8 with the address of the first byte of ALPHAS. Register 8 is used as the base register for incrementing through the nine bytes of ALPHAS, one byte at a time.

Statement 02411 compares a single byte of ALPHAS to a single byte of AUDITFLD. Each time the processing enters this instruction statement from Statement 02410, the address generated by 0(1,6) points to the first character in the ALPHAS table. Each time the processing enters this instruction as a result of the branch taken from Statement 02414, the address generated by 0(1,6) points to the EBCDIC character of ALPHAS to the right of the one previously tested. The loop LITTLOOP is considered to be all of the instruction statements from Statement 02411 through Statement 02414.

Statement 02412 is a conditional branch instruction statement. It specifies that if the single byte of AUDITFLD, as pointed to by register 6, contains the same character as the single byte

Data Validation

SYSTEM / 370 ASSEMBLER CODING FORM

NAME	OPERATION	OPERAND	COMMENTS	IDENTIFICATION SEQUENCE NO.
*				02400
AUDITFLD	DC	CL200' '		02401
ALPHAS	DC	CL9'ABCDEFGHI'		02402
*				02403
*				02404
AUDIT8	MVC	AUDITFLD,INFIELD		02405
	LA	5,25		02406
	LA	6,AUDITFLD		02407
BIGLOOP	LA	7,9		02408
	LA	8,ALPHAS		02409
LITTLOOP	CLC	0(1,6),0(8)		02410
	BC	8,OKALPHA		02411
	AH	8,=H'1'		02412
	BCT	7,LITTLOOP		02413
	MVI	0(6),C'Z'		02414
OKALPHA	AH	6,=H'8'		02415
	BCT	5,BIGLOOP		02416
	BC	15,GETDATA		02417
*				02418
*				02419
GETDATA	- -	- -	- -	02420
	- -	- -	- -	02430
				02440

FIGURE 174

of ALPHAS pointed to by register 8, the program logic should branch to OKALPHA. If the two bytes do not contain identical characters, the program logic should fall through to Statement 02413.

Statement 02413 increases the address in general register 8 by adding a fixed-point halfword literal of +1 to it. General register 8 should now point to the next byte of ALPHAS that is higher than the one tested by Statement 02411. If the loop should be processed all nine times, the last time through the loop general register 8 will point one byte beyond the right end of ALPHAS. This does not matter because the logic drops through Statement 02414 and a comparison is never made using that address.

Statement 02414 is the Branch on Count loop control statement for LITTLOOP. The branch to LITTLOOP is taken until general register 7 is decremented to zero or until the conditional branch in Statement 02412 is taken.

Statement 02415 uses a Move Immediate instruction to move an EBCDIC alpha 'Z' character into the address within AUDITFLD that is pointed to by general register 6. The fact that the processing logic entered this statement indicates that the single byte of AUDITFLD currently being checked does not contain one of the EBCDIC alpha characters that form the constant ALPHAS.

Statement 02416 adds a halfword fixed-point literal value of +8 to the current address contained in general register 6, which now contains an address that points to the next byte of AUDITFLD to be tested. This statement may be entered either through Statement 02415 or via the branch from Statement 02412.

Statement 02417 is the Branch on Count loop control statement for BIGLOOP. The branch to BIGLOOP is taken until general register 5 is decremented to zero, after which the logic execution falls through to Statement 02418.

Statement 02418 is a forced branch to a routine labeled GETDATA, which, although it does not exist within the example itself, is assumed to consist of the necessary instruction statments to obtain a new set of data and re-enter the AUDIT8 routine.

Whenever a new set of 200 bytes of data is ready to be audited, the AUDIT8 subroutine is entered. BIGLOOP checks every eighth byte of the 200-byte field, AUDITFLD. For each byte of AUDITFLD to be audited, LITTLOOP is entered. Each time the logic passes through LITTLOOP, it compares the current byte of AUDITFLD against a table of valid alpha characters, looking for a match. The processing leaves the LITTLOOP routine whenever a character has been found in ALPHAS that corresponds to the current byte of AUDITFLD or if the entire ALPHAS table has been scanned without finding a match. In the latter instance, this would indicate that the current character in AUDITFLD is invalid and the program logic replaces it with a character 'Z'.

Task 2. This particular task requests that the program finds several special hex representations within a continuing source of input. The input to the program is passed to the routine, as requested, by a remote terminal application that transmits the data in 80-byte sections from a storage device. Throughout this data are two special one-byte hex representations—X'37' and X'26'. The hex '26' byte is an END OF BLOCK symbolic; the hex '37' is an END OF TASK indicator. Although the data is passed to the problem program in 80-byte increments, that same data is accumulated in a continuous stream until a X'26' byte is encountered. At that point, the program passes the accumulated stream of data to an output routine that places the variable length records on a direct access storage device. The program must count the number of bytes in each output record and pass that value along in the high-order two bytes of a four-byte field that immediately precedes

Data Validation

the record itself. If an X'37' byte is encountered, it indicates that all available data has now been supplied to the program and this subroutine may be terminated. The implication of this routine is that variable-length records of data, stored at another location, are being transmitted in 80-byte segments and that any one segment may contain the logical end of one record and the beginning of the next.

Before analyzing this routine, it should be mentioned that this does not necessarily represent the optimum method of accomplishing the required task. It does, however, provide some insight into the logic process of an audit of this type.

The instruction statements for the subroutines performing this task and the definitions of the fields are given in Figure 17-5 a, b, c, and d.

Statement 03004, PRESET, would only be entered once during each execution of the program. The functions of Statements 03004 and 03005 are subsequently accomplished by Statements 03204 and 03205 in the BLOCKEND subroutine. This statement loads the address of the first byte of the data portion of the output record area into general register 3. Note that general register 3 has been referred to as R3—this is possible inasmuch as Statements 05003 to 05007 have set up symbolic references for some of the general registers.

Statement 03005 uses the Load Address instruction to set register 7 to a +0 value. This could also have been accomplished by coding—SR 7,7.

Statement 03006, NEWSEGMT, is a Branch & Link to a subroutine that accomplishes the I/O task necessary to supply SEGFIELD with 80 bytes of incoming data. When the data is received, the program logic should return to continue processing at Statement 03007 because this statement has loaded that address into general register 6 before branching to GETSEGMT. This statement is reentered from Statement 03020 each time the current 80-byte segment has been exhausted.

Statement 03007 loads general register 4 with a fixed-point value of +80. Register 4 is the loop control register for stepping through the 80-byte segment one byte at a time.

Statement 03008 loads the address of the first byte of SEGFIELD into general register 5. Each time that a new segment is obtained, this address is reset to the first byte.

Statement 03009 compares a single byte within SEGFIELD, as pointed to by the address in general register 5, to a hexadecimal literal of X'26'. This checks for an EOB (End-of-Block) indicator.

Statement 03010 is a conditional branch. If Statement 03009 results in an "equal" condition, a branch would be generated from this statement to the BLOCKEND routine.

Statement 03011 compares the single byte of SEGFIELD that is addressed by general register 5 to a hexadecimal literal of X'37'—an EOT (End-of-Task) indicator.

Statement 03012 causes a branch to ALLDONE if Statement 03011 results in an equal condition, indicating that all available data has been received from the sending operations.

Statement 03013 moves a single byte of data from the incoming segment to the output record build-area. This byte is moved because it was determined not to be an EOB or an EOT indicator byte. General register 5 points to an address within SEGFIELD and general register 3 points to an address within OUTRECRD.

Statement 03014 adds a fixed-point value of +1 to the address contained in general register 5. That address now points to the next sequential byte in SEGFIELD.

Statement 03015 adds a fixed-point value of +1 to the address in general register 3. That address now points to the next byte in OUTRECRD that is to receive a data byte from SEGFIELD.

Statement 03016 adds a fixed-point value of +1 to the value in general register 7. This value represents the number of bytes of data that have been moved to the output record being built in OUTRECRD.

SYSTEM / 370 ASSEMBLER CODING FORM

Name	Operation	Operand	Comments	Seq
*				03001
*		*	MAIN-LINE AUDITING LOGIC	03002
*		*		03003
PRESET	LA	R3,OUTRECRD		03004
	LA	R7,0		03005
NEWSEGMT	BAL	R6,GETSEGMT		03006
	LA	R4,80		03007
	LA	R5,SEGFIELD		03008
SEGLOOP	CLI	0(R5),X'26'		03009
	BC	8,BLOCKEND		03010
	CLI	0(R5),X'37'		03011
	BC	8,ALLDONE		03012
	MVC	0(1,R3),0(R5)		03013
	AH	R5,=H'1'		03014
	AH	R3,=H'1'		03015
	AH	R7,=H'1'		03016
	C	R7,=F'500'		03017
	BC	2,ERROR		03018
	BCT	R4,SEGLOOP		03019
	BC	15,NEWSEGMT		03020
*				03021
*				03022

FIGURE 17-5a

Data Validation

SYSTEM / 370 ASSEMBLER CODING FORM

Name	Operation	Operand	Comments	Identification Seq. No.
*		ROUTINE FOR END-OF-OUTPUT-BLOCK CONDITION		03200
*				03201
BLOCKEND	STH	R7,PREREC		03202
	BAL	R6,PUTRECRD		03203
	LA	R3,OUTRECRD		03204
	LA	R7,0		03205
	AH	R5,=H'1'		03206
	BCT	R4,SEGLOOP		03207
	BC	15,NEWSEGMT		03208
*				03209
*			(ASSUMED TO CONTAIN THE CLOSING	03400
ALLDONE			ROUTINES OF THE PROGRAM.)	03401
				03402
				03403
				03404
*				03405
*				03600
GETSEGMT			(ASSUMED TO CONTAIN THE INSTRUCTION	03601
			STATEMENTS NECESSARY TO BRING IN	03602
			A NEW 80-BYTE DATA SEGMENT.)	03603
				03604
	BCR	15,R6		03605
				03606
*				03607

FIGURE 17-5b

Name	Operation	Operand	Comments	Identification
* *				03800
PUTRECRD			(ASSUMED TO CONTAIN THE STATEMENTS	03801
			NECESSARY TO WRITE OUT THE CURRENT	03802
			VARIABLE-LENGTH OUTPUT RECORD JUST	03803
			COMPLETED.)	03804
	BCR	15,R6		03805
* *				03806
* * *				03807
ERROR			(ASSUMED TO CONTAIN THE STATEMENTS	03808
			NECESSARY TO ADVISE THE PROGRAMMER	04000
			THAT AN OUTPUT RECORD IN EXCESS OF	04001
			500 BYTES WAS RECEIVED VIA THE	04002
			80-BYTE SEGMENTS.)	04003
	BC	15,BLOCKEND		04004
* * *			*	04005
* * *			* CONSTANTS AND WORK AREAS	04006
			*	05000
R3	EQU	3		05001
R4	EQU	4		05002
R5	EQU	5		05003
R6	EQU	6		05004
R7	EQU	7		05005
				05006
				05007

FIGURE 17-5c

Data Validation

SYSTEM / 370 ASSEMBLER CODING FORM

PAGE 4 OF 4
ASSIGN NO. 17-5D

NAME	OPERATION	OPERAND		IDENTIFICATION SEQUENCE NO.
SEGFIELD	DC	CL80' '		05008
PREREC	DC	H'0'		05009
PRESYS	DC	H'0'		05010
OUTRECRD	DC	2CL250' '		05011
				05012
				05013
				05014
*				05015
*				05016
				05017
				05018

FIGURE 17-5d

Statement 03017 compares the fixed-point value in general register 7 to a fullword fixed-point literal of +500. This is to determine whether or not 500 bytes of data (the maximum allowable size) have been supplied to OUTRECRD without encountering an EOB condition.

Statement 03018 indicates that as a result of the preceding comparison, the program logic should branch to a routine labeled ERROR if general register 7 contains a value greater than +500. This condition would indicate that the maximum length of OUTRECRD, 500 bytes, has already been filled.

Statement 03019 is the loop control Branch on Count instruction. It reduces the value contained in general register 4 by one each time the BCT is executed and branches to SEGLOOP each time until general register 4 is reduced to zero. At that time, the branch will not be taken and the processing will fall through to Statement 03020. This instruction statement controls the reentry to SEGLOOP to a maximum of 80 times—the number of bytes in each segment of data.

Statement 03020 is a forced branch back to NEWSEGMT. If this statement is entered, it indicates that the preceding BCT instruction has signified that all bytes of the current segment have been processed; it is now time to request another segment of data.

Statement 03202, BLOCKEND, is the first instruction within the subroutine that is to handle the output of a completed variable-length record. The statement itself stores the length count of the record, accumulated in the low-order two bytes of general register 7, into the first of two halfwords that immediately precede the OUTRECRD field.

Statement 03203 is a Branch & Link instruction to the subroutine that actually generates the I/O task for writing the output record, OUTRECRD. It places the address of Statement 03204 into general register 6 and then branches to PUTRECRD. After completion of the I/O task subroutine, the processing logic should return to Statement 03204.

Statement 03204 reinitializes the address pointer in general register 3 so that it once again points to the first byte of OUTRECRD in preparation for building a new output record.

Statement 03205 reinitializes general register 7 to a zero value. Register 7 is used to keep count of the total number of bytes supplied to the record being built in OUTRECRD.

Statement 03206 adds a value of +1 to the address contained in general register 5. When this set of instructions was entered, register 5 was pointing to a byte containing X'26' within SEGFIELD. Because the processing leaves this subroutine and goes directly to either NEWSEGMT or SEGLOOP without passing through Statement 03014, it is necessary to adjust the address pointer to the byte immediately following the EOB byte containing X'26'.

Statement 03207 is a Branch on Count instruction using the same register and logic as used in Statement 03019. This is done because the processing logic does not pass directly through Statement 03019 after leaving this subroutine, and it is necessary to reduce the value in general register 4 to determine whether or not all 80 bytes in the current segment have been processed. If the byte containing a X'26', which brought the processing into this subroutine, is the 80th byte of the current segment, this instruction results in general register 4 being reduced to zero and the processing falls through to Statement 03208 rather than branching at this point.

Statement 03208 is a forced branch to NEWSEGMT. If this statement is entered, it indicates that the current segment of data has been exhausted and the processing should go to the statement that arranges to bring a new segment into storage.

Statement 03401, ALLDONE, would be the first instruction of a set of statements that closes the files and performs any other functions necessary to complete the normal program termination.

Statement 03601, GETSEGMT, would be the opening instruction of a set of statements that creates the input I/O task and actually receives the data record from the terminal operation.

Data Validation 575

Statement 03606 is a forced branch to the address contained in general register 6. In this phase of the program, that address should point to Statement 03007, the instruction statement immediately following the BAL that routed the processing logic to the GETSEGMT subroutine.

Statement 03802 is the initial instruction in the subroutine that creates the I/O task for writing out the output record created in OUTRECRD. Because these are considered to be variable-length records, the I/O task would have to specify that the output record is 504 bytes in length—the 500-byte data record preceded by the two halfword areas.

Statement 03806 is a forced branch to the address contained within general register 6. This address should point to Statement 03204, the one immediately following the BAL that brought the processing logic into Statement 03802.

Statement 04001 is the initial statement in a subroutine that must make a decision as to what action is to be taken as a result of the output record area being filled without encountering an EOB indicator. The program logic might include the instruction statements necessary to write a message on the console typewriter for reference by the programmer or the computer operator. On the other hand, it might only want to keep a count of how many records of this type were received by the program. The logic of this program is that since the output record area is now full, write out the completed record by branching to the BLOCKEND routine and then continue processing any remaining bytes as an entirely new record.

Statement 04005 is the forced branch to take the processing logic to the BLOCKEND routine just described.

Statements 05003 through 05007 equate certain general registers to symbolic references. Any of these five general registers may, therefore, be referred to by their symbolic reference (such as R4) or by their actual representation (4).

Statement 05010 is a Define Constant statement that creates an 80-byte field of blanks. As each 80-byte data segment is requested by the program, that segment is placed into this area by the I/O tasks.

Statements 05011 through 05013 define the maximum area (500 bytes preceded by a four-byte count area) for the variable length output record.

Statement 05011 creates a halfword constant containing a fixed-point value of zero. The length of each completed record is stored into this halfword from general register 7, as shown in Statement 03202.

Statement 05012 creates a second halfword constant of zero. This represents the two bytes used by the system when creating variable-length output records.

Statement 05013 creates a 500-byte string of blanks by specifying a duplication factor of two for a 250-byte constant. This constant constitutes the output record field.

This particular set of routines has indicated more of the "housekeeping" tasks than represented in most of the previous examples. Many other instructions that would be required to make this a complete program are not shown. The omitted statements would be the base register assignments, opening the data sets, I/O task macroinstructions for obtaining the input records, I/O tasks for the output records, closing the data sets, the beginning and ending program housekeeping functions, and many others. These have been intentionally omitted because of the wide variance available in the expression of this type of item between the various operating systems. Once again, it will have to be the responsibility of the computer installation with which you are working to provide the proper education on these items. If an OS or OS/VS system is being used, there is an example of creating many of these functions within the section entitled "Basic Program Initialization."

Although the latter two tasks within this particular section did not employ either of the Translate instructions, it would have been entirely possible and practical to use them in solving these tasks. It would be merely a matter of choice on your part as to which way you would prefer to code the statements. Hopefully, you would have chosen the way that represented the most expedient processing of the data, regardless of the amount of coding effort that this required.

REVIEW EXERCISES

1. A single byte within a translate table is accessed by adding the binary value of the hexadecimal contents of the source field byte to the address of the beginning of the _____ _____.
2. A translate table would normally consist of a total of _____ bytes.
3. Whenever the Translate & Test instruction encounters an "exception byte" in the translate table, it loads general register _____ with the address of the source data byte that pointed to the exception byte.
4. When the same type of exception occurs as was specified in the preceding statement, the TRT statement loads the hexadecimal contents of the translate table exception byte into the low-order byte of general register _____.
5. The contents of the individual translate table segment pointed to by a source byte is used to replace the contents of the _____ _____.
6. The programmer may configure the contents of the translate table in any manner that meets the logic requirements of the individual program. (True) (False)
7. In the Translate & Test instruction processing, the binary value of the hexadecimal configuration of the source data byte is used as an _____ value to the address of the _____ byte of the translate table.
8. In a Translate instruction statement the second operand represents the address of the _____ _____.
9. The Translate & Test instruction does not alter the configuration of the data field being tested. (True) (False)
10. The _____ operand of the Translate instruction statement represents the field of data to be translated.
11. When executing the Translate & Test instruction, the processing of that instruction terminates if a translate table segment is encountered whose contents are other than X'_____'.

The remainder of the problems within this review relate specifically to the translation of data using the Translate instruction. Using Table 17-10, apply the coded instruction statement in each problem against the original source field configuration. Then supply the character and hexadecimal configuration of each byte of the translated version of the source field as it would appear after execution of the Translate statement. Remember that the translate table, as shown here, indicates the contents of each of the segment bytes; the hexadecimal contents of each of those segment bytes do not necessarily represent the hex configuration that will represent the address of those same bytes. The translate table is assumed to be defined by the label TRANTABL.

Data Validation

TABLE 17-10. Translate Table—Indicating the Hex Contents of Each Byte Segment

ADDRESS RANGE	_0	_1	_2	_3	_4	_5	_6	_7	_8	_9	_A	_B	_C	_D	_E	_F
0 _	00	01	02	03	04	05	06	07	08	09	0A	0B	0C	0D	0E	0F
1 _	10	11	12	13	14	15	16	17	18	19	1A	1B	1C	1D	1E	1F
2 _	20	21	22	23	24	25	26	27	28	29	2A	2B	2C	2D	2E	2F
3 _	30	31	32	33	34	35	36	37	38	39	3A	3B	3C	3D	3E	3F
4 _	40	41	42	43	44	45	46	47	48	49	4A	4B	4C	4D	4E	4F
5 _	50	51	52	53	54	55	56	57	58	59	5A	5B	5C	5D	5E	5F
6 _	60	61	62	63	64	65	66	67	68	69	6A	6B	6C	6D	6E	6F
7 _	70	71	72	73	74	75	76	77	78	79	7A	7B	7C	7D	7E	7F
8 _	80	81	82	83	84	85	86	87	88	89	8A	8B	8C	8D	8E	8F
9 _	90	91	92	93	94	95	96	97	98	99	9A	9B	9C	9D	9E	9F
A _	A0	A1	A2	A3	A4	A5	A6	A7	A8	A9	AA	AB	AC	AD	AE	AF
B _	B0	B1	B2	B3	B4	B5	B6	B7	B8	B9	BA	BB	BC	BD	BE	BF
C _	C0	C7	D6	C2	E9	D4	E3	C9	E4	D7	CA	CB	CC	CD	CE	CF
D _	D0	D9	F6	C4	F0	F5	C8	F2	C3	C5	DA	DB	DC	DD	DE	DF
E _	E0	E1	D3	F3	F1	D1	E2	E5	D8	D2	EA	EB	EC	ED	EE	EF
F _	F4	D5	C6	F7	E6	F8	C1	E8	F9	E7	FA	FB	FC	FD	FE	FF

12. DATAFLDA

character	F	H	E	C	S	R
hex	C 6	C 8	C 5	C 3	E 2	D 9

    TRANSA   TR   DATAFLDA (6) , TRANTABL

DATAFLDA

hex						
character						

13. DATAFLDB

character	P	J	B	C	S	R	M
hex	D 7	D 1	C 2	C 3	E 2	D 9	D 4

    TRANSB   TR   DATAFLDB+1 (5) , TRANTABL

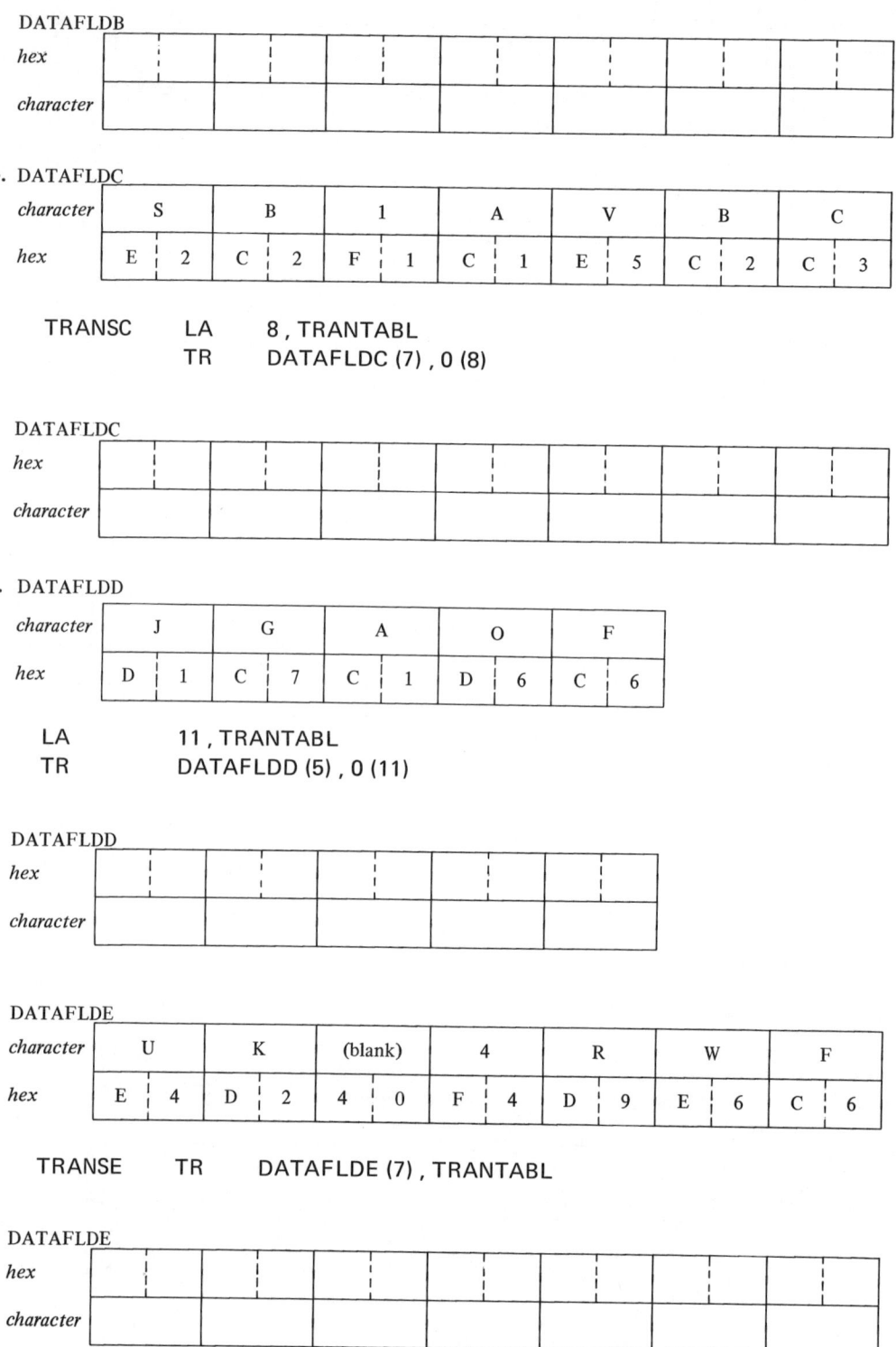

Data Validation

17. DATAFLDF

character	A		P		A		U		A		4	
hex	C	1	D	7	C	1	E	4	C	1	F	4

DATAFLDG

character	6		F		9		Z		R	
hex	F	6	C	6	F	9	E	9	D	9

```
TRANSRTE    LA    5,TRANTABL
            TR    DATAFLDF(6),0(5)
            MVC   DATAFLDG(5),DATAFLDF+1
            TR    DATAFLDG(5),0(5)
```

DATAFLDF

hex												
character												

DATAFLDG

hex										
character										

18

Interpreting Hexadecimal-Formatted Storage Dumps

Each operating system, and even the various control programs within any one system, creates a dump listing that is unique in some way from all others. Because of this fact, the entire process of problem program interpretation and debugging within a dump cannot be completely defined within this text. Technical manuals relative to the exact operating system being used should be utilized in order to determine the control blocks and error condition pointers available to you. As an alternative to this exact information, this section will attempt to aid you in your efforts to interpret the data fields contained within the problem program portion of the dump listing.

To begin with, the hexadecimal dump listing does not describe the format interpretation of the data that it represents. Hexadecimal representation is the highest level of common expression for any and all types of data; binary-expression shares equal commonality but is considerably more cumbersome to interpret. Therefore, it is necessary that you know the intended representation of the hex digits which form the data bytes you are looking at. In order to know the intended representation, you must relate the listed main storage position addresses to the portion of the problem program source listing that they represent.

Most listings of main storage are printed out in lines of data such as:

   007B20 D5C3C540 E6C9E3C8 40E3C8C5 C9D940D9 C5E2D7C5 C3E3C9E5 C540D5E4 D4C5D9C9

The left-most six hex digits represent the beginning address of the storage bytes listed within this line of data:

   <u>007B20</u> <u>D</u>5C3C540 E6C9E3C8 40E3C8C5 C9D940D9 C5E2D7C5 C3E3C9E5 C540D5E4 D4C5D9C9
   ↑
   Address, in hex,
   of this storage byte

Because the system cannot determine the intended representation of each storage byte, each byte is printed out as a two-digit hexadecimal configuration. Every pair of hexadecimal digits has a storage address one byte (+1) greater than the address of the preceding pair of hexadecimal digits.

581

In the illustrations of hexadecimal dump listings used here, there are 32 one-byte positions represented on each line, or a total of 64 hexadecimal digits of storage representation. The hex digits are in groups of eight, equal to four bytes per group. The address of any byte-aligned pair of hex digits can easily be determined by incrementing (in hex) from the address of the first pair of hex digits on the dump listing.

In order to become familiar with the hexadecimal formatting of different types of data fields, study Figure 18-1, an illustration of a partial dump listing that contains the lines with the addresses 007A20 through 007CA0. The first portion of this listing has been interpreted into the character representation of the hexadecimal digits. Note that a hex configuration of X'40' is a valid "blank"; therefore, there is no character representation indicated for such bytes.

Starting at address 007B80, there are nine arithmetic fields that will be subsequently defined. Addresses 007BA0 through 007C11 contain more character data. Addresses 007C12 through 007C51 contain program instruction statements in machine-language form. The remaining portion of the listing contains additional character-interpreted data.

Assume that the arithmetic fields in this illustration have been defined by the programmer as shown within the following statements. At the time that the hexadecimal dump has taken place, these fields have not yet been altered.

```
        FIELD1    DC    PL6 ' 14539 '
        FIELD2    DC    H ' 19 '
        FIELD3    DC    F ' 243621 '
        FIELD4    DC    PL4 ' -25 '
        FIELD5    DC    PL8 ' 213116478 '
        FIELD6    DC    PL1 ' 5 '
        FIELD7    DC    PL3 ' 0 '
        FIELD8    DC    H ' 1365 '
        FIELD9    DC    H ' -1 '
```

The interpretation of the arithmetic fields would be as follows:

FIELD1—Address 007B80 through 007B85.

This field contains a six-byte packed decimal value of +14,539. The hex 'C' in the right-most half-byte of this field indicates that this amount is a positive value and the remaining high-order hex numeric digits indicate the value itself.

FIELD2—Address 007B86 through 007B87.

This is a fixed-point two-byte halfword value of +19. In the instance of fixed-point and binary values, the hex digits themselves are not self-defining as to the assumed decimal value of the field. By using the Hexadecimal/Decimal Conversion Table, you can determine that the hex digit '3' has a value of +3 and the hex digit '1' to its left has a value of +16—or +16 plus +3 equals +19. The overall value is considered to be a positive (+) value because the left-most bit position of the two-byte field contains a zero-digit. This position is the high-order bit position of the left-most hex '0' digit of the field. If this field were represented in bit-format it would appear as:

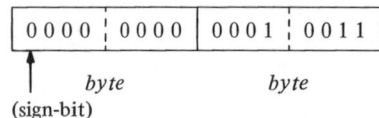

Interpreting Hexadecimal-Formatted Storage Dumps 583

```
                 T H I S     I S     T H E       W A Y       T H A T     A   D A T A       D U M P
        007A20   E3C8C9E2  40C9E240  E3C8C540  E6C1E840  E3C8C1E3  40C140C4  C1E3C140  C4E4D4D7

                 M I G     H T   A   P P E A     R   I N       H E X   A D E C I M A L       F O R
        007A40   40D4C9C7  C8E340C1  D7D7C5C1  D940C9D5  40C8C5E7  C1C4C5C3  C9D4C1D3  40C6D6D9

                 M A T .       D     A T A     A P P E     A R I N     G   I N       S T R   A I G H
        007A60   D4C1E34B  404040C4  C1E3C140  C1D7D7C5  C1D9C9D5  C740C9D5  40E2E3D9  C1C9C7C8

                 T   E B     C D I C       C H A     R A C T     E R   F     O R M       C O U L   D   B E
        007A80   E340C5C2  C3C4C9C3  40C3C8C1  D9C1C3E3  C5D940C6  D6D9D440  C3D6E4D3  C440C2C5

                 I N T     E R P R E T E D       I N       T H E       S A M E       M A N     N E R
        007AA0   40C9D5E3  C5D9D7D9  C5E3C5C4  40C9D540  E3C8C540  E2C1D4C5  40D4C1D5  D5C5D940

                 A S     T     H I S       L I N E       Y O U       A R E       R E A     D I N G   .
        007AC0   C1E240E3  C8C9E240  E3C9D5C5  40E8D6E4  40C1D9C5  40D9C5C1  C4C9D5C7  4B404040

                 F I X E       D - P O     I N T       A N D       P A C K     E D   D E C I M A L     V
        007AE0   C6C9E7C5  C460D7D6  C9D5E340  C1D5C440  D7C1C3D2  C5C440C4  C5C3C9D4  C1D340E5

                 A L U E       S   A R E     I N       T E R P     R E T E     D   I N       A C C   O R D A
        007B00   C1D3E4C5  E240C1D9  C540C9D5  E3C5D9D7  D9C5E3C5  C440C9D5  40C1C3C3  D6D9C4C1

                 N C E       W I T H       T H E       I R   R     E S P E       C T I V   ·E   N U   M E R I
        007B20   D5C3C540  E6C9E3C8  40E3C8C5  C9D940D9  C5E2D7C5  C3E3C9E5  C540D5E4  D4C5D9C9

                 C   R E     P R E S     E N T A     T I O N       A S       I N D I     C A T E     D   W I
        007B40   C340D9C5  D7D9C5E2  C5D5E3C1  E3C9D6D5  40C1E240  C9D5C4C9  C3C1E3C5  C440E6C9

                 T H I N       T H E       F O L     L O W I     N G   F     I E L D   S .
        007B60   E3C8C9D5  40E3C8C5  40C6D6D3  D3D6E6C9  D5C740C6  C9C5D3C4  E24B4040  40404040

                    #1       #2       #3       #4          #5       #6  #7        #8  #9
        007B80   ͡00000014  ͡539C0013  ͡0003B7A5  ͡0000025D   ͡00000021  ͡3116478C  ͡5C00000C  ͡0555FFFF

                 P R O G     R A M     I N S T     R U C T     I O N       S T A T     E M E N     T S     A
        007BA0   D7D9D6C7  D9C1D440  C9D5E2E3  D9E4C3E3  C9D6D540  E3E3C1E3  C5D4C5D5  E3E240C1

                 R E     S     H O W N       I N       M A C H     I N E       L A N G     U A G E       F O R
        007BC0   D9C540E2  C8D6E6D5  40C9D540  D4C1C3C8  C9D5C540  D3C1D5C7  E4C1C7C5  40C6D6D9

                 M A T       A S   R     E P R E     S E N T     E D   B     Y   T H     E   F O     L L O W
        007BE0   D4C1E340  C1E240D9  C5D7D9C5  E2C5D5E3  C5C440C2  E840E3C8  C540C6D6  D3D3D6E6

                 I N G     E X A M     P L E S     .                      #1       #2        #3
        007C00   C9D5C740  C5E7C1D4  D7D3C5E2  4B404040  4040D20D  ͡A0056E4B  ͡4AA0568A  ͡58806C98

                   #4       #5       #6       #7       #8       #9       #10
        007C20   ͡58906C9C  ͡FA106CB0  ͡56BFF911  ͡6CB0568C  ͡4770449C  ͡95E76CB3  ͡47804462  ͡92E76CB3

                   #11      #12      #13      #14
        007C40   ͡41A07B01  ͡4AA0568E  ͡F8106CB0  ͡56BA47F0  449C4040  40404040  40404040  40404040

                 E A C H       2   H E X   D     I G I T     S   A P     P E A R     I N G       I N   T
        007C60   C5C1C3C8  40F240C8  C5E740C4  C9C7C9E3  E240C1D7  D7C5C1D9  C9D5C740  C9D540E3

                 H E   D     A T A     D U M P     R E P     R E S E     N T S     1   B Y     T E   O
        007C80   C8C5440C4  C1E3C140  C4E4D4D7  40D9C5D7  D9C5E2C5  D5E3E240  F140C2E8  E3C540D6

                 F   M A     I N   S     T O R A     G E .
        007CA0   C640D4C1  C9D540E2  E3D6D9C1  C7C54B40  40404040  40404040  40404040  40404040
```

FIGURE 18-1

This field could be considered to be an unsigned binary value. Because it resides on a halfword address boundary (any address that is divisible by two) it is also a valid signed fixed-point halfword value.

FIELD3—Address 007B88 through 007B8B.

This field is intended as a signed fixed-point fullword value of +243,621. It is aligned on a fullword boundary (an address divisible by four). It could also be interpreted as an unsigned binary value. The bit representation of this field would be:

byte	byte	byte	byte
0000 ¦ 0000	0000 ¦ 0011	1011 ¦ 0111	1010 ¦ 0101

↑
(sign-bit)

If this field were interpreted as a fixed-point fullword it would be defined as a positive value—the sign-bit position contains a zero-bit.

FIELD4—Address 007B8C through 007B8F.

Although this field could be interpreted as a fixed-point fullword (because it is on a fullword boundary) containing a value of +605, assume that the programmer has defined it as a four-byte packed decimal field. Therefore, the contents of this field must be interpreted as a packed decimal value of –25. The negative condition of the value is indicated by the hex 'D' digit in the right-most half-byte of the field.

FIELD5—Address 007B90 through 007B97.

This field contains an eight-byte packed decimal value of +213,116,478. The right-most hex digit of 'C' within this field has defined the positive (+) characteristic of the value.

FIELD6—Address 007B98.

This is a one-byte packed decimal value of +5. If the programmer had not declared this single byte as a packed decimal field, this particular configuration could have been interpreted as a character-byte. In the latter instance, the hex configuration of X'5C' represents a valid EBCDIC character of an asterisk (*).

FIELD7—Address 007B99 through 007B9B.

This field has been defined as a packed decimal field by the programmer. As such it may be interpreted as a packed decimal value of +0.

FIELD8—Address 007B9C and 007B9D.

Because the programmer has defined this field as a fixed-point halfword value, it is interpreted here as containing an integer value of +1365. The bit configuration of this field would be:

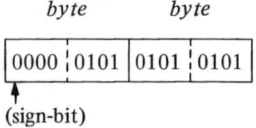

byte	byte
0000 ¦ 0101	0101 ¦ 0101

↑
(sign-bit)

The high-order sign-bit, consisting of a zero-bit, assigns a positive representation to the integer value. The assigned value of this field, +1365, can be verified by summing the "Powers-of-Two"

Interpreting Hexadecimal-Formatted Storage Dumps

values of the bit positions containing one-bits, or by converting the hexadecimal configuration of X'0555' through the use of the Hexadecimal/Decimal Conversion Table.

FIELD9—Address 007B9E and 007B9F.

This field has also been defined by the programmer as a fixed-point halfword value. In this instance, the value content of the halfword is -1. The bit configuration of this field would appear to be:

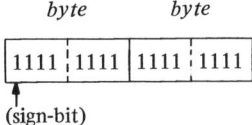

(sign-bit)

The one-bit sign-bit indicates that this fixed-point value has a negative representation—in Two's Complement form. If the programmer inadvertently interprets this field as a binary value, rather than as a fixed-point value, it would be considered to be an unsigned integer value of 65,535.

The instruction statements shown within this dump listing, beginning at address 007C12, have been coded within the problem program as:

```
MVC    0+5 (14 , 10) , BOLE        001
AH     R10 , =H ' 133 '            002
L      R8 , HOLDP8                 003
L      R9 , HOLDP9                 004
AP     PECON , =PL1 ' 1 '          005
CP     PECON , =PL2 ' 030 '        006
BC     7 , NOTWANTA                007
CLI    MINT2 , C ' X '             008
BC     8 , TAP60                   009
MVI    MINT2 , C ' X '             010
LA     R10 , PAVE1                 011
AH     R10 , =H ' 66 '             012
ZAP    PECON , =PL1 ' 0 '          013
BC     15 , NOTWANTA               014
```

While reviewing these statements, it must be assumed that elsewhere within the program there has been coding created to equate some registers to symbolic labels—register 8 equated to R8, register 9 equated to R9, etc.

The fields of data and the labels referenced by these instruction statements are not shown within this particular portion of the dump listing. However, the machine-language format of these statements may be interpreted by their hexadecimal representation as follows:

Statement 001—Address 007C12 through 007C17.

    Instruction code   D2 or MVC (Move Characters)
    Length of move   0D or 13 (machine-language code for 14 bytes)
    First operand address   A005
        A states that register 10 is the base register.
        005 is the displacement from that address.
    Second operand address   6E4B
        6 states that register 6 is the base register.
        E4B is the displacement from that address.

This statement specifies: "Move 14 bytes of data from the field addressed by the label BOLE into an area that is addressed by the contents of general register 10 plus five bytes." The address of BOLE is the contents of general register 6 plus the decimal value of X'E4B', the displacement.

Statement 002–Address 007C18 through 007C1B.
    Instruction code   4A or AH (Add Halfword)
    First operand   A or general register 10
    Second operand address   0568A
        0 is the indexing register; a zero value.
        5 is the base register.
        68A is the displacement.
The statement is: "Take the fixed-point value of the halfword literal constant (located at the address generated by the sum of the contents of general register 5 plus a displacement of X'68A') and add it to the contents of general register 10."

Statement 003–Address 007C1C through 007C1F.
    Instruction code   58 or L (Load)
    First operand   8 or general register 8
    Second operand address   06C98
        0 is the indexing register; a zero value.
        6 is the base register.
        C98 is the displacement.
The statement is: "Take the contents of the fullword HOLDP8 (located at the address generated by the sum of the contents of general register 6 plus a displacement of X'C98') and load those four bytes into general register 8."

Statement 004–Address 007C20 through 007C23.
    Instruction code   58 or L (Load)
    First operand   9 or general register 9
    Second operand address   06C9C
        0 is the indexing register; a zero value.
        6 is the base register.
        C9C is the displacement.
The statement is: "Take the contents of the fullword HOLDP9 (located at the address generated by the sum of the contents of general register 6 added to a displacement of X'C9C') and load those four bytes into general register 9."

Statement 005–Address 007C24 through 007C29.
    Instruction code   FA or AP (Add Packed)
    Length of first operand   1 (machine-language code for two bytes)
    Length of second operand   0 (machine-language code for one byte)
    First operand address   6CB0
        6 is the base register.
        CB0 is the displacement.
    Second operand address   56BF
        5 is the base register.
        6BF is the displacement.

Interpreting Hexadecimal-Formatted Storage Dumps

The statement is: "Take the packed decimal value of the one-byte literal constant (located at the address generated by the sum of the contents of general register 5 added to a displacement of X'6BF') and add it to the two-byte packed decimal field PECON (located at the address generated by the sum of the contents of general register 6 added to the displacement of X'CB0')."

Statement 006—Address 007C2A through 007C2F.
Instruction code	F9 or CP (Compare Packed)
Length of first operand	1 (machine-language code for two bytes)
Length of second operand	1 (machine-language code for two bytes)
First operand address	6CB0

    6 is the base register.
    CB0 is the displacement.

Second operand address	568C

    5 is the base register.
    68C is the displacement.

The statement is: "Take the packed decimal value of the two-byte literal constant (located at the address generated by the sum of the contents of general register 5 added to a displacement of X'68C') and compare that to the two-byte packed decimal field PECON (located at the address generated by the sum of the contents of general register 6 added to a displacement of X'CB0')."

Statement 007—Address 007C30 through 007C33.
Instruction code	47 or BC (Branch on Condition)
Mask value for condition code	7
Second operand address	0449C

    0 is the indexing register; a zero value.
    4 is the base register.
    49C is the displacement.

This statement specifies: "Take the mask value of the first operand and use it to test the configuration of the Condition Code bits within the Program Status Word for an 'unequal' condition. If the Condition Code reflects an unequal condition setting as a result of Statement 006, then branch to NOTWANTA (located at the address generated by the sum of the contents of general register 4 plus a displacement of X'49C')."

Statement 008—Address 007C34 through 007C37.
Instruction code	95 or CLI (Compare Logical Immediate)
Immediate character	E7 or alpha character 'X'
First operand address	6CB3

    6 is the base register.
    CB3 is the displacement.

The statement is: "Take the single eight-bit character that is contained in the second byte of this machine-language statement and compare it to the single byte of data located at MINT2 (the address generated by the sum of the contents of general register 6 added to a displacement of X'CB3')."

Statement 009—Address 007C38 through 007C3B.
Instruction code	47 or BC (Branch on Condition)
Mask value for condition code	8

Second operand address   04462
    0 is the indexing register; a zero value.
    4 is the base register.
    462 is the displacement.

This statement indicates: "Use the mask value of the first operand to test the configuration of the Condition Code bits within the Program Status Word for an 'equal' condition. If the Condition Code reflects an equal comparison setting as a result of Statement 008, then branch to TAP60 (located at the address generated by the sum of the contents of general register 4 added to the displacement of X'462')."

Statement 010–Address 007C3C through 007C3F.

Instruction code   92 or MVI (Move Immediate)
Immediate character   E7 or alpha character 'X'
First operand address   6CB3
    6 is the base register.
    CB3 is the displacement.

This statement specifies: "Take the single eight-bit character that is contained in the second byte of the machine-language statement and move it into the single storage byte addressed by the label MINT2 (the address generated by the sum of the contents of general register 6 plus a displacement of X'CB3')."

Statement 011–Address 007C40 through 007C43.

Instruction code   41 or LA (Load Address)
First operand   A or general register 10.
Second operand address   07B01
    0 is the indexing register; a zero value.
    7 is the base register.
    B01 is the displacement.

The statement is: "Take the address of PAVE1 and load it into general register 10." (The address of PAVE1 is the sum generated by adding the displacement of X'B01' to the address contained in general register 7.)

Statement 012–Address 007C44 through 007C47.

Instruction code   A4 or AH (Add Halfword)
First operand   A or general register 10.
Second operand address   0568E
    0 is the indexing register; a zero value.
    5 is the base register.
    68E is the displacement.

The statement specifies: "Take the fixed-point value of the halfword literal value constant (located at the address generated by the sum of the contents of general register 5 added to the displacement of X'68E') and add it to the contents of general register 10."

Statement 013–Address 007C48 through 007C4D.

Instruction code   F8 or ZAP (Zero and Add Packed)
Length of first operand   1 (machine-language code for two bytes)
Length of second operand   0 (machine-language code for one byte)

Interpreting Hexadecimal-Formatted Storage Dumps 589

    First operand address   6CB0
       6 is the base register.
       CB0 is the displacement.
    Second operand address   56BA
       6 is the base register.
       6BA is the displacement.

The statement is: "Set the first operand field, PECON, to a zero content and then add the second operand, a packed decimal literal constant to PECON. PECON is located at the address generated by adding together the displacement of X'CB0' and the contents of general register 6. The packed decimal literal is addressed by the sum of the addition of the displacement of X'6BA' and the contents of general register 5."

Statement 014—Address 007C4E through 007C51.

    Instruction code   47 or BC (Branch on Condition)
    Mask value for condition code   F or 15
    Second operand address   0449C
       0 is the indexing register; a zero value.
       4 is the base register.
       49C is the displacement.

This statement forces the program logic to branch. It states: "Use the mask value of the first operand to test the configuration of the Condition Code bits. Because this mask encompasses all conceivable Condition Code settings, the program logic will branch to NOTWANTA (located at the address generated by the addition of the displacement X'49C' to the address contained in general register 4)."

If the entire dump listing was presented as an illustration, you would be able to find all of the addresses indicated by these statements.

Although the dump listing contains the complete coding statement of the problem program, the address of these statements, constants, and areas will no longer be the same as the addresses indicated on the program source code listing. The problem program, as it resides within storage of the computer, will be offset from the beginning addresses of zero by some quantity of bytes. This offset could be 10,000, 45,000, 300,000 bytes, or any amount within the range of the available storage capacity of the computer. The number of bytes of this offset not only varies between the different types of operating systems, but also between similar computer systems. This latter variance would be created by the difference between the options specified at system generation time for each individual computer system.

Although there generally is not a predetermined storage starting point of the problem program that is necessarily consistent between the different systems, the dump listing does provide an address pointer to the first byte of the program. Once again, unfortunately, this is another item that cannot be completely defined at this time—the dumps generated by different versions of the various operating systems are not alike in format. For now, it is sufficient to say that the dump listing will provide you with the means of locating the problem program coding.

The offset of the problem program from the beginning address of storage is referred to as a *relocation* factor. For example, assume that a particular problem program actually resides in storage beginning at an address of X'0035A6'. If you want to check the storage contents of a field of data that resides at a source listing address of X'124', you would add that address to the relocation factor of X'0035A6'—X'124' plus X'0035A6' equals X'0036CA'. The field to be analyzed would be located within the dump listing at address X'0036CA'.

The previous illustration of a dump listing indicates that instruction statements are contained in machine-language form, generally referencing storage addresses as a "base register and displacement" combination. Most dump listings provide you with special analysis of the contents of the general registers at the time that the dump function was invoked. You can refer to the contents of a base register, add the desired displacement and use the sum of that addition to find the point within the problem program referenced by the statement you are examining. For example, assume that the instruction statement—BC 8,GOTO—appears within the dump listing in machine-language format as:

   47806390

In this instance:

   47 is the machine instruction code for BC.
   8 is the mask value for testing the Condition Code.
   0 is the indexing value.
   6 is the base register.
   390 is the displacement.

If, at this point, general register 6 contains a value of X'0000380D' the actual relocated address of GOTO within the dump listing could be determined by adding X'390' (the displacement) to X'0000380D' (the base register contents), the sum of which would be X'00003B9D'. This sum would be the address at which GOTO would be found within the dump listing.

In Figure 18-2, another illustration of a dump listing, there are constants of varying lengths and configurations. These represent tables, work areas, switches, and general types of constants. The contents of some of these areas have been altered from the configuration they had when the problem program was loaded; other areas still contain their original values. The instruction statements represented in this dump listing are coded within the problem program as:

```
WORKAREA    DC    CL55 ' ␢ '
BYTESWIT    DC    CL1 ' ␢ '
TABLE4      DC    30PL3 ' 0 '
FULLWD      DC    F ' 10 '
HAFWD1      DC    H ' 0 '
HAFWD2      DC    H ' 20 '
BITSWIT     DC    X ' 00 '
TABLE5      DC    16F ' 0 '
COUNTER1    DC    PL3 ' 0 '
LETTERS     DC    14XL2 ' 0C '
SWITCHNO    DC    CL1 ' ␢ '
```

The contents of this portion of the dump listing are arranged in the same sequence as the DC statements shown preceding it.

WORKAREA—Storage addresses 010F60 through 010F96.

This field consists of 55 bytes, each byte containing the hexadecimal configuration of a valid blank (X'40'). Even though the constant indicates only one blank (which would appear in the first position of the field), the remaining bytes of the field to the right of the first byte were also

Interpreting Hexadecimal-Formatted Storage Dumps

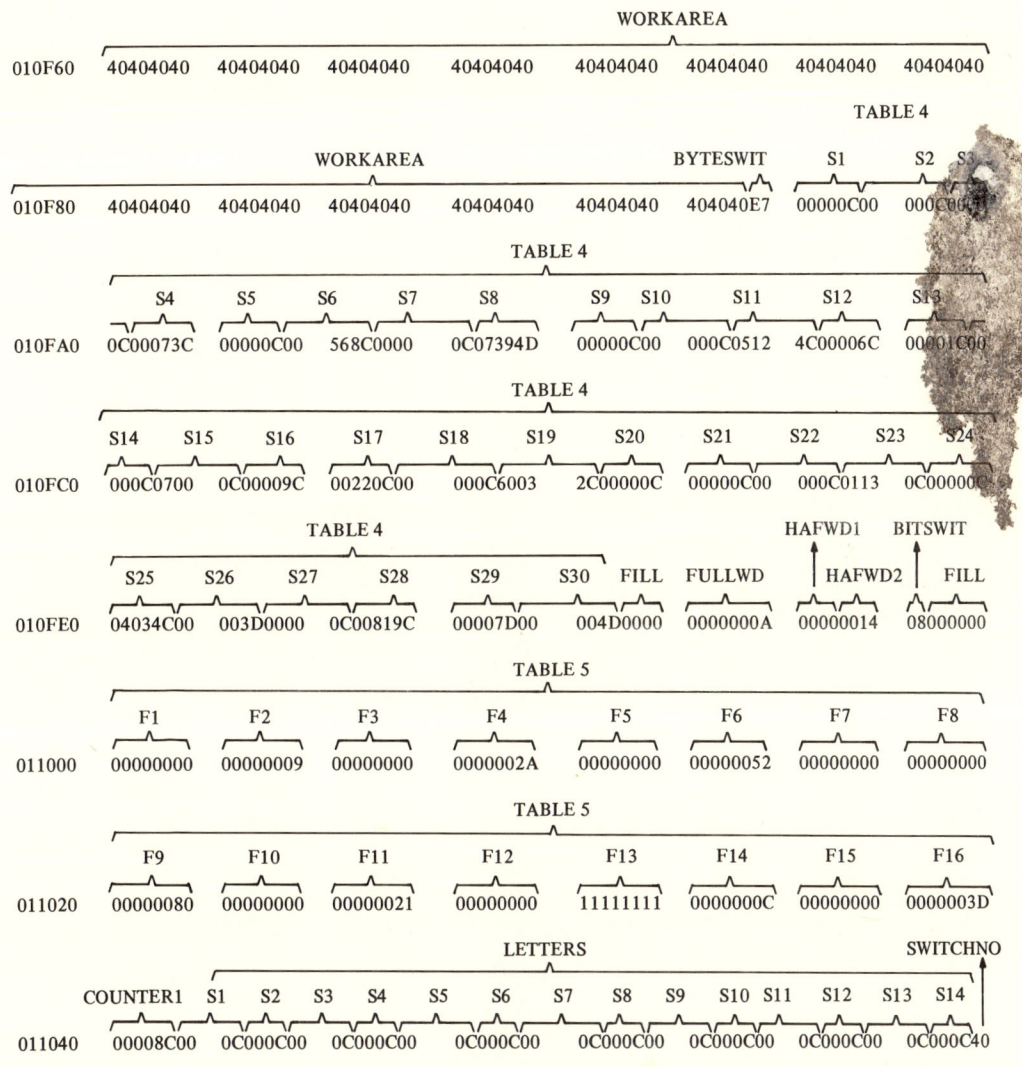

FIGURE 18-2

supplied with the configuration of a blank. This results from the fact that if a character constant is given a length attribute that is greater than the number of characters specified as the constant, then all bytes remaining to the right are supplied with the X'40' configuration of a blank.

BYTESWIT—Storage address 010F97.

This is a one-byte character constant that now contains the hex configuration of an alpha 'X' character. It would be implied that the program logic had moved the 'X' into this byte some time between the point at which the program was initialized and the time when the dump was invoked.

TABLE4—Storage address 010F98 through 010FF1.

This area was originally defined as a table consisting of 30 three-byte packed decimal segments, each segment containing a packed decimal value of +0. Once the program began executing, some of the table segments were supplied with packed decimal values. The current contents of the segments are:

segment number	address	value
S1	010F98	+0
S2	010F9B	+0
S3	010F9E	+0
S4	010FA1	+73
S5	010FA4	+0
S6	010FA7	+568
S7	010FAA	+0
S8	010FAD	-7,394
S9	010FB0	+0
S10	010FB3	+0
S11	010FB6	+5,124
S12	010FB9	+6
S13	010FBC	+1
S14	010FBF	+0
S15	010FC2	+7,000
S16	010FC5	+9
S17	010FC8	+220
S18	010FCB	+0
S19	010FCE	+60,032
S20	010FD1	+0
S21	010FD4	+0
S22	010FD7	+0
S23	010FDA	+1,130
S24	010FDD	+0
S25	010FE0	+4,034
S26	010FE3	-3
S27	010FE6	+0
S28	010FE9	+819
S29	010FEC	-7
S30	010FEF	-4

FULLWD—Storage addresses 010FF4 through 010FF7.

This is a fullword fixed-point constant containing a value of +10. Because the DC statement that created this field specified it as a fullword, the first byte was aligned on the next available fullword boundary. As a result of this alignment, there are two unused storage byte locations between the last byte of the previous constant and the first byte of this one.

HAFWD1—Storage addresses 010FF8 through 010FF9.

This is a halfword fixed-point constant containing a value of +0. It was not necessary to skip any storage bytes inasmuch as the next available byte was on a halfword boundary.

HAFWD2—Storage addresses 010FFA through 010FFB.

This halfword fixed-point constant contains a value of +20. It is aligned properly immediately adjacent to the preceding halfword.

BITSWIT—Storage address 010FFC.

This one-byte storage is assumed to consist of eight bit-switches. Although this byte was initialized as all zero-bits, it now contains a one-bit in the fifth bit position from the left. You would be able to determine the implied logic conditions based on the setting of these switches.

TABLE5—Storage addresses 011000 through 01103F.

This table consists of 16 fixed-point four-byte segments. As specified by the DC statement that created this table, each segment is aligned on a fullword boundary. In order to align the first fullword segment of the table, it was necessary for the compiler to skip the three bytes immediately following the preceding constant. Originally, each table segment contained a value of +0. During the execution of the program, several of the segments received fixed-point values. The current contents of the segments are shown here in detail:

fullword segment number	address	value
F1	011000	+0
F2	011004	+9
F3	011008	+0
F4	01100C	+42
F5	011010	+0
F6	011014	+82
F7	011018	+0
F8	01101C	+0
F9	011020	+128
F10	011024	+0
F11	011028	+33
F12	01102C	+0
F13	011030	−1
F14	011034	+12
F15	011038	+0
F16	01103C	+61

COUNTER1—Storage address 011040 through 011042.

As implied by the label, this three-byte packed decimal field is used as a counter by the programmer. Although originally defined as containing a value of +0, it now contains a value of +8. Whatever event, or item, was being counted, that situation has occurred eight times before the core dump listing was obtained.

LETTERS—Storage addresses 011043 through 01105E.

This area has been defined as consisting of 14 two-byte segments. In the DC statement, however, only the actual contents of one byte (two hex digits) for each segment have been defined. Because the characteristics of the constant have been stated as being in hexadecimal form, the Assembler Language compiler placed the single byte of specific constant into the low-order position of each segment and has supplied hex zero-digits to the remaining portion of each segment. There is no absolute indication of the intended use of these segments, but the total 28 storage bytes allocated to this constant have the acceptable form of 14 two-byte fields, each containing a packed decimal value of +0.

SWITCHNO—Storage address 01105F.

This is a one-byte constant containing a valid blank. This particular constant could be used to reset the byte-switch referred to by the label BYTESWIT.

The material presented in this chapter is only a portion of the overall knowledge required to fully interpret a dump listing. It will provide you with the necessary concepts for interpreting problem data. In addition, it will be necessary for you to obtain the exact format of the dump listings provided by the particular system you are working with and to study the technical manuals available for that system.

Part IV

ACCESS METHODS AND DATA SET FORMATS

19

Data Sets and Data Set Record Formats

A *data set* is a collection of logical data records. The format and data content of these records consist of an organization and information required to provide input data to one or more specific tasks. In this context a data set is considered to reside on a magnetic tape file, a direct access volume, or a similar storage device. The data records of the data set may each be similar in form, size, and data content, or they may vary from record to record. Each record is generally considered to be unique from other records, containing one or more data fields that create the unique identity of the record. For example, a personnel department would probably maintain a data set that consists of one or more records for each employee. Within each record there would be data regarding the employee's name, address, age, dependents, job classification, pay grade, and countless other items. Assuming that in this instance there is one record per employee, each record would be considered to be unique on the basis of the Employee Number contained within that record. In a large corporation or organization, there are many similar or identical proper names—hence the necessity to identify the employee by a unique number rather than by name.

A number of data sets may exist in which the same type of record identifiers are used, but the records within each data set contain a different type of information than that of the other data sets. Referring once again to personnel files, several data sets might exist, in all of which the Employee Number is used to distinguish unique records. One data set could consist of records containing historical or background information for each employee; a second data set might have records containing current year payroll information for each employee, such as gross earnings, withholding taxes, Social Security deductions, net earnings, etc.; a third data set would possibly comprise records containing a history of the supervisor's evaluation of the employee's performance over certain periods of time. Each of these data sets contains records that may be uniquely identified by the Employee Number, yet each is considered to be a separate collection of records due to the different type of data contained within them.

The manner in which each data set is organized is referred to as the *file organization*. For example:

- A data set that consists of records that are recorded in a sequential manner, either logically and/or physically sequential, without any built-in or external referencing indexes, is considered to be a sequential data set.

- A data set that has been created by the data management routines of the Indexed Sequential Access Method is referred to as an indexed sequential data set. This type of data set organization has several levels of internal indexing created by the Access Method. The index structure is used as a reference to the identity key field of the records contained in the data set.

- A data set that is considered to be formatted in a direct organization mode may have a number of different physical attributes. The records themselves may appear within the data set in a logical sequential order, in a physically sequential by random logical order, or in a "spaced" logically sequential order in which dummy records appear between records whose identity field keys are not of a contiguous sequence. The sequence of records for this latter type might appear as, for example, 1, 2, 3, D, D, 6, D, 8, 9, 10, D, 12, etc. A dummy record resides where a data record with a logical key of 4, 5, 7, and 11 should be inasmuch as no data records with those actual identities exist.

- A partitioned data set consists of groups of logically sequential records, each group appearing anywhere within the data set where space is available for its records. In this organization, each group of records is called a *member*, and for each member there is an entry within the *directory* of the partitioned data set. The directory consists of a series of entries, one for each member in the data set. The directory entry contains a name for the member and a *pointer* (an address) to the location where the first record of the member may be found.

Of these various types of data set organizations, all types may be applied to direct access devices. Magnetic tape, however, is generally restricted to a sequential data set organization.

RECORD FORMATS

A record is considered to be a logical set of data fields that provides information directly related to a unique identifier. The identifier provides the ability to distinguish that set of data fields from other sets of data fields, or other records. Depending on the type of data contained within the records, or on the logic of the problem program, the records do not absolutely require an identifier —in the greater number of data sets, however, a record identifier or key is present.

When the records are actually recorded, or *written* on the data set, they may be written in a single record configuration or as a group of records recorded in one Input/Output operation. This latter method is referred to as *blocking*, or creating *blocked* records. To the device that contains the data, there is no difference between a single record or a block of records—either one is treated by the hardware as a logical block of data. It is the data management routines of certain access methods that decide whether or not a *read* or *write* operation results in manipulating data consisting of a single record or a group of records. In order to distinguish the beginning and end of logical data blocks, regardless of whether they are single records or blocks of multiple records, the data storage device skips a certain amount of usable recording space between each block of data. Although this is technically referred to as an *Inter-Record Gap* (IRG), it could be more properly referred to as an inter-block gap—it physically exists between blocks of data. Note the slight difference in terminology here, which might be somewhat confusing—the storage device considers every section of data passed to it by an I/O task to be a block of data; the program logic or access method that passes the data to the device may interpret it as a block of records or as a single record. In other words, either a single record or a block of records is treated identically by the storage device—as a logical block of data.

To provide a graphic concept of a record and the elements it comprises, it is necessary to visualize what the same information would appear to be like if it were printed out on a roll of paper tape.

Data Sets and Data Set Record Formats

For example, the following illustration might represent a portion of a typical personnel record in an Employee Record data set.

Employee number	Employee name			Sex	Age	M or S	Dep	Ins. class	Etc.
	Last name	First name	MI						

one record

The fields within the record cannot be independently identified by the data management routines, access methods, or operating system. These fields have significance only to the problem program(s) that might use the records. The major fields shown within this record are:

Employee number	M or S (Marital status)
Employee name	Dep (Dependents)
Sex	Ins class (Insurance classification)
Age	

and any other field that might appear in the remainder of the record. Within the Employee Name field there are subfields to define the length limitations of Last Name, First Name, and MI (Middle Initial). These subfields, like the major fields, are known only to the problem program. The small blocks shown under each field and subfield represent the variable byte area allocated for the data that is to be contained within that field. The layout of this record is for visual representation only—when the record is either written or read, only the actual data bytes themselves exist. The descriptions of the fields, or the field titles, do not exist within the record on the storage device.

Assuming that the terms "record," "block of records," and "data block" or "block of data" are now understood, it is time to interpret the physical structure of these items as they would be considered to exist on a storage device. Single unblocked records would appear to be located on the recording surface of a storage device as:

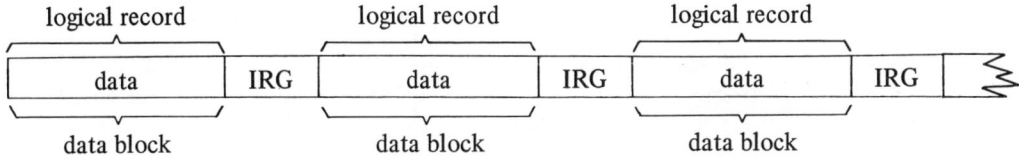

To the storage device, the data contained between two IRG's is a data block; to the problem program, this same data is considered to consist of one logical record.

When the data is formatted in "blocked record" mode, it is considered to appear on the storage device in the following manner:

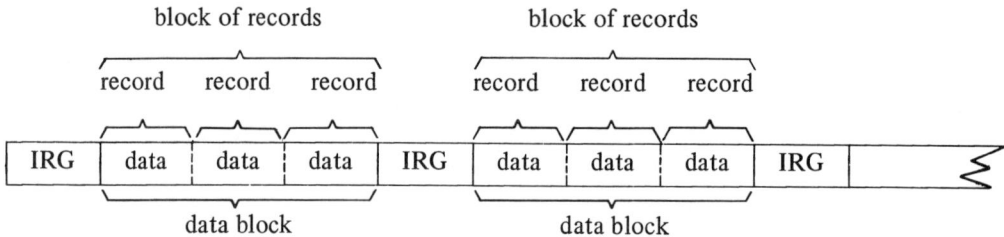

Once again, the storage device interprets the data contained between two IRG's as a data block. However, either the problem program or a portion of the data management routines (if they have been advised accordingly), or perhaps both, will interpret the same data as three unique data records per block. These illustrations are a general interpretation of the appearance of data on a storage device; there are some differences in the manner in which this data would appear on either a magnetic tape or a direct access storage device.

Whenever an access method is used that handles the blocking and unblocking of blocked data records, the program does not need to be concerned when a new block of records has become filled and ready to be physically written onto a data set. The program merely gives an I/O macroinstruction for each record and proceeds with its normal processing. These I/O requests are intercepted by the access method and the records are placed into the block one at a time. When sufficient records have been completed to fill a block, the access method processes the I/O command to write that completed block onto the data set. It then proceeds to start all over again to fill the block with the next set of records as they are passed from the program. If the records are being read from a storage device, the access method routines work in almost the exact opposite manner. An entire block of records is first brought into main storage and then, as the problem program issues each I/O request for a read operation, the access method passes a record from that block to the program, one record at a time. When that block has been emptied, another block of records is provided to the access method for it to pass those records to the problem program.

The individual records may consist of one of three forms—fixed-length, variable-length, or undefined records. Each of these three record forms are described in the subsequent paragraphs.

Fixed-Length Records

When the record form of a data set is described as containing fixed-length records, it is specifying that every individual record consists of exactly the same number of bytes of data. For example, if a data set is described as consisting of fixed-length 300-byte records, every record in that data set is exactly 300 bytes in length. Although the record length is fixed, the interpretation of the data fields within the records does not need to be. The access method data management routines are primarily concerned with the arrangement and the form of the records themselves— the problem program is concerned with the arrangement of the data within the records. Consequently, a data set containing fixed-length records may actually consist of a number of different types of data. The problem program would then be responsible for determining the type of record that it was processing. This can be illustrated by simulating a data set that contains records related to a purchase order reporting system. The data set might contain four types of records, such as:

Type 1 A requisition record
Type 2 A purchase order record
Type 3 A receiving report record
Type 4 An accounts payable record

The internal format of each of these types of records might be:

Type 1—Requisition record

P.O. #	RC	Reqn. #	Reqn. date			Dept.	Expense #	Qty.	etc.
			Mo.	Day	Year				
	1								

Type 2—Purchase order record

P.O. #	RC	Reqn. #	Reqn. date			Vendor code	Buyer code	Item #	etc.
			Mo.	Day	Year				
	2								

Type 3—Receiving report record

P.O. #	RC	Vendor code	Date recd.			Order quantity	Quantity received	Descrip.
			Mo.	Day	Year			
	3							

Type 4—Accounts payable record

P.O. #	RC	Vendor code	Terms	Cost per unit		Quantity	Invoice amount	
				$	¢		$	¢
	4							

These examples display the beginning portion of each of the various types of records within the data set. The access method used to create the data set or to retrieve the records would not distinguish the difference between the various internal configurations; the fixed-length record attribute of the data set would only require the system data management routines to assure that each record was the correct length. It would probably be a function of the problem program to look at the RC (Record Code) byte of each record in order to determine the type of record configuration applied to that set of data, and then to execute the logic applicable to that type of data.

When the problem program logic calls for sequential processing of data set records, it is a definite advantage to block the records. The size of the blocks should be as large as is convenient and practical with the system configuration and storage available to the problem program. Each time that a physical read/write operation is performed, it processes an entire block of data—regardless of whether or not that data consists of a single record or a block of fifteen records. As can be assumed, it takes considerably less time to read or write a block of data containing fifteen records than it does to accomplish fifteen read or write operations of one record each.

When blocked records are used to create a data set containing fixed-length records, all blocks will be the same length with the possible exception of the last block on the file. If the number of records remaining to constitute the final block are not sufficient to create a full block, they are written as a *short block*. The operating system automatically checks for short blocks and makes allowance for them.

Variable-Length Records

Variable-length records may be composed of different amounts of data and types of data fields. Each record may be any minimum valid length allowable by the device on which it is stored, and may be as long as the maximum-size record specified for the data set. In order for the operating system to determine the length of any single record, whether blocked or unblocked, each record must include a four-byte prefix that supplies the length of the record to which it is attached. This four-byte prefix consists of two low-order bytes used by the operating system and two high-order bytes that contain the binary-expressed length of the record. When the data set is being created, the problem program must provide this length for each record. Whenever the record is being retrieved or accessed from the data set, the system uses the existing record length information for length-checking procedures and deblocking functions when applicable.

A single variable-length data record extracted from a data set would appear as:

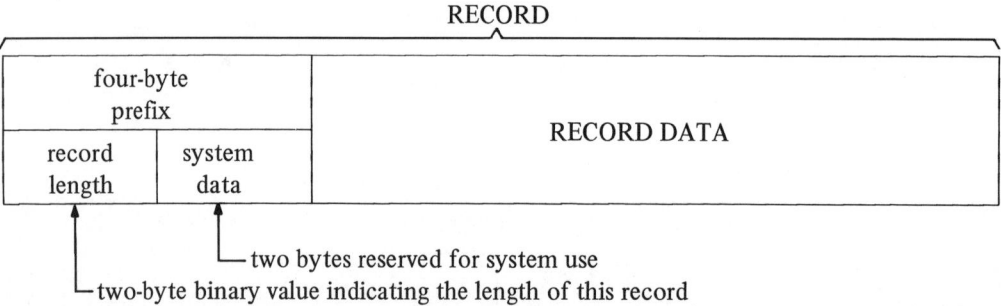

Each and every variable-length record must have the four-byte prefix containing the length specification.

In addition, every block of data that is to be read or written using variable-length records must have a similar four-byte prefix. The block prefix must be present regardless of whether the data block consists of a single record or multiple records. As in the application of the record prefix, the block prefix contains a high-order two-byte binary value and a two-byte field reserved for the use of the operating system. If the access method used to create a data set provides automatic record blocking, the system will compute the length of the block of records and place that value, in binary form, into the high-order two bytes of the block prefix. If the problem program handles the blocking functions within its own logic, then it must also calculate the block length and supply that value to the prefix of the block.

Blocked variable-length records would appear as:

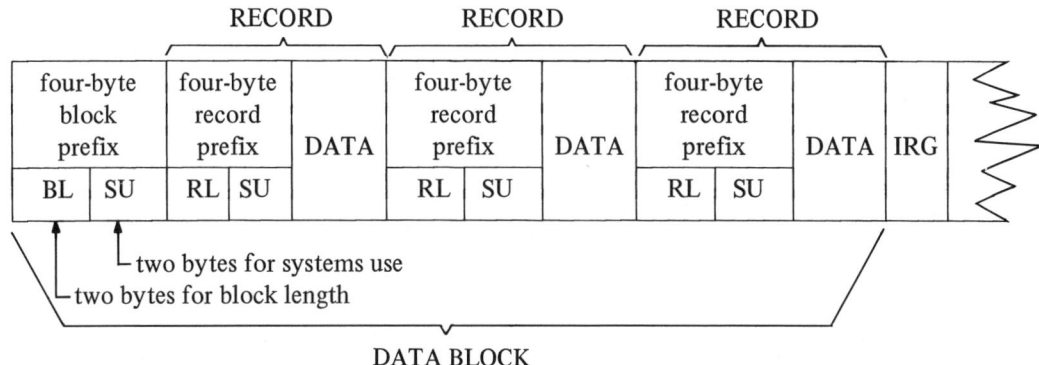

Unblocked variable-length records require a four-byte block count field even though the data block consists of only one record. These would appear as:

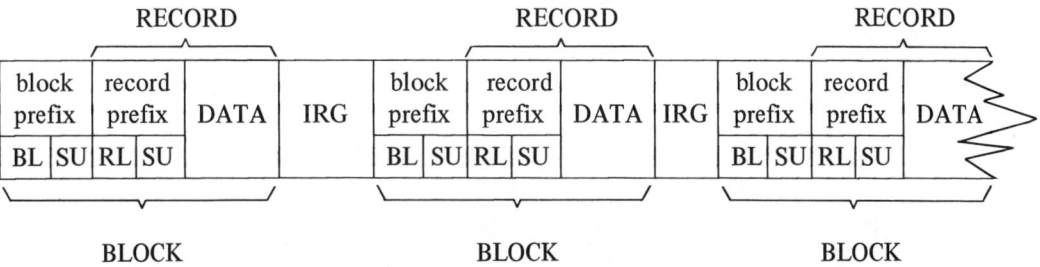

In the latter illustration, the system considers each record to also be a data block, therefore requiring the use of the four-byte block descriptor prefix in addition to the four-byte record descriptor prefix.

Undefined Records

Undefined records are described in some technical manuals as being records that do not conform to the fixed-length or variable-length form. This description does not properly imply the application for interpreting undefined records. If a program is going to create data records, you would have a choice of all records being the same length or being of varying lengths—both types being classified by either fixed-length or variable-length forms. What is an undefined record then? The practical explanation of an undefined record, and its application, is that it is "any block of data that is to be read from an existing data set, wherein the record form and length is not known." The system treats each logical block of data as a single record, regardless of whether or not that block actually consists of fixed-length or variable-length records, blocked or unblocked. If you do not specify a block size large enough to contain the full length of an undefined record, the system only reads in as much data as space has been provided for.

The appearance of an undefined record on a storage device, regardless of its real organization, is interpreted by the operating system as:

| RECORD/BLOCK | IRG | RECORD/BLOCK | IRG | RECORD/BLOCK | IRG | ⋛ |

Data is read into storage until an IRG (Inter-Record Gap) is sensed, or until the programmed data storage area is filled, whichever occurs first. The data records are treated much the same as unblocked variable-length records except that the block prefix and record prefix are not necessarily in evidence with undefined records. If true variable-length records have been read into the problem program as undefined records, the two four-byte prefixes are treated as a part of the data record.

PRINTED, PUNCHED, OR DISPLAYED RECORDS

In some instances, a general reference to the term "data set" is used to indicate sets of records that are directed to a nonstorage type of output device such as a printer, card punch unit, or display unit. The correctness of this use of the term "data set" is a matter of interpretation by the user's installation. As a rule, however, a data set is construed to consist of records stored in an Input/Output device that allows the data to remain there for an indefinite period and to be retrieved, altered, or added to.

The data transmitted to these nonstorage types of devices is properly defined as consisting of records. These records may be either blocked or unblocked as allowed by the system and data management routines under which the data is being processed. The reference is made to this type of data at this point only for the purpose of defining the use of a system function that allows the inclusion of a record *Control Character*. The Control Character referred to in this instance is not a part of the general processing logic of the problem program, although it is the responsibility of the problem program to create that character and place it in the outbound records. If a control character of this type is to be used, the programmer must advise the system of this fact through a specific Data Control Block (DCB) parameter. The one-byte character will appear as the first byte of the data record; therefore, the logical record length must be specified as the logical data length plus one byte.

The purpose of the control character is:

- If the output data is to be punched, the control character specifies the punched card output bin that is to be selected.

- If the output data is to be printed, the control character specifies the line spacing that is to be in effect for each line of printed output.

In the event that you have indicated to the system that a control character is to be included within the output record and then do not provide for one, the system considers the first byte of the data record to be the control character. Conversely, if you create a control character within the first byte of each record and then do not advise the system it should look for that character, that single byte is considered to be a part of the data fields forming the length of the record.

If a record that contains a control character is transmitted to a device that does not utilize, nor recognize, the function of that character, the single byte will again be considered to be a part of the data fields comprising the overall record.

MAGNETIC TAPE DATA SETS

Data sets recorded on magnetic tape are stored on reels that are referred to by the system as *volumes*. Each volume, or reel of tape, usually has been assigned a unique serial number that is indicated on the external surface of the reel itself. Magnetic tape internal labeling procedures, when used, also create an internal label containing the volume serial number. Data sets may then be readily located by both the computer operator and the operating system—the operator using the external serial number for reference, the system using the internal label serial number for reference. One magnetic tape volume may contain a single data set or multiple data sets; a single data set may reside on a series of volumes.

A specific analysis of the construction of the internal magnetic tape labels will not be presented within this text due to the variations employed by different computer installations and operating systems. In general, however, a magnetic tape volume label contains a label identifier, a label-type number, the volume serial number, and other system data. In addition to the volume label, each data set on a magnetic tape may have its own set of labels—system header labels, "users" labels, and system trailer labels. The system header labels and trailer labels contain information regarding the data set; such as record format, block length, record length, tape density, and other information necessary for the system to process the data contained within that data set. Standard users' labels are generally formatted according to the procedures set by the individual computer installation. They are normally used to provide additional information to the program that will utilize those data sets.

When a magnetic tape data set occupies more than one reel of tape, the standard trailer labels advise the operating system whether or not there are subsequent volumes to be processed as a part of this data set. This is accomplished by indicating an EOV (End of Volume) condition in the trailer label. When an EOV condition is encountered, it advises the system that the physical end of the recorded portion of the tape has been reached, but that the data set itself is continued on a successive volume or volumes. In order that the system knows when all data contained within a data set has been passed, the trailer label contains an EOF (End of File) indication.

Admittedly, this has been a brief explanation of what could be a rather extensive subject. It is recommended that you determine the types of labels and label processing utilized by your computer installation and then become familiar with those label types by referring to the manufacturers' technical manuals.

DIRECT ACCESS DATA SETS

Direct access devices, such as disks, use the "volume" concept in much the same manner as magnetic tape volumes. Each pack, in the instance of removable disk packs, is identified externally and internally with a unique volume serial number. This identification is on an internal label called a volume label, usually appearing on the first track of the first cylinder. Unlike magnetic tape, however, direct access volumes maintain a special small data set that provides an indexing service to the operating system. This special data set is referred to as a Volume Table of Contents (VTOC). It is a series of reference entries referred to as Data Set Control Blocks (DSCB), which are created one at a time as new data sets are added to the volume. The DSCBs contain information relative to each existing data set such as the location address, name and general description, as well as information relevant to the volume itself—remaining space available on the volume, space occupied by the VTOC, and other information of this nature.

The initialization of the direct access volume and the creation of a VTOC data set is not an automatic function of the operating system. For example, a new disk pack for a 3330 DSF unit cannot be unpackaged, mounted, and immediately used to store regular data. It must first be initialized through the use of a utility program which performs a Direct Access Storage Device Initialization (DASDI). This utility program has different names among the various operating systems, but herein it is referred to as DASDI. The utility program, and the action that it generates on the volume, also differs among the various operating systems. The general functions of a DASDI-type utility program are:

- Create the volume label and the identity of the volume itself.

- Create the VTOC data set based on the information supplied on control card statements regarding such variables as quantity of tracks to be supplied to the VTOC and the beginning location of the VTOC.

- Do a surface analysis of all standard recording tracks that normally can be addressed by the programmer. In the event that a defective recording surface is found, the DASDI assigns an alternate track from one of the spare tracks on the volume. This is done in such a manner that the programmer does not even need to know that the replacement track has been assigned. A pointer is set within the volume so that any reference to the defective track will automatically be directed to the alternate track.

During the life-span of direct access device recording surfaces, one or more tracks might become defective because of deterioration of the oxide recording surface. In such an event the existing data sets may all be recopied to another device and that volume can be reinitialized by the DASDI program. After the defective tracks have been analyzed and the alternate tracks assigned as their replacements, the volume may once again be loaded with data. Direct access device volumes have unique physical limitations that are not existent in magnetic tape volumes. Recording tracks for certain direct access storage devices are often defined as being capable of containing a maximum number of bytes of data. The real use of this available storage space depends almost entirely on the programmer's specification of the data set format parameters. For example, 100 unblocked records of 30 bytes each would require considerably more storage space than a single data block consisting of 100 30-byte records. This results from the presence of the inter-record gap (IRG) between each logical data block.

Certain direct access devices contain special features, or have optional features available, that permit a data block to begin on one logical track and continue for one or more successive tracks without interruption. This is generally referred to as a "track overflow" feature. What this means is that you are no longer restricted to a record length or block length that is less than or equal to the maximum byte length of a single recording track. The standard byte capacity of a single track on the disk pack for an IBM 3330 DSF is 13,030 bytes—but by utilizing the track overflow feature available with this equipment, the problem program could write a 31,472 byte data block without concern for the physical limitations of a single track. Assuming that such a data block began in the first byte of any single track, the system would record 13,030 bytes on that track, another 13,030 bytes on the following track, and finally 5412 bytes on the third successive track. It should be noted that the track overflow feature functions only when the data set consists entirely of a contiguous quantity of assigned tracks. Any attempt to write a record that would be required to overflow to a noncontiguous track, or to overflow to another volume, creates an error condition.

The allocation of space on a direct access device is provided at the time that a data set is created. Under OS or OS/VS this service is performed by the Job Control Language and the respective job control cards. The request for a certain amount of space, expressed in quantities of tracks, cylinders, or blocks, is coded with the "SPACE=" parameter of the Job Control Language on the Data Definition (DD) card. Whenever space is requested, one of the options provided is the ability to request an initial amount of space and then to indicate an increment of additional quantities of storage space to be provided in the event that the initial allocation is not sufficient to contain the entire data set. In this type of allocation, whenever the space requested by the initial space parameter request has been exhausted, whether during the creation of the data set or during subsequent additions to the data set, the system allocates additional space to the data set in quantities equal to the secondary increments requested. The areas allocated under these conditions are referred to as secondary extents; the original space provided is referred to as the primary extent. Unless specifically stated within the Job Control Language, the secondary extents are not necessarily assigned contiguously with the primary extents or even with each other. The address of each of the extents of a data set is contained within the DSCB (Data Set Control Block) entries in the volume VTOC.

The information provided within this section has been considerably general in nature because variations occur among the different operating systems. It will be necessary for you to obtain copies of the technical manuals that pertain to the type of operating system you will be working with and review them in their entirety. In addition, there are numerous educational courses available through commercial training centers and computer manufacturers educational centers on these subjects.

20
The General Access Methods

This portion of the text is provided for those readers who wish to become somewhat more involved with the concepts of data set organization and the data management routines that create and access data sets. It is written in relation to OS and OS/VS because they are probably the most powerful and versatile of all of the available operating systems at this time. The data contained within this section is presented as an overview of the various access methods and the optional variations available. It is intended to provide a general overall concept of the relationship of the access methods to the file organizations systems and input/output devices without requiring the detailed study of the individual logic modules and macroinstructions of an operating system. However, this data *is not* intended as sufficient educational material to provide the proficiency and knowledge required to apply these concepts, but rather should allow you to grasp the fundamentals of access methods and file organization systems.

As implied, and in some instances specified, throughout this section the decision of which access method to use is based on the following considerations.

- The I/O devices to be utilized.
- The logical format of the data sets involved.
- The requirements of the problem program.

The access method used by the problem program need not be restricted to one particular method. Multiple access methods, or versions of a single method, may be used by the problem program in order to perform its required functions in an orderly, efficient manner.

GENERAL TERMINOLOGY AND DESCRIPTIONS

An access method may be literally defined as " . . . a group or groups of macroinstructions that will interface for the computer Central Processing Unit (CPU) to a particular device, or devices, in order to accomplish input/output tasks for a problem program." In many instances this includes the I/O completion-checking functions, error handling, data formatting, validity checking, seeking and locating data records, etc. Because of the extensive range of device peculiarities, as well as the unlimited scope of uniqueness in problem programs, it is logical that a number of different access methods have been made available to the programmer. This allows the choice of the access method best suited to the task, and the execution of that task within a minimum of parameter coding.

At "systems generation" time, the computer installation has the option of specifying whether or not to include resident access method load modules in the system nucleus each time this system loads into the CPU. If they specify that the resident access method options are to be included within the system, the computer operator might be given a choice of three options at IPL (Initial Program Load) time. Some possible options are listed below.

- The computer operator may advise the operating system, via the console typewriter, that no access method load modules are to be made resident at this time. This would normally provide additional main storage for the problem programs to operate within.

- The computer operator might allow the system to extract, and make resident, a specified list of access method modules. This list would be contained within the "procedure library" of the operating system. That list may be created or altered at any time by the systems programmer responsible for that particular computer operating system. Because of the storage allocations required for these resident modules, discretion and experienced judgement must be used in determining which modules would be on the "resident list" and which ones would not. The systems programmer responsible for creating the list must analyze them in order to determine their priority to be made resident. This would be based on storage size requirements, frequency of usage, time to be saved in having them resident, and similar considerations.

- Another potential option available to the computer operator is to enter the name of an alternate list, or lists, of access method load modules to be made resident for a special system run or test. An example of this could be related to testing telecommunications techniques. During normal system operation, it might be advantageous to have any telecommunications access method modules resident. However, if a special, lengthy telecommunications test was to be made, it would be correct for the operator to reinitialize the system and make resident only the telecommunications access method modules along with any other modules required by this test.

The access methods generally discussed herein are:

BDAM	Basic Direct Access Method
BISAM	Basic Indexed Sequential Access Method
BPAM	Basic Partitioned Access Method
BSAM	Basic Sequential Access Method
QISAM	Queued Indexed Sequential Access Method
QSAM	Queued Sequential Access Method
EXCP	Execute Channel Program

The last method on this list, EXCP, will not be covered except to recognize its inclusion here. It is indeed an access method, but one that would not normally be used by regular programming personnel. As a rule, the EXCP macroinstruction should only be used by systems analysts and systems programmers who are thoroughly familiar with the internal structure of their particular operating system and who have a peculiar task to perform in which they must rely on the "manual" interrogation and manipulation of the I/O devices and channels. You should also be aware that there are numerous other data management access methods not included within this text (TCAM, VSAM, QTAM, BTAM, and others).

The decision regarding what particular version of which access method to use is often, although not always, a compromise. In many instances a preestablished standard or existing data field dictates the use of a particular access method. If this is not the case, then the compromise is entered into, based partially on the knowledge and capability of the programmer. It is entirely possible that an experienced programmer can manipulate a basic access method more efficiently than the performance of the queued version of an access method. The additional effort of detailed instruction and macro coding expended to obtain this control is rewarded by increased efficiency. Consequently, someone not as thoroughly experienced in the dictates of a basic access method could find it advantageous to use a queued access method wherever possible. Inefficient use of an access method, or the use of an access method that is poorly matched to the task, can result in excessive degradation of the performance of the problem program.

BASIC VERSUS QUEUED ACCESS METHODS

A graphic comparison between the basic and queued versions of access methods would be the action of preparing a cup of coffee, brewed to your particular liking, adding the measured ingredients, and stirring (Basic)—as opposed to pushing a button on a vending machine and having a prepared cup of coffee poured for you (Queued). The results may be coincidentally the same, but this is not likely the case.

In the one instance (Basic), it is the programmer's responsibility to determine that all of the necessary parameters are supplied and functions performed in order to achieve the desired result; in the other instance (Queued), many of the detail functions are performed for the programmer, leaving only the responsibility of controlling the major parameter functions.

The five "manual versus automatic" functional differences between basic and queued access methods are the I/O Overlap Synchronization, Anticipatory Buffering, Blocking and Unblocking of Records, I/O Completion Checking, and Error Analysis and Exits. A comparison of these items follows.

I/O Overlap Synchronization

Basic: Each time that the problem program issues an I/O request, that request is passed on to the system to await execution. However, control is returned to the problem program immediately. If it is logically necessary for the physical I/O task to be completed before additional processing may take place, the program is required to wait for the termination of that I/O event and to test for its successful completion. It is conceivably possible for the programmer to anticipate the need for an I/O request and to consequently issue such a request prior to that point where the logic would depend on completion of that I/O event. If the I/O request is dependent on the result of the logic to determine which record should be retrieved or created next, or which device should be accessed next, this technique would be impractical.

Queued: The issuance of an I/O request does not necessarily result in a processing delay at the time that the request is issued by the problem program, as will be explained in the discussion of Anticipatory Buffering. However, if an I/O request should happen to result in an immediate physical I/O task, control might not be returned to the problem program until all functions of the task have been completed.

Anticipatory Buffering

Basic: Because an operating system cannot predict the sequence in which records are to be processed under a basic access method, anticipatory buffering is not accomplished. The programmer does, however, have macroinstructions available to aid in manipulating buffer control. Buffers are filled, or emptied, in their entirety each time the problem program initiates an I/O request.

Queued: Buffer processing is controlled by the operating system in such a manner that an I/O request by the problem program need not result in a physical I/O task at that time. If it does, an entire buffer of data may be filled, or emptied by the one physical I/O task, deferring the need for a separate physical I/O task each time the problem program requires another single unit of data. The status and location of the next selective buffer of data to be processed is automatically controlled.

Blocking and Unblocking

Basic: The basic access method macros process blocks of data only. Therefore, a block of data that consists of more than one logical record must be blocked or unblocked by the responsible problem program.

Queued: The macroinstructions provided with the queued access methods automatically manipulate the blocking and unblocking of records. This action is based on parameters specified in the problem program DCB (Data Control Block) or from data supplied by the Job Control Language or data set labels. The problem program needs only to request a record for processing, upon which request the combined operating system/access method provides it with the next logically sequential record that should be processed. The programmer never needs to be concerned with which block, or even which buffer, has passed the record; or whether or not a physical I/O task was performed at that time. The reverse action is appropriate when the problem program is creating records to place onto an output data set. The created records are passed to the access method data management routines and thereafter it is the responsibility of those routines to determine when an actual physical I/O task is to be accomplished in order to place those records on the data set.

I/O Operation Completion and Error Exits

Basic: In order to be assured of proper I/O completion, the problem program may issue a CHECK macroinstruction that, in turn, will:

1. Cause the problem program to enter a "wait" condition until that physical I/O task is ended.
2. Test the Event Control Block for successful I/O completion.
3. Return control to the problem program if the I/O was successfully completed; or,
4. Reroute control to an error analysis routine if the I/O completion was not normal.

In lieu of the CHECK macroinstruction, the problem program may issue its own WAIT macroinstruction and then test the condition of the Event Control Block in order to determine the status of the condition codes returned as a result of the I/O task.

Queued: The access method data management routines automatically handle all functions of completion status checking, error conditions and error routine routing, end-of-file conditions, and end-of-volume conditions. Control is not returned to the problem program until these functions have been completed.

It should be noted at this point that there is not a queued access method counterpart for each of the basic access methods. Although the basic access methods being discussed include direct, indexed sequential, partitioned and sequential, the queued access methods include only indexed sequential and sequential. The direct and partitioned access methods contain inherent variables that preclude the use of a queued access method. For example, as discussed previously within this section, the anticipatory buffering provided by a queued access method depends on a predictable sequence of record accessing. This predictable sequence does not exist in a direct or partitioned access method, hence they have no queued versions at this time.

DIRECT ACCESS METHODS

As implied by the title, a direct access method is used to access or create data sets residing on a direct access storage device.

The intent and purpose of direct addressing via direct accessing techniques is to be able to locate randomly organized records within the data set without reading or writing through multiple records that might precede, or follow, the record position that is being sought. This objective can be obtained with reasonably little overhead by using one of three addressing methods—direct addressing, direct addressing via the use of cross-reference tables, and indirect addressing with a randomizing/numerical conversion base. In these methods, identification of any particular record can be expressed in a number of ways: by relative record number, by relative track and actual record number, by relative record and actual identity key, by relative track and actual record number, by relative track and actual identity key, and by an actual address that consists of the unit, cylinder, track, and record numbers. In addition, there is an extended search option that scans a specified number of records or tracks in an effort to locate the desired record position. Three of these methods of specifying the address of a record should be further defined as follows.

Relative record number. This type of addressing indicates the relative location of the record within the entire data set; relative to the point immediately prior to the first record within the data set. The access method then computes the actual track and record position based on the physical number of records per track. This reference is applicable only when used with fixed-length unblocked records.

Relative track and actual key. The addressing here is the relative location of the track containing the record (in relationship to the beginning of the data set) and an address of a program defined field containing the value of the identity key that represents the identification of the record to be located. The system computes the actual track address and then searches that track for the record with the matching key value.

Relative track and actual record number. This type of address represents the relative location of the track containing the record (in relationship to the beginning of the data set) and the actual record number on the track. The system computes the actual track address and then goes to the actual record number on that track.

Direct addressing uses the principal that each record, record identifier, or key reflects a sequential/contiguous numbering system that represents the relationship of that record to its relative position within the data set. This is the technique utilized by Relative Record addressing. One example of this might be that if a set of data records contains key identities whose values range contiguously from 1 to 500, a record with a key identity of 236 would be construed to be the 236th record within that data set.

Direct address via the use of a cross-reference table may be interpreted as a form of indexing. In utilizing this technique, it is necessary to create a table containing the actual address (or a relative track and record number) at the time at which the data record is written and stored on the device. The building of that table is the responsibility of the problem program. When attempting to access the data records, it is then necessary for the problem program to search the table for the identifier of this record, find the actual or relative address associated with it, and then use that information to direct the I/O request to the data record desired. Under normal considerations, this scheme of direct addressing would appear to be prohibitive for any large-volume files. However, it is entirely possible to use subtables for records containing identifiers with similar attribute groupings, somewhat in the same manner as the index levels of a dictionary might be arranged. For example, if the record identifiers consist of alphabetic characters, a set of subtables could be organized for the letters from A to F, from G to K, from L to Q, from R to U, and from V to Z. Consideration should be given to the possibility of frequency grouping of certain characters or values. That is, the majority of records may possibly be grouped under a relatively small percentage of the identifier characters, resulting in extremely unbalanced subtables.

Indirect addressing via randomizing or numerical conversion can become quite complex. Generally, it is performed by a mathematical manipulation of the record identity key in such a manner as to create a unique identifier that relates to the address of the track containing the record. There are many such randomizing/conversion procedures that may have considerable merit. The majority of technical manuals make no attempt to completely define or to recommend a particular procedure of this type because of the quantity of different types of techniques that are available. It is the user's option to select the one that is most adaptable to his needs.

In essence, then, a direct access method is used to address and access any position within a data set comprising records that may appear in a nonsequential, noncontiguous identity pattern.

SEQUENTIAL ACCESS METHODS

Sequential access methods have the widest range of device-independent applications of any of the access methods. They can be applied to magnetic tape, paper tape devices, printers, card reader/punches, and direct access devices. It is this latitude of performance that allows the sequential access methods to increase computer facility capabilities through the concepts of *device independence*.

Sequential file organization is the common link between data sets and device independence. The problem program itself may omit all reference to device-dependent characteristics. At execution time, such references may be inserted via the job stream or by computer operator intervention. If the problem program requests 80-character data records, it can be designed to accept such records from any device capable of passing them to it—card reader, magnetic tape, or direct access device. This can prove to be a valuable aid in efficient computer scheduling and utilization.

Although it might be normal to assume that a sequential access method is used only to process sequentially-organized data sets, this is not a factual assumption. A data set residing on a direct access device can be processed sequentially, regardless of the data set organization pattern. Generally, however, the realistic interpretation of a sequential access method is to *sequentially access* a stream of data (one block or record of data following another) in a contiguous manner, whether or not the data is in a logically sequential order of value or identity.

Conversely, a sequential data set is usually considered to be in a logical sequential order based on the criteria of a particular identity or value arranged in an ascending or descending sequence.

In addition, data sets with a format of other than sequential organization may be created by a sequential access method and later interrogated by an altogether different access method, depending on the format in which it was arranged.

When the Queued Sequential Access Method (QSAM) is used in conjunction with multiple buffering, the most efficient use of processing overlap with I/O tasks is realized. If a problem program specifies three buffer areas, each of which would contain a block of data consisting of 20 data records, a physical I/O task might be accomplished for every 20 data records processed—each time all of the data in a single buffer area is used. This would mean that the problem program would still have data records to be processed, during which time a physical I/O task could be completed and the recently emptied buffer(s) could be replenished with data and requeued for usage. It must be pointed out, however, that each buffer occupies storage within the problem program partition; three 2000-byte buffers would occupy 6000 bytes of storage. The decision must be made as to which factor is the more important—process time or storage availability.

INDEXED SEQUENTIAL ACCESS METHODS

The indexed sequential data set format is an arrangement of records in a logical order, based on the criteria of sequence of a particular value or identity related to each record. As each block of records or record is written, the system precedes that block of data with an identity key. This key contains the identity value of the highest-value record within that block. In a logical sequence mode, this would be the value of the last record within a block of records—if the records were unblocked, this would be the key of the single, unblocked record.

In order to easily find a particular record, up to three unique levels of index are created by the data management routines at the time that the data set is generated. These are the track index, the cylinder index, and the master index. Depending on the size of the data set, it is usually quite practical to use only two of these index levels—the track index and the cylinder index. The master index level appears to be practical only when the data set is exceptionally large. Through the use of parameters of Job Control Language, any index other than the track index can be positioned in chosen areas—embedded in the middle of the data set, embedded at the beginning or end of the data set, or assigned to an entirely different volume.

For the purpose of further definition of an indexed sequential data set, assume that the following discussion relates to a data set that contains a "parts-list" master file. The file has been organized in ascending sequential order, from the lowest-value part-number record to the highest-value part-number record. During the creation of the data set, as each block of part-number records was written, the system initialized a key containing the high-value part-number for that data block and then wrote that key immediately preceding that particular block of data.

For each cylinder of data that is created, the Indexed Sequential Access Method generates a *track index* on the first track of that cylinder. The track index contains one entry for every track of data within that cylinder. In this instance, then, there would be an entry for each track, each entry containing the highest-value part-number key on that track along with the address of the referenced track. If this data set had been created on a 3330 DSF, which contains 19 tracks per cylinder, there would be 18 tracks of part-number data records and one track for the track index. The track index would normally contain 19 track entries—one for each of the data tracks, and one for the track index.

For each track index created (referencing the data records in one complete cylinder), the system creates an entry for a *cylinder index*. The cylinder index contains one entry for each cylinder occupied by the data set. This entry would contain the address of the track index for a cylinder (the cylinder number and track number zero) and the highest-value part-number contained on that track index. Consequently, if the data set physically occupies 50 cylinders, the cylinder index would contain 50 entries—each entry containing the address of a track index and the highest-value part-number related to that index.

If the data set is large enough to create many tracks of cylinder index entries, the programmer has the option of creating a master index level. In line with the step-by-step scheme demonstrated by the lower-level index structures, the master index may contain an entry for each track of cylinder index entries created—giving the address of each of the cylinder index tracks and the high-value part-number contained on that track. The master index level itself may also consist of three levels of index if the data set is large enough and the programmer deems this to be necessary. Each level of master index can create entries for the next higher level of master index, for a maximum total of three levels.

In describing the procedure that takes place in retrieving a data record, assume that a data record is to be accessed for part-number 32967. From the master index down to the part-number record desired, the action could be represented as follows:

1. Scan the master index (from low value to high value) for the cylinder index address whose highest part-number is greater than or equal to 32967.
2. Go to that cylinder index track and scan it (from low value to high value) for the track index entry whose highest value part-number is greater than or equal to 32967.
3. Go to that track index track and scan it (from low value to high value) for the address of the data track whose highest value part-number is greater than or equal to 32967.
4. Access that data track and scan the block keys (from low value to high value) for the block of data whose highest value part-number is greater than or equal to 32967.
5. Access and extract that block of data records and find the single data record for part-number 32967.

Although this chain of action taken to locate a single record might seem lengthy, it performs rather expediently. This type of file accessing is of particular value when used in an environment wherein a particular "header record" is to be located and then a subsequent series of sequential "trailer records" are to be accessed.

Among the various capabilities of the indexed sequential access method are the following:

- Reading or writing of the data set sequentially or randomly.
- Processing of individual records in any order.
- Deletion of records.
- Addition of new records.
- Automatic logical positioning of new records within the data set.
- Automatic handling of overflow conditions for new records inserted into the area in which they belong, when such an insertion expands that area beyond the track capacity.

The General Access Methods

The queued and basic versions of the Indexed Sequential Access Method (QISAM and BISAM) are used interactively for overall performance. Their particular responsibilities are:

- Create the data set—QISAM only
- Process or update new data records—QISAM or BISAM
- Insert new records—BISAM only

Continual insertions of new records are likely to cause the use of numerous overflow areas, resulting in a slowdown of record retrieval speeds. For this reason, the indexed sequential data set should be reorganized periodically, depending on the size and activity of the file.

BASIC PARTITIONED ACCESS METHOD

This access method, applicable only in conjunction with direct access devices, is used to create and access a partitioned data set. It is necessary, therefore, to understand the format concept of a partitioned data set and its general applications.

The partitioned data set has the general characteristics of both the indexed sequential and the sequentially organized data sets, although it is logically sequential and physically random. It is frequently used to store groups of programs similar to, and often referred to as, a "library." The two basic sections of a partitioned data set are the *directory* and the data area occupied by the *members* of the data set.

The members: A member is a sequentially organized set of records referred to within the data set by a symbolic label or name. One or more members, in addition to the directory, form the partitioned data set. Although the records within a member are considered to be sequentially arranged, the location of the members themselves (within the overall data set) is random. In order to readily locate a particular member by its given name, the system builds a directory that is quite similar to simple indexing. By referencing the directory, which appears at the very beginning of the data set, the system is able to locate any member within its data set boundaries. A member may be added, deleted, or updated in its entirety. However, when a member is deleted from the data set, only the directory entry is actually removed. The space used by that member is not made available for reuse and cannot be utilized again until the data set is completely reorganized.

The directory: The directory itself consists of a series of 256-byte blocks. Each block is made up of variable-length directory records, which may be considered to be entries similar to an index. Of the 256 bytes allocated for a directory block, up to 254 bytes may be used by the directory records. Each block is immediately preceded by an eight-byte field that contains the name of the last member record entry within that block. Each 256-byte block of directory records (entries) contains (for each entry):

1. A field containing the name of the member that it is referencing.
2. A three-byte field containing the address of the first record in that member. This address is in the form of a relative track number (relative to the beginning of the data set) and a relative block number within that track.

3. A one-byte field, in binary format, containing information regarding:
   - A code to indicate if the data in the name field is an "alias" for this member.
   - The number of halfwords of user data within this entry.
   - Whether one or more user pointers reference this particular member.
4. Up to 62 bytes of user data, in halfword increments, pertaining to the additional entry pointers for this member.

Because of the unique characteristics of a partitioned data set the Operating System provides special macroinstructions for manipulating the members and directory entries. These macros are:

BLDL—to construct an entry list for the directory.

FIND—to find the starting address of a specified member, and place that address into the Data Control Block so that a subsequent READ operation will access that member.

STOW—to add an entry for a member to an existing directory; or to delete, replace, or change a member name within a directory entry.

Members of a partitioned data set may be retrieved by the QSAM, BSAM, or BPAM access methods.

Part V
TABLES AND GLOSSARY

Tables

A. Table of Contiguous Bit Position Values and Respective "Powers-of-Two" Values

Bit Position	"2" to the Nth Power	Decimal Value of Bit Position
1	0	1
2	1	2
3	2	4
4	3	8
5	4	16
6	5	32
7	6	64
8	7	128
9	8	256
10	9	512
11	10	1,024
12	11	2,048
13	12	4,096
14	13	8,192
15	14	16,384
16	15	32,768
17	16	65,536
18	17	131,072
19	18	262,144
20	19	524,288
21	20	1,048,576
22	21	2,097,152
23	22	4,194,304
24	23	8,388,608
25	24	16,777,216
26	25	33,554,432
27	26	67,108,864
28	27	134,217,728
29	28	268,435,456
30	29	536,870,912
31	30	1,073,741,824
32	31	2,147,483,648

The implied bit positions are considered to be numbered from right to left, from low-order to high-order. The "Powers-of-Two" value of any given bit position is not considered to be effective unless it is occupied by a one-bit.

B. Hexadecimal/Decimal Conversion Table

FOUR-BYTE FULLWORD															
HALFWORD #2								HALFWORD #1							
BYTE 4				BYTE 3				BYTE 2				BYTE 1			
HALF-BYTE 8		HALF-BYTE 7		HALF-BYTE 6		HALF-BYTE 5		HALF-BYTE 4		HALF-BYTE 3		HALF-BYTE 2		HALF-BYTE 1	
hex	decimal	hex	decimal	hex	decimal	hex	decimal	hex	decimal	hex	decimal	hex	decimal	hex	decimal
0	0	0	0	0	0	0	0	0	0	0	0	0	0	0	0
1	268,435,456	1	16,777,216	1	1,048,576	1	65,536	1	4,096	1	256	1	16	1	1
2	536,870,912	2	33,554,432	2	2,097,152	2	131,072	2	8,192	2	512	2	32	2	2
3	805,306,368	3	50,331,648	3	3,145,728	3	196,608	3	12,288	3	768	3	48	3	3
4	1,073,741,824	4	67,108,864	4	4,194,304	4	262,144	4	16,384	4	1,024	4	64	4	4
5	1,342,177,280	5	83,886,080	5	5,242,880	5	327,680	5	20,480	5	1,280	5	80	5	5
6	1,610,612,736	6	100,663,296	6	6,291,456	6	393,216	6	24,576	6	1,536	6	96	6	6
7	1,879,048,192	7	117,440,512	7	7,340,032	7	458,752	7	28,672	7	1,792	7	112	7	7
8	2,147,483,648	8	134,217,728	8	8,388,608	8	524,288	8	32,768	8	2,048	8	128	8	8
9	2,415,919,104	9	150,994,944	9	9,437,184	9	589,824	9	36,864	9	2,304	9	144	9	9
A	2,684,354,560	A	167,772,160	A	10,485,760	A	655,360	A	40,960	A	2,560	A	160	A	10
B	2,952,790,016	B	184,549,376	B	11,534,336	B	720,896	B	45,056	B	2,816	B	176	B	11
C	3,221,225,472	C	201,326,592	C	12,582,912	C	786,432	C	49,152	C	3,072	C	192	C	12
D	3,489,660,928	D	218,103,808	D	13,631,488	D	851,968	D	53,248	D	3,328	D	208	D	13
E	3,758,096,384	E	234,881,024	E	14,680,064	E	917,504	E	57,344	E	3,584	E	224	E	14
F	4,026,531,840	F	251,658,240	F	15,728,640	F	983,040	F	61,440	F	3,840	F	240	F	15

C. Table of Condition Code Settings

This table contains the various Condition Code settings that might occur as a result of the execution of the Assembler Language instructions. The headings over each of the result columns represent the mask value that would agree with the configuration of the PSW Condition Code bits. This mask value is the one that would be used within the instruction statement, i.e., BC 8, LABEL. The condition indicated relates to the result within the first operand or the condition of the first operand as compared to the second operand.

Instruction	Op Code	8 = Mask	4 = Mask	2 = Mask	1 = Mask
ADD	A	Zero	Negative	Positive	Overflow
ADD REGISTERS	AR	Zero	Negative	Positive	Overflow
ADD PACKED	AP	Zero	Negative	Positive	Overflow
ADD HALFWORD	AH	Zero	Negative	Positive	Overflow
ADD LOGICAL	AL	Zero, no carry	Not zero, no carry	Zero, carry	Not zero, carry
AND LOGICAL	N	Zero	Not zero	—	—
AND LOGICAL	NC	Zero	Not zero	—	—
AND LOGICAL	NR	Zero	Not zero	—	—
AND LOGICAL IMMEDIATE	NI	Zero	Not zero	—	—
COMPARE	C	Equal	Low	High	—
COMPARE REGISTERS	CR	Equal	Low	High	—
COMPARE PACKED	CP	Equal	Low	High	—
COMPARE HALFWORD	CH	Equal	Low	High	—
COMPARE LOGICAL	CL	Equal	Low	High	—
COMPARE LOGICAL CHARACTERS	CLC	Equal	Low	High	—
COMPARE LOGICAL CHARACTERS UNDER MASK	CLM	Equal	Low	High	—
COMPARE LOGICAL LONG	CLCL	Equal	Low	High	—
COMPARE LOGICAL REGISTERS	CLR	Equal	Low	High	—
COMPARE LOGICAL IMMEDIATE	CLI	Equal	Low	High	—
EDIT	ED	Zero	Negative	Positive	—
EDIT & MARK	EDMK	Zero	Negative	Positive	—
EXCLUSIVE OR	X	Zero	Not zero	—	—
EXCLUSIVE OR	XC	Zero	Not zero	—	—
EXCLUSIVE OR	XR	Zero	Not zero	—	—
EXCLUSIVE OR IMMEDIATE	XI	Zero	Not zero	—	—
INSERT CHARACTERS UNDER MASK	ICM	Zero	First bit one	First bit zero	—
LOAD & TEST REGISTER	LTR	Zero	Negative	Positive	—
LOAD COMPLEMENT REGISTER	LCR	Zero	Negative	Positive	Overflow
LOAD NEGATIVE REGISTER	LNR	Zero	Negative	—	—
LOAD POSITIVE REGISTER	LPR	Zero	—	Positive	Overflow
MOVE LONG	MVCL	Count equal	Count low	Count high	Destructive overlap
OR LOGICAL	O	Zero	Not zero	—	—
OR LOGICAL	OC	Zero	Not zero	—	—
OR LOGICAL	OR	Zero	Not zero	—	—
OR LOGICAL IMMEDIATE	OI	Zero	Not zero	—	—
SHIFT & ROUND PACKED DECIMALS	SRP	Zero	Negative	Positive	Overflow
SHIFT LEFT DOUBLE ALGEB.	SLDA	Zero	Negative	Positive	Overflow
SHIFT LEFT ALGEBRAICALLY	SLA	Zero	Negative	Positive	Overflow
SHIFT RIGHT DOUBLE ALGEB.	SRDA	Zero	Negative	Positive	—
SHIFT RIGHT ALGEBRAICALLY	SRA	Zero	Negative	Positive	—
SUBTRACT	S	Zero	Negative	Positive	—
SUBTRACT REGISTERS	SR	Zero	Negative	Positive	Overflow
SUBTRACT PACKED	SP	Zero	Negative	Positive	Overflow
SUBTRACT HALFWORD	SH	Zero	Negative	Positive	Overflow
SUBTRACT LOGICAL	SL	—	Not zero, no carry	Zero, carry	Not zero, carry
SUBTRACT LOGICAL REGISTERS	SLR	—	Not zero, no carry	Zero, carry	Not zero, carry
TEST UNDER MASK	TM	All zero-bits	Mixed bits	—	All one-bits
TRANSLATE & TEST	TRT	Zero	Incomplete	Complete	—
ZERO & ADD PACKED	ZAP	Zero	Negative	Positive	Overflow

D. Table of Program Interrupt Conditions

Instruction	op code	ADDR	SPEC	OVFL	PROT	OPERN	OTHER
ADD	A	X	X	F			
ADD HALFWORD	AH	X	X	F			
ADD LOGICAL	AL	X	X				
ADD PACKED	AP	X		D	X	X	DATA
ADD REGISTERS	AR			F			
AND	N	X	X				
AND	NC	X			X		
AND IMMEDIATE	NI	X			X		
COMPARE	C	X	X				
COMPARE HALFWORD	CH	X	X				
COMPARE LOGICAL	CL	X	X				
COMPARE LOGICAL CHARACTERS	CLC	X	X				
COMPARE LOGICAL CHARACTERS UNDER MASK	CLM	X					
COMPARE LOGICAL LONG	CLCL	X	X				
COMPARE LOGICAL IMMEDIATE	CLI	X					
COMPARE LOGICAL REGISTERS	CLR	X					
COMPARE PACKED	CP	X			X		DATA
CONVERT TO BINARY	CVB	X	X				DATA, F
CONVERT TO DECIMAL	CVD	X	X		X		DATA, F
DIVIDE	D	X	X				F
DIVIDE PACKED	DP	X	X		X	X	DATA, D
DIVIDE REGISTERS	DR		X				F
EDIT	ED	X			X	X	DATA
EDIT & MARK	EDMK	X			X	X	DATA
EXCLUSIVE OR	X	X	X				
EXCLUSIVE OR	XC	X			X		
EXCLUSIVE OR IMMEDIATE	XI	X			X		
INSERT CHARACTER	IC	X					
INSERT CHARACTERS UNDER MASK	ICM	X	X				
LOAD	L	X	X				
LOAD COMPLEMENT REGISTER	LCR			F			
LOAD HALFWORD	LH	X	X				
LOAD MULTIPLE	LM	X	X				
LOAD POSITIVE REGISTER	LPR			F			
MOVE CHARACTERS	MVC	X			X		
MOVE LONG	MVCL	X	X		X		
MOVE IMMEDIATE	MVI	X			X		
MOVE NUMERIC	MVN	X			X		
MOVE WITH OFFSET	MVO	X			X		
MOVE ZONE	MVZ	X			X		
MULTIPLY	M	X	X				
MULTIPLY HALFWORD	MH	X	X				
MULTIPLY PACKED	MP	X	X		X	X	DATA
MULTIPLY REGISTERS	MR		X				
OR	O	X	X				
OR	OC	X			X		
OR IMMEDIATE	OI	X			X		
PACK	PACK	X			X		
SHIFT & ROUND PACKED DECIMALS	SRP	X		D	X	X	DATA
SHIFT LEFT ALGEBRAICALLY	SLA			F			
SHIFT LEFT DOUBLE ALGEB.	SLDA		X	F			
SHIFT LEFT DOUBLE LOGICAL	SLDL		X				
SHIFT RIGHT DOUBLE ALGEB.	SRDA		X				
SHIFT RIGHT DOUBLE LOGICAL	SRDL		X				
STORE	ST	X	X		X		
STORE CHARACTER	STC	X			X		
STORE CHARACTERS UNDER MASK	STCM	X					
STORE HALFWORD	STH	X	X		X		
STORE MULTIPLE	STM	X	X		X		
SUBTRACT	S	X	X	F			
SUBTRACT HALFWORD	SH	X	X	F			
SUBTRACT LOGICAL	SL	X	X				
SUBTRACT PACKED	SP	X		D	X	X	DATA
SUBTRACT REGISTERS	SR			F			
TEST UNDER MASK	TM	X					
TRANSLATE	TR	X			X		
TRANSLATE & TEST	TRT	X			X		
UNPACK	UNPK	X			X		
ZERO & ADD PACKED	ZAP	X		D	X	X	DATA

Explanation of Interruption Codes

ADDR	Addressing	OVFL	Overflow:	PROT	Protection
SPEC	Specification		D—Decimal	OPERN	Operation
			F—Fixed-point	OTHER	D—Decimal divide
					F—Fixed-point divide

Note: The Interrupt Conditions listed above have been grouped into general categories. Further definitions and breakdowns of these categories are detailed in full in the appropriate "Principles Of Operation" manuals published by IBM.

E. EBCDIC Character Table

This table contains the graphic representations of alphabetics, numerics, and symbols that are available as an EBCDIC character set. The lowercase alphabetics are not standard characters, but are available as special characters on printer units and other graphic devices.

Hex	Graphic	Bit Config.	Hex	Graphic	Bit Config.	Hex	Graphic	Bit Config.
40	(blank)	0100 0000	84	d	1000 0100	C8	H	1100 1000
4A	¢	0100 1010	85	e	1000 0101	C9	I	1100 1001
4B	.	0100 1011	86	f	1000 0110	D1	J	1101 0001
4C	<	0100 1100	87	g	1000 0111	D2	K	1101 0010
4D	(	0100 1101	88	h	1000 1000	D3	L	1101 0011
4E	+	0100 1110	89	i	1000 1001	D4	M	1101 0100
4F	|	0100 1111	91	j	1001 0001	D5	N	1101 0101
50	&	0101 0000	92	k	1001 0010	D6	O	1101 0110
5A	!	0101 1010	93	l	1001 0011	D7	P	1101 0111
5B	$	0101 1011	94	m	1001 0100	D8	Q	1101 1000
5C	*	0101 1100	95	n	1001 0101	D9	R	1101 1001
5D	)	0101 1101	96	o	1001 0110	E2	S	1110 0010
5E	;	0101 1110	97	p	1001 0111	E3	T	1110 0011
5F	¬	0101 1111	98	q	1001 1000	E4	U	1110 0100
60	-	0110 0000	99	r	1001 1001	E5	V	1110 0101
61	/	0110 0001	A2	s	1010 0010	E6	W	1110 0110
6B	,	0110 1011	A3	t	1010 0011	E7	X	1110 0111
6C	%	0110 1100	A4	u	1010 0100	E8	Y	1110 1000
6D	_	0110 1101	A5	v	1010 0101	E9	Z	1110 1001
6E	>	0110 1110	A6	w	1010 0110	F0	0	1111 0000
6F	?	0110 1111	A7	x	1010 0111	F1	1	1111 0001
7A	:	0111 1010	A8	y	1010 1000	F2	2	1111 0010
7B	#	0111 1011	A9	z	1010 1001	F3	3	1111 0011
7C	@	0111 1100	C1	A	1100 0001	F4	4	1111 0100
7D	'	0111 1101	C2	B	1100 0010	F5	5	1111 0101
7E	=	0111 1110	C3	C	1100 0011	F6	6	1111 0110
7F	"	0111 1111	C4	D	1100 0100	F7	7	1111 0111
81	a	1000 0001	C5	E	1100 0101	F8	8	1111 1000
82	b	1000 0010	C6	F	1100 0110	F9	9	1111 1001
83	c	1000 0011	C7	G	1100 0111			

F. Table of Assembler Language Instructions by Hexadecimal Code

hex code	mnemonic	instruction
05	BALR	Branch & Link Registers
06	BCTR	Branch on Count to Register
07	BCR	Branch on Condition to Register
0E	MVCL	Move Long
0F	CLCL	Compare Logical Long
10	LPR	Load Positive Register
11	LNR	Load Negative Register
12	LTR	Load & Test Register
13	LCR	Load Complement Register
14	NR	And (RR Format)
15	CLR	Compare Logical Registers
16	OR	Or Logical (RR Format)
17	XR	Exclusive Or (RR Format)
18	LR	Load Register
19	CR	Compare Registers
1A	AR	Add Registers
1B	SR	Subtract Registers
1C	MR	Multiply Registers
1D	DR	Divide Registers
40	STH	Store Halfword
41	LA	Load Address
42	STC	Store Character
43	IC	Insert Character
45	BAL	Branch & Link
46	BCT	Branch on Count
47	BC	Branch on Condition
48	LH	Load Halfword
49	CH	Compare Halfword
4A	AH	Add Halfword
4B	SH	Subtract Halfword
4C	MH	Multiply Halfword
4E	CVD	Convert to Decimal
4F	CVB	Convert to Binary
50	ST	Store
54	N	And (RX Format)
55	CL	Compare Logical
56	O	Or (RX Format)
57	X	Exclusive Or (RX Format)
58	L	Load
59	C	Compare
5A	A	Add
5B	S	Subtract
5C	M	Multiply
5D	D	Divide
5E	AL	Add Logical

hex code	mnemonic	instruction
5F	SL	Subtract Logical
86	BXH	Branch on Index High
87	BXLE	Branch on Index Low or Equal
88	SRL	Shift Right Logical
89	SLL	Shift Left Logical
8A	SRA	Shift Right Algebraically
8B	SLA	Shift Left Algebraically
8C	SRDL	Shift Right Double Logical
8D	SLDL	Shift Left Double Logical
8E	SRDA	Shift Right Double Algebraically
8F	SLDA	Shift Left Double Algebraically
90	STM	Store Multiple
91	TM	Test Under Mask
92	MVI	Move Immediate
94	NI	And Immediate (SI Format)
95	CLI	Compare Logical Immediate
96	OI	Or Immediate (SI Format)
97	XI	Exclusive Or Immediate (SI Format)
98	LM	Load Multiple
BD	CLM	Compare Logical Characters Under Mask
BE	STCM	Store Characters Under Mask
BF	ICM	Insert Characters Under Mask
D1	MVN	Move Numeric
D2	MVC	Move Characters
D3	MVZ	Move Zone
D4	NC	And (SS Format)
D5	CLC	Compare Logical Characters
D6	OC	Or (SS Format)
D7	XC	Exclusive Or (SS Format)
DC	TR	Translate
DD	TRT	Translate & Test
DE	ED	Edit
DF	EDMK	Edit & Mark
F0	SRP	Shift and Round Packed Decimals
F1	MVO	Move with Offset
F2	PACK	Pack
F3	UNPK	Unpack
F8	ZAP	Zero & Add Packed
F9	CP	Compare Packed
FA	AP	Add Packed
FB	SP	Subtract Packed
FC	MP	Multiply Packed
FD	DP	Divide Packed

Answers to Review Exercises

CHAPTER 3
1. Zero and One (0 and 1)
2. Sign-bit Integer
3. Thirty-one (31)
4. Hexadecimal
5. Eight (8)
6. Twelve (12)
7. Hexadecimal
8. Zoned decimal

9a. | 0000 | 0000 | 1011 | 1110 | 0111 | 1011 |

9b. | 0000 | 0000 | 0000 | 0011 | 0101 | 1001 | 0100 | 1001 |

9c. | 0000 | 0000 | 0010 | 1101 | 0010 | 0101 |

10a. +28,781
10b. +2,216,797
10c. +2,686
10d. +10,438,659
10e. −7,659
10f. −277,522

11a. | s | | | | |
     | 0 | 110 | 1000 | 0101 | 1011 |

11b. | s | | | | |
     | 1 | 101 | 1101 | 0011 | 1011 |

11c. | s | | | | | | | |
     | 0 | 000 | 0000 | 1101 | 1000 | 1101 | 1001 | 1101 | 0000 |

11d. | s | | | | | | | |
     | 1 | 111 | 1111 | 1111 | 1001 | 1110 | 1101 | 1111 | 1101 |

12a. 9,552,023
12b. 65,535
12c. 22,764
12d. 6,784,601
13a. Hex ... 5CCA   Decimal ... 23,754
13b. Hex ... 3621   Decimal ... 13,857
13c. Hex ... DAAC   Decimal ... 55,980
13d. Hex ... D1F4   Decimal ... 53,748
13e. Hex ... 65F2   Decimal ... 26,098

13f. Hex ... BB8A   Decimal ... 48,010
13g. Hex ... 76D6   Decimal ... 30,422
13h. Hex ... 5010   Decimal ... 20,496

14a. | 0011 | 1111 | 1010 | 0110 | 1100 | 0001 |

14b. | 0000 | 0000 | 1101 | 0101 | 1000 | 0111 |

14c. | 0000 | 1111 | 0011 | 0100 | 0111 | 1110 |

14d. | 0001 | 1000 | 1001 | 1100 | 0100 | 1011 |

15a. Hex ... F25F   Decimal ... 62,047
15b. Hex ... 2EF3   Decimal ... 12,019
15c. Hex ... 70EA   Decimal ... 28,906
15d. Hex ... 38C6E   Decimal ... 232,558
16a. +400
16b. -30,970
16c. +65,002
16d. -8,700
16e. 10,786,039 (assumed to be positive value)
17a. -3,022,570,649
17b. -7,034
17c. +5,581
17d. -40,067,997

CHAPTER 4
1. Four (4)   Fullword
2. Statement
3. Label, tag, or symbol
4. Sixteen (16)
5. Alphabetic
6. 0, 1, 2, 3, 4, 5, 6, 7, 8, 9, 10, 11, 12, 13, 14 and 15
7. Eight (8)
8. Op code
9. Hexadecimal
10. Positive
11. Four (4)
12. Operands
13. Positive Negative
14. Two (2)
15. One (1)
16. +32,767   -32,768
17. Four (4)
18. Asterisk, (*)
19. Explicit
20. Register

Answers to Review Exercises

CHAPTER 6

1. *character format*

A	B	C	X	Y	Z

hex format

C 1	C 2	C 3	E 7	E 8	E 9

2. *character*

7	8	9

hex

F 7	F 8	F 9

3. *character*

7	8	I	7	8	I	7	8	I

hex

F 7	F 8	C 9	F 7	F 8	C 9	F 7	F 8	C 9

4. *character*

$	.	.	/	/

hex

5 B	4 B	4 B	6 1	6 1

5. *character*

␢	␢

hex

4 0	4 0

6. *character*

$	6	1	0	$	6	1	0

hex

5 B	F 6	F 1	F 0	5 B	F 6	F 1	F 0

7. *character*

A	B	C

hex

C 1	C 2	C 3

8. *character*

9	9	9	9	9

hex

F 9	F 9	F 9	F 9	F 9

9. *character*

A	␢	B	␢	A	␢	B	␢

hex

C 1	4 0	C 2	4 0	C 1	4 0	C 2	4 0

10. *character*

$	-

hex

5 B	6 0

11. *character*

A	D	H	L	P	T

hex

C 1	C 4	C 8	D 3	D 7	E 3

12. character

1	3	1	3	1	3	1	3

hex

F1	F3	F1	F3	F1	F3	F1	F3

13. character

ƀ	ƀ	ƀ	ƀ	ƀ
ƀ	ƀ	ƀ	ƀ	ƀ
ƀ	ƀ	ƀ	ƀ	ƀ

hex

40	40	40	40	40
40	40	40	40	40
40	40	40	40	40

14. hex

22	5C	22	5C	22	5C	22	5C

15. hex

00	00	00	05	19	83	3D

16. hex

00	61	0C

17. hex

15	98	76	2C	15	98	76	2C

18. hex

9D	9D	9D	9D	9D

19. hex

59	87	7C	59	87	7C

20. character

0	0	2	1	5	Q

hex

F0	F0	F2	F1	F5	D8

21. character

7	8	I	7	8	I

hex

F7	F8	C9	F7	F8	C9

22. character

0	0	3	3	C

hex

F0	F0	F3	F3	C3

23. character

0	N	0	N	0	N

hex

F0	D5	F0	D5	F0	D5

24. character

4	1	7	B

hex

F4	F1	F7	C2

Answers to Review Exercises

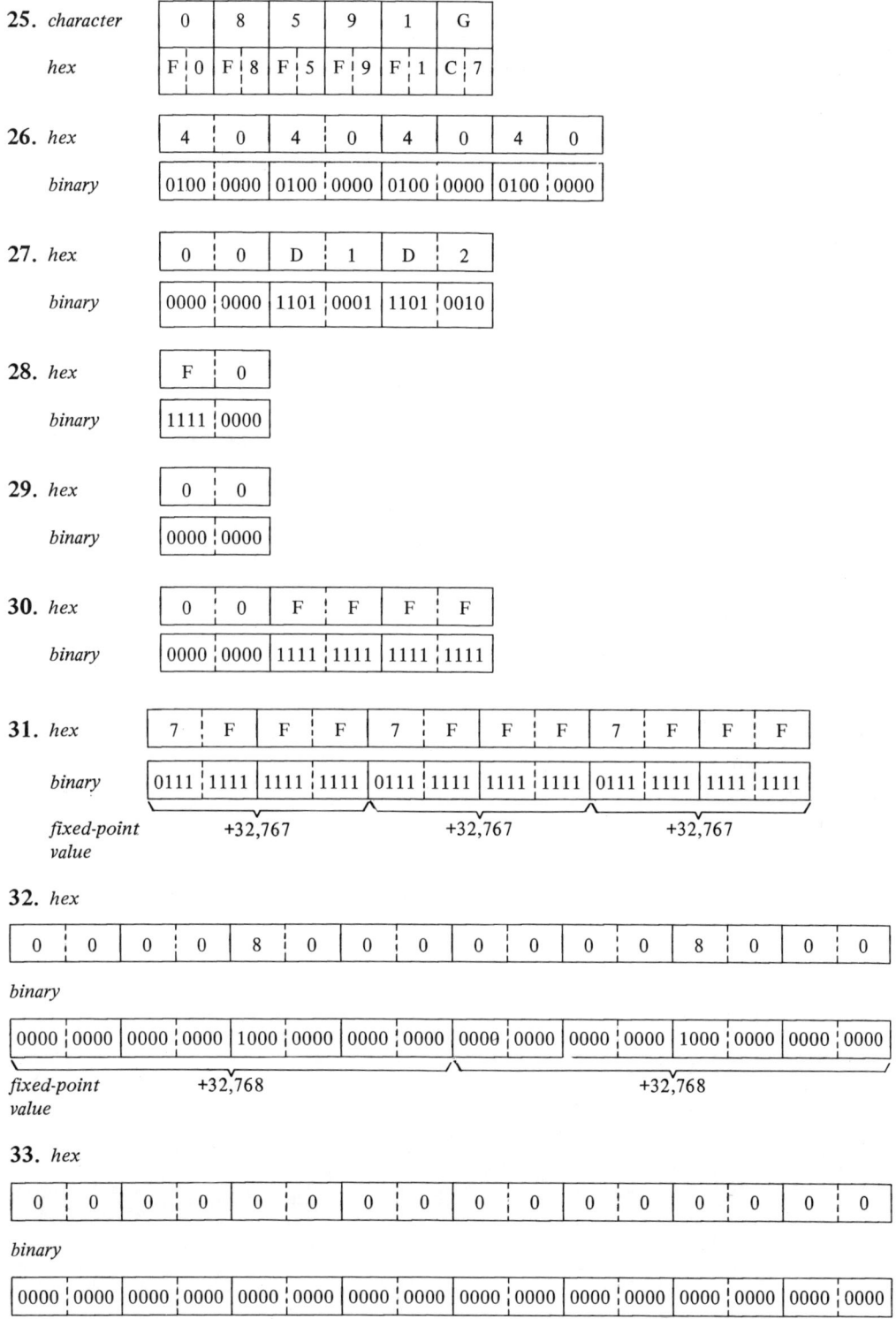

634 Assembler Language for Application Programming

34. hex | 1 | 1 | 9 | A | 2 | 8 | B | F |

binary | 0001 | 0001 | 1001 | 1010 | 0010 | 1000 | 1011 | 1111 |

35. hex | E | 7 | F | 7 |

binary | 1110 | 0111 | 1111 | 0111 |

36. hex

| F | F | F | A | 1 | 8 | 4 | D | F | F | F | A | 1 | 8 | 4 | D |

binary

| 1111 | 1111 | 1111 | 1010 | 0001 | 1000 | 0100 | 1101 | 1111 | 1111 | 1111 | 1010 | 0001 | 1000 | 0100 | 1101 |

fixed-point value: −386,995   −386,995

37. DC (Define Constant)
DS (Define Storage)
38. Does not
39. True
40. False (The label will only address the first 50-byte field. Subsequent fields of 50 bytes must be accessed by address adjusting.)
41. Sixty (60) bytes
42. Fullword
43a. Eighteen (18)
43b. Sixty (60)
43c. Zero (0)
44. SETDATA1   R6SET
    DC   Y
    FLDA1   Z32MSG
    G   ORG
45. 256
46. Three (3)
47. X'40'
48. Thirteen (13)

49. | S | T | A | R | T | ∅ | ∅ | ∅ |

50. Zero (the label contains 9 bytes and is therefore invalid)

51. | 0 | 0 | 5 | C | 0 | 0 | 5 | C | 0 | 0 | 5 | C |

52. | 0001 | 0001 | 0001 | 0001 | 0001 | 0001 |

53. | 3 | E | 7 | F |

Answers to Review Exercises

54. Sixteen (16)

55.

| 0 | 0 | 0 | 1 | 5 | C | 0 | 0 | 0 | 1 | 5 | C |

CHAPTER 7
1. High Low Bit
2. "Immediate"
3. "Padding"
4. Fixed-point
5. Four bytes
6. B D
7. 16 bytes
8. False
9. Equal
10. High
11. False
12. 256

13.

| 0000 | 1010 | 1100 | 0100 | 1101 | 1011 | 1111 | 1000 |

↕

| 0000 | 1010 | 1100 | 0100 | 1101 | 1010 | 1111 | 1000 |

14. Equal
15. No
16. Less than
17. False
18. False
19. Valid
20. Valid
21. Valid
22. Valid
23. Invalid
24. Valid
25. Invalid
26. Invalid
27. Invalid
28. Valid
29. Valid
30. Invalid
31. Valid
32. Valid
33. Invalid
34. Invalid
35. Valid
36. Valid
37. Valid
38. Invalid
39. Valid
40. Invalid
41. Invalid
42. Valid
43. Invalid
44. Valid
45. Invalid
46. Invalid
47. Valid
48. Valid
49. Invalid
50. Invalid
51. Invalid
52. Invalid
53. Valid
54. Valid
55. Invalid
56. Invalid
57. Valid
58. Invalid
59. Valid
60. Invalid
61. Valid
62. Valid
63. Invalid
64. Valid

CHAPTER 8
1. Program linkage
2. Branch on Condition (BC)   Branch on Condition to Register (BCR)
3. 15   forced
4. 8 4 2 1
5. 1st +1
6a. The first operand would be less than or equal to the second operand.
6b. The first operand would not be equal to the second operand; or: The first operand would be greater than or less than the second operand.
6c. The first operand would be greater than or equal to the second operand.
6d. The first operand would be greater than the second operand.
6e. The first operand would be equal to the second operand.
6f. The first operand would be less than, equal to, or greater than the second operand.
6g. The first operand would be greater than the second operand.
6h. The first operand would be less than the second operand.
7. +2,147,483,647
8. Register
9. Three
10. Zero
11. Address
12. Registers
13. 0 (zero)
14. 74 (seventy-four)
15. +3,250 -25 +50
16. The address of the statement labeled BACK.
17. CONTIG
18a.   BC   4,SUBRT1
18b.   BC   2,SUBRT5
18c.   BC   8,SUBRT7
18d.   BC   4,SUBRT10
18e.   BC   6,SUBRT12A
18f.   BC   15,SUBRT14
18g.   BC   2,SUBRT17

CHAPTER 9
The "Move" Instructions
1. SI and RR
2. 4
3. MVCL (Move Long)
4. MVI (Move Immediate)
5. MVZ (Move Zone)
6. "Sliding" first
7. False
8. MVZ
9. MVN (Move Numeric)
10. First

Answers to Review Exercises 637

11. MVC (Move Characters)
12. 7
13. "Chaining"
14. False

15a. FIELD3 — | G | A | 3 | 9 | 5 |

15b. FLD4 — | D | A | T | E |

15c. DATASET — | C2 | D9 | C1 | D5 | C4 | E8 |

15d. COUNTFLD — | 9 | 8 | 7 | 6 | 5 |

15e. CHEXFLD — | FF | 20 | 20 |

15f. CFLD — | E | A | S | T |

15g. FLD1G — | R | S | M | I | T | H |

15h. SET2 — | H | A | P | P | Y |

15i. SETPAK — | 40 | 5C |

15j. INFIELD — | 9 | 9 | 9 | 9 | 9 | 9 |

15k. DATAREV — | R | E | A | R | E | D |

16. False
17. STH (Store Halfword)
18. False
19. STM (Store Multiple)
20. ST (Store)
21. False
22. STC (Store Character)
23. Two high-order
24. Four bytes
25. Nine
26. Ten
27. −319,771
28. One-bits
29. Eight

30a. FULLWD6 — | 25 | 31 | 09 | 7D |

30b. SETWD1 | 0 0 0 3 9 5 6 C |

SETWD2 | 0 0 0 0 0 F C 3 |

SETWD3 | 0 0 6 9 2 1 C 6 |

SETWD4 | 0 0 0 C 0 7 4 2 |

30c. DAFLD | 4 C 0 0 0 0 0 0 |

30d. DATA8 | 0 0 0 0 0 5 C 6 |
| F F 2 9 0 0 6 C |

The "Load" and "Insert" Instructions
31. LH (Load Halfword)
32. False
33. LA (Load Address)
34. LPR (Load Positive Register)
35. One   Sixty-four (64)
36. Positive   Negative
37. L (Load)
38. IC (Insert Character)
39. LNR (Load Negative Register)
40. +32,767
41. True
42. Thirty-two (32)
43. LR (Load Register)
44. LTR (Load & Test Register)
45. X'00'
46. X'712400FF'
47. LCR (Load Complement Register)
48. LM (Load Multiple)
49. Unaltered

50. register 8 | F F F F C 1 C 2 |

51. X'FCFBFAFA'
52. X'003D0E46'

53a. register 3 | 0 0 0 F 3 9 0 0 |

53b. register 11 | 0 0 0 0 0 F F F |

53c. register 5 | F F F 2 0 5 9 F |

53d. register 3 | 0 0 0 0 D E 0 D |

53e. register 4 | 0 6 3 9 0 0 F F |

Answers to Review Exercises

53f. register 6 | F | F | F | 9 | F | 0 | 6 | 9 |

53g. register 8 | F | 0 | F | F | 0 | C | 0 | C |

53h. register 3 | 0 | 0 | C | 6 | A | B | D | 3 |

53i. register 2 | 0 | 0 | 0 | 6 | 5 | 1 | F | F |

53j. register 3 | F | 0 | F | A | C | D | 6 | B |

register 4 | F | F | 3 | 9 | F | B | D | F |

register 5 | F | F | F | 2 | 9 | A | A | 6 |

53k. register 12 | 0 | 0 | 0 | 0 | 7 | 6 | 5 | 4 |

53l. register 12 | 0 | 0 | C | 6 | F | 9 | D | 9 |

The "Shift" Instructions

54. Second
55. Eight
56. SLL (Shift Left Logical)
57. Sign-bit
58. SRA (Shift Right Algebraic)
59. Even-numbered
60. SLDL (Shift Left Double Logical)
61. Even-numbered
62. SRL (Shift Right Logical)
63. Unlike
64. SLDA (Shift Left Double Algebraic)
65. Odd-numbered
66. SRA (Shift Right Algebraic)
67. Zero-bits
68. SRDL (Shift Right Double Logical) zero-bits
69. Thirty-two (32)
70. SRDA (Shift Right Double Algebraic) sixty-three
71. Zero

72a. register 5 *binary*

| 1111 | 1111 | 0000 | 0001 | 1101 | 1111 | 0000 | 1110 |

hex

| F | F | 0 | 1 | D | F | 0 | E |

72b. registers 2 and 3 *in binary and hex*

| 1111 | 1111 | 1000 | 0000 | 0011 | 1111 | 1111 | 1001 | 0110 | 0110 | 0001 | 0000 | 0000 | 0000 | 0000 | 0000 |
| F | F | 8 | 0 | 3 | F | F | 9 | 6 | 6 | 1 | 0 | 0 | 0 | 0 | 0 |

72c. register 10 binary

0000	0000	0000	0000	0000	0000	0000	0000

hex

0	0	0	0	0	0	0	0

72d. register 9 binary

0000	0000	0000	1111	0100	1110	0101	1101

hex

0	0	0	F	4	E	5	D

72e. registers 6 and 7 binary and hex

1000	0111	1011	1010	0000	1110	0101	0000	0000	0100	1101	1001	1111	0101	1011	0000
8	7	B	A	0	E	5	0	0	4	D	9	F	5	B	0

72f. registers 10 and 11 binary and hex

1111	1111	1111	1111	1111	1111	1111	1111	0000	0000	0000	0000	0000	0001	0000	0010
F	F	F	F	F	F	F	F	0	0	0	0	0	1	0	2

72g. register 2 binary

0100	0110	0000	1110	1010	0001	0000	0000

hex

4	6	0	E	A	1	0	0

72h. registers 8 and 9 binary abd hex

0000	0000	0000	0000	0010	1000	0000	1100	1111	1101	0001	1000	1111	1101	0001	1000
0	0	0	0	2	8	0	C	F	D	1	8	F	D	1	8

CHAPTER 10
1. PACK
2. 1000
3. CVD (Convert to Decimal)
4. Length
5. False

6. PAKFLD

0	0	0	0	2	5	9	F

7. OUTFLD

F	0	F	0	F	0	F	0	F	3	F	9	C	6

8. PKFA

6	0	5	5	6	6	6	C

9. INPACK

1	1	2	3	3	C

10. PACKRA

0	5	4	0	9	5	4	C

Answers to Review Exercises

11. DATAFLD | 0 | 6 | 5 | 9 | 2 | 3 | V |

12. PKSETB | 0 | 0 | 0 | 3 | 6 | 5 | 1 | 2 | 4 | D |

13. PKFLD | 0 | 0 | 0 | 0 | 8 | 6 | 5 | 8 | 9 | 5 | 4 | C |

14. At all times
15. Eight (8)
16. Ten (10)
17. Eight   doubleword
18. Left
19. "12345F"
20. Divisor
21. Second
22. True (depending upon the contents of register 3)
23. CVD (Convert to Decimal) UNPACK
24. High-order
25. Left
26. X'F0'
27. No

28. PAKFLDA | 0 | 1 | 3 | 4 | 4 | 8 | 5 | C |

29. DATAPAK | 6 | 0 | 0 | 6 | 0 | 0 | 3 | C |

30. QUOREM | 0 | 0 | 1 | 0 | 4 | 0 | 5 | C | 0 | 0 | 6 | C |

31. SETPAKA | 0 | 1 | 3 | 5 | 4 | 7 | 4 | 0 | 2 | C |

32. MULTPAK | 0 | 0 | 0 | 0 | 5 | 5 | 3 | 5 | 6 | C |

    ANSWER | 0 | 0 | 5 | 5 | 3 | 5 | 6 | C |

33. PAKONE | 0 | 0 | 0 | 0 | 0 | 0 |

    PAKTWO | 0 | 0 | 0 | 0 | 9 | 3 | 4 | C |

34. PAKRECV | 0 | 3 | 2 | 3 | 4 | 5 | 8 | C |

    DATASFLD | 3 | 2 | 3 | 4 | 5 | H |

35. QUOREM | 0 | 0 | 4 | 8 | 4 | C | 0 | 0 | 2 | C |

    ANSW | 0 | 0 | 4 | 8 | 4 | C |

36. REPACK | 0 | 0 | 0 | 0 | 9 | 2 | 6 | 0 | 8 | C |

37. MULTAREA | 0 | 0 | 0 | 4 | 5 | 5 | 0 | 6 | 0 | C |

    ANSWR | 0 | 0 | 0 | 0 | 4 | 5 | 5 | C |

CHAPTER 11

1. False
2. Subtract Logical Registers (SLR)
3. Multiply Divide
4. One-bit
5. Complemented added
6. Even-numbered
7. +4096
8. True
9. First

10. | F | F | F | F | 8 | 0 | 0 | 0 |

11. True
12. Logical
13. False

14. register 3

hex	0	0	0	0	2	6	2	5
binary	0000	0000	0000	0000	0010	0110	0010	0101

15. register 11

hex	0	0	0	6	7	B	E	8
binary	0000	0000	0000	0110	0111	1011	1110	1000

16. register 7

hex	0	1	E	E	3	7	0	C
binary	0000	0001	1110	1110	0011	0111	0000	1100

17. register 9

hex	0	2	5	B	9	9	8	6
binary	0000	0010	0101	1011	1001	1001	1000	0110

18. register 10

hex	0	0	0	2	6	3	3	C
binary	0000	0000	0000	0010	0110	0011	0011	1100

19. register 4

hex	0	0	0	0	0	0	0	0
binary	0000	0000	0000	0000	0000	0000	0000	0000

20. register 12

hex	0	0	0	0	9	1	F	7
binary	0000	0000	0000	0000	1001	0001	1111	0111

Answers to Review Exercises

21. register 7

hex	0	0	0	4	F	F	0	F
binary	0000	0000	0000	0100	1111	1111	0000	1111

22. register 10

hex	0	1	4	8	E	2	E	D
binary	0000	0001	0100	1000	1110	0010	1110	1101

23. register 3

hex	0	0	2	F	3	4	8	D
binary	0000	0000	0010	1111	0011	0100	1000	1101

24. register 2

hex	0	0	0	0	0	0	0	0
binary	0000	0000	0000	0000	0000	0000	0000	0000

register 3

hex	0	7	3	C	D	A	4	8
binary	0000	0111	0011	1100	1101	1010	0100	1000

25. register 4

hex	0	0	0	0	0	0	0	0
binary	0000	0000	0000	0000	0000	0000	0000	0000

register 5

hex	0	3	F	5	7	5	0	8
binary	0000	0011	1111	0101	0111	0101	0000	1000

26. register 6

hex	0	0	0	0	0	0	0	0
binary	0000	0000	0000	0000	0000	0000	0000	0000

register 7

hex	0	0	0	5	E	3	7	6
binary	0000	0000	0000	0101	1110	0011	0111	0110

27. register 8

hex	0	0	0	0	0	0	3	9
binary	0000	0000	0000	0000	0000	0000	0011	1001

register 9

hex	0	0	0	0	0	0	8	4
binary	0000	0000	0000	0000	0000	0000	1000	0100

28. register 4

hex	0	0	0	0	0	0	5	7
binary	0000	0000	0000	0000	0000	0000	0101	0111

register 5

hex	0	0	0	0	0	3	5	8
binary	0000	0000	0000	0000	0000	0011	0101	1000

CHAPTERS 3-11 – ADDITIONAL REVIEW

1. Correct
2. Correct
3. Correct
4. Correct
5. Correct
6. Correct
7. Correct
8. Correct
9. Correct
10. Correct
11. Incorrect
12. Correct
13. Incorrect
14. Incorrect
15. Correct
16. Correct
17. Correct
18. Incorrect
19. Incorrect
20. Incorrect
21. Incorrect
22. Incorrect
23. Correct
24. Incorrect
25. Correct
26. Incorrect
27. Correct
28. Correct
29. Incorrect
30. Correct
31. Correct
32. Incorrect
33. Correct
34. Correct
35. Incorrect
36. Correct
37. Incorrect
38. Incorrect
39. Incorrect
40. Incorrect
41. Incorrect
42. Correct
43. Correct
44. Correct
45. Incorrect
46. Incorrect
47. Correct
48. Correct
49. Incorrect
50. Correct
51. Correct
52. Correct
53. Correct
54. Correct
55. Correct
56. Correct
57. Correct
58. Correct
59. Correct
60. Incorrect
61. Correct
62. Correct
63. Incorrect
64. Correct
65. Incorrect
66. Correct
67. Incorrect
68. Incorrect
69. Incorrect
70. Incorrect
71. Correct
72. Correct
73. Incorrect
74. Correct
75. Correct
76. Correct
77. Incorrect
78. Incorrect
79. Correct
80. Correct
81. Correct
82. Incorrect
83. Correct
84. Correct
85. Correct
86. Incorrect
87. Correct
88. Correct
89. Correct
90. Correct
91. Incorrect
92. Incorrect
93. Incorrect
94. Incorrect
95. Correct
96. Correct
97. Correct
98. Correct
99. Incorrect
100. Incorrect
101. Incorrect
102. Incorrect
103. Incorrect
104. Correct
105. Correct
106. Correct
107. Correct
108. Incorrect
109. Correct
110. Incorrect
111. Incorrect
112. Correct
113. Correct
114. Correct
115. Correct
116. Incorrect
117. Incorrect
118. Incorrect
119. Correct
120. Incorrect
121. Incorrect
122. Incorrect
123. Incorrect
124. Correct
125. Incorrect

CHAPTER 12

1. Bits   bits
2. And

Answers to Review Exercises

3. "Add"
4. Zero-bit   one-bit
5. XC
6. "Mask"
7. One-bit
8. 32
9. One-bit   zero-bit
10. Register   Fullword
11. Immediate
12. "Times"   Multiplication
13. And   256
14. Register
15. Register   Register
16. "On" (or) "yes"
17. Zero-bit
18. One-bits

19. register 3

binary	0010	0000	1111	0011	0100	0101	0101	1111
hex	2	0	F	3	4	5	5	F

20. register 8

binary	0001	0001	0111	0011	0111	0111	1111	1111
hex	1	1	7	3	7	7	F	F

21. DATAFLD

binary	1101	0001	1100	0010	1110	0011
hex	D	1	C	2	E	3

22. DATASET

binary	1100	0100	1111	0011	1100	0100	0011	1100	1110	1001
hex	C	4	F	3	C	4	3	C	E	9

23. register 12

binary	0000	0000	1100	0111	0101	0110	1001	1100
hex	0	0	C	7	5	6	9	C

24. DATASET

binary	1100	0111	1100	1000	0000	0010	0000	0000	0000	0000
hex	C	7	C	8	0	2	0	0	0	0

25. CHKFLD

binary	0010	1101	1011	1111	1111	0010	1101	0101	1111	0011
hex	2	D	B	F	F	2	D	5	F	3

26. FLDSET

binary	1110	0011	0110	1011	0101	1011	1001	1100
hex	E	3	6	B	5	B	9	C

27. register 4

binary	0000	0000	0011	1001	0010	0110	0111	1000
hex	0	0	3	9	2	6	7	8

28. SWITCHES

binary	0000	0000	0010	1010	0101	1111	0000	0001
hex	0	0	2	A	5	F	0	1

29. register 8

binary	0000	0000	0000	0000	0011	0010	0110	0000
hex	0	0	0	0	3	2	6	0

30. DATASW

binary	1000	0110	1110	0011	1000	0010	1010	0011	1100	0110
hex	8	6	E	3	8	2	A	3	C	6

31. WORDBASE

binary	1111	0011	1111	0101	1100	0100	1100	0001	1101	0111
hex	F	3	F	5	C	4	C	1	D	7

32. register 6

binary	1100	0010	1100	0111	1100	0101	1100	1000
hex	C	2	C	7	C	5	C	8

33. register 5

binary	0000	0000	0000	0000	0000	0000	0000	1100
hex	0	0	0	0	0	0	0	C

CHAPTER 13
1. Eight
2. Compare Logical Immediate (CLI)
3. Test Under Mask
4. Character
5. One-bit
6. Move Immediate (MVI)
7. 256

8. ABITS | 1 1 1 0 | 1 0 1 0 | OI   ABITS,X'A8'

9. KBITS | 0 0 0 0 | 0 0 0 0 |

10. HBITS | 0 0 0 1 | 0 0 0 0 | NI   HBITS,X'10'

Answers to Review Exercises 647

11. BBITS | 1 0 0 1 | 0 1 1 1 | OI BBITS,X'97'

12. EBITS | 0 1 0 0 | 1 0 1 0 | NI EBITS,X'5E'
                                   OI EBITS,X'48'

13. CBITS | 0 0 0 0 | 1 0 0 1 | NI CBITS,X'AB'

14. FBITS | 1 0 1 0 | 0 1 0 1 | XI FBITS,X'3A'

15. GBITS | 0 1 1 0 | 0 0 0 1 | TM GBITS,X'4B'

16. DBITS | 0 0 1 0 | 1 0 0 0 | NI DBITS,X'38'

CHAPTER 15

1. *a.* Fill character
   b. Significant Start character
   c. Digit Select character
   d. Field Separator character
2. Register 1
3. Significant Trigger (or) S-Trigger
4. X'21'
5. Plus-sign
6. Significant Start
7. Packed decimal
8. Five
9. X'20'
10. Significant Start
11. Left to right (or) High-order to low-order
12. X'22'
13. Edit pattern
14. Field Separator
15. Fill character (or) Insertion character
16. Digit select
17. Significant Trigger (or) S-Trigger
18. Field Separator
19. Fill character (or) Insertion character
20. RESULTA

hex	C	1	4	0	4	0	4	0	4	0	F	0	F	9
character	A		(blank)		(blank)		(blank)		(blank)		0		9	

21. RESULTB

hex	D	1	4	0	F	3	F	8	F	7	F	8
character	J		(blank)		3		8		7		8	

22. RESULTC

hex	5	B	4	0	F	0	F	0	4	B	F	2	F	5
character	$		(blank)		0		0				2		5	

23. RESULTD

hex	4	0	4	0	F	3	F	6	4	0	4	0	4	0
character	(blank)		(blank)		3		6		(blank)		(blank)		(blank)	

24. RESULTE

hex	4	0	F	7	4	B	F	4	F	8	C	3	D	9
character	(blank)		7				4		8		C		R	

25. RESULTF

hex	5	C	5	C	5	C	F	6	F	2	F	9	6	0
character	*		*		*		6		2		9		—	

26. RESULTG

hex	4	0	5	B	F	6	F	1	4	B	F	1	F	7
character	(blank)		$		6		1				1		7	

27. RESULTH

hex	4	0	4	0	4	0	5	B	4	B	F	3	F	3
character	(blank)		(blank)		(blank)		$		.		3		3	

CHAPTER 17

1. Translate table
2. 256
3. General register 1
4. General register 2
5. Source byte
6. True
7. Increment First
8. Translate table
9. True
10. First
11. X'00'

Answers to Review Exercises

12. DATAFLDA

hex	E	3	E	4	D	4	C	2	D	3	C	5
character	T		U		M		B		L		E	

13. DATAFLDB

hex	D	7	D	9	D	6	C	2	D	3	C	5	D	4
character	P		R		O		B		L		E		M	

14. DATAFLDC

hex	D	3	D	6	D	5	C	7	D	1	D	6	C	2
character	L		O		N		G		J		O		B	

15. DATAFLDD

hex	D	9	C	9	C	7	C	8	E	3
character	R		I		G		H		T	

16. DATAFLDE

hex	F	1	F	6	4	0	E	6	C	5	E	2	E	3
character	1		6		(blank)		W		E		S		T	

17. DATAFLDF

hex	C	7	F	2	C	7	F	1	C	7	E	6
character	G		2		G		1		G		W	

DATAFLDG

hex	C	6	C	9	D	5	C	9	E	2
character	F		I		N		I		S	

Glossary of Terms and Nomenclature

absolute value A value that is self-defining, one whose decimal characteristics denote its intended arithmetic value.

adcon An address constant; any one of the particular group of constants that have an address as their contents.

address The absolute identity of a position of storage.

address adjusting The action of modifying an address; to modify the address pointed to by a label by stating that label name in conjunction with an increment, i.e. FIELDA +6 which would address a point in storage six bytes beyond FIELDA.

alphameric Alphanumeric.

alphanumeric A mixture of alphabetic and numeric digits, usually in 8-bit character form.

base-2 (See Powers of-Two) A number system composed of ones and zeros. These digits are arranged in a contiguous row in order to express a numeric value. Each digit position has a potential value of twice that of the digit position to its right. The actual value range of each position is effective only if it contains a one-bit.

base-16 The hexadecimal number system, represented by a total of sixteen digits consisting of 0 through 9 and A through F. When multiple digits are expressed, each digit has a value range sixteen times greater than the digit position to its right.

base register A general register that has been assigned as an addressing base within a program. This base is used as part of a "base and displacement" addressing form for referencing any point within the next contiguous 4096 bytes of storage.

BDAM Basic Direct Access Method. It is used to randomly or directly retrieve data records from a data set that resides on a direct access storage device.

binary A number system consisting of ones and zeros, the representation of the base-2 number system. Values are expressed in a contiguous row of ones and zeros.

A data configuration in which the data is expressed in the bit form of ones and zeros. This configuration represents character data, numeric values, or special representations.

binary comparison A type of comparison in which the data is compared on the basis of the contents of each bit position, regardless of the intended interpretation of the data field itself. Thus, a numeric value in any form could be compared against a field that is considered to contain alphanumeric characters.

binary format The bit-by-bit configuration of any field regardless of the intended representation or interpretation of that field.

BISAM Basic Indexed Sequential Access Method. The basic version of the access method that is capable of contiguous sequential, random sequential, or random processing of data records. The access method creates its own indexing structures based on keys associated with each record.

bit A single bit is the smallest definable segment of any type of data. Multiple bits compose the binary system of data representation. A single bit may be represented within a bit position by either a one or a zero.

bit configuration The configuration of any data as expressed in individual bits.

bit position The individual position of bits within any data when it is expressed in binary or bit form.

bit switch An indicator or logic switch consisting of one bit position. It is considered to represent one of two conditions, such as yes/no, on/off, etc.

block of records A group of records considered to be one physical segment of data for the purpose of recording that data on a storage device. Certain data management routines can collect these records into blocks or extract them individually from the blocks.

boundary alignment Any position of main storage that constitutes a valid alignment for a fixed-point field of a halfword, a fullword, or a doubleword. An address which is evenly divisible by 2, 4 or 8.

BPAM Basic Partitioned Access Method of System/360.

branch To redirect the route of the program logic to a given instruction statement, as opposed to the natural flow of logic through sequential statements.

BSAM The Basic Sequential Access Method of System/360.

byte A measurement of space. A byte consists of eight binary bit positions, representing the size of an EBCDIC alphanumeric character or symbol. The combinations of bit configurations for a byte can be any one of 256 possible configurations. A byte is also the smallest addressable segment of storage.

byte-switch An indicator or logic switch requiring one byte of storage within the problem program. Its contents may represent one of several conditions such as yes/no, on/off, etc., but it can represent 256 different conditions, the maximum number of bit configurations for a single byte.

call A program function that requests, extracts, or activates an external logic module or routine. An independent program or routine may be available to, and called by, any other program that wishes to use it.

Carriage Control Symbol A one-byte EBCDIC character, appearing as the first byte of a data field to be printed, that is used to control the vertical spacing and skipping on the printed output form.

channel A data transmission channel; an electrical cable over which pulses, representing data, may be passed between units of hardware of the computer system.

character Any one of the standard EBCDIC character representations; alphabetics, numerics, and other characters and symbols such as $, #, *, %, &, ?, etc.

character-switch A byte-switch.

compiler A program that takes in the source coding of a programming language, interprets the coded statements, and creates a program module or deck containing the machine-language equivalent of the source language statements.

complement The opposite value (negative or positive) of a value or configuration. The complement of +250 is −250, the complement of −786 is +786, etc.

conditional branch A branch within the program logic that is taken only when certain processing conditions have been met.

Condition Code An internal indicator of the computer operating system, consisting of two bit positions within the Program Status Word. Any one of the four possible bit configurations (00, 01, 10, 11) may reside within the Condition Code bit positions as a result of the execution of an instruction.

constant A labeled field of data defined for the purpose of multiple references throughout the program. Unless the contents of that field are explicitly altered by the program, the data within the defined constant will not change.

control block A logical collection of specific parameter data, formatted and used by an operating system.

CPU Central Processing Unit of a computer system; that portion of the hardware containing the basic memory units, logic modules, and arithmetic function modules.

DASD A direct access storage device.

DASF A direct access storage facility.

Data Control Block An operating system control block containing the identifying attributes of a data set. Such information is provided by the DCB parameters specified by the program and consists of the record length, blocking factor, record form, system options, buffering techniques to be used, etc.

data management routines Supporting software programs that provide the functions of file organization, file structure, and input/output tasks.

data set One or more data records forming a logical grouping of information that may be referred to by a unique name. Data sets are usually considered to reside on a storage device such as a disk or magnetic tape.

Data Set Control Block A control block entry of the Volume Table of Contents (VTOC) on a direct access storage device. The Data Set Control Block contains information regarding the location and organization of a single data set. Each data set has its own DSCB within the overall Volume Table of Contents.

DCB Data Control Block.

delimiter card A card used to signal either the end of a function or the end of input card data.

delimiter segment A segment within a problem program table or index, indicating the end of data or space assigned to that area.

Digit Select Character One of the unprintable characters that are a functional part of the editing process generated by the Edit and the Edit & Mark instructions. It is represented by the hexadecimal digits "20". The Digit Select Characters, residing within the edit pattern, indicate those one-byte position within the pattern that are to be supplied with numeric characters from the source field or with fill characters from the edit pattern.

direct access device Any one of a group of data storage devices capable of performing random or direct data retrieval and access.

direct access volume A unit of data storage; a portion of a direct access device. When used to refer to a disk pack of a disk storage unit, the direct access volume is considered to have a unique volume serial number or identity by which it may be addressed or referred to.

directory The internal index of a Partitioned Data Set, pointing to the associated data set members.

direct processing A mode of data record processing. Records are sent to or retrieved from a direct access device via a relative location and/or identity key. One or more records may be written on the file without regard to their logical or physical sequence.

disk (disc) Any one of the storage devices that record data on platters resembling phonograph records.
A single platter within a disk storage device.

displacement The actual distance, measured in bytes, between two locations of storage.

display unit A device used to enter or retrieve and visually display data being transmitted between that unit and another device. Although it can be a typewriter-style of device, a display unit is usually thought of as presenting the data on a cathode ray tube similar to a television picture tube.

DOS Disk Operating System of System/360 and System/370.

doubleword An eight-byte field residing at a decimal address evenly divisible by eight. Although a doubleword may contain data of any type, they are primarily intended for floating-point arithmetic purposes.

doubleword boundary Any storage position address which, in decimal form, is evenly divisible by 8.

DSCB Data Set Control Block

DSD A disk storage device; a general reference to any of the group of disk storage devices.

dummy records Format records; pseudo-records; simulated records created for the purpose of formatting or padding a data set, used particularly on those data sets that are created or retrieved by direct access techniques.

dump A storage dump; a printed listing of the partial or complete contents of main storage.

duplication factor A specification element of a Define Constant (DC) or Define Storage (DS) statement. It indicates how many copies (duplicates) of the defined constant or storage area should be created by the language complier.

EBCDIC Extended Binary Coded Decimal Interchange Code. A system of bit representations for standard alphanumeric characters, punctuation symbols, and special characters, using eight bit positions to represent each character or symbol.

edit pattern A field containing an arrangement of the control characters that are used by the Edit and the Edit & Mark instructions. The packed decimal data is edited into this field, replacing the pattern in its entirety.

end-of-file condition A condition that exists whenever the end of a data set (file) volume is encountered. The condition setting is activated by the data management routines whenever an I/O task detects an end-of-volume marker or trailer label on a storage device.

end-of-volume condition A condition that exists whenever the end of a storage device volume is encountered. The condition setting is activated by the data management routines whenever an I/O task detects an end-of-volume marker or trailer label on a storage device.

EOF The end-of-file condition or the situation resulting from encountering an end-of-file.

EOV The end-of-volume condition or the situation resulting from encountering an end-of-volume.

equate An Assembler Language instruction that defines a label (symbol) so as to represent a decimal value or expression, either of which may be absolute (self-defining) or relocatable. The equate statement might appear as. . . REG2 EQU 2. In this case the label REG2 could now be used anywhere that the decimal "2" might be used as a register symbol. REG2 could be used equally as well wherever the programmer desires to indicate a parameter value of 2, such as. . . MVC FIELD (REG2,REG2), INPUT. In this instance the first REG2 indicates the length of the data being moved and the second REG2 specifies the base register assigned to FIELD.

even-numbered register Any one of the general registers whose reference is an even number, such as register 2, register 4, register 6, register 8, etc.

explicit attributes The specified characteristics of a constant as stated within a Define Constant (DC) statement.

fall through The action of the program logic processing encountering a conditional branch statement and passing on to the next sequential statement without taking the branch.

Field Separator Character One of the control characters used by the Assembler Language instructions of Edit and Edit & Mark. The Field Separator Character is used in multiple field edits to reset the Significant Trigger to an "off" condition between adjoining edited fields.

file organization The organization or structure of a data set. In most instances the file organization is directly related to the access method used to create the data set. For example, an indexed sequential file organization is created by the Indexed Sequential Access Method (ISAM).

fill character The first (left-most) character in an edit pattern. The editing function uses the fill character to replace those Digit Select Characters in the edit pattern that do not receive digits from the source field. The fill character is only transmitted to those pattern positions when the Significant Trigger (S-Trigger) is in an "off" condition.

fixed-length records Describing the contents of a data set or collection of data records in which all records are of equal fixed size.

fixed-point Specifically, the fixed-point arithmetic concept. Fixed-point numeric values are expressed in binary Powers-of-Two bit configuration wherein the single high-order bit position identifies the negative or positive representation of that value.

forced branch A branch statement which, when encountered, always causes an effective branch. The processing logic never falls through a forced branch unless the branch itself is to that next sequential instruction statement.

fullword A four-byte data field residing at a storage position address evenly divisible by 4. The contents of a fullword are considered to be in fixed-point arithmetic form, although the fullword may contain data of any type.

fullword boundary Any storage position which, in decimal form, is evenly divisible by 4.

half-byte Either half of a byte; either the left-most or right-most four bit positions of a byte; a nibble.

halfword Two bytes of data having a storage position address evenly divisible by 2. The contents of a halfword are considered to be in a fixed-point arithmetic form, although the halfword may contain data of any type.

halfword boundary Any storage position address which, in decimal form, is evenly divisible by 2.

hardware Any of the computer system units or related devices which form the overall physical portion of the computer. This would include the central processing unit, magnetic tape drives, storage devices, printers, and appropriate control units, as well as many other physical units.

header label A data set label that appears at the beginning of a data set or at the beginning of a continuation of a data set residing on one or more separate storage volumes.

hex A general reference to the hexadecimal configuration of a field or to a single hexadecimal digit.

hexadecimal The complete base-16 number system or any one of the hexadecimal digits that are a part of that system.

hexadecimal digit A single digit of the base-16 hexadecimal number system. Four bit positions (one half-byte) form one hexadecimal digit, creating a configuration that provides a range of digits from 0 through 9 and A through F.

high-order The single position within a field that is to the extreme left of that field; that portion of a configuration that is to the left of the right-most position or positions of a field.

housekeeping A set of instruction statements or logic usually performed at the beginning of a program. These statements perform base register initialization, save initial register contents, initialize data areas, and other functions that the programmer may wish to accomplish prior to entering the main logic of the program.

immediate character A self-expressing byte of data used as an operand in any one of the Assembler Language "immediate" instruction statements. An immediate character may be expressed as a character, as two hexadecimal digits, or as eight binary bits.

implied attributes The attributes or characteristics of a Define Constant (DC) statement, which, by their omission, are implied by the data contents of the constant.

insertion character The fill character of an edit pattern.

instruction A keyword or logical operator of a programming language; identifies a specific type of action that is to be accomplished.

integer The decimal value expressed by a fixed-point numeric field; it is construed to consist of all of the bit positions of that field except for the single high-order sign-bit position.

integer-bit Any one of the bits composing the integer portion of a fixed-point value or field.

inter-record gap A nonrecorded area separating physical groups of data on a storage device.

I/O Input/output; used in reference to transmitting or receiving data between devices.

K A symbol used to represent a decimal value of 1024; an expression of "4K" is interpreted to represent a decimal value of 4096. There are some exceptions in technical manuals where "K" is used to represent an even value of 1000.

key The identity field or identifier of a record. A name or value associated with a particular record for the purpose of unique identification of that record or to synonomously associate it with other records.

label A symbolic reference to an address within a program.

A data set label; the unique name identifying a particular data set.

language In computer terminology a language is a written code, words, or statements that are used to program the action of a computer. The language is written according to the action desired, entered into the computer, and translated into executable machine-coding by a compiler (translator) program for that particular language. The results of this translation, an object module or object deck, are used as the executable program.

length modifier The length specification for a Define Constant (DC) statement or a Define Storage (DS) statement. The specified length attribute assigned to a constant, literal, or storage area.

literal A constant created as the second operand of an executable instruction statement, rather than by a Define Constant statement. The format of this type of constant is the same as for regular constants except that it must be preceded by an equal sign (=).

logical comparison A comparison, between two characters or fields, in which the compare is made between corresponding bit positions of each field, from left to right. The comparison terminates as soon as two unlike bits are compared. The signed arithmetic value or character representation of the fields are not taken into consideration.

looping The technique for contiguous repetition of the execution of a group of instruction statements for a controlled number of times. The number of times that the loop is executed is determined by a "count control" or by one or more conditions that are tested within the loop. This technique is often used in performing table searches and scanning data fields.

low-order The single position within a field that is to the extreme right; that portion of a configuration to the right of the left-most position or positions of the field; the units position of a whole decimal value.

machine-language The level of coding that may be directly executed by the computer without further translation; the type of coding generated by a language compiler. System/360 and System/370 machine-language code is represented in hexadecimal form and may be directly interpreted by the operating system.

macro A macroinstruction; a type of language used to write macroinstructions.

macroinstruction A keyword, label, or name that activates a macro-language routine as identified by that reference. The macro-language routine contains a group of statements for performing a specific function. Macro-language routines generally reside in a macro-library; their use may be invoked within a program by stating the name of the routine to be performed.

magnetic tape A data storage media. A reel of magnetic tape consists of a plastic film base coated on one side with an oxide compound. Data is magnetically stored on the oxide surface in groups of parallel bits which are represented by the magnetic rearrangement of the oxide material.

mask A field of data (one or more bytes) used to test or alter another data field. The bit or byte representation of the mask causes a reaction upon each corresponding bit or byte of the field being acted upon.

mask operand An instruction statement operand used as a mask by that statement.

member A logical group of records within a partitioned data set; the member name that identifies a particular set of data records.

module A self-contained set of program instructions which may be in source, object, or executable form; a program, routine, or subroutine.

nibble The left-most four bits or right-most four bits of a byte; one-half byte.

object deck A deck of punched cards containing the machine-language interpretations of a program; the output deck from a compiled program.

object module The machine-language coding, either in card deck form or in stored data form, that results from a program compilation.

odd-numbered register Any of the general registers whose reference is an odd number, such as register 1, register 3, register 5, register 7, etc.

one-bit A binary bit represented by a digit of 1.

op code The mnemonic representation of an Assembler Language instruction. More generally, the logical operator or keyword of any computer language.

operand A label, value, or symbolic reference used within an instruction statement to identify a field or value.

operating system Any one of the supervisory systems that control the operation of a configuration of computer hardware.

overflow Arithmetic overflow; the result of an arithmetic operation in which the resulting field value is larger than the field allotted to that result.

overflow record A record that has been moved into one of the overflow areas of an indexed sequential data set.

pack To compress an EBCDIC numeric character value into packed decimal form.
A disk pack for a direct access storage device.

packed decimal One of the arithmetic systems of System/360 and System/370. Numeric values are represented in multiple hexadecimal digits, each with a potential self-defining value of 0 through 9. The hexadecimal digits, as expressed, represent the decimal interpretation of the value. The value may be signed by the existence of a hex digit of "A" through "F" in the rightmost half-byte of the field.

parameter A field, a value, or a set of characters that must be stated explicitly in order to supply a set of characteristics to a language statement. Such items would be the operands of an Assembler Language instruction statement, the operand fields of a macroinstruction, or the control information on a Job Control Language card.

Partitioned Data Set A data set that has been created by the Basic Partitioned Access Method data management routines. The physical organization of the data set consists of a directory (an index) and the data set members (the collections of records). The directory entries point to the location of current data set members.

PDS Partitioned Data Set.

pointer An address, symbol, or label used for the purpose of specifying any given address point within storage or on a storage device.

Powers-of-Two The ascending scale of value of the base-2 (binary) numeric system, used to define the potential value of contiguous bit positions from right to left. Each bit position to the left of its right-hand neighbor has a potential value equal to twice as much as that neighboring bit position.

printer Any one of a group of output devices that create printed output. This group includes system typewriters, but the term "printer" is more often used to define a device that uses a type-bar or type-chain and prints several complete lines in less than one second.

problem program A program that is executed to perform a particular task or service as an end in itself. Although this program may call or invoke other programs and routines, the calling program is considered to be the main program or the problem program.

program interrupt The interruption of a program as a result of planned or unplanned circumstances that prevent logic processing from continuing without additional intervening program logic or operator action.

Program Status Word A doubleword field (64 bit positions) within the controlling section of an operating system. It contains status indicators, addresses, error indicators, and other data regarding the status of the executing program. The Program Status Word is reset each time a machine instruction is executed.

PSW Program Status Word.

QISAM Queued Indexed Sequential Access Method; an access method or set of data management routines used in creating and accessing a data set arranged in an indexed sequential mode of organization.

QSAM Queued Sequential Access Method; an access method used to process a sequentially organized data set in a contiguously sequential manner.

query byte A byte used to create an argument (comparator) for a comparison; a byte that references an address point within a translate table.

quorem A programmer-created work area for an arithmetic divide operation. After the divide operation is completed, the *quo*tient and *rem*ainder occupy this work area, hence the name "quorem."

record overflow Track overflow; a hardware/software feature that allows the automatic continuance of a data record between two contiguous tracks on a direct access device.

register A fixed-location 32-bit field (one fullword) used for address storage and address reference. There are 16 general registers, numbered from 0 through 15. These registers are also available to the Assembler Language programmer for use as data retention units, work areas for fixed-point arithmetic operations, and as address bases for problem program addressing linkage.

relative position The location of any item in relationship to some other point. If a set of data consists of "ABCDE" in character form, then the relative position of "B" to "A" would be 1, the relative position of "E" to "A" would be 4, etc. This is used to refer to the position or address of a record within a data set residing on a direct access device, in lieu of using a true physical address. Such reference would be that although record "XYZ" was the 3296th record within the data set, it would actually be the 3295th record relative to the beginning of the data set. The first physical record in the data set would be relative record 0 (zero), relative to the beginning of the data set.

relocation factor A value representing the difference between the first addressable byte of storage and the address of the storage point at which a program or routine is physically located; a value representing the number of bytes of storage between two specific addresses.

segment A portion of a table or index, representing the groups of data within that set of data. Any one of the entries or values within a table or index.

self-defining A value or character that is presented in the form that it is intended to represent. Data whose intended character representation or value can be visually understood without further interpretation.

sequential processing The mode of processing data records in which each successive record is examined or processed in the sequence of its physical storage or input location.

short block A block of data that contains fewer logical records or bytes than specified for blocks on the data set to which it belongs.

sign That portion of an arithmetic field that defines the plus/positive or minus/negative value of that field.

sign-bit The single high-order bit of a fixed-point value, used to define the positive or negative configuration of that value.

significant digit A bit, a hexadecimal digit, or a numeric character whose individual decimal value is greater than zero.

Significant Start Character One of the non-printable characters that are a functional part of the editing process. It is represented by the hexadecimal digits '21'. The Significant Start Character is placed into the edit pattern to signal the termination of zero suppression. If zero suppression has not been terminated prior to encountering a Significant Start Character in the edit pattern, the editing process inspects that character and sets the Significant Trigger to an "on" condition.

Significant Trigger A logic switch that is a part of the editing function. It has a setting of either "on" or "off." If the Significant Trigger is "off," zero suppression takes place and fill characters are used to replace non-significant source digits in the Digit Select Character positions of the edit pattern. If the Significant Trigger is "on," source field digits replace the Digit Select Characters in the edit pattern.

software Any program or series of programs designed to aid in the execution of a problem program; the supervisory control programs of an operating system; a program designed to perform special functional operations for any other program that requires those services.

source deck A deck of punched cards containing the EBCDIC character representation of the uncompiled coded statements for a program.

source field A data field that supplies information, characters, or values to an instruction during the execution of a statement. If data is being moved from field "B" to field "A", then the source field is field "B", the sending field.

statement An instruction statement; a language instruction presented in its operational form along with any or all operands or keywords required for the execution of that instruction.

storage area The areas of main storage utilized by executable programs or routines.

storage dump A listing of the data contents of main storage at any given point in time. A storage dump is usually created whenever the abnormal termination of a program occurs; it is then used by the programmer as an aid in interpreting the problem area within the program that might have caused the termination.

S-Trigger The Significant Trigger of the editing functions.

subroutine One or more instruction statements forming a logic portion of a program, usually set apart from the straight-line coding logic of the body of the program. A logic routine that is secondary to the main logic of the program.

switch A bit, a byte, or a data field of storage used to signal a condition or situation of processing. It may be logically altered or configured by the program logic, by the result of the processing action, or by the operating system of the computer.

symbol A label, tag, name, or reference; an identifier that represents a value. A symbol may be used to represent the address of a field, a register, a statement, or any other addressable point within the program.

symbolic label A name, tag, or identity used to reference an address point within a program. The symbolic label effectively creates an address in base and displacement form, corresponding to that segment of the program to which it was assigned.

Sysgen A system generation; the process of creating an operating system or a version of an operating system.

system generation The process of creating (generating) an operating system; a merge and organization of the data management routines, supervisory programs, and related computer systems programs, all arranged and defined for a specific hardware configuration on which the operating system is to be used.

table A group of data, often arranged in some type of logical pattern, containing specific information or a cross-reference to other data. A table usually consists of a quantity of data segments of equal length.

table segment One of the sections or elements of a table, usually containing a unique value or set of characters in order to identify it from the other segments within the table.

tape A general reference to magnetic tape; a means of data storage.

tape volume A single reel of magnetic tape, normally assigned a unique serial number. Although one reel of tape is considered to be an individual tape volume, a logical set of data, identified by one name, may reside contiguously across several reels of tape.

terminal Any type of input/output device that is used for entering, receiving, trans-

Glossary of Terms and Nomenclature

mitting and/or interpreting data, rather than for the purpose of storing data. Such terminal units would be cathode ray display units, computer typewriter units, etc.

track overflow Record overflow; a feature that allows a logical data block to commence on one physical track and extend through one or more contiguous tracks.

trailer label A data set label or control block that appears at the end of the data set. It contains information relative to the data set including the number of data blocks within that file.

translate table A 256-byte table used by the Translate and the Translate & Test instructions.

truncated block A recorded data block that contains a lesser quantity of data bytes than the quantity stated as the block length for that data set. A short block.

Two's Complement notation A value expressed in negative fixed-point binary form.

unconditional branch A forced branch; an instruction statement, which, when entered, always creates a logic branch to another portion of the executing program or programs.

undefined records Data records whose length and format are not known.

variable-length records Data set records whose record length is not necessarily consistent throughout the overall data set. Each record contains a four-byte prefix specifying the total length of that record including the prefix bytes.

volume The quantity of records within a data set.
A complete unit of storage for a data storage device; such as a disk pack or a reel of magnetic tape.

volume label An identity control block for a data storage volume. The volume label usually appears as the first data on such a volume. It contains the volume serial number in order to create a unique identity for that particular volume.

volume table of contents The data set labels for a direct access storage volume, also known as a VTOC. The volume table of contents serves as an informational data reference and index for the data sets residing on the volume. Each uniquely-named VTOC entry consists of Data Set Control Blocks for that specific data set.

VTOC The volume table of contents for a data storage volume.

word A measure of data or storage, equal to four bytes; a shortened form of reference to a fullword.

zero-bit A zero digit representing a binary bit.

zero-suppression The means or technique of creating an EBCDIC numeric value in which all non-significant leading zeros are replaced by either a blank or by a special character.

zoned decimal A decimal value in EBCDIC character form; the units position consists of an alphabetic character representing the sign of the value.

Index

A address constants, 112, 114, 132
ABEND, 286
Abnormal termination, 286
Absolute decimal values, 92
Absolute values, 92
Access arm mechanism, 23
Access Method, Basic Direct, 610
Access Method, Basic Indexed Sequential, 610, 617
Access Method, Basic Partitioned, 617
Access Method, Basic Sequential, 610
Access Method, Queued Indexed Sequential, 610, 617
Access Method, Queued Sequential, 610, 615
Access methods, 610
Access methods, basic vs. queued, 611
Access methods, direct, 613
Access methods, indexed sequential, 615
Access methods, partitioned, 610, 617
Access methods, queued, 611
Access methods, sequential, 614
Access methods, the general, 609-618
Accumulator register, 181
Add (A) instruction, 333, 342-344
Add Halfword (AH) instruction, 333, 344
Adding bit values, 34-40
Adding hexadecimals, 49, 50
Addition, fixed-point, 36-40, 333-335, 342-354
Addition, hexadecimal, 49, 50
Addition, packed decimal, 274, 289-291
Add Logical (AL) instruction, 334, 347-349
Add Logical Registers (ALR) instruction, 334, 349
Add Packed (AP) instruction, 274, 289-291
Add Registers (AR) instruction, 334, 345-347
Address, 77
Address adjusting, 78
Address constants, 112-116, 132, 133
Address increment values, 77
Addressing, direct, 613
Addressing, instruction, 77
Addressing, relative record, 613
Addressing, relative track and actual record, 613
Addressing, relative track and key, 613
Address, modified, 78
Address values, 77, 112-116, 132, 133
AH (Add Halfword) instruction, 333, 344
A (Add) instruction, 333, 342-344

AL (Add Logical) instruction, 334, 347-349
Algebraic comparisons, 146, 147, 159-165
Algebraic shifts, 203-205, 251-258
ALGOL language, 14
Aligned coding, 64-66
Alignment, establishing fullword boundary, 107-109
Alignment, fullword boundary, 107-109
Alignment, halfword boundary, 107-109
Alignments, boundary, 107-109
Alpha characters, EBCDIC, 71, 625
Alphameric, 71
Alphanumeric, 71, 625
Alphanumeric characters, EBCDIC, 71, 625
Alphanumeric representation, 71
ALR (Add Logical Registers) instruction, 334, 349
Ampersands within constants, 117
And Immediate (NI) instruction, 92, 399, 407-409
And instructions, the, 399-401, 406-413
And (N) instruction, 399, 409
And (NC) instruction, 400, 410
And (NR) instruction, 401, 412
Anticipatory buffering, 611
AP (Add Packed) instruction, 274, 289-291
Apostrophes within constants, 117
Application of switches, 435-451
Application of the "Compare" instructions, 147-166
Application of the editing instructions, 498-523
Applications, register concepts and, 69
Areas, establishing storage, 101-132
Areas, fullword storage, 107, 112, 113, 116, 124
Areas, "save", 94, 109
Areas, storage, 101-132
Areas, subdefined, 101-107
AR (Add Registers) instruction, 334, 345-347
Arguments, search, 466
Arithmetic data, fixed-point 35, 73, 333-390
Arithmetic instructions, fixed-point, 333-339
Arithmetic instructions, packed decimal, 271-327
Arithmetic operations, fixed-point, 333-390
Arithmetic operations, logical, 334, 336, 337, 347-349, 359-361
Arithmetic operations, packed decimal, 71-74, 277-327
Arithmetic values, binary, 33, 73, 74

ASCII code, 543
Assembler Language Instructions, Table of, 626, 627
Assignments, base register, 70, 94
Assignments, register, 70, 94
Assumed decimal point logic, 315-327, 381-390
Assumed decimal points within constants, 129, 381-390
Assumed decimal points, fixed-point logic with, 381-390
Assumed decimal points, packed decimal logic with, 129, 315-327
Asterisks, comment line, 65
Attribute, DS non-reserving, 101
Attribute, explicit length, 62, 83
Attributes, fixed length, 83
Attributes, implied, 83
Attributes, implied length, 83, 111
Attributes, length, 62, 83, 111
Auditing data, 551-576
Auditing for special characters, 551-576

B constants, 112, 113, 116, 123, 124
BAL (Branch and Link) instruction, 173, 187
BALR (Branch and Link Registers) instruction, 173, 188
Base and displacement addressing, 62-64, 69, 70, 585-589
Base register, 62, 69, 94
Base register assignments, 94
Base registers, stringing, 94
Base-2, 33
Base-2 number system, 33
Base-16, 41
Base-16 number system, 41
Base-16 unit of increment, 42
Basic access methods, 611
Basic Direct Access Method (BDAM), 610
Basic Indexed Sequential Access Method (BISAM), 610, 617
Basic Partitioned Access Method (BPAM), 617
Basic program initialization, 94
Basic Sequential Access Method, 610
Basic vs. queued access methods, 611
BC (Branch on Condition) instruction, 171, 174
BCR (Branch on Condition to Register) instruction, 171, 177
BCT (Branch on Count) instruction, 171, 178
BCTR (Branch on Count to Register) instruction, 171, 179
BDAM, 610
Binary, 17, 33, 73
Binary arithmetic values, 33, 73
Binary bit configurations, 17, 33, 73

Binary bits, 33
Binary-configured, integer, 73
Binary constant, 112, 113, 116, 123, 124
Binary format, 73
Binary literals, 124
Binary notation, powers-of-two, 73
Binary notation, true, 33-35
Binary representation, 33
Binary representation, powers-of-two, 33, 73
Binary representation true, 33-35
Binary value representation, 33, 73
BISAM, 610-617
Bit arrangements, 15
Bit-by-bit comparisons, 143-145, 148, 158
Bit configuration, 33
Bit configurations, binary, 17, 33, 73
Bit-length modifier, 111
Bit-length specification, 111
Bit positions, 33
Bit position values, 33, 621
Bits, 15, 33
Bits, binary, 33
Bits, Condition Code, 69, 143-166
Bits per inch (BPI), 15
Bits, significant digit, 35-42, 240-256
Bit switches, 74, 442-449
BLDL macroinstruction, 618
Block, Data Control, 98
Block, Data Set Control, 605
Block delimiter, 210
Blocked records, 598, 602
Blocking and unblocking records, 612
Blocks, control, 98, 605
Blocks, data, 598, 602
Blocks, short, 602
Boolean Algebra logic instructions, 399-406
Boolean binary logic, 406-428
Boolean logic, 406-428
Boolean logic applications, 399-428
Boolean logic instructions in data searches, 424-428
Boundary, doubleword, 107-109
Boundary, fullword, 70, 107-109
Boundary, halfword, 107-109
Boundary alignment, establishing fullword, 70, 107-109
Boundary alignment, fullword, 70, 107-109
Boundary alignment, halfword, 107-109
Boundary alignments, 70, 107-109
BPAM, 610, 617
BPI, 15
Branch, 173
Branch, forced, 173, 176
Branch and Link (BAL) instruction, 173, 187

Index

Branch and Link Registers (BALR) instruction, 173, 188
Branches, conditional, 171, 172, 174-186
Branches, program linkage, 173, 187, 188
Branches, unconditional, 173, 176, 187, 188
Branching, 171-191
Branching, program logic, 173-191
Branch instruction, NOP (No-op), 176
Branch instructions, conditional, 171, 172, 174-186
Branch Instructions, Extended Mnemonics for, 188, 189
Branch on Condition (BC) instruction, 171, 174
Branch on Condition to Register (BCR) instruction, 171, 177
Branch on Count (BCT) instruction, 171, 178
Branch on Count to Register (BCTR) instruction, 171, 179
Branch on Index High (BXH) instruction, 172, 181-184
Branch on Index Low or Equal (BXLE) instruction, 172, 184-186
Branch statement, no-operation, 176
BSAM, 610
Buffering, anticipatory, 611
Buffers, 25, 611
BXH (Branch on Index High) instruction, 172, 181-184
BXLE (Branch on Index Low or Equal) instruction, 172, 184-186
Byte, 33, 652
Byte-length modifier, 111
Byte, query, 424-428
Byte-switch, character or, 436-442

Call, 59
Card punch, 17, 19
Card reader, 17, 18
Card reader/punch, 17
Cards, control, 439-442
Cards, punched, 17
Cards, source statement, 13
Carriage Control Symbol, 532-542
Cathode ray tube display devices, 24
C constants, 112, 116-120
Central Processing Unit (CPU), 6, 15
Chained moves, 208-212
Chained MVC statements, 208-212
Channel, 15
Character, control, 604
Character, immediate, 90
Character, insertion, 500-523
Character constants, 112, 116-120
Character, Field Separator, 500-523
Character data, 71, 117-120
Character data, EBCDIC, 71, 625

Character-formatted data, 71
Character-formatted screen display, 25
Characteristics, length attribute, 62, 83
Character literals, 90, 120
Characters, 71, 625
Characters, digit select, 500-523
Characters, EBCDIC, 52, 71, 625
Characters, EBCDIC numeric, 52, 625
Characters, fill, 501
Characters, self-defining, 89
Character switches, 436-442
Character table, EBCDIC, 625
CH (Compare Halfword) instruction, 146, 162
C (Compare) instruction, 146, 159
CL (Compare Logical) instruction, 143, 148
CLC (Compare Logical Characters) instruction, 144, 150
CLCL (Compare Logical Long) instruction, 145, 153
CLI (Compare Logical Immediate) instruction, 92, 144, 153
CLM (Compare Logical Characters Under Mask) instruction, 145, 157
CLR (Compare Logical Registers) instruction, 144, 153
COBOL language, 14
Coded instructions, 59, 67
Codes, component, 62
Coding, aligned, 65
Coding, program, 64
Coding format, instruction statement, 60
Coding sheet conventions, 64
COM, 28
Command, 59
Comment entry, 65
Comment headings, 65
Comment line asterisk, 65
Comment lines, 65
Comments, program, 65
Compare (C) instruction, 146, 159
Compare Halfword (CH) instruction, 146, 162
Compare instructions, the, 143-166
Compare Logical (CL) instruction, 143, 148
Compare Logical Characters (CLC) instruction, 144, 150
Compare Logical Immediate (CLI) instruction, 92, 144, 152
Compare Logical Long (CLCL) instruction, 145, 153
Compare Logical Characters Under Mask (CLM) instruction, 145, 157
Compare Logical Registers (CLR) instruction, 144, 153
Compare Packed (CP) instruction, 147, 165
Compare Registers (CR) instruction, 147, 163

Comparing data and conditions, 143-166
Comparisons, algebraic, 146, 147, 158-165
Comparisons, bit-by-bit, 143-145, 148-158
Comparisons, fixed-point, 146, 147, 158-165
Comparisons, logical, 143-145, 148-158
Comparisons, packed decimal, 147, 165
Compiler, 13
Compiler, language, 13
Complement, 40, 341
Complement configuration, 341-342
Complement negative form, 341
Complement, two's, 36, 341
Complement value, 40
Completion checking, I/O, 611-612
Component codes, 62
Components, 62
Composition of Edit statements, 500-502
Compound hexadecimals, 42
Compressing numeric data, 73
Computer control programs, 6
Computer generations, 4
Computer Output Microfilmer (COM), 28
Concepts, magnetic tape, 15
Concepts of switches and indicators, 435-451
Concepts, register, 69
Conditional branches, 174-186
Conditional branch instructions, 171, 172, 174-186
Condition Code, 69, 174-178
Condition Code bits, 69, 143-166, 174-178
Condition Code Settings, Table of, 623
Conditions, Comparing data and, 143-166
Conditions, end-of-file, 605
Conditions, multiple switch, 450
Configurations, binary bit, 17, 33, 73
Configurations, bit, 17, 33, 73
Configurations, half-byte (nibble), 51, 52
Configurations, hardware, 5, 6
Configurations, hexadecimal digit, 41-52
Configurations, negative, 36, 38, 51, 71, 73
Constant, B, 112, 113, 116, 123
Constant, C, 112, 116, 117
Constant, D, 107, 116, 127
Constant, F, 107, 112, 113, 116, 124
Constant, H, 107, 112, 113, 116, 126
Constant, P, 112, 114, 116, 127
Constant, X, 116, 120
Constant, Z, 116, 130
Constant fields, 103-132
Constants, 103-132
Constants, A Address, 112, 114, 116, 132
Constants, address, 112, 114, 116, 132
Constants, binary, 112, 113, 116, 123
Constants, bit-length modifier of, 111
Constants, byte-length modifier of, 111

Constants, character, 112, 116, 117
Constants, doubleword, 107, 116, 127
Constants, exponent modifiers of, 112
Constants, expressing, 110, 116-132
Constants, fullword fixed-point, 107, 112, 113, 116, 124
Constants, halfword fixed-point, 107, 116, 126
Constants, hexadecimal, 112, 113, 116, 120
Constants, length modifiers of, 110
Constants, literal versions of, 114, 120, 123, 124, 126, 127, 130, 132
Constants, packed decimal, 112, 114, 127
Constants, S address, 116, 133
Constants, scale modifiers of, 112
Constants, the "L" component of, 110
Constants, V address, 116, 132
Constants, Y address, 116, 132
Constants, zoned decimal, 116, 130
Constants and literals, defining, 109, 116
Contiguous Bit Position Values, Table of, 621
Contiguous fullword storage areas, 109
Continuation lines, coding sheet, 117
Control Block, Data, 98
Control Block, Data Set, 605
Control blocks, 98, 605
Control character, 604
Control function keyboard, 25
Control, page, 534
Control programs, 6
Control programs, computer, 6
Controls, loop, 178, 455
Control Symbol, Carriage, 532-542
Conventions, coding sheet, 64
Conversion, decimal-to-hexadecimal, 43
Conversion, hexadecimal-to-decimal, 46, 622
Conversion, packed decimal/fixed-point, 278
Convert to Binary (CVB) instruction, 273, 283
Convert to Decimal (CVD) instruction, 273, 284
Counter, page, 534
CP (Compare Packed) instruction, 147, 165
CPU (Central Processing Unit), 6, 15
Creating work areas, 101
Crash, head, 24
CR (Compare Register) instruction, 147, 163
CRT Terminal, 25
CVB (Convert to Binary) instruction, 273, 283
CVD (Convert to Decimal) instruction, 273, 284
Cycles, loop, 178-186, 455-466
Cylinder index, 616

D constant, 107, 116, 127
DASD, 20
DASDI, 606
DASF, 21
Data and conditions, comparing, 143-166

Index

Data auditing, 543-576
Data, character, 71
Data, character-formatted, 71
Data, compressing numeric, 73
Data, editing, 497-523
Data, fixed-point arithmetic, 35, 73
Data, relocating, 206-223
Data blocks, 598
Data Control Block (DCB), 98
Data formats, 70
Data listings, printing, 529-542
Data management routines, 597-600, 609-618
Data movement instructions, 206-223
Data records, 597
Data searches, 424-428
Data searches, Boolean logic in, 424-428
Data segment, 210
Data set, 597
Data sets, 597-607
Data sets, indexed sequential, 597
Data sets, partitioned, 598
Data sets, sequential, 597
Data Set Control Block (DSCB), 605
Data set directory, partitioned, 598
Data set record formats, 597-607
Data sets, direct access, 605
Data sets, direct organization, 598
Data sets, magnetic tape, 605
Data tables, mixed, 493-495
Data validation, 543-576
Date, forms of expressing a, 537
DCB, 98
DC (Define Constant) instruction, 110
Decimal self-defining expressions, 92
Decimal self-defining terms, 92
Decimals, zoned, 53, 130
Decimal-to-hexadecimal conversion, 43
Decimal values, absolute, 92
Deck, 65
Deck, object, 13
Decrement registers, 178, 179, 181
Define Constant (DC) instruction, 110, 116-132
Defined areas, 101
Defined subfields, 101
Define Storage (DS) instruction, 101
Defining constants and literals, 109-132
Defining output areas, 529-532
Defining storage areas, 101
Definitions, multiple field, 104-107
Definitions, subfield, 101
Delimiter, block, 210
Delimiter card, 461
Delimiter, end-of-table, 210
Delimiter, table segment, 210
Delimiter, segment, 210

Density, recording, 15, 23
Destructive overlap by the MVCL instruction, 215
Device independence, 614
Devices, direct access, 20
Devices, disk storage, 20
Devices, display, 24
Devices, graphic output, 24-28
Digit bits, significant, 35-42, 240-256
Digit configurations, hexadecimal, 41
Digit select characters, 500-523
Digits, hexadecimal, 41, 278-327
Digits, packed decimal, 51, 71, 278-327
Digits, packed decimal numeric, 51, 71, 278-327
Digits, significant hex, 42-51, 72
D (Divide) instruction, 338, 377-380
Direct access data sets, 605
Direct access devices, 20
Direct access methods, 613
Direct access storage devices, 20
Direct Access Storage Facility, IBM 2314, 5
Direct Access Storage Unit, IBM 3350, 21
Direct access volume, 605
Direct addressing, 484-493, 613
Direct addressing of table segments, 484-493
Directory, partitioned data set, 598, 617
Disk Operating System, 6
Disk packs, 23
Disk Storage Facility, IBM 3330, 5, 21, 606
Disk Storage Devices, 5, 21
Displacement, 62, 80
Displacement addressing, base and, 62-64, 69, 70, 585-589
Displacement parameter, 62, 80, 92, 94
Display devices, 24
Display stations, 24
Display Station, IBM 3278 CRT, 27
Display units, 24
Divide (D) instruction, 338, 337-380
Divide Packed (DP) instruction, 276, 299-308
Divide Registers (DR) instruction, 338, 380
Division, fixed-point, 338, 377-381
Division, packed decimal, 276, 299-308
Documentation, 65
Documentation, instruction statement, 65
Documenting the program, 65
Dollar-sign, floating, 498, 518-521
DOS, 6
DOS/VS, 6
Dot matrix screen, 25
Doubleword, 654
Doubleword boundary, 107
Doubleword constant (D), 107, 116, 127
Doubleword storage location, 107
DP (Divide Packed) instruction, 276, 299-308
DR (Divide Registers) instruction, 338, 380

DSCB (Data Set Control Block), 605
DS (Define Storage) instruction, 101
DS non-reserving attribute, 101
DS statement, the, 101
DS statement, non-reserving, 101
Dummy records, 654
Dump, 67, 581-594
Dumps, interpreting hexadecimal-formatted storage, 581-594
Dumps, hexadecimal storage, 67, 581-594
Duplication factor, 110

EBCDIC, 17, 52
EBCDIC alpha characters, 71, 625
EBCDIC alphanumeric characters, 71, 625
EBCDIC character data, 71, 625
EBCDIC characters, 52, 71, 625
EBCDIC Character Table, 625
EBCDIC graphic characters, 71, 625
EBCDIC numerals, 52, 625
EBCDIC numeric characters, 52, 625
ED (Edit) instruction, 497, 516-518
Edit (ED) instruction, 497, 516-518
Edit and Mark (EDMK) instruction, 497, 518-523
Editing, 497-523
Editing, functional characteristics of, 502-523
Editing, the necessity of, 498-500
Editing data, 497-523
Editing instructions, the, 497-498
Editing instructions, the application of the, 498-523
Editing multiple fields, 514-516
Edit instruction statements, composition of the, 500-502
Edit pattern, 500-523
EDMK (Edit and Mark) instruction, 497, 518-523
"Elastic" indexes, 210
Embedded switches, 450
End-of-file, 449, 605
End-of-file conditions, 449
End-of-table delimiter, 210
End-of-volume, 605
END statement, 98
EOF, 605
EOV, 605
Equate, 98
Equate statement, 98
EQU (Equate) instruction, 98
Equipment, peripheral, 4, 14
Establishing fullword boundary alignments, 107-109
Establishing storage areas, 101
Even-numbered registers, 243-248, 253, 254, 256-258

Even/odd pairs of general registers, 213, 243-248, 253, 254, 256-258
Exception segment, 560-565
Exclusive Or Immediate (XI) instruction, 92, 404, 419-421
Exclusive Or instructions, the, 404-406, 418-424
Exclusive Or (XR) instruction, 405-423
Exclusive Or (X) instruction, 404-421
Exclusive Or (XC) instruction, 405, 421-423
EXCP (Execute Channel Program) instruction, 610
Execute Channel Program, 610
Expansion, halfword, 146, 162, 163, 199, 232, 333, 335, 338, 344, 356, 372
Explicit attributes, 83
Explicit length modifier, 85, 111
Exponent modifier, 111, 124
Expressed constant values, 116-132
Expressing constants, 110, 116-132
Expression language, 14
Expressions, decimal self-defining, 92
Extended Binary-Coded Decimal Interchange Code (EBCDIC), 17, 52
Extended Mnemonics for Branch instructions, 188, 189
External serial number, 605

F constant, 107, 112, 113, 116
Factor, relocation, 589
"Fall through", 655
Field, source, 500
Field definitions, multiple, 103
Field descriptions, overlaying, 102, 104
Fields, constant, 103
Fields, data, 597
Fields, editing multiple, 514-516
Fields, packed decimal, 72, 278-327
Fields, subdefined, 102
Field Separator Character, 500-523
File organization, 597, 609-618
Fill characters, 501
FIND macroinstruction, 618
First generation computers, 4
Fixed-head devices, 23
Fixed length attributes, 83
Fixed-length records, 600-602
Fixed-point, 33, 73
Fixed-point addition, 38, 333-335, 342-354
Fixed-point arithmetic data, 35, 73, 339-390
Fixed-point arithmetic instructions, 333-339
Fixed-point arithmetic operations, 333-390
Fixed-point compares, 146, 158
Fixed-point constants, fullword, 107, 112, 113, 116, 124

Index

Fixed-point constants, halfword, 107, 116, 126
Fixed-point division, 338, 377-381
Fixed-point instructions, 333-390
Fixed-point literals, 126
Fixed-point logic with assumed decimal points, 381-390
Fixed-point multiplication, 337, 338, 366-377
Fixed-point signs, 35, 73, 339-390
Fixed-point subtraction, 40, 335-337, 354-366
Fixed-point value, maximum fullword, 38
Fixed-point value, maximum halfword, 38
Fixed-point value representation, 35, 73, 339-390
Fixed-point values, 35, 46, 73, 339-390
Fixed-point values, hexadecimal representation of, 46
Fixed-point values, interpreting, 35-41
Fixed-point values, negative, 36, 73, 339
Fixed-point values, positive, 35, 73, 339
Flag, 13
F literals, 126
Floating dollar-sign, 498, 518-521
Floating-point, 59
Floating-Point Feature Instruction Set, 59
Floating-point logic, 59
Floating-point registers, 69
Forced branch, 173, 176
Format, hexadecimal, 42
Format, instruction statement coding, 60
Format descriptions, 62
Formats, binary, 73
Formats, instruction, 59
Formats, machine-language instruction, 67
Formats, operand, 62
Formats, record, 598-604
Formats, zoned decimal, 53
Forms, date, 537
FORTRAN language, 14
Fullword, 35, 655
Fullword boundary, 70, 107-109
Fullword boundary alignment, 107-109
Fullword fixed-point constants, 107, 112, 113, 116, 124
Fullword fixed-point value, maximum, 38
Fullword literals, 126
Fullword sign-bit, 38, 73
Fullword storage areas, 107-109
Fullword storage areas, contiguous, 109
Fullword storage location, 107
Fullword value, maximum negative, 38
Fullword value, maximum positive, 38
Functional characteristics of editing, 502-523

Garbage, 3
General access methods, the, 609-618

General registers, 64, 69
General registers, even/odd pairs of, 213
General register sets, odd-even-odd, 172, 173, 181-186
Generation, 4
Generations, computer, 4
Glossary of Terms and Nomenclature, 651-661
Graphic characters, EBCDIC, 71, 625
Graphic output devices, 24-28
Grid-formatted screen, 25

H constant, 107, 112, 113, 116, 126
Half-byte, 5, 655
Half-byte configurations, 51-52
Halfword, 35
Halfword boundary, 107
Halfword boundary alignment, 107
Halfword expansion, 146, 162, 163, 199, 232, 333, 335, 338, 344, 356, 372
Halfword fixed-point constants, 107, 112, 113, 116
Halfword fixed-point value, maximum, 38
Halfword literal, 127
Halfword sign-bit, 38, 73
Halfword storage location, 107, 109
Halfword value, maximum negative, 38
Halfword value, maximum positive, 38
Hard-copy, 17
Hardware, 10
Hardware, peripheral I/O, 14
Hardware configurations, 5, 6
Head crash, 24
Header label, 605
Headings, comment, 65
Headings and subheadings, 539-542
Hex, 41
Hexadecimal, 17, 33, 41
Hexadecimal addition, 49, 50
Hexadecimal computation of fixed-point values, 46
Hexadecimal constants, 112, 113, 116, 120
Hexadecimal conversion to fixed-point, 46
Hexadecimal-formatted storage dumps, interpreting, 581-594
Hexadecimal/Decimal Conversion Table, 622
Hexadecimal digit configurations, 41-52
Hexadecimal digits, 41-52
Hexadecimal format, 42
Hexadecimal literals, 123
Hexadecimal notation, 42
Hexadecimal number system, 33, 41
Hexadecimal representation, 41-52
Hexadecimals, 41
Hexadecimals, adding, 49
Hexadecimals, compound, 42
Hexadecimals, subtracting, 50

Hexadecimal-to-decimal conversion, 46, 159–164
Hex digits, high-order, 46–48
Hex digits, significant, 42–51, 72
High-level language, 13
High-order, 78
High-order hex digits, 46–48
High-order integer-bits, 35–38
Housekeeping, 94

IBM System/370 Model 168 Computer, 7
IBM System/370 3033 Processor, 8
IBM 129 Card Data Recorder (Keypunch), 11
IBM 3278 CRT Display Station, 27
IBM 3330 Disk Storage Facility, 22
IBM 3340 Disk Storage Facility, 24
IBM 3350 Direct Access Storage Facility, 22
IBM 3420 Magnetic Tape Drive, 16
IBM 3505 Card Reader, 18
IBM 3525 Card Punch, 19
IBM 3741 Data Entry Station, 12
IBM 3800 Printing Subsystem, 21
IBM 3850 Mass Storage System, 25
IBM 8775 CRT Terminal, 26
IC (Insert Character) instruction, 198, 229
ICM (Insert Character Under Mask) instruction, 199, 230–232
Immediate character, 62, 90
Immediate character representation, 62, 90
Implied attributes, 83
Implied length attributes, 83, 111
Implied lengths, 83, 111
Increment, base-16 unit of, 42
Incrementing, register, 62
Increment register, 181
Increment values, address, 77
Independence, device, 614
Index, cylinder, 616
Index, track, 615
Indexed sequential, 597
Indexed sequential access method, 597, 615
Indexed Sequential Access Method, Basic, 610, 617
Indexed sequential data sets, 597
Indexes, "elastic", 210
Indexing register, 62
Index searches, 455–466
Initialization, basic program, 94
Initializing the program, 94
Input/output storage areas, 101, 104
Insert Character (IC) instruction, 198, 229
Insert Characters Under Mask (ICM) instruction, 199, 230–232
Insertion character, 500–523
Instruction, 59, 67
Instruction formats, 59, 67

Instruction formats, machine-language, 67
Instruction op codes, 60, 65
Instructions, machine-language, 59
Instructions, Table of Assembler Language, 626
Instruction statement, specifying the, 77
Instruction statement coding format, 60
Instruction statement documentation, 65
Instruction statements, 59
Instruction statements, modifying, 223
Integer-bits, 35
Integer-bits, high-order, 35–38
Integer-bits, significant, 35–41, 339–342
Integers, 35
Integers, binary-configurated, 35
Integers, signed, 35–41
Integer value, 35–41
Integer values, negative, 37–41
Integer values, positive, 35–41
Internal labeling, 605
Interpreting storage dumps, 581–594
Interpreting fixed-point values, 35–41
Interpreting hexadecimal-formatted storage dumps, 581–594
Interrecord gap, 15, 598
Interrupt, program, 624
Interrupt conditions, table of program, 624
Invalid symbollic labels, 101
I/O (Input/Output), 611
I/O completion checking, 611, 612
I/O overlap synchronization, 611
I/O task, 611
IRG (Interrecord gap), 15, 598

Job Control Language (JCL), 98, 607

K, 8, 15, 656
KBS, 15
Key, 613–616
Keyboard, control function, 25
Keyed records, 613–616

L (Load) instruction, 199, 232
Label, 60, 65, 78
Label, header, 605
Label, volume, 605
Labeling, internal, 605
Label references, nonmodified, 78
Labels, invalid symbollic, 60
Labels, modified, 78
Labels, trailer, 605
LA (Load Address) instruction, 200, 234
Language, 13
Language, low-level, 13, 59
Language, high-level, 13
Language, programming, 13

Index

Language, statement, 14
Language assembler, 13
Language compiler, 13
Language, expression, 14
L component of constants, the, 85, 111
LCR (Load Complement Register) instruction, 201, 236
Length attribute characteristics, 62, 83
Length attribute characteristics, explicit, 62, 83
Length attributes, 62, 83
Length attributes, fixed, 83
Length attributes, implied, 83
Length attribute specification, 62
Length modifier of constants, 85, 111
Lengths, implied, 85
LH (Load Halfword) instruction, 199, 232
Library, 13, 59, 617
Library, program, 13, 617
Light-pen, optic-fiber, 28
Line, comment, 65
Line control, printed, 532-534
Line, coding sheet continuation, 117
Line spacing, printed, 532-534
Linkage branches, program, 173, 187, 188
Linkage register, 188
Listings, printing data, 529-542
Literal, the B, 124
Literal, the C, 90
Literal, the F, 126
Literal, the H, 127
Literal, the P, 90, 130
Literal, the X, 90, 123
Literal, the Z, 132
Literal org, 98
Literals, 89, 114, 120, 123, 124, 126, 127, 130, 132
Literals, binary, 124
Literals, character, 90
Literals, defining constants and, 109
Literals, fixed-point, 126
Literals, fullword, 126
Literals, halfword, 127
Literals, hexadecimal, 123
Literals, packed decimal, 90
Literals, zoned decimal, 132
Literal versions of constants, 89, 114, 120, 123, 124, 126, 127, 130, 132
LM (Load Multiple) instruction, 200, 234
LNR (Load Negative Register) instruction, 202, 239
Load (L) instruction, 199, 232
Loadable tables, 461
Load Address (LA) instruction, 200, 234
Load Complement Register (LCR) instruction, 201, 236

Load Halfword (LH) instruction, 199, 232
Load and Insert instructions, the, 199-202, 229-239
Load Multiple (LM) instruction, 200, 234
Load Negative Register (LNR) instruction, 202, 239
Load Positive Register (LPR) instruction, 201, 237-239
Load Register (LR) instruction, 200, 233
Load and Test Register (LTR) instruction, 201, 235
Local mode operation, CRT, 27
Logic, assumed decimal point, 315-327, 381-390
Logic, Boolean, 406-428
Logic, floating-point, 59
Logic, program branching, 171
Logical arithmetic operations, 334, 336, 337, 347-349, 359-361
Logical compares, 143, 148
Logical page breaks, 535
Logical shifting, 202, 203, 240-249
Logical shifts, 202, 203, 240-249
Logic branching, program 171
Logic paths, multiple, 173, 174
Look-ups and scans, sequential, 455-466
Look-ups, table, 178, 455-495
Look-up techniques, sectored, 466-484
Loop control register, 178-186
Loop controls, 178-186, 455-466
Loop controls and table look-ups, 455-495
Loop cycles, 178-186, 455-466
Looping, 178-186, 455-466
Looping techniques, 178-186, 455-466
Loop routines, 178-186, 455-466
Loop within a loop, 178-186
Low-level, 13, 59
Low-level language, 13, 59
Low-order, 78
LPR (Load Positive Register) instruction, 201, 237-239
LR (Load Register) instruction, 200-233
LTR (Load and Test Register) instruction, 201, 235

M (Multiply) instruction, 337, 366-369
Machine-language, 13, 59
Machine-language instruction formats, 67
Machine-language instructions, 13, 59
Macros, 59
Macroinstructions, 59, 65
Magnetic tape, 15
Magnetic tape concepts, 15, 16
Magnetic tape data sets, 605
Magnetic tape drives, 15
Main storage, 8
Mask, 62, 145, 157, 171
Mask operand, 62, 145, 157, 171, 224, 230, 435, 337-449

Mask value, 62, 157, 175, 224, 230, 435, 447–449
Mass Storage System, IBM 3850, 24
Master index, 616
Maximum four-byte binary value, 38
Maximum fullword fixed-point value, 38
Maximum halfword fixed-point value, 38
Maximum negative fullword value, 38
Maximum negative halfword value, 38
Member, 617
Members, partitioned data set, 598, 617
MH (Multiply Halfword) instruction, 338, 372–374
Microfiche, 29
Microfilm, 28
Microfilm readers, 28
Microfilm viewers, 28
Micrographics, 28
Mixed data tables, 493–495
Mnemonic, 61
Modified labels, 78
Modifier, bit-length, 111
Modifier, byte-length, 111
Modifier, exponent, 112, 124
Modifier, scale, 112, 124
Modifying instruction statements, 223
Modular concept, 5
Module, 657
Monitor, 6
MOSFET transistors, 4
Moveable-head devices, 23
Move Characters (MVC) instruction, 195, 207–212
Move Immediate (MVI) instruction, 92, 195, 206
Move instructions, the, 195–197
Move Long (MVCL) instruction, 195, 212–218
Move Numeric (MVN) instruction, 196, 218–220
Moves, chained, 208–212
Moves, sliding, 208–212
Move With Offset (MVO) instruction, 276, 308–310
Move Zone (MVZ) instruction, 196, 220–223
Moving data within the problem program, 206–223
Moving, storing and loading data, 195–258
MP (Multiply Packed) instruction, 275, 293–299
MR (Multiply Registers) instruction, 338, 369–372
Multiple field definitions, 104–107
Multiple field editing, 514–516
Multiple logic paths, 173, 174
Multiple switch conditions, 450
Multiplication, fixed-point, 337, 338, 366–377
Multiplication, packed decimal, 275, 293–299
Multiply (M) instruction, 337, 366–369
Multiply Halfword (MH) instruction, 338, 372–374
Multiply Packed (MP) instruction, 275, 293–299
Multiply Registers (MR) instruction, 338, 369–372
MVC (Move Characters) instruction, 195, 207–212
MVCL (Move Long) instruction, 195, 212–218
MVC statements, chained, 208–212

MVI (Move Immediate) instruction, 92, 195, 206
MVN (Move Numeric) instruction, 196, 218–220
MVO (Move With Offset) instruction, 276, 308–310
MVZ (Move Zone) instruction, 196, 220–223

Nanoseconds, 4
NC (And) instruction, 400, 410
Negative configuration, 36
Negative fixed-point values, 36, 46, 339–390
Negative form, complement, 341
Negative fullword value, maximum, 38
Negative halfword value, maximum, 38
Negative integer values, 37–41
Negative-signed values, 36, 339–390
Negative sign-bit, 36, 339–390
"New Page" routine, 536
Nibble, 71, 218–223
NI (And Immediate) instruction, 92, 399, 407–409
N (And) instruction, 399, 409
Non-labeled storage positions, 78
Nonmodified label references, 78
Nonreserving DS statement, 101
No-operation branch statement, 176
NOP branch instruction, 176
Notation, hexadecimal, 42
Notation, powers-of-two, 340
Notation, true binary, 33–35
Notation, two's complement, 341
NR (And) instruction, 401, 412
Number, serial, 605
Numbers, sequence, 65
Number system, base-2, 33
Number system, base-16, 41, 51
Number system, binary, 33
Number system, hexadecimal, 33
Number system, fixed-point, 33
Number system packed decimal, 33, 51
Number systems, 33
Numerals, EBCDIC, 52
Numeric character representation, 52
Numeric characters, EBCDIC, 52
Numeric data, compressing, 73
Numeric data, packed decimal, 51
Numeric data, validation of, 545–551
Numeric digits, packed decimal, 51
Numeric representation, 33, 51, 53
Numeric values, rounding, 315
Numeric values, validation of, 545–551

Object deck, 13
Object module, 13
OC (Or) instruction, 402, 416
Odd-even-odd register sets, 172, 173, 181–186
Odd-numbered registers, 657
OI (Or Immediate) instruction, 92, 401, 414

Index

O (Or) instruction, 402, 415
One-bit, 33
Op codes, 60, 65
Op codes, instruction, 60, 65
Operand formats, 62
Operand parameters, 61
Operands, 60, 65
Operands, mask, 62, 145, 157, 171, 175
Operating system, 6, 657
Operating System (OS), 6
Operating System with Virtual Storage (OS/VS), 6
Operating System, Disk (DOS), 6
Operating System with Virtual Storage, Disk (DOS/VS), 6
Operations, packed decimal, 127, 278-327
Optic-fiber light-pen, 28
Organization, file, 597, 609-618
ORG instruction, 98, 104
ORG statement, 98, 104
Or Immediate (OI) instruction, 92, 401, 414
OR (Or) instruction, 403, 417
Or instructions, the, 401-403, 413-418
Or (OR) instruction, 403, 417
Or (O) instruction, 402, 415
Or (OC) instruction, 402, 416
OS, 6, 98
OS/VS, 6, 98
Output areas, defining the, 529-532
Output devices, graphic, 24-28
Output, hard-copy, 17
Overlap, destructive, 215
Overlap synchronization, I/O, 611
Overlaying field descriptions, 104

PACK Instruction, 271, 278-280
Packed decimal arithmetic instructions, 271-327
Packed decimal arithmetic operations, 72, 277-327
Packed decimal comparison, 147, 165
Packed decimal constants, 112, 114, 116, 127
Packed decimal data, 71, 277-327
Packed decimal digits, 51, 278-327
Packed decimal digits, significant, 72
Packed decimal fields, 72, 278-327
Packed decimal/fixed-point conversion, 278, 284
Packed decimal literal, 130
Packed decimal logic with assumed decimal points, 129, 315-327
Packed decimal number system, 51
Packed decimal numeric data, 51, 72, 277-327
Packed decimal numeric digits, 51, 71, 277-327
Packed decimal operations, 127, 278-327
Packed decimals, 33, 71, 278-327
Packed decimal sign-digits, 51, 71, 278-327
Packed decimal signs, 51, 71, 278-327
Packed decimal values, 51, 71, 278-327

Packed decimal values, signed, 51, 71, 278-327
Packs, disk, 23
Page breaks, logical, 535
Page control, 534
Page counter, 534
Paging, concept of, 9
Parameter, displacement, 62, 80, 92, 94
Parameter, RECFM, 532
Parameters, 61
Parameters, operand, 61
Partitioned access method, 610, 617
Partitioned Access Method, Basic, 617
Partitioned data set, 598
Pattern, edit, 500-523
P Constant, 112, 114, 116, 127
PDS, 598
Peripheral equipment, 14
Peripheral hardware, 14
Peripheral I/O hardware, 14
Peripheral support equipment, 4
PFK's, 25
Picoseconds, 4
Platters, 21
PL/I language, 14
Positive fixed-point values, 35, 46, 339-390
Positive fullword value, maximum, 38
Positive halfword value, maximum, 38
Positive integer values, 35-41
Powers-of-two, 33, 42, 73
Powers-of-two binary notation, 33, 73
Powers-of-two binary representation, 33, 73
Powers-of-two notation, 34, 73
Powers-of-two table, 35
Print bar, 17, 20
Printed line control, 532-534
Printed records, 604
Printers, 5, 17
Printers, laser, 20
Printer units, 5, 17
Print hammer, 20
Printed data listings, 529-542
Printing Subsystem, IBM 3800, 20
Print-out, main storage, 67
Processing, sequential, 614
Program, compiler, 13
Program branching logic, 170
Program coding, 64
Program comments, 65
Program function keys, 25
Program initialization, 94
Program interrupts, 624
Program Interrupt Conditions, Table of, 624
Program library, 13, 617
Program linkage branches, 171-191
Program linkage operations, 173, 186-188

Program logic branching, 170
Programming languages, 13
Programs, computer control, 6
Programs, control, 6
Program Status Word (PSW), 69
Pseudo-character representation, 503
PSW, 69
Punch, card, 5, 17
Punched cards, 17
Punched records, 604
Punch record, 5, 17, 19

QISAM, 610, 617
QSAM, 610, 615
Query byte, 424-428
Queued access methods, 610, 611, 615, 617
Queued Indexed Sequential Access Method, 610, 617
Queued Sequential Access Method, 610, 615
Quorem, 299-308, 658

Reader, card, 5, 17, 18
Reader unit, 5, 17, 18
Read/write heads, 23
Real storage, 8
RECFM parameter, 532
Record formats, 598-604
Record formats, data set, 597-607
Recording density, 23
Recording paths, 21
Records, blocked, 598, 602
Records, blocking and unblocking, 612
Records, data, 597
Records, displayed, 604
Records, dummy, 654
Records, fixed-length, 600-602
Records, keyed, 613-616
Records, printed, 604
Records, punched, 604
Records, undefined, 603
Records, variable-length, 602
Reel, tape, 605
Regions, 8
Registers, 62, 69, 80
Registers, comparison value, 181
Registers, decrement, 178, 179, 181
Registers, increment, 62, 80, 181
Registers, indexing, 62
Registers, linkage, 188
Registers, loop control, 178-186
Register concepts and applications, 69
Register assignment, 70
Register assignments, base, 70
Register concepts, 69
Registers, accumulator, 181

Registers, base, 62, 69
Registers, decrementing, 178, 179
Registers, even-numbered, 243-248, 253, 254 256-258
Registers, even-odd pairs, 213, 243-248, 253, 254, 256-258
Registers, floating-point, 69
Registers, general, 62, 69
Registers, incrementing, 62, 80
Registers, odd-numbered, 657
Registers, stringing base, 70
Register set, odd-even-odd, 172, 173, 181-186
Relative position, 659
Relative record addressing, 613
Relative track addressing, 613
Relative track and actual record addressing, 613
Relative track and key addressing, 613
Relocation factor, 589
Remote mode operation, CRT, 28
Report dating, 537
Representation alphanumeric, 71
Representation, binary, 33
Representation, fixed-point value, 35, 73, 339-390
Representation, hexadecimal, 41-52
Representation, immediate character, 62, 90
Representation, numeric character, 52, 625
Representation, pseudo-character, 503
Representation, true binary, 33-35
Review exercises—Chapter 3, 55-58
Review exercises—Chapter 4, 75-76
Review exercises—Chapter 6, 133-141
Review exercises—Chapter 7, 166-169
Review exercises—Chapter 8, 192-194
Review exercises—Chapter 9, 258-270
Review exercises—Chapter 10, 327-331
Review exercises—Chapter 11, 390-398
Review exercises—Chapter 12, 428-433
Review exercises—Chapter 13, 451-453
Review exercises—Chapter 15, 524-528
Review exercises—Chapter 17, 576-579
Review exercises, Answers to—Chapter 3, 629
Review exercises, Answers to—Chapter 4, 630
Review exercises, Answers to—Chapter 6, 631
Review exercises, Answers to—Chapter 7, 635
Review exercises, Answers to—Chapter 8, 636
Review exercises, Answers to—Chapter 9, 636
Review exercises, Answers to—Chapter 10, 640
Review exercises, Answers to—Chapter 11, 642
Review exercises, Answers to—Chapter 12, 644
Review exercises, Answers to—Chapter 13, 646
Review exercises, Answers to—Chapter 15, 647
Review exercises, Answers to—Chapter 17, 648
Rounding numeric values, 315
Routines, data mangement, 597-600, 609-618
Routines, loop, 178-186, 455-466

Index

RR instruction format, 62, 67
RS instruction format, 62, 68
RX instruction format, 64, 67

S address constant, 116, 133
Save areas, 94, 109
Scale modifier, 111, 124
Scans, sequential look-ups and, 455-466
Screen display, character-formatted, 25
Screen, dot matrix, 25
Screen, grid-formatted, 25
Search, table, 182-184, 455-495
Search arguments, 466
Search criteria, selective, 424-428
Searches, data, 424-428
Searches, index, 455-466
Second Generation Computers, 4
Sectored look-up techniques, 466-484
Segment, 659
Segment, data, 210
Segment, delimiter, 210
Segment, exception, 560-565
Segments, direct addressing of table, 484-493
Segments, table, 80, 210, 455-495
Selective search criteria, 424-428
Self-defining characters and values, 62, 89
Self-defining expressions, decimal, 92
Self-defining terms, decimal, 92
Sequence numbers, 65
Sequential Access Method, Basic, 610
Sequential access methods, 614
Sequential data set, 597
Sequential look-ups and scans, 455-466
Sequential processing, 614
Serial number, 605
Serial number, external, 605
Serial number, volume, 605
Shift and Round Packed Decimals (SRP) instruction, 276, 310-315
Shifting, 202-205, 240-258
Shifting, algebraic, 249-258
Shifting, logical, 240-249
Shift instructions, the, 202-205, 240-258
Shift Left Algebraically (SLA) instruction, 203, 251-253
Shift Left Double Algebraically (SLDA) instruction, 204, 253
Shift Left Double Logical (SLDL) instruction, 202, 243
Shift Left Logical (SLL) instruction, 202, 240-242
Shift Right Algebraically (SRA) instruction 204, 254-256
Shift Right Double Algebraically (SRDA) instruction, 205, 256-258

Shift Right Double Logical (SRDL) instruction, 203, 246-249
Shift Right Logical (SRL) instruction, 203, 244-246
SH (Subtract Halfword) instruction, 335, 356-358
Short block, 602
SI instruction formats, 64, 68
Sign, 35
Sign-bit, 35, 46, 73, 339
Sign-bit, fullword, 38, 73
Sign-bit, halfword, 38, 73
Sign-bit, negative, 35, 46, 73, 339
Sign-bit, positive, 35, 46, 73, 339
Sign-digits, 51, 72
Sign-digits, packed decimal, 51, 72
Signed EBCDIC numerals, 52
Signed integer expressions, 35-41, 73
Signed integers, 73
Signed packed decimal values, 51, 72
Significant digit-bits, 35-42, 240-256
Significant hex digits, 42-51, 72
Significant integer-bits, 35-41, 339-342
Significant packed decimal digits, 72
Significant Start Character, 500-523
Significant Trigger, 500-523
Signs, fixed-point, 35, 38, 46, 51, 72, 73
Signs, packed decimal, 51, 71, 278-327
S (Subtract) instruction, 335, 354-356
Sliding moves, 208-212
"Sliding table" concept, 210
"Sliding table" routine, 210
SLA (Shift Left Algebraically) instruction, 203, 251-253
SLDA (Shift Left Double Algebraically) instruction, 204, 253
SLDL (Shift Left Double Logical) instruction, 202, 243
SL (Subtract Logical) instruction, 336, 359-361
SLL (Shift Left Logical) instruction, 202, 240-242
SLR (Subtract Logical Registers) instruction, 337, 361
Software, 10
Source deck, 66, 67
Source field, 500
Source statement cards, 13
Source statements, 13
Spacing, printed line, 532-534
Special characters, auditing for, 551-576
Special data, 74
Specification, bit-length, 111
Specification, length attribute, 62
Specifying the instruction statement, 77
SP (Subtract Packed) instruction, 274, 291-293
SRA (Shift Right Algebraically) instruction, 204, 254-256

SRDA (Shift Right Double Algebraically) instruction, 205, 256-258
SRDL (Shift Right Double Logical) instruction, 203, 246-249
SR (Subtract Registers) instruction, 336, 358
SRL (Shift Right Logical) instruction, 203, 244-246
SRP (Shift & Round Packed Decimals) instruction, 276, 310-315
SS instruction formats, 64, 68
Statement, 59
Statement, DC, 110
Statement, DS, 101
Statement, END, 98
Statement language, 14
Statements, instruction, 59
Statements, source, 13
Statements, storage definition, 101
STC (Store Character) instruction, 197, 223
STC (Store Character Under Mask) instruction, 197, 224
STH (Store Halfword) instruction, 197, 225
ST (Store) instruction, 198, 226
STM (Store Multiple) instruction, 198, 227, 229
Storage, main, 8
Storage areas, 101-132
Storage areas, contiguous fullword, 109
Storage areas, defining, 101
Storage areas, establishing, 101
Storage ares, fullword, 107-109
Storage areas, input/output, 101, 104
Storage definition statements, 101
Storage devices, disk, 5, 21
Storage dumps, interpreting hexadecimal-formatted, 581-594
Storage location, doubleword, 107
Storage location, fullword, 107
Storage location, halfword, 107
Storage, real, 8
Storage, virtual, 9
Store (ST) instruction, 198, 226
Store Character (STC) instruction, 197, 223
Store Characters Under Mask (STCM) instruction, 197, 224
Store Halfword (STH) instruction, 197, 225
Store instructions, the, 197, 198, 223-229
Store Multiple (STM) instruction, 198, 227, 229
STOW macroinstruction, 618
S-Trigger, 500-523
Stringing base registers, 94
Subdefined areas, 101-107
Subdefined fields, 101-107
Subfield definitions, 101-107

Subheadings, headings and, 535-542
Subroutines, 660
Subtract (S) instruction, 335, 354-356
Subtract Halfword (SH) instruction, 335, 356-358
Subtracting hexadecimals, 50
Subtraction, fixed-point, 40
Subtraction, packed decimal, 274, 291-293
Subtract Logical (SL) instruction, 336, 359-361
Subtract Logical Registers, (SLR) instruction, 337, 361
Subtract Packed (SP) instruction, 274, 291-293
Subtract Registers (SR) instruction, 336, 358
Supervisor, 6
Suppression, zero, 498, 510
Switch conditions, multiple, 450
Switches, 435-451
Switches, program, 435-451
Switches, applications of, 435-451
Switches, bit, 74, 442-449
Switches, character, 436-442
Switches, embedded, 450
Switches, general applications of, 449-451
Switches, using, 435-451
Switches and indicators, concepts of, 435-451
Symbol, 60
Symbol, Carriage Control, 532-542
Symbollic labels, 60, 78, 110
Symbollic labels, invalid, 110
Sysgen, 6, 609
System generation, 6, 609
System/360, 5
System/370, 4

Table, EBCDIC Character, 625
Table, Hexadecimal/Decimal Conversion, 622
Table look-ups, 80, 178, 455-495
Table look-ups, loop controls and, 455-495
Table of Assembler Language Instructions, 626
Table of Condition Code Settings, 623
Table of Contiguous Bit Positions, 621
Table of Program Interrupt Conditions, 624
Table, Powers-of-two, 621
Table searching, 182-184, 455-495
Table segment delimiter, 210
Table segments, 80, 210, 455-495
Table segments, direct addressing of, 484-493
Tables, loadable, 461
Tables, mixed data, 493-495
Tables, translate, 552-565
Table of values, 621
Tag, 78
Tape, 15, 16
Tape, magnetic, 15, 16

Index

Tape data sets, magnetic, 605
Tape drives, 5
Tape volume, magnetic, 605
Task, I/O, 611
Techniques, looping, 178-186, 455-466
Techniques, sectored look-up, 466-484
Terminal, 26
Terminal, IBM 8775 CRT, 26
Termination, Abnormal Program (ABEND), 286
Terms, decimal self-defining, 92
Terms and Nomenclature, Glossary of, 651-661
Test Under Mask (TM) instruction, 92, 435, 447-449
Third Generation computers, 4, 13
Titles, report, 535-542
Titles, headings and subheadings, 535-542
TM (Test Under Mask) instruction, 92, 435, 447-449
Track index, 615
Tracks, 21
Trailer label, 605
Transistors, MOSFET, 4
Translate (TR) instruction, 543, 552-560
Translate and Test (TRT) instruction, 72, 543, 560-565
Translate tables, 552-565
TR (Translate) instruction, 543, 552-560
TRT (Translate and Test) instruction, 72, 543, 560-565
True binary notation, 33-35
True binary representation, 33-35
True binary value, 33-35
Two's complement, 35, 341
Two's complement notation, 36, 341
Type-bar, 17, 20
Type-chain, 17, 20
Types of constants, 111
Type-train, 20

Unblocking records, blocking and, 612
Unconditional branches, 173, 176, 187, 188
Undefined records, 603
Unit of increment, base-16, 42
Unpack (UNPK) instruction, 272, 281-283
UNPK (Unpack) instruction, 272, 281-283
Unsigned EBCDIC numerals, 54
Unsigned packed decimal values, 51
Using switches, 435-451

V address constants, 116, 133
Validation of data, 543-576
Validation of numeric values, 545-551
Valid symbolic labels, 110

Value, complement, 40
Value, integer, 35-41
Value, true binary, 33-35
Value representation, fixed-point, 35, 73, 339-390
Values, absolute, 92
Values, address, 77, 112-116, 132, 133
Values, binary arithmetic, 33, 73
Values, bit position, 33, 621
Values, main storage address, 78, 581-594
Values, expressed constant, 116-132
Values, fixed-point, 35, 46, 73, 339-390
Values, immediate, 90
Values, mask, 62, 157, 175, 224, 230, 435, 447-449
Values, negative fixed-point, 36, 73, 339
Values, negative integer, 37-41
Values, negative signed, 36, 339-390
Values, packed decimal, 51, 71, 278-327
Values, positive fixed-point, 35, 73, 339-390
Values positive integer, 35
Values, self-defining, 89
Variable-length records, 602
VDU's (Visual Display Units), 25
Virtual storage, 9
Volume, 605
Volume, direct access, 605
Volume label, 605
Volume serial number, 605
Volume Table Of Contents (VTOC), 605
VTOC, 605

Word, 661
Work areas, creating, 101

XC (Exclusive Or) instruction, 404, 421-423
X constants, 116, 120
XI (Exclusive Or Immediate) instruction, 92, 404, 419-421
X (Exclusive Or) instruction, 404, 421
XR (Exclusive Or) instruction, 404, 423

Y address constants, 116, 132

ZAP (Zero and Add Packed Decimals) instruction, 273, 286-289
Z constants, 116, 130
Zero and Add Packed Decimals (ZAP) instruction, 273, 286-289
Zero-bit, 33
Zero-suppression, 498-510
Zoned decimal constants, 116-130
Zoned decimal format, 53, 130
Zoned decimal literals, 132
Zoned decimals, 53, 130